SELECTED SHORTER WRITINGS
OF
BENJAMIN B. WARFIELD–II

SELECTED SHORTER WRITINGS

OF

BENJAMIN B. WARFIELD–II

Professor of Didactic and Polemic Theology
Princeton Theological Seminary
1887-1921

Edited by
JOHN E. MEETER

PRESBYTERIAN AND REFORMED PUBLISHING COMPANY
NUTLEY, NEW JERSEY

LIBRARY OF CONGRESS CATALOG CARD NUMBER: 76-110499

Second Printing, November 1976

PRINTED IN THE UNITED STATES OF AMERICA

To
GRACE

COMPANION
in

LIFE
LOVE
STUDY
WORSHIP
SERVICE
PARENTHOOD
GRANDPARENTHOOD

FOREWORD

I

I may have owned a book or two by Dr. Benjamin B. Warfield earlier, but I first came to know him as a scholar and writer in the academic year 1928–1929 when I was a graduate student at Princeton Seminary. In working for my Master's degree I took what was known as a ten-hour thesis course under Dr. Caspar Wistar Hodge: in the fall the student was given a bibliography and in the spring he submitted his paper. I chose as my subject "Redemptive Religions and Christianity as The Redemptive Religion," and found included in my bibliography such B. B. Warfield articles as "Redemption," "Redeemer and Redemption," "The New Testament Terminology of Redemption," "Christless Christianity," "The Essence of Christianity and The Cross of Christ": an encyclopaedia article, two articles from the *Princeton Theological Review*, and two from the *Harvard Theological Review*, the last two considered by many (including Dr. Ethelbert Warfield) to be Dr. Warfield's finest and noblest writings. They made a deep impression on me and more than any of the other books or articles in the bibliography shaped my thinking for my paper and I may add for my life.

Some twenty years later, after teaching ten years at Wilson College and at this time serving the Christian Reformed Church of West Park, Cleveland, as its minister, I wrote this account and appreciation of Dr. Warfield for the *Banner*, the official weekly of the Christian Reformed Church (I quote part of it):

> I like especially the tribute paid Dr. Warfield by his successor in the Chair of Systematic Theology at Princeton

vii

Seminary, Dr. Caspar Wistar Hodge Jr. (in 1921): "We think today of Archibald Alexander, that man of God, the first professor in this Seminary; of Charles Hodge, whose *Systematic Theology* today remains as probably the greatest exposition of the Reformed theology in the English language; of Archibald Alexander Hodge, a man of rare popular gifts and of unusual metaphysical ability; and last but not least, excelling them all in erudition, of Dr. Warfield. . . . At the time of his death he was, I think, without an equal as a theologian in the English-speaking world. With Drs. Kuyper and Bavinck of the Netherlands he made up a great trio of outstanding exponents of the Reformed faith."

Is this comparison warranted?

Let it be said at once that Dr. Warfield did not found a Free University, or give leadership to a Calvinistic political party, or undertake a systematic exposition of the Reformed faith such as is found in Kuyper's *Encyclopaedie* or Bavinck's *Gereformeerde Dogmatiek*.

Here, in summary form, is the story of his life. Benjamin Breckinridge Warfield was born into a godly Presbyterian home at "Grasmere," near Lexington, Kentucky, November 5th, 1851. When only nineteen years of age he was graduated from what is now Princeton University, with the highest honors of his class. After two years of further study and travel abroad he entered Princeton Seminary, graduating in the class of 1876. In 1878 he was appointed instructor, and in 1879 installed as professor of New Testament Exegesis and Literature at Western Theological Seminary, Allegheny. In 1887 he received, and accepted, the appointment to the Charles Hodge Chair of Didactic and Polemic Theology at Princeton Seminary; and for thirty-three years, from 1887 to the time of his death in 1921, he served Princeton Seminary and the Presbyterian Church U. S. A. in the Chair made famous by the Alexander-Hodge succession.

The Rev. F. T. McGill of the Southern Presbyterian Church, of the Seminary class of 1920, writes: "Personally, Dr. Warfield has had a greater influence in my life and ministry than any other man I have ever met. . . . After thinking through the great theological truths under this master thinker and teacher, my mind has never been bothered with religious doubts. . . . Dr. Warfield made such indelible impressions upon me while I was in the Seminary, his figure and influence still stand before me as I prepare sermons; while the recollection of his personal piety helps me to live a more Christ-like life."

Dr. George L. Robinson, himself a distinguished scholar, teacher, and author, a graduate of the class of 1893, writes: "Dr. Warfield was the best teacher I ever had either in America or Germany. I took notes under him assiduously; and the notes I took I have used more than those of all other professors together. He taught us with rare clarity and persuasiveness. He combined quizzing and lecturing in a most marvelous way. He kept a man on his feet from twenty to thirty minutes, interrogating him and in Socratic style informing him."

It is good to be reminded of the influence of Dr. Warfield as a man and as a teacher, since the emphasis usually falls on Dr. Warfield as a scholar. Nor is this strange; for in all his writings, whether for religious weeklies or theological quarterlies or international encyclopaedias, his scholarly method and spirit are apparent. And to say this is to say much: for the quantity of Dr. Warfield's writings is as impressive as its quality. From 1880, when his first article appeared in the *Presbyterian Review*, to the time of his death when three series of articles on Perfectionism were being run in three different quarterlies, his pen was incessantly busy. He was for many years editor of or chief contributor to, first the *Presbyterian and Reformed Review* (1890–1903), and then its successor the *Princeton Theological Review*. He wrote a number of books, including *Introduction to the Textual Criticism of the New Testament* (1886), *The Right of Systematic Theology* (1897), *The Lord of Glory* (1907), and *The Plan of Salvation* (1915). He will be best remembered, perhaps, for some of his articles for such Biblical encyclopaedias as the *International Standard Bible Encyclopaedia*, Hastings' *Dictionary of the Bible,* Hastings' *Dictionary of Christ and the Gospels*, Hastings' *Encyclopaedia of Religion and Ethics*, and the *New Schaff-Herzog Encyclopaedia of Religious Knowledge*. After Dr. Warfield's death, in accordance with instructions left in his will, the more important articles contributed by him to journals and encyclopaedias were collected and published in book form: ten large attractive volumes put out by the Oxford University Press.

These ten volumes were reduced to five handsome volumes and published, with omissions and additions (particularly sermons) and helpful introductions, by the Presbyterian and Reformed Publishing Company during the 1950's, with the titles

The Inspiration and Authority of the Bible
The Person and Work of Christ
Biblical and Theological Studies
Calvin and Augustine
Perfectionism.

The fact that the more recent collection has more than ten times as many copies in print as the earlier set and that it is still in constant demand suggests that interest in Dr. Warfield's writings is greater now than it was at the time of his death more than fifty years ago.

II

This volume, like *Selected Shorter Writings of Benjamin B. Warfield* I, published in 1970, is a collection largely of shorter articles by Dr. Warfield not even considered for inclusion in the ten-volume Oxford edition, and of some longer articles not selected for inclusion because less important for the purpose in hand than those selected. I have also included a small book, *The Right of Systematic Theology*, long since out of print, and a few introductions to books also out of print, which is a departure from the principle of selection followed by the committee responsible for preparing the Oxford collection. As a result this volume contains a wide variety of articles: sermons, book reviews, introductions to books, articles published in encyclopaedias or theological journals, and about two dozen short articles that appeared in such papers as the *Presbyterian,* the *Presbyterian Journal*, the *Presbyterian Messenger*, the *Westminster Teacher*, the *Independent*, and the *New York Observer*.

Part I is made up of five articles, one on the Bible as a whole and four on the New Testament, a felicitous arrangement when it is remembered that Dr. Warfield taught New Testament Exegesis and Literature at Western Theological Seminary, Allegheny, from 1878 to 1887, before beginning his lifework at Princeton Theological Seminary. The opening article gives a masterful survey of Biblical scholarship during the nineteenth century: selection and evaluation of those books that most contributed to the progress of knowledge and learning with respect to the Bible as a whole during one of the truly great centuries in the history of thought. In teaching a college course on Apostolic History I read a number of introductions to the book Acts, but none as helpful or well ordered as Dr. Warfield's "Some Characteristics of the Book of Acts." The fourth article, "The Canonicity of Second Peter," written in 1882, is said by Dr. John R. Mackay (*Expositors*, July 1922, p. 31) to have been "among the first of Dr. Warfield's contributions to New Testament studies which brought its author to the notice of British New Testament scholars." The fifth article, on the book Revelation and written in 1884, is valuable in itself and a worthy representative of the many writings (in the New Testament field) of the opening decade of Dr. Warfield's teaching; it may be compared with the article, "The Millennium and the Apocalypse," in *Biblical Doctrines*, 1929, pp. 643-664.

Part II consists of seven articles ordinarily included in what Dr. Charles Hodge designates the Introduction to Systematic Theology, Dr. Herman Bavinck the *Principia* of Systematic Theology, and Dr. Valentine Hepp the *Pars Formalis* as distinguished from the *Pars Materialis* of Dogmatics. They are of interest mainly for elaborating more fully than does the article "Apologetics" in *Studies in Theology*, 1932, pp. 3-21, the things that differentiate the Princeton Apologetic from that of Professors Kuyper and Bavinck of the Free University of Amsterdam.

Part III is composed of fourteen articles dealing with Systematic Theology in general and with specific doctrines in the field of Systematic Theology. Articles 13-19 may be placed alongside the articles, "The Idea of Systematic Theology" and "The Task and Method of Systematic Theology," pp. 49-105 of *Studies in Theology*, 1932 (which like the article "Apologetics" mentioned in the preceding paragraph are not included in the later five-volume edition); all of these articles are important because setting forth Dr. Warfield's conception of Systematic Theology as a science, its relation to science in general, its importance as a discipline despite declining interest in it, its importance for the minister of the gospel in his work as a preacher. The most important article certainly in Part III is "The Right of Systematic Theology," first published in the *Presbyterian and Reformed Review* and then as a small book in Edinburgh, with an introduction by Professor James Orr. I included the short articles "Regeneration" and "Sanctification" and the rather long article "Calvinism" for several reasons: they were written in the first instance by Dr. Warfield's predecessor in the Chair of Systematic Theology, Dr. Archibald Alexander Hodge, and revised for a later edition of the encyclopaedia by Dr. Warfield, exemplifying therefore the fine way in which these men worked together; the shorter articles give us a brief but systematic presentation of specific doctrines; and the longer article, on Calvinism, invites comparison with the later article which appeared in the *New Schaff-Herzog Encyclopaedia of Religious Knowledge* in 1908 (see *Calvin and Calvinism*, 1932, pp. 353-369, and *Calvin and Augustine*, 1956, pp. 287-300) and the three articles, "John Calvin the Theologian," "The Theology of Calvin," and "Present-Day Attitude to Calvinism," published together as a pamphlet with the title *Calvin as a Theologian and Calvinism Today* (see *Calvin and Augustine*, 1956, Appendix, pp. 481-507).

Part IV is a miscellany of four articles: a sermon on incarnate truth, a very learned article on "Africa and the Beginnings of Christian Latin Literature," and two down-to-earth articles on the perils missionaries face in their work and on the devotional life of seminary students. Of these articles I like the last-named one best, both as revealing the kind of man Dr. Warfield was or wanted to be and as speaking to my own heart on the high level of life one should strive to achieve as a minister of the gospel. I think I am moved and stimulated more by this article than I am by the similar article included in *Selected Shorter Writings of Benjamin B. Warfield* I, which is saying a whole lot: at the request of the administrations of several seminaries "The Religious Life of Theological Students" (the article in Volume I) has been made available in pamphlet form to secure for it a wider circulation among students.

Parts V and VI are made up, mainly, of very short articles that appeared in such papers as the *Presbyterian,* the *Independent,* the *Westminster Teacher.* To the editorial committee responsible for preparing the ten-volume Oxford set of Dr. Warfield's writings they were, necessarily so, inconsequential; but I like them, I was impressed by them when first I found them in Dr. Warfield's *Scrapbooks,* I think they are altogether delightful and so do my friends who have read Volume I of the *Selected Shorter Writings.* When dealing with familiar material they present it in a simple clearcut non-technical way; in addition they touch upon subjects not dealt with elsewhere and so reveal not only Dr. Warfield's views in these areas but also another facet of his mind and interest. If I may single out a few of these gems I should like to mention "Why Four Gospels?," "The Gospel of John," "The Dogmatic Spirit," "Authority, Intellect, and Heart," and the two articles on the race problem in the United States in 1887 and 1888.

As was the case in Volume I, here too the footnotes are by Dr. Warfield himself, except for the opening footnote for each article, marked by an asterisk. In this opening footnote I indicate the source of the article, and also the date and place of publication, and sometimes I give a bit of additional information gleaned from the *Scrapbooks.* I have not always succeeded in making the style and arrangement of the footnotes contemporary, which is not all loss; the footnotes to the articles "The Canonicity of Second Peter" and "Africa and the Beginnings of Christian Latin Literature," for example, are much (I refer to spelling, abbreviation, punctuation) as they came from Dr. Warfield's hand.

It has been a pleasure and a privilege to edit these volumes,

Selected Shorter Writings I and II: exploring the *Scrapbooks* and the *Opuscula,* and in general the material not included in the ten-volume Oxford or the five-volume Presbyterian and Reformed Publishing Company collections. I am grateful to the staff at Princeton Seminary Library, particularly Mr. James S. Irvine, the assistant librarian, who was most helpful in securing copies of articles I needed in preparing the manuscript for the publisher; and Miss Virginia Cranstoun, secretary to the librarian, who Xeroxed most of the very short articles for me. I am also much indebted to Miss Lillian Staiger, reference librarian at the Library of St. Aquinas Institute and Dubuque Theological Seminary, for her helpfulness in providing the tools needed to verify dates or name spellings as I read the galley proofs; to Dr. Peter Kjeseth, professor of New Testament at Wartburg Lutheran Seminary, for reviewing the footnotes and Greek quotations in the article "The Canonicity of Second Peter"; and to Dr. John McDonnell, professor of Old Testament at Aquinas, for helping me with some of the footnotes to the article "Africa and the Beginnings of Christian Latin Literature." I wish also to express my appreciation to Mr. Charles H. Craig, Director of the Presbyterian and Reformed Publishing Company at Nutley, New Jersey, for his kindness and encouragement and specifically for his willingness to publish this two-volume set of Dr. Warfield's *Selected Shorter Writings.* It is my prayer that God may use these volumes not only to give a larger and more complete picture of Dr. Warfield as a scholar and a theologian, but also to deepen or renew interest in the system of doctrine presented in them, "the only system," to use Dr. Warfield's words, "in which the whole order of this world is brought into a rational unity with the doctrine of grace," to the exposition and defense of which, to use the words he applied to Dr. Charles Hodge, "every jot of Dr. Warfield's learning was consecrated."

JOHN E. MEETER

2129 Carter Road
Dubuque, Iowa 52001

CONTENTS

PART I

1

THE CENTURY'S PROGRESS
IN BIBLICAL KNOWLEDGE*

We have been accustomed to look upon this nineteenth century of ours with pardonable, because honest, pride, as preeminently the century of Biblical research and advancing knowledge of the Scriptures. On the whole, this impression is doubtless justified; but it is not difficult to exaggerate it into an unmeasured admiration of the Biblical attainments of our own age and a corresponding depreciation of the labors of the preceding centuries, by standing on the shoulders of which alone the Biblical learning of our time has been able to reach its present height. After all, the nineteenth century did not invent the Bible, nor did it even discover it. The merit of discovering the Bible, after its long occultation through the Middle Ages, belongs rather to the sixteenth century, and that century made this its reasonable boast. "We may most truly declare," says Calvin, "that we have brought more light to bear on the understanding of Scripture than all the authors who have sprung up among Christians since the rise of the papacy; nor do they themselves venture to rob us of this praise."

The light that was then turned upon the Word of God has been shining steadily upon it ever since. From the moment when Judea and Greece rose from the grave, in the persons of Reuchlin and Erasmus, with the Hebrew and Greek Testaments in their hands, the treasures that they brought back to the world have been kept continuously under the scrutiny of men. There has been no flagging in the labor of investigating them; there has been no pause in the advancing understanding of

*This article is from the *Homiletic Review*, March, 1900, pp. 195-202.

them; there has been almost no limit to the accumulations of knowledge concerning them. No doubt there have been fluctuations in the point of view from which the Scriptures have been approached, and gradations in the value of the contributions of each period to their understanding. The Reformation age grasped at the heart of Scripture; the age of systematization investigated its substance; the age of rationalism occupied itself with its shell. But each point of view and each age had its own contribution to make to the common store of ascertained fact, and still knowledge grew. And this accumulated mass of learning was laid at last in the lap of the nineteenth century. It would be ingratitude indeed were she to forget those by whose labors she has profited and the measure of whose individual attainments often no one of her own sons has surpassed, or perhaps even equaled. To mention no more than a few typical names, John Calvin still reigns acknowledged king of all Biblical students; men still turn to John Lightfoot as a guide in the intricacies of Jewish learning; and no one thinks of disputing the supremacy of John Albert Bengel in his own special sphere.

I. If we may approach the matter from this point of view, the first remark which falls to be made in attempting to estimate the century's progress in Biblical knowledge would seem to be obvious. It is this: the nineteenth century has vigorously entered into the various lines of work begun by the preceding ages and carried them to a higher stage of completeness. It is rather remarkable, when we come to look at it, how much of the accomplishment of the nineteenth century has been of the nature of the perfecting of lines of labor successfully inaugurated in the preceding periods.

This is true, for example, of the task of establishing the Biblical text. In the case of the Old Testament, there seemed indeed for long to be a disposition abroad to rest content with the eighteenth century Masoretic studies of Kennicott and De Rossi; but, at last, as the century draws to its close, we have in the works of Baer and Delitzsch and of Ginsburg a worthy continuation of their labors; while even yet we have no critical edition of even the Septuagint Version, though the hope of this is now held out to us by Dr. Swete and his coadjutors. Meanwhile scholars of the regnant school of Old Testament criticism, neglecting the warning of experience in other departments, are preferring, in their emendation of the text, the primrose path of conjecture, diligently endeavoring (like Mr. Shandy) "to scratch some better sense into it." Things have gone better in the case of the New Testament text. The way here, too, was blazed out by the eighteenth century scholars, Mill and Bentley, Bengel and Wetstein and Griesbach; but the work fell in the nineteenth century into extraordinarily good hands, and through the labors of Lachmann and Tischendorf and Tregelles, of Westcott and Hort and Weiss, the tasks of collecting and weighing the evidence have gone on *pari passu,* until it is safe to say we have today a better New Testament text in our hands than has been currently read since the opening years of the second century.

Something of the same sort is no less true with regard to the study of the Biblical languages. From the end of the sixteenth century on, the philological study of the Biblical texts had been prosecuted with the greatest diligence in a cloud of monographs, and it was largely these labors which made possible the work of a Gesenius and an Ewald, of a Winer and a Grimm. The task of the nineteenth century has been largely that of sifting and systematizing and reducing to exact and compact form the results of this long continued philological study of the Bible. The outcome has been the production of a series of works, both in the grammatical and lexical spheres, which place the student in a position to prosecute his investigations with an ease and accuracy unknown to any former age. It is here, in the production of a multitude of compact and well digested "instruments of precision" for the study of the Bible text—grammars like Kautzsch–Gesenius in Hebrew, and Schmiedel–Winer in Greek; lexicons like Brown–Gesenius in Hebrew, and Thayer–Grimm in Greek; concordances like Mandelkern in Hebrew, Hatch–Redpath in the LXX, and Moulton–Geden in the Greek New Testament—that the nineteenth century makes the next age her special debtor. Positively new acquisitions are marked in this sphere chiefly in matters of detail, always excepting, of course, the recovery of the languages hidden beneath the cuneiform texts, which is perhaps the greatest achievement of our century in the linguistic sphere, and the results of which for the better understanding of Old Testament philology have only begun to be garnered.

Much the same may be said again of all that large department of investigation that may be classed under the broad rubric of Biblical archaeology. The foundations of this group of sciences were laid and the edifice well begun upon them by older writers; the nineteenth century has systematized and perfected their work and compressed it into condensed exhibits which place it in all its details within the reach of every Bible student, however humble. One has but to glance, for example, through our Bible dictionaries—Smith's, which has been the companion of English-speaking students for a generation, or Hastings', which essays to take its place at the close of the century—in order to realize what treasures have been collected and how fairly they have been brought within the reach of all. In this sphere of labor, however, the nineteenth century can boast also of great and even revolutionary discoveries; as never before, the spade has become the interpreter of Scripture, and the recovery of the ancient civilizations, of the Euphrates valley in particular, marks a new epoch in the understanding of the life of the Oriental peoples, and is bearing fruit of the richest kind for Biblical investigation.

If we look upon the progress of Biblical knowledge, thus, merely from the point of view of the continuation of the lines of research already begun and well begun in the previous centuries, the nineteenth century can give a good account of itself.

II. The main thing that calls for remark in the domain of Biblical criticism is the rise within the nineteenth century of a new form of critical assault upon the documentary *origines* of the Christian religion, in the successful withstanding of which a vast mass of Biblical knowledge has accumulated and the understanding of the Scriptures has been placed on quite a new plane.

At the opening of the century vulgar rationalism was still leading the attack against Christianity; the main effort was still to save the husk, with an entire discarding of the kernel. Those were the days in which Dr. Paulus, for example, reigned supreme, and men were gravely going through the Bible narrative explaining away every miraculous occurrence by a "psychological interpretation" which sought to represent the thing narrated to have occurred, but in a form stripped of its miraculous coloring. Thus, for example, Jesus did indeed feed the five thousand, but it was by setting a good example to the crowd by bringing unreservedly out his own meager store, whereupon all the rest did the like and there was abundance for all; Jesus did indeed provide the wedding feast at Cana with wine, but it was by producing at the critical moment the present of wine he had brought with him to the festival. Thus in the name of rationalism the supernatural history was violently transformed into probably the most unnatural history ever conceived by man. Already the end of all this was preparing, however, by the rise of the idealistic philosophy, which had at least the merit of possessing an eye for ideas; and the dénouement came quite dramatically on the simultaneous publication in 1835 of three books, which, as Pfleiderer says, contained the germs of all subsequent criticism of the Biblical writings—Strauss's *Life of Jesus*, Baur's work on *The Pastoral Epistles*, and Vatke's *Religion of the Old Testament*.

The shell with which the old rationalism exclusively busied itself was now cast entirely aside in the professed interests of the kernel; and from that time on criticism has consistently represented itself as occupied with the effort to disengage essential Christianity from the accidents of form in which it was originally clothed. There is no reason to doubt that Strauss was at first as honest as his less extreme followers have been ever since, when he explained "the essence of the Christian faith to be perfectly independent of his criticism." "The supernatural birth of Christ, his miracles, his resurrection and ascension," he adds, "remain eternal truths, whatever doubts may be cast on their reality as historical facts." The echoes of this declaration are sounding around us until today, and it contains indeed the keynote of the nineteenth century assault on Christianity, under the soothing music of which it would fain substitute its own conceptions for the historical religion of Christ.

It does not fall within our present scope to trace the stages through which this new form of attack on the Christian documents and their contents has passed as it has run its course, or through which rather it has been forced by the splendid resistance offered to it by the Christian scholarship of our time. Everybody knows how quickly, in the sphere of the New Testament, Strauss's construction was superseded by that of Baur; and how Baur's more solidly built edifice has gradually crumbled of its own weight until the adherents of the once arrogantly dominant "Tübingen School" have fallen into insignificance— either on the one hand by repeated concessions to the conservative attack, until they have left themselves no ground to stand on, or on the other by growing extremity of denial in the vain effort to resist the inevitable end. At the end of the century the "tendency hypothesis" is so well dead that it is already almost forgotten; and its place is taken by a Ritschlian rationalism, which still flies the old banner of "the kernel at the cost of the husk," but can find no better justification of its inconsistent radicalism in the criticism of the apostolic documents than is supplied by an ungrounded charge of fanatical enthusiasm brought against the first followers of Christ. Old Testament criticism was slower in falling into the new line and has not yet so fully run its course. The end of the century finds its point of view still dominating the mass of professed students of the subject; and even by the height of its flood able to send back an eddy into the sphere of New Testament criticism, where its methods have already been fully tested and found wanting. Already, however, the discerning eye may perceive the same disintegration preparing for it which has met its companion movement in the New Testament; and although the nineteenth century must needs commit its decent burial to the twentieth century, it does this with entire confidence that this function will be thoroughly, perhaps speedily, performed.

Meanwhile in conflict with these new modes of assault the Biblical learning of our own day has been greatly enriched. This mode of statement is not intended to imply that Biblical learning has not been at all directly advanced by the labors of the neologists themselves. The contrary is true. There is no student of the New Testament who will not confess deep indebtedness to the works of Baur, for example, both for facts in abundance and for generalizations and points of view of the most stimulating character; and though the lesser balance of many of Baur's followers has rendered their labors less helpful, yet the contribution made by the Tübingen School and its successors to the knowledge of the Scriptural deposit is nothing less than immense. And the same is true in their own measure of the Old Testament scholars who have prosecuted their work under the spell of the new construction of the history of the religion of Israel and its record in the Old Testament books—from Graf and Reuss to Kuenen and Wellhausen and Stade. And if we take into consideration the men who have occupied a more or less intermediate position between the advocates of the new construction and the conservative defenders of the Biblical revelation, it must be confessed that a great part of recent Biblical investigation has been done by them. But the material as it lies on the pages of these writers is presented not merely in a connection, but also in a form and with a coloring, which is more or less unassimilable by a truly Christian consciousness, so that even this material becomes the permanent possession of Christendom only as it is tested and cleansed and built into the fabric of really Christian thought by its more consistent exponents; while, in opposition to the deflected point of view of the destructive criticism, truly Christian scholarship has been forced to explore more deeply its records and to draw from them ever more purely their treasures of truth. In the course of this process, a great host of scholars have deepened and widened our acquaintance with the Scriptures, until we feel as if the nineteenth century had introduced a quite new era in the knowledge of the Bible.

III. We do not touch the center of the matter, however, until we observe that, in the course of its Biblical study, the nineteenth century has attained a distinctly fuller and more completely defined detailed exegetical result than meets us in the work of any previous century.

It is, after all, ultimately to the continuous exegesis of the Biblical text that we must look for the soundest measure of the Biblical attainments of any age; and tried by that standard, the nineteenth century registers a distinct advance. To this have cooperated the systematization of the results of the labors of preceding ages in the auxiliary sciences, and the accessibility given to these results in the numerous helps to students that have poured from the press; the interest awakened in Biblical studies by the learned assaults made by the new critical schools upon the traditional opinion; and above all the ever increasing demands made on Biblical science by advancing general culture and the increasing dispersion of knowledge. The result has been an incredible flood of exegetical treatises which have poured through all the conduits for the distribution of learning —the work now of single authors, now of small coteries of like-minded scholars, now of larger companies associated for the task in hand—addressed now to a purely scholastic audience, now to the people at large—now exhausting all the accumulated learning of the ages in the exposition of a single book, now spreading a moderate supply of information over the whole Biblical library.

The world has probably never seen the like of this output of exposition for abundance; and, as a mass, its quality has been as remarkable as its quantity. Such a huge composite work as Lange's Bible Work, transplanted to America and swelled there to even larger proportions, is characteristic of the age. So are also the numerous attempts of smaller circles to set forth the results of exegesis after their own conceptions. Thus, a body of scholars in the Church of England has given us what is known as the *Speaker's Commentary*. Thus the "great

Cambridge triumvirate" projected a commentary on the New Testament, which cannot be said to have failed when we owe to it Dr. Lightfoot's commentaries on Paul's Epistles, and Dr. Westcott's on the writings of John and the Epistle to the Hebrews. Thus the Liberals of Oxford also undertook a like task, the outcome of which was Stanley on Corinthians and Jowett on Paul's Epistles; and the Biblical students of Princeton, essaying something similar, produced on one plane Alexander on Isaiah and Hodge on Romans, and then on a more popular one, Alexander on the Psalms, the Gospels of Matthew and Mark, and the Book of Acts, and Hodge on Corinthians and Ephesians. And what can be said of the individual commentaries of this century, beginning with De Wette and running to seed in the innumerable expositions that have fallen still-born on the world during the last decade?

Judgments will differ as to where the cream of this rich body of exegesis is to be found. But who will not think at once of at least De Wette and Ewald and Luecke and Hengstenberg and Hävernick and Tholuck, of Hoffmann and Delitzsch and Dillmann and Keil, of Fritzsche and Rueckert, of Meyer and Weiss? Of Reuss and Godet, also; and of Alford, Lightfoot, and Westcott? For ourselves, we should be willing to hang the credit of this century's work in exegesis on the single commentary of Meyer on the New Testament, continued after Meyer's death under the admirable editorship of Weiss; and in the Old Testament on the various volumes issued by Dillmann, Delitzsch, and Keil. In these works the sobriety and the learning of the age are certainly fairly exhibited; and after the critical theories that have vexed our day are forgotten and the literature dominated by them has become a curiosity or a puzzle, it may well be that the eyes of students will turn back to the class of works represented by such learned, careful, and penetrating expositions as the most characteristic and permanently useful products of nineteenth century Bible study.

IV. It is interesting to note, finally, how large a portion of this Bible study of the nineteenth century has issued in distinctively theological results. For, despite a current impression to the contrary, our age has been in comparison with its immediate predecessor decidedly a theological one. It owes this characteristic, in part, of course, to the renewed interest in ideas which came in naturally with the idealistic philosophy and has been powerfully fostered in theological investigation by the spiritualizing stream which has flooded the whole theological thinking of our time. One characteristic result of it has been the development in our day of an entirely new theological discipline. This new discipline of "Biblical Theology" came to us indeed wrapped in the swaddling-clothes of rationalism, and it was rocked in the cradle of the Hegelian recasting of Christianity; it did not present at first, therefore, a very engaging countenance, and seemed to find for a time its chief pleasure in setting the prophets and apostles by the ears. But already in the hands of men like Schmid and Oehler it began to show that it was born to better things. And now as it grows to a more mature form and begins to overtake the tasks that belong to its adulthood, it bids fair to mark a new era in theological investigation by making known to us the revelation of God genetically—that is, by laying it before us in the stages of its growth and its several stadia of development. If men have hitherto been content to contemplate the counsel of the Most High only in its final state—laid out before them, as it were, in a map—hereafter it seems that they are to consider it by preference in its stages, in its vital processes of growth and maturing. Obviously a much higher form of knowledge is thus laid open to us; and were this discipline the sole gift of the nineteenth century to the Christian student, she would by it alone have made good a claim on his permanent gratitude.

It is scarcely possible to survey, however cursorily, the march of Biblical study throughout the nineteenth century without being impressed by the magnitude of the contribution that has been made by it to the better knowledge of the Bible. But as we have said that Biblical study did not originate with this century, so now we must admit that neither is it to cease with it. We are accordingly impressed with the evidences all about us that the nineteenth century has brought no single branch of Biblical investigation to its definite completion. It has done its part; but it hands on an unfinished task to its successor. It is a great thing to say of it, that it hands on all its tasks in completer shape than it received them. It received the Bible from the dead hands of eighteenth century rationalism into hands that were cold with fear; it hands it on to the twentieth century with the courage of assured conviction. It has not been a century of quiet and undisturbed study of the Bible. Fierce controversies have raged throughout its whole length. But fierce controversies can rage only where strong convictions burn. And amid, or rather by means of, all these controversies knowledge has increased; and after them all we can only lay our hands on our mouths and say: "God fulfils himself in many ways." The very wrath of man has come to praise him in this sphere too; and the Bible has emerged from these fires, as out of all others, without so much as the smell of smoke upon its very garments. It is the whole Bible that is committed to the twentieth century—to receive from it, as we believe, an even deeper reverence and an even completer obedience.

INTRODUCTORY NOTE TO
JOHN H. KERR'S
Introduction to the Study of
the Books of the New Testament*

I feel very deeply the honor which Mr. Kerr has done me in inscribing to me this book—the first fruits, but we all hope by no means the last fruits, of his studies in the New Testament. Certainly it is a pleasure to be allowed to commend to the wide public of Bible students for which it is designed, this sober and serious attempt to popularize the study of the human origin and characteristics of that body of literature which God has made the repository of his gospel.

The New Testament is far more than a body of literature. It is the Word of God. It is not simply the literary product of the Church of the first age. It is the gift of God to the Church of all ages. Neither in the composition of its individual books, nor in the collection of those books into a "canon," can it be justly looked upon as the creation of the literary genius or of the selective instincts of the Church. The books were given one by one by the authoritative founders of the Church—the apostles whom Christ had chosen and whom the Spirit had endowed—to the Church which they founded, as its authoritative Rule of Faith and Practice, its *corpus juris;* and the Book formed itself out of these authoritative books and differentiated itself by this simple fact from all other books or collections of books. The principle of the canon has ever been apostolic gift, never fitness to edify or adaptation to the Christian con-

---

*The Introductory Note to John H. Kerr's book, *An Introduction to the Study of the Books of the New Testament*, 1892, pp. ix-xvi.

sciousness: authoritativeness is its note. And when a Christian approaches it, he approaches it not merely as a book which he finds spiritually helpful, far less, merely as one which he finds literarily interesting, but as the Oracles of God.

Nevertheless, God did not give us these books, as he gave Moses the Ten Words, written without human intermediation, by his own finger, on the tables of stone. He gave them not only by, but through men. They are the Oracles of God, and every word of them is a word of God. But they are also the writings of men, and every word of them is a word of man. By a perfect confluence of the divine and human, the one word is at once all divine and all human. So then, for their proper and complete understanding, we must approach each book not only as the Word of God, but also as the words of Peter, or of Paul, or of John. We must seek to understand its human author in his most intimate characteristics, in his trials, experiences, and training, in the special circumstances of joy or sorrow, of straits or deliverance, in which he stood when writing this book, in his relations to his readers, and to the immediate needs and special situation of his readers which gave occasion for his writing—in all, in a word, which went to make him an author, and just the author which he was—in order that we may understand the Word of God which these words of his servants are. And we must approach the Book as a whole, with our eyes open to the relations borne by part to part—their chronological order, their mutual interdependencies and interrelations, their several places in the advancing delivery of doctrine, in the development of Christian life, in the elaboration of Church or-organization and worship—in order that we may understand the method of God in creating his Church through the labors of these, his servants. This vast field is embraced in that literary study of the New Testament to which, it is to be hoped, Mr. Kerr's book will introduce many to whom it may have hitherto seemed too remote or too recondite.

Let us look for a moment at the chronological list of New Testament books which Mr. Kerr gives us in the table on page xx:

TABLE

Showing the date and place of composition, and the authors of the books of the New Testament

Book	Date	Place	Author
James	45	Jerusalem	James, the brother of our Lord
1 Thessalonians	52	Corinth	Paul, the apostle
2 Thessalonians	52	"	" " "
Galatians	57	Ephesus	" " "
1 Corinthians	57	"	" " "
2 Corinthians	57	Macedonia	" " "
Romans	58	Corinth	" " "
Matthew	c 58	Jerusalem	Matthew
Luke	58–60	Caesarea	Luke, the beloved physician
Colossians	62	Rome	Paul, the apostle
Philemon	62	"	" " "
Ephesians	62	"	" " "
Philippians	63	"	" " "
Acts	63	"	Luke, the beloved physician
Hebrews	c 64	"	Paul, the apostle
1 Peter	64	Babylon	Peter, the apostle
Jude	c 66	Jerusalem(?)	Jude, the brother of our Lord
1 Timothy	66	Macedonia	Paul, the apostle
Titus	67	Ephesus	" " "
2 Timothy	68	Rome	" " "
2 Peter	68	Enroute to Rome	Peter, the apostle
Mark	68	Rome	Mark
John	90	Ephesus	John, the apostle
1 John	90	"	" " "
2 John	91	"	" " "
3 John	91	"	" " "
Revelation	96	Patmos	" " "

Note how interesting even such "a dry list" may become through what it suggests as to the relations of the books to one another, when they are viewed organically as a body of literature. Consider the obvious domination of Paul throughout nearly the whole list, until Paul passes out of view at the close of the seventh Christian decade, and John fills the spacious time of the end of the century with his Spirit-attuned voice. And, then, consider the grouping of the books. We observe the first light of the early dawn of Christian literature in the Epistle of James; and we cannot fail to remark the aroma of "beginning-ness" which rises from every verse of that beautiful relic of really primitive Christianity, in which the Church is a syna-gogue, and the sins that break its purity and peace are still the sins of Jewish temperament and Jewish inheritance. Then we have a long series of Paul's Epistles—from Thessalonians to Romans—and observe already the ascendancy of this apostle in early Christian literature, leading us to think of its first epoch as the first Pauline period. Then come the first Gospels; and here, at the end of the sixth decade of the century, we may draw a deep line, and say that the beginnings are over. What we may call the central literary period now emerges into view. How Pauline it is! First, there is a central body of Paul's letters; and then a sequence of histories and epistles deeply imbued (with the exception of Jude) with the Pauline spirit, and ex-hibiting with striking clearness the supremeness of Paul's in-fluence throughout the whole formative age of the Church. The central period closes, and is followed by a remarkable series of writings which have this common feature—that they all may be looked upon as the leave-taking of the apostles from the churches which they have established. We may consider them the legacy to the Church, in order, of Paul, of Peter, and of John—the whole closing with that long, steady glow in the western heavens, illuminating the whole pathway of the Church through time, which is fitly called the Apocalypse.

On the [following] page, I have sought to represent this group-ing in diagram. It is sufficiently striking to add likelihood to the chronological scheme on which it is founded. And if we will look a little deeper, we may perceive lines of development running through the sequence of writings, which go far toward

TABLE

Showing the periods of New Testament literature

Book	Date	Period		
James	45	Dawn	The Beginnings of Apostolic Literature	The Founding of the Church
1 Thessalonians	52	First Pauline Period		
2 Thessalonians	53			
Galatians	57			
1 Corinthians	57			
2 Corinthians	57			
Romans	58			
Matthew	c 58	First Gospels		
Luke	c 60			
Colossians	62	Central Pauline Period	The Central Period of Apostolic Literature	The Establishing of the Church
Ephesians	62			
Philemon	62			
Philippians	63			
Acts	c 64			
Hebrews	64			
1 Peter	64			
Jude	c 66			
1 Timothy	67	Paul's Legacy	The Closing of Apostolic Literature	The Leaving of the Church
Titus	67			
2 Timothy	68			
2 Peter	68	Peter's Legacy		
Mark	68			
John	90	John's Legacy		
1 John	90			
2 John	91			
3 John	91			
Revelation	96			

demonstrating the general correctness of the order which has been assigned them. All the books which I have classed under the caption of "The Beginnings of Apostolic Literature" share with the Epistle of James the primitive flavor. The Epistles to the Thessalonians obviously belong to the infancy of the Church, when men were learning the first principles of the faith—God and the Judgment. The questions connected with the mode and ground of salvation, with which the great Epistles to the Galatians, Corinthians, and Romans are busied, were characteristic of the transition from Judaism to Christianity. And the supplying of both the Jewish and Gentile sections of the Church with their appropriate Gospel was a necessary element in the foundation of these churches. The Church having once been founded, new needs arose and new questions pressed for solution. The faith had been delivered; now it needed establishing. The discussions as to the Person of Christ and his relation to his Body, the Church, which occupy the foreground in the central group of Paul's letters, could not have sprung up in the first infancy of the Church. It belongs to manhood to wrestle with the philosophy of its faith. Nor are histories of the foundation of a society, such as we have in the book of Acts, written, until the society is conscious that the foundations are already laid. Hebrews, First Peter, and Jude are as distinctively not evangelizing, but confirming literature. All the writings of this central period, thus, correspond with the place assigned to them chronologically: they are characteristic of the early maturity of the Church. Equally loudly do the contents of the remaining books proclaim themselves to belong to the period of the departure of the apostles. It is not arbitrarily that Paul busies himself in the Pastoral Epistles with the organization of the churches: it is because the churches had grown so numerous and so large that questions of organization had become pressing—it is because the time was drawing near when they should be left to self-government, without his inspired guidance. And as Paul wrote Second Timothy when he was already being poured out and the time of his departure was come, so Peter wrote Second Peter in full realization that the putting off of his tabernacle was coming swiftly, and in order to promise to his readers the memoirs of an eye-witness to Christ's majesty: it is Peter's swan-song. John's whole body of writings bears witness to a Church long established, and may be justly looked upon as the farewell of the apostolate to the churches they had founded. Hence the Gospel of the Spirit, the final Gospel, and its strengthening accompanying letter. Hence the typical messages to the churches, opening that immortal vision which uncovers to glad eyes the course of the great conflict through time, by which Christ is putting his enemies under his feet, and the glories of the final victory. Only with these is the deposit of faith made complete, the basis of hope impregnable, and the revelation of God's love perfect.

This meager hint may serve as some sort of a sample of how, as we study the literary history of the New Testament, we may gain broader and deeper conceptions of God's method in giving his Word to man, and so also a fuller apprehension of the supreme value of these precious books and their fitness to meet every human need. May Mr. Kerr's excellent volume prove to many, an introduction not only to the study of the human conditions and methods by which these books came to man, but also to a fuller understanding of the loving care of our God and Savior for his flock.

SOME CHARACTERISTICS OF
THE BOOK OF ACTS*

I

The book which we know as "The Acts of the Apostles," or, by a very natural abbreviation, simply as "The Acts," has borne this title from at least the middle of the second century. It is the only title for it, in fact, that has been transmitted to us. Nevertheless, it is not a perfectly appropriate title. The book is nothing so little as a narrative of the deeds of the apostles. The very names of most of them occur in its pages only in the list incorporated in its first chapter. The fortunes of no one of them are recounted with anything like completeness. The acts of only two of them fill any large place in its story. Even a cursory reading will make it clear that the task to which the author addressed himself was something quite different from the recital of either the labors of the apostles severally, or even their collective work. The fact probably is that he gave the book no title at all. To him it was no separate "treatise," as it is miscalled in our English version of its first verse, needing therefore a particularizing title; but only a Second Book of a larger treatise, sharing with the First Book the common title of the whole work. What this common title was, we have now, to be sure, no means of confidently determining. When the two Books of which the work consisted (at least so far as it was ever completed) were torn asunder and assigned in the current copies of the New Testament, each to the place among

---

*From the *Bible Student*, Jan., Feb., Mar., 1902, pp. 13-21, 72-80, 130-136. See also the very similar Introduction to the little book in the Temple Bible series: *Acts and the Pastoral Epistles*, London, 1902, pp. v-xxvii.

the Sacred Books suggested by the nature of its contents, a separate title was necessarily given to each, and the general title common to the two (if such a formal general title ever existed) passed out of use and out of memory. The preface to the whole work still stands at the head of its First Book, and from it we may learn the author's purpose in writing; and from the preface to the Second Book we may obtain a notion how the two Books are related to one another. Any reconstruction of the general title to the whole is, however, purely conjectural; although (what is of chief importance) we may still read the two Books in the light of the author's conception of them.

The First Book of the extended historical treatise of which our so-called Book of Acts is the Second is the book that has come down to us under the name of "The Gospel according to Luke." This is not only assured by the unbroken testimony of antiquity which ascribes both books to the same author; but is evidenced by many internal proofs of the most convincing kind. It counts for something that both books are addressed to the same patron, a certain Gentile Christian of high rank, named Theophilus. But it counts for much more, that in the preface attached to Luke much more is promised to Theophilus than that book provides, while what is lacking is actually found in Acts; and Acts explicitly puts itself forward, in the preface attached to it, as the Second Book of a treatise to the First Book of which is ascribed the compass and contents of the Gospel of Luke. Moreover, the Gospel of Luke closes somewhat abruptly and apparently points forward to something yet to come; and the Book of Acts so opens as to supply precisely what seemed thus left untold, and this affords the only satisfactory explanation of the manner of the Gospel's closing. Still, again, the two books are bound together by such kinship not only in language and style and historical method, but also in tone, point of view, and underlying purpose, as to suggest that they are not merely products of a single hand, but parts of a single whole. It is difficult, in short, to refuse to recognize in these two books consecutive portions of a large historical work written throughout with a single aim and on a carefully adjusted plan, and intended to make a definite impression as a whole.

Whether in these two books we have the whole of this great historical treatise as projected by its author is more doubtful. It may fairly be contended, indeed, that the two, taken together, meet all that is required by the terms of the general preface (Luke i. 1-4). What seems to be promised there is, briefly, a comprehensive, accurate, orderly history of the origins of Christianity brought down to date—such a history (to use its own words) as will supply a satisfactory basis for confidence with respect to those matters which had been (at the time of writing) consummated among Christians. Clearly the writer's mind was occupied with a feeling that Christianity had accomplished great things in the world. It had reached a stage of development which could be looked upon as a consummation, and back from which its history could be surveyed as a process leading up to this goal. His point of sight, accordingly, cannot be supposed to be taken merely from the ascension of our Lord: this marked rather the time of the entrance of Christianity into the world than an advanced stage of its progress. He was evidently looking back over a considerable past in which much that was notable had occurred, in which Christianity had wrought out a history in some sense complete, worth the labor of ascertaining with exactitude, and worthy of a grateful record. There seems no such stringent reason, however, why his point of sight may not be supposed to be taken from the completion of the great work of Paul, as apostle of the Gentiles, as marked, say, at least potentially, by his arrival at Rome and his two years of unhindered preaching of the gospel in the capital of the world. The spectacle laid before us in the Book of Acts, of the rapid advance of the gospel from its starting-point, and the progressive establishment of the Christian Church in the great centers of population and influence from Jerusalem to Rome, may well be thought accomplishment enough to satisfy whatever sense of the attainment of great things may be thought to underlie the calm but pregnant words of this preface.

Nevertheless, on closer scrutiny, it does not seem likely

that these two books constitute the whole treatise which the author had it in mind to write. We observe the Book of Acts to come to a close after a fashion quite similar to the closing of the Gospel of Luke; and it has all, and more, of the same suggestion of something yet to follow. In fact, if the manner in which the Gospel ends would seem abrupt and unsatisfying on the supposition that it was the absolute end of the story, much more is this true of the manner in which Acts ends. Here the reader has had his expectation kept on the strain through many chapters for the climax of the visit to Rome (xix. 21; xxiii. 11; xxv. 11, 21, 25; xxvii. 24; xxviii. 14-16; cf. Rom. i. 10-15; xv. 22-29) and his interest has been apparently purposely fixed especially upon the approaching trial of Paul before the emperor of the world (xxv. 10; xxvii. 24). Yet when the culmination of the whole story is reached—absolutely nothing is made of it. Paul reaches Rome, calls the leaders of the Jewish community there to a conference—apparently with a view to ascertaining whether they had been primed from Jerusalem to press for his condemnation—and then the trial itself is not even mentioned; and all that the reader had been led to believe the attainment of his long cherished desire to reach Rome meant to Paul drops utterly out of sight. The book closes abruptly with a brief notice that he preached two whole years in Rome without molestation. These two years, it must be remembered, were already over when this account was written: a change in Paul's condition had taken place; the author knew whether the issue had been the release or the execution of his hero. Could he have intended to leave his readers uninformed of this issue by even the slightest hint? It seems incredible that the work should close thus. But that the Book should so close lies quite in the nature of the case and is in the closest analogy with the way in which the Gospel of Luke, the First Book of this history, is brought to its close. It seems exceedingly probable, therefore, that a Third Book was to follow, opening—somewhat after the fashion in which Acts opens with reference to Luke—with a detailed account of Paul's work in Rome, of his trial and release; and thence carrying the story of the foundation of Christianity in the world on up to the consummation originally intended and hinted at in the preface set at the head of the Gospel of Luke. All that is strange in this otherwise very strange ending of the book passes away on the simple hypothesis that it is only the Second Book of the history, and not the history itself, that closes with the close of Acts.

And now we observe that in his description of this Book, the author has himself really told us that it does not bring the whole work to a conclusion. For, in the opening verse of Acts, he does not, as our English version misrepresents him, speak of the *"Former* Book" but rather of the *"First* Book" of his treatise as already in the hands of Theophilus: and there is no reason to suspect that this language is not employed with sufficient precision to distinguish between the implication of "former" and "first." Let us add, further, that the hints in this preface of the scope of the remainder of the history seem to hold out a broader promise than the Book of Acts meets; so that we should be justified on this ground in believing that a Third Book was probably to follow the two we have, in order that there might be recorded in it the rest of what Jesus continued to do and to teach through his servants, after he was received up, until witness had been borne him even "unto the uttermost part of the earth." It is idle, of course, to speculate minutely as to the proposed contents of this projected Third Book. We can be sure it was to begin with an account of Paul's work in Rome and of his trial there and its issue. We can be sure also that it was to continue with such a narrative of the work of Jesus in establishing his Church in the world as would not only bring the story "up to date," but round it out as a complete whole, calculated to convey the impression of a definite attainment of Christianity, as is suggested in the preface to Luke. But it is hidden from us whether this continued narrative was to follow in the main the work of Paul and throw its stress on the development of the Church in organization and efficiency (which seems most probable); or whether (as is at least possible) it was to revert to the work of the other apostles and exhibit the extension of the Church to the east and south of Jerusalem through their labors, thus giving us a completer view of the place occupied by Christianity in the world at the point of time set by the writer as his *terminus ad quem*. It is enough, meanwhile, to be assured that a Third Book was contemplated; and that our Book of Acts is not to be looked upon as a complete treatise upon even apostolic history, but only as the middle section of a great historical work, projected but never completed, which was to contain the story of the beginnings of Christianity, with a view especially to exhibiting its divine origin and mission and its divine fitting for the great work committed to it.

It is only a particular portion of this comprehensive program, that the section of the work included within its Second Book— our Book of Acts—is intended to carry out. Speaking *sub specie temporis*, we may perhaps say that the First Book—our Gospel of Luke—was devoted to the preparation for the Church of Christ: the Second Book—our Book of Acts—to the establishment of the Church in the Roman Empire with its center in the capital city: while, perhaps, we may not unfitly suppose that the Third Book was to exhibit the equipment of that Church for its great function in the world. But the author of the work, it must be clearly noted, does not himself look at the matter *sub specie temporis*. By him the whole development is conceived *sub specie aeternitatis*. Accordingly, he puts the matter thus (Acts i. 1): The First Book treats of all that Jesus began to do and to teach until the day on which he was taken up; the two subsequent Books were, therefore, to treat of all that Jesus continued to do and to teach after his ascension. To him, thus, this second section of his history was not the "Acts of the Apostles," except in so far as the apostles may be conceived as the instruments through whom Jesus prosecuted his work of establishing his Church in the world. It was specifically the Acts of the Risen Christ. It is, therefore, that it begins with an account of the forty days which Jesus spent with his disciples after his resurrection, and of the ascension itself, which brought them to a close by his session on the throne of his power; this whole account having been purposely held over from the Gos-

pel, and here so ordered as to throw into relief the relation of
the events recorded rather to what was yet to come than to
what was already past. It is therefore, also, that the baptism
of the Holy Spirit is particularly dwelt upon in this account,
and that the narrative hastens on to the record of the descent
of the Spirit on the great day of Pentecost, when "the promise
of the Father" came and the nascent Church was endowed for
its work with a supernatural power, or rather with a supernatural
Agent. It is therefore, again, that at every step in the progress of
the history, explicit stress is laid upon its divine direction; and
not only is the course of the narrative studded with references
to the hand of God as the real factor operative in the production
of the several stages of advance, but the whole course of the
history itself is represented as in every step a product of direct
divine leading. It has been sometimes imagined that the
miraculous element might be sifted out from the Book of Acts
and a residuum for a natural history of the origins of Christianity left. Nothing could be more impossible. This, not
merely because the miracles recorded are inseparably interwoven with the narrative, and the whole must be taken or the
whole left; but much more because the whole history is conceived from a supernatural point of view, and developed as a
distinctively supernatural product. To the author of Acts the
Church was not established in the Roman Empire by the self-
directed efforts of men who wrought no doubt with the divine
approval, and enjoyed a high measure of the divine favor, and
were, therefore, aided in their arduous labors by the divine
power, intruded here and there to rescue them from special dangers or to give them at particular crises special acceptance in the
eyes of men. It was established by the constant and unintermit-
tent activity of the Lord Jesus, sitting on the throne of the universe and ordering the course of history according to his will, so
that the whole development is to be conceived as a supernatural
work.

It cannot surprise us, therefore, that the program of the work
is derived from a heavenly source, and that it seeks to present
the history as the sheer unfolding of the announced purpose of

the risen Lord. It does not seem to be going too far to discover
something very like the formal announcement of its theme in
Luke xxiv. 47 and Acts i. 8—our Lord's prophetic announcement that after "the promise of the Father" had been received
by his followers, repentance and remission of sins were to be
preached in his name "unto all the nations, beginning with Jerusalem"; or, more specifically, that his followers should receive
power when the Holy Ghost had come upon them, and should
be his witnesses, "both in Jerusalem and in all Judea and
Samaria, and unto the uttermost part of the earth." It is
certainly much in the manner of this author to prepare the way
for his detailed treatment by anticipatory communications of
this sort; and the more specific of these announcements seems
to supply, in the transformed shape of narrative, the place
of the second member of the sentence in which he had begun
to contrast the two Books of his treatise, and therefore appears
to be in effect a formal description of his intention with reference to the Second Book. In fine, there is every reason to
suspect that, by his careful and prominent record of these predictions of the risen Jesus, the author wished to forecast the
outline of the narrative upon which he was about to enter. And
certainly the actual contents of the Book as it lies before us encourage this suspicion, and justify us at least in saying (as it has
been admirably phrased) that the terms of our Lord's promise
"implicitly involve a table of contents" of the Book. "Ye shall
receive power when the Holy Ghost is come upon you (Acts
ii. 1-13), and ye shall be my witnesses—both in Jerusalem
(ii. 14–viii. 1); and in all Judea and Samaria (viii. 1–xii. 25);
and unto the uttermost part of the earth" (xiii. 1–xxviii. 31).
The last of these topics, to be sure, is not exhausted in this
Book. There is a sense, no doubt, in which even it, though
not "actually," is yet "potentially" carried to its conclusion.
In Paul's journey to Rome and unhindered preaching there and
in the consequent firm footing obtained for Christianity "in the
metropolis of the human race, the stronghold of heathendom,"
we may unquestionably see such an earnest of the end afforded
as will "leave no doubt of its ultimate accomplishment." But

there is a certain subtlety in so conceiving the author's meaning which appears foreign to his method. We seem to be pointed by this forward look not so much to history as yet incompletely unrolled as to a Third Book of records, in which, we can scarcely doubt, a course of events was set down which afforded at least a fuller earnest of the complete accomplishment of the great promise. In any event, however, the purpose of the author seems to have been to portray the history of the Christian Church as the fulfilment of our Lord's prophetic outline.

The common view of the disposition of the book, therefore, is a very close transcript of the author's intention. It seems naturally to fall into three parts, the narrative revolving in turn about Jerusalem, Antioch, and Rome, as the opening, middle, and end points in the development of the history. The progress thus runs in ever widening circles—at each shifting of the center a point on the periphery of the preceding circle becoming the center of its enlarged successor. The circle swept from Rome as a center is left, indeed, for the Third Book; the narrative of the Second Book closing with the attainment of this new center. Within its limits the whole progress of the movement up to the establishment of the Church in this third center of its development—which was at the same time the center of the world—is unfolded. The Book of Acts, then, in effect, gives us not so much the history of the spread of the Church—much that would necessarily enter into such a history is omitted—as the history of the establishment of the Church successively (or perhaps we should say, progressively) in the three great centers, Jerusalem, Antioch, Rome; and the movement of the narrative falls into complete order only when it is looked at from this point of view. First we have explained to us the process by which the Church was firmly established in Jerusalem (i. 1–viii. 1). Then the radiation of the Church from Jerusalem is described, working up to the firm establishment of a new center for its activities at Antioch (viii. 1–xii. 25). Lastly, the missionary circuits from Antioch as a center are described, culminating in the establishment of a new center at Rome (xiii. 1–xxviii. 31). The author's effort seems to be in each case, to trace out the factors that co-operated in obtaining for the Church a firm footing and center of development in these three great centers in turn. His narrative thus advances in something like a spiral movement steadily upwards towards its goal.

Following out this conception of the general scheme more into detail, we shall obtain something like the following table of contents for the book:

II

In the January number of *The Bible Student*, we obtained some insight into the outline of the Book of Acts. In filling out this outline the author fulfils his promise of an orderly narrative. The order of narration is not always, to be sure, chronological. He permits himself, for instance, freely to illustrate a period by parallel instances (e.g., viii–xi); and he uses the device of general statements afterwards illustrated in one or more of their parts by particular instances. Yet he is careful of chronological sequences and writes with a clear and firm grasp upon the actual line of development. Very few points of contact occur with the course of events in the secular world, from which we may calculate an absolute chronology for the history. The whole action of the Book is included between the ascension of our Lord and the release of Paul from his first imprisonment: and these two events may be dated with some confidence A.D. 30 and 63 respectively. The time actually covered by the story, therefore, is just that 33 year period which we conventionally ascribe to a generation, and corresponds as nearly as possible with the time covered by the First Book of this history—the life of Jesus having extended to about 33 years. Just at the close of the second period of the history as here depicted, when the establishment of a new church-center at Antioch had been accomplished and the series of events was about to begin which ended in the shifting of the center finally to Rome (Acts xii), there is introduced an account of the death of Herod Agrippa I, which fell in A.D. 44. Between A.D. 30 and A.D. 44, therefore, the action of the first twelve chapters is to be distributed. Of more importance in fixing the chronology, would be the accession of Festus to the procuratorship of Judea, which is mentioned toward the close of the book (Acts xxv. 1), if we could only be absolutely sure of the date of that event. On the whole, A.D. 60 seems its most probable date. From this point we can work back by the aid of fairly continuous notices of time-intervals to the Council of Acts xv; and for the period before that we receive aid from certain chronological hints in the Epistle to the Galatians (i. 18; ii. 1). Other allusions to events of secular history—such as the dominion of Aretas over Damascus (ix. 25), the great famine (xi. 28), the edict of Claudius expelling the Jews from Rome (xviii. 2), the proconsulship of Gallio in Achaia (xviii. 12), supply only a series of general checks to the adjustments thus arrived at. The following chronological scheme for the history here recorded is thus suggested:

A.D. 30.   The Ascension of the Lord .... Acts i
A.D. 34-35.   The Conversion of Paul .... Acts ix
A.D. 44-45.   Paul's (Second) Visit to Jerusalem .... Acts xii
A.D. 47-48.   Paul's First Missionary Journey .... Acts xiii, xiv
A.D. 50-51.   The Council at Jerusalem .... Acts xv
A.D. 51-53.   Paul's Second Missionary
             Journey .... Acts xv. 40–xviii. 22
A.D. 54-58.   Paul's so-called Third Missionary
             Journey .... Acts xviii. 23
A.D. 58.   Paul's Arrest .... Acts xxi. 27
A.D. 60.   The Accession of Festus .... Acts xxiv. 27
A.D. 61.   Paul's Arrival at Rome .... Acts xxviii. 16
A.D. 63.   End of Paul's Imprisonment .... Acts xxviii. 30

It is immediately evident from even a cursory survey of the plan and contents of the book, that it is no dry and colorless chronicle, recording the facts as they occurred without further interest in any of them. Not all the facts that took place during the period covered by this narrative have been given a place in it; nor even all that came under the notice of the author. The Epistles of Paul, for example, supply facts in his life of the utmost interest, which are not recorded in Acts. It is quite plain that a very rigid selection has been employed and only those facts have been made use of that fell in with the purpose the writer had in view; and those that have been made use of have been given prominence according to a very keen sense of proportion and value, measured again, of course, with respect to this purpose. If this is what is intended by ascribing "tendency" to a book, this book is undoubtedly a tendential writing— as is every historical work whose author rises above the mere mechanical cataloguing of events and seeks to understand them and to convey his convictions as to their significance to his readers. It is more usual to speak of a book written out of so clear a conception of the drift of the history as Acts exhibits, and marshaling its material with such skill with a view to conveying this conception to its readers, as a historical treatise of the first rank, whose view of the progress and meaning of the stretch of history it records is worth inquiring into.

The conception which this author entertained of the history of the apostolic age is too clearly conveyed to be easily missed, and in its main traits has been already cursorily suggested. He saw in it, above everything else, the continued activity of the Lord Jesus Christ, establishing his Church in the Roman Empire. Nothing is more characteristic of his presentation of it than his supernaturalism. It is primarily this that gives unity to his view of its course, and color to his handling of its details. The whole history is unfolded by him as the evolution of the divine plan, under the immediate direction of the divine hand. Closely connected with this pervasive supernaturalism is the universalism of the narrative. The divine plan of which the history is treated as the unfolding is announced at the outset as involving a distinct universalism (Luke xxiv. 47; Acts i. 8); and the writer makes it his business—we might almost say his primary concern—not only carefully to trace the steps by which this universalism was actually realized, but also to exhibit with the utmost clearness its essential implication in every stage of the developing history. This involves, naturally, a theological attitude, since the universalism of the gospel depends on a conception of the terms of salvation. It is, therefore, not surprising that an attachment to the Pauline doctrine of justification is traceable in the very fabric of the history.

Three further traits of the author's conception of the history stand in close relation to this fundamental design. The most important of these is what has been miscalled his "conciliatory tendency." He undoubtedly conceived the history as having developed in a right line, and the final universal outcome as having lain implicitly in the situation from the beginning. And it lay in the very nature of an attempt to exhibit this orderly development that the implicit universalism of the early stages and of the early teachers should be drawn out as clearly as possible. The inevitable effect of this is to throw the differences in details that may have existed between the several stages of growth, or between the successive leaders of the movement, more or less into the background in comparison with their more important agreements; and so, perhaps, to produce a superficial appearance of an attempt to harmonize conflicting elements or views. A similar origin has produced also the trait which has sometimes been spoken of as an "apologetical tendency." It is so far real that the narrative is undoubtedly directed to supply a historical account, and therefore justification, of the course of development taken by the Church under the leading of Paul. To the author, Paul is unquestionably the great hero of the early Church as it was formed and given shape and character by Paul's teaching. The Pauline Church in the Roman Empire is, in a word, the consummation whose divine origin and formation he has undertaken historically to exhibit; and of course, he makes it his business to justify every step by which this consummation was attained, as the divinely led explication of what was implicit in the Church from the beginning. This naturally makes his history in a sense an apology for Gentile Christianity—for the Christianity of Paul: only he obviously conceives himself as exhibiting this as the teaching of the facts simply and truly related, and not as artificially imposing it upon them. Somewhat more remotely is what has been called the "political tendency" of the book also the outgrowth of its fundamental standpoint. It was not from the universalizing empire, but from narrow racialism that the Church was at first in danger. A certain implicit sympathy existed between the universalism of Rome and the universalism of the Pauline Church, by which they were made in some sense natural allies. A sense of this seems impressed upon the narrative, which appears to lay some stress on the fact that the Church had spread through the Roman Empire without coming into serious conflict with it, and was thus exhibiting itself as an affair of the empire—that is, not a provincial but a world phenomenon, proclaiming a gospel to be preached "in all creation under heaven." The apparent care with which the freedom of the Church from all complications with the Roman state, and even a favorable attitude toward it on the part of the Roman officials is suggested, may, to be sure, have had an immediate apologetic intent, and may be meant to carry a plea for continued relations of amity, if not of alliance, between the two. If so, however, this is assuredly secondary. The main significance of this phenomenon lies, we may be sure, in the recognition on the author's part of the contrasting effects of the Church's actual universalism on the representatives of national exclusiveness, on the one side, and of universal empire, on the other.

There is one further trait, not so much of the author's conception of the history, as of his presentation of it, which attracts attention at this point. We refer to his strong artistic instinct. This has, no doubt, conditioned somewhat both his selection and his use of his materials, and has thus become a not unimportant factor in the molding of his narrative. We see it at work, for example, in the choice of the incidents by which, in his opening chapters, he seeks to convey a vivid impression of the "formation and maturing of a mother church, a model church within the precincts of the Holy City." This is accomplished by an artistically arranged alternating series of disturbances and trials, from without and from within, by which the infant Church was purified and hardened (chaps. iii–vii). We may see it at work, again, in the parallel which can be traced to a certain very obvious extent (but by no means throughout) in the recorded experiences of Peter and Paul, suggestive somewhat of the art of Plutarch's *Parallel Lives*. It is particularly visible, however, in the multitude of graphic details which are introduced, in the incorporation of the very speeches delivered by the actors on this or that important occasion, and in the vigorous touches that enliven and give force to the whole narrative. There lies in these graphic touches a hint of the intense personal interest with which the author prosecuted his task of composition; and it is not surprising that he sometimes seems to have inserted details or lingered over incidents, for all that appears, chiefly because of his own lively interest in them. From a strictly aesthetic point of view (as also from the point of view of strictly "scientific" history), this tendency to permit his own interest, now and then, so to speak, to run away with him, to the injury of a nicely calculated proportion, may possibly be considered a flaw; but it adds a trait of naturalness to the narrative which is as charmingly human as it is calculated to increase the reader's confidence in a narrative so obviously written out of the heart.

Considered merely as a piece of literary composition, thus, the work shows a breadth of conception, a grasp of the historical situation, a command of its material, a firmness of handling, a faculty of graphic narration, and an artistic instinct and human interest which must place it among the world's great examples of historical composition. Considered, on the other hand, as a historical document, it evinces itself by every test we can apply to be a remarkably accurate transcript of the facts with which it deals, and a thoroughly trustworthy account of the course of the events which it portrays. The geographical, historical, and topographical tests for which its subject-matter affords opportunity are exceptionally numerous and varied; and the result of their application is to evince what must be called a wonderful exactitude both of formal statement and of incidental allusion. The narrative carries us into the intimate life of a multitude of communities scattered through the whole East—Palestine, Syria, Asia Minor, Greece—and then to Rome. Amid all the complicated conditions and changeable circumstances of the times it portrays, it moves with firm and sure step. Geographical, topographical, political details positively swarm in his pages; but the author seems never to have been betrayed into an error. The personages he introduces act thoroughly in character, and, when known from other sources, are recognizably themselves in his pages. The speeches, for example, which he records, reproduce not only the characteristic ideas of their authors, but their very diction and linguistic peculiarities. James, Peter, Paul speak in the Acts, each with the same accent with which we are made familiar by their extant epistles. This is the more remarkable as there is no trace of the use of these epistles by the author of the Acts. So far as his narrative is concerned, we should not know that a single one of them was in existence. Nevertheless, there is room for all of them that were written during the time covered by it, within the compass of his narrative; and a comparison of their incidental allusions to events with the narrative of Acts exhibits such a mass of what are called "undesigned coincidences" as affords a fresh basis of confidence in its trustworthiness. In short, the ability of Acts as a literary composition is fairly matched by its value as a record of facts; and its claim to recognition as a history of the first rank is rooted no more firmly in its clear conception of its task and strong and artistic handling of its material than in its evident possession and faithful use of excellent first-hand sources of information.

Inquiring more closely into the nature of the sources which the author had at his command, our attention is, of course, called in the first instance to the circumstance that certain passages occur in the course of the narrative which are couched in the first person, as if the author were also an actor in the scenes described. These famous "we-passages" embrace sections in the narrative of Paul's second and (so-called) third missionary journeys, including the final journey to Jerusalem and to Rome (xvi. 10-17; xx. 5-15; xxi. 1-18; xxvii. 1–xxviii. 16); and their contents fully bear out the natural implication of the use of the first personal pronoun. They are obviously the description by an eye-witness of experiences in which he had borne a personal part, written with all the vividness and detailed exactness natural in these circumstances. The author of the Book of Acts, at the least, therefore, certainly had access to what may not unfitly be called a journal of one of the companions of the Apostle Paul. These sections of his narrative excerpted from this journal (if that is the proper way to account for them) are the immediate composition of an eye-witness of the events recorded: and the mere fact of the author's access to such a journal raises the query whether he may not have derived much more of his material, especially that concerned with the work of Paul, from the same, or from some equally good source. But here another fact of the first importance imposes itself upon our notice. It develops upon examination that these "we-passages" not only contain cross-references to other parts of the narrative, but in manner, diction, stylistic, and linguistic peculiarities, differ in no respect from the remainder of the Book of Acts or the Gospel of Luke. Despite minor distinctions, obviously arising from variations in subject and underlying differences of sources, the whole book, from a literary point of view, is of a piece; and it is unreasonable to doubt that the author of the "we-passages" is the author also of the entire book. It becomes at once clear, therefore, that the author of the book comes forward in these "we-passages" as himself a companion of Paul, and marks by the change of person his presence at or absence from the transactions described. All the phenomena support this certainly eminently reasonable—or perhaps we should say, almost necessary—supposition.

But in the recognition of this fact the problem of the sources of information for the history takes on a new complexion. For a considerable portion of the work of Paul—the portion described in the "we-passages"—the author was himself an eyewitness and a primary source. For the remainder of the work of that apostle, his long and intimate companionship with Paul, and his association with others of Paul's companions, provided him with the best conceivable means of information. Nor need we stop here. We learn that the author of the "we-passages," who is also the author of the whole book, accompanied Paul on his last visit to Jerusalem; abode, along with him, "many days" in the house of Philip at Caesarea; lodged with him with one of the "primitive disciples" named Mnason, on the way up to the city; was taken by Paul with him "unto James" and made known to "all the elders" of the Church at Jerusalem; and was still with him when, two years later, he sailed from Caesarea for Rome—apparently having lived with him in the cradle-region of Christianity throughout the whole intervening time. Nor must we forget the opportunities he must have had, as a companion of Paul for so long a period, for intercourse with others of his companions (say, for example, John Mark, the "interpreter" of Peter) who were intimately acquainted with the history of the Church from the beginning. He enjoyed, in short, every conceivable opportunity to collect from the actors themselves authentic information as to the origins of the Christian Church.

The Book of Acts comes to us, therefore, from the hand of one whom we know to have been in long-continued and intimate contact with the primary sources of information for the matters with which it deals, and who, according to his own account, borne out by the results, made it his business to "trace the course of all things accurately from the first." It is in the strictest sense of the word, therefore, history at first hand. This is curiously illustrated by a fact which would otherwise be puzzling—the fact, to wit, already incidentally alluded to, that the epistles of Paul, for example, are not put under contribution by the author as a source for his history. Only a writer in possession of more immediate, and, so to say, better sources of information could have ventured to neglect Paul's own letters in drawing up an account of his missionary labors. A late writer could not possibly have done so: or had he essayed it, could not possibly have avoided contradicting their data. Thus a phenomenon seemingly strange in itself receives its adequate explanation from the circumstances of the case. Paul's letters were not used by this author, for the very sufficient reason that they were not needed. He had even more direct means of information at his command, and comes before us as a co-witness with Paul's letters to the life and labors of the apostle, rather than as dependent on their testimony for knowledge of the events of his life.

III

In the February number of *The Bible Student*, we learned that the Book of Acts was certainly written by a close companion of the Apostle Paul. Who this companion of Paul was, we could scarcely learn from Acts itself. But the unanimous voice of early tradition identifies him with "the beloved physician, Luke," of whom the apostle speaks in his later epistles as a specially trusted fellow laborer (Col. iv. 14; Philem. 24; 2 Tim. iv. 11); and to this must be added the weight of the equally consistent tradition that its companion book, the Gospel of Luke, came from Luke's hands. The very obscurity of Luke increases the credibility of this tradition. Pure invention might well have selected an apostle, or at least "some great one" to whom to attribute the authorship of so substantial a portion of the New Testament. But it would scarcely have singled out a person who would have been unknown even by name, save for passing allusions in the closing words of two or three later epistles. Still further weight is added to it by the thorough fitting in of the allusions to Luke in these epistles with the implications of the "we-passages"—a thing that cannot be said of either Timothy or Silas or Titus, to whom modern speculation has pointed as alternative possibilities. It would seem that if we do not assign the book to Luke, there is no one to whom we can assign it; and it does not appear likely that the authorship of such an important duad of works could have utterly perished from the memory of the early Church. Let us add that the diction of these books is redolent of the phraseology in vogue among the Greek medical writers; which again points to Luke, "the beloved physician," as its author. There are thus no internal considerations to break the force of the historical attestation; but all the internal indications, on the contrary, fall well in with it. The matter is not of the first importance; but a natural interest attaches to singling out the very person to whom we owe so important a portion of the New Testament.

Little is added by the passages in Paul's epistles in which Luke is mentioned, to what is revealed to us of his personality in his own writings. We learn that he was of Gentile origin, a native possibly of Philippi, a physician by profession—and, let it be noted, apparently a practising physician during the period of his companionship with Paul, and therefore the first medical missionary. He seems to have joined Paul first at Troas, in the midst of the second missionary journey, and to have accompanied him to Philippi. There he appears to have remained until Paul's return to Philippi in the course of his so-called third missionary journey (A.D. 58), and to have gone with him to Jerusalem and thence to Rome. He seems to have remained with the apostle at Rome until his release. During the second imprisonment of the apostle he is again found by his side at Rome (2 Tim. iv. 11)—but this is beyond the limits of the history as presented to us in the two Books which alone he was enabled to finish. Tradition adds nothing trustworthy to these meager facts.

A good deal of the significance of an inquiry into the date at which the Book of Acts was written is evacuated by the identification of its author with a companion of Paul, who had enjoyed exceptional advantages for informing himself of the details of the early history of Christianity. No matter when he actually worked his *collectanea* into this highly organized treatise, it is first-hand information he is giving us, wrought into shape by one who had not only been at pains to trace the course of all things accurately from the first, but had meditated deeply on the sequences and significances of the history as a whole. Nevertheless, it is not merely an idle question when the book was written. Certain difficulties in understanding it—as, for example, its relation to the epistles of Paul—seem to be increased by carrying it down to a late date. It would become very hard, if not impossible, to account for the entire absence of allusions to their very existence, to say nothing of the omission of many details of Paul's experiences recorded in these epistles, if the book be thought to have been put into shape at a time when these epistles had for nearly a generation been the sole source of information about Paul's work accessible to the churches, which had long been lovingly studied and had created a tradition concerning it. It is far easier to understand Luke's entire detachment from them as sources of his narrative, if he wrote not merely as a contemporary, but actually contemporaneously with them—knowing of them, of course, so far as they were in existence when he wrote, but looking upon them rather as sent out from his circle than to his circle.

There is very little in the Book of Acts itself to suggest a date for its composition, and what there is certainly does not point to one late in the century. It contains no allusion to any event whatever occurring later than the scope of its own narrative. We cannot, to be sure, infer from its abrupt close, with a bare reference to Paul's two years' preaching in Rome, that it was written immediately at the expiry of those two years: for this abrupt close is only a finger-post pointing us to a Third Book which was to carry the narrative further. But there is little in the Book to suggest a much later date for it. Almost the only hint that has weight in this direction is derived from the character of the "we-passages." These are so full of detail of an inherently unimportant kind as to create a suspicion that they may be excerpts from a journal, incorporated without substantial alteration into a later narrative. There is a problem raised by this phenomenon which has not yet received a perfectly satisfactory solution. Perhaps the key to it is to be found in recognizing a trait of the author's manner which has already been adverted to—a tendency, that is, to permit the keenness of his own personal interest sometimes to sway his choice of material. Possibly, this tendency being fully allowed for, we need not suspect that these passages rest at all on written sources: and the passing over of such written sources as Paul's letters in favor of oral means of acquiring information, fall in with this supposition. It is questionable whether a very few years—six or seven, say—may not, in any event, suffice to meet the whole force of this consideration.

Everything else, certainly, points to a date of composition only a few years at most removed from the events last recorded. The considerations leading may critics to seek a later date are derived chiefly from the supposition that the record in the Gospel of Luke of our Lord's prophecy of the destruction of Jerusalem, is so phrased as to imply that this had already taken place when the record was made. And as the Second Book of the treatise must have been written subsequently to the First, this would carry its composition down to a date not earlier than, say, A.D. 80. This argument appears, however, to be somewhat strained, and, one may suspect, rests ultimately on a certain chariness in allowing the reality of very detailed predictive prophecy. There seems to be in Luke's record of this prediction really nothing to suggest a date for it later than A.D. 70, which could not be applied similarly to Matthew's record, or indeed to Daniel's original prophecy. On the other hand, it seems that a reference to Luke's Gospel can scarcely be eliminated from 1 Tim. v. 18, without resort to very artificial interpretation; and if this reference be allowed, it is quite certain that Luke's Gospel was written prior to the date of that epistle— say, A.D. 68. Acts would naturally follow after no very extended interval. On the whole it seems not unlikely that the Gospel was written either during the long stay of Paul and his companions at Caesarea, when leisure would naturally be found for much that would have been difficult to accomplish during the course of the more active years that immediately preceded; or else during the two years of imprisonment at Rome: and that Acts was written possibly before Paul's death, say, during the second imprisonment at Rome; or at all events, not long after it, as certain early Christian writers (Irenaeus, for example) affirm. The manner in which the book closes renders it certain that it was not written until after Paul's release from his first imprisonment: but there is no hint of his death. At the time when it was written a Third Book was in contemplation; and it is natural to suppose that enough time had elapsed since Paul's arrival in Rome to supply the material which it was intended to incorporate in it. But events hastened in those formative days. And it would appear that from a standpoint of A.D. 67 or 68, there would be accumulation enough to justify the contemplation of another Book. In any event, we cannot argue confidently from the conjecture that the Third Book was to be differentiated from the Second chiefly by the period covered by it. The possibility lies open that the difference lay in the main in the topics treated—say, the organization of the churches and their fitting for their function as permanent wit-

nesses of Christ in the world; or the progress of the gospel in
the rest of the world through the labors of the rest of the
apostles. On the whole, the earlier the date assigned to the
book, the better are its phenomena accounted for; and the
most likely time would seem to be the months just preceding
or just succeeding Paul's execution.

The revelation of the author's personality on the other hand
adds zest to the observation of the literary manner, style, and
diction of the book, which correspond rather remarkably with
what might be expected of the person who wrote it. Occasion
has already arisen for speaking of the strong flavor of medical
phraseology which pervades its whole language. It is scarcely
possible that anyone but a physician would have written just
as this book is written. It is just as obviously the production
of a Greek, and of an educated gentleman. The Greek instinct
for the sea, for example, is continually in evidence. It is clearly
a landsman that is writing; but a landsman habituated to think
of human intercourse in the terms of a seafaring people. Thus,
for example, he is always careful to mention the ports of the
towns which he visited. On the other hand, he describes the
management of a ship, the incidents of a voyage, and the be-
havior of a vessel in the sea after a fashion that suggests one
dependent on what he heard about him for his terms and modes
of expression. The ease with which he takes up the language of
sailors is perhaps a hint of the versatile talent of his race.
Certainly, throughout the book there is apparent what we may
perhaps call a remarkable transparency of diction; through
which continually shine the traits of the particular sources
(oral or written) which are for the time being drawn upon.
Thus a great variety is introduced into the underlying tint of
the narrative, despite its essential unity in language and diction.
The contrast thus induced, for example, between the opening
and the closing chapters is very marked and corresponds with
the change of moral and spiritual atmosphere (as it has been
happily phrased) from the Hebrew beginning to the Hellenic
end of the history. These variations of tone, nicely adjusted
as they are to the gradually changing conditions of the Church,

are obviously not due to calculated artifice, but to the sensitiveness of the author's feeling for language, under the influence of which his own speech insensibly takes on the tint of the sources used.

Were the book written in the formal language of the schools, no doubt the influence of its sources upon its diction would have been far less marked. But this is not at all the case. Of the fashionable rhetorical devices of the day—the elaborate structure of sentences, the parallelisms and rhythms of clauses —that had been set in vogue by the Greek Sophists, it exhibits no trace. It is written throughout rather in the simple language of educated conversation, and exhibits all the flexibility and transparency of that most versatile of vehicles. The English version scarcely does justice to it in this respect, and throws over it a veil of far too formal, not to say stately, diction. To revert from it to the Greek often brings a little shock, until adjustment is made anew to the clear, rapid, flexible, but somewhat familiar tone of its more conversational manner.

Another trait of the method of the book is possibly due in part to the author's mental habits as an educated physician. We refer to the place accorded in his presentation to the mere hard facts. He is not much given to reflections; nor does he often pause to point out the working of causes or their nexus with their effects. He appears to feel that if the facts are duly and clearly set down in their proper relations, they may be safely left to tell their own story. Few books at all events, even among historical treatises, have ever been written which are so compact of the bare facts. And it is a great testimony to Luke's genius that he has been able to produce by this method not a chronicle, or dry body of collections, but a treatise of the first rank, vivid, vital, and vitalizing, conveying with clearness and force the conception of the historical development which he had himself formed. The essentials of the highest dramatic talent are latent in such a performance.

The value of the Book of Acts is not exhausted, however, when we note its excellence as a piece of literature or its importance as a historical document. It commands our admiration as literature. It is precious to the student of ancient history, and preserves for him probably the most trustworthy and vivid picture that has come down to us of the conditions of social life in the Eastern provinces at about the middle of the first century of our era. To the sacred historian it is inestimable, as the sole authentic history of the planting and early training of the Church. But above all these claims upon our attention, it can urge this supreme one—that it has come down to us as a portion of those sacred writings, which are able to make men wise unto salvation, through faith in Christ Jesus. From the very beginning of its history it has held a secure place in the Christian canon. The First Book of the treatise of which it is a part is, indeed, attested by Paul himself (1 Tim. v. 18), as standing along with Deuteronomy among the "Scriptures" which bring the Word of God to man; and there is sufficient independent evidence of its own assured place in the same collection to preclude all hesitation in extending this attestation to it also.

In its internal characteristics it justifies the character thus attributed to it. For it is not ordinary history that it offers us. In the strictest sense of the word, it is sacred history. It is even obviously written less in the interests of pure history, than in those of religious edification. The interest Luke feels in the events he recounts, the emotions they arouse in him, communicate themselves to his narrative; he clearly seeks to produce the same emotions in his readers, to set before them examples for their imitation, to communicate to them a religious view of history. The book, as we have seen, takes its standpoint not from earth but from heaven. What it essays to inform us is not how the Church spread from Jerusalem to Antioch and from Antioch to Rome; it is to reveal to us how the risen Jesus has established his Church in the world, and how he is fulfilling his promise to be with his followers to the end of time. As truly as is done by the Apocalypse itself, this book draws aside the veil that we may see in the events of earth, who are the real actors and to what end all things are really tending. This is "revelation." And as the vehicle of such a revelation, the Book of Acts takes its fitting place between the Gospels and the Epistles, and we read it, with no sense of incongruity, within the complex of the Word of God. He who reads it with the heart and understanding also will be led by it to know God better; will by it be more fully taught his power and purpose to save the world; and will be made to feel more profoundly that Jesus Christ is God over all, blessed forever, and that God is in him reconciling the world with himself. And as he reads and ponders, it will be no fault of the book if he does not set his seal to it, as a book which speaks of God, and leads to God, and which doubtless also came from God.

4

THE CANONICITY OF SECOND PETER*

The question which we propose is a purely historical one.
The Canon of the New Testament is a definite collection of
books; 2 Peter is found to occupy a place in it. The question
is, Was it always there, or has it been foisted unrighteously into
a place to which it has no claim? This is a historical question,
and is to be settled on appropriate historical evidence. It is
a question, however, of vast dogmatic interest. Perhaps it may
be said that the settlement of it means the settlement of the
Canon. It is admitted on all hands that the evidence for the
canonicity of 2 Peter is less cogent than that for any other New
Testament book—not, perhaps, less in amount (2 John and
Philemon have less)—but less proportionately to its length
and importance. If the evidence for 2 Peter can be shown to be
sufficient and convincing, therefore, the greater evidence capable of being adduced for the other books will be readily seen to
be of overwhelming power. It is thus of special importance
that we examine with particular care the testimony for it, both
that we may hold correct opinions as to its own authority, and
that we may obtain a practical standard by which to estimate
the strength of the evidence for the other books.

It is essential to the canonicity of a New Testament book
that it should have been given to the Church by the apostles
as of divine authority. But we cannot at this day hear the
apostolic voice in its authorization. Beyond what witness one
apostolic book was to bear to another—as Paul in 1 Tim.

*Southern Presbyterian Review, Jan., 1882, pp. 45-75. Dr. John R.
Mackay says of this "able article" that it was "among the first
of Dr. Warfield's contributions to New Testament studies which
brought its author to the notice of British New Testament scholars"
(Expositors, July, 1922, p. 31).

v. 18 authenticates Luke—and what witness an apostolic book may bear to itself, we cannot appeal at this day to immediate apostolic authorization. In the case of 2 Peter the first of these testimonies fails, and the second is not of itself and by itself sufficient to satisfy doubt, but only when connected with some external presumption that the Epistle may be what it asserts. We have no resource, then, but to seek to resolve the question of its apostolic gift to the Church indirectly. To do this we must make two queries: Is the letter old enough to have been written by an apostle? Has the Church from its beginning held it as a part of the authoritative rule of faith? If these two questions are answered in the affirmative, the presumption is over-whelming that the Church thus from the apostolic age held it to be divine only because it had received it from the apostles as divine. If the internal evidence is found to corroborate this, and no adequate rebutting evidence is produced, the position of the Epistle in the Canon will be seen to be so secure that it will amount to self-stultification to oppose it.

I. EXTERNAL EVIDENCE FOR THE EARLY DATE OF 2 PETER

It is admitted on all hands that the veritable 2 Peter which we now have was, at the opening of the third century, in the hands of Origen. This, indeed, is reiteratedly plain. He not only quotes its words, but he quotes them as Peter's,[1] and as Scripture,[2] he distinguishes it from 1 Peter[3] and combines it as equally Peter's with the first Epistle,[4] he clearly and distinctly names both together.[5] Although, therefore, he mentions the fact that there were some doubts abroad with reference to the Epistle's genuineness, the way in which Origen speaks of the

---

[1]*Comm. in Ep. Ro.* (Migne, IV. 1179): "*Et Petrus in epistola sua dicit* (2 P. i. 2)."

[2]*In Numer. Hom.* (II. 676): "*Et ut ait quodam in loco scriptura* (2 P. ii. 16)."

[3]*Comm. in Matt.*, T. 15 (III. 1333): Ἀπο τε τῆς πρώτης ἐπιστολῆς (1 P. i. 8).

[4]Add to footnote 2 above: "*Et iterum alibi* (1 P. iv. 10)."

[5]Eus. *H. E.*, VI. 25: "Peter left behind one epistle that is ὁμολογουμέ-νην· ἔστω δέ καὶ δευτέραν· ἀμφιβάλλεται γαρ. So also in *Lib. Jesu*, Nov. Hom. 8 (Migne II. 857).

letter and uses it clearly indicates this fact—that it was generally received at this time as Peter's and Scripture. Now, it is not possible to believe that a book so dealt with by Origen was manufactured or first became widely known in his own day. We would *a priori* expect his older contemporary and preceptor, Clement of Alexandria, to have also known it. We are consequently not surprised to find that this was the fact. Eusebius[6] tells us that "Clement, in his 'Outlines,' has given, to speak generally, concise explanations of all the Canonical Scriptures without omitting the disputed books—I mean the Epistle of Jude, and the other catholic Epistles; as well as the Epistle of Barnabas and the so-called Revelation of Peter." This testimony is supported by Cassiodorus[7] and Photius.[8] It may, therefore, be accepted as indubitable and the conclusion drawn confidently that Clement had our 2 Peter probably (or, rather, according to Eusebius, certainly) among the Scriptures, and that he even wrote a commentary on it.

The mass of modern critics would have us believe that this is as far as we can go, and that Clement marks the earliest trace of our Epistle. So Credner and Hilgenfeld expressly, while Bleek and Reuss would go further and throw doubt even on Clement's testimony, and even such men as Alford and Westcott are in uncertainty. Hence Credner can assign its origin, at the earliest, to the beginning of the second century, and Hilgenfeld, at the earliest, to its middle; while Bleek wavers between the two opinions, although inclining to the former. That the later date, as assigned by Hilgenfeld and the majority of his school, is untenable, however, is abundantly evident

---

[6]*H. E.*, VI. 14.

[7]*Institutio Divinarum Scripturarum*, praef. (Cf. c. 8, which must be explained by praef.)

[8]*Bibl. Cod.* 109. He calls the Hypotyposes (or "Outlines") of Clement: Expositions τοῦ θείου Παυλοῦ τῶν ἐπιστολῶν καὶ τῶν καθολικῶν καὶ τοῦ ἐκκλησιαστικοῦ· All sorts of conjectures have been hazarded to explain this last term; plainly it includes the Epistle of Barnabas and Revelation of Peter given in Eusebius' statement. May it be simply a scribe's error for τῶν ἐκκλησιαστικῶν, meaning "the ecclesiastical books" in Rufinus' sense?

from the data already before us. The basis of the opinion is simply the asserted silence of earlier writers; but the precariousness of the argument from silence may be learned from Clement of Alexandria himself. He possessed the letter and wrote a commentary on it—the proof of this is irrefragable; and yet no mention of it, no evidence of his knowledge of it at all secure,[9] can be found in any of his extant writings. This should teach us a lesson as to the value of the argument from silence. On the other hand, it is impossible to square the mere fact that Clement has written a commentary on Second Peter—a book bearing the name of Peter and hence either considered genuine by him, or else a malicious forgery—with the assertion that it was first published during Clement's own lifetime. We may go still further. The usage of the book by Origen is of such a character as, taken in connection with the fact of Clement's commenting on it, to exhibit it as a part of Clement's Canon of Scripture. The further evidence in the case points to the same conclusion. But Clement's Canon was not a private collection, but the same that was held by the whole Church; and the mere fact that the book formed a part of the Church Canon of the later part of the second century throws a strong probability on the supposition that it had always been part of it, and hence was as old as the apostolic age. To feel this we have only to listen to Clement's professions. He declares that he had traveled far and sat under many teachers of many names, and he holds only those books which he had found everywhere clung to as those which had come down from the apostles. If we had no further evidence than Clement's, therefore, a probability of the apostolical origin of 2 Peter would already exist, such as would require some weighty evidence to overturn. The burden of proof would certainly rest on those who denied its canonicity.

---

[9]The passage often adduced, *Cohort. ad Gentes*, p. 66, ed. Sylb., would be a most probable reference, except that it occurs also in Clement of Rome, whence Clement of Alexandria, who used freely the works of his namesake, may have obtained it. See below (the passage adduced from Clement Ro. XXXV. 5).

The question still remains, however, whether the assertion is true that there is no earlier evidence than Clement's for 2 Peter. Reuss hints that "apologists" have gone so far in seeking older witnesses as, in reality, to refer any trace of Christianity in the second century to this Epistle, as if "that century could have obtained Christianity from no other source than 2 Peter." How far this sarcasm is deserved may be best determined by examining the parallels actually adduced by "apologists."

We begin, then, with Irenaeus, an older contemporary of Clement's. In the third book (chapter 1) of his great work against Heresies, we meet with the first seeming allusion. Peter (2 Peter i. 15) had spoken of something that he intended to have done μετὰ τὴν ἐμὴν ἔξοδον. Irenaeus, speaking of *Peter* and Paul, remarks on what happened μετὰ δὲ τὴν τουτῶν ἔξοδον. Now this is a very unusual expression, and in Irenaeus' mouth it has been repeatedly misunderstood. Does it not seem to have been suggested by Peter's words? Reading further, we come in the fourth book (chapter xxxvi. 4) to another passage in which he adduces Noah, then Sodom and Gomorrah, and Lot, to show that God will punish the wicked and save the holy. Our minds go immediately to 2 Peter ii. 4-7, whence the framing of this passage seems to have been derived. Already a presumption for Irenaeus' use of our Epistle is raised. This is lifted to an exceedingly high degree when we read his fifth book (chapter xxviii. 3) and read that the world shall last a thousand years for every day consumed in its creation— ἡ γὰρ ἡμέρα Κυρίου ὡς χίλια ἔτη—a passage which irresistibly suggests 2 Peter iii. 8. There the creation of the world had been discoursed upon (vs. 5), and its destruction (vss. 6 and 7); ὅτι μία ἡμέρα παρὰ Κυρίῳ ὡς χίλια ἔτη. We are told, indeed, that the resemblance is due not to dependence of one upon the other, but a mutual dependence on Ps. xc. 4. But Ps. xc. 4 reads: ὅτι χίλια ἔτη ἐν ὀφθαλμοῖς σου ὡς ἡ ἡμέρα ἡ ἐχθὲς ἥτις διῆλθε, which presents a very diverse, not to say directly opposite thought. The passage in 2 Peter depends on this Psalm and the next clause to that quoted above becomes a quotation from the Psalm. But Irenaeus' statement follows, not the Psalm nor

Peter's quotation from the Psalm, but Peter's *inference* from the Psalm, and that almost verbally; and it seems morally certain that it must have come, directly or indirectly, from 2 Peter. The argument is strengthened by the fact that in V. 23, 2, Irenaeus repeats the same statement, and as coming from a respected source. It seems clear that we are justified in modestly asserting that the probability that Irenaeus possessed 2 Peter amounts to a moral certainty.

It is, indeed, replied that a phrase which occurs in IV. 9, 2, where Irenaeus quotes 1 Peter with the formula, *"Petrus ait in epistola sua,"* excludes any knowledge on the part of the writer of a 2 Peter also. We may waive any question of the genuineness of the words, and answer simply that this may be a very convincing argument against Irenaeus' care and scholarly accuracy in distinguishing the special epistle he meant, but it cannot disprove his knowledge of an epistle which he has elsewhere quoted. It may be astounding to the critics, and yet it is true, that just such a loose method of quoting was most common in Irenaeus' day. Irenaeus certainly knew 2 John—he quotes it explicitly and by name (I. 16, 3, and III. 16, 8)—and yet he quotes 1 John (III. 16, 5 and 8) just as he quotes 1 Peter (*in epistola sua*, ἐν τῇ ἐπιστολῇ). Shall we say that this excludes the knowledge of 2 John? Then again, Cyprian quotes 1 Peter after the same fashion, and yet his correspondent, Firmilian, has no difficulty in quoting 2 Peter in a letter to him. Did these two old hob-nobbing bishops possess distinct and different canons? Still again, at the seventh Council of Carthage, at which Cyprian was present, one bishop is found quoting 1 John as "his epistle," and immediately afterwards Aurelius is represented as quoting 2 John after the same fashion: *"Johannes apostolus in epistola sua poscit, dicens"* (2 John x. 11), so that it appears that not only 1 John but 2 John also, and both together at the same time and place, could be cited in these obnoxious words. Other evidence of the same kind is abundant; but we need only adduce further a clinching fact from Origen, who is able to quote both 1 Peter and 2 Peter with the same formula, as may be seen by referring to the first quotation given from him at the beginning of this paper. The fact is, these ancient brethren were very much like us moderns, and used very free and general forms of speech. Certainly no argument from Irenaeus' use of the phrase can be drawn to weaken the evidence for his knowledge of 2 Peter.

Going a few years further back into the second century, we find a passage in the writings of Theophilus of Antioch which bears all the appearance of being a reminiscence from 2 Peter. We do not refer to *Ad Autolycum*, II. 9, which is usually quoted as parallel to 2 Peter i. 21, but to the following passage from *Ad Autolycum*, II. 13: "The διάταξις of God, therefore—this is *his* word, φαίνων ὥσπερ λύχνος ἐν οἰκήματι συνεχομένῳ, ἐφώτισεν τὴν ὑπ' οὐρανόν." The resemblance of this to 2 Peter i. 19 is too great to be overlooked, and cannot be wholly vitiated by an appeal to 4 Esdras xii. 42 (*tu enim nobis superasti ex omnibus prophetis—sicut lucerna in loco obscuro*). We may at least claim that we have here a probable reference.

In some writings of a still older contemporary of Irenaeus', Melito of Sardis, preserved to us in a Syriac translation, we meet with a striking passage which seems to show dependence on 2 Peter iii. 5-7 and 10-12. In the translation of Dr. Westcott it runs as follows: "There was a flood of waters. . . . So also shall it be at the last time; there shall be a flood of fire, and the earth shall be burnt up together with its mountains, and men shall be burnt up together with their idols which they have made and the graven images which they have worshiped; and the sea together with its isles shall be burnt up; and the just shall be delivered from the fury like their fellows in the ark from the waters of the deluge."[10] Perhaps it is within the bounds of moderation to hold that this *probably* is a reminiscence of 2 Peter.

During the period which stretches back between Melito and A.D. 120, we find parallels between 2 Peter and three writers: Hermas, Justin, and Pseudo-Clement. That from 2 Clement,

---

[10]*On the Canon*, 3d ed., p. 202, note 2.

however, is scarcely worth pleading (2 Clem. xvi. 3, and 2 Peter iii. 7); at best this may possibly depend on that. Those from Hermas are much more striking and are certainly sufficient to raise a very strong presumption that Hermas had 2 Peter. They are three: *Vis.* iv. 3, 4, "Ye who have escaped from this world." Compare 2 Peter ii. 20. *Vis.* iii. 7, 1, "abandoned the true way." Compare 2 Peter ii. 15 (ii. 2). And much more important, *Simil.* vi. 4, last part: τῆς τρυφῆς καὶ τὰ ἀπατῆς ὃ χρόνος ὥρα ἐστὶ μία· τῆς δὲ βασάνου ὥραι τριάκοντα ἡμερῶν δύναμιν ἔχουσαι. Ἐὰν οὖν μίαν ἡμέραν τις τρυφήσῃ καὶ ἀπατηθῇ. Compare 2 Peter ii. 13: τὴν ἐν ἡμέρα τρύφην . . . . . . ἐντρυφῶντες ἐν ταῖς ἀπάταις αὐτῶν. Much stronger still are those urged from Justin. In *Dial.* c. 81, we read: Συνήκαμεν καὶ τὸ εἰρήμενον ὅτι Ἡμέρα Κυρίου ὡς χίλια ἔτη, εἰς τοῦτο συνάγειν, which, like the parallel passage in Irenaeus, must be assigned to 2 Peter iii. 8 as its source. Again in *Dial.* c. 82, we read: "In the same manner also as there were ψευδοπροφῆται among the holy prophets that were with you, so also among us now are also many ψευδοδιδάσκαλοι, of whom our Lord forewarned us." But where can this forewarning be found? Does it exist anywhere but in 2 Peter ii. 1 (cf. i. 21): "But there were ψευδοπροφῆται among the people, as also among you shall be ψευδοδιδάσκαλοι, who shall subintroduce damnable heresies"? It is exceedingly difficult to see how there can be any reasonable doubt but that these passages are drawn from 2 Peter. And if so, it is noticeable that Justin refers to 2 Peter with respect, as Scripture, as, practically, the words of the Lord— in a word, as an authoritative book giving the Lord's teaching. All that was said above about the value of Clement's testimony may, therefore, be transferred now to Justin's, with this difference, that the period now before us is the years before A.D. 147, instead of after 195. It will not be surprising, therefore, if we find testimonies for 2 Peter in the next earlier age.

From this next age—called the sub-apostolic, because the next succeeding to that in which the apostles lived—and stretching from the apostolic age to A.D. 120, parallels have been adduced with 2 Peter from the *Testaments of the Twelve Patri-*

archs, Polycarp, Barnabas, and Clement of Rome. That from
Polycarp (iii. 2, with 2 Peter iii. 15, 16) may be passed over as
only possibly derived from 2 Peter. Those from the *Test. XII
Patt.* are more striking and render it probable that the author
had and used 2 Peter. They are such as the very rare phrase
μιασμοῖς [Oxford MS.—μιάσμασι] τῆς γῆς in Benj. 8, cf. 2 Peter
ii. 20—a phrase found in 2 Peter only in the New Testament
and in the *Test. XII Patt.*, only in its age; the rare phrase τοῦ
πλάττειν λόγους in Reuben 3, which seems to have been suggested by 2 Peter ii. 3; the use of τήρειν in Reuben 5, just as
it is used in 2 Peter ii. 9, and some peculiarities of vocabulary
common to the two writings; all of which combined raise a
probability of some force of dependence on 2 Peter.[11]

The parallel with Barnabas seems decisive as to the earlier
existence of 2 Peter; and it is difficult to see how assent can
be withheld from the statement, that we have here a plain
reference to 2 Peter. We read in *Barn.* xv. 4: ἡ γὰρ ἡμέρα παρ'
αὐτῷ χίλια ἔτη, αὐτὸς δὲ μοι μαρτυρει λέγων· Ἰδοὺ σήμερον ἡμέρα
ἔσται ὡς χίλια ἔτη. It is to be observed that the closeness of
Barnabas to 2 Peter iii. 8, is greater than was the case in the
like parallel in either Irenaeus or Justin. What was said there
is therefore *a fortiori* strong here. Nor can the difference of
context in Barnabas be urged against his dependence on 2
Peter;[11a] this is too characteristic of Barnabas elsewhere to be
of any importance here.

The case with the parallels in Clement of Rome is not quite

---

[11]These points are fully stated in *The Presbyterian Review*, January,
1880, p. 65.

[11a]There is a great deal of error abroad as to what and how much is
needful to prove literary dependence. We need greatly a full, well-
thought-out essay on the general question of literary dependence—its
proofs, marks, and signs. Dr. Sanday in his *Gospels in the Second
Century* has made a fair beginning as to the question, With how much
looseness may a second century Father be allowed to quote and his
quotation be recognized? But all is not done yet that is essential. Something is wrong or insufficient in the general understanding of this subject
when men will universally and immediately recognize this passage as
exhibiting dependence on Matthew—"All this preliminary ferment,
then [speaking of the brood of American poets in the second quarter of
the nineteenth century], was in some way needful. The experiments

so plain. We have, first, Noah and Lot adduced in vii. 5, and xi. 1, similarly to what is done in 2 Peter ii. 5-9. And then we have two passages: ix. 2, "Let us fix our eyes on them that ministered perfectly τῇ μεγαλοπρεπεῖ δόξῃ αὐτοῦ, compared with 2 Peter i. 17; and xxxv. 5, τῇ ὁδῷ τῆς ἀληθείας, compared with 2 Peter ii. 2—the strength of which rests in this fact: that in each case a very rare and peculiar phrase occurs, peculiar in the New Testament to 2 Peter, and in the sub-apostolic age to Clement. Certainly this is enough to raise some probability that as early as A.D. 97, Clement had and borrowed a peculiar phraseology from 2 Peter.

Now, it must have been already observed that these parallels do not turn, as Reuss sneers, on Christian commonplaces, but that they contain marked peculiarities of phraseology and thought. Some of them seem insoluble save by—all of them easiest soluble by—the assumption of dependence on 2 Peter. If we had, earlier than Clement of Alexandria, only the probable references of Theophilus, Melito, Hermas, *Test. XII. Patt.*, and Clement of Rome, the only rational course would be to ascribe 2 Peter to the first century and to the apostolic period. The presumption of its early date thus raised would be convincingly strong. Yet this is but the weaker half of our evidence. To a moral certainty 2 Peter was used by Irenaeus (A.D. 175), Justin Martyr (*c.* 147), and Barnabas (*c.* 106). One probable quotation from the early second century would have so supported the inference flowing from the first testimony of

---

of many who thought themselves called, enabled the few who were chosen to find motives and occasions for work of real import." (Mr. Stedman in *Scribner* for October, 1881, p. 821), and yet at the same time will doubt or deny any dependence on the same passage in the following—'Ὡς γέγραπται, πολλοὶ κλητοί, ὀλίγοι δὲ ἐκλεκτοὶ εὑρεθῶμεν—(*Ep. of Barnabas*, iv. 14), or doubt or deny a dependence on 2 Peter in the passages in the text. Is Mr. Stedman's *context* a voucher for his borrowing from Matthew? Or is there something in being a nineteenth century writer, and English, which renders it more probable that he should quote from the New Testament, than if he were a second century writer and a Greek? Certainly something is wrong with the critics. *Or is it that Mr. Stedman's passage does not help the "apologists," while Barnabas' does?* We are ashamed to even think such a thing.

Clement of Alexandria and Origen as to render the first century origin of the book the only probable hypothesis. Instead of that we have fifteen or sixteen quotations. The two earliest of the post-apostolic writers both furnish references: the one such as almost demonstrates his use of the book, the other such as raises his use of it to a high degree of probability. There are no earlier witnesses to call. How can we fail to see that to a moral certainty 2 Peter came from the first century, and may very well, therefore, have sprung from the bosom of the apostolical circle?

II.　EXTERNAL EVIDENCE OF THE EARLY ACCEPTANCE OF THE EPISTLE AS CANONICAL

In seeking to discover the attitude of the early Church toward 2 Peter, too much cannot possibly be made of the fact that this Epistle was finally accepted as genuinely Peter's and part of the Canon by the whole Church. On the theory of its ungenuineness (which implies uncanonicity) this is exceedingly difficult to account for. And this agreement as to its canonicity extends back certainly to the *fourth century,* in which, with the exception of one branch of the Church only, 2 Peter was universally accepted as part of the Canon. The Byzantine, Alexandrian, and Western branches of the Church had at this time all accepted and were all holding confidently to this Epistle as of divine authority. The Syriac Church alone had omitted it from her canon. Not only is it found in those great monuments of the New Testament text as it existed in the fourth century, without a word or sign to distinguish it from the other books,[12] codices B and X; but it is witnessed to as existing in the Church Canon by the great writers of the day—by Eusebius, Cyril of Jerusalem, Gregory Nazianzen, Epiphanius, by Athanasius, by Augustine, Rufinus, Jerome, Philastrius, by the third Council of Carthage, by the [Canons of Laodicea], Adamantius, Synopsis Athanasii, the

---

[12]In B the marginal marks of division are lacking.

Decreta of Damasus, Gelasius, and Hormisdas, the apostolical canons, and so on, down to our own time. Now, it has been well said that such a general support yielded to a book in the fourth century is an antecedent proof of the truth of its claims, so that with regard to it the question is not, What further proof have we for its canonicity? but rather, What proof have we which will justify us in putting it out of the Canon, authenticated as the Canon of the fourth century, as a whole, is?[13] Beyond all controversy this is a true position. That a book held so firm a position in the fourth century Canon is presumptive proof that it belonged of right in it; and this presumption is valid to determine our faith and rational assent unless it be set aside by cogent reasons. The question, therefore, is *not*, Independently of this presumption, what sufficient grounds have we for placing 2 Peter in the Canon? *but*, What sufficient grounds have we for putting it out of the Canon, where it seems so firmly instated?

Three facts have been and may be pleaded as such grounds: (1) the absence of the book from the Syriac Canon; (2) the doubts expressed concerning it by fourth century and earlier writers; and (3) the small amount of very early evidence for the existence of the book. Some remarks on each of these assertions will be proper.

(1) It is to be admitted that 2 Peter was absent from the Syrian Canon current in the late fourth century, and after. Chrysostom accepts only three catholic epistles; Amphilochius of Iconium, in his catalogue, while mentioning that some accepted seven, mentions also that some accepted only three. Junilius himself accepts only two, though he admits that *quamplurimi* in his day accepted seven. Even as late a writer as Ebed Jesu (14th century) confines the catholic epistles to only three. Still further the Peshito version, as it comes down to us, in all its copies of any weight of evidence, omits the same four catholic epistles (together with the Apocalypse) which all these writers omit. And the loose and manifestly exaggerated

---

[13]Westcott on the Canon, p. 319.

remarks of Leontius of Byzantium[14] are doubtless to be understood as classing Theodore of Mopsuestia with this Syriac school. It is clear, therefore, that from the fourth century the Syriac Church omitted 2 Peter from her Canon. On the other hand, however, it is remarked that, even if this truly represented the original Syriac Canon, it would be the testimony of only one corner of the Church and could not overbear the testimony of the whole of the rest; but in truth it is more than doubtful whether the early Syriac Church rejected these epistles. Chrysostom is the earliest witness to the shorter form of the Syriac Canon, while earlier than his time that Canon seems to have included all of our New Testament books. Thus Ephraem Syrus, of the preceding generation, confessedly possessed all seven catholic epistles and the Revelation in an older Syriac translation of ecclesiastical authority.[15] He is our earliest witness to the Peshito. The original Peshito is therefore admitted by such critics as Thiersch, Lücke, and even Hilgenfeld, to have doubtless contained the omitted books, while the form in which it was possessed by Chrysostom represents the result of a critical Antiochene revision of the fourth century.[16] This conclusion, sound in itself and in its own right, is yet still further borne out by two further considerations: The later Syriac Church was not agreed as to the number of the catholic epistles—the school of Nisibis (represented by Junilius) accepting only two; and this diversity can be best accounted for by the supposition that the objection proceeded on critical grounds, and critical grounds were for each individual to determine also how much was to be rejected. And the earlier Syrian writers certainly possessed and esteemed the

---

[14]*Contra Nestor. et Eutych. lit. III* (Galland, *Biblio.* XII. 686 f.). Compare also the wild statements of Kosmas' *Indicopleustes.*

[15]See Hilgenfeld's *Einleitung in das N. T.,* pp. 111, 112, 122, and the authorities there quoted. Ephraem's use of 2 Peter may be noted in *Opp. Syr.,* T. II. p. 342, *Graec.,* T. II. p. 387.

[16]It has been customary to say that Ephraem witnesses to a Greek, not the Syrian Canon (so Westcott). But it is clear that his Canon all existed in Syriac, and it is doubtful how far his knowledge even of the Greek language extended. See Smith and Wace's *Dict. of Christ. Biog.,* II. 142 and 143, for a just estimate of his Greek learning.

rejected books. Thus Theophilus of Antioch (168–180) had 2 Peter and Revelation,[17] Malchion had Jude,[18] and Pamphilus had Revelation[19] (which he assigned to John), and seemingly also the whole seven of the catholic epistles.[20] The testimony of the early Syrian Church, therefore, is for our completed Canon; and the omission of 2 Peter from the later fourth century Syrian Canon resolves itself simply into another case of fourth century critical doubts.

(2) The doubts expressed by certain of the fourth century writers constitute the most serious objection to the force of the fourth century evidence for the genuineness of the Epistle. Reported by Eusebius at Constantinople and Didymus at Alexandria—acted on, as we have seen, by the Syrian Church —repeated by Jerome in Italy—the air seems heavy with them. Nor were they of late origin. Early in the third century, Origen, in one brief statement, lets us see that they existed even then. It is necessary, therefore, that we should give them detailed attention.

In his catalogue of New Testament books,[21] which, as a formal passage, must take precedence of all others, Eusebius arranges 2 Peter among the Antilegomena or disputed books. This, however, does not imply more than that it had not passed thus far without having been disputed, and, therefore, adds nothing to our knowledge. He moreover distinctly states that it was among those that had been "recognized by most," and betrays the fact that his own opinion as to its genuineness was favorable. In brief, therefore, his testimony is that the book is genuine and was held to be such by the Church, although it had been disputed by unnamed individuals on unmentioned grounds.[22] It cannot be said, therefore, that he raises doubts as

---

[17]Eus. *H. E.*, IV. 24.   [20]Westcott, p. 362.
[18]Eus. *H. E.*, VII. 30.   [21]*H. E.*, III. 25.
[19]Pamph. *Apol.*, VII.

[22]Canon Westcott has shown (pp. 388 ff.) that this formal statement must explain the other looser statements of Eusebius. Elsewhere (III. 3) he declares that the book current under the name of 2 Peter had not been handed down (παρειλήφαμεν) as ἐνδιάθετον—"still, since it appeared useful to many, it had been diligently read *with the* OTHER

to the genuineness of 2 Peter; he simply recognizes and records
the doubts that had already been raised. Born probably and
brought up certainly at Caesarea, he had been from his earliest
childhood in contact with the Syrian Church, and could not but
be deeply affected by their critical opinions. He had the writings of Origen in his hands, and quotes the passage in which he
communicates the fact that there were doubters of 2 Peter's
genuineness in his day. There is no reason to believe that what
he says of the position of 2 Peter has anything further than this
at its base; he had promised to tell us whatever was said by
earlier writers about the Antilegomena; and he tells us only of
Origen's remarks against 2 Peter. We may with considerable
confidence, therefore, affirm with respect to Eusebius, that he
witnesses to the canonical position of 2 Peter in the Church of
his day—that his own opinion was favorable to its genuineness
—that while he recognizes the fact that it had been disputed,
he yet tells us nothing of the grounds on which it had been
disputed, and does not imply that he had knowledge of a
greater or more widespread doubt than we have the items of.
In other words, his remarks add nothing to the evidence against
the Epistle, but do add to the argument for the genuineness
of the Epistle. The shadows of the doubts whose complete
selves could not shake his faith, need not shake ours.

The state of the case with reference to the doubts expressed
by Didymus of Alexandria is much the same. He wrote a commentary on this Epistle—which is itself a significant fact—at
the close of which we find a sentence which in the Latin
translation (which has alone come down to us) appears to
read as follows: "It ought not, then, to be unknown that the
epistle is accounted spurious [*falsatam*, probably a rendering
of νοθεύεται], which although it is in public use, is nevertheless

---

Scriptures." And later, he says somewhat unguardedly and inconsistently: "I recognize only one Epistle [of Peter] as genuine and acknowledged by the ancient presbyters"; though doubtless he meant the
whole predicate here to be taken as one single thought, which would
void the inconsistency. However difficult it may be to us to harmonize
all this perfectly, it is clear that the passage given in the text, as being
the only formal statement, must be the one followed.

not in the Canon."[23] Like the statement of Eusebius, this only recites a fact without giving the grounds on which it is based. But, unlike the case of Eusebius, the fact here stated, if taken strictly, is demonstrably false, and Didymus' personal opinion seems to be involved in the statement. If the original Greek stated, as the slovenly Latin seems to imply, that in Didymus' day 2 Peter was not generally considered canonical, then Didymus has simply misinformed his readers. For, after the middle of the fourth century, when he flourished (born 309 or 314) it is confessed on all sides that 2 Peter was in the Church Canon. It is difficult to believe, however, that the Latin accurately represents the original Greek. Didymus uses 2 Peter most fully as Petrine and Scripture, in his work on the Trinity,[24] and this proves either that he himself held it to be genuine, or that he was so accustomed to see it used and to use it as genuine that his critical opinion to the contrary was apt to be forgotten in practice—that is, that it was generally considered genuine, and had been so considered through a long past. In all probability, Didymus simply repeats his master Origen; and at all events his own use of 2 Peter in his work on the Trinity sucks the poison out of his adverse statement. At the worst, it can only represent the personal opinion of Didymus supported by an anonymous minority, and therefore cannot stand against the faith of the mass of the Church.

Jerome, at last, informs us of the grounds of the early doubts. "Peter wrote," he tells us,[25] "two epistles which are called catholic; the second of which is denied by very many (*plerisque*) to be his *on account of dissonance of style with the first*." Jerome is not himself a doubter. His notice is valuable only

[23]Migne, XXXIX. p. 1,774.
[24]In *De Trinitate* he calls it a catholic epistle (ed. Mingarell, p. 234), ascribes it distinctly to Peter (pp. 21, 28, 99, 151, 234), and cites it just like the other Scriptures (pp. 90, 115). Moreover, he cites 1 Peter under that name, thus implying 2 Peter (99, 182, 276, 340). It is worth while to note further that he seems to use 2 Peter as genuine, also in the *Enarratio in Ep. Judae*, in defiance of his (seeming) adverse statement at the end of the *Enarratio* on 2 Peter. It may, perhaps, be worth noting further that the *Enarrationes* were a youthful work.
[25]*De Vir. Ill.*, c. 1.

because it assures us that the doubters of the early Church based their objections on purely *internal*, not *historical* considerations. From this hint we can understand the whole history. This explains why it is that these objections first appear at Alexandria, and why it is that they bore their fruit away in Syria. The Alexandrian school was notable above all others for internal criticism. It was in it that the style of Hebrews and Revelation was first discussed and inferences drawn from the discussion. If this was the source of objection to 2 Peter, it is not strange that objections are first heard of there. The Antiochene school, on the other hand, was the legitimate heir of Alexandrian speculation, and was the first to drive in many matters the critical hints of its predecessor to a practical end. It is not strange that this same course was followed in this matter also. Jerome thus unties the whole knot for us, and in doing so voids these early objections of their terror. Let there have been many or few affected by them (and Jerome's *"very many"* doubtless refers to the numbers involved in the rejection by the Syrian Church), they are, as founded on internal considerations, of no value to us. We appeal to the Fathers not for internal but for external arguments; and we can, when all the external testimony is in, examine opinions as to style at our leisure.

Origen, finally, was the earliest writer who mentions doubts as to our Epistle; and his words are not unambiguous: "Peter . . . has left behind one epistle which is ὁμολογουμένην; perhaps also a second, for it is disputed."[26] Perhaps no more colorless words could have been chosen. Origen's own opinion cannot be gathered from them, and must remain in doubt. When this statement is taken in connection with Origen's own practice in regard to the Epistle, it is plain, (1) that some in Origen's day disputed the genuineness of this Epistle, and yet, (2) it was the usual if not universal habit to think and speak of it as Scripture and Peter's. It is clear from this that it was individuals who doubted, but the Church that re-

---

[26]Eus. *H. E.*, VI. 25.

ceived, and that the Church had received it through a long past.

Taking a general review of the early doubts expressed, we are justified in saying that, except the later Syrians, it is difficult to put our finger exactly on the doubters. Didymus possibly, Origen possibly, were among them; but most probably they were not. They are an anomymous body. And they are a minority and a hopelessly small one; in Jerome's day they are very many—before that, plainly few. The grounds of their doubt were purely internal, perhaps solely questions of style. It is plain, therefore, that they are by no means of sufficient importance to rebut the presumption already raised for the genuineness and canonicity of the Epistle. The testimony of the Church, as the Church, rings clear and strong above all doubt in favor of the letter.

(3)   While it may be confessed that the evidence for the existence of 2 Peter drawn from writers earlier than Origen is not as copious as could be desired, it has already been shown that it exists in abundant quantity to prove the letter to be as old as the apostolic times. Further evidence might make this proof more overwhelming, but could not alter its import. It is only where one shuts his eyes to this array of passages and refuses to consider really its meaning and strength, that he can allow himself to speak of an insufficiency of early references to that book. The amount of evidence for it seems small, and is in danger of appearing insufficient, only when it is viewed in comparison with the remarkable mass which God has preserved for the chief books of the New Testament. When compared with what is thought—and justly so—amply sufficient to authenticate any other early writing, it looms up before us great and invincible. 2 Peter is to a moral certainty quoted by two writers, and most probably by three or four more, within the first century after its composition; and long before the next century has rolled away, it is fully witnessed to as occupying an assured position in a Canon held all-holy, and thoroughly witnessed to as a whole. Now, Herodotus is quoted but once in the century which followed its composition, but once in the next, not at all in the next, only twice in the next, and not until

its fifth century is anything like as fully witnessed to as 2 Peter
is in its second. Again, Thucydides is not distinctly quoted,
until quite two centuries after its composition; while Tacitus
is first cited by Tertullian.[27] Yet no one thinks of disputing
the genuineness of Herodotus, Thucydides, or Tacitus. Clement of Alexandria's testimony alone puts 2 Peter on a par
with Tacitus; Origen's testimony alone would put it on a better
basis than Thucydides stands securely on. Save for the contrast between the testimony for it, and that amazing abundance
which stands for the greater New Testament books, it would be
simply astonishing how anyone could speak of insufficient witness; and that contrast is due not to insufficiency of evidence for
2 Peter, but to astounding over-sufficiency of evidence for the
other books.

Thus no one of these lines of argument, nor all together, are
able to raise any cogent rebutting evidence against the presumption from the attitude of the fourth century in favor of the
book. A strong presumption still remains untouched, that this
book thus accepted by the great writers and the Church in
general, in that century, was always in the Canon—not to be
set aside save on cogent grounds. And, resting on this presumption, we might here rest the case, asking simply for
reasons why this book should be ignominiously cast out of the
Canon of the fourth century. This question clamors in vain for
an answer. Yet the fourth century evidence is not all that can
be adduced, and it will be instructive to go further. We have
seen incidentally that the notices of Origen prove that the book
was a part of the Church Canon of the early years of the third
century. And corroborative witness is at hand. Firmilian, in
Asia Minor (†270), quotes it as an authoritative letter of
Peter "the blessed apostle," when writing to Cyprian in North
Africa; whence it is hard not to conclude that he could naturally
count on Cyprian esteeming it just as he did—in other words,
that at this period 2 Peter was part of the Canon of the universal Church. That it was part of the North African Canon of

---

[27]See for these facts Rawlinson's *Hist. Evidences*, p. 376 (American
edition).

the third century is certain from the fact that it is included in
the Claromontanian Stichometry.[28] In Italy, Hippolytus at the
same time seems to quote it.[29] It cannot be denied, therefore,
that it was a part of the Church Canon of the early third century; and the evidence goes further· and proves that it was
naturally in the Canon at this time—that the men of the early
third century did not *put* it in, but *found* it in the Canon. It
was, therefore, in the Canon of the later years of the second
century. And indeed this is independently proved. Not only
was it known to several authors of the time, but it was commented on by Clement of Alexandria, and has a place in both
the Egyptian versions and in the early form of the Peshito, all
of which date from the second century.[30] No stronger evidence of its canonical authority at the time could be asked.
We must shift our question back two centuries then, and ask,
What reason exists to degrade 2 Peter from the Canon of the
late second century? Known all over the Church at this period
and securely fixed in the Canon, we find it quoted here and
there, back to the very earliest Christian writers; nay, Justin
Martyr, before 147, quotes it in such a way as to prove that
he esteemed it authoritative. What evidence is there which will
compel us to revise the decision of the late second century and
put the letter out of its Canon? Absolutely nothing is hazarded
in asserting that its position in the Canon of this period
peremptorily authenticates· it as divine. Even were there no
trace of it earlier, this would be enough; how much more so,
with the traces we have of its earlier possession and estimation!
One has but to catch the grounds on which this age held its
Canon, to be convinced of this. Irenaeus tells us that he holds
only to what has been handed down from the elders, the companions of the apostles; Clement appeals as boldly to tradition

---

[28]See the proof that this represents the African Canon of the third
century in Credner's *Einleitung*, p. 175, and Hilgenfeld's, p. 107.

[29]*De Antichristo*, c. 2.

[30]This is the old opinion as to the Peshito; and Dr. Lightfoot has ren-
dered it the most probable date for the others. See also the opinion of
Dr. Schaff and of Drs. Westcott and Hort in their new edition of the
New Testament.

as his only dependence. Now, the teachers of these men were these very companions of the apostles. Polycarp was Irenaeus' teacher, and he was the pupil of John. Clement had studied under many masters of the previous generation in all parts of the Church. The one *sine qua non* with all the writers of this age, for the reception of a book as canonical, was that it should come to them from these Fathers as having come to them from the bosom of the apostolical circle. That a book was a recognized part of the New Testament of this period, therefore, authenticates it as having come from the elders who could bear personal witness to its apostolicity. So that the witness of the age of Irenaeus alone, if fairly widespread, is amply sufficient to authenticate any New Testament book. 2 Peter has that witness. And it has more than that: it is independently witnessed to as coming from the apostolic times (Barnabas, Clement of Rome, etc.), and as being esteemed authoritative (Justin). Surely the presumption of its canonicity amounts to a moral certainty.

III. The Internal Evidence in Favor of its Genuineness

But what witness does the letter bear to itself? The Church has from the beginning held it to be an authoritative letter from Peter; that it is its own witness in this direction. It bears on the forefront the name of Peter, and this is the first thing we note in asking after internal evidence: the letter asserts itself to be by Peter (i. 1, 14, 16). It is, therefore, either Peter's, or else a base and designing forgery. It cannot be held to be an innocent production which by some mistake has found its way into the Canon; it is either genuinely Peter's, or else it is an embodied lie. Now this raises a very strong presumption in favor of its genuineness. For it is apparent on any reading of it that a very "holy and apostolic spirit breathes through this letter." Not a false note is struck throughout the whole of it. "We feel," says Froumüller with as much truth as eloquence, "that the author stands in the grace and knowledge of Jesus Christ; that he loves truth above all things (i. 12; i. 3); that he is thoroughly in earnest about Christianity (i. 5); that he fears the judgments of eternity (ii. 1); that he believes in God's justice (ii. 9); that he despises cunningly-devised fables and speaks from a sure and personal autoptic knowledge (i. 16)." The Epistle's claim to be by Peter is thus reinforced by every mark of honesty in its form and matter.

We note next that what it tells us about its author is in striking harmony with its assertion that he was Peter. Not only does the double name Symeon Peter (with its Hebraic sound) fit, and the character of the writer reflect itself as the impulsive, quick, outspoken Peter of the evangelists, but there are some minute points of coincidence brought out which certainly identify him. Thus, only three of the disciples witnessed our Lord's transfiguration. The author of this Epistle was one of them (i. 16-18). Can this natural reference to his own experience be the trick of a forger? That seems scarcely credible on the face of it, but it is rendered quite impossible by some minute signs in the context which prove that that scene had burnt itself into the writer's heart. His mind is full of it; it is retransacting itself before his very eyes as he writes; its smallest details are in his mouth as he speaks. We remember that it was Peter who said, "Lord, let us make here three *tabernacles*," and in verse 13 we see a reminiscence of this creeping out: "As long as I am in this *tabernacle*." Immediately after that wonderful scene the Lord had spoken of his ἔξοδος; and in verse 15 we find a reminiscence of this: "after my exodus." No forger could have introduced these reminiscences. Clearly, as the writer approaches the mention of the scene, his mind and heart are full of it, and he naturally lets fall these minute reminiscences. The author of this letter seems certainly to have witnessed the transfiguration. Again, only seven of the disciples at most, very likely only two (xxi. 20), possibly only one, heard our Lord's prediction recorded in John xxi. 18. The author of this Epistle is one to whom Jesus had predicted a violent death (i. 14), and this must refer to this prediction. The author of this Epistle was again, therefore, Peter; who could have placed this reminiscence here but Peter?

Still again, the writer of this Epistle is the same as the Peter of the Acts. The style of the Epistle is the same as that of the speeches of Peter recorded in the Acts, as is proved by a long series of parallels capable of being adduced between the two,[31] the greater number of which turn on the usage of peculiar (that is, rare) words or phrases, and therefore present evidence of great convincingness.

Once again, the author of this Epistle was the writer of 1 Peter. In the face of all that has been urged as to the difference of style between the two, we still insist on this. The same character underlies both writings; both are the outflow of an ardent, impulsive, yet chastened heart. The writers of both bear the same relation to Paul and are anxious equally to express approval and recommendation of his teaching; the one quotes his words to a remarkable extent, and has evidently, as one object of his writing, to commend his doctrine (1 Peter v. 12 *et passim*); the other expressly declares its position on this point (2 Peter iii. 2). The writers of both are apt to draw their language from previous sources, not mechanically, but so as to show adoption by, and transmission through, a mind which has grasped at once all that has been said, has felt it through and through, and been so affected by it that it naturally repeats it in its own striking fashion. Thus 1 Peter depends on Romans and Ephesians; thus 2 Peter depends on Jude. The writers of both exhibit a tendency to adduce the *mysteries* of the truth in illustration of their arguments; thus compare 1 Peter iii. 19; iv. 6; iii. 6, 21, on the one hand, and on the other such passages as 2 Peter iii. 5, 10. That the *same* mysteries are not dwelt on by both does not void the argument, which turns on a quality of mind, the tendency found in both writers to bring forward incidentally the deep things of the kingdom. Still further, the doctrinal teaching of both writers, although adduced for different purposes and therefore expressed in different forms, is precisely the same, not only in ground principles but in modes of presentation, as even Schwegler feels forced to

---

[31]Alford adduces, e.g.: i. 1=Acts i. 17; i. 3, 6, 7=Acts iii. 12; i. 21= Acts ii. 23; ii 8=Acts ii. 29; ii. 8=Acts ii. 23; ii. 9=Acts x. 2, 7; ii. 9=Acts iv. 21; iii. 2=Acts v. 32; iii. 10=Acts. ii. 20, etc.

admit.[32] Even minute points of teaching, exhibiting favorite tenets, pass over from one Epistle to the other; this is true of the view as to prophecy (cf. 1 Peter i. 10-12 and 2 Peter i. 19-21; iii. 2), of the views of the new birth *through the divine word* (cf. 1 Peter i. 22; ii. 2; and 2 Peter i. 4); of the teaching given as to submission to worldly rulers (1 Peter ii. 13, and 2 Peter ii. 10); of the dread expressed of false teachers, etc. The likeness extends even to the use of special words such as κρίμα (1 Peter iv. 17 and 2 Peter ii. 3); ἀρετη (1 Peter ii. 9 and 2 Peter i. 3), etc. So that working one further step we may say that the two Epistles exhibit striking resemblances of style, resemblances much more striking and far-reaching than the differences so freely adduced by many critics. These resemblances are seen not only in peculiar phrases, such as the form of salutation, "Grace and peace *be multiplied*," found in these two Epistles and nowhere else; but also in the recurrence in both of rare combinations, such as ἀμώμου καὶ ἀσπίλου, 1 Peter i. 19, repeated 2 Peter ii. 13 and iii. 14 and nowhere else, and also the common possession of a very peculiar vocabulary such as is represented by the occurrence in both of ἐποπτεύσαντες (1 Peter ii. 12; 2 Peter i. 16), ἰσότιμος (1 Peter i. 7, 19; 2 Peter i. 1, 4), reinforced by the like community in such as φιλαδελφία (1 Peter i. 22; 2 Peter i. 7); χορηγεῖν (1 Peter iv. 11; 2 Peter i. 5, 11); ἀπόθεσις (1 Peter iii. 21; 2 Peter i. 14); ἀρετη (1 Peter ii. 9; 2 Peter i. 3); ἀναστροφή (1 Peter i. 15; 2 Peter ii. 21); ἀλήθεια in a peculiar sense (1 Peter i. 22; 2 Peter i. 12); κομίζεσθαι (1 Peter i. 9; 2 Peter ii. 13), etc.;[33] all of which are rare words in the New Testament. In the face of such considerations as these, it would certainly require very cogent rebutting evidence to convince us that 2 Peter did not come from the same hand which gave us 1 Peter.

Before leaving this general subject, however, we must present two other internal considerations which cannot be passed over, and which possess considerable weight as evidence:

(1) The relation of our Epistle to the Gospel of Mark must

---

[32]*Nachapost. Zeitalter,* I. 512 f.
[33]See Plumptre's *Christ and Christendom,* p. 345.

be considered. All antiquity tells us that Mark's Gospel bears a special relation to Peter. Now compare 2 Peter ii. 1 and Mark xiii. 22; 2 Peter iii. 17 and Mark xiii. 23; 2 Peter iii. 10 and Mark xiii. 36; 2 Peter iii. 4 and Mark xiii. 19. These are certainly striking parallels; and if 2 Peter preceded Mark in time we may say they are conclusive that Peter wrote this Epistle. Yet there is a still more striking connection between the two which seems to have all the force of a complex undesigned coincidence. All antiquity tells us that Mark wrote down what Peter orally taught of the Lord's life and teaching; and internal criticism of Mark's Gospel corroborates this external testimony. In 1 Peter v. 13, we find Mark on intimate terms with Peter (cf. also for an earlier period, Acts xv. 12). Now in 2 Peter i. 15 the author promises his readers that he will see to it that they shall be in a position after his death to have his teaching always in remembrance, and in this he has special reference to the *facts* of Christ's life, witnessed to by him, as is proved by the purpose which he expresses for so arranging, namely, that they may know that they have not followed cunningly devised fables, but facts autoptically witnessed. Surely this seems to promise a Gospel. And we have this series: 1 Peter testifies to Mark's intimacy with Peter; 2 Peter promises a Petrine Gospel; antiquity tells us that Mark was but Peter's mouthpiece. Who could have invented that middle term and so delicately inserted it into 2 Peter? 2 Peter thus appears a link in a natural chain which is complete with it and incomplete without it. All three of these sources from which the links are drawn are therefore genuine.[34]

(2) 2 Peter witnesses to its own date. Whoever wrote it, it belongs to a time when Peter was living, and consequently he might well have written it. We need do nothing more than consider the teaching and character of the false teachers condemned in it to prove this. They occupy a place intermediate between those condemned by Paul and those condemned by John. This has been clearly shown by Thiersch and repeatedly

---

[34]Cf. Plumptre, *loc. cit.*

exhibited since, as for example, by Froumüller and Guerike; so that we may content ourselves with simply mentioning it here.[35]

Conclusive independently or not, for the Petrine authorship of this Epistle, the internal evidence, considered as corroborative to the external testimonies already adduced, is certainly conclusive and ought to compel assent.

IV. THE REBUTTING EVIDENCE

The evidence thus presented in favor of the canonicity of 2 Peter would seem to be almost overwhelming. It certainly raises a presumption of immense force in its favor, such as cannot be overturned except by equally cogent rebutting evidence. Yet, of late years, many have been found able to resist its force, such as Schmidt, Eichhorn, De Wette, Richter, Schott, Neander, Credner, Mayerhoff, Magnus, Andemars, Reuss, Daumas, Bleek, Huther, and the whole Tübingen school, from Schwegler to Hilgenfeld. It is necessary to ask, On what rebutting evidence do these writers rely? Hilgenfeld, indeed, hardly deigns to assign a reason for his action, but sets aside the Epistle summarily as, (1) presupposing the ungenuine 1 Peter as well as Jude; (2) plainly belonging to the later Gnostic period (250†); and (3) having insufficient external support. But most of the other writers named are less high-handed—Credner, especially, entering fully into the argument; and from them we may obtain some idea of the rebutting evidence on which they rely. It may be briefly stated as follows:

(1) There was a known tendency in the early Church to forge Peter's name.

(2) The external support of 2 Peter is insufficient.

---

[35]Another rather remarkable coincidence in the use of language may be adduced here, as having some bearing on the genuineness of 2 Peter. At a time when every word and act was permanently burning itself in on Peter's heart, our Lord had said to him: "Strengthen ($\sigma\tau\eta\rho\ell\zeta\omega$) the brethren." Now it is noticeable that there are reminiscences of this word in both 1 and 2 Peter: cf. 1 Peter v. 10; 2 Peter i. 12; iii. 17. Does not this look as if he who had received that command had written this Epistle? The word is not rare enough to found any secure inference upon; but its use in 2 Peter may count as one small item of evidence.

(3) It has plainly borrowed largely from Jude, which is judged unworthy of an apostle by some, and by others is held a proof that 2 Peter belongs to the second century, on the ground of the assumed ungenuineness of Jude.

(4) The author exhibits too great a desire to make himself out to be Peter.

(5) Yet betrays the later time in which he wrote by many minute anachronisms.

(6) The style of the Epistle is divergent from that of 1 Peter, and the differences amount at times to inconsistencies, such as the assumption that its readers (which are assumed to be the same as 1 Peter's) were personally taught by Peter (i. 15; iii. 2).

The first of these points might raise a suspicion against an unsupported claim to Petrine authorship, but only a *suspicion*, which would, moreover, give way before any evidence. The second has already been disproved. The third, again, is clearly invalid. One inspired writer frequently quotes the words of another, which is but the Spirit's authentication of himself; and the genuineness of Jude rests on a stronger array of proof than that of Second Peter, while the argument can be pleaded only on the assumption of the spuriousness of Jude. The other three arguments, (4), (5), and (6), are purely internal and sub- jective—depend for their force on the mental attitude and state of the critic, and cannot rebut the array of external and internal evidences for the Epistle, even if allowed just as urged. Think of really allowing more weight to these three opinions than to all that has been adduced—external and internal—in favor of the Epistle! Still, it will be instructive for us to note the details that are urged under these heads.

The fourth argument is strongly urged alike by Credner, Neander, and Reuss. But wherein is this great anxiety seen? In i. 1, iii. 1, 2, 15, say some; in the adduction of Christ's proph- ecy, in i. 14, "in an unsuitable manner," and the unapostolic appeal to the transfiguration, in i. 17, as a proof of apostleship, say others. But how these natural passages can be alleged to prove forgery, it requires a very advanced critic to see. They are not *lugged in*, but *fallen into*. Who can see (except Neander) how the prophecy of Christ that Peter should die a violent death, is introduced "in an unsuitable manner"? It is barely alluded to, and that obscurely: is that the way with forgers, who introduce such allusions for a purpose? The transfiguration is not adduced to prove the apostleship of the writer, but to prove the truth of the teaching which the readers had received as to the divinity of Christ by an autoptic testimony. The other passages can be paralleled from 2 Corinthians, which is allowed to be genuine; and could not fail if 2 Peter be a *second* letter of the *Apostle Peter's*. How then can this be urged against this authorship? The items adduced under the fifth head are equally unsatisfactory, and conclusive as to nothing but the hypercriticism of their adducers. (4) and (5) are moreover mutually destructive; such a consummate forger as (4) requires could not have fallen into such easy traps as (5) adduces—the fault must be the critic's, not the author's. The points actually adduced are the mixing of the presents and futures in ii. 12-15, 17-22; Gnostic traces; references to myths (i. 16); the blending of Petrinism and Paulinism (iii. 15, 16); the use of the term "Holy Mount" (i. 18), which is said to be a designation which could only have supplanted the proper name of the mountain at a comparatively late date; the mode of citing St. Paul's epistles as Scripture, which they are not esteemed to be at first; the evidences of disappointed hopes as to the speedy second coming of Christ, and the peculiar adduction of apostolic testimony in iii. 2. The basis of most of these is pure assumption. The so-called Gnostic tendencies opposed belong clearly to an earlier age than those opposed by John, while Irenaeus is our witness to the contemporaneity of John and Cerinthus, who, he tells us, held the advanced doctrines controverted in John. The discovery of a blending of Petrinism and Paulinism, and a consequent betrayal of a reconciling purpose, grows simply out of a Tübingen dream; what happens if it be true that Peter and Paul were never opposed to one another? The "Holy Mount" is not introduced as a name, but as a descriptive designation of a well-known spot. Who says St. Paul's epistles were not esteemed Scripture at the beginning? and who will undertake to prove it? Paul so quotes Luke in Timothy; why not Peter Paul? Shall we bend our theories to fit the facts, or the facts to fit the theories? The peculiarity of iii. 2 depends only on a false reading, and disappears on the restoration of the true ancient text. Why presents and futures are mixed in the repetitions from the earlier Jude, the careful exegete will not need to ask. And who shall say how soon fanatics in the early Church needed correcting as to our Lord's second coming? Evidence such as this certainly rebuts itself rather than the opposing considerations.

The latter half of the sixth head will need no reply, as it turns on a misinterpretation of plain passages. 2 Peter iii. 2 can be pleaded here only before being corrected in its reading; when we read ὑμῶν, with the best authorities, the opposite is implied; i. 15 only implies that there were close relations between the readers and Peter, such as might have been indicated by the first Epistle; the "we" of i. 16 includes all preachers of the gospel, some of whom had preached to these Christians. Much more stress is, however, usually laid on the simple argument from diversity of style. But how the details adduced can bear any weight, it is exceedingly difficult to see. Credner has probably presented this argument as strongly as it admits of— certainly more strongly than anyone else as yet. The list of the "most remarkable differences," which he urges, is as follows:[36] 2 Peter's common use of κύριος for Christ, which 1 Peter never does, except i. 13 (borrowed from Ephesians), while on the other hand 2 Peter always so uses it, except in passages derived from Jude or the Old Testament; 2 Peter's frequent application of the term σωτήρ to Jesus, which 1 Peter never does; 2 Peter's application to Christ of what 1 Peter applies to God, and its seldom mention of God; the failure in 2 Peter of the common words ἀποκάλυψις, ἀποκαλύπτω, when speaking of the second advent, which are common in 1 Peter, while ἡμέρα is the com-

---

[36]See his *Einleitung in das Neue Testament*, 1836, pp. 660 ff.

mon term in this connection in 2 Peter; the Hebraistic or
pleonastic use of the preposition ἐν in 2 Peter, a usage not
found at all in 1 Peter; the failure in 2 Peter of the common
1 Peter usage of an unessential ὡς; the substitution for the titles
by which the Christian teaching is called in 1 Peter, viz., ἐλπις,
χάρις, πίστις, ἀλήθεια, λόγος, εὐαγγέλιον τοῦ Θεοῦ, etc., of quite
distinct designations in 2 Peter, such as Χριστοῦ δύναμις καὶ
παρουσία (i. 16), "the way of righteousness" (ii. 21), the "holy
commandment" (ii. 21), the "commandment of the apostles"
(iii. 2), etc; the failure in 2 Peter of the common and frequent
quotation of the Old Testament as found in 1 Peter; and finally,
broadly, the diffuse, heavy, languid style of 2 Peter, as distinguished from the easier, synthetic, irregular, fresh style of
1 Peter.

Are these worth the stating, except as an interesting inquiry as to the special peculiarities of two writings from the
same hand? Will they bear any weight, considered as rebutting
evidence against sufficient testimony? Reuss speaks wise, even
if obvious, words when he says: "On the theological and linguistic differences between the two Epistles, which the later criticism
has so emphasized, we lay no stress. The two Epistles are too
short, have to do with wholly different circumstances; and
especially there are no direct contradictions to be found. Only
if the Epistle is on other grounds proved to be ungenuine, can
this also be brought into account."[37] In other words, the argument from style is not valid against the genuineness of the
Epistle. We say, Amen! What, then, are we to do with this
long list of Credner's? Only note the following points: (1) The
list of differences is nothing like as striking as the list of resemblances; so that the problem is *not* to find a theory which
will account for the differences alone, *but* to find a theory which
will account for the coexistence of differences with still more
striking resemblances. Diversity of authorship will not do this.
(2) The differences are mere contradictions, and usually not
uniform, but only *prevailing* differences—some parallels being

---

[37]*Geschichte*, etc., *Neue Testament*, pars. 270-272.

found in the other Epistle. (3) Credner fails to take account of the very distinct occasions, objects, spirits, on, for, and in which the two letters were written. These determine the style of speech in this case, and will account for most if not all of the differences adduced. The fact that 2 Peter is specifically a letter of reproof and warning will account for its general tone as different from 1 Peter (a letter of exhortation and comfort); the character of the errors opposed will account for the fact that it dwells on the majesty and lordship of Christ, his saving power, his authority and love, and substitutes him for God in most passages. This goes like a destroying brand straight through Credner's list. (4) Still further, Credner forgets that it is characteristic of Peter to rest on and write out of a previous document. The fact that Paul lay at the root of 1 Peter, and Jude at the root of 2 Peter, will account for much divergence in style; still the community of authorship of both accounts for their resemblances. The theory of diversity of authorship will thus not account for the phenomenon; we have unity in diversity to account for, and must assume unity of authorship in the account we render.

The state of the argument, then, really is this: a mountain mass of presumption in favor of the genuineness and canonicity of 2 Peter, to be raised and overturned only by a very strong lever of rebutting evidence; a pitiable show of rebutting evidence offered as lever. It is doubtless true that we can move the world if the proper lever and fulcrum be given. But if the lever is a common quarryman's tool and the fulcrum thin air! Then, woe only to the man who wields it. What can such rebutting evidence as we have here really injure, except its own cause?

V. The History of the Epistle

We are surely in a condition now to assert that the canonicity of the letter is secure. We pause only to add briefly its history. Sent forth by Peter soon after the middle of the first century (say in A.D. 67), it soon found its way as an authoritative part of the Canon of faith over the whole Christian world.

Already with the beginning of uninspired Christian literature, it is found everywhere. Clement has it in 97 at Rome; Barnabas in 106 at Alexandria; at the same time the Jewish Christian author of the *Testaments of the Twelve Patriarchs* was reading it at Pella. Throughout the second century the Church enjoyed the peaceful possession of it; and before the close of that age was demanding and receiving commentaries upon it. In the meantime the acute school of internal criticism at Alexandria was scrutinizing its peculiarities, and by the beginning of the third century some were found able to magnify them into inconsistencies with 1 Peter. On these internal grounds some were now led to question its genuineness and consequently its canonicity; but no one was yet bold enough to exscind it from the Canon. The fourth century found a critical school in Syria, daring above all precedent; and here at last, but only here, the subjective judgment of minute, one-sided scholarship won the victory over the external evidences for the Epistle. The common sense of the Church at large, however, refused to be thus led, and preserved it from the heresy; and soon, as the value of the subjective criticism was better understood, the doubts that had been raised died away, and the Epistle's place in the Canon became once more undoubted. So matters stood until the Reformation. Then once more individual doubts revived, while once more the Church stood firm. Erasmus, Cajetan, Luther, even Calvin, spoke doubtfully of its genuineness and consequent canonicity; but even such names could not lead the Church astray. That storm was also weathered, and once more the waters seemed quiet. Once more, in these modern times, we see the attack begun; but once more we witness the same phenomena as of old repeated—*individuals* doubt, the *Church* stands firm. In the whole history of the Church, the Syrian Church alone among the churches has ever, as a body, doubted the Epistle. From the beginning, the Church as a Church has always held it without fear and without dubiety. With the evidence as it is, so it ought to be. We think we hazard nothing in adding, so it will ever be.

THE BOOK OF REVELATION*

The Book of Revelation is also called, by adoption, instead of translation of the Greek title, the Apocalypse, a term which, according to its original sense, would denote the future glorious revelation of Christ, and only by a later idiom the prophecy of it, and which is now commonly used to designate that specific kind of prophecy, of which this book is the most perfect example, which expresses itself in symbolical visions rather than in simple predictive words. According to the usual arrangement, it stands at the end of the New Testament, a position appropriate to its contents, and probably also to its date. It is the only prophetic book of the New Testament Canon and, with the partial exception of Daniel, the only prophetic book of either Testament which is planned and written in the form of a carefully ordered and closely concatenated whole. The boldness of its symbolism makes it the most difficult book of the Bible: it has always been the most variously understood, the most arbitrarily interpreted, the most exegetically tortured.

Any question of its *genuineness, authenticity,* or *canonicity* may be considered excluded by the strength of the external evidence. The book asserts itself to be by John in terms which forbid our understanding another than the John of the other New Testament books (i. 1, 4, 9; xxii. 8). "An unknown John, whose name has disappeared from history, leaving hardly a trace behind it, can scarcely have given commands in the name of Christ and the Spirit to the seven churches"; and it is indubitable that "all this was generally understood in the first two centuries of the apostle John" (Hilgenfeld). Traces of the

---

*From the *Schaff-Herzog Cyclopaedia*, Vol. III, 1884, pp. 2034-2038. I have omitted the bibliography.

use of the book are found as early as Barnabas, Ignatius, and the *Test. XII Patt.*; John's pupil, Papias, witnessed to its credibility; Justin (147) declares it an inspired prophecy of the apostle John. No church writer expresses a different opinion (Gaius of Rome has been misunderstood) until Dionysius of the third century, who, on purely internal grounds, denies it to the author of the Gospel, although asserting it to be certain that its author was some holy and inspired John, who saw a revelation and received knowledge and prophecy. Nor did doubt, when it had thus once entered the Church, spread rapidly. The third century closes without giving us the name of another doubter; and although Eusebius himself wavers, and tells us that opinion in his day was much divided, and soon afterwards the Syrian Church rejected it—not without affecting the judgment of individual writers in Jerusalem, Asia Minor, and Constantinople—yet Eusebius himself believed it to be inspired and canonical, the doubts were purely of an internal kind, the Church at large was never affected by them, and the storm, even in the East, was soon weathered. Objection was renewed in the Reformation era by Erasmus, Carlstadt, Luther, Zwingli: but the churches refused to follow their leading; and, so soon as the subject of controversy changed, the book was used authoritatively by all parties. Modern objection began with W. Mace, 1729, and especially with the party of Semler in Germany. The latest opinion is divided into four classes. The moderate theologians, chiefly of the school of Schleiermacher, just because John wrote the Gospel, deny to him the Apocalypse, which they assign to some other John. The Tübingen school, on the other hand, rightly judging the evidence for the apostolical authorship of the Apocalypse decisive, just on that account deny to him the Gospel. Several extremists wish to pronounce both books forgeries. The Church at large, on the other hand, together with the great majority of critics, defends the common apostolical authorship of both books; although some feel compelled to place them as far apart in date as possible, in order to account for their internal unlikeness: so, for example, Hase, Réville, Weiss (1882), Farrar, Niermeyer. The grounds of modern objection are almost wholly internal, turning on divergences between the Gospel and Apocalypse in doctrinal conception, point of view, style, language. But Gebhardt has shown that no argument against unity of authorship can be drawn from the doctrinal relations of the two books; and every new investigation into the differences of style and language renders it more and more plain that it is consistent with unity of authorship. "The difference in the language can . . . have no decisive weight attached to it" (Reuss).

The *integrity and unity* of the book are not in dispute. Grotius, Vogel, Schleiermacher, Völter, and (at one time) Bleek and De Wette stand almost alone in doubting them. Today "the assumption of the unity of the Apocalypse forms the uniform basis of all works upon it" (Völter). Its *text,* because of the comparatively few manuscripts which contain it, remains in an uncertain state in comparison with the other New Testament books, though not so in comparison with other ancient works, or to any such degree as to impair our confidence in its use.

Its *date* has been much disputed; although the testimony of the early Church, which is ancient, credible, and uniform, would seem decisive for A.D. 94–95. Irenaeus, who was not only brought up in Asia Minor, and there knew several apostolical men, but was also the pupil of John's pupil, Polycarp, explicitly testifies that it was seen towards the close of Domitian's reign; and he is supported in this by Clement of Alexandria, according to Eusebius' understanding of his words, as well as by Victorinus, Jerome, and later writers generally. Eusebius drops no hint that any other opinion was known to him. Even those who denied the book to the apostle, yet assigned it to this time. Not the slightest trace (except, perhaps, an obscure one in Origen) of another opinion is found until the late fourth century (the Muratori canon has been misunderstood), which the notoriously inaccurate Epiphanius, not without self-contradiction, places the banishment and prophecy of John under Claudius (41–54). Some few writers adopt interpretations of special passages which might appear to imply their writing before the destruction of Jerusalem, but this inference is sometimes clearly excluded. No early writer assigns John's banishment, or the composition of the Apocalypse, to the times of Nero or his immediate successors. The earliest direct statement to this effect is found in the Syriac Apocalypse of the sixth century, which declares that John was banished to Patmos by Nero Caesar. (Is this due to a clerical error for Nerva?) This is thought to be supported, (1) by Theophylact (eleventh century), who places the writing of John's Gospel at Patmos thirty-two years after the ascension, but at the same time assigns John's condemnation to Trajan, and (2) by a false reading (*Domitiou* [understood of Nero] for *Domitianou*) in one passage of Hippolytus Thebanus (tenth or eleventh century), which is corrected in another. Certainly, if historical testimony is ever decisive, it assigns the Apocalypse to the closing years of the first century. Nor are supporting internal considerations lacking. (1) The natural implication of i. 9 is, that John was banished to Patmos; and this is in accordance with Domitian's, and not with Nero's, known practice. (2) The churches are addressed after a fashion which suggests intimate, perhaps long-standing, personal acquaintance between them and the author; yet it is certain that, up to A.D. 68, John was not their spiritual head, and was probably unknown to them. Neither in Second Timothy nor in Second Peter (both sent to this region) is there the remotest hint of the relation between John and these churches, which seems to have been of long standing when Rev. ii and iii were written. (3) The internal condition of the seven churches appears to be different from that pictured in Ephesians, Colossians, First and Second Timothy, First and Second Peter; and the difference is such as seems to require not only time, but a period of quiet time, succeeded by a persecution, for its development. (4) The ecclesiastical usages of the churches seem to have made an advance. The term "the Lord's Day," for Sunday, is unique in the New Testament; the office of "pastor," found elsewhere clearly marked in the New Testament only in the case of James, is here assumed as universal in Asia Minor, and well settled; the public reading (i. 3) of the Christian writings in the churches is spoken of as a usage of long standing, and a matter of course.

On the other hand, it has of late become the ruling opinion among critics that the book comes from a time previous to the destruction of Jerusalem. The chief arguments which are urged in its support are: (1) The whole tradition of the Domitianic origin of the Apocalypse hangs on Irenaeus; and it is quite conceivable that Irenaeus has fallen into an error, either as to time alone (e.g., Stuart), or as to matter as well— the banishment, and hence the time of it, and hence the date of the Apocalypse, all depending on a misunderstanding of Rev. i. 9 (e.g., Düsterdieck). But Rev. i. 9 seems most naturally to imply a banishment. Irenaeus does not depend on any inference from the book, but mentions excellent independent sources of information in the matter. It does not follow, because all the evidence of the first three centuries and a half is consentient, that it is dependent on Irenaeus. Eusebius, on the contrary, understands Clement to the same effect, and appeals as well to a plurality of sources.[1] (2) There is not even an obscure reference in the book to the destruction of Jerusalem as a past event —a catastrophe of too great importance in God's dealings with his Church to be passed over in silence in a book of this kind. This would probably be a valid argument if the book were thought to be a history or practical treatise written about 70–80; but if a prophecy written about 95, it is too much to demand that it should contain reference to a catastrophe the lessons of which had been long since learned, and which belonged to a stadium of development as well as date long past. (3) Jerusalem is spoken of in it as still standing, and the temple as still undestroyed (xi. 1, 2, 3, and even i. 7; ii. 9; iii. 9; vi. 12, 16)—a statement which proceeds on a literalistic interpretation confessedly not applicable throughout the book, or in the parallel case of Ezek. xl. (4) The time of writing is exactly fixed by the description of the then reigning emperor in xiii. 13 and xvii. 7-12. Until, however, it be agreed who this emperor

---

[1]*Historia Ecclesiastica*, **III**. 20.

is—whether Nero (Berthold, Bruston), or Galba (Reuss, Ewald, Hilgenfeld, Gebhardt), or Vespasian (Bleek, De Wette, Düsterdieck, Weiss)—this reasoning is not strong; and the interpretation on which it is founded (implying the assumption that the ideal date of any vision can be the actual date of the book itself) is exceedingly unnatural in itself, cannot be made to fit the description, except by extreme pressure of its language, and seems to fasten false expectations on the prophet, if not, indeed, the invention of what is known as the "Nero fable." (5) The chief argument with evangelical men, however, is that derived from the literary differences between the Apocalypse and Gospel of John, which are thought by many to be too great to be explained, except on the supposition that a long period of time intervened between the writing of the two books. The differences in dogmatic conception and point of view will hardly, however, after Gebhardt's investigations, be asserted to be greater than may be explained by the diverse purposes and forms of the two writings; and it is perfectly vain to contend that the differences in style and language are such as are explicable by lapse of time. The Apocalypse betrays no lack of knowledge of, or command over, Greek syntax or vocabulary: the difference lies, rather, in the manner in which a language well in hand is used, in style, properly so called; and the solution of it must turn on psychological, and not chronological, considerations. Every new investigation diminishes the amount and significance of the difference on the one hand, and on the other renders it more and more clear that its explanation is to be sought in the different requirements of the well-marked types of composition and the divergent mental condition of the writer. The evangelist, dealing freely with his material, takes pains to write better Greek than was customary with him; the seer is overwhelmed with visions crowding upon him, and finds no other speech fit for their expression than that of the old prophets, and therefore rightly yields himself to a prophetic, antique, Ezekiel-like, Hebraizing form of speech (Ebrard).[2]

---

[2] At this point the editor of the *Schaff-Herzog Cyclopaedia* inserts a

The *plan and structure* of the book, the whole of which seems to have been seen by John in one day (i. 10), are exceedingly artistic, and are based on progressive repetitions of sevenfold visions. It thus advertises to us at once its copious use of numerical symbolism, and the principle underlying its structure. Ewald, Volkmar, Rinck, Weiss, Farrar, have further correctly seen that the whole consists of seven sections, and thus constitutes a sevenfold series of sevens, and symbolizes the perfection and finality of its revelation. Five of these sections are clearly marked: it is more difficult to trace the other two. But, if we follow the indications of the natural division of the matter, we shall find the separating line between them at xix. 11 (so De Wette, Weiss, Godet, Hilgenfeld). The plan of the whole, then, is as follows: Prologue, i. 1-8; (1) The seven churches, i. 9–iii. 22; (2) The seven seals, iv. 1–viii. 1; (3) The seven trumpets, viii. 2–xi. 19; (4) The seven mystic figures, xii. 1–xiv. 20; (5) The seven bowls, xv. 1–xvi. 21; (6) The sevenfold judgment on the whore, xvii. 1–xix. 10; (7) The sevenfold triumph, xix. 11–xxii. 5; Epilogue, xxii. 6-21. The sevenfold subdivision of each section is easy to trace in all cases except in (5), (6), and (7), where it is more difficult to find, and is more doubtful.

Within this elaborate plan is developed the action of a prophetic poem unsurpassed in sacred or profane literature in either the grandeur of its poetic imagery, or the superb sweep of its prophetic vision. It is of the first importance to its correct

---

footnote (J.E.M.): The early date is now accepted by perhaps the majority of scholars. In its favor, besides the arguments mentioned by the author of the article, may be urged the allusion to the temple at Jerusalem (xi. 1 ff.), in language which implies that it yet existed, but would speedily be destroyed; and, further, that the nature and object of the Revelation are best suited by the earlier date, while its historical understanding is greatly facilitated. With the great conflagration at Rome, and the Neronian persecution fresh in mind, with the horrors of the Jewish war then going on, and in view of the destruction of Jerusalem as an impending fact, John received the visions of the conflicts and the final victories of the Christian Church. His book came, therefore, as a comforter to hearts distracted by calamities without a parallel in history. Cf. Schaff, *History of the Christian Church*, rev. ed., Vol. I, pp. 834-837.

understanding, that we should grasp the fact that its prime *design* is not chronological, but ethical. It was not intended to write history beforehand, but, by tracing the great outlines of the struggle between Christ and the enemy, to keep steadily before the eye of the believer the issue to which all tends, and thus comfort him in distress, encourage him in depression, and succor him in time of need. It has always been the recourse of a persecuted church. In proportion as a church has waxed cold, and settled upon her lees, in that proportion has she neglected this book; but, whenever earthly help and hope have slipped from her grasp, she has addressed herself to it, and found in it all she could need to comfort, encourage, and enhearten. As Luke adjoined to his Acts of the earthly Christ Acts also of the risen Christ, conquering the world from Jerusalem to Rome, and establishing his Church in the face of all opposition, so John, to his Acts of the God become man, adjoins the Acts of the man become God, triumphing not only over one age, but over all ages, not only establishing, but perfecting, his Church; and thus he brings to the New Testament and the Bible its capstone and crown. "If the Gospels are principally intended to lay the foundations of faith, and the Epistles to enkindle love, the Apocalypse gives food to hope. Without it, we should perhaps see in the Church only a place across which believers pass in order to attain individually to salvation. But by its help we recognize in her a body which develops and which struggles until, with all its members, it attains the full stature of Christ" (Godet).

It is evident that all attempts at the *interpretation* of such a book are foredoomed to failure, unless they proceed in full recognition of its special peculiarities. Certain guiding principles to its exegesis emerge from a general view of its form and scope. (1) The primarily ethical purpose of the book, which at once determined the choice and treatment of its matter, and which gives it a universal and eternal application and usefulness, forbids us to expect in it what we might otherwise have looked for, a continuous or detailed account of the events of future ages. All expositions are wrong which read it as a history framed with chronological purpose and detailed minuteness, and seek to apply its main portions to events of local or temporal interest, or to recognize the vast outlines of the future as drawn in it in the minute and recondite details of past or contemporary crises. We might as well see in Michelangelo's Last Judgment a county assize. This were to make John a pedant, puzzling his readers with his superior knowledge of petty details, instead of a comforter, consoling and strengthening their hearts by revelation of the true relations and final outcome of things. He is dealing with the great conflict of heaven and earth and hell, not with such facts as the exact time when Roman emperors began to wear diadems, or that Turcomans used horse-tail standards, or that the arms of old France were three frogs. (2) Like the other Biblical books, the Apocalypse was intended to be, for the purpose it was meant to subserve, a plain book, to be read and understood by plain men. No more than elsewhere are we to find here a hidden and esoteric wisdom, but must labor to avoid the two opposite errors—of considering the book an elaborate puzzle, or refusing to find any mystery in it at all. It would be difficult to determine which notion is the more hopelessly wrong—that which supposes that the original reader readily understood its whole meaning in every particular, and which thus refuses to allow here the brooding shadow which hangs over all unfulfilled prophecy, especially if only broadly outlined; or that which supposes that, in delineating each prophetic picture, the seer chose emblems appropriate, not to his own age or all ages, but specifically to that in which this special prophecy was to be fulfilled, and which thus condemns him to write in enigmas unintelligible to all ages alike—a concourse of meaningless symbols enclosing one single spot of lucidity for each era. Both the analogy of other Scripture and the experience of all time have disproved both fancies. Notwithstanding the naturalists, no one has ever understood all the details of these visions unto perfection; notwithstanding the pedants, the unlettered child of God has found them always open to his spiritual sight, and fitted to his spiritual need. (3) The Apocalypse is written in a language of its own, having its own laws, in accordance with which it must be interpreted. There is such a thing as a grammar of apocalyptical symbolism; and what is meant by the various images is no more a matter for the imagination to settle than are points of Greek syntax. This is not the same as calling the book obscure, in any other sense than a writing in a foreign language is obscure to those ignorant of it. "As all language abounds in metaphor and other materials of imagery, imagery itself may form the ground of a descriptive language. The forms of it may become intelligible terms, and the combination of them may be equivalent to a narrative of description" (Davison). The source and explanation of this symbolism are found in the prophets of the Old Testament (especially Daniel, Ezekiel, and Zechariah) and our Lord's eschatological discourses, which, moreover, furnish the model on the lines of which the Apocalypse is composed. The study of apocryphal apocalypses has also its uses, since their symbolism is also drawn from the canonical prophets; but it is best to draw water directly from the fountain. (4) The question of the fulfilment of the prophecy is totally distinct from and secondary to that of the sense of the prophecy. Nowhere is it more necessary to carry out the processes of exegisis free from subjective preconceptions, and nowhere is it more difficult. There seems no way, except to jealously keep the exegesis of the prophecy and the inquiry after its fulfilment sharply and thoroughly separated. It is only after we know fully what the book says that we can with any propriety ask whether, and how far, these sayings have been fulfilled. (5) As the very structure of the book advises us, and numerous details in it make certain, it is exegetically untenable to regard it as one continuously progressive vision: it is rather a series of seven visions, each reaching to the end, not in mere repetition of each other, but in ever-increasing clearness of development.

Doubtless it is because of failure to note and apply these and like simple principles that the *actual exegesis* of the book has proceeded after such diverse fashions, and reached such entirely contradictory results. No book of the Bible has been so much commented on: the exegesis of no book is in a more unsatisfactory state. It is impossible here to enter upon the *history of its interpretation*: the works of Lücke and Elliott, mentioned below, treat the subject in detail. In general, the schemes of interpretation that have been adopted fall into three roughly drawn classes. (1) *The Preterist*, which holds that all, or nearly all, the prophecies of the book were fulfilled in the early Christian ages, either in the history of the Jewish race up to A.D. 70, or in that of pagan Rome up to the fourth or fifth century. With Hentensius and Salmeron as forerunners, the Jesuit Alcasar (1614) was the father of this school. To it belong Grotius, Bossuet, Hammond, LeClerc, Wetstein, Eichhorn, Herder, Hartwig, Koppe, Hug, Heinrichs, Ewald, De Wette, Bleek, Reuss, Réville, Renan, Desprez, S. Davidson, Stuart, Lücke, Düsterdieck, Maurice, Farrar, etc. (2) *The Futurist*, which holds that the whole book, or most of it, refers to events yet in the future, to precede, accompany, or follow the second advent. The Jesuit Ribera (1603) was the father of this school. To it belong Lacunza, Tyso, S. R. and C. Maitland, DeBurgh, Todd, Kelly, I. Williams, etc. (3) *The Historical*, which holds that the book contains a prophetic view of the great conflict between Christ and the enemy from the first to the second advents. It is as old as the twelfth century, when Berengaud, followed by Anselm and the Abbot Joachim, expounded it. It has received in one form or another, often differing extremely among themselves, the suffrages of most students of the book. It is the system of DeLire, Wiclif, the Reformers generally, Fox, Brightman, Pareus, Mede, Vitringa, Sir I. Newton, Flemming, Daubuz, Whiston, Bengel, Gaussen, Elliott, Faber, Woodhouse, Wordsworth, Hengstenberg, Ebrard, Von Hofmann, Auberlen, Alford, W. Lee, etc. The last six of these writers will be found nearest the truth.

PART II

6

INTRODUCTION TO
FRANCIS R. BEATTIE'S *Apologetics**

It gives me great pleasure to respond to Dr. Beattie's request that I shall say a few words by way of introduction to his
comprehensive work on Apologetics. I am purposely laying
stress on the comprehensiveness of the work. It is always a
satisfaction to have placed in our hands a treatise on one of
the theological disciplines, which develops with serenity and
sanity its entire content. In the case of Apologetics, however, such an achievement is particularly to be welcomed. We
have had many apologies; perhaps no branch of scientific
theology has been more fruitful during the past two centuries.
But we have had comparatively few surveys of the whole field
of Apologetics. Perhaps Dr. Beattie's is the first to be produced
by an American Presbyterian.

The fact is, despite the richness of our apologetical literature,
Apologetics has been treated very much like a stepchild in
the theological household. The encyclopaedists have seemed
scarcely to know what to do with it. They have with difficulty been persuaded to allow it a place among the theological
disciplines at all. And, when forced to recognize it, they have
been very prone to thrust it away into some odd corner, where
it could hide its diminished head behind the skirts of some of
its more esteemed sisters.

This widespread misprision of Apologetics has been greatly
fostered by the influence of two opposite (if they be indeed
opposite) tendencies of thought, which have very deeply
affected the thinking even of theologians who are in principle

---

*Introduction to Francis R. Beattie's *Apologetics: or the Rational
Vindication of Christianity*, Richmond, Va., 1903, pp. 19-32.

antagonistic to them. I mean Rationalism and Mysticism. To Rationalism, of course, Apologetics is an inanity; to Mysticism, an impertinence. Wherever, therefore, rationalistic presuppositions have intruded, there proportionately the validity of Apologetics has been questioned. Wherever mystical sentiment has seeped in, there the utility of Apologetics has been more or less distrusted. At the present moment, the rationalistic tendency is perhaps most active in the churches in the form given it by Albrecht Ritschl. In this form it strikes at the very roots of Apologetics by the distinction it erects between religious and theoretical knowledge. Where religion is supposed to seek and find expression only in value-judgments—the subjective product of the human soul in its struggle after personal freedom—and thus to stand out of all relation with theoretical knowledge, there, obviously there is no place for a vindication of Christian faith to reason and no possibility of Apologetics. In a somewhat odd parallelism to this (though, perhaps, it is not so odd after all) the mystical tendency is showing itself in our day most markedly in a widespread inclination to decline Apologetics in favor of the so-called *testimonium Spiritus Sancti*. The convictions of the Christian man, we are told, are not the product of reasons addressed to his intellect, but are the immediate creation of the Holy Spirit in his heart. Therefore, it is intimated, we can not only do very well without these reasons, but it is something very like sacrilege to attend to them. Apologetics, accordingly, is not merely useless, but may even become noxious, because tending to substitute a barren intellectualism for a vital faith.

We need not much disturb ourselves over such utterances when they are the expression, as they often are in our modern Church, of the intellectual distress of those whose own apologetic has proved too weak to withstand the rationalistic assault, and who are fain, therefore, to take refuge from the oppressive rationalism of their understandings in an empty irrationalism of the heart. In these cases the extremes have met, and the would-be mystic preserves nothing but his dialect to distinguish him from the Ritschlite rationalist. What he needs for his cure is clearly not less Apologetics, but more Apologetics—lacking which he must ever remain of a "double mind," clinging with the desperation of a drowining man to a faith on which his own intellect has passed the sentence of irrationality. The case is very different, however, when we encounter very much the same forms of speech on the lips of heroes of the faith, who deprecate Apologetics because they feel no need of "reasons" to ground a faith which they are sure they have received immediately from God. Apologetics, they say, will never make a Christian. Christians are made by the creative Spirit alone. And when God Almighty has implanted faith in the heart, we shall not require to seek for "reasons" to ground our conviction of the truth of the Christian religion. We have tasted and seen, and we know of ourselves that it is from God. Thus, the sturdiest belief joins hands with unbelief to disparage the defenses of the Christian religion.

Dr. Abraham Kuyper, one of the really great theologians of our time, is a very striking instance of thinkers of this tendency. It is not to be supposed that Dr. Kuyper would abolish Apologetics altogether. He has written an *Encyclopaedia of Sacred Theology*, and in it he gives a place to Apologetics among the other disciplines. But how subordinate a place! And in what a curtailed form! Hidden away as a subdivision of a subdivision of what Dr. Kuyper calls the "Dogmatological Group" of disciplines (which corresponds roughly to what most encyclopaedists call "Systematic Theology"), one has to search for it before he finds it, and when he finds it, he discovers that its function is confined closely, we might almost say jealously, to the narrow task of defending developed Christianity against philosophy, falsely so called. After the contents of Christianity have been set forth thetically in Dogmatics and Ethics, it finds itself, it seems, in a threefold conflict. This is waged with a pseudo-Christianity, a pseudo-religion, and a pseudo-philosophy. Three antithetic dogmatological disciplines are therefore requisite—Polemics, Elenchtics, and Apologetics, corresponding, respectively, to heterodoxy, paganism, philosophy. The least of these is Apologetics, which concerns itself only with the distinctively philosophical assault on Christianity. Meanwhile, as for Christianity itself, it has remained up to this point—let us say it frankly—the great assumption. The work of the exegete, the historian, the systematist, has all hung, so to speak, in the air; not until all their labor is accomplished do they pause to wipe their streaming brows and ask whether they have been dealing with realities, or perchance with fancies only.

Naturally it is not thus that Dr. Kuyper represents it to himself. He supposes that all these workers have throughout wrought in faith. But he seems not quite able to conceal from himself that they have not justified that faith, and that some may think their procedure itself, therefore, unjustified, if not unjustifiable. He distributes the departments of theological science into four groups, corresponding roughly with the Exegetical, Historical, Systematic, and Practical disciplines which the majority of encyclopaedists erect, although for reasons of his own, very interestingly set forth, he prefers to call them, respectively, the Bibliological, Ecclesiological, Dogmatological, and Diaconological groups of disciplines. Now, when he comes to discuss the contents of these groups in detail, he betrays a feeling that something is lacking at the beginning. "Before dealing separately with the four groups of departments of study into which theology is divided," he says, "we must give a brief resumé from the second part of this *Encyclopaedia*, of how the subject arrives at the first group. Logical order demands that the first group bring you to the point where the second begins, that the second open the way for the third, and that the third introduce you to the fourth. But no other precedes the first group, and it is accordingly in place here to indicate how we arrive at the first group."[1] Just so, surely!

Dr. Kuyper proceeds to point out that the subject of theology is the human consciousness; that in this consciousness there is implanted a *sensus divinitatis,* a *semen religionis,* which impels it to seek after the knowledge of God; that in the sinner this

---

[1] *Encyclopaedie der Heilige Godgeleerdheid,* Deel III, pp. 4 ff.

action is renewed and quickened by the palingenesis, through which the subject is opened for the reception of the special revelation of God made first by deed, culminating in the Incarnation, and then by word, centering in the Scriptures. Thus, by the *testimonium Spiritus Sancti*, the subject is put in possession of the revelation of God embodied in the Scriptures, and is able to proceed to explicate its contents through the several disciplines of theological science. Now, what is it that Dr. Kuyper has done here except outline a very considerable— though certainly not a complete—Apologetics, which must precede and prepare the way for the "Bibliological Group" of theological departments? We must, it seems, vindicate the existence of a *sensus divinitatis* in man capable of producing a natural theology independently of special revelation; and then the reality of a special revelation in deed and word; and as well, the reality of a supernatural preparation of the heart of man to receive it; before we can proceed to the study of theology at all, as Dr. Kuyper has outlined it. With these things at least we must, then, confessedly, reckon at the outset; and to reckon with these things is to enter deeply into Apologetics.

As the case really stands, we must say even more. Despite the attractiveness of Dr. Kuyper's distribution of the departments of theological science, we cannot think it an improvement upon the ordinary *schema*. It appears to us a mistake to derive, as he does, the *principium divisionis* from the Holy Scriptures. The Scriptures, after all, are not the object of theology, but only its source; and the *principium divisionis* in this science, too, must be taken, as Dr. Kuyper himself argues,[2] from the object. Now, the object of theology, as Dr. Kuyper has often justly insisted, is the ectypal knowledge of God. This knowledge of God is deposited for us in the Scriptures, and must needs be drawn out of them—hence "Exegetical Theology." It has been derived from the Scriptures by divers portions and in divers manners, for the life of the Church through the ages, and its gradual assimilation must needs be traced in its

---

[2]*Encyclopaedia*, E. T., p. 629.

effects on the life of the Christian world—hence "Historical Theology." It is capable of statement in a systematized thetical form—hence "Systematic Theology." And, so drawn out from Scripture, so assimilated in the Church's growth, so organized into a system, it is to be made available for life—hence "Practical Theology." But certainly, before we draw it from the Scriptures, we must assure ourselves that there is a knowledge of God in the Scriptures. And, before we do that, we must assure ourselves that there is a knowledge of God in the world. And, before we do that, we must assure ourselves that a knowledge of God is possible for man. And, before we do that, we must assure ourselves that there is a God to know. Thus, we inevitably work back to first principles. And, in working thus back to first principles, we exhibit the indispensability of an "Apologetical Theology," which of necessity holds the place of the first among the five essential theological disciplines.

It is easy, of course, to say that a Christian man must take his standpoint not *above* the Scriptures, but *in* the Scriptures. He very certainly must. But surely he must first *have* Scriptures, authenticated to him as such, before he can take his standpoint in them. It is equally easy to say that Christianity is attained, not by demonstrations, but by a new birth. Nothing could be more true. But neither could anything be more unjustified than the inferences that are drawn from this truth for the discrediting of Apologetics. It certainly is not in the power of all the demonstrations in the world to make a Christian. Paul may plant and Apollos water; it is God alone who gives the increase. But it does not seem to follow that Paul would as well, therefore, not plant, and Apollos as well not water. Faith is the gift of God; but it does not in the least follow that the faith that God gives is an irrational faith, that is, a faith without grounds in right reason. It is beyond all question only the prepared heart that can fitly respond to the "reasons"; but how can even a prepared heart respond, when there are no "reasons" to draw out its action? One might as well say that photography is independent of light, because no light can make an impression unless the plate is prepared to receive it. The

Holy Spirit does not work a blind, an ungrounded faith in the heart. What is supplied by his creative energy in working faith is not a ready-made faith, rooted in nothing and clinging without reason to its object; nor yet new grounds of belief in the object presented; but just a new ability of the heart to respond to the grounds of faith, sufficient in themselves, already present to the understanding. We believe in Christ because it is rational to believe in him, not though it be irrational. Accordingly, our Reformed fathers always posited in the production of faith the presence of the "*argumentum propter quod credo*," as well as the "*principium seu causa efficiens a quo ad credendum adducor.*" That is to say, for the birth of faith in the soul, it is just as essential that grounds of faith should be present to the mind as that the Giver of faith should act creatively upon the heart.

We are not absurdly arguing that Apologetics has in itself the power to make a man a Christian or to conquer the world to Christ. Only the Spirit of Life can communicate life to a dead soul, or can convict the world in respect of sin, and of righteousness, and of judgment. But we are arguing that faith is, in all its exercises alike, a form of conviction, and is, therefore, necessarily grounded in evidence. And we are arguing that evidence accordingly has its part to play in the conversion of the soul; and that the systematically organized evidence which we call Apologetics similarly has its part to play in the Christianizing of the world. And we are arguing that this part is not a small part; nor is it a merely subsidiary part; nor yet a merely defensive part—as if the one end of Apologetics were to protect an isolated body of Christians from annoyance from the surrounding world, or to aid the distracted Christian to bring his head into harmony with his heart. The part that Apologetics has to play in the Christianizing of the world is rather a primary part, and it is a conquering part. It is the distinction of Christianity that it has come into the world clothed with the mission to *reason* its way to its dominion. Other religions may appeal to the sword, or seek some other way to propagate themselves. Christianity makes its appeal to right reason, and stands out among all religions, therefore, as distinctively "the Apologetic religion." It is solely by reasoning that it has come thus far on its way to its kingship. And it is solely by reasoning that it will put all its enemies under its feet. Face to face with the tremendous energy of thought and the incredible fertility in assault which characterizes the world in its anti-Christian manifestation, Christianity finds its task in thinking itself thoroughly through, and in organizing, not its defense only, but also its attack. It stands calmly over against the world with its credentials in its hands, and fears no contention of men.

It is a standing matter of surprise to us that the brilliant school of Christian thinkers, on whose attitude toward Apologetics we have been animadverting, should be tempted to make little of Apologetics. When we read, for instance, the beautiful exposition of sin and regeneration to science which Dr. Kuyper has given us in his *Encyclopaedie*, we cannot understand why he does not magnify, instead of minifying, the value of Apologetics. Perhaps the explanation is to be found in a tendency to make too absolute the contrast between the "two kinds of science"—that which is the product of the thought of sinful man in his state of nature, and that which is the product of man under the influence of the regenerating grace of God. There certainly do exist these "two kinds of men" in the world —men under the unbroken sway of sin, and men who have been brought under the power of the palingenesis. And the product of the intellection of these "two kinds of men" will certainly give us "two kinds of science." But the difference between the two is, after all, not accurately described as a difference in *kind—gradus non mutant speciem*. Sin has not destroyed or altered in its essential nature any one of man's faculties, although—since it corrupts *homo totus*—it has affected the operation of them all. The depraved man neither thinks, nor feels, nor wills as he ought; and the products of his action as a scientific thinker cannot possibly escape the influence of this everywhere operative destructive power; although, as Dr. Kuyper lucidly points out, they are affected in different degrees in the several "sciences," in accordance with the nature of their objects and the rank of the human faculties engaged in their structure. Nevertheless, there is question here of perfection of performance, rather than of kind. It is "science" that is produced by the subject held under sin, even though imperfect science—falling away from the ideal here, there, and elsewhere, on account of all sorts of deflecting influences entering in at all points of the process. The science of sinful man is thus a substantive part of the abstract science produced by the ideal subject, the general human consciousness, though a less valuable part than it would be without sin.

It is well that it is so; for otherwise there would be no "science" attainable by man at all. For regeneration is not, in the first instance, the removal of sin: the regenerated man remains a sinner. Only after his sanctification has become complete can the contrast between him and the unregenerate sinner become absolute; not until then, in any case, could there be thought to exist an absolute contrast between his intellection and that of the sinner. In the meantime, the regenerated man remains a sinner; no new faculties have been inserted into him by regeneration; and the old faculties, common to man in all his states, have been only in some measure restored to their proper functioning. He is in no condition, therefore, to produce a "science" differing in *kind* from that produced by sinful man; the science of palingenesis is only a part of the science of sinful humanity, though no doubt its best part; and only along with it can it enter as a constituent part into that ideal science which the composite human subject is producing in its endless effort to embrace in mental grasp the ideal object, that is to say, all that is. Even if the palingenesis had completed its work, indeed, and those under its sway had become "perfect," it may be doubted whether the contrast between the science produced by the two classes of men could be treated as absolute. Sinful and sinless men are, after all, both men; and being both men, are fundamentally alike and know fundamentally alike. Ideally there is but one "science," the subject of which is the human spirit, and the object all that is. Meanwhile, as things are, the human spirit attains to this science only in part and by slow accretions, won through many partial and erroneous constructions. Men of all sorts and of all grades work side by side at the common task, and the common edifice grows under their hands into ever fuller and truer outlines. As Dr. Kuyper finely says himself,[3] in the conflict of perceptions and opinions, those of the strongest energy and clearest thought finally prevail. Why is not the palingenesis to be conceived simply as preparing the stronger and clearer spirits whose thought always finally prevails? It is not a different kind of science that they are producing. It is not even the same kind of science, but as part of a different edifice of truth. Through them merely the better scientific outlook, the better scientific product, are striving in conflict with the outlook and product of fellow workers, to get built into the one great edifice of truth ascertained, which is rising slowly because of sin, but surely because of palingenesis.

Only in the divine mind, of course, does science lie perfect— the perfect comprehension of all that is in its organic completeness. In the mind of perfected humanity, the perfected ectypal science shall at length lie. In the mind of sinful humanity, struggling here below, there can lie only a partial and broken reflection of the object, a reflection which is rather a deflection. The task of science is, therefore, not merely quantitative, but qualitative; the edifice must be built up to its completion, and the deflection induced by sin must be corrected. This cannot be accomplished by sinful man. But he makes the effort continuously, and is continuously attaining his measure of success—a success that varies inversely with the rank of the sciences. The entrance of regeneration prepares men to build better and ever more truly as the effects of regeneration increase intensively and extensively. The end will come only when the regenerated universe becomes the well-comprehended object of the science of the regenerated race. It would seem, then, a grave mistake to separate the men of the palingenesis from the race, a part of which they are, and which is itself the

---

[3]*Encyclopaedia*, E. T., p. 151.

object of the palingenesis. And no mistake could be greater than to lead them to decline to bring their principles into conflict with those of the unregenerate in the prosecution of the common task of man. It is the better science that ever in the end wins the victory; and palingenetic science is the better science, and to it belongs the victory. How shall it win its victory, however, if it declines the conflict? In the ordinance of God, it is only in and through this conflict that the edifice of truth is to rise steadily onwards to its perfecting.

In the fact thus brought out, the ultimate vindication of the supreme importance of Apologetics lies, and as well the vindication of its supreme utility. In the prosecution of the tasks of Apologetics, we see the palingenesis at work on the science of man at its highest point. And here, too, the "man of stronger and purer thought"—even though that he has it is of God alone —"will prevail in the end." The task of the Christian is surely to urge "his stronger and purer thought" continuously, and in all its details, upon the attention of men. It is not true that he cannot soundly prove his position. It is not true that the Christian view of the world is subjective merely, and is incapable of validation in the forum of pure reason. It is not true that the arguments adduced for the support of the foundations of the Christian religion lack objective validity. It is not even true that the minds of sinful men are inaccessible to the "evidences," though, in the sense of the proverb, "convinced against their will," they may "remain of the same opinion still." All minds are of the same essential structure; and the less illuminated will not be able permanently to resist or gainsay the determinations of the more illuminated. The Christian, by virtue of the palingenesis working in him, stands undoubtedly on an indefinitely higher plane of thought than that occupied by sinful man as such. And he must not decline, but use and press the advantage which God has thus given him. He must insist, and insist again, that his determinations, and not those of the unilluminated, must be built into the slowly rising fabric of human science. Thus will he serve, if not obviously his own generation, yet truly all the generations of men.

We may assure ourselves from the outset that the palingenesis shall ultimately conquer to itself the whole race and all its products; and we may equally assure ourselves that its gradually increasing power will show itself only as the result of conflict in the free intercourse of men.

Thinking thus of Apologetics and of its task, it is natural that we should feel little sympathy with the representation sometimes heard, to the effect that Apologetics concerns itself only with "the *minimum* of Christianity." What is "the *minimum* of Christianity"? And what business has Apologetics with "the *minimum* of Christianity"? What Apologetics has to do with is certainly not any "*minimum*," but just Christianity itself, whatever that may prove to be. Its function is not to vindicate for us the least that we can get along with, and yet manage to call ourselves Christians; but to validate the Christian "view of the world," with all that is contained in the Christian "view of the world," for the science of men. It must not be permitted to sink into an "apology" for the Christian religion, in the vulgar sense of that word, which makes it much the synonym of an "excuse"; and much less into an "apology" for what is at best an "apology for the Christian religion"—possibly nothing more than "a couple of starved and hunger-bitten dogmas," which for the purposes of the moment we may choose to identify with "the essence of Christianity." The function of Apologetics is not performed until it has placed in our hands God, religion, Christianity, and the Bible, and said to us, Now go on and explicate these fundamental facts in all their contents. When men speak of "the Apologetical *minimum*," we cannot help suspecting that they have for the moment lost sight of Apologetics itself altogether, and are thinking rather of some specific "Apology" which they judge might usefully be launched in behalf of Christianity, in the conditions of thought for the moment obtaining. If such an "Apology" were identifiable with "Apologetics," we might well sympathize with those who consider Apologetics a department of "Practical Theology," and it is doubtless because they do not rise above such a conception of it that many encyclopaedists have so classified it. But the

Apologetics with which we are concerned is a much more fundamental, a much more comprehensive, and a much more objective thing. It does not concern itself with how this man or that may best be approached to induce him to make a beginning of Christian living, or how this age or that may most easily be brought to give a hearing to the Christian conception of the world. It concerns itself with the solid objective establishment, after a fashion valid for all normally working minds and for all ages of the world in its developing thought, of those great basal facts which constitute the Christian religion; or, better, which embody in the concrete the entire knowledge of God accessible to men, and which, therefore, need only explication by means of the further theological disciplines in order to lay openly before the eyes of men the entirety of the knowledge of God within their reach.

It is because Dr. Beattie's treatise conceives Apologetics after this fundamental, comprehensive, and objective fashion, and develops its contents from that point of view, that we accord it our heartiest welcome.

7

A REVIEW OF *De Zekerheid des Geloofs**

DE ZEKERHEID DES GELOOFS. By PROF. DR. H. BAVINCK (8 VO, pp. 78), Kampen: J. H. Kok, 1901.

In this delightful booklet Dr. Bavinck gives us not so much a scientific investigation into the nature and sources of certitude in religion as a popular discussion of the whole matter of certitude with reference to Christianity. "Inquiry into the certainty of faith," he tells us, "is of importance not merely for scientific theology but also for practical religion. It concerns not only the theologian but equally the layman; it has a place not alone in the study but in the household sanctuary as well. It is a question not more of theory and the schools than eminently also of practice and life." The particular subject of investigation which he proposes to himself in this discussion is the determination of "where and how that divine authority is to be found which has the right to demand from us recognition and obedience" (p. 50). In the interests of orderly development, however, he prefixes to the answer offered to this main inquiry some account of "what is to be understood by this certainty of faith, and how it has been sought by various schools of thought" (p. 12).

The first part of the discourse is devoted therefore to defining

---

*From the *Princeton Theological Review*, Jan. 1903, pp. 138-148. In his *Opuscula*, Vol. IX, Dr. Warfield notes that Dr. Bavinck "very graciously referred to" this review "in the second edition of his book." It is hoped that the reader will not object to the repetition here of a few paragraphs found in the previous article; both articles are important in evaluating the "Princeton apologetic" as contrasted with the viewpoint of the Amsterdam school of thought represented by Drs. Kuyper and Bavinck. See *Jerusalem and Athens*, 1971, edited by E. R. Geehan, pp. 154 ff., 275 ff., 420 ff., for the continuing interest in the issues raised here.

the nature of the certitude of faith that is under discussion. Certitude, we are told, is the complete resting of the spirit in an object of knowledge. Even the Greeks recognized various varieties of it—distinguishing between the certitude produced by sense-perception and that produced by thought, and in the latter further between the immediate certainty we possess of the first principles of science and the mediate certainty we attain by reasoning and demonstration. Alongside of these universally recognized varieties must be placed, he urges, the further variety known as the certitude of faith—which is not the result of either sense-perception or of scientific proof, but differs from all certainty so reached in two respects: it is objectively weaker, it is subjectively stronger. Objectively weaker, because it does not rest on grounds of common reason, valid for all, to which therefore compelling appeal may be made; but is the fruit of a faith, the possession of the individual alone. Subjectively stronger, because it is rooted in the very heart of man and is intertwined with all the fibers of his being, expressing not merely an intellectual judgment but a movement of the whole soul.

In the second part a rapid but illuminating survey is given of the history of certitude of faith in the Church. Here come under review Rome's renunciation of all individual assurance of salvation; the recovery of it by the Reformers, and its gradual loss again in the seventeenth century; pietistic legalism with its renewed renunciation of personal assurance; the different one-sided efforts of Moravians and Methodists to regain it; its virtual disappearance from modern Christendom. This section is notable for the genial and yet clear-sighted judgments it expresses. Apropos of the effort to attain a sense of safety through an ascetic life, which is represented as one side of the Romish development, for example, Protestants are sharply warned not to content themselves with the facile condemnation that it all is the result of a false principle—the false principle of work-righteousness. This is true enough, Dr. Bavinck remarks, but it becomes Protestants to consider that Romish work-righteousness is at least preferable to that doctrine-

righteousness to which Protestants are prone: work-righteousness, usually at least, advantages somebody, while doctrine-
righteousness produces no fruit but loveless pride.

Again, nothing could be more just than the criticism passed
upon the diverse attempts of the Moravians and Methodists
to restore assurance to the Christian heart. "Both movements,"
we read, "have exerted a strong influence on the Christian life.
They have aroused believers out of their self-engrossment and
recalled them from their retirement to the conflict with the
world. Home and foreign missions have been vigorously taken
in hand under their direction. Sunday schools and associations
of all kinds and for all sorts of purposes have been established
through their initiative. Bible and tract distributions, evangelizing and philanthropic enterprises and numerous other Christian activities have been since their rise set on foot for the
extension of God's Kingdom. The whole of Christendom has
been aroused from its slumber and awakened to a new and
energetic life." "Nevertheless," he adds, "both movements
indubitably suffer from a great one-sidedness. Neither of them
reckons sufficiently with the first article of our common undoubted Christian faith, that God the Father Almighty is the
Maker of heaven and earth. The earthly spheres of art and
science, of literature and politics, of domestic and social economy are underestimated in value and significance by them, and
are consequently not reformed and regenerated by the Christian
principle. To 'rest in the wounds of Jesus' or 'to be converted
and then go forth to convert others' seems to constitute the
entire content of the Christian life. Sentimentality and un-
healthy emotion seem often to mark the one, excitement and
zeal without knowledge frequently to characterize the other
movement. The intellect is repressed in the interests of the
feelings and will, and the harmony of all the faculties and
powers is destroyed. The liberty of the children of God, their
dominion over the world, the thankful enjoyment of every good
gift that comes down from the Father of lights, the faithful
discharge of the earthly vocation—the open eye, the wide outlook, the expanded heart—these things do not come to their

rights. The Christian life stands here alongside of—sometimes above, in some instances even hostilely in opposition to—human life. Christianity is here not like the leaven that transfuses the whole lump and leavens it all" (pp. 45-46).

This wide-minded conception of the mission of Christianity in the world is, as it should be, characteristic of Dr. Bavinck's teaching as of that of the whole school to which he belongs. He has given beautiful expression to it in a separate tractate on *De Algemeene Genade*, published in 1894 and reviewed in this *Review* for January, 1897 (Vol. VIII, p. 155); and Dr. A. Kuyper has sought to work it out in all its details in a long series of articles on Common Grace printed in *De Heraut* and just now being gathered into volume form. It is reverted to more than once in the present brochure, and especially most eloquently near its close, where the pietist is blamed for withdrawing from the world and treating all earthly employment— even the care of husband, wife, or family—as only so much time and effort withdrawn from "the one thing needful"; and the Christian is exhorted to remember that all things are his, because he is Christ's and Christ is God's, and to enter into his dominion as king of the whole earth—loving the flowers that bloom at his feet and admiring the stars that shine above his head, not despising art, which is a noble gift from God, or sneering at science, which is a bequest from the Father of lights, but believing that every creature of God is good and is not to be rejected but received with thanksgiving. We miss in this only the explicit correlation of this noble and truly Reformed conception of the Christian's relation to the world with the organic character of the redemptive work and its eschatological outlook. For it is only as we realize that God is saving the world and not merely one individual here and there out of the world, that the profound significance of the earthly life to the Christian can be properly apprehended. And the deepest distinction between the attitude to the world alike of the Pietist, Moravian, and Methodist and that of the Reformed Christian turns just on the fact that the point of view of the former is individualistic and atomistic and that of the latter is organic.

Missing explicit reference to the organic character of the redemptive process, in the reformation of the world after the plan of God and its gradual transmutation into his Kingdom in which his will shall be done even as in heaven, the uninstructed reader may fail to catch the ground of the significance to the Christian of the earthly life which is so eloquently described, and may even mentally pass the unintelligent criticism which is so often pressed against the Reformed conception, that with its doctrine of predestination it leaves the earthly life without significance—a criticism which obviously is without meaning save on the extremest individualistic presuppositions.

To the third part of the essay is committed the task of explaining how Christian certitude is to be attained. Here the stress of the exposition is thrown on the assumption that it is to be reached in neither of the two ways in which it is most commonly sought—which may be called the apologetical and the experimental ways. Men cannot reach Christian certitude, we are told, as the result of a process of reasoning—proving first of all on rational grounds that God exists and there is such a thing as the soul and it is immortal; and then that the apostles are trustworthy witnesses of truth, that the prophecies of Scripture were really spoken and its miracles really occurred, and that Jesus really lived and worked and taught as he is represented to have done; and the like. All such reasonings leave the truth of Christianity not yet raised above all doubt and cannot be said to supply ground for an absolute certitude. Neither can it be attained, however, by the method introduced by Schleiermacher, which throws men back for certitude on what each has individually experienced. The greater part of what enters into the Christian religion has not been and cannot be "experienced" by the individual Christian: it comes to him from without, and only as so coming to him works "experiences" in him—and somewhat similar "experiences," including the experience of passionate conviction, are wrought by the teachings of every religion. It is very easy to say with Zinzendorf, "My heart tells me it is true; it is true for me." But what is there that the human heart may not, under appropriate circumstances, tell us is true? And how can a scientific certitude be attained along this pathway?

How then is certitude of faith to be attained? There remains nothing to be said except that it is the fruit of faith itself. Faith, it must be remembered, is a moral act and not merely an intellectual assent. It is the response of the whole being to its appropriate object: and when the soul of man thus goes out to and finds satisfaction in an object presented to it, it carries its assurance in the very act. How the believer comes to this act, he cannot himself explain. He only knows that an object is presented to him, to which his whole being goes out in loving trust. This is not to make faith the ground on which the truth rests, or the fountain from which the knowledge of it comes, but only the organ of the soul by which truth, which is in itself objective and rests on itself, is recognized. There is always a correlation between the object and the faculty by which it is laid hold of. The eye in perceiving the sun knows that the sun exists no less than that it perceives it. So the believer in receiving the truth knows that it is the truth that he receives. There is involved in this obviously also an assurance of salvation. Here, too, it is with faith as with knowledge. It belongs to knowledge to be assured not only of its object but also of itself. When we know something, we know along with this that we know it. Real, true knowledge excludes all doubt of itself; not by a logical process but directly and immediately. "So it is also with faith. The faith that really deserves the name brings its own assurance with it. When we from the heart believe the promises of God revealed in the gospel, say, for example, the forgiveness of sins, we believe at the same time that we are ourselves personally by grace sharers in the blessing of forgiveness; the former is impossible without the latter. Certitude as to the truth of the gospel is never to be attained except along the path of personal saving faith. And just like knowledge, faith does not come to certitude regarding itself by logical reasoning, by making itself the object of investigation and meditating on its own nature: the 'criticism of pure reason' is seldom useful for establishing our certitude. But certitude flows to us immediately and directly out of faith itself; certitude is an essential quality of faith, it is inseparable from it and belongs to our nature." The practical rule for acquiring certitude of faith is, then, to keep our thought on the object of faith. It is this object that works through faith on our nature and produces certitude. "Let the plant of faith then only root itself in the soil of the promises of God and it will of itself bear the fruit of certitude. And the deeper and faster its roots are buried in the soil, the more strongly will it shoot up, the higher will it grow and the richer will be the fruitage."

We are not sure we have done full justice to Dr. Bavinck in this transcript of his exposition. We are sure the practical advice he gives is sound: it is the object of faith that is the main thing, not the faith itself; and it is on that object that we must keep the eyes of our heart set would we grow in strength of faith and in the joy that comes of believing. But we are not at all sure we have fully apprehended his analysis of the rise of certitude in the soul. Indeed we must confess to a certain confusion of mind as to the exact sense in which the word certitude is to be taken here and there. If we understand Dr. Bavinck, he considers that the two things most commonly connoted by the term go always together: that "certitude of the truth of the Christian religion'" and "assurance of faith" imply one another, and neither is ever present without the other—both being the fruit indeed of one single act of faith. This is itself a debatable point: and in any case it will conduce to clearness if we endeavor to keep separate the two, certainly very separable, inquiries of how men can reach certainty as to the truth of the Christian religion and how they can reach assurance as to their own participation in the benefits secured by the work of Christ. For ourselves, we confess we can conceive of no act of faith of any kind which is not grounded in evidence: faith is a specific form of persuasion or conviction, and all persuasion or conviction is grounded in evidence. And it does not seem obvious on the face of it that the evidence adapted to ground the conviction that the Christian religion is true, and the evidence adapted to ground the conviction that I am myself in Christ

Jesus, need be the same: so that the resulting acts of faith must necessarily occur together or even coalesce. It is quite legitimate, of course, to endeavor to point out that there is nevertheless a point in which the two do coalesce: to urge, for instance, that certitude of the truth of Christianity involves, if it does not consist in, assurance that God is in Christ reconciling the world with himself; and that likewise assurance that I am in Christ is at bottom nothing other than the conviction that God is in Christ reconciling the world with himself, given a personal form: so that it is only by the direct act of faith laying hold of Jesus as redeemer that we may attain either conviction of the truth of the Christian religion or the assurance of salvation. We have no wish to minimize the value of this suggestion—which, if we understand him, expresses more or less crudely Dr. Bavinck's position. But it seems to involve certain assumptions that stand in some need of explication.

For one thing, the assumption that the direct act of saving faith underlies and is the necesary prerequisite of certitude of the truth of the Christian religion appears to reverse the natural order. On the face of it, conviction of the truth of the Christian religion would appear to be the logical *prius* of self-commitment to the Founder of that religion—who is also its Heart—as the redeemer of my soul. So to hold would not necessarily be to say that a man must be a learned apologist before he can become a Christian, and entrance into the Kingdom of Heaven can be had only through the lofty gateway of Science. There are other evidences of the truth of the Christian religion besides the philosophical and historical ones; and the appeal to faith may not be an appeal to an unjustified and therefore irrational faith, because it does not require the marshaling of all the evidence by which it may be supported before it is obeyed. We do not believe in the existence of the sun without evidence because we are not learned in astronomical science. My conviction that the handwriting that lies before me is that of my dear friend is not a groundless conviction, because I am not capable of analyzing the nature of the evidence on which it is founded, and the conviction may seem to me therefore to be direct and without mediation through "reasons." Our believing response to the appeal of the gospel may similarly not be ungrounded in sufficient evidence of the truth of the Christian religion merely because the evidence on which it is grounded is not all the evidence which might be adduced and works its affect of conviction in our hearts by so direct and subtle an operation that we do not stop, perhaps do not possess the skill, to analyze it. Surely we believe in Christ because it is rational to believe in him, though it be irrational.

It is a natural result of the view we are discussing to make little of "the evidences." It is therefore characteristic of the school of thought of which Dr. Bavinck is a shining ornament to estimate the value of Apologetics somewhat lightly. This is apparent in this essay also, although Dr. Bavinck is careful in it to point out the esteem in which he holds it and the high estimate he puts upon it. The prophets, the apostles, Jesus himself, he tells us, used the method of "proofs." It is wrong, therefore, in a spirit of doubt and suspicion, to abstain from them and retire behind the bulwarks of mysticism and agnosticism. "Believers are rather called to give an account of the hope that is in them even in the domain of science, and in firm trust in the justice of their cause, to stop the mouths of opponents and to repel their assaults" (p. 58). But he goes on to intimate at once that all the "proofs" that the Christian can marshal are nevertheless insufficient to place the truth of Christianity beyond doubt (pp. 56 and 57): and he elsewhere expresses his conviction of the secondary place of Apologetics sententiously, in the form that "Apologetics is the fruit, not the root of faith" (p. 24). We cannot help believing there is some slight confusion here. No one is in danger of believing that "the evidences" can produce "faith": but neither can the presentation of Christ in the gospel produce "faith." "Faith" is the gift of God. But it does not follow that the "faith" that God gives is not grounded in "the evidences." Of course it is only the prepared heart that can fitly respond to the force of the "evidences," or "receive" the proclamation: just as it is only the eye that can see, as Dr. Bavinck explains, to which the sun can reveal itself. But this faith that the prepared heart yields—is it yielded blindly and without reason, or is it yielded rationally and on the ground of sufficient reason? Does God the Holy Spirit work a blind and ungrounded faith in the heart? What is supplied by the Holy Spirit in working faith in the heart surely is not a ready-made faith, rooted in nothing and clinging without reason to its object; nor yet new grounds of belief in the object presented; but just a new power to the heart to respond to the grounds of faith, sufficient in themselves, already present to the mind. Our Reformed fathers did not overlook this: they always posited the presence, in the production of faith, of the "*argumentum, propter quod credo,*" as well as the "*principium seu causa efficiens a quo ad credendum adducor.*" From this point of view, the presence to the mind of the "grounds" of faith is just as essential as the creative operation of the Giver of faith itself.

Perhaps we should say even more. The Holy Spirit does not produce faith without grounds. But the "grounds" may and do produce a faith without that specific operation of the Holy Spirit by which alone saving faith can be created in the soul. In saying this we have the fullest support from Dr. Bavinck's own exposition. He tells us that the rational arguments which are urged in favor of the truth of Christianity are of great use in silencing gainsayers. How can they so operate if they are adapted to produce no conviction in the minds of the gainsayers? He remarks again that these rational arguments can of themselves produce nothing more than "historical faith." This is true. But then "historical faith" is faith—is a conviction of mind; and it is, as Dr. Bavinck elsewhere fully allows, of no little use in the world. The truth therefore is that rational argumentation does, entirely apart from that specific operation of the Holy Ghost which produces saving faith, ground a genuine exercise of faith. This operation of the Spirit is not necessary then to produce faith, but only to give to a faith which naturally grows out of the proper grounds of faith, that peculiar quality which makes it saving faith.

Perhaps we may make this clear by an illustration drawn

from the specific instance of "faith in God." Even as sinner, man cannot but believe in God: the very devils believe—and tremble. But as sinner, man cannot have faith in God in the higher sense of humbly trusting in him. Precisely what sin has done to man is to destroy the root of this trust by altering the relation to God in which man stands. Man as sinner is, of course, just as truly and just as entirely dependent on God as he was in his unfallen state: and because he is self-conscious he remains conscious of this, his relation of dependence on God; so long as he remains human he cannot escape the consciousness of dependence on God. But this consciousness no longer bears the same character as in the unfallen state. In the unfallen state consciousness of dependence on God took the "form" of glad and loving trust. By destroying the natural relation that exists between God and his creature and instituting a new relation—that proper to God and sinner—sin has introduced a new factor into the functioning of all human powers. The sinner instinctively and by his very nature, as he cannot help believing in God, in the intellectual sense, so cannot possibly exercise faith in God in the fiducial sense. On the contrary, faith in this sense has been transformed into its opposite—faith has passed into unfaith, trust to distrust. Faith now takes the "form" of fear and despair. The reëstablishment of it in the "form" of loving trust cannot be the work of the sinner himself. It can result only from a radical change in the relation of the sinner to God, brought home to the sinner by that creative act of the Holy Ghost which we call the *testimonium Spiritus Sancti.* Of course this restored "faith of trust" is not precisely the same thing as the "faith of trust" in unfallen man: it differs from that as a forgiven sinner differs from one who has never sinned. But this difference is not the important thing for our present purpose. That is the outstanding fact that "faith in God" is natural to man, belongs to him in all his states alike, and rests throughout them all on its proper grounds. What differs from state to state is the "form" taken by this faith—whether it is "formed" by trust or by fear. It cannot be hopeless, therefore, to produce in the sinner that form of conviction we call faith, by the presentation of the evidence on which it rests. What is hopeless is to produce by this evidence the "form" which faith takes in the regenerated sinner. That comes only by the operation of the Spirit of God. But faith without this is not therefore useless and of little worth.

It is a standing matter of surprise to us that the school which Dr. Bavinck so brilliantly represents should be tempted to make so little of Apologetics. When we read, for instance, the really beautiful exposition which Dr. Kuyper has given us in his *Encyclopaedia of Theology* of the relation of sin and regeneration to science, we cannot understand why he does not magnify instead of minifying the value of Apologetics. Perhaps the explanation is to be found in a tendency to make the contrast between the "two kinds of science"—that of nature and that of palingenesis—too absolute. There are "two kinds of men"—men under the power of sin and men under the power of the palingenesis; and the product of their intellection will naturally give us "two kinds of science": but the difference between the two is after all not properly described as a difference in *kind—gradus not mutant speciem*. For a critical estimate of Dr. Kuyper's view on this matter we should obviously take our start from an exact conception of the effects of sin on man. Sin clearly has not destroyed or altered in its essential nature any one of man's faculties, although (since it has affected *homo totus et omnis*) it has affected the operation of them all. The depraved man neither reasons, nor feels, nor wills as he ought. The products of his action as a scientific thinker cannot possibly escape this influence, though they are affected in different degrees and through different channels, as Dr. Kuyper lucidly points out, in the several "sciences," in accordance with the nature of their object. Nevertheless there is question here rather of perfection than of kind of performance: it is "science" that is produced by the sinful subject even though imperfect science—falling away from the ideal, here, there, and elsewhere, on account of all sorts of deflecting influences, entering it at all points of the process. The science of sinful man is thus a substantive part of the abstract science

produced by the ideal subject, the general human consciousness, though a less valuable part than it would be without sin.

Regeneration, now, is not in the first instance the removal
of sin; the regenerated man remains a sinner. It is only after
his sanctification is completed that the contrast between him
and the sinner can be thought to become absolute, and not till
then could in any case the contrast between the intellection of
the one and of the other become absolute. Meanwhile the regenerated man remains a sinner: no new faculties have been
inserted into him by regeneration; and the old faculties common
to man in all his states have been only measurably restored to
their proper functioning. He is in no position therefore to
produce a science different in *kind* from that produced by
sinful man: the science of palingenesis is only a part of the
science of sinful humanity, though no doubt its best part: and
only along with it can it enter as a constituent part into that
ideal science which the composite human subject is producing
in its ceaseless effort to embrace in mental grasp the ideal
object, that is to say, all that is. Indeed, even if palingenesis had
completed its work it may be doubted whether the contrast between the science produced by the two classes of men could
be absolute. Even sinful men and sinless men are alike fundamentally men; and being both men, they know fundamentally
alike. There is ideally but one science, the subject of which is
the human spirit, and the object, all that is. Meanwhile, as
things are, the human spirit attains to this science only in part
and by slow accretions and through many partial and erroneous
constructions. Men work side by side at the common task, and
the common edifice takes gradually fuller and truer outlines. As
Dr. Kuyper finely says himself (p. 151), in the conflict of
perceptions and opinions those of the strongest energy and
clearest thought finally prevail. Why is not the palingenesis to
be conceived simply as preparing those stronger and clearer
spirits, whose thought shall finally prevail? It is not a different
kind of science that they are producing: it is not even the same
kind but as part of a different edifice of truth. It is only the
better scientific outlook, and the better scientific product,

striving in conflict with the product of fellow workers to build itself into one edifice of truth, which rises slowly because of sin but surely because of palingenesis.

Only in God's mind, of course, does science lie perfect—the perfect comprehension of all that is, in its organic completeness. In the mind of perfected humanity, the perfected ectypal science shall lie. In the mind of sinful humanity struggling here below, there can lie only a broken reflection of the object, a reflection which is rather a deflection. The great task of science lies in completing the edifice and correcting this deflection. Sinful man cannot accomplish it. But he makes the effort and attains his measure of success, a success that varies inversely with the rank of the sciences. The intrusion of regeneration prepares man to build better, and ever more truly as the effects of regeneration increase intensively and extensively, until the end comes when the regenerated universe becomes the well-comprehended object of the science of the regenerated race. Now it would seem a grave mistake to separate the men of the palingenesis from the race, a part of which they are, and which is itself the object of the palingenesis. And no mistake could be greater than to lead them to decline to bring their principles into conflict with those of the unregenerate in the prosecution of the common task of man. They will meet with dull opposition, with active scorn, with decisive rejection at the hands of the world: but thereby they shall win their victory. Just as the better science ever in the end secures its recognition, so palingenetic science, which is the better science, will certainly win its way to ultimate recognition. And it is in this fact that the vindication of Apologetics lies. Here too the "man of stronger and purer thought"—even though that he has it is of God alone—"will prevail in the end." The task of the Christian is surely to continue hopefully to urge "his stronger and purer thought" in all its details on the attention of men. It is not true that he cannot soundly prove his position. It is not true that the arguments he urges are not sufficient to validate the Christian religion. It is not even true that the minds of sinful men are inaccessible to his "evidences": though, in the sense of the proverb, "convinced against their will they remain of the same opinion still." On the contrary, men (all of whose minds are after all of the same essential structure with his own, though less illuminated than his) will not be able to resist or gainsay his determinations. He must use and press the advantage that God has given him. He must insist and insist again that his and not the opposing results shall be built into the slowly rising fabric of truth. Thus will he serve, if not obviously his own generation, yet truly all the generations of men.

We are not, we repeat, absurdly arguing that Apologetics will of itself make a man a Christian. But neither can it be said that the proclaimed gospel itself can do that. Only the Spirit of life can communicate life to a dead soul. But we are arguing that Apologetics has its part to play in the Christianizing of the world: and that this part is not a small part: nor is it merely a subsidiary or a defensive part—as if its one end were to protect an isolated body of Christians from annoyance from the great surrounding world. It has a primary part to play and a conquering part. The individual, to be sure, does not need to become a trained apologist first, and only after and as a result of that a Christian. The individual is prone vastly to overestimate himself: it ordinarily does not require the whole "body of evidences" to convince him. But surely he does require that kind and amount of evidence which is requisite to convince him before he can really be convinced: and faith, in all its forms, is a conviction of truth, founded as such, of course, on evidence. And this kind and amount of the evidences constitutes "Apologetics" for him and performs the functions of Apologetics for him. When we speak of Apologetics as a science, however, we have our eye not on the individual but on the thinking world. In the face of the world, with its opposing points of view and its tremendous energy of thought and incredible fertility in attack and defense, Christianity must think through and organize its, not defense merely, but assault. It has been placed in the world to *reason* its way to the dominion of the world. And it is by reasoning its way that it has come to its kingship. By reasoning it will gather to itself all its own. And by reasoning it will put its enemies under its feet.

Let it not be imagined that with all this we have done away with the "certainty of faith" as distinguished from "certainty of knowledge." We have only opened the way to a proper appreciation of the difference between the two. This difference is obviously the difference between faith and knowledge. And the difference between faith and knowledge is not that knowledge rests on evidence and faith does not, or that knowledge rests on sufficient evidence and faith does not, or that knowledge rests on grounds objectively or universally valid and faith does not. The difference is only that they rest on different kinds of evidence—knowledge on "sight" and faith on "testimony." The whole question of a "certainty of faith" turns, therefore, simply on the question whether testimony is adapted to produce conviction in the human mind, and is capable of producing a conviction which is clear and firm—a *firma certaque persuasio*. If we judge that it is, we shall have no choice but to range alongside of the various forms of "certainty of knowledge," whether resting on sense-perception, immediate intuition, or rational demonstration, a "certainty of faith" also, resting on convincing testimony. This "certainty of faith" has nothing in it particularly mysterious; it is no more "incommunicable than the "certainty of knowledge" and no more "subjective." Testimony that is "objectively" valid for the establishment of any fact should be "subjectively" valid to establish it in the forum of any mind; and only such testimony should be valid to any mind whatever. But a conviction grounded on testimony is obviously of a different variety from a conviction grounded on "sight" and will have characteristics of its own. Chief among these is that in it the element of "trust," which is of course present in all forms of conviction (for knowledge itself rests on trust), is peculiarly prominent. In this fact only, so far as we can see, lies whatever relative justification it is possible to give to the notion that the certainty of faith is of a "lower" order than the certainty of knowledge, and bears a "more subjective" character. It does not appear, however, that either of these epithets is properly applied to it. There seems to be no reason why—if testimony is adapted to produce conviction at all—the conviction produced by testimony may not be as strong and as "objectively valid" as that produced by "sight" itself; that is, why it should not rise into "certainty." For "the certainty of faith" is obviously no more the product of faith than "the certainty of knowledge" is the product of knowledge. Strictly speaking it is just that faith itself raised to its eminent degree. No doubt, if by "certainty," "assurance," we mean the emotional accompaniments of the conviction—the rest, confidence, comfort, happiness, we find in it—it would be the product of faith; but so would the "certainty of knowledge" under such an understanding be the product of knowledge. In itself, however, it is just the conviction itself, and its validity depends only on the validity of the testimony on which it is grounded. If that testimony is really adequate to the establishment of the fact, the conviction founded on that testimony is as valid as any knowledge founded on "sight" can be.

We have wandered far from our text in Dr. Bavinck's apparent subordination of the function of the "evidences" in assuring us of the truth of the Christian religion. We should be sorry to be supposed in all this to be arraying ourselves polemically against his teaching. We are not sure that he would not give a hearty assent to all—or most—of what we have urged. The inherent interest and comparative novelty of the subject must be our excuse for taking so slight an occasion for such extended remarks. We shall hope to atone for it by extreme brevity as to the other point as to which we have signalized doubt, viz., Dr. Bavinck's apparent assumption of the invariable or normal implication of "assurance of salvation" in the direct act of faith. This is an old subject and one which has been much debated. Its solution seems ultimately to turn on our conception of the object of faith. If faith terminates on a proposition—however precious—it would seem necessary to look upon assurance as of its very essence. If it terminates rather on a person, this necessity is not apparent and the way lies open to treat assurance rather as a reflex of faith which may or may not manifest itself. All this is familiar ground.

We must not close without emphasizing the delight we take in Dr. Bavinck's writings. In them extensive learning, sound thinking, and profound religious feeling are smelted intimately together into a product of singular charm. He has given us the most valuable treatise on *Dogmatics* written during the last quarter of a century—a thoroughly wrought out treatise which we never consult without the keenest satisfaction and abundant profit. And the lectures and brochures he from time to time presents an eager public are worthy of the best traditions of Reformed thought and Reformed eloquence. Not least among them we esteem this excellent booklet on "the certitude of faith."

8

CHRISTIAN EVIDENCES: HOW AFFECTED BY RECENT CRITICISMS*

In any age of intellectual activity and rapid growth of knowledge, like our own, a continuous process of adjustment is
necessary between our mental inheritance and our constantly
increasing acquisition. Except to such excessively hospitable
minds as can without discomfort entertain together contradictory propositions, advancing knowledge, involving this continuous adjustment, unavoidably brings a perpetual criticism
of the whole body of knowledge already held, both in its statement and in its ground. An age of investigation is therefore
also an age of criticism. The total body of old knowledge is
tested and tried afresh when confronted with each new discovery; and we cannot avoid the questions, What effect has
this new fact on the old facts? What place can it find among
them? Which of them must give place for it? But we must not
fail to remember—what is sometimes forgotten—that the
criticism is reciprocal, and that we must equally ask on each
occasion, What effect has the body of established facts on this
so-called new fact? What place can they find for themselves
in union with it? What in it must give way before their pressure? We must, moreover, have our eyes wide enough open to
distinguish between the turmoil of the process—the fermenta-
tion of the limpid liquid mass of knowledge when the new element is cast into it—and the final product. We must not
mistake the battle for the victory. We must rather possess
our souls in sufficient patience to note the condition of the
field after the conflict; to observe what has been eliminated

*The Homiletic Review, Aug. 1888, pp. 107-112.

and cast out in the strife of the elements, whether some part or all of the old or some part or all of the new, or neither the one nor the other. Thus we shall be able to distinguish between the queries, What has been criticized? and What has been affected by the criticism?

Nowhere is it more necessary to make this distinction than when we are inquiring concerning recent criticism of the Christian evidences. If we mean to ask what in them has been subjected to searching criticism by recent thinkers, we may shortly answer, everything. Nothing has been allowed to escape. The validity of all the proofs of the existence of God is questioned. The very capacity of man's mind, not only to attain to the idea of God, but to receive it when presented to it, is denied. Historical criticism has been as busy and as radical as philosophical and scientific. Not only are we told, for example, that miracle is impossible, and that no evidence would suffice to prove it, but we are told that there is no evidence, worth the name, which can be presented for the Christian miracles—that, as respects historicity, they stand on a similar level with those of the mediaeval saints, if not with those of Mr. Anstey's *A Fallen Idol*. No single book of either Old or New Testament has been left unassailed. Even such a liberal as Prof. Robertson Smith has felt called upon to rebuke the wildness of some of the recent Grafian critics. While, as regards the New Testament, grave scholars are telling us that even those books which Baur left us are all late compositions— the word is used literally—made up of fragments of ancient Jewish writings ignorantly pieced together. If we are of such sensitive disposition that we dare not assert or believe to be true what some acute or learned critic affirms to be impossible, we may as well strip off at once all our Christian garments: there are no Christian evidences. Nay, we must in such case strip off still more, and, wrapping our heads in our discarded raiment, plunge, in complete intellectual nakedness, into the gulf of nescience. There is nothing that has not been criticized.

But if what we ask is how the presentation of the Christian evidences has been affected by recent criticism, we have another story to tell. "The Christian Evidences" are an essentially persuasive science: they undertake to prove something and to prove it to somebody. They are, therefore, especially sensitive to changes in current thinking. Not only does every attack call out its appropriate defense, but every new point of view must map out for itself the whole prospect of the world of fact as seen from its vantage ground. Hence every type of thought which takes hold upon men's minds, sooner or later creates an apologetic for itself, suited to its needs and calculated for its meridian, by which its adherents feel their way to God and to Christ. So ineradicable is belief in divine things, so inseparable a part of human nature is it, that no sooner has a philosophy removed, to its own satisfaction, all rational foundations of faith, than forthwith faith begins to arise again out of the ruins and to frame for itself a new basis for belief. Accordingly, we already see building, stone by stone, before our eyes, a series of entirely new systematic natural theologies, based on the teachings of our current philosophies. Take such a book, for instance, as *Faith and Conduct*, recently published anonymously; here a new apologetic lays its foundations in philosophical skepticism, and then builds a temple out of the material furnished by a thoroughgoing evolutionism, into which it invites all Christian men to come and worship their God and their Savior. More constructive work of this kind, valuable as showing us how much can go and yet Christianity not go, may be expected from the adherents of the newer trends of thought every year.

From the other side, the mode of presentation of the evidences by the opponents of each new hypothesis is deeply affected by its nature and its claims. And in this way, every criticism creates against itself, so far, a new order of apologetic. The richness of the new apologetic which has thus been beaten out by the controversies of the last half-century is almost incredible. The scientific attack on the supernatural, based on the idea of invariable law, for example, has quickened in the apologete the sense of order, and plan, and relation, until a new conviction of divine power and presence has grown up which bids permanently to banish deistic conceptions from the minds of men. So the efforts of the naturalistic school of historical criticism, to bring into doubt the genuineness and unity of the books of the Bible, with a view to rearranging their material in an order for which a plausible plea for natural development might be put in, has not only called forth a mass of direct evidence for the authenticity of the books, such as was undreamed of before, but has also given birth to a whole library of more indirect argumentation of a nature and amount sufficient almost to revolutionize the science of "the evidences." For example, the attack of the Tübingen school on the New Testament has developed a direct historical apologetic, which has well nigh made a separate science of the history of the second century, and at the same time has called out a body of reasoning, based on Paul's four chief epistles, which has almost itself grown to the stature of a complete and satisfying "system of Christian evidences." The effort to reconstruct Old Testament history in the same naturalistic interest bids fair to perform a similar service for it. In particular, reply to modern criticism has developed a system of evidences, built around and resting upon the unique personality of Jesus, which almost constitutes a new science. It was in answer to Strauss that the argument (best known through Prebendary Row's *Jesus of the Evangelists*) based upon the literary portraiture of the perfect God-man presented in the evangelists was first given vogue among us; and since then it has been successfully adapted, not only to the proof that the evangelical records are true records of a truly supernatural life which was truly lived in the world, but also to the proof that the writers of these records were divinely aided in their record of such a life, and not only they, but all those who in the books of the Old and New Testaments alike "testify of him"; and thence again to the proof of the divine origin and divine truth of the whole Christian record and system. It is in opposition to the reconstruction of the Old Testament by the presently prevailing school of negative criticism that appeal is being ever made sharper and sharper to the authority of the God-man when

testifying to the origin and meaning of the Scriptures which
he himself revealed and inspired. If it be a fact that he lived
and taught as God-man, and being thus the very Word from
heaven, made assertions as to matters of fact: then there is
an end of all dispute as to the reality of the facts asserted by
such lips. He asserted, for instance, the reality of miracle; his
very life in the world was an assertion of the intrusion of the
supernatural into this world of sense. He asserted the supreme
evidential authority of miracles—representing them as in such a
degree faith-compelling as to detract somewhat from the value
of faith as evidence of a right heart. He asserted the divine authority of the Scriptures—declaring that no word of them
should ever be broken. He asserted the Mosaic authorship
of the Pentateuch—affirming that Moses spoke its laws and
wrote its prophecies of him. Men may, and men do, deny these
facts; but when they deny them, they deny them in the face of
the assertions of the God-man, and they can save themselves
from blasphemy only by taking refuge in a purely humanitarian
or in an extreme kenotic theory of the person of Christ, such
as reduces his life in the world to the limits of a simple human
life, but which is already abundantly refuted in advance by
the facts on which the argument from the portraiture of the
God-man in the Gospels is built. It is just because this Being
is obviously represented as living and acting not as a mere
man; it is just because he is obviously and consistently represented to us as "God *manifested* in the flesh"; that we must
believe that he really lived and taught in order to account for
the record: and this argument, once developed for this literary
purpose, is equally valid to compel us to bow before all his
utterances. Thus, about the central figure of Jesus an entirely
new apologetic is organizing itself, which in its own strength
is able to hold the field.

It is, of course, not to be understood that the sole way in
which the presentation of the Christian evidences has been
affected by recent criticism has been in the way of addition to
them of new lines of thought. Apologetes, too, are but men;
and many unsound arguments have been put forward in de-

fense of truth which the keen criticism of our critical age has exposed. Prof. Huxley tells us that "extinguished theologians lie about the cradle of every science as the strangled snakes beside that of Hercules." It is easy to retort that they keep company there with an interesting body of scientific lights. But it is wiser to confess the fact and profit by the lesson. Apologetics is wiser than apologetes, even as calm-eyed science is wiser than any of her votaries. Many a crude argument has been put forth in her name which she has learned to repudiate; many an absurd position she has found it for her best interests to desert. But it is no more desirable to exaggerate this side than the other. Recent criticism has correctingly affected the details and modes of presentation of the old evidences; but it would be beyond the truth to say that it has at all invalidated their essence. Every one of the old lines of proof of the truth of the Christian religion stands today with its validity and cogency unimpaired. The new scientific conception of the world, for example, has not at all either diminished the evidential value of miracles or rendered their occurrence incredible. They were always marvels, and they owed their evidential value to their marvelousness. But with respect to their relation to physical law, there is not one whit more of difficulty connected with conceiving the intrusion of a divine will into the chain of physical causation than there is in allowing our daily intrusion into it of a human will. We must still within us the ineradicable witness of our consciousness to the spontaneity of our activity, and wipe out from the world around us all the manifestations of our directing energy, before we dare deny the possibility of miracle, which differs from our own activity chiefly in the stupendousness of the effect, witnessing to the all-mightiness of the source. The only difficulty of believing in their reality arises from the difficulty of believing that such a power can really exist in the universe; and this difficulty they were intended to raise that they might direct our eyes above the universe for their source. Historical criticism has, in like manner, completely failed to invalidate, in the least degree, the old argument from prophecy, although it may be freely admitted that it has

set aside many old arguments from prophecies. All the resources of a numerous body of nobly gifted and splendidly
equipped critics have been exhausted in a vain endeavor so to
arrange the dates of origin of the Biblical books as to eliminate
the proofs of prediction from their pages. With a truly Herod-
like indifference they have murdered a host of innocent facts
which stood in the way of their purposes, and yet the reconstruction still always fails. After all, the Old Testament books
were written before Christ, and these are they which testify of
him. Through them all, one increasing purpose runs, which
proclaims them a preparation for something to come; and this
something actually does come in the New Testament, and is
found to be the center to which hundreds of typical and
prophetic fingers, which cannot be obliterated until we blot
out the Old Testament record, convergingly point.

The success of negative criticism in the closely allied attempt
to discredit the authenticity and genuineness and consequent
historical credibility of the Biblical books has been no greater.
Every new unearthing of lost documents but drives a new nail
into the coffin of unbelief. The discovery of Hippolytus' *Refutation of All Heresies* in 1842, of the complete Greek copy of
the *Clementine Homilies* in 1853, of the full text of Barnabas in
1859, of the complete text of the *Letters* of Clement of Rome in
1875, of the *Diatessaron* of Tatian in 1876 and 1887—each
marks the final settlement of a distinct issue with skepticism in
a victory for the old line of the "Christian Evidences." Critical
investigation has had a similar history: the import of the Basili-
dean quotations in Hippolytus, the relation of Marcion's Gospel
to Luke, the source of the evangelical quotations in Justin, the
meaning of the "Logia" in Papias—these are but samples of
the heated controversies which have, one after the other,
issued in decisive victories for the old line of the "Christian
Evidences." The discoveries of archaeology have walked in
the same path with those of literary research. Every new illustration from the monuments of either the Old or the New Testament has strengthened the old apologetic. A mere list of the
statements of either Testament which have been paraded as

inaccuracies, but which archaeology has proved to be rather subtle indications of supreme accuracy, would constitute a telling sermon in defense of Scripture. These examples must, however, suffice. It must be already apparent that recent criticism has not so affected the old line of "Christian Evidences" as to set them aside or to evacuate them of their force. It has rather, by detecting and uncovering their points of weakness, led to the filling up of their gaps, and thus to a large increase in their strength.

The single question that is left to ask has already received its reply in the last remark. What has been, then, the effect of recent criticism on the validity and force of the Christian evidences? Is there, on the whole, less cogent reason now available for accepting Christianity on rational grounds than has seemed to be within reach heretofore? A thousand times no. Criticism has proved the best friend to apologetics a science ever had. It is as if it had walked with her around her battlements and, lending her its keen eyes, pointed out an insufficiently guarded place here and an unbuttressed approach there; and then, taking playfully the part of the aggressor, made feint after feint towards capturing the citadel, and thus both persuaded and enabled and even compelled her to develop her resources, throw up new defenses, abandon all indefensible positions, and refurbish her weapons, until she now stands armed *cap-a-pie*, impregnable to every enemy. The case is briefly this: recent criticism has had a very deep effect upon the Christian evidences in modernizing them and so developing and perfecting them that they stand now easily victor against all modern assaults.

9

DARWIN'S ARGUMENTS AGAINST CHRISTIANITY AND AGAINST RELIGION*

Science has not broken with religion. But a large number of the scientific thinkers of our generation have. When we ask why, the reason returned is apt to be colored by the personal feelings of the answerer. One attributes it to the bondage into which what he speaks of as "so-called modern science" has fallen, to materialistic philosophy, or even to Satanic evil-heartedness. Another finds its explanation in the absorption of scientific workers, in this busy age, in a kind of investigation which deadens spiritual life and spiritual aspirations within them, and totally unfits them for estimating the value of other forms of evidence than that obtained in the crucible or under the microscope. Others suppose that it is the crude mode in which religion is presented to men's minds, in these days of infallible popes and Salvation Armies, which insults the intelligence of thoughtful men and prevents their giving to the real essence of faith the attention which would result in its acceptance. Others, still, conceive that it is advancing knowledge itself which in science has come to blows in religion with the outworn superstitions of a past age. In such a Babel of discordant voices it is a boon to be able to bend our ear and listen to one scientific worker, honored by all, as he tells us what it was that led him to yield up his Christian faith, and even, in large measure, that common faith in a God which he shared not with Christians only but with all men of thought and feeling.

---

*From the *Homiletic Review*, Jan. 1889, pp. 9-16. For a longer treatment of Darwin's "spiritual biography," with notes, see "Charles Darwin's Religious Life: A Sketch in Spiritual Biography" (written in 1888), in *Studies in Theology*, 1932, pp. 541-582.

A rare opportunity of this sort has been afforded us by the publication of the *Life and Letters of Charles Darwin*, by his son, in which is incorporated a very remarkable passage, extracted from some autobiographical. notes written by this great student of nature, as late as 1876, with the special purpose of tracing the history of his religious views. Certainly no one will hesitate to accord to him a calm hearing; and we cannot but be instructed by learning by what processes and under the pressure of what arguments so eminently thoughtful a mind was led to desert the faith in which he was bred, and gradually to assume a position toward the problem of the origin of the world which he can call by no more luminous name than that of agnosticism.

The history of the drift by which Mr. Darwin was separated from faith in a divine order in the world, divides itself into two well-marked periods. The first of these, which was completed at about the time when he reached his fortieth year, ends with the loss of his Christianity. During the second, which extended over the remainder of his life, he struggled, with varying fortunes, but ever more and more hopelessly, to retain his standing at least as a theist. At the end of the first he no longer believed that God had ever spoken to men in his Word; at the end of the second he more than doubted whether the faintest whisper of his voice could be distinguished in his works. He was never prepared dogmatically to deny his existence; but search as he might he could not find him, and he could only say that if he existed he was, verily, a God that hides himself.

Let us take up the matter in the orderly form which Mr. Darwin has himself given it, and inform ourselves seriously what were the objections to Christianity and the difficulties in the way of a reasoned theism which led him to such sad conclusions.

His account of his loss of Christianity takes the shape of a personal history. He gives us not so much an argument against Christianity as a record of the arguments which led him to discard it. These fall into two classes: in the first stands the single decisive argument that really determined his anti-

Christian attitude; while in the second are gathered together the various supporting considerations which came flocking to buttress the conclusion when once it was attained. The palmary argument depends for its weight on a twofold peculiarity of his personal attitude. He had persuaded himself not only that species originated by a process of evolution, but also that this process was slow, long continued, and by a purely natural development. And he held, with dogmatic tenacity, the opinion that the Book of Genesis teaches that God created each species by a separate, sudden, and immediate fiat. If both these positions were sound, it followed necessarily that either his theory or Genesis was in error; and to him, in his naturally enthusiastic advocacy of his theory, this meant that Genesis must go. Now he was ready for another step. Genesis is an integral part of the Old Testament, and the Old Testament is not only bound up with the New Testament in a single volume, but is in such a sense a part of Christianity—as its groundwork and basis—that Christianity cannot be true if the Old Testament record is untrustworthy. To give up Genesis is, therefore, to give up Christianity. Thus his chief argument against Christianity reduces itself to a conflict between his theory of evolution and his interpretation of Genesis, about the accuracy of both of which there are the gravest of doubts. Here is the form in which he himself describes the process: "I had gradually come by this time, that is, 1836 to 1839, to see that the Old Testament was no more to be trusted than the sacred books of the Hindus. The question then continually rose before my mind, and would not be banished: is it credible that if God were now to make a revelation to the Hindus he would permit it to be connected with the belief in Vishnu, Siva, etc., as Christianity is connected with the Old Testament? This appeared to me as utterly incredible."

It was impossible, however, to deal with Christianity as if it came claiming our acceptance uncommended by evidence of its own. The assumed conflict with Genesis would be fatal to the theory of evolution if the Christianity in vital connection with Genesis were confessed to be truth demonstrated by its own appropriate historical evidence. Mr. Darwin could not, therefore, rest in this short refutation without calling to its aid other more direct arguments, such as would suffice to place Christianity at least on the defensive and thus allow the palmary argument free scope to work its ruin. Thus we read further: "By further reflecting that the clearest evidence would be requisite to make any sane man believe in the miracles by which Christianity is supported, and that the more we know of the fixed laws of nature the more incredible do miracles become; that the men at that time were ignorant and credulous to a degree almost incomprehensible by us; that the Gospels cannot be proved to have been written simultaneously with the events; that they differ in many important details, far too important, as it seemed to me, to be admitted as the usual inaccuracies of eye-witnesses—by such reflections as these . . . I gradually came to disbelieve in Christianity as a divine revelation. The fact that many false religions have spread over large portions of the earth like wildfire had some weight with me."

This is Mr. Darwin's arraignment of the Christian evidences. A close scrutiny will reveal the important place which miracles occupy in it. It may almost be said that Mr. Darwin concerns himself with no other of the evidences of Christianity, except miracles. It looks as if, in his objection to Christianity, arising from the conflict that existed in his opinion between Genesis and his theory of evolution, he felt himself faced down by the force of the miracles by which, as he says, "Christianity is supported," and felt bound to throw doubt on this evidence or yield up his theory. In one word, he felt the force of the evidence from miracles. It is instructive to observe how he proceeds in the effort to break the weight of their evidence. He does not shortly assert, as some lesser scientific lights are accustomed to assert, that miracles are impossible. He merely says that they need clear evidence of their real occurrence to make us believe in them, and that this is increasingly true as the reign of law is becoming better recognized. And then he tries to throw doubt on the evidence of their occurrence: they profess to have been wrought in a credulous age; the documents in which they are recorded cannot be proved to be contemporaneous with their asserted occurrence, and are marred by internal contradictions in detail which lessen their trustworthiness; and it is not necessary to assume the miraculous origin of Christianity in order to account for its rapid spread. In a word, Mr. Darwin deserts the metaphysical and what may be called the "scientific" objections to miracles, in order to rest his case on the historical objections. He does not say miracles cannot have occurred; he merely says that the evidence on which they are asserted to have occurred falls something short of demonstration.

Were our object here criticism rather than exposition, it would be easy to show the untenableness of this position: it was not in the field of the historical criticism of the first Christian centuries that Mr. Darwin won his spurs. There are also many more sources of evidence for Christianity than its miracles. It is enough for our present purpose, however, to take note of the form which the reasoning assumed in his own mind. It has a somewhat odd appearance, and was about as follows: The miracles by which Christianity is supported are not demonstrably proved to have really occurred; therefore the conflict of my theory with Genesis, and through Genesis with Christianity, is not a conflict with miraculous evidence; therefore my theory may as well be true as Christianity. The validity of the inference seems to rest on the suppressed premise that none but miraculous evidence would suffice to set aside his theory. And there is a droll suggestion that his state of mind on the subject was not very far from this: "I was very unwilling to give up my belief," he writes; "I feel sure of this, for I can well remember often and often inventing day-dreams of old letters between distinguished Romans, and manuscripts being found at Pompeii or elsewhere, which confirmed in the most striking manner all that was written in the Gospels. But I found it more and more difficult, with free scope given to my imagination, to invent evidence which would suffice to convince me. Thus unbelief crept on me at a very slow rate, but was at last complete. The rate was so slow that I felt no distress." Nothing short of a miracle would, then, have convinced him; and nothing short of a miracle could have convinced him of a miracle. Surely a man in such a state of mind would be refused as a juror in any case. In lesser causes we should speak of him as under bondage to an invincible prejudice; in this great one we are certainly justified in saying that his predilection for his theory of the origin of species, and that in the exact form in which he had conceived it, lay at the root of his rejection of Christianity. If both Christianity and it could not be true, why then Christianity certainly could not be true, and a full examination of the evidence was unnecessary.

It was some years after his giving up of Christianity before his belief in the existence of a personal God was shaken. But as time went on this also came. The account given in his autobiography of this new step in unbelief is not thrown into the form of a history so much as of ordered reasoning. So that we have, strangely enough, as part of a brief body of autobiographical notes, a formal antitheistic argument. The heads of theistic proof, which Mr. Darwin treats in this remarkable passage, are the following: (1) "The old argument from design in nature as given by Paley"; (2) "the general beneficent arrangement of the world"; (3) "the most usual argument for the existence of an intelligent God at the present day, drawn from the deep inward conviction and feelings which are experienced by most persons"; and (4) the argument "from the extreme difficulty or rather impossibility of conceiving this immense and wonderful universe, including man with his capacity of looking far backwards and far into futurity, as the result of blind chance or necessity." The full development of these propositions, while it would be far, no doubt, from exhausting the argument for the existence of God, would afford quite a respectable body of theistic proof. In offering a refutation of, them, one by one, Mr. Darwin evidently feels that he is sufficiently treating the whole fabric of theistic argumentation; and he draws an agnostic conclusion accordingly. It will be very instructive to note his answers to them, in as much detail as space will allow.

To the first—the argument from design as developed, say, by Paley—he replies that it "fails, now that the law of natural selection has been discovered." "We can no longer argue," he adds, "that, for instance, the beautiful hinge of a bivalve must have been made by an intelligent being, like the hinge of a door by man. There seems to be no more design in the variability of organic beings and in the action of natural selection than in the course which the wind blows." By this he means that the adaptations of means to ends, as observed in nature, are the necessary result of the interaction of the purely mechanical forces of nature, and would result from them whether there is a God or not; and that therefore they cannot be pleaded as a proof that there is a God. This conception of the working of nature is the result of the stringency with which he held to his theory of evolution by natural selection, in the exact naturalistic form in which he first conceived it. The second argument, that drawn "from the general beneficent arrangement of the world," he meets by a reference to the great amount of suffering in the world. As a sound evolutionist he believes that happiness decidedly prevails over misery; but he urges that the existence of so much suffering is an argument against the existence of an intelligent first cause; "whereas the presence of much suffering agrees well with the view that all organic beings have been developed through variation and natural selection," which he appears to assume to be a necessarily anti-theistic conception. In treating the third argument, derived from man's "deep inward conviction and feelings" that there is a God, to whom his aspirations go out, on whom he is dependent and to whom he is responsible, Mr. Darwin confuses the "conviction" with the "feelings," and sets the whole aside as no more valid an argument for the existence of God than "the powerful, though vague, and similar feelings excited by music." He sorrowfully recalls the time when he too had such feelings rise within him in the presence of grand scenery, for instance— when he could not adequately describe the "higher feelings of wonder and admiration and devotion which filled and elevated his mind"; but confesses that they no more visit him, and that he might truly be said to be like a man who has become color-blind and whose loss of perception is therefore of no value as evidence against the universal belief of men. But he denies that the "conviction of the existence of one God" (why "*one*" God?) is universal among men; and hints that he believes that all these feelings can be reduced to the "sense of the sublime," which, could it only be analyzed, might be shown not to involve the existence of God any more than the similar emotions raised by music. The confusion here is immense—confusion of a conviction that accompanies, or rather begets and governs, feelings with the feelings themselves—confusion of the analysis of an emotion into its elements with the discovery of its cause, and the like. But the confusion and Mr. Darwin's method of seeking relief from his puzzlement, are characteristic traits which may teach us somewhat of the value of his testimony as to the scientific aspects of faith. The fourth argument, that which rests upon our causal judgment, is the only one to which he ascribes much value. He does not hesitate to speak of the "impossibility of conceiving this immense and wonderful universe as the result of blind chance or necessity." But the question arises: Impossibility to whom? And here again Mr. Darwin's theory of the origin of man, by a purely natural process of development from brute ancestors, entered in to void the unavoidable conclusion. "But then," he adds, "arises the doubt, Can the mind of man, which has, as I fully believe, been developed from a mind as low as that possessed by the lowest animals, be trusted when it draws such grand conclusions?" Or, as he writes later, after having again confessed to "an inward conviction that the universe is not the result of chance": "But then with me the horrid doubt always arises whether the convictions of man's mind, which has been developed from the mind of the lower animals, are of any value or at all trustworthy. Would anyone trust in the convictions of a monkey's mind, if there are any convictions in such a mind?" Thus the last and strongest theistic proof fails, not because of any lack in its stringent validity to the human mind, but because so brute-bred a mind as man's is no judge of the validity of proof.

We are tempted to turn aside and ask, Why, then, are the theistic proofs so carefully examined by Mr. Darwin? Why is so much validity assigned to the judgment of his human mind as to the value of the argument from design, for instance? Why does he trust that brute-bred mind through all the devious reasonings by which the theory of development by natural selection, on the basis of which the value of its conclusions are now challenged, was arrived at? In a word, is it not certain, if man's mind is so brutish that its causal judgment is not trustworthy when it demands a sufficient cause for this universe, that it is equally untrustworthy in all its demands for a sufficient cause, and that thus all the fabric of our knowledge tumbles about our ears, all our fine theories, all our common judgments by which we live? When Mr. Darwin chokes down this "inward conviction" and refuses to believe what he confesses to be "impossible" to him not to believe, he puts the knife at the throat of all his convictions, even of his conviction that he exists and his conviction that a world lies about him, such as he sees with his eyes and theorizes about with his "bestial" mind; and there necessarily goes out into the blackness of nescience all thought, all belief, all truth.

But we remember that we are not now criticizing, but only trying to understand Mr. Darwin's reasons for refusing to believe in "what is called a personal God." This much is plain, that the root of his agnosticism, as of his rejection of Christianity, was his enthusiastic acceptance of his own theory of evolution, in the mechanical naturalistic sense in which he conceived it. We raise no question whether this was an inevitable result; there have been many evolutionists who have been and have remained theists and Christians. But this was the actual course of reasoning with him. It was because he conceived of each organic form as liable to indefinite variation in every direction, and to development into other forms by the natural reaction of the environment on these variations, through the struggle for existence, that he denied that the hand of God could be traced either in the line of variation or in the selection of the types to live. It was because he included all organic phenomena, mental and moral as well as physical, in this natural process, that he found himself unable to trust the convictions of the mind of man, which was after all nothing but the brute's mind beaten and squeezed into something of a new form by an unmoral struggle for existence stretching through immemorial ages. In a word, Mr. Darwin's rejection of Christianity and loss of faith in a personal God were simply the result of his enthusiastic adoption of a special theory of the origin of organic differentiation, and of ruthless subjection of all his thought to its terms.

And now, returning to our original query, we are prepared to answer why one scientific man broke with faith. Mr. Darwin was honest in deserting the faith of his childhood and the theistic convictions of his manhood. But was he logically driven to it? He himself, despite himself, confesses that he was not. To the end his "conviction" remained irreconcilable with his "conclusion." Yet he was logical, if the evidence in favor of the extremely naturalistic form of the evolutionary hypothesis is more convincing than that for God and the Bible; but logical with a logic which strips the very logic on which we are depending for our conclusion of all its validity, and leaves us shiveringly naked of all belief and of all trustworthy faculty of thought. If we are to retain belief in our own existence, Mr. Darwin himself being witness, we must believe also in that God who gave us life and being. We can only account for Mr. Darwin's failure to accept the guidance of his inextinguishable conviction here, by recognizing that his absorption in a single line of investigation and inference had so atrophied his mind in other directions that he had ceased to be a trustworthy judge of evidence. Whatever may be true in other cases, in this case the defection of a scientific man from religion was distinctly due to an atrophy of mental qualities by which he was unfitted for the estimation of any other kind of evidence than that derived from the scalpel and the laboratory, and no longer could feel the force of the ineradicable convictions which are as "much a part of man as his stomach or his heart."

10

ST. PAUL'S USE OF THE ARGUMENT
FROM EXPERIENCE*

The place of the opening verses of the fifth chapter of Romans in the general argument of the Epistle has always presented a crux to interpreters. The problem has sometimes been complicated by the intrusion of the textual question of whether the verbs in this passage are to be read as indicatives or subjunctives. The difference in reading is, however, a matter of itacism, and of an itacism from which none of the great witnesses to the text are free. To condition the solution of the problem of the logical sequence of thought upon the discrimination of omicron from omega by such witnesses, would be somewhat like suspending higher concerns upon the correctness of the pronunciation of "s" by lisping lips. Manifestly, the textual question here must itself be resolved by the demands of the thought sequence; that is, it is the internal and not the external evidence which must here rule. We are safe in throwing ourselves back upon the main problem of the place of these verses in the argument of the Epistle, without allowing ourselves to be confused by the textual question, which is of no more than secondary interest.

The general disposition of the matter of the Epistle is tolerably clear. In the opening chapters, the necessity of a justification by faith and not works was exhibited (i. 18–iii. 20). Then the nature and working of this method of justification was expounded (iii. 21-31). Then the Apostle presents a series of considerations designed to show that this method of justifica-

---

*From the *Expositor*, March 1895, pp. 226-236. Adapted from a sermon written Jan. 29, 1894, afterward printed in *The Power of God unto Salvation*, Philadelphia, 1903, pp. 57-90.

tion by faith is indeed God's method of saving men (iv. 1–
v. 21). It is in this section that our present passage falls. The
first consideration offered is drawn from the case of Abraham,
and operates to show that God has always so dealt with his
people. For that Abraham, the father of the faithful, was justified by faith and not by works, the Scriptures expressly testify,
saying that "Abraham believed God, and it was reckoned to
him unto righteousness." This is the immediately preceding
paragraph (iv. 1-25) to our present passage. In the immediately succeeding paragraph (v. 12-21) appeal is made to the
analogy of God's dealings with men in other matters. It was
by the trespass of one that men were brought into sin and
death: does it not comport with his methods that by the righteousness of One, men should be brought into justification and
life? Our present passage (v. 1-11) lies between, and ought
to furnish an intermediate argument that justification by faith
is God's own method of saving sinners.

It is because commentators have not seen such an argument
in it, that they have found it so difficult to discover the progress
of thought at this point. If we are to read the verbs as subjunctives, it is no doubt impossible to understand them as
propounding an argument. But if they be read as indicatives,
just the intermediate argument for which we are in search will
emerge as the most natural sense of the passage, when looked
at in the light of the contextual indications. The Apostle had
not presented the argument from the case of Abraham in a
purely historical spirit. His preoccupation was with its bearing
upon the case of his readers. Its relation to them is therefore
very richly drawn out, and culminates in the closing declaration
that it was not written for Abraham's sake only that his believing was imputed to him unto righteousness, "but also for
our sakes to whom it is to be imputed, who believe on him
who raised Jesus our Lord from the dead, who was delivered
up for our trespasses, and was raised for our justification."
Here is the point of attachment for the new argument. "It is
because, then, we have been justified out of faith," the Apostle
begins, throwing the participle forward to the head of the

sentence, with, as Meyer puts it, "triumphant emphasis": "it is because, then, we have been *actually and truly justified* out of faith, that we have peace with God through our Lord Jesus Christ, and exult in hope of the glory of God." There is obviously an appeal to the experience of his Christian readers here, strengthened by its indicated relation to the normative case of Abraham. The Apostle is not arguing that a Christian ought to have peace and joy. Far less is he exhorting Christians to have peace and joy. He is appealing to their conscious peace and joy. And on their conscious possession of this peace and joy, he is founding his argument. They had sought justification, not on the ground of works of righteousness which they had wrought, but, like Abraham, out of faith; and the turmoil of guilty dread before God which had filled their hearts had sunk into a sweet sense of peace, and the future to which they had hitherto looked shudderingly forward in fearful expectation of judgment had taken on a new aspect—they "exult in hope of the glory of God." It is on this their own experience that the Apostle Paul fixes their eyes. They have sought justification out of faith. They have reaped the fruits of justification. Can they doubt the reality of the middle term? No: it is because we have been justified, says the Apostle—*really and truly justified* —out of faith, that we have this peace with God which we feel in our quieted souls, and exult in this hope of the glory of God in which we are now rejoicing. Not only the case of Abraham, but their own experience as well, will teach them then that it is out of faith and not out of works that God justifies the sinner.

If this be the meaning of the passage, it will be observed that the argument which is here employed is what has of late obtained great vogue among us under the name of "the argument from experience." It is not without interest that we note the prominent use which the Apostle makes of an argument which some appear to fancy one of the greatest discoveries of the nineteenth century, while others seem to look upon it with suspicion as an innovation of dangerous tendency. Like other forms of argumentation, it is no doubt capable of misuse. It is to misuse it to confuse it with proof by experiment. By his

use of the argument from experience, Paul is far from justifying
the position of those who will accept as true only those elements of Christian teaching the truth of which they can verify
by experiment. There is certainly a recognizable difference
between trusting God for the future because we have known
his goodness in the past, and casting ourselves from every pin-
nacle of the temple of truth in turn to see whether he has really
given his angels charge concerning us, according to his Word.
It is to misuse it, again, to throw the whole weight of the evidence of Christianity upon it, or to seek to enhance its value
by disparaging all other forms of evidence. Such exaggeration
of its importance is a symptom of that unhappy subjectivism
which is unfortunately growing ever more widespread among
us, which betrays its weakened hold upon the objective truth
and reality of Christianity by its neglect or even renunciation
of its objective proofs. When men find the philosophical or
critical postulates to which they have committed their thinking
working their way subtly into every detail of their thought, and
gradually taking from them their confidence in those supernatural facts on which historical Christianity rests, it is no
wonder that they should despairingly contend that "the essence
of Christianity," being vindicated by the immanent experiences
of their souls, is independent of its supposed supernatural history. It is needless to say that this desperate employment of
the argument from experience has no analogy in the usage of
Paul. With him, it does not take the place of other arguments,
but takes its place among them. He appeals, first, to God's
announced intention from the beginning so to deal with his
people, and to the historic fact of his so dealing with them.
He appeals, last, to the analogy of God's dealings with men in
other matters. Between these he adduces the argument from
experience, and twists the cord of his proof from the three fibers
of God's express promise, our experience, and the analogy of
his working. When we unite the Scriptural, experiential, and
analogical arguments, we are followers of Paul.

But though it may interest us, it cannot surprise us to find
Paul employing the argument from experience here. It is an

argument which is repeatedly given a capital place in his writings. It is to it for example that he appeals, when he cries to the foolish Galatians, "This only would I learn from you, Received ye the Spirit by works of law or by the hearing of faith?" (Gal. iii. 2). They had received the Spirit: of that, both he and they were sure. And they had sought him, not by works of law, but out of faith: that too they knew very well. Were they so foolish as to be unable to draw the inference thrust upon them, that the seeking that found was the true and right seeking? The Apostle, then, will draw it for them: "He, therefore, that supplieth the Spirit to you and worketh powers in you, doeth he it by law-works or by the hearing of faith? Even as Abraham believed God, and it was reckoned to him unto righteousness. Ye perceive therefore that they which be of faith, the same are Abraham's sons" (Gal. iii. 5-7). A humbler servant of Christ than Paul, and a far earlier one, had indeed long before pressed this argument with matchless force (John ix). Blind unbelief alone could say to him who once was blind but now did see, "This man was not from God . . . give glory to God; we know that this man is a sinner." The one, the sufficient answer was, "Whether he be a sinner, I know not; one thing I know, that, whereas I was blind, now I see. . . . Why, herein is the marvel, that ye know not whence he is, and he opened mine eyes!" Greater marvel than the opening of the eyes of one born blind, that men should shut their eyes to who, and what, and whence he is, who opens blind eyes: "If this man were not from God, he could do nothing." What, after all, is "the argument from experience" but an extension of our Lord's favorite argument from the fruits to the tree which bears the fruits? He who is producing the fruits of the Spirit has received the Spirit; he who is reaping the fruits of justification has received justification; and he who has received these fruits by the seeking of faith, knows that he has received out of faith the justification of which they are the fruits, and may know therefore that the way of faith is the right and true way of receiving justification. We must not pause in the midst of the argument and refuse to draw the final conclusion. If the presence of the fruits of justification proves that we are justified, the presence of the justification thus proved, proves that justification is found on the road by which we reached it. This is the Apostle's argument.

The validity of such an argument lies on the surface. It is useless to tell the famishing wanderer that the pool into which he has dipped his cup is but a mirage of the desert, when the refreshing fluid is already moistening his parched lips. Nevertheless, the validity of the argument has its implications; and this is as much as to say that it rests on presuppositions without which it would not be valid. Men may draw water from a well and be content with this practical proof that the pump yields water, without stopping to consider the theory of suction by which the pump acts. But no pump will yield water if it be not constructed in accordance with the principles of suction: and the understanding of these principles not merely increases the intelligence but also adds to the confidence with which we credit the refreshing floods to its gift. In a somewhat analogous way Paul's argument from experience will grow in force in proportion to the clearness with which its implications are apprehended and the heartiness with which they are accepted. What are these implications?

In the first place, it is implied in this argument, that there is a natural adaptation in the mode of salvation which he is commending to us for the production of peace and joy in the heart of the sinner who embraces it. Whoever seeks justification by faith will find peace and joy; but this could not be if this mode of salvation had no natural adaptation to produce peace and joy; and the perception of this adaptation, while not necessary to receiving its benefits, will greatly increase the confidence with which we assign the benefits received to their proper source. No doubt the peace which steals into the heart and the exultation which cannot keep silence upon the lips of him who is justified out of faith, are the work of the Holy Spirit in his soul. But there is a distinction between the efficient cause and the formal ground of our emotions. The Holy Spirit does not here, any more than elsewhere, work a blind, an ungrounded, an irrational set of emotions in the heart. A set of emotions arising in the soul no one knows whence, no one knows on what grounds, especially if they were persistent and in proportion as they were strong, would only vex and puzzle the soul. A rational account of them must be possible if they are to be probative of anything. The mode of justification propounded by God through the Apostle is one which is adapted to the actual condition of man: one which is calculated to allay his sense of guilt, to satisfy his accusing conscience, and to supply him with a rational ground of conviction of acceptance with God and of hope for the future. It is because this mode of justification is thus adapted to provide a solid ground for peace and joy to the rational understanding that those who seek justification thus and not otherwise, under the quickening influences of the Spirit, acquire a sense of peace with God and an exalting hope for the future. And it is only because these Spirit-framed emotions thus attach themselves rationally to the mode of justification by faith, that they can point to it as their source and prove that they who have sought their justification by faith have surely found.

The gist of the matter, then, is that the justification which comes out of faith is experienced as actual justification and bears its appropriate fruits, because it alone, of all the methods by which men have sought to obtain peace with God, is adapted to satisfy the conscience and to supply a sufficient ground of conviction of acceptance with God. How many ways there are in which men vainly seek peace, need not be enumerated here: by works, by repentance, by offerings to God of precious possessions or of dedicated lives. They give no peace, because men can find in them no sufficient ground for confidence that they are accepted by God. When they have performed all of which they are capable, they recognize that they are but unprofitable servants. The soul's fierce condemnation of itself in its awakened sense of sin cannot instil peace into the soul. They know that the judgment of God is true and righteous altogether. It is only on the ground of an adequate expiation of sin and a perfect righteousness, wrought out by a person capable of bearing to the uttermost the penalty and fulfilling to the uttermost the requirement of the law, and justly made ours, that conscience may be appeased and peace once more visit the guilty soul. This is what Paul offers in his doctrine of justification by faith. And observe how the whole Epistle on to this fifth chapter operates like a bent bow to give force to the appeal to personal experience which is there shot like an arrow into the soul, and to evoke an immediate and deep response. For what is that proof with which the Epistle opens, that all men are sinners and under the wrath of God, but a faithful probing of conscience, awakening it to a sense of guilt and to a consciousness of helplessness? And what is that explanation of God's method of justification by means of a righteousness provided in Christ, laid hold of by faith, with which the third chapter closes, but a loving presentation of the work of Christ to the apprehension of faith? And what is that exposition of the Old Testament narrative of the acceptance of Abraham, the father of the faithful, with which the fourth chapter is occupied, but a gracious assurance that it is thus that God deals with his children? And what now is this appeal to his readers' own experience as they have humbly sought God's forgiveness and acceptance out of faith in Christ, but an assault upon their hearts that they may be forced to realize all the satisfaction they have found in believing in Christ? It is to this satisfaction that the Apostle now appeals in evidence of the reality of the justification of which it is the fruit. The argument is from the internal peace to the external peace. You have sought justification out of faith, he says in effect; you have appropriated the work of Jesus Christ; you rest upon him; and your conscience at last says, It is enough. Your guilty pangs and fears subside, and the serenity of peace and the exultation of hope take their place. Is not this new-found satisfaction of conscience a proof of the reality of your justification? This is the Apostle's argument.

There is yet a deeper implication in the argument which we would do well explicitly to recognize, in order that we may feel its full force. External peace with God is inferred from internal peace of conscience. This involves the assumption that the deliverances of the human conscience are but shadows of the divine judgment, that its imperatives repeat the demands of God's righteousness and its satisfaction argues the satisfaction of his justice. Such an assumption can scarcely be called in question; for were this correspondence not actual, no valid peace could ever visit the human heart, no grounded hope could ever brighten its outlook upon the future. If our moral sense were so entirely out of analogy with the moral sense of God that what fully meets and satisfies that indignation which rises in us upon the realization of sin as sin should stand so wholly out of relation with God's moral sense as to leave it unmoved, we should be utterly incapacitated to know God, and the foundation of morality and religion alike for us would be destroyed. If there be a God at all, the Author of our moral nature, it is just as certain as his existence that the moral judgment which he has implanted in us is true to its pole in the depths of his own moral being; that its deliverances are but the transcripts of his own moral judgments; and that we may hearken to its voice with the assurance that it is but the echo of his decision. The sense of guilt by which the awakened conscience accuses us, speeding on into the remorse that bites back so fiercely on the sinking soul, is but the reflection of God's judgment against sin. But this could not be if an appeased conscience were not the reflection of God's judgment of acquittal. For if conscience could cease to accuse, while God continued to condemn, it would no longer be true that God's condemnation is repeated in our accusing conscience, and our sense of guilt is but the shadow of his overhanging wrath. Conscience must be conceived, therefore, as a mirror hung in the human breast, upon which man may read the reflection of the divine judgment upon himself. When frowns of a just anger conceal his face, the clouds gather upon its polished surface: and surely when those shades pass away and the unclouded sun gleams once more from its surface, it cannot be other than the reflection of God's smile. Certainly a peace which is so firmly grounded as the reality of this correspondence is rooted so deeply in the nature of man that humanity itself must perish before that peace can be taken away.

We seem now to have Paul's argument fully before us. Man's conscience reflects God's judgment upon the soul. What satisfies man's conscience satisfies God's justice. Paul's presentation to faith of an expiating and obedient God-man, paying the penalty of our sin and keeping probation before God's law in our stead, satisfies the demands of conscience. The peace that steals into the heart of him who rests upon this Savior in faith, and the joy that exults upon his lips as he contemplates standing in him before the judgment-seat of God, are but the proper emotions of the satisfied conscience, and as such are the proof to us that God's wrath is really appeased, his condemnation reversed, and his face turned upon us in loving acceptance in his beloved Son. Lastly, then, his experience of peace and joy is an irrefutable proof that this and no other is the just God's method of justifying the sinner.

11

DREAM*

The interest of the student of the Gospels in dreams turns upon the occurrence in the opening chapters of Matthew of the record of no fewer than five supernatural dreams (i. 20; ii. 12, 13, 19, 22). Later in the same Gospel mention is made of a remarkable dream which came to the wife of Pilate (xxvii. 19). There is no reference to dreams elsewhere in the New Testament except in a citation from the Old Testament in Acts ii. 17 and in an obscure verse in Jude (vs. 8).

No allusion is made in the Gospels, or indeed in the whole New Testament, to dreams as phenomena forming part of the common experience of man. Any such allusions that may occur in Scripture are, of course, purely incidental; they are therefore in the whole extent of Scripture very infrequent. Barely enough exist to assure us that dreams were thought of by the Hebrews very much as they are by men of average good sense in our own day. Men then, too, were visited with pleasant dreams which they knew were too good to be true (Psalm cxxvi. 1), and afflicted with nightmares which drove rest from their beds (Job vii. 14). To them, too, dreams were the type of the evanescent and shadowy, whatever suddenly flies away and cannot be found (Job xx. 8; Psalm lxxiii. 20). The vanity and deceptiveness of dreams were proverbial (Eccles. v. 7; Isa. xxix. 8). The hungry man may dream that he eats, but his soul continues empty; the thirsty man may dream that he drinks, but he remains faint (Isa. xxix. 8). Their roots were set in the multitude of cares, and their issue was emptiness (Eccles. v. 3, 7).

---

*From Hastings' *Dictionary of Christ and the Gospels*, I. 1908, pp. 494-498. I have omitted the bibliography. See also the *Bible Student*, Nov. 1901, pp. 241-250.

When the Son of Sirach (xxxiv. 1, 2) represents them as but reflections of our waking experiences, to regard which is to catch at a shadow and to follow after the wind, he has in no respect passed beyond the Biblical view.[1]

The interest of the Bible in dreams is absorbed by the rare instances in which they are made the vehicles of supernatural revelation. That they were occasionally so employed is everywhere recognized, and they therefore find a place in the several enumerations of the modes of revelation (Num. xii. 6; Deut. xiii. 1-5; 1 Sam. xxviii. 6, 15; Joel ii. 28; Acts ii. 17; Jer. xxiii. 3, 25, 28, 32; xxvii. 9; xxix. 8; Zech. x. 2: Job iv. 13; xxxiii. 15 stand somewhat apart). In this matter, too, the Son of Sirach retains the Biblical view, explicitly recognizing that dreams may be sent by the Most High in the very passage in which he reproves the folly of looking upon dreams in general as sources of knowledge (xxxiv. 6). The superstitious attitude characteristic of the whole heathen world, which regards all dreams as omens and seeks to utilize them for purposes of divination, receives no support whatever from the Biblical writers. Therefore in Israel there arose no "houses of dreams," there was no place for a guild of "dream-examiners" or "dream-critics." When on rare occasions God did vouchsafe symbolical dreams to men, the professed dream-interpreters of the most highly trained castes stood helpless before them (Gen. xxxvii, xl, xli; Dan. ii, iv). The interpretation of really God-sent dreams belonged solely to God himself, the sender, and only his messengers could read their purport. There could be no more striking indication of the gulf that divides the Biblical and the ethnic views of dreams. If there is a hint of an overestimate of dreams among some Israelites (Jer. xxiii. 25; xxvii. 9), this is mentioned only to be condemned, and is obviously a trait not native to Israel, but, like all the soothsaying in vogue among the ill-instructed of the land, borrowed from the surrounding heathenism.[2] If there are possible suggestions that there

---

[1] Cf. Delitzsch, *Biblical Psychology*, p. 328, Orelli, art. "Träume" in Herzog-Hauck, *Prot. Realencyclopädie*, ed. 2.

[2] Cf. Lehmann, *Aberglaube und Zauberei*, p. 56.

were methods by which prophetic dreams were sought (Jer. xxix. 8; 1 Sam. xxviii. 6, 15), these suggestions are obscure, and involve no commendation of such usages as prevailed among the heathen. All the supernatural dreams mentioned in the Bible were the unsought gift of Jehovah; and there is not the slightest recommendation in the Scriptural narrative of any of the superstitious practices of either seeking or inter- preting dreams which constitute the very nerve of ethnic dream-lore.[3]

Very exaggerated language is often met with regarding the place which supernatural dreams occupy in Scripture. The writer of the article "Songes" in Lichtenberger's *Encyclopedique des Sciences Religieuse* (Vol. XI, p. 641), for example, opens a treatment of the subject dominated by this idea with the statement that, "as everywhere in antiquity, dreams play a pre- ponderant rôle in the religion of the Hebrews." Even M. Bouché-Leclercq, who usually studies precision, remarks that "the Scriptures are filled with apparitions and prophetic dreams."[4] Nothing could be more contrary to the fact. The truth is the supernatural dream is a very uncommon phe- nomenon in Scripture. Although, as we have seen, dreams are a recognized mode of divine communication, and dream- revelations may be presumed therefore to have occurred throughout the whole history of revelation; yet very few are actually recorded, and they oddly clustered at two or three critical points in the development of Israel. Of each of the two well-marked types of supernatural dreams[5]—those in which direct divine revelations are communicated (Gen. xv. 12; xx. 3, 6; xxviii. 12; xxxi. 10, 11; 1 Kings iii. 5; Matt. i. 20; ii. 12, 13, 19, 22; xxvii. 19) and symbolical dreams which receive divine interpretations (Gen. xxxvii. 5, 6, 10; xl. 5-16; xli. 1, 5; Judges vii. 13-15; Dan. ii. 1, 3, 26; iv. 5; vii. 1)—only some half-score of clear instances are given. All the symbolical dreams, it will be observed further, with the exception of the

---

[3]Cf. F. B. Jevons in Hastings' *Dictionary of the Bible*, Vol. I, p. 622.
[4]*Histoire de la divination dans l'antiquité*, Vol. I, p. 278.
[5]Cf. Baur, *Symbolik und Mythologie*, II. i. 142.

one recorded in Judges vii. 13-15 (and this may have been only a "providential" dream), occur in the histories of Joseph and Daniel; and all the dreams of direct divine communication, with the exception of the one to Solomon (1 Kings iii. 5), in the histories of the nativity of Israel or of the nativity of Israel's Redeemer. In effect, the patriarchal stories of the Book of Genesis, the story of Daniel at the palace of the king, and the story of the birth of Jesus are the sole depositions of supernatural dreams in Scripture; the apparent exceptions (Judges vii. 13-15; 1 Kings iii. 5; Matt. xxvii. 19) may be reduced to the single one of 1 Kings iii. 5.

The significance of the marked clustering of recorded supernatural dreams at just these historical points it is not easy to be perfectly sure of. Perhaps it is only a part of the general tendency of the supernatural manifestations recorded in Scripture to gather to the great historical crises; throughout Scripture the creative epochs are the supernaturalistic epochs. Perhaps, on the other hand, it may be connected with the circumstance that at just these particular periods God's people were brought into particularly close relations with the outside world. We have but to think of Abraham and Abimelech, of Jacob and Laban, of Joseph and Pharaoh, of Daniel and Nebuchadnezzar, of Joseph and the Magi, to observe how near at hand the suggestion lies that the choice of dreams in these instances as the medium of revelation has some connection with the relation in which the recipient stood at the moment to influences arising from the outer world, or at least to some special interaction between Israel and that world.

In entertaining such a conjecture we must beware, however, of imagining that there was something heathenish in the recognition of dreams as vehicles of revelation; or even of unduly deprecating dreams among the vehicles of revelation. It has become quite usual to speak of dreams as the lowest of the media of revelation, with the general implication either that the revelations given through them cannot rise very high in the scale of revelations, or at least that the choice of dreams as their vehicle implies something inferior in the qualification of the recipients for receiving revelations. There is very little Scriptural support for such representations. No doubt, there is a certain gradation in dignity indicated in the methods of revelation. Moses' pre-eminence was marked by Jehovah speaking with him "mouth to mouth," manifestly, while to others he made himself known "in a vision," or "in a dream" (Num. xii. 6). And it is possible that the order in which the various methods of revelation are enumerated in such passages as Deut. xiii. 1; 1 Sam. xxviii. 6, 15; Joel ii. 28; Acts ii. 17 may imply a gradation in which revelation through dreams may stand at the foot. But these very passages establish dreams among the media statedly used by God for the revelation of his will, and drop no word deprecatory of them; nor is there discoverable in Scripture any justification for conceiving the revelations made through them as less valuable than those made through other media.[6]

It is very misleading to say, for example,[7] that "the greater number" of the recorded supernatural dreams "were granted, for prediction or for warning, to those who were aliens to the Jewish covenant"; and when they were given to God's "chosen servants, they were almost always referred to the periods of their earliest and most imperfect knowledge of him"; and, "moreover, they belong especially to the earliest age, and became less frequent as the revelations of prophecy increase." As many of these dreams were granted to Israelites as to aliens; they do not mark any particular stage of religious development in their recipients; they do not gradually decrease with the progress of revelation; they no more characterize the patriarchal age than that of the exile or the opening of the new dispensation. If no example is recorded during the whole period from Solomon to Daniel; so none is recorded from the patriarchs to Solomon, or again from Daniel to our Lord. If the great writing prophets assign none of their revelations to dreams, they yet refer to revelations by dreams in such a way as to manifest their

---

[6]Cf. König, *Offenbarungsbegriff*, I. p. 55, II. pp. 9 f., 63 f.

[7]Barry in Smith's *Dictionary of the Bible*, Vol. I, p. 617; cf. Orelli, *op. cit.*

recognition of them as an ordinary medium of revelation (Jer. xxiii. 25, 28, 32; xxvii. 9; xxix. 8; Zech. x. 2). These passages are often adduced, to be sure, as suggesting that appeal especially to dreams was a characteristic of the false prophets of the day; and it is even sometimes represented that Jeremiah means to brand dream-revelations as such as lying revelations. Jeremiah's polemic, however, is not directed against any one particular method of revelation, but against false claims to revelation by any method. His zeal burns no more hot against the prophet that "hath a dream" than against him that "hath the Lord's word" (xxiii. 28); no more against those that cry, "I have dreamed, I have dreamed," than against those who "take their tongue and say, he saith" (xxiii. 25, 31). Nor does Zechariah's careful definition of his visions as received waking, though coming to him at night (i. 8; iv. 1), involve a deprecation of revelations through dreams; it merely calls our attention to the fact, otherwise copiously illustrated, that all night-visions are not dreams (cf. Gen. xv. 12; xxvi. 24; xlvi. 2; Num. xxii. 20; 1 Chron. xvii. 3; 2 Chron. vii. 12; Job iv. 13; xx. 8; xxxiii. 15; Dan. ii. 19; Acts xvi. 9; xviii. 9; xxiii. 11; xxvii. 24).

The citation in Acts ii. 17 of the prediction of Joel ii. 8 suffices to show that there rested no shadow upon the "dreaming of dreams" in the estimation of the writers of the New Testament. Rather this was in their view one of the tokens of the messianic glory. Nevertheless, as we have seen, none of them except Matthew records instances of the supernatural dream. In the Gospel of Matthew, however, no fewer than five or six instances occur. Some doubt may attach, to be sure, to the nature of the dream of Pilate's wife (xxvii. 19). The mention of it was certainly not introduced by Matthew idly, or for its own sake; it forms rather one of the incidents which he accumulates to exhibit the atrocity of the judicial murder of Jesus. Is his meaning that thus God himself intervened to render Pilate utterly without excuse in his terrible crime (so Keil, *in loc.*)? Even so the question would still remain open whether the divine intervention was direct and immediate, in the mode of a special revelation, or indirect and mediate, in the mode of a providential determination. In the latter contingency, this dream would take its place in a large class, naturally mediated, but induced by God for the guidance of the affairs of men— another instance of which, we have already suggested, may be discovered in the dream of the Midianitish man mentioned in Judges vii. 13, 15 (so Nösgen, *in loc.*). In this case, the five instances of the directly supernatural dream which Matthew records in his "Gospel of the infancy" stand alone in the New Testament.

In any event, this remarkable series of direct divine revelations through dreams (Matt. i. 20; ii. 12, 13, 19, 22) forms a notable feature of this section of Matthew's Gospel, and contributes its share to marking it off as a section apart. On this account, as on others, accordingly, this section is sometimes contrasted unfavorably with the corresponding section of the Gospel of Luke. In that, remarks, for example, Reuss,[8] the angel visitants address waking hearers, the inspiration of the Spirit of God renews veritable prophecy, "it is a living world, conscious of itself, that appears before us"; in this, on the contrary, "the form of communication from on high is the dream— the form the least perfect, the least elevated, the least reassuring." Others, less preoccupied with literary problems, fancy that it is the recipients of these dream-revelations rather than the author of the narrative to whom they are derogatory. Thus, for example, we are told that, like the Magi of the East and the wife of Pilate, Joseph "was thought worthy of communion with the unseen world and of communications from God's messenger only when in an unconscious state," seeing that he was not ripe for the manifestation of the angel to him, as to Zacharias and Mary, when awake.[9] Of course, there is nothing of all this in the narrative, as there is nothing to justify it in any Scripture reference to the significance of revelation through dreams. The narrative is notable chiefly for its simple dignity and directness. In three of the instances we are merely told that "an angel of the Lord appeared to Joseph," and in the

[8]*La Bible* (N.T.), Vol. I, p. 138.
[9]Nebe, *Kindheitsgeschichte*, p. 212, cf. p. 368.

other two that he or the Magi were "warned of God" in a dream, that is, either by way of, or during, a dream. The term employed for "appearing" ($\varphi\alpha\acute{\iota}\nu\omega$) marks the phenomenal objectivity of the object: Joseph did not see in his dream-image something which he merely interpreted to stand for an angel, but an angel in his proper phenomenal presentation.[10] The term translated "warned of God" ($\chi\rho\eta\mu\alpha\tau\acute{\iota}\zeta\omega$) imports simply an authoritative communication of a declaration of the divine will (so, e.g., Weiss, Keil, Alexander, Broadus, Nebe), and does not presuppose a precedent inquiry (as is assumed, e.g., by Bengel, Meyer, Fritzsche). The narratives confine themselves, therefore, purely to declaring, in the simplest and most direct manner, that the dream-communications recorded were from the Lord. Any hesitancy we may experience in reading them is not suggested by them, but is imported from our own personal estimate of the fitness of dreams to serve as media of divine communications.

It is probable that the mere appearance of dreams among the media of revelation recognized by Scripture constitutes more or less of a stumbling-block to most readers of the Bible. The disordered phantasmagoria of dreams seems to render them peculiarly unfit for such a use. The superstitious employment of them by all nations in the lower stages of culture, including not only the nations of classical antiquity, but also those ancient peoples with whom Israel stood in closest relations, suggests further hesitancy. We naturally question whether we are not to look upon their presence in the Scripture narrative just as we look upon them in the Gilgamesh epic or the annals of Assurbanipal, on the stêle of Bentrest or the inscriptions of Karnak, in the verses of Homer or the histories of Herodotus. We are not without temptation to say shortly with Kant,[11] "We must not accept dream-tales as revelations from the invisible world." And we are pretty sure, if we begin, with Witsius, with a faithful recognition of the fact that "God has seen fit to reveal

---

[10]See Grimm-Thayer, *sub voc.* $\delta o\kappa\acute{\epsilon}\omega$, *ad fin.;* Trench, *Synonyms of the New Testament,* par. lxxx; Schmidt, *Griech. Syn.,* c. 15.

[11]*Anthropologie,* Vol. I, sec. 29.

himself not only to the waking, but sometimes also to the sleeping," to lapse, like him, at once into an apologetical vein, and to raise the question seriously, "Why should God wish to manifest himself in this singular way, by night, and to the sleeping, when the manifestation must appear obscure, uncertain, and little suited either to the dignity of the matters revealed or to the use of those to whom the revelation is made?"[12]

We have already pointed out how little there is in common between the occasional employment of dreams for revelations, such as meets us in Scripture, and the superstitious view of dreams prevalent among the ancients. It is an understatement when it is remarked that "the Scriptures start from a spiritual height to which the religious consciousness of the heathen world attained only after a long course of evolution, and then only in the case of an isolated genius like Plato" (Jevons, *loc. cit.,* p. 622). The difference is not a matter of degree, but of kind. No special sacredness or significance is ascribed by the Scriptures to dreams in general. No class or variety of dreams is recommended by them to our scrutiny that we may through this or that method of interpretation seek guidance from them for our life. The Scriptures merely affirm that God has on certain specific occasions, in making known his will to men, chosen to approach them through the medium of their night-visions; and has through these warned them of danger, awakened them to a sense of wrong-doing, communicated to them his will, or made known his purposes. The question that is raised by the affirmation of such an occasional divine employment of dreams is obviously not whether dreams as such possess a supernatural quality and bear a supernatural message if only we could get at it, but rather whether there is anything inherent in their very nature which renders it impossible that God should have made such occasional use of them, or derogatory to him to suppose that he has done so.

Surely we should bear in mind, in any consideration of such

---

[12]See "de Prophetis et Prophetia," ch. v in *Miscell. Sacra,* Vol. I, pp. 22-27; cf. also Spanheim, *Dubia Evangelica,* Part II, Geneva, 1700, pp. 239-240, and Rivetus, *In Gen. Exercit.,* cxxiv.

a question, the infinite condescension involved in God's speaking to man through any medium of communication. There is a sense in which it is derogatory to God to suppose him to hold any commerce with man at all, particularly with sinful man. If we realized, as we should, the distance which separates the infinite and infinitely holy God from sin-stricken humanity, we should be little inclined to raise questions with respect to the relative condescension involved in his approaching us in these or those particular circumstances. In any revelation which God makes to man he stoops infinitely—and there are no degrees in the infinite. God's thoughts are not as our thoughts, and the clothing of his messages in the forms of human conception and language involves an infinite derogation. Looked at *sub specie aeternitatis*, the difference between God's approaching man through the medium of a dream or through the medium of his waking apprehension, shrinks into practical nothingness. The cry of the heart which has really seen or heard God must in any case be, "What is man, that thou art mindful of him? or the son of man, that thou visitest him?"

It should also be kept clearly in view that the subject of dreams, too, is, after all, the human spirit. It is the same soul that is active in the waking consciousness which is active also in the dream-consciousness—the same soul acting according to the same laws (cf. Lehmann, *op. cit.*, p. 397). No doubt there are some dreams which we should find difficulty in believing were direct inspirations of God. Are there not some waking thoughts also of which the same may be said? This does not in the least suggest that the divine Spirit may not on suitable occasion enter into the dream-consciousness, as into the waking, and impress upon it, with that force of conviction which he alone knows how to produce, the assurance of his presence and the terms of his message.

Dr. G. T. Ladd writes:

The psychology of dreams and visions, so far as we can speak of such a psychology, furnishes us with neither sufficient motive nor sufficient means for denying the truth of the Biblical narratives. On the contrary, there are certain grounds for confirming the truth of some of these narratives. . . . Even in ordinary dreams, the dreamer is still the human soul. The soul acts, then, even in dreaming, as a unity, which involves within itself the functions and activities of the higher, even of the ethical and religious powers. . . . The possibility of even the highest forms of ethical and religious activities in dreams cannot be denied. . . . There is nothing in the physiological or psychical conditions of dream-life to prevent such psychical activity for the reception of revealed truth. . . . It remains in general true that the Bible does not transgress the safe limits of possible or even actual experience.[13]

So little, indeed, do emptiness and disorder enter into the very essence of dreaming, that common experience supplies innumerable examples of dreams thoroughly coherent and consequent. The literature of the subject is filled with instances in which even a heightened activity of human faculty is exhibited in dreams, and that throughout every department of mental endowment. Jurists have in their dreams prepared briefs of which they have been only too glad to avail themselves in their waking hours; statesmen have in their dreams obtained their best insight into policy; lecturers have elaborated their discourses; mathematicians solved their most puzzling problems; authors composed their most admired productions; artists worked out their most inspired motives. Dr. Franklin told Cabanis that the bearings and issues of political events which had baffled his inquisition when awake were not infrequently unfolded to him in his dreams. It was in a dream that Reinhold worked out his table of categories. Condorcet informs us that he often completed his imperfect calculations in his dreams; and the same experience has been shared by many other mathematicians, as, for example, by Maignan, Göns, Wähnert. Condillac, when engaged upon his *Cours d'Études*, repeatedly developed and finished in his dreams a subject which he had broken off on retiring to rest. The story of the origin of Coleridge's *Kubla Khan* in a dream is well known. Possibly no more instructive instance is on record,

---

[13]*The Doctrine of Sacred Scripture*, Vol. II, p. 436.

however, than the account given by Robert Louis Stevenson, in his delightful *Chapter on Dreams*,[14] of how "the little people" of his brain, who had been wont to amuse him with absurd farragos, harnessed themselves to their task and dreamed for him consecutively and artistically when he became a craftsman in the art of story-telling. Now, they trimmed and pared their dream-stories, and set them on all fours, and made them run from a beginning to an end, and fitted them to the laws of life, and even filled them with dramatic situations of guileful art, making the conduct of the actors psychologically correct, and aptly graduating the emotion up to the climax.[15]

Instances of this heightened mental action in dreams are so numerous and so striking in fact, that they have given rise to a hypothesis which provokes Wundt's scoff at those "who are inclined to think that when we dream the mind has burst the fetters of the body, and that dream fancies transcend the activity of the waking consciousness, with its narrow confinement to the limitations of space and time."[16] The well-known essay of Lange "On the Double Consciousness, especially on the Night-Consciousness and its polar relation to the Day-Consciousness of Man," printed in the *Deutsche Zeitschrift für christliche Wissenschaft und christliches Leben* for 1851 (nos. 30, 31, and 32), still provides one of the most readable and instructive statements of this theory. But English readers will be apt to turn for it first of all to the voluminous discussions of the late Mr. Frederic W. H. Myers, *Human Personality and Its Survival of Bodily Death* (London, 1903), where it is given a new statement on a fresh and more empirical basis. In Mr. Myers' view, the sleeping state is more plastic than the waking, exhibiting some trace "of the soul's less exclusive absorption in the activity

---

[14]Thistle ed. of *Works*, Vol. XV, pp. 250 ff.

[15]See Abercrombie, *Inquiries Concerning the Intellectual Powers*, Part III, sec. iv, esp. pp. 216-221; Carpenter, *Principles of Mental Physiology*, pp. 524 f.; Lehmann as cited, p. 411; Volkelt, *Die Traumphantasie*, no. 15; Myers, *Human Personality*, nos. 417, 418, 430, with corresponding Appendices.

[16]*Vorlesungen über die Menschen-und Thierseele*, Lect. xxii. pp. 360-370, E.T. pp. 323 f.

of the organism," by which is possibly increased "the soul's power of operating in that spiritual world to which sleep has drawn it nearer."[17] Accordingly, "these subliminal uprushes" which we call dreams, these "bubbles breaking on the surface from the deep below," may be counted upon to bring us messages, now and again, from a spiritual environment to which our waking consciousness is closed. On hypotheses like these it is often argued that the sleeping state is the most favorable for the reception of spiritual communications. It is not necessary to commit ourselves to such speculations. But their existence among investigators who have given close study to the phenomena of dreams strongly suggests to us that those phenomena, in the mass, are not such as to exclude the possibility or the propriety of the occasional employment by the divine Spirit of dreams as vehicles of revelation.

That powerful influences should occasionally arise out of dreams, affecting the conduct and the destiny of men, is only natural, and is illustrated by numerous examples. Literature is crowded with instances of the effect of dreams upon life, for good and evil; and the personal experience of each of us will add additional ones. There is no one of us who has not been conscious of the influence of night visions in deterring him from evil and leading him to good. The annals of religion are sown with instances in which the careers of men have been swayed and their outlook for time and eternity altered by a dream. We may recall the dream of Evagrius of Pontus, recorded by Socrates, for example, by which he was nerved to resist temptation, and his whole life determined. Or we may recall the dream of Patrick, given in his *Confession*, on which hung his whole work as apostle of the Irish. Or we may recall the dream of Elizabeth Fry, by which she was rescued from the indecision and doubt into which she fell after her conversion. The part played by dreams in the conversion of John Bunyan, John Newton, James Gardiner, Alexander Duff, are but well-known instances of a phenomenon illustrated copiously from

---

[17]Vol. I, pp. 151-152; cf. p. 135.

every age of the Church's experience. "Converting dreams"
are indeed a recognized variety,[18] and are in nowise stranger
than many of their fellows. They are the natural result of the
action of the stirred conscience obtruding itself into the visions
of the night, and, as psychological phenomena, are of precisely
the same order as the completion of mathematical problems
in dreams, or the familiar experience of the invasion of our
dreams by our waking anxieties. In the providence of God,
however, they have been used as instruments of divine grace,
and levers by which not only individual destiny has been determined, but the very world has been moved.[19]

With such dreams and the issues which have flowed from
them in mind, we surely can find no difficulty in recognizing
the possibility and propriety of occasional divine employment
of dreams for the highest of ends. Obviously dreams have not
been deemed by Providence too empty and bizarre to be used
as instruments of the most far-reaching effects. Indeed, we
must extend the control of divine Providence to the whole world
of dreams. Of course, no dream visits us in our sleep, any
more than any occurrence takes place during our waking hours,
apart from the appointment and direction of him who himself
never either slumbers or sleeps, and in whose hands all things
work together for the execution of his ends. We may, now and
again, be able to trace with special clearness the hand of the great
Potter, molding the vessel to its destined uses, in, say, an unusual
dream, producing a profoundly arresting effect upon the consciousness. But in all the dreams that visit us, we must believe the
guidance of the universal Governor to be present, working out his
will. It will hardly be possible, however, to recognize this providential guidance of dreams, and especially the divine employment of particularly moving dreams in the mode of what we
commonly call "special providences," without removing all
legitimate ground for hesitation in thinking of his employment
of special dreams also as media of revelation. The God of

---

[18]See Myers as cited, no. 409, i. pp. 126, 127.

[19]Cf. Delitzsch, as cited, and "Dreams and the Moral Life" [by
B.B.W.], in the *Homiletic Review*, Sept. 1890.

providence and the God of revelation are one God; and his providential and revelational actions flow together into one harmonious effect. It is not possible to believe that the instrumentalities employed by him freely in the one sphere of his operation can be unworthy of use by him in the other. Those whom he has brought by his providential dealings with them into such a state of mind that they are prepared to meet with him in the night watches, and to receive on the prepared surface of their souls the impressions which he designs to convey to them, he surely may visit according to his will, not merely by the immediate operation of his grace, but also in revealing visions, whether these visions themselves are wrought through the media of their own experiences or by his own creative energy. It is difficult to perceive in what the one mode of action would be more unfitting than the other.

12

THE QUESTION OF MIRACLES*

I

One would think it a principle too obvious to require insisting upon that every discussion of miracles should begin with a clearly defined conception of what a miracle is and what is asserted to have occurred when it is affirmed that a miracle has taken place. Nevertheless, this is a principle which has not been universally acted upon. Many of the debates which have been held as to the possibility and the actual occurrence of miracles have been vitiated *ab initio* by lack of agreement between the parties as to what it is they are talking about. If the question of miracles is only a question of size, as "theologians," according to Prof. Borden T. Bowne,[1] are apt to think —and so, a raising from the dead would be a miracle because it is so stupendous a thing and "an answer to prayer of moderate dimensions" would not—the question could easily be settled by the simple use of a spiritual tape line. If the question is only a question of God's manifest presence and activity, then it is settled at once in the personal experience of every Christian, who in his closet or in his hours of danger or distress has "met with God." If it is only a question of whether God's hand is outstretched for the governing of the universe, so that nothing occurs without his ordering and direction, then it is settled for everyone having an eye for final causes, who will observe the course of nature or the progress of history at all; everything that occurs is a miracle. But if it is a question of

---

*The Bible Student, Mar. 1903, pp. 121-126; Apr. 1903, pp. 193-197; May 1903, pp. 243-250; June 1903, pp. 314-320.
[1] *The Independent* for January 15, 1903, p. 151.

something more specific than these things, we must surely begin by defining just what it is, that we may know precisely what to look for. Nor ought it to be so extremely difficult to say what we mean by a miracle that we should be justified in declining the task. Certainly, it may cost us some care. As Dr. C. M. Mead points out in his admirable discussion of the definition of a miracle included in his volume of Stone Lectures, our definition may err either by overstatement or by understatement.[2]

"It is an overstatement," he says, truly, "when a miracle is spoken of as a violation, or suspension, or transgression of the laws or forces of nature." A miracle is not performed by or through the forces of nature or according to its laws: but is, as Mill accurately defines it, "a new effect supposed to be produced by the introduction of a new cause."[3] It does not "violate" any law of nature that a new cause should produce a new effect. It does not "suspend" any law of nature that the intrusion of a new force should be followed by the appearance of a new result. It does not "transgress" any law of nature that the new force is productive of new effects. The mark of a miracle, in a word, is not that it is contra-natural, but that it is extra-natural and more specifically that it is super-natural. It is not conceived as a product of nature, different from or contrary to the ordinary products of nature; but as the product of a force outside of nature, and specifically above nature, intruding into the complex of natural forces and producing, therefore, in that complex, effects which could not be produced by the natural forces themselves. These effects reveal themselves, therefore, as "new"—but not as neo-natural but rather as extra-natural and specifically as super-natural.

It is, therefore, on the other hand, an understatement when a miracle is spoken of as the product of the ordinary and known forces of nature under the manipulation of the infinite intellect of God, or even as the product of occult and so-called "higher" natural forces brought into action by the omniscient control

---

[2]*Supernatural Revelation*, New York, 1889, pp. 96 ff.
[3]*Logic*, Book III, ch. xxv, p. 32.

over nature exercised by God. By such definitions miracles are reduced to the category of the natural. For the forces of nature, under whatever guidance, can produce nothing but natural effects. They are thus confused with what we know as "special providences." The mark of a miracle is, on the contrary, just that it is not the product of "second causes," under whatever wise and powerful government: that it is not analogous, therefore, to the effects which we produce in our intelligent adaptation of the forces of nature; but that it is the product of a new force introduced into the complex of natural forces and producing in that complex a new effect.

No doubt this effect thus produced is an effect in the complex of nature, and exhibits itself, in that sense, as a "natural" effect. But it is nevertheless an effect to the production of which—when conceived barely, in itself alone—the natural forces working along with the force which really produces it, contribute nothing whatever. These natural forces are continually operative during the whole process of the production of the miracle. The miracle takes place in and among them, not "violating," "suspending," or "transgressing" them. And therefore the new force acts in harmony with the natural forces operative at the time and place where the effect is produced; and the product of the new force appears thus without wrench in the complex of natural effects, and takes its place in this complex, as amenable to these forces so far as they are operative upon it, and, therefore, subject to all natural law. The wine made at Cana, for example, was true wine, and produced all the effects of wine; it was made under the conditions of the natural forces then and there operative, and became at once on its production subject to them; but it was not made by them, nor with their co-operation. The complex of nature furnishes thus the condition of a miracle; but in this sense only, that a miracle occurs in nature, and its product takes its place in the complex of nature; but it is in no sense, in whole or in part, the product of nature. It is of the *differentia* of a miracle in a word, that it is, as distinguished from a subjective effect, objectively real, and takes place in the external world. And thus are set aside the attempts sometimes made to explain miracles "by transposing the marvels from the physical to the mental world"—as if the wine at Cana, for example, was not really wine, but men's sense of taste was so affected as to make what was really water seem wine to them.

A miracle then is specifically an effect in the external world, produced by the immediate efficiency of God. Its *differentiae* are: (1) that it occurs in the external world, and thus is objectively real and not a merely mental phenomenon; and (2) that its cause is a new super-natural force, intruded into the complex of nature, and not a natural force under whatever wise and powerful manipulation. Robert Browning has caught the idea when he cries:

> Here is the finger of God, a flash of the will that can—
> Existent behind all laws, that made them, and lo! they are!

The question as to miracles, therefore, is simply whether any such events as this have ever occurred. Have there ever occurred effects which are just a "flash of the will that can," of the will that exists behind all laws, that made them, and that acts at discretion through, along with, or apart from them? The question as to miracles is, therefore, not precisely the question of the supernatural. There are modes of the supernatural that are not miracles. There is the subjective supernatural: and miracles are objective occurrences in the external world. There are objective supernatural occurrences in the external world, the proximate causes of which are to be found in what we know as "second causes," though these "second causes" are so utilized by God as to produce results to which they are inadequate when left to their "natural working": these we call "special providences." There is the supernatural, of the entire world-order, due to the immanent concursus of God, by virtue of which the world order is a providential order. The question is whether over and above all these, there is another mode of the supernatural—the mode we call miracle—the mode of the immediate as distinguished from all mediate operations of God's power in the external as distinguished from the subjective world.

There are many, of course, who answer this question at once and emphatically in the negative. And the number of these, we are told, is increasing. The grounds taken up by such are generically three. They usually declare that such events are impossible; or that they are, though abstractly possible, incapable of being proved to have taken place; or that though, of course, sufficient evidence of their occurrence would be conceivable, as a matter of fact sufficient evidence of the occurrence of such events has never been produced. We have enumerated these three grounds in what seems their natural order, and the order moreover in which they probably actually lie in the minds of objectors. It may cheerfully be admitted, however, that they are ordinarily explicitly defined in the consciousness of objectors in the reverse order. When the evidence for a miracle presents itself before their minds it scarcely finds hospitable reception; and when that evidence is exceptionally abundant and cogent, they are compelled to face the question, What kind and amount of evidence would avail to convince them that an event outside of the natural order had actually taken place. Honesty compels them to reply that no amount of evidence would convince them of the real occurrence of such an event, and they thus discover their real position to be that a miraculous event is as such incapable of proof. Why such an event should be incapable of proof, however, is not immediately obvious. If it occurs, it ought to be capable of being shown to have occurred. Ultimately, therefore, this ground will exhibit itself as incapable of occupation, except on the postulate that the occurrence of such an event is in itself impossible. The assumption of the impossibility of an event outside of the natural order may be believed, therefore, to underlie and condition, consciously or unconsciously, the thought of all those who at once and emphatically deny the existence of such events, whether they base their denial explicitly on this postulate, or on one of the other grounds enumerated. Logically, at all events, it seems to come to that.

That this is true is naïvely allowed, indeed, with sufficient frequency. Mr. Alfred W. Benn, for example, published some years ago in *The New World* (September, 1895) a paper, the whole purpose of which was to contend that disbelief in the supernatural, among historical investigators, is *a posteriori*—the result, not the cause, of modern destructive Biblical criticism. The "science of historical evidence," he tells us, "refuses to accept any story not intrinsically probable, except on the testimony of eye-witnesses, or, at the very least of contemporaries" (pp. 43 f.). Whence it would seem to follow that "the science of historical evidence" would accept even intrinsically improbable stories—that is, in this context, accounts of miracles—on the testimony of eye-witnesses; that it would be at least conceivable that the testimony of eye-witnesses could be so strong and convincing that it would compel the acceptance of such stories. Yet shortly afterwards (pp. 440 f.) Mr. Benn with great naïveté drops the remark: "If the evidence of eye-witnesses could convert the rationalists to a belief in miracles, incredulity on this point would long ago have ceased to trouble the apologist." The confession here that the testimony of eye-witnesses, as formerly demanded, is available for miracles; but that the rationalist is inconvincible of the reality of miracles by any testimony whatever—that is, that the possibility of miracles is *a priori* denied by him—is flagrant. Let us turn, however, from the incidental to a formal confession that this is the real state of the case. Dr. William Mackintosh finds himself unable to admit that any supernatural events lie at the origin of the Christian religion. He says:

> With a large and ever increasing number of cultivated men we hold that miracles not only "do not" but cannot happen. . . . We confess that as here stated in synthetic form, this assumption has all the appearance of an unwarranted begging of the whole question in dispute, and a summary setting aside of the claims of Christianity to be a supernatural revelation. This has been so strongly felt, that in order to avoid the appearance of a *petitio principii*, many even of those critics who deny the supernatural nature of Christianity, set out by admitting the possibility of miracles

in the abstract, while maintaining that the alleged miracles of Christianity do not satisfy their canons of credibility: and no doubt this intermediate position has a certain air of judicial candor, and of dispassionate consideration. But it cannot be concealed that this mode of treatment opens the door to endless controversy and gives no hope of a conclusive settlement. . . . It is impossible to determine the amount of evidence which is necessary to prove the reality of an alleged miracle, or to say when it is that the presumption against such an abnormal occurrence is overcome. . . . Indeed, it is easy to see that to grant the possibility of miracle in the abstract, is to surrender the whole position to the orthodox theologian. To say the very least, it is to place the supernatural character of Christianity among the things which cannot be disproved, and to throw the door open to a never-ending because resultless controversy between the scientific and the religious spirit. . . . Nothing more need be said to demonstrate what an inconclusive procedure it is to rest the denial of the miraculous element of the Gospels, as Kuenen in Holland and Huxley in this country are disposed to do, on the inadequacy of the historical evidence. When a critic like Kuenen professes to believe, or not to dispute, the possibility of miracle in the abstract, and to be willing to leave that as an open and unsettled question, but at the same time shows himself very exacting as to the evidence for the miraculous element in Christianity as a whole, or for the miraculous works recorded of Jesus in particular, and declares that the evidence for these does not satisfy his canons of credibility; the likelihood is that unconsciously to himself, there is an *arrière pensée* in his mind equivalent to the denial of the possibility of miracles; at least, that is the impression which the rigor of his criticism will make on the minds of others.[4]

We may suspect, then, that a more or less clearly formulated assumption of the impossibility of miracles underlies the strenuous opposition to the admission of their reality, of all this class of writers: as we may contend that only on this assumption may the denial of their reality be made good.

When we ask for the grounds of this assumption, however, we shall seek long for a satisfactory answer. Certainly Dr.

---

[4]*The Natural History of the Christian Religion*, p. 20.

Mackintosh himself, who insists that the whole case must be based on this assumption, has no sufficient reason to give for making this assumption. He tells us that, in his own mind, the origin of the conviction of the impossibility of miracle was mediated by a general view of what he calls the "religious relation" (p. 20): that is to say, he first came to believe that man's relation to God was that of a child to his father, and this "led him on to the position that miracle is impossible." How it did so extraordinary a thing he does not stop to tell us. He defends this position, however, solely by an appeal to what he considers the implications of scientific research.

> Science [he tells us] has brought into view certain considerations which strongly imply the impossibility of any infraction of the immanent laws of existence. . . . Science has pushed its investigations into almost every department of existence, and in every one, physical and psychological, to which it has gained access, it has found that all occurrences, phenomena, and sequences bear invariable witness to the control of law and to the sway of order—that what is called divine action never operates irrespective of such order, or otherwise than naturally—that is, through, or in accordance with such order. The inference is irresistible that the same thing holds true in those departments also, if such there be, which science has not yet invaded, and the tendency is fostered in the scientific mind to assume that every fact or event, however strange, and apparently exceptional or abnormal, admits of being subsumed under some general law or laws, either already ascertained or yet ascertainable (p. 23).

Accordingly—

> Modern thought holds, in the form of a scientific conviction, what was matter of surmise or divination to a few of the leading minds in ages past, viz., that the universe is governed by immutable laws inherent in the very nature and constitution of things—by laws which are "never reversed, never suspended, and never supplemented in the interest of any special object whatever."

So far as we are able to apprehend this reasoning, it appears to lay down as a premise, the discovery by science of the uni-

form order of nature and the conviction arising from that, that
the forces of nature are adequate for all the ends of nature;
and then to draw from this premise, as intermediate conclusion,
that this order of nature is never invaded by its author "for any
special object whatever" not provided for in its own forces
and laws; and then further, as ultimate conclusion, that miracles
are "impossible."

The stringency of the steps in this reasoning does not readily
appear. How we can infer from any study of the ordinary
course of things, however protracted, profound, or complete,
that an extraordinary event never occurs; and how we can infer
from the conviction that such an extraordinary event never
occurs, that it is impossible; it is not easy to see. An extraordinary event is by definition outside the ordinary course.
Whether it occurs or not is, then, not a matter of inference
from the ordinary course, however completely investigated or
understood; but a matter of simple observation. And whether
in the absence of such observed extraordinary events, they are
"impossible," is again not a matter of inference from their non-
occurrence; but must rest on some principle deeper than experience can furnish. The fact is, in other words, that the
impossibility of miracles can be affirmed only on *a priori*
grounds: Dr. Mackintosh's attempt to supply an *a posteriori*
ground for it was predoomed to failure. The atheist, the ma-
terialist, the pantheist are within their rights in denying the
possibility of miracle. But none other is. So soon as we adopt
the postulate of a personal God and a creation, so soon miracles
cease to be "impossible" in any exact sense of the word. We
may hold them to be improbable, to the verge of the unprov-
able: but their *possibility* is inherent in the very nature of God
as personal and the author of the universal frame.

But if possible, then, as Dr. Mackintosh admits, their actual
occurrence is a matter of experience and is a proper subject
for testimony. The question of miracles, then, is after all just a
question of evidence. There may still remain room for dispute
with reference to the kind and amount of evidence which should
be held requisite to establish their actual occurrence. It is

possible to say—men have said—that only miraculous evidence could establish the actual occurrence of a miracle. But it is also very possible to show that this is a position at least as untenable as the *a priori* denial of their possibility. For—but that is another story, and too long a story to be entered upon here and now. Let it suffice for the present that the *a priori* assertion of the impossibility of miracles is shown to be an untenable position, and that, therefore, all denial of their actual occurrence based explicitly or implicitly on that assumption (and according to Dr. Mackintosh all denial of it is based at least implicitly upon that assumption) falls to the ground.

II

The bald assertion that miracles are "impossible" is, for the theist, obviously mere unreasonable dogmatism. There are very many, therefore, who, while habitually acting on no other supposition, are yet unwilling to take up this position openly. An amusing instance is afforded by Prof. Paul W. Schmiedel in the course of his much talked of article, "Gospels," in the *Encyclopedia Biblica*. He opens his discussion of "the miracle-narratives" included in the Synoptics, with the eminently just remark: "It would clearly be wrong, in an investigation such as the present, to start from any such postulate or axiom as that 'miracles' are impossible" (p. 1876). But he is soon found reasoning on precisely this "postulate." He believes himself able to point out "two cases in which even one strongly predisposed to believe in miracles would find it difficult to accept a narrative of this kind on account of the time to which it is assigned." The first of these cases he describes as follows: "Luke xxiii. 44 expressly, and Mark xv. 33, Matt. xxvii. 45, also to all appearance, allege an eclipse of the sun, a celestial phenomenon which, however, is possible only at the period of New Moon—that is, shortly before the first of Nisan—and cannot happen on the 15th or 14th of a month" (p. 1878). That is to say, we must without ado pronounce a darkening of the sun "impossible" unless it occurred at the time of the month when such things can happen—naturally.

A "miracle" in other words is "impossible." If "even one strongly disposed to believe in miracles" cannot accept a simple account of a miraculous occurrence except by transposing it to a time when the event "could happen"—that is, naturally—and so become "possible"; what shall one who is indisposed to believe in miracles hold as to their possibility?

A very common refuge for thinkers of this type—thinkers, that is, who are unwilling to assert miracles to be impossible, and are yet equally unwilling to act on the presumption of their possibility—lies in drawing a distinction between the objective and the subjective. They will not assert miracles to be objectively impossible: but they are quite ready to declare them to be subjectively incredible. They may happen or they may not happen, they say: but it is all one to us—since they cannot be accredited to us as having happened.

Its classical expression has been given to this mode of thought by David Hume in the famous tenth section of his *Enquiry Concerning the Human Understanding*:

> A miracle is a violation of the laws of nature; and as a firm and unalterable experience has established these laws, the proof against a miracle, from the very nature of the fact, is as entire as any argument from experience can possibly be imagined. . . . The plain consequence is (and it is a general maxim worthy of our attention), "that no testimony is sufficient to establish a miracle, unless the testimony be of such a kind, that its falsehood would be more miraculous, than the fact which it endeavors to establish. . . ." When anyone tells me that he saw a dead man restored to life . . . if the falsehood of his testimony would be more miraculous than the event which he relates; then, and not till then, can he pretend to command my belief or opinion.

This statement is obviously marred by a number of logical faults, which even those who agree with it in the main are not slow to recognize. The grossest of these is the assumption underlying its very first clause that no miracles have ever occurred—that there lies against their occurrence the record of a uniform and unbroken—nay an unbreakable—experience.

This is the very thing in dispute. Accordingly John Stuart Mill has properly objected that the evidence for the unbroken uniformity of nature is diminished by whatever weight belongs to the evidence that certain miracles have taken place (*Logic,* II. p. 155); and Prof. Huxley that "all we know of the order of nature is derived from an observation of the course of events of which the so-called miracle is a part" (*Hume,* p. 131). Both of these writers, however, and many others who, like them, criticize the form Hume has given it, consider the essence of the argument sound. For exceptional events, they say, in effect, exceptional evidence is required; for unexampled events, unexampled evidence; for truly miraculous events— must we not demand truly miraculous evidence? It would need therefore a miracle to authenticate a miracle, and we are thus delivered to an endless chain of miracles. Suppose the abstract possibility of miracles, therefore, if you choose: their actual reality remains, they say, in the nature of the case, incapable of validation.

There is much that appears exceedingly plausible in this argument. But a sound estimate of its value will require the making of certain distinctions. When we ask for testimony to a miracle, what is it, primarily, that we are asking testimony to? A miracle is an event in the external world produced by the immediate efficiency of God. Now, what is it that we expect testimony to establish in the first instance? That an event that has occurred in the external world has been produced by the immediate efficiency of God? Or that an event which must be due to the immediate efficiency of God has occurred in the external world? Certainly the second rather than the first. We are not saying that testimony to the nature of the causality involved is illegitimate or cannot carry conviction. Such testimony may exist and may deserve our attention or command our assent: it may even be of "miraculous" quality and cogency and so meet the express requirements of Hume's dilemma. But this is not the testimony to which in the first instance we appeal; and it is not necessary for us to confuse the issue by attending to it here. What we seek testimony for, in the first instance, is assuredly not the miraculous nature of the activity, but the real occurrence of the alleged effect. If the real occurrence of the alleged effect is established, our causal judgment can ordinarily be trusted to do the rest. If it is credibly testified to me, for example, that a man died, and was laid in his grave until corruption had set in, and then arose well and strong at the call of another, I need no express evidence to that effect to prove to me that here is "a flash of the will that can." If indeed the event testified to were that the sun rose as usual on the Galilean hills one April morning, I might ask further evidence than the mere proof of its occurrence, to convince me that this was due to a special supernatural intrusion of the divine will: and one might well hold that only miraculous testimony could establish the miraculous character of such an effect. We must operate under the guidance of our causal judgment and on the principle of an adequate cause. If we perceive an effect to belong to the natural order we shall find it hard to credit any amount of testimony affirming it to belong to the supernatural order. But on the other hand if we perceive the effect to lie outside the natural order, we require no testimony to assure us that it must find its account in an extra-natural, or specifically a supernatural causation. The thing to be established by testimony, therefore, is in the first instance, not the nature of the cause but the occurrence of the effect—simply and solely the phenomenal occurrence.

Now all phenomenal occurrences are surely, in themselves considered, much of the same order. It makes no difference what the implication of this or that one may be—in themselves considered they are all just phenomenal occurrences and nothing else. Butler, we take it therefore, is so far quite right, despite the sharp criticism to which he has been subjected, in contending that the fact of the occurrence of an event which we must judge to be miraculous in its cause, stands, as regards the matter of testimony to its occurrence, much on the same plane with the fact of the occurrence of any other event whatever (*Analogy*, II. p. 2). At this point the cause of the event does not enter into consideration at all: the only matter to be considered is its phenomenal occurrence: and no more testimony can be demanded to establish its phenomenal occurrence than the testimony which is adequate to that single result. We may be more disposed to accept on uncriticized testimony a fact that falls in with our preconceived notions than one that confounds all our previous habits of thought. But after all, the actual evidence that establishes a fact is just the criticized evidence; and not that evidence reinforced or evacuated, as the case may be, by our existing prejudices. This criticized evidence, if it is sufficient to establish a fact that we should like to believe, is equally sufficient to establish one that we should prefer not to believe. In any event, it is surely illegitimate to say that miraculous evidence is requisite to establish the occurrence of a simple objective fact. That Lazarus was dead; that he had lain three days in the tomb; that he came forth at Christ's mere command: surely something less than miraculous testimony can assure us of simple facts like these—level to any man's comprehension, open to any man's investigation, liable to any man's contradiction. Or take the man born blind, whose story we read in the ninth chapter of John. Was he blind, born blind? Did he see again? Did this occur on "the man that is called Jesus making clay and anointing his eyes and saying unto him, 'Go to Siloam and wash' "—which doing, he received his sight? What single occurrence in all this narrative is there, which the testimony offered, if it prove sound upon criticism, is not sufficient to establish? Whether it be a miracle or not that is here detailed to us, we can judge for ourselves— as indeed the happy healed one challenges us to judge. But if we hold it a miracle it is primarily the consent of our minds to his reasoning and not the weight of his testimony that determines our conviction. For the facts we are dependent on the witnesses, and they are assuredly competent to establish them. But for our conclusion as to the cause of these facts, we are standing, in the first instance at least, upon our own rational judgment.

What, then, can be the source of the demand that "miraculous" evidence should be produced for the occurrence of miracles before they can be believed to have occurred? Obviously, nothing more than this: that we feel so assured of the absolute validity of a world-view which excludes miracles, that no evidence can accredit a fact to us which does not fall in with that world-view. We have formed our conviction that the universe is a closed system admitting of no intrusion from without: and we assume that this conviction is so solidly established that we can admit the occurrence of no event which is inconsistent with it. But this is just to say that we deny *a priori* the possibility of miracles. And what is that but to drop back onto the rejected principle that miracles are of themselves impossible, while pretending to admit their abstract possibility and to deny only that they can be proved? In all such demands we are really making the major premise in the examination of the credibility of any alleged fact of a miraculous nature, the precedent assumption of its impossibility. And, of course, if we begin with assuming that miracles are impossible, we shall find little difficulty in concluding that no conceivable evidence will accredit the occurrence of a miracle to us. The validity of this reasoning clearly depends, however, on the validity of our assumption of the irreformability of our non-miraculous world-view. And the question presses, Have we a right to assume that no event can possibly have occurred, which, if it occurred, would compel a revision of the conception we have formed of the universe? The real dilemma, then, is clearly between the world-view we have formed for ourselves and the facts that come to us, accredited by testimony sufficient in itself to prove their reality—apart, that is, from the presumption cherished against them in our minds on the credit of our world-view. In other words, are the facts that are to be permitted to occur in the universe to be determined by our precedently conceived world-view? Or is our world-view to be determined by a due consideration of all the facts that occur in the universe? This is the simple dilemma that is raised. And it is clearly just the dilemma between an *a priori* determination of facts or an *a posteriori* determination of theory.

From the point of view of the truly scientific spirit it cannot be doubtful on which side our decision should fall. We have the highest scientific authority for affirming indeed that no theory of the universe—or of any part of it—has any claim to finality. In a famous address, delivered at Belfast in 1874, Professor Tyndall declared: "Every system which would escape the fate of an organism too rigid to adjust itself to its environment, must be plastic to the extent that the growth of knowledge de- mands."[5] Twenty-eight years afterwards, speaking from the same platform, Prof. Dewar announces the same principle of "the plasticity of scientific thought," as the very condition of scientific investigation. The scientific investigator, it seems, "does not claim for his best hypotheses, more than a pro- visional validity." "He does not forget that tomorrow may bring a new experience compelling him to recast the hypotheses of today." These are wise sayings. And on this doctrine of the plasticity of all truly scientific theories the door is thrown wide open for the admission of miracles—on the sole condition that the occurrence of such fact-phenomena as find no explanation in the current anti-miraculous theories is established on ap- propriate and sufficient evidence. A demand for extraordinary evidence for the establishment of the occurrence of such fact- phenomena is the measure of the non-plasticity of our hy- potheses: and if this demand rises so high as to require "miracu- lous" evidence before a "miraculous" fact will be admitted to have occurred—that is to say, so high as practically to affirm the impossibility of miracles, their incredibility to the pass that no evidence could establish them—that is but the proclamation of the absolute non-plasticity of our theories. Or are we to con- tend that our hypotheses are to be plastic on all other sides, but absolutely rigid on this: that they may be corrected, revolu- tionized, replaced on the emergence of facts infringing on them in every other respect, but never in this respect: that no phe- nomenon can possibly be allowed to have occurred—whatever the evidence of its occurrence may be—which would entail the confession that God has intervened in nature, and would there-

---

[5]*Forty-fourth Report of the British Association*, p. xcv.

fore compel such a revision of our theories as to the relation
of God to the universe as would involve the confession that law
is not the sole sphere of his activity? Obviously this amounts
merely to the arbitrary imposition of a dogmatic naturalism
upon scientific theory. All revisions of scientific theory are to
be welcomed, forsooth, except such a revision as will provide
for the theistic conception of the free relation of the Creator of
all to the product of his handiwork! Such an arbitrary imposition of naturalistic limitations upon our theory of the universe
can certainly have no claim to be called scientific. It is simply
the culminating instance of a mode of procedure which Prof.
Tindall truly declared (with a different application in his mind, no
doubt) has always "proved disastrous in the past, and is simply
fatuous today." Not even the "scientist" can be permitted to
erect his arbitrary theorizing into the rigid test of fact.

There seems to exist no sufficient reason, therefore, why we
should pronounce a miracle incapable of being proved to have
occurred. A miracle in itself is just an occurrence in the external world. And it is hard to see why if it occurs it may not
be shown to have occurred. Whether it occurs or not is just a
matter of experience, and all actual experience is assuredly
capable of being authenticated as actual. Unless there lies behind the assertion a veiled assumption of the impossibility of
miracles, there is really no meaning, then, in the assertion
that miracles are incapable of being proved to have occurred.
There is along this pathway, therefore, no escape from the simple
truth that whether miracles have occurred or not is just a matter
of experience; and that means, just a matter of testimony.

III

Professor Ménégoz, a few years ago (1894), delivered a
remarkable "opening lecture" before the faculty of the Protestant School of Theology at Paris, on "The Biblical Notion of
Miracles." He began by determining with unusual accuracy
just what the Biblical notion of a miracle is, and ended by
recommending his audience to adopt quite a different notion
for their own. In the course of his lecture he reproaches "apolo-

gists" with too often contenting themselves with vindicating "the possibility of miracles in a theoretical abstract manner, without applying their principle to the texts of the Bible as they stand." The establishment of the abstract possibility of an immediate intervention of God, he justly rejoins, is no proof of the reality of the miraculous facts recounted in the Bible (p. 32).

Certainly "apologists" cannot plead the example of the assailants of miracles as an excuse for any half-measures in dealing with the subject. Even those who intrench themselves in the assertion that miracles are impossible are seldom inclined to rest their case on that apparently sufficient reason for rejecting the Biblical miracles. David Hume, for example, who begins by assuming that miracles are impossible and proceeds by striving to demonstrate that they are incapable of proof, yet is not satisfied until he pronounces directly upon the actual evidence submitted for the occurrence of the alleged miraculous events lying at the foundation of the Christian revelation. As the result of his *a posteriori* examination he declares roundly that "there is not to be found in all history, any miracle attested" sufficiently to give us assurance that it happened; nay, that "no testimony for any kind of miracle has ever amounted to a probability, much less to a proof." Mr. Huxley follows Hume in this. After having explained that no amount of testimony could ever prove to him that a miracle had occurred; but at the most would only enlarge his conception of the powers of nature; he nevertheless closes by adducing Hume's *a posteriori* declaration as the pronouncement of a historical expert, and therefore conclusive in the case. Perhaps the most striking illustration of this "thorough" method is provided, however, by the author of *Supernatural Religion.* In the First Part of the book he argues quite on the line of Hume that miracles are impossible and incapable of validation *per se.* But then he suddenly turns and devotes much the larger part of his bulky work to a labored and detailed examination of the trustworthiness of the documentary evidence for the miracles of the Gospels. There is certainly something very odd in this procedure. The appearance is very strong that these reasoners do not themselves thoroughly trust their *a priori* reasoning, and feel the necessity of assailing the direct evidence adduced for the actual occurrence of miracles, before their case against them acquires solidity. In any event, it is made very clear to the Christian student that his task is not completed until he has faced fairly the assertion that no miracle has as a matter of fact ever been shown to have occurred.

We may perhaps wisely take a hint from the author of *Supernatural Religion* in approaching the consideration of the evidence for the actual occurrence of miraculous events. "Now it is apparent," he observes, on the last page of his First Part, "that the evidence for miracles requires to embrace two distinct points: the reality of the alleged facts, and the accuracy of the inference that the phenomena were produced by Supernatural Agency." That is as much as to say that the rejection of the miraculous element in the *origines* of Christianity, say for example—and it is with this that we are primarily concerned—may proceed on two distinct lines. It may either be affirmed that the extraordinary events recorded in the Scriptural narrative never occurred. Or it may be admitted that these events occurred; but it be at once denied that they are in the strict sense miracles. Both lines of attack are actually in use, and they are sufficiently distinct to demand separate treatment. We shall take them up, therefore, in their order.

Is it possible, then, we may ask, first, to deny that the establishment of Christianity in the world was accompanied, or perhaps we may even say effected, by a series of extraordinary occurrences which were looked upon, at the time at any rate, and by the agents by whom Christianity was established and propagated, as "the wonderful works of God"? We do not ourselves see that it is possible to deny this. And we are gratified to observe that we have the fullest support in this judgment of so excessively cautious a writer (the epithet is used advisedly) as Dr. William Sanday. In a recent paper Dr. Sanday lays down at the outset of his study of the question of miracles "the proposition that miracles, or what were thought to be miracles, certainly happened." "The proof of this," he adds, "seems to me decisive": and again, "the evidence is nothing short of stringent." "There is then, I conceive," he concludes, "practically no doubt that at the time when the miracles are said to have been wrought there really were phenomena which those concerned in them with one consent believed to be miraculous."[6]

Of course the evidence on which this historical judgment rests cannot be drawn out in detail here. This evidence consists, it may be briefly said, not only in detailed and formal accounts of extraordinary occurrences narrated with a sanity and sobriety, a combined restraint and confidence, which is unique in all the literature of marvels. It includes also numerous incidental allusions to the occurrence of such events, as notorious matters of facts, such as implicate the whole community in the testimony in the most natural and convincing way. And it includes further historical sequences from these events such as interweave them so into the very fabric of all subsequent history, that history becomes inexplicable save on the assumption of their actual occurrence. Dr. Sanday, in the brevity he required to study, contents himself with adducing the testimony of Paul, of Christ himself, and of the Gospel narrative, reinforced by the exceptionally good historical quality of the evidence given in each case. That such incidental allusions to his own extraordinary works as Paul lets fall in, say, Rom. xv. 18, 19; 1 Cor. xii. 5, 8-10; xiv. 18-19; 2 Cor. xii. 12; Gal. iii. 5, should be otherwise than true, Dr. Sanday justly pronounces simply impossible. Such narratives as that of the Temptation, which turn just on the assumption of Jesus' power to work miracles, are wholly inexplicable if he wrought no miracles at all; and the whole character of these narratives negatives the hypothesis of invention. The detailed evidence of the Gospel narratives cannot be set aside on any critical hypothesis of the origin of the Gospels: for these narratives are on any theory of the composition of the Gospels imbedded in the sources that lie behind our Gospels, whatever these sources

---

[6]*The Expository Times*, Nov. 1902.

may be conceived to be. The hypothetical Ur-Marcus, the problematical Matthean *Logia,* the supposed Lucan "Special Sources," the "triple tradition" operated with by Dr. Abbott— any and every "source" of the Gospel narratives conceived or conceivable—are all alike in this. They all give us not only a miracle-working Jesus, but a Jesus whose miracle-working is an essential element in his manifestation, and yet whose miracle-working is of a sort peculiar in its restraint and fitness to himself. The consistent historical portraiture that is the result of this varied representation is, as Dr. Sanday well argues, of itself a crowning testimony to the reality of the details. Add that the very existence of Christianity, founded as it is on the preaching, say, of the resurrection of Christ, adds its cogent evidence to the same effect. We do not think that Dr. Sanday goes too far in saying that the proof in some of its elements is "as stringent as a proposition of Euclid," and in its entirety must carry conviction to every reasonable judgment. It really cannot be rationally doubted that such extraordinary events did happen.

As over against this overwhelming weight of testimony to these extraordinary facts, those who are "set to oppose" their reality have really nothing to urge, except on the one hand an alleged cloud upon the authenticity of the witnessing documents, and on the other an *a priori* presumption against the occurrence of a series of facts so extraordinary. It would be idle to close our eyes to the vigor with which these lines of assault have been exploited. But it would be a crime to close our eyes to the futility of them at their best—and worst. The critical assault on the genuineness and authenticity of our Biblical books has been a dismal failure. After a century's conflict and the lavish expenditure of nothing less than splendid scholarship and the brilliancy of genius itself upon the assault, things remain just as they were before. As regards the New Testament, indeed, this has long been apparent to even the dullest apprehension; and we must not permit our perception of it to be clouded by the recent recrudescence of the turmoil of the hopeless battle. But even were the matter different, and

the explosion of criticism that has filled all the nineteenth century with its noise, had really scattered the New Testament
documents into fragments, the case for the real occurrence of
these facts would remain essentially the same. For, as we have
already pointed out, the testimony of these documents to the
extraordinary accompaniments of the origin of Christianity
is pervasive, and survives in the very fragments. Leave us only
the four major epistles of Paul; leave us only the hypothetical
Logia—leave us only the "triple tradition"—and we have
essentially the same quiet, constant, and convincing testimony
to the occurrence of these extraordinary events. The fact is,
this testimony is not the testimony of a document here and
there only—much less of a passage here and there scattered
sparsely through the documents: it is the testimony of all the
remains of primitive Christianity, and you would have to destroy the entire body of remains of primitive Christianity to be
rid of it. You would have to represent Christianity as having
no *origines*: as growing out of nothing: as appearing suddenly
full-fledged in the second century without historical beginnings:
if you would be rid of its extraordinary foundations. It is safe
to say that so far as the critical assault is concerned, the
extraordinary events belonging to the first Christian age stand
unassailable.

What, then, shall we say of the presumption against the
actual occurrence of such extraordinary events? It may well
be enough to say that this presumption is *a priori;* and as such
must pass away in the presence of the actually authenticated
events. Such a presumption can be treated as a bar to the
admission of facts, thoroughly authenticated, only when pressed
beyond a presumption and turned into an *a priori* assertion of
the impossibility of the extraordinary. It may not be without its
uses, however, to examine a little into the nature and force of
the presumption that can be said to lie against the actual occurrence of the extraordinary facts testified to in the Biblical
record—say, for instance, in the pages of the New Testament.
To estimate this with any precision there are a number of
distinctions which imperatively demand to be noted.

We must, then, in the first place, distinguish between the general presumption that lies against the anticipated occurrence of extraordinary events, and the particular presumption that lies against the attested occurrence of a particular extraordinary event. The improbability that a given extraordinary event will occur, considered in itself alone, is something very different from the improbability of a given extraordinary event having actually occurred which is testified to as having really occurred. We may calculate the chances, say, against a dead man's rising from the dead in the abstract, and appal ourselves by their immensity. Suppose, however, that such a rising from the dead is actually attested as having really taken place. We cannot carry our abstract calculation of chances over to this case. The matter is now very different. We have not the bare probability of the fact occurring to consider, but, in addition to that, the probability of the testimony offered to it being true. Nor is there here to be considered merely the abstract probability of the truthfulness of testimony in general; but the concrete probability of the particular testimony in hand for the special case under consideration being true. And the probability of this testimony being true rests in part on the known or presumable trustworthiness of the witnesses available in the case, anterior to their testimony to the particular fact now under consideration. To operate in such an instance with the bare abstract presumption against extraordinary events is in effect to deny *a priori* the value of testimony altogether.

And now, another distinction claims our attention: the distinction, to wit, between the presumption against extraordinary facts presented to our acceptance upon the credit of uncriticized testimony, and the presumption against these same facts presented to our acceptance on the credit of criticized testimony. There does lie a presumption against the occurrence of extraordinary events, as such, because of their very character as extraordinary. And this presumption is not wholly lifted by the mere circumstances that a fact is brought before us not merely as a possible fact, with the query, what is the likelihood or unlikelihood of the occurrence of such a fact; but as an alleged fact, which is reported as having actually occurred. It is the natural effect of this presumption that the testimony to its occurrence should be carefully scrutinized and subjected to a thorough criticism. Until this is done, we naturally and properly receive the alleged fact with a certain suspension of judgment. But the case is very different when the testimony stands the scrutiny, and comes forth from the criticism intact. We have no right in this case to speak autocratically of its being a common experience for testimony to be mistaken, or worse. We are no longer dealing with testimony in the abstract, but with this particular piece of testimony; and it must be estimated not on general maxims applying to testimony on the average, but must be accorded the particular degree of credit established as its right by this scrutiny. Otherwise we withhold *a priori* from a special piece of testimony the character it has vindicated for itself under tests—it may be under stringent and most convincing tests.

Nor is this all. We must distinguish further between the presumption that lies against extraordinary events in general and the presumption that can be held to lie against the particular extraordinary events we have under consideration. The special character of the extraordinary events under consideration has its bearing also, on the estimate we should form of the likelihood of their actual occurrence. Extraordinary events witnessed as actually occurring; and witnessed as occurring by exceptionally good testimony, which on testing approves itself as not likely to be mistaken or misleading; may yet raise a presumption against themselves by their character—or, on the other hand, may powerfully commend themselves to us by their inherent character, as events which assuredly ought to have occurred. We may not arbitrarily withhold from the series of extraordinary events which are witnessed to us in the Biblical record, for example, the advantage that accrues rightly to them from their exceptional nobility. "It is true," says J. H. Newman—though Dr. Newman had exceptionally strong temptations not to see this—"it is true, that the miracles of Scripture, viewed as a whole, recommend themselves to our reason, and claim our veneration, above all others, by a peculiar dignity and beauty." We have only to compare the miracles ascribed to Jesus in our canonical Gospels, for example, with those ascribed to him in even the soberest of the apocryphal Gospels: or the miracles accredited to the apostles in the Book of Acts with those accredited to them in the numerous apocryphal Acts; or in general the miracles described in the Biblical narratives with the marvels that crowd the pages either of the Greek romances or of their doubles, the early Christian hagiographies; to be smitten in the face with the unspeakable elevation of the former above the latter. If the latter may be taken as typical inventions of the mythopoeic faculties, the former are immeasurably removed above their powers. This contrast is in no wise destroyed by the rare presence in the Biblical record of an isolated instance of a miracle in some degree assimilable to the type of the marvels of human imagination; or in the mass of frivolous or bizarre marvels that elbow one another in the uncanonical narratives, of a rarer instance of a marvel that in some degree approaches the Biblical miracles in dignity or appropriateness. The contrast is too striking to escape even the most careless eye; and it can scarcely be contended that the presumption against the occurrence of the one type of extraordinary events is as great as that that lies against the other.

Nor yet can it be fairly contended that there is no distinction between the presumption that lies against the occurrence of an isolated marvel, and the presumption that can be held to lie against an extraordinary event which is a constituent part of a body of extraordinary events that are bound together in a system. It certainly would require far more evidence to accredit an extraordinary event lying off to itself out of connection with others, than it would to accredit an extraordinary event standing in close relation with others like itself, which unite with it in a system creating a kind of "nature" within the limits of which each of the individual events—extraordinary as each is in itself—acquires a certain naturalness. The Biblical miracles are anything but a simple mass or congeries of unrelated marvels: they are organically related and constitute as a whole a sort of a

penumbra around a great central fact which lends a kind of necessity to them all. They lead up to, manifest, and lead down from
the incarnation, and in its light appear as in a sense natural events.
One might as well expect a lamp to burn without rays extending
from it into the surrounding darkness, as the Son of God to descend from heaven without trailing clouds of glory as he came.
We have gone beyond our purpose in the concrete manner in
which we have stated this fact. We mean now only somewhat abstractly to call attention to the organic relation which the
whole body of Biblical miracles bear to one another, sustained
as a whole by a great central event, and to point out that in
such circumstances the presumption against the occurrence of
each of the constituent facts is something very different from
the presumption that might be held to lie against an isolated
marvel standing off to itself.

Finally, we must assuredly distinguish between the presumption that lies against a meaningless marvel and the presumption that can be held to lie against an extraordinary event
that serves an obvious purpose, apparently not to be served
except by it. A series, or let us rather say a system, of extraordinary events that serve a high purpose; that are, so to speak,
needed; and that find their excuse—if we can make use of so
low a term where we ought rather to say, their necessity—in
a lofty end which they attain; surely any presumption that lies
against an isolated and meaningless marvel has no application
to them. If we conceive of the universe as a machine made by
God, and just because made by the All-wise and All-powerful
One, perfect in its structure and in all its functioning; we shall
hardly find adequate occasion for any extraordinary activities
on his part. Within the limits of its operation why should he
intervene to do of himself what he surely might leave his machine to do of itself? Any fancied need of interference might
seem at bottom even an arraignment of the perfection of
the great Artificer. Or leaving to one side this mechanical
conception, if we think of the march of history through time
as following a right line of development from the first creative
impulse, working out its destiny without departure in any

respect from its inherent and increate character, it might be difficult to credit the interposition of extraordinary events into the complex of its steady and straightforward movement. But conceive the entrance into this process of any deflection of movement from the straight line of onward progress. Then, the interposition of corrective, that is to say, of extraordinary measures, becomes at once fully comprehensible. The entrance of sin into the world is in this sense the sufficient occasion of the entrance also of miracle. Extraordinary exigencies (we speak as a man) are the sufficient explanation of extraordinary expedients. If, then, we conceive the extraordinary events of the Scriptural record as part and parcel of the redemptive work of God—and this is how they are uniformly represented in the Scriptural record itself—surely the presumption which is held to lie against them merely as extraordinary events is transmitted into a presumption in their favor, as appropriate elements in a great remedial scheme, by means of which the broken scheme of nature is mended and restored.

A peculiarly happy expression is given to this essentially Biblical conception of the place of the extraordinary in the economy of God, by Dr. A. Kuyper. We cannot refrain from quoting a few sentences here:

A miracle is not to be conceived as an isolated phenomenon, which appears without causal connection with all that exists; but as the victorious continuous working of the divine energy, by which God breaks through all opposition, and in despite of disorder, brings his cosmos to that end which was determined for his cosmos in his eternal counsel. It is out of the deeper basis in his will, whereon the whole cosmos rests, that this mysterious power works up into the cosmos; breaks to pieces the bonds of sin and disorder which hold the cosmos in their grasp; and so influences the whole life of the cosmos, out of the center of humanity, that in the end it must attain the glory predestined for it by God, in order in that glory to render to God the purpose God had in mind in the very creation of the cosmos. All interpretations of miracles as arbitrary incidents, out of connection with the palingenesis of the whole cosmos, to which our Lord refers in Matt. xix. 28, and thus as standing in no relation to the whole metamorphosis which awaits the cosmos at the last judgment, so far from exalting the honor of God, degrade the Recreator of heaven and earth to the proportions of a juggler. The whole recreative action of the divine energy is a continuous miracle that shows itself in the radical life-renewal of men through regeneration, in the radical life-renewal of humanity in the new Head which it receives in Christ, and shall finally produce a similar life-renewal of all nature. And it is only because these three effects do not run disconnectedly side by side, but are organically bound together, so that the mystery of the regeneration, incarnation, and *apocatastasis* forms one whole, that this wondrous energy of recreation exhibits itself in one extended history, in which what once were considered incidental wonders could not be lacking.[7]

If there is any validity in this noble outlook, the presumption against the extraordinary events of the Biblical record seems fairly to be transferred to the other side of the account. It would be strange if in the process of the redemption of the world from sin, there were not thrown up in extraordinary occurrences signs of the extraordinary renewal in process. There appears to be no reason then why we should not affirm with all emphasis that the extraordinary events of the Biblical record must be accepted on their own appropriate evidence as facts that actually occurred. But we are no sooner preparing to claim the results of this conclusion than we find the hand of the author of *Supernatural Religion*—and not his hand alone, but with it that of many others—laid on our arm, and hear him saying, "Stop! Supposing it be granted that these extraordinary facts occurred: you must yet face the further question whether they were in the strict sense of your definition miracles. Establishment of the reality of the alleged occurrences still leaves open the accuracy of the inference that the phenomena were produced by direct supernatural agency." We are not so sure that this is at all the case. But to humor these who suppose it to be so, we shall, on a subsequent occasion, seek to give this specific question also some grounded reply, asking the question:

---

[7]*Encyclopaedia of Sacred Theology*, E.T., p. 414; cf. pp. 420-428.

Are the extraordinary facts of the Biblical record to be held to be miracles in the strict sense?

IV

Goethe is reported to have remarked once to Lavater, "A voice from heaven would not convince me that water burned or a dead man rose again." This sufficiently energetic expression of invincible skepticism is the index of the strength of the prejudice against the supernatural, which leads many into the adoption of any expedient rather than to admit the occurrence of real miracles. Mr. Huxley's expedient is not, like Goethe, to deny that the event happens, no matter what the evidence for it may be; but to deny that any event that happens, no matter how extraordinary it may be, is beyond the powers of nature. "Nature," he says, "means neither more nor less than that which is; the sum of phenomena presented to our experience; the totality of events, past, present, and to come. Every event must be taken to be a part of nature, until proof to the contrary is supplied. And such proof is, from the nature of the case, impossible."[8] "No event," he explains, "is too extraordinary to be possible" (p. 131). "Every wise man will admit that the possibilities of nature are infinite" (p. 133). "In truth, if a dead man did come to life, the fact would be evidence, not that any law of nature had been violated, but that these laws, even when they express the results of a very long and uniform experience, are necessarily based on incomplete knowledge, and are to be held only as grounds of more or less justifiable expectation" (p. 131). The most apparently impossible event, "for aught we can prove to the contrary," "may appear in the order of nature tomorrow" (p. 134). Accordingly, on the happening of anything extraordinary Mr. Huxley would not infer "miracle," but only "enlarge his experience and modify his hitherto unduly narrow conception of the laws of nature"; that is, he would "frame new laws to cover our extended experience" (p. 133). To men of this mind, it is

---

[8]*Hume*, p. 129.

clear, the proof that the extraordinary events recorded in the Biblical narration really happened would never prove the occurrence of "miracles." They would assume at once only that they had hitherto misconceived the capabilities of the powers inherent in nature, and proceed to "frame new laws to cover the extended experience."

A position not essentially different from this is occupied by many Christian theologians of the "liberal" type. For example, Prof. Ménégoz in his address on *The Biblical Idea of Miracle* argues that little toward the validation of "miracles" has been accomplished when it has been proved that the alleged facts are really historical—as he is frank to admit can be proved in the case of very many of them. It still remains to be proved that these historical occurrences are "miracles."

> When it has been demonstrated to us that all the facts related in the Bible are *historical,* it has not yet been proved that they are due to a special and miraculous intervention of God. In certain cases it is possible to prove absolutely conclusively the reality of an extraordinary phenomenon; but the proof stops there; it cannot proceed further; it is impossible to demonstrate that this extraordinary fact is due to a supernatural divine action, that it is not the effect of a natural cause. We must make full account of the impossibility of proving a miracle. If the Academy of Medicine sees a leper healed by a word, it will seek for the natural causes of this effect, and will not regard itself as in any way bound to see in this cure the finger of God. Facts exceedingly extraordinary may be observed among the fakirs of India, the secret of which our Christian missionaries seek after, but in which, despite their miraculous character, they refuse to recognize supernatural phenomena (p. 40).

To men like Prof. Ménégoz, therefore, the establishment of the actual occurrence of the extraordinary events narrated in the Scriptures still leaves the question open whether "miracles," strictly so-called, have ever occurred. They are predisposed to refer all such events to natural causes, and to assume beforehand that they happen along the lines of natural law.

This attitude of dogmatic rejection of the very idea of a

"miracle" it is scarcely worth while to turn aside to reason with. Essentially unreasonable in itself, it is not accessible to reason. To demand that, in all our investigations of the miraculous, we shall take with us, as our major premise, the proposition that the truly miraculous is impossible, is the foreclosure of all discussion. It is the arbitrary imposition of an *a priori* theory of the relation of God to the universe upon all investigation, and therefore the fatal limitation of the results of the investigation to the bounds of the preconceived theory. Only foregone conclusions can be reached under such conditions, and, as we start with our conclusion, we may as well save ourselves the labor of the journey by which we pretend to reach it. If it were only these theoretical deniers of the possibility or provableness of miracles that we had to deal with, we might suitably decline the task, therefore, of inquiring whether the extraordinary facts recorded in Scripture and validated as actually occurring, may not be subsumed under the category of natural law. But as Dr. Mozley points out,[9] this question is raised by a very different class of persons also, and in a very different spirit. There are many who have not foreclosed the question of the possibility or of the provableness of "miracles," and who do not approach the study of the Biblical "miracles," therefore, with the foregone conclusion that they must be subsumed under the category of "natural law"—though they stretch that category beyond the breaking point—who yet in their legitimate efforts to understand the real character of these "miracles" moot the question whether they may not be, and are not to be conceived of as wrought through the medium of natural forces and therefore within the domain of natural law. This is a perfectly legitimate question to raise at this point, and it deserves a candid consideration and a fair solution before it can be affirmed with confidence that any events deserving the name of "miracles" in the strict sense have ever occurred.

In approaching the consideration of the question thus raised, in this candid spirit, the first fact of importance that meets us

---

[9]*Lectures on Miracles*, p. 113.

is that the agents in the performance of the wonderful works recorded for us in the Scriptures, and the agents in recording their occurrence for us in the pages of the Scriptures are unanimous in viewing them, not as extraordinary events performed through the medium of natural forces, but as the immediate products of the energy of God. We have already had occasion to refer to Prof. Ménégoz' lecture on *The Biblical Idea of Miracle*. To Prof. Ménégoz' own notion of what a miracle is, we attach very little value: it is a notion which grows naturally out of his peculiar theological position in general. But the very peculiarity of his theological position (which involves, among other things, emancipation from the authority of Scripture) has perhaps conduced to his reading Scripture, on a point in which it is not quite at one with the so-called "modern spirit," with open eyes. At all events he seems to us to have caught and stated the Biblical idea of a miracle with unusual exactness and accuracy, and we shall avail ourselves of his words to state what we believe that idea to be.

> In all these narratives the miracle is invariably considered a phenomenon contrary to the natural order of things. It is precisely this that gives it its peculiar character, its character of miracle. I have no wish to contend that these facts, so far as they are historically established, really took place contrary to the laws of nature. This is a question we are to discuss later. What I wish to say is that the Biblical writers saw in the miracles which they recount, not facts which are natural, and simply surprising, astonishing, extraordinary, but phenomena which are contrary to the natural course of things, or as we should say, today, contrary to the laws of nature.[10] I have reached the assurance that the Biblical notion differs in nothing from our current notion, from the popular and historical notion, which sees in miracle a violation of the laws of nature, or, if you prefer it, a suspension of those laws, or a derogation from those laws. . . . The miracle is always considered a supernatural intervention of God in the natural order of things. This conception of the writers of the Old and New Testaments was also that of Jesus Christ. That is made clear to

---

[10]*The Biblical Idea of Miracle*, p. 25.

us by that word of his to his disciples—which was no doubt hyperbolical but very characteristic of Jesus, "If you had faith as a grain of mustard seed, you would say to this mountain, Remove hence and be cast into the sea, and it would be cast thither." It could scarcely be declared more clearly that a miracle is contrary to the natural order. And I add that I am convinced that Jesus and the apostles firmly believed in the reality of all the miracles recounted in the Old Testament—as the authors of the New Testament did not for a moment doubt the reality of the miracles that they reported in their writings (p. 27). We see that in reducing the miracle to a natural fact, produced by laws of which we are ignorant today but which may be discovered tomorrow, we destroy the Biblical idea of the miracle, and shake instead of strengthening, as we imagine, faith in the miracle itself. This is one of the minor causes of the feebleness of an apologetic which, while asseverating its orthodoxy, nevertheless more or less deserts the doctrines. In contrast with the apostles, who *accentuate* the miraculous character of the working of Jesus, in order to throw the greatness of his person into relief, these apologists in the effort to obtain from our contemporaries the admission of the truth of the evangelical accounts, endeavor to *attenuate* their miraculous character, and even to efface it as far as possible. This tendency will suffice to reveal to us the difference between their conceptions and those of the Biblical writers (p. 30).

Now, of course, the value we attach to the idea of the nature of a miracle entertained by the Biblical writers and by the workers of the miracles recorded in the Bible, will naturally vary very much. There are some of us who look upon the authority of these teachers as so high, that the ascertainment of their view of the matter will settle the question for us. Others, no doubt, will, like Prof. Ménégoz himself, attach no more importance to the ascertainment of their view than they would to the ascertainment of the conception of Plato as to the origin of the world. Surely this is, however, an extreme position. Surely, even on the lowest estimate of their authority as teachers, some significance should be attached to the conception of the nature and mode of a miracle characteristically held by all those through whom these works have been wrought.

The notion of a miracle entertained by Jesus and Paul, say, by whom these extraordinary works were certainly wrought, if the historicity of any of the Biblical miracles be granted, is certainly worthy of our highest respect, and should not be set aside except on the most decisive grounds. So much weight as this, in any event, should surely be accorded to the Biblical notion of a miracle.

The next thing that strikes us regarding the extraordinary events recorded in the Scriptures is that some of them, at all events, cannot possibly be conceived to have been wrought through the medium of second causes. If they be adjudged historical and to have actually occurred, they must needs be conceived as the immediate product of the divine energy. Descartes says crisply: "*Tria mirabilia fecit Dominus; res ex nihilo, liberum arbitrium, et hominem Deum.*" We may for our own purpose be permitted to amend this, by saying there are three of the extraordinary works of God recorded in Scripture which can by no finessing be subsumed under the category of natural law: creation, the incarnation, and the resurrection of Christ. And the admission of the truly miraculous character of these three will not only itself suffice to fill the category "miracle," taken in its strictest sense, with an undeniable content, and so to vindicate the main proposition that miracles have happened; but will tend to drag into that category others in their train. Says a solid writer, with much point:

> The history of the Old Testament commences with the first miracle on record—that of a creation by a Creator. The history of the New Testament begins with the incarnation of the Son of God for the salvation of man. The former of these two is the distinctive article in the creed of the theist, and denied by none but the atheist. The latter of the two is the distinctive article in the creed of the Christian, and denied by none except those who must forfeit that name. Between, or intimately connected with, these two commencing and crowning miracles of the Bible, so strangely alike and so strangely unlike, are found arranged all the other miracles on record, deriving from these two an explanation and a meaning which nothing else can furnish. It is not enough to say that the man who, on the authority

of the Bible, believes in the creation and the incarnation—
that is to say, the man who is not an atheist or an infidel—
is bound in consistency to believe, on the same authority,
every other miracle of Scripture. That is true. But much
more than this is implied in those two grand manifestations
of almighty power, that stand as sentinels at the commencement and the close of the record of God's supernatural acts
upon the earth; and much more that is fitted to cast light
on the proper nature and evidential character of miracles.[11]

That the act of creation was an immediate operation of God's
power without all means is inherent in the very nature of
the case. The matter is scarcely less clear in the case of the
incarnation, which consists in the intrusion of the very person
of the Son of God himself into the sphere of law. Nor can
there lie more doubt in the instance of the resurrection of Jesus.
If on his death he really "descended into hell"—that is to say,
both the divine Spirit and the human soul that had hitherto
been clothed in the body that hung on the tree, departed into
"the other world"—then, his resurrection involved something
over which "natural forces" could have no power—namely, the
return of the departed spirit and soul to the clay. And if this
be true, it would seem to carry with it the truly miraculous
character of all resuscitations from the dead, whether recorded
in the Old or in the New Testament. It may not be a matter
of surprise when Prof. Huxley speaks of a resuscitation of a
dead man as capable of possible subsumption under a law of
nature. But we are confounded when a Christian theologian
writes: "With our imperfect knowledge of the conditions of
life, we are not justified in saying with confidence that the dead
could not be restored to life by some, to us, unknown combination of physical forces."[12] Are then life and death questions
of merely physical forces? Can physical forces in any conceivable combination be accorded the power to compel the
soul to return from Hades and reinhabit its earthly tenement?
One would like to know what conception Dr. Bernard entertains
of life—especially human life—and of the restoration of life

---

[11]Bannerman, *Inspiration*, p. 58.
[12]Dr. J. H. Bernard of Dublin in Hastings' *Bible Dictionary*, III. p. 383.

to a dead body. Certainly he never learned from Scripture to treat matter as the Lord of life, or to see in physical forces the source of human vitality. From the resurrection of the dead we may advance to other miracles which have to do with spiritual entities, such as, for example, the cure of demoniacs, which can scarcely be subsumed under the operation of natural forces. And by another line of advance we would proceed to all miracles of a distinctively creative nature, such as the multiplication of the loaves and fishes, and the turning of water into wine—in both of which the production of artificial products due ordinarily to manufacture and man's device are in question. But we need not go far into detail. It is enough to call attention here to the certainty that some of the miracles recorded in the Scriptures—however many, however few, makes now no difference—are veritable "miracles," "flashes of the will that can," without possibility of explanation on any other basis; and to the natural tendency that exists to work out from them as a center to the inclusion in the same category of others more or less like them. Just because some are certainly miracles of this order, a presumption is raised that others also may be of this order; and this presumption may not unnaturally grow upon us until we are inclined to assign to the same group many which in themselves would never have suggested this classification.

A third important fact now claims our attention. This is that we have no right to apply our abstract categories to the Biblical miracles in a mechanical manner. The question is not, in the case of each of them, whether such an effect as that produced can possibly be produced by natural forces; but rather whether it was on the occasion recorded probably produced by natural forces. The conditions and circumstances must be taken into account; and it is whether the effect recorded can be believed to have been produced by the natural forces present and active at the place and time of its production that we need to investigate, and not the merely academic question whether a similar effect is capable of being produced by natural forces in other times and circumstances than those that then obtained. Telegraphs, telephones, wireless telegraphy did not exist in Biblical times and cannot be utilized to explain the Biblical marvels: nor can any other appliances not then existent and in use. Men seem often to proceed in their reasoning on the assumption that, if any possible way can be imagined in which natural forces can be made to simulate the effects of miraculous action recorded in Scripture, it is fair to assume that these effects were produced by means of these natural forces operating in this way. Nothing could be more hopelessly academic than such an abstract manner of dealing with concrete facts. At this rate, the tricks of the magicians of Egypt would be made to confound the miracles of Moses. We have no right to call in for the explanation of these marvels any other natural forces than those that can be shown to have been present and operative at the time and place of the performance of the marvel. We have no right to assume that Jesus made use of wireless telegraphy to ascertain that Lazarus was dead: that the secrets of chemistry were utilized by him in the making of the wine at Cana: that a hidden magnet was employed to make the axe-head rise in the water; and the like. The point never is, whether natural forces may not be made to simulate these effects. The question is, what were the actual forces really employed for their production. It is remarkable how many of the so-called natural explanations of the miracles of Scripture become absurd when they are confronted with the conditions of time and place.

So true is this that probably the very best refutation possible of the notion that the Biblical miracles may be the product of natural forces would be supplied by just the attempt to apply it throughout the whole list. Attempts to do this were actually made, as all know, by the rationalistic interpreters of the end of the eighteenth and opening of the nineteenth century. The classical instance is the explanation of the Gospel miracles which was essayed by Dr. Paulus. Each miracle was carefully expounded as a natural occurrence: and in the effort to carry this method of exposition through, a mass of improbabilities, of bizarreries, was accumulated which presented a greater impossibility to belief than the supernatural itself. Probably no such series of interpretations invented today could exhibit the gross bad taste and crass absurdities of that of Paulus. But it is certain that none would succeed any better. The strength of the suggestion that the Biblical miracles may have been the product of natural forces lies in its vagueness; once attempt to explicate it in detail, and it is sure to break down of its own weight. Strauss himself executed justice on Paulus and pointed out that his stories involved a greater miracle of inaptitude than the miracles themselves could involve of power. Such experiences certainly should teach us at least that either the recorded miracles were veritable miracles, or else the events never occurred as recorded. No middle ground is tenable.

But, it may be said, even when full allowance is given to these considerations there yet remain some among the marvels of Scripture which may be believed to have been wrought through the medium of second causes. Indeed, there are some in connection with the working of which second causes are explicitly mentioned as their proximate causes. This is no doubt true. We can have no interest in contending that all the marvels of Scripture are, without exception, miracles in the strict sense. It is enough to show that some of them are such beyond question, and that the presumption is that many more belong to this variety of marvels. Let it be conceded that others may possibly belong to the order of "special providences"—that is, events brought to pass obviously by God, indeed, but through the medium of second causes. And let it be conceded that between these two classes there may stand certain others of the correct classification of which—whether as "miracles" or "special providences"—we may justly cherish some doubt. This is a natural state of affairs with reference to a series of wonderful works, recounted to us in popular rather than in scientific language. Meanwhile it stands firm that "miracles" in the strict sense have happened; that accounts of them are given us in the Scriptural record; and that the class tends to grow ever greater in number as we attend more closely to the details of the accounts as they are set down in the record, to the obvious convictions of their narrators regarding them, and to the limitations of time, place, and circumstances of their occurrence.

PART III

13

THEOLOGY A SCIENCE*

Our common definitions of Theology are of the logical order, and begin by assigning it to its genus, viz., Science, and then seek its *differentia*, by which it is distinguished from other sciences, in its subject matter. Theology, we say, is that science which treats of God in himself and in his relations. This appears orderly and entirely satisfactory. It refers Theology to its class, and discriminates it from other members of this class in the same way that each of them is discriminated from its fellows. It has not given universal satisfaction, however—chiefly through an unwillingness, for one reason or another, to recognize Theology as a Science.

Sometimes this unwillingness is the result of nothing more than too low a conception of "Science." If, for example, we mean by "Science" the study of phenomena, merely—then to be sure, theology is not a "science," just as philosophy is not a "science," because, to wit, it is something immensely more. This is the point of sight, for example, of Professor William Knight, who writes:

> It is outside the province of science to investigate the nature of substance. That is the province of philosophy; and when we raise the question of the ultimate essence of all things, it is a problem of philosophical theology. Theology is not a science. If theology were a science, God would be a phenomenon. There is a science of Religion, because the phenomenon of the human mind, in its effort to apprehend that which lies beyond Nature, can be classified and so far sustained: but there can be no Science of the Infinite. It is true that we might scientifically explain the results of any

---

*This article is from the *Bible Student*, Jan. 1900, pp. 1-4, under the heading "Editorial Notes."

manifestation of the Infinite in Nature or in History; and, therefore, to that extent, we might have a Science of Theology; but we cannot place it within the circle of those sciences which have for their object-matter the phenomena of the universe.[1]

On the other hand, there is often apparent a low view of theology which denies to it, in principle, all scientific character, and sets it, indeed, over against Science as its very antipodes. A specially gross form of this misconception may be found in Dr. Andrew D. White's *History of the Warfare of Science with Theology*, the very truth of which sets aside without a word of justification all claim of theology to be itself a science. If Theology be itself a "Science," it is as absurd to talk of warfare between Science and Theology as of warfare between Science and Astronomy. The finding of the various sciences may, indeed, come into temporary apparent conflict; the biologists and the physicists are today at serious odds as to the age of the habitated earth—the physicists (as represented by Lord Kelvin, for example) refusing to allow the time demanded for the development of animal life ordained by the biologists (as represented by Haeckel, for example). But neither party has assumed the exclusive name of "Science" for itself, Science with a big "S" being identified with its own special views. But it is just as absurd to talk of "Science having evidently conquered Dogmatic Theology," as Dr. White does, as to talk of "Science having evidently conquered Biology or Physics."

More reasonably than in either of these cases, a difficulty is sometimes raised against recognizing theology as a science, on the ground that it is a practical discipline with its end outside itself. This is in accordance with a dictum which is thus laid down by Paul de Lagarde:

Everybody who knows Science knows that it has its end purely in itself, and seeks its own method accordingly, receiving presumptions, laws, points of view from no power in heaven or earth. What it wishes is to know, nothing but

---

[1]Essay on "The Classification of the Sciences," in *Essays on Philosophy*, pp. 80, 81.

to know, and that only in order to know. It knows that it knows nothing where it has proved nothing. It is to any man of science a matter of complete indifference what results from his investigations, if only one thing results from them—that is, if only some new truth is discovered.[2]

Therefore, the theologian, who is not indifferent to the outcome of his work, but wishes to conduce to the eternal welfare of man, is no man of science; and theology, which has as its end not merely to make wise but "to make wise unto salvation," is no science. And conversely, the theologian, were he a man of science, would and must be careless as to the outcome of his work; and theology, were it scientific, would have no concern with the practical value of the truths with which it deals.

Let men of science say whether Professor Lagarde has declared the whole truth about them. Must, indeed, one cease to be a man, when he gives himself to science? Certainly, from the point of view of theology, it is not hard to see that there has entered into this point of view a certain leaven of confusion which may be dispersed by one or two not very recondite distinctions. There is, first of all, the distinction between "Theology" and "Systematic Theology." "Theology" is a broader thing than any one of its constituent parts. It includes "Apologetical Theology," "Exegetical Theology," "Historical Theology," "Practical Theology," as well as "Systematic Theology." The scientific character of "Theology" culminates in "Systematic Theology"; which is, therefore, by eminence *the* scientific theological discipline. There may be a sense, therefore, in which it might be said of "Systematic Theology," with better right than of Theology at large, that it has its end in itself and seeks nothing but knowledge. But even here, this can be said only when Systematic Theology is abstracted from its sister disciplines and conceived sharply from the point of sight of the specific part committed to it in the general theological task. To "Systematic Theology" is committed that part of the common theological task which is expressed by the phrase "to make wise"; while to "Practical Theology" is committed that

---

[2]*Deutsche Schriften*, 1892, p. 37.

other part, which is expressed in the phrase "unto salvation." The intellectualistic motive may thus be said to dominate in "Systematic Theology." But "Systematic Theology" does not exist by itself or for itself. It is a member of an organism, and it exists for the organism of which it is a part and in which it plays its part for the benefit of the whole. And the action of the whole culminates in, and all the functioning of the parts press on toward, the vital effect made operative in "Practical Theology." The scientific character of Theology, so far from clashing with its practical issue, therefore, is one of the elements working toward this practical issue.

A far more fruitful distinction encourages us, however, in the twofold meaning of the word "knowledge." Theology has for its end the "knowledge of God." But there is a shallower and a deeper sense of the word "knowledge"—a purely intellectualistic sense, and a sense that involves the whole man and all his activities. "To know God" in the deeper sense is not the act of the mere understanding, nor can theology fulfil its function of making man "to know God" simply by framing propositions for the logical intellect. As Aesthetics or Ethics cannot fulfil its calling without calling into action something much deeper than the mere understanding, no more can Theology. For Ethics there is requisite a moral nature and that not merely in possession, but in use; Aesthetics does not consist in a series of propositions about beauty, but in the active functioning of the sense of beauty; and similarly Theology does not exist when only the intellect is busied with the apprehension of logical propositions about God, but can come into existence only in beings that possess religious natures and through the actions of the religious faculty. The knowledge of God, accordingly, which it is the end of Theology to produce, is that vital knowledge of God which engages the whole man; it can terminate only in distinctively *religious* knowledge—and this adjective must needs describe the quantity of knowledge as well as its sphere. As well say that a being without a moral nature can produce a scientific ethic, or a being without a sense of beauty can produce a scientific aesthetic, as to say that a being without a religious nature, or without his religious nature stirred and in action, can produce a Scientific Theology. "Science" in no one of these cases consists of a bare series of intellectual propositions, however logically constructed.

It is but a corollary from this to say that the Science of Theology, that it may be a Science, must produce a religious effect—or, in more popular language, "a practical effect." It is rooted in the very nature of Theology as a Science that it should involve and impinge on the religious life: and the function of "Theology" is not completed as a science until this practical end is subserved. It is evident, therefore, that a department of "Practical Theology" is essential to the *scheme* of Theology, and indeed constitutes its culmination and goal. Were there no department of "Practical Theology," provision for the application of the truths philosophically contemplated in "Systematic Theology" would need to be made within the limits of Systematic Theology itself, that it should not hang incompletely in the air. There is no "Theology" that does not touch and move that religious nature by the movement of which alone may God be really known.

It follows, still further, that there is much that passes current as "Theology" that is not Theology at all. All that does not naturally take its place in the general scheme of investigation which tends to produce a true and vital knowledge of God—a truly *religious* knowledge of God—lies outside of the limits of "Theology." Says a recent French writer, Mr. Varicher, with great justice:

> We recognize the possible existence of profane sciences treating of the same material (with theology)—of an exegesis which strikes the primitive Christian documents independently of their religious value—of a history of the church which is only a branch of general history. Theology loses nothing by the recognition of the possibility of these sciences; it rather gains by not considering as theological certain works which today pretend to be such, but in their whole tendency and point of view have no right to that honor.[3]

[3]*Methodologie*, p. 261.

Nothing could be more true. It is against good taste to suppose that a work belongs to the domain of "Theology" merely because it deals with a topic with which Theology may deal, or that a man has earned a title to the great name of "Theologian" because he has written, say, the life of some mediaeval monk, or even a life of Christ. There are purely secular lives of Christ; purely secular investigations of the text and even contents of Scripture.

Theology, therefore, not only may remain a science while yet "practical" in aim; it cannot even exist without this "practical" aim. As long as we remain in the region of the pure intellect we remain out of the proper region of Theology. Theology is the product of, appeals to, and impinges on the religious elements in man's nature, and nothing is "Theology" which does not move in this sphere.

14

CHRISTIANITY THE TRUTH*

It is the primary claim of Christianity that it is "the truth." Jesus Christ, its founder, calls himself significantly "the truth" (John xiv. 6), and sums up his mission in the world as a constant witness-bearing to "the truth" (John xviii. 37). It is accordingly as "the truth" that the gospel offers itself to men; and it seeks to propagate itself in the world only as "truth," and therefore only by those methods by which "truth" makes its way. Not the sword but the word is Christianity's weapon of defense and instrument of conquest. "Cut me off that old man's head" was Caliph Omar's answer to the arguments with which the aged Christian priest met him as he triumphantly entered Jerusalem: and in this scene we have revealed the contrast between Christianity and all other religions. "That old man," says Dr. James Macgregor, "with no shield but faith, no sword but the word, setting himself alone to stem the then raging lava-torrent of fanaticism, with its brutish alternative of the Koran or death, is typical of the fact that Christianity is an *apologetic* religion." Confident that it is the only reasonable religion, it comes forward as pre-eminently the reasoning religion. The task it has set itself is no less than to *reason* the world into acceptance of the "truth."

If the world were only as eager to receive the truth as the truth is to win the world, the function of Christian men might well be summed up in the one word, *proclamation*. But the typical responses of the world to the proclaimed truth are the cynical sneer of Pilate, "What is truth?" and the brutal command of Omar, "Cut me off that old man's head!" So, procla-

The Bible Student, Jan. 1901, pp. 1-5, under the heading "Editorial Notes."

mation must needs pass into asseveration, and asseveration into contention, that the truth may abide in the world. "Bear witness to the truth"; "contend earnestly for the faith which was once for all delivered to the saints": these are the twin exhortations by which every Christian man's duty is declared for him. How early did the Christian proclamation produce its double fruitage of martyrdom and controversy! The old Greek word "martyr," "witness" soon took on a specific Christian meaning, and became more and more confined to those who had sealed their testimony with their blood; and everywhere the irritated world complained of these persistent reasoners that they were turning the world upside down.

"Martyrdom" and "controversy!" If the collocation sounds strange in our ears it can only be because we have failed to realize how inevitable is their connection, how necessarily they appear as twin fruits of the one fair tree of faithfulness. There never was a martyrdom save as the result of controversy. The spirit which would still contention for the truth never yet went to the stake. There is a sentiment abroad indeed which decries controversy. The same sentiment should certainly decry martyrdom also. An anemic Christianity which is too little virile to strive for the truth can never possess the nerve to die for it. And the contradiction of loving the one and hating the other is glaring. Says Dr. Mandell Creighton strikingly: "The age of the martyrs has a powerful attraction even to the casual reader; the age of the heresies leaves him bewildered and distressed. Yet the agents in both were discharging an equally necessary function. Both were upholding the truth of the gospel; the one against the power of the world, the other against the wisdom of the world. The martyrs had this advantage, that the force of their testimony was concentrated in one supreme moment, was expressed in one heroic act, which commands universal sympathy. The controversialists had to live through a protracted struggle and are judged by all their utterances, and all their human weaknesses which the conflict remorselessly revealed."

The spirit of the martyr and the spirit of the controversialist are therefore one. Both alike are the sport of the indifferent, and the scorn of the worldly-wise to whom opportunism is the last word of wisdom, and "convictions" the disease of fools. "Conviction," cries the "Master-Devil" of Gilbert Parker's *The Seats of the Mighty*—"conviction is the executioner of the stupid. When a man is not great enough to let change and chance guide him he gets convictions and dies a fool." Christian men may call him a martyr: but the world at best a fanatic, at worst a well-punished disturber of the peace. The issue does not seem to the world worth fighting for and certainly not worth dying for. If it did, the verdict would assuredly be different. At least whenever the issue seems to it worth fighting and dying for, even the worldly-wise can find ground enough for admiration and praise of that spirit of faithfulness, by which it is that the martyr and the controversialist alike are dominated. We find this anecdote in General Sir John Adye's *Recollections of a Military Life*: "An English soldier coming on duty was heard to say to his comrade, 'Well, Jim, what's the orders at this post?' Jim replied, 'Why, the orders is you're never to leave it till you're killed, and if you see any other man leaving it, you're to kill him.' " There burns (in its own coarse form) the spirit both of the martyr and of the controversialist—or, to put it in one word, the spirit of the faithful man ready to do his duty, all his duty, and his duty to the end. Let us permit one who himself trod the thorny path to its goal make for us the application. "In Tynedale, where I was born, not far from the Scottish border," writes Nicholas Ridley, "I have known my countrymen watch night and day in their harness, such as they had, that is, in their jacks, and their spears in their hands (you call them northern gads), especially when they had any privy warning of the coming of the Scots. And so doing, although at every such bickering some of them spent their lives, yet by such means, like pretty men, they defended their country. And those that so did, I think that before God they died in a good quarrel, and their offspring and progeny, all the country loved them the better for their fathers' sakes. And in the quarrel of Christ our Savior, in the defense of his own divine ordinances, by the which he giveth us life and immortality, yea, in the quarrel of faith and Christian religion, wherein resteth our everlasting salvation, shall we not watch? Shall we not go always armed, ever looking when our adversary (which, like a roaring lion, seeketh whom he may devour) shall come upon us by reason of our slothfulness? Yea, and woe be unto us, if he can oppress us unawares, which undoubtedly he will do, if he find us sleeping."

Nicholas Ridley would fain persuade us then, of the duty of controversy. He walked in that path himself and it led him to the stake. Was he a "martyr"? Or, as many prudent men of his day declared, only an inextinguishable firebrand? It is greatly to be feared that today also he would be judged by the wise among us merely "a stirrer up of strife." It is certain that there are many in our midst who fear controversy more than error. These assuredly do not stay to remember that Christianity's sole weapon is reasoning, its supreme effort to reason itself into the acceptance of the world. What then will happen if it renounces the duty of reasoning? To be sure constant reasoning is a weariness to the flesh, and the temptation lies very close to purchase longed-for and needed peace by calling a halt for a time and resting on what is already attained. This were much like seeking rest from the labors of life by ceasing to breathe for a season. Let us learn here from a remark of Coleridge's. "For a nation to make peace only because it is tired of war," he says, "in order just to take breath is in direct subversion to the end and object of the war, which was its sole justification. 'Tis like a poor waysore foot-traveler getting up behind a coach that is going the contrary way to his." Christianity is in its very nature an aggressive religion; it is in the world just in order to convince men; when it ceases to *reason,* it ceases to exist. It is no doubt the truth; but the truth no longer proclaimed and defended rots quickly down. The lawyers have a very instructive maxim which it will do us all no harm to heed: "A lie well stuck to," they say, "is better than the truth abandoned." "I have often asked my Radical friends," Mr. Froude writes in one of his latest books, "what is to be done if out of every hundred enlightened voters two-thirds will give their votes one way but are afraid to fight, and the remaining third will not only vote but will fight too if the poll goes against them. Which has the right to rule? I can tell them," he adds, "which will rule. . . . The brave and resolute minority will rule. The majority must be prepared to assert their Divine Right *with their hands*, or it will go the way that other Divine Rights have gone before." Mr. Froude is dealing with political matters, and speaks of that strife with the sword which the Christian religion has renounced. But strife it has not renounced: and whenever it shall have renounced strife against its perennial foe with its own appropriate weapon—the Word—it will have renounced hope of ruling over the hearts and thoughts of men. Controversy is in this sense and to this degree the vital breath of a really living Christianity.

Are there then to be no limits set to the controversial spirit? Assuredly there are. These limits are, however, not to be sought in motives of convenience or prudence. Christianity thrives on controversy, and exists only by virtue of it—it is in the world to *reason* the world into acceptance of itself, and it would surely be vain to expect the world to take its reasonings without reply. "It is the native property of the divine word," says Calvin, rather "never to make its appearance without disturbing Satan, and rousing his opposition. This is the most certain and unequivocal criterion by which it is distinguished from false doctrines, which are easily broached since they are heard with general attention and received with the applause of the world." "If the presence of controversy," therefore, adds Vinet, "is not in itself the criterion of the truth of a doctrine, a doctrine which arouses no contradiction lacks one of the marks of truth." And surely subjective motives cannot exonerate us from bearing our witness to the truth. Indeed it may be fairly argued that even subjective considerations would rather bid us advance valiantly to the defense of the truth, if it be at all the case as Dr. Hort tells us it is, that "smooth ways" in this sphere too "are like smooth ways of action: truth is never reached or held fast without friction and grappling." And surely we will give quick assent to the same writer's dictum that "there are other and better kinds of victory than those that issue in imperial calm." Even a certain amount of heat in controversy may thus find its justification— in the consideration, to wit, that it is not merely the chill logical intellect which may well be enlisted in this war. The poet's line, "And God's calm will was their burning will," is no libel on the spirit of God's true martyrs and saints.

The limits of controversy for the saving truth of God must be sought then solely in objective considerations. Aristotle perhaps as well as another, lays down the principles which should gov- ern the matter. "It is not necessary," he remarks, in his formal manner, "to examine every proposition or every thesis; but only those concerning which there really exists doubt in someone's mind, so that it is instruction and not rather rebuke or sense that is needed; for (for example)," he adds, "it is rebuke that is needed when doubt is expressed whether the gods should be served, and it is sense that is lacking when doubt is expressed as to whether snow is white." His meaning is apparently that there are some opinions which are so senseless that those who broach them proclaim themselves by that very fact beyond the reach of argument; and some so immoral that those that broach them exhibit in them an evil heart beyond the cure of reason: with these controversy may well be declined because from the outset useless. But whenever opinions are broached which do not argue utter depravity or utter senselessness—they claim, of right, instruction from those who are in the world for the express purpose of bearing witness to the truth. Questions beyond this concern only the manner of controversy and the tone of controversy: they cannot touch the duty of controversy. He that declines controversy "on principle," or from motives of convenience or prudence, has thereby renounced his confidence in the truth—that truth of which it has been truly said, that it is "like a torch, the more it's shook, it shines."

THE RIGHT OF SYSTEMATIC THEOLOGY*

The question of the right of such a thing as Systematic Theology to exist may be regarded as a question in general philosophy or as one within the limits of the theological disciplines themselves. If the former alternative be taken, we are confronted at once with such problems as these: Does God exist? May God be known? Have we trustworthy means of learning concerning him, his nature, his works, his purposes? In other words, all the great questions with which Apologetics busies itself immediately loom before us. Theology is the science of God, and the right of a science of God to exist will depend on a favorable solution of such problems. They are, therefore, in every sense of the words, the fundamental problems with which the theologian has to deal. If we pass them by at present it is because of no underestimation of their supreme importance. We may fairly be allowed, however, to assume at this point, the existence and the knowableness of God and the accessibility of credible sources of knowledge of him—in a word, the possibility and right of a theology, generically so called. This is after all not a very large assumption to make. It amounts only to asking to be permitted to raise a question to be discussed between men professing to be Christians, instead of one in debate between the Christian and non-Christian worlds.

The question, then, that we propose to consider lies within the limits of the theological disciplines. It assumes the right of

---

*Originally published as an article in the *Presbyterian and Reformed Review*, July 1896, pp. 412-458; then as a book, *The Right of Systematic Theology*, Edinburgh, 1897, with an introduction by Prof. James Orr.

theology at large, and inquires concerning the right of Systematic Theology in particular. He who says "Systematic Theology" says theological discipline, and calls to mind its correlates in the other theological disciplines. We may not find that the distinction is kept carefully in mind by all who raise objection to the right of Systematic Theology. We shall certainly find, on the contrary, that many of the objections urged against it would, if valid, cut deeper still and destroy Christianity itself. But this is a common incident in debate. And the clear recognition at the outset of the limits of the discussion will conduce to a proper estimate of those forms of objection to Systematic Theology in the mouths of Christian men, which, if really insisted upon, would render Christianity itself nugatory. Such arguments prove so much that for Christian men they prove nothing at all. They are disproved, in other words, by the whole mass of evidence which gives us Christianity.

We are accustomed to regard theology as the queen of the sciences, and Systematic Theology as queen among the theological disciplines. But these are not days in which lofty claims are readily allowed; and we need not be surprised to discover that those which Systematic Theology advances are not permitted to pass unchallenged. It is little that her sister theological disciplines are sometimes found resisting her high pretensions and declaring that they will no longer have her to rule over them: although no more here than elsewhere is the spectacle of conflict between sisters edifying, nor more here than elsewhere is it likely that a family will add much to its strength by becoming divided against itself. Systematic Theology may look on with an amused tolerance and a certain older-sister's pleased recognition of powers just now perhaps a little too conscious of themselves, when the new discipline of Biblical Theology, for example, tosses her fine young head and announces of her more settled sister that her day is over. But these words have a more ominous ring in them when the lips that frame them speak no longer as a sister's but as an enemy's, and the meaning injected into them threatens not merely dethronement but destruction. The right of Systematic Theology to reign is not the only thing that is brought into question in these days: its very right to exist is widely challenged. There are few phenomena in the theological world which are more striking indeed than the impatience which is exhibited on every hand with the effort to define truth and to state with precision the doctrinal presuppositions and contents of Christianity.

The basis of this impatience is often a mere latitudinarian indifferentism, which finds its expression in neglect of formulated truth and is never weary of girding at what it represents as the hair-splitting ingenuity of theologians and the unprofitableness of theological discussion. But this indifference is at root dislike; and the easy affirmation that doctrines are useless passes very readily into the heated assertion that they are noxious. Now, the contemptuous smile gives way to the flush of anger, and instead of an unconcerned expression of the opinion that theology is a more or less amiable weakness, we have the passionate assertion that theology is killing religion.

A certain relief often comes with the outbreak of open war. Dead indifference is frequently more difficult to deal with than the most lively assault. This is doubtless true in the present case also. It is not hard to show the folly of theological indifferentism: but just because it is indifferent, indifferentism is apt to pay little attention to our exhibition of its folly. If we only could get it to care! But let us reduce it to ever so much absurdity—it calmly goes on in indifference. This indifference to its own refutation by no means extends, however, to its own propagation. It has developed, on the contrary, a most widespread, persistent, and earnest propagandism. We cannot escape its wooing. Turn where we may, we are met with appeals, suggestions, assaults. The air is full of it. It presides over great religious enterprises; it colors the daily life and thought of social intercourse; it entrenches itself behind philosophical barriers; it finds a voice for itself in the lightest of current literature. It may not be surprising that it is the dominant note among the purveyors to the mere amusement of an idle hour, though the seriousness is worthy of note with which it is commended to us alike in even such novels of contemplation as

Lanoe Falconer's *Cecilia de Noël*, and such novels of adventure as Dr. Conan Doyle's *Micah Clark*. It certainly is not surprising that a bright Jewish writer like Mr. Zangwill[1] should include among the sparkling stories which he has gathered into his *King of the Schnorrers* a pathetic appeal to us to recognize that all the differences which divide Jew and Gentile, Romanist and Protestant, fade into nothingness before the spectacle of human suffering and in presence of "the eternal mystery" of death.[2] But we cannot miss its significance when, in the midst of the stirrings of soul with which we read of the doings in dear Drumtochty of those men of sturdy hearts whom "Ian Maclaren" has taught us to love, we find it slowly borne in upon us that the main purpose of this evangelical minister is to wring from us the confession that the Christianity approved of Rousseau is good enough for the world.[3] Much

---

[1]Mr. Claude G. Montefiori, for example, tells us that modern "Judaism teaches that God looks to character and conduct, and to these only, in his capacity as Judge. The religious dogmas which a man happens to be taught and to believe are of no account or importance in this regard: the good life is all. 'The righteous of all nations shall have a share in the world to come'; that, according to the Jewish divine, is the doctrine of the Talmud and of modern Judaism."—*The Jewish Quarterly Review*, January, 1896, p. 202; cf. pp. 210, 211.

[2]The story referred to is that entitled "A Tragi-Comedy of Creeds," pp. 176 ff. of the volume. It is only another form of the celebrated apologue of the Three Rings which Lessing made the core of his *Nathan the Wise*, concerning which it is worth while to consult Cairns's *Unbelief in the Eighteenth Century*, Lecture V. ii, *ad finem*.

[3]Let it not be thought that we do injustice to this delightful and profoundly religious writer. An editorial in *The British Weekly* for October 31, 1895, puts most strikingly just what we conceive the attitude of his stories toward Christianity to be: "A parallel of profound interest is to be found in the place assigned to religion by the older sentimentalists and the new. The position of Ian Maclaren and Mr. Barrie seems to us exactly to coincide with Rousseau's. Rousseau always professed to be religious. He thought there was a certain want of moral depth and grandeur wherever religion was left out, and he would probably have said that this was necessary, for without religion the loftiest reaches of conduct were a form of insanity. At the close of his life Rousseau rejoiced that he had remained faithful to the prejudices of his childhood, and that he had continued a Christian, *up to the point of membership in the Universal Church*. The words in italics precisely describe the religion that is glorified in Ian Maclaren's books. He is not unjust to

of even the professed literature of religion and its reflection
on platform and in too many pulpits enforces the same lesson.
When we read good Georgie Hesperton's description of the
"conference at Honchester," we find ourselves recalling many
another conference which it would fit without the need of her
finessing. "Of course"—so runs her picture—"there was a
tremendous crowd on the day when the Imperial High Com-
missioner gave his address, and everybody was so delighted
with it. I am afraid I do not exactly remember what his subject was, but I know he said it seemed probable that nothing
in particular was true, but that people could go on believing
whatever they liked, which did just as well. And all the
Bishops said it was perfectly satisfactory. I hear his address
is to be printed as a sort of tract, and no doubt you will read it;
it was very earnest and convincing."[4] The whole mass of
popular religious literature seems surcharged with attacks on
"Intellectualism" and "Dogmatism," and glowing with highly

Evangelicalism, and one of his noblest characters is Burnbrae, a Free
Church elder. But he lingers with most love and understanding on
the Moderates—Drumsheugh, Dr. Davidson, Dr. Maclure, and James
Soutar. Maclure, who has the best means of knowing, declares that if
there be a judgment, and books be opened, there will be one for Drumtochty, and the bravest page in it will be Drumsheugh's. There is very
little sympathy here for modernity; the ministers who talk about two
Isaiahs are laughed at. But there is just as little sympathy for extreme
Evangelicalism. Plymouthism is treated as if it were hypocrisy of the
grossest kind, and high Calvinism as almost too monstrous to be mentioned. The particular forms in which the religion of revivals expresses
itself are described with evident dislike. All this is, of course, Ian
Maclaren's limitation. We should not care to lend him our cherished
volumes of the *Earthen Vessel*. Still the heart of things is here. 'Say
the NAME,' that is enough—the name of Jesus, in which every knee
shall bow. Beyond that nothing is needed to create the noblest character.
Mr. Barrie does not glorify Moderatism, but, like Ian Maclaren, he
declines a dogmatic religion, and is gently apologetic or humorous when
speaking of what goes beyond the essence. Therein he differs from
George Macdonald, whose books are full of *theologoumena*, and have
suffered in consequence. But they side with Rousseau, who was wont
to insist that the Christianity which appeals only to the moral conscience
is alone conformable to the Spirit of Christ. Conduct, character—
these were with him and are with them the great results and tests
of true religion.

[4]Jane Barlow's *Maureen's Fairing*, p. 148.

colored portraitures of "good Christians" of every name and no name, of every faith and no faith, under each of which stands the legend written that since good Christians arise under every form of faith or no faith alike, it cannot be of much importance what men believe. "Let others wrangle over this or that," is the common cry—"it is all of no consequence: let us leave them to their disputes and for ourselves be Christians." The late Prof. John Stuart Blackie's lines quite embody the sentiment of the hour:

> Creeds and confessions? High Church or the Low?
>   I cannot say; but you would vastly please us
> If with some pointed Scripture you could show
>   To which of these belonged the Saviour, Jesus.
> I think to all or none. Not curious creeds
>   Or ordered forms of churchly rule He taught,
> But soul of love that blossomed into deeds,
>   With human good and human blessing fraught.
> On me nor priest nor presbyter nor pope,
>   Bishop nor dean, may stamp a party name;
> But Jesus with His largely human scope
>   The service of my human life may claim.
> Let prideful priests do battle about creeds,
> The church is mine that does most Christ-like deeds.

The inconsequence of this reasoning is, of course, colossal, and the line of thought that is thus lightly adopted, when pushed to its legitimate conclusion, would obviously banish Christianity from the earth. For if doctrine be of no value, because some, who theoretically deny or neglect it, nevertheless exhibit the traits of a good life, what truth will remain to which we can attach importance? It would not be difficult to discover good men who deny severally every doctrine of even the most attenuated Christianity; and we should soon find ourselves forced to allow that not only those doctrines which divide Christian sects but those also which constitute the very elements of Christianity are of no real moment. But let us ask a brilliant young French theologian to make this clear to us. Says M. Henri Bois:

Doctrine is of little importance, what is of importance is

life, we are told. But, it being admitted that life is the essential thing—a matter which is as incontestable as it is uncontested, and which, when it is admitted, saves us from Intellectualism in the only censurable sense of the word— the question is precisely whether certain doctrines are not necessary for the production and maintenance of a certain life. Doctrines are not life! Assuredly not. No one ever said they were. But does it follow from that that they are not indispensable to life? Doctrines are not the cause of life! On that we are agreed. Does it follow from that that they are not one of the conditions of life?

Here recourse is had to a notable argument. Such and such a great Christian is adduced who does not profess some doctrines which we profess. And at once the consequence is drawn to the uselessness of these doctrines. You see this scholar, as pious as he is learned: he rejects these doctrines, and that does not prevent him from being pious. Therefore these doctrines serve no purpose—or else, you must refuse to see a Christian in your brother, you must anathematize him, condemn him.

It will be wise to observe whither this argument leads. Apply it well and it will not be easy to discover what it will leave subsisting: for, after all, who of us does not know rationalists who lead a life as moral and spiritual as some evangelicals—sometimes more so? Therefore, since it is conduct, life, sentiment, which is of supreme importance, there is no need to be evangelical. More than that, who of us does not know free-thinkers, unbelievers, superior in morality at least, if we hesitate to say in spirituality, to such and such Christians? Therefore, there is no need to be a Christian.

"Well, yes," our honorable opponents will reply, "there is no need to be a Christian, in the sense you mean; there is no need to be evangelical in the sense you mean—that is, in the doctrinal sense. True religion is life." And then, if you press them, they will tell you with a fine air that they know perfectly what they mean by "life," however little you may believe it. Well, tell us then what it is, if you know it, we reply; communicate your happy knowledge to us! But take good care! If you open your mouth you will become at once Intellectualists—Intellectualists on your own account!

> This exaggerated aversion to Intellectualism leads logically
> to rendering incapable of transmission and to isolating in
> the silence of the individual consciousness, a life which
> doctrines alone have rendered possible and which without
> them would not exist.[5]

In one word, the whole latitudinarian position is built up upon
the fancy that the product of the religious sentiment is Christianity; and it is destined to a rude awakening whenever it discovers that religious sentiment is the natural possession of man
and performs its appropriate work in every atmosphere and
under the tutelage of every faith. The fetish-worshiper, no
less than the vested priest serving at some gorgeous altar at
Rome or Moscow, possesses his religious nature, and may
through it attain a high degree of religious development. If,
then, we take the ground that nothing is needed but a deep
religious sentiment and its fruits, we have cut up Christianity,
in any intelligible sense, by the roots. So poor Francis W.
Newman found when in his half-taught zeal he stood before the
Moslem carpenter at Aleppo,[6] and his heart was forced to
recognize in him a man of deeper religious nature and of higher
religious attainments than he himself possessed—he who had
come to teach to him and such as him the "true religion." With
the premises which had taken possession of his mind, what
could he do but what he did—give distinctive Christianity up?
What, after all, is peculiar to Christianity is not the religious
sentiment and its working, but its message of salvation—in a

---

[5] *Le Dogme Grec* (Paris, 1893), pp. 40-42. We shall have occasion
during the course of this paper to draw very largely from two admirable
books by Prof. Henri Bois—his *Le Dogme Grec* and his *De la Connaissance Religieuse*. Let us express here our appreciation of the value of
these works as well as our indebtedness to them.

[6] The striking scene is described in *Phases of Faith* (London, 1870),
p. 32. The reader of Mr. James Macdonald's *Religion and Myth* (London, 1893) will feel that Mr. Macdonald has gone through some such
experience, in a less acute form, as Mr. Newman's. He, too, has discovered that even the lowest savages have a religious consciousness and
exercise religious faith and enjoy religious certitude, and is led by it to
a theory of the origin of Christianity which amounts to pure naturalism.
Cf. J. Macbride Sterrett's *Reason and Authority in Religion* for some
good remarks on this point.

word, its doctrine. To be indifferent to doctrine is thus but another way of saying we are indifferent to Christianity.

It is of course easy to say that in reasoning thus we have pressed the latitudinarian idea to an unwarrantable extreme. It is quite possible to look with indifference upon doctrinal differences within the limits of essential Christianity, without thinking of no consequence those great fundamental truths which constitute essential Christianity. But the answer is equally easy. To refuse to follow the latitudinarian idea to this extreme is to abandon altogether the principle of the uselessness, the indifference of doctrines. If there be some doctrines to which, as Christian men, we cannot be indifferent, then it is no longer true that doctrines as such are matters of indifference. There may be some doctrines which we esteem as less important than others, or even as of no importance in the framing of a specifically Christian life; but so long as there remain others, the maintenance of which we esteem essential to the very existence of Christianity, our attitude toward doctrine as such cannot be that of amused contempt. The very center of the debate is now shifted. And so little can doctrine be neglected on this new ground, that a serious attempt becomes at once imperative to distinguish between essential and unessential doctrines. Men may conceivably differ as to the exact point at which the line of discrimination between these classes should be drawn. But the very attempt to draw it implies that there are doctrines which are useful, important, necessary. And the admission of this yields the whole point in debate. If there be any doctrines, however few, which justly deserve the name of essential doctrines and stand at the root of the Christian life as its conditions, foundations, or presuppositions, it surely becomes the duty as well as the right of the Christian man to study them, to seek to understand them in themselves and in their relations, to attempt to state them with accuracy and to adjust their statement to the whole body of known truth—in a word, the right and function of Systematic Theology is vindicated.

The extent of this Systematic Theology may remain an open

question; but a content is already vindicated for it and a place and function among the necessary theological disciplines, so soon as the conception of "essential doctrines," however limited, once emerges into thought. He who goes only so far, in a word, becomes at once an "Intellectualist" in the only sense in which the Systematic Theologian is an Intellectualist—that is, he recognizes that Christianity is truth as well as life, and as such addresses itself to the intelligence of men and has claims upon their belief as well as upon their obedience. He becomes at once a "Dogmatist" in the only sense in which the Systematic Theologian is a Dogmatist—that is, he recognizes the objective validity of a body of religious truth and its imperative claims upon all for acceptance, and is therefore prepared to press this truth upon the attention of all alike as the condition of their religious life. In fine, he who only goes so far becomes in spite of himself, himself a Systematic Theologian: and once having come to look upon any doctrines as "essential," and to attempt to set them forth in an orderly manner, he will hardly fail gradually to enlarge the circle of truths which he will admit to his systematic treatment. Let us say that only the "essential" doctrines are to be included: but surely, in a systematic treatment of these, we cannot exclude the statement and development of those other truths which, while not "essential" in and of themselves, are yet necessary to the integrity and stability of these "essential" doctrines, and so are, in a secondary and derived sense, themselves "essential." And so on in the tertiary and quarternary rank. Thus the body of doctrine will grow until it will be hard if we do not find ourselves at last in possession of a pretty complete Systematic Theology.

It would seem, then, that a mere doctrinal indifferentism cannot sustain itself as over against the claims of Systematic Theology. If the right of theology to exist is to be denied, it must be on some more positive ground than that which merely affirms that doctrines lack all significance. It is only when the widely diffused dislike of doctrines takes the more directly polemic form of declaring them not merely useless but actively noxious, that the real controversy begins. And of late this stronger assertion has become exceedingly common. Christ, we are told, did not come to teach a doctrine or to institute a hierarchy; he came to found a religion. To his simple followers, to whose pious hearts his holy living communicated a deep religious impulse, the elaborate ecclesiastical machinery of Rome was no more foreign than the equally elaborate theological constructions of the dogmatists. In their toils faith is imprisoned, straitened, petrified: if it is ever to regain its freedom and flexibility, its primitive fecundity and power of reproduction, it must be stripped of all the artificial envelopes in which it has been swathed by the perverse ingenuity of men, and permitted once more to work on men in its naked simplicity, as faith and not dogma. Theology is killing religion, we are told; and the hope of the future rests on our killing theology first that religion may live.

There are naturally many forms taken by this somewhat violent hostility to doctrine—or to "dogma," as its opponents like to call it—and many grounds on which it seeks to support itself. No doubt it is often only the expression of an innate antipathy to clear thinking and of a not very rare incapacity for truth—a sort of color-blindness to truth. The late Mr. James Anthony Froude, for example, suffering from what Mr. Andrew Lang speaks of as his "lamented and constitutional inaccuracy,"[7] exhibited a similar antipathy to formulated truth in the spheres in which he dealt. "Truth itself," he wrote, "becomes distasteful to me when it comes in the shape of a proposition. Half the life is struck out of it, in the process."[8] How much more trustworthy he would have been as a historian

---

[7]"In Mr. Froude's wine there were no dregs. To the last he had the same captivating power, despite his lamented and constitutional inaccuracy" (Andrew Lang, *The Cosmopolitan* [magazine], September, 1895, p. 576).

[8]"The *Fortnightly Review*, about which you ask, is an advanced radical publication. Many good men write in it. But it is too doctrinaire for my taste. The formulas of advanced English politicians are as stiff and arrogant as the formulas of theology. Truth itself becomes distasteful to me when it comes in the shape of a proposition. Half the life is struck out of it in the process" (J. A. Froude, letter to Gen. Cluseret, in *The Independent*, August 8, 1895).

if he could only have had more taste for exact fact! There are many theologians to whom truth in propositional form is in like manner distasteful, and half, or all, its life seems dissipated, for the same reason—because they too are afflicted with a "lamentable and constitutional inaccuracy." No wonder that upon such minds exact statement seems to act like an irritant, and theology appears to be an enemy of religion. Men like these must be classified as deficient; and we can no more yield the right of theology in obedience to their outcries than the physicist can consent to refuse all discussion of color to please the color-blind, or the musician all study of harmony lest he should bore those who have no ear for music. Men who have no faculty for truth will always consider an appeal to truth an evil. But the assault upon doctrinal Christianity is far from being confined to those whom we must believe to possess reason, indeed, for they too are men, but who seem very chary of using it. On the contrary, it is being carried on today by the very leaders of Christian thought—by men whose shining intellectual gifts are equaled only by their trained dialectical skill and the profundity of their theological learning. "Theology is killing religion" is not merely the wail of those who are incapable of theology and would nevertheless fain preserve their religion. It is the reasoned assertion of masters of theological science whose professed object is to preserve Christianity in its purity and save it from the dangers which encompass it in this weak and erring world. It is a position, therefore, which deserves our most respectful consideration, and if we still feel bound to refuse it, we owe it to ourselves to give a reason for the faith that is in us.

There are two chief points of view from which the right of doctrinal Christianity is denied by leading theologians of our day. The watchword of one of these schools of thought is that Christianity consists of facts, not dogmas: that of the other is that Christianity consists of life, not doctrine. Let us see in turn what is meant by these phrases and what is to be said with reference to the modes of conceiving Christianity which they represent.

Christianity, then, we are told, consists of facts, not of dogmas. What we rest upon for our salvation is not a body of theories, intellectual constructions, speculative ideas, but a series of mighty acts of God, by which he has entered into the course of human history and wrought powerfully for the salvation of our lost race. Thus, he chose for himself a people in Abraham and gradually molded them into a matrix in which salvation might be prepared for all the world; and when the fulness of time had come, he descended into their midst in the person of his Son, was born of a woman, lived and suffered and died for our salvation, and having died for our sins, rose again for our justification, and now ever lives to make intercession for us. This—this mighty series of divine acts—this is Christianity: by the side of these facts all human theories are only so many impertinences. It is not by any theory of the person of Christ that we are saved—it is by the great fact of the incarnation; it is not by any theory of the atonement that we are saved—it is by the great fact of Christ's death for us; it is not by any theory of his heavenly high-priesthood that we are saved, but by the great fact that he sits at the right hand of the Majesty on High and reigns over all things for his Church. Let us, then, renounce all our wire-drawn theories and take our stand once for all upon these great facts which really constitute Christianity. Christianity consists of these facts, not of dogmas: and it is the sole business of the theologian to establish these facts, not to invent dogmas.[9] In this, moreover, he will be imitating the writers of Scripture: for "the Bible simply recounts the facts without pretending to the least shadow of authority."[10]

The truth that underlies these representations is very obvious; and we cannot wonder that they have exercised an influence far beyond the limits of the class of thinkers whose watchword they are intended to justify. Accordingly nothing

---

[9]"La théologie doit peutêtre se borner à constater des faits" (Stapfer, *Jésus de Nazareth et le développement de sa pensée sur lui-même*, p. 156; quoted by H. Bois, *Le Dogme Grec*, p. 225).

[10]"La Bible raconte simplement les faits, sans prétendre à la moindre ombre d'autorité" (Astié, in *Évangile et Liberté*, Dec. 26, 1890; quoted by H. Bois, *De la Connaissance Religieuse*, p. 342).

has become more common of late than an appeal from the doctrines of Christianity to its facts. All revelation is reduced to the patefaction of God in the series of his great redemptive acts, to the exclusion—entire or partial—of revelation by word, which is sometimes represented, indeed, as in the nature of the case impossible. Churches are exhorted to lay aside their "theological" creeds and adopt "religious" ones—that is, creeds which consist in the mere enumeration of the great facts which lie at the basis of Christianity, the advocates of this procedure usually having something like the Apostles' Creed in mind. In still broader circles, it has become very customary to distinguish between what is called the fact and the theory when dealing with special doctrines, and to profess belief in the fact of sin, of the incarnation, of the atonement, and the like, while despairing of discovering any tenable explanation of them. A recent example of this now fashionable mode of dealing with fundamental elements of Christianity may be found in the essay on the Atonement which was contributed to the volume called *Faith and Criticism*, by Mr. Robert F. Horton, of London—a brilliant preacher, who, however, must not be taken too seriously as a theologian.[11] Such a mental attitude, as Dr. James Denney points out,[12] in a striking passage in the lectures

---

[11]*Faith and Criticism*, Essays by Congregationalists, New York: E. P. Dutton, 1893, V. The Atonement, pp. 188, 222, 237: "It is the object of the present essay to advocate this sobriety of assertion in dealing with the question of the Atonement. It may be a duty on the one hand to maintain that the death of Christ is the means by which sin is pardoned and reconciliation between God and man effected; and yet, on the other, to own that no real explanation of it can be found." "*The New Testament has no theory about the Atonement* . . . nor is the case fully stated when we deny that the New Testament contains a theory; there is strong reason for suspecting that the several New Testament writers . . . differed," etc.

[12]*Studies in Theology*, p. 106: "In spite, too, of confident assertions to the contrary," he adds, "this distinction of fact and theory—this pleading for the fact as opposed to the theory—is very far from finding support in the New Testament. For my own part, I have no doubt the New Testament does contain a theory, or, as I should prefer to say, a doctrine of the Atonement," etc. One may suspect that Dr. Denney had precisely Mr. Horton's essay in mind in penning this portion of his discussion; certainly he traverses with very great convincingness the contentions

which he recently delivered before the students of the Chicago
Theological Seminary, is certainly not easy to understand and
cannot possibly be final: but it is an attitude in which not only
do many acquiesce, today, but some even seem to glory. Mr.
John Watson, for example, in a delightful "little book on
religion," in which, like Mr. Horton, he emphasizes the importance of Christ's death for salvation, yet seems to take
considerable pride and to find great comfort in the idea that it
is entirely inexplicable how his death could make for salvation.
"Had one questioned the little band that evening"—the evening of the Last Supper—he says in his customarily striking
way, "how Christ's death would be of any good unto them or
the world, then it is probable that St. John himself had been
silent. Much has been written since by devout scholars, and
some of their words have helped and some have hindered, and
the reason of the great mystery of sacrifice has not yet been
declared. . . . There is one modern crucifixion which is perfectly satisfying because it leaves everything beyond Jesus
and the soul to the imagination. It is a space of black darkness,
with some dim strokes of light, and as you try to pierce the
gloom they suggest the form of a crucified Man. The face is
faintly visible and a ray from the forehead striking downwards reveals a kneeling figure at the foot of the cross. Within
the secret place of this mystery the human soul and Jesus meet
and become one."[13] Is it, then, indeed true that Christianity

and illustrations alike put forward by Mr. Horton. The statement in the
late Dr. Henry B. Smith's *System of Christian Theology*, p. 460, may
well be compared. "When we say that the death of Christ was instead
of our punishment, and that it made expiation for our sins, we are not
stating theories but revealed facts. . . . We do not suppose that anything which can properly be called a theory is involved in any one of the
points that we have presented in respect to the doctrine of sacrifices."
[13]*The Upper Room*, New York: Dodd, Mead & Co., 1895, p. 75. "A
mystic," says Mr. Watson, admiringly (p. 60), "gathers truth as a plant absorbs the light, in silence and without effort." It is certainly easy enough
to refuse to make the requisite effort to obtain the truth: and were it only
indubitable that thus the truth would be absorbed, the pathway to knowledge would be royal indeed. It seems to be the characteristic of our
modern mystics, however, to stop short of obtaining the truth and to
proclaim it to be unnecessary, if indeed not positively undesirable.

loves darkness more than light, and thrives best where it is least understood?

If, indeed, it were necessary to distinguish, as sharply as this theory bids us, between the doctrines and facts of Christianity, there is none who would not find the essence of Christianity in the facts. The fact of the incarnation, the atonement, the heavenly high-priesthood—here undoubtedly is the center of Christianity, about which its doctrines revolve. And if it were possible not merely to distinguish between them, but to separate the doctrines from the facts, then of course it would be to the facts alone that we could flee. We may cherish doubts as to the value of facts without their interpreting doctrines, but we cannot but be sure that doctrines to which no facts correspond can be nothing other than myths—let us say it frankly, lies. It is to the force of this suggestion that the representations under discussion owe their influence. But the antithesis thus drawn is a wholly false one. No one would contend that Christianity consists in doctrines as distinguished from facts, far less that it consists in doctrines wholly unrelated to facts. But neither ought anyone contend that it consists in facts as distinguished from doctrines, and far less that it consists in facts as separated from doctrines. What Christianity consists in is facts that are doctrines, and doctrines that are facts. Just because it is a true religion, which offers to man a real redemption that was really wrought out in history, its facts and doctrines entirely coalesce. All its facts are doctrines and all its doctrines are facts. The Incarnation is a doctrine: no eye saw the Son of God descend from heaven and enter the virgin's womb: but if it be not a true fact as well, our faith is vain, we are yet in our sins. The Resurrection of Christ is a fact: an occurrence in time level to the apprehension of men and witnessed by their adequate testimony: but it is at the same time the cardinal doctrine of Christianity. Dr. James Orr, in his noble Kerr Lectures, brings out the truth here in a most satisfactory manner. He says:

> Christianity, it will be here said, is a *fact-revelation*—it has its center in a living Christ and not in a dogmatic creed.

And this in a sense is true. . . . The gospel is no mere proclamation of "eternal truths," but the discovery of a saving purpose of God for mankind, executed in time. But the doctrines are the interpretation of the facts. The facts do not stand blank and dumb before us, but have a voice given to them and a meaning put into them. They are accompanied by living speech, which makes their meaning clear. When John declares that Jesus Christ is come in the flesh and is the Son of God, he is stating a fact, but he is none the less enunciating a doctrine. When Paul affirms, "Christ died for our sins according to the Scriptures," he is proclaiming a fact, but he is at the same time giving an interpretation of it.[14]

It will be of use to us to consider for a moment the effect of the sharp antithesis which is drawn in the declaration that Christianity does not consist in dogmas, but in facts. What is a fact that is wholly separated from what is here called "dogma"? If doctrines which stand entirely out of relation to facts are myths, lies, facts which have no connection with what we call doctrine could have no meaning to us whatsoever. It is what we call doctrine which gives all their significance to facts. A fact without doctrine is simply a fact not understood. That intellectual element brought by the mind to the contemplation of facts, which we call "doctrine," "theory," is the condition of any proper comprehension of facts. It constitutes the elements of what the Herbartians call "apperception," and by means of it alone is a fact capable of passing into our minds as a force and in any measure influencing our thought and life. And therefore Dr. James Denney, in the passage to which we have already had occasion to allude—where he is expressing his surprise that anyone should seem to glory and triumph in inability to discover the theory of a fact fundamental to Christianity—adds with the most complete justice:

A fact of which there is absolutely no theory is a fact which stands out of relation to everything in the universe, a fact which has no connection with any part of our experience;

[14]Cf. Dr. James Orr's *The Christian View of God and the World*, p. 25.

it is a blank unintelligibility, a rock in the sky, a mere irrelevance in the mind of man. There is no such thing conceivable as a fact of which there is no theory, or even a fact of which *we* have no theory; such a thing could not enter *our* world at all; if there could be such a thing, it would be so far from having the virtue in it to redeem us from sin that it would have no interest for us and no effect upon us at all.[15]

So closely welded are those intellectual elements—those elements of previous knowledge, or of knowledge derived from other sources—to facts as taken up into our minds in the complex act of apperception, that possibly we have ordinarily failed to separate them, and consequently, in our worship of what we call so fluently "the naked facts," have very little considered what a bare fact is, and what little meaning it could have for us. M. Naville has sought to illustrate the matter by an incident from his own experience. Even, he says:

The things which we ourselves see have their meaning and their import only through the adjunction of *ideas* taken upon testimony. One day, at Paris, I saw on the quay which runs alongside the Tuileries, the Emperor Napoleon III pass by in a cabriolet which he himself was driving. Here is a fact which I verified for myself. But let us reduce this fact to

[15]*Studies in Theology*, p. 106. Cf. the remark of Coleridge, in *Anima Poetae*, p. 125: " 'Facts—stubborn facts! None of your theory!' A most entertaining and instructive essay might be written on this text, and the sooner the better. Trace it from the most absurd credulity— e.g., in Fracastorius' *De Sympathiâ*, Cap. i, and the Alchemy Book— even to that of your modern agriculturists, relating their own facts and swearing against each other like ships' crews. O! it is the relations of the facts—not the facts, friend!" From the point of view of the historian, Prof. Woodrow Wilson (*The Century Magazine*, September, 1895, pp. 787, 788) speaks to somewhat the same effect: " 'Give us the facts, and nothing but the facts,' is the sharp injunction of our age to its historians. Upon the face of it, an eminently reasonable requirement. To tell the truth, simply, openly, without reservation, is the unimpeachable first principle of all right living; and historians have no license to be quit of it. Unquestionably they must tell us the truth. . . ." But "an interesting circumstance thus comes to light. It is nothing less than this, that the facts do not of themselves constitute the truth. The truth is abstract, not concrete. It is the just idea, the right revelation of what things mean. It is evoked only by such arrangements and orderings of facts as suggest meanings."

the elements of personal perception, separated from the *ideas* which came from another source. I saw a large building: how did I know that this building bore the name of the Tuileries, and that it was the residence of the sovereign of France? By the testimony of others. I saw a man pass: how did I know that this man was called Napoleon III and that he was the Emperor of the French? By testimony. If I reduce the fact to the data of my personal perceptions, here is what is left: I saw, near a large building, a man who drove a cabriolet—nothing more. The facts that pass under our eyes have their meaning and value only by the intervention of *ideas* which we owe to the affirmations of our fellows.[16]

If, then, we are to affirm that Christianity consists of facts, wholly separated from those ideas by which these facts obtain their significance and meaning and which it pleases us to call "dogmas"—what shall we do but destroy all that we know as Christianity altogether? The great facts that constitute Christianity are just as "naked" as any other facts, and are just as meaningless to us as any other facts, until they are not only perceived but understood, that is, until not only they themselves but their doctrinal significance is made known to us. The whole Christianity of these facts resides in their meaning, in the ideas which are involved in them, but which are not independently gathered from them by each observer, but are attributed to them by those who interpret them to us—in a word, in the doctrines accompanying them. For what are the great facts that constitute Christianity? Strip them free from "dogma," from that interpretation which has transformed them into doctrine, and what have we left at the most but this: that once upon a time a man was born, who lived in poverty and charity, died on the cross and rose again. An interesting series of facts, no doubt, with elements of mystery in them, of the marvelous, of the touching: but hardly in their naked form constituting what we call Christianity. For that they require to receive their interpretation. This man was the Son of God,

---

[16]*Le témoignage du Christ et l'unité du monde Chrétien*, pp. 293, 294; quoted by H. Bois, *De la Connaissance Religieuse*, p. 343.

we are told; he came in the flesh to save sinners; he gave himself to death as a propitiation for their sins; and he rose again for their justification. Now, indeed, we have Christianity. But it is not constituted by the "bare facts," but by the facts as interpreted, and indeed by the facts as thus interpreted and not otherwise. Give the facts no interpretation, and we cannot find in them what we can call Christianity; give them a different interpretation and we shall have something other than Christianity. Christianity is constituted, therefore, not by the facts, but by the "dogmas"—that is, by the facts as understood in one specific manner. Surely it is of importance therefore to the Christian man to investigate this one Christian interpretation of the great facts that constitute Christianity: and this is the task of Systematic Theology.

We must not fail to emphasize that the conclusion at which we have thus arrived implies that there lies at the basis of Christianity not only a series of great redemptive facts, but also an authoritative interpretation of those facts. Amid the perhaps many interpretations possible to this series of facts, who will help us to that one through which alone they can constitute Christianity? In the ordinary affairs of life we are enabled to arrive at the true interpretation of the facts that meet us, by the explanations of those who have knowledge of their meaning and who have a claim upon our belief when they explain them to us. For example, in the instance cited from M. Naville, he could be assured that the man he saw driving the cabriolet was Napoleon III by anyone whose knowledge of the Emperor he could trust. These great facts of Christianity—is there anyone who has knowledge of their meaning and who has a right to our belief when he explains them to us?—who, in a word, has authority to declare to the world what this series of great facts means, or in other words, what Christianity is? It is evident that we are face to face here with an anxious question. And it means nothing less than this, that the existence of a doctrinal authority is fundamental to the very existence of Christianity. We find that doctrinal authority ultimately, of course, in Christ. In him we discern one in whose knowledge of the meaning of the great series of Christian facts in which he was chief actor, we can have supreme confidence; and to whom, with the apostles whom he appointed to teach all nations, we may safely go for the interpretation of the Christian facts. In the teachings of Christ and his apostles therefore we find authoritative Christian doctrine—"dogma" in the strictest sense of the word: and this "dogma" enters into the very essence of Christianity.[17]

But, we are told, as may perhaps be remembered, that the Bible does not contain "dogmas." M. Astié, for example, has allowed himself to affirm, in a passage already quoted, that "the Bible simply recounts the facts without pretending to the least shadow of authority." It is a question of fact; and every Bible reader may be trusted to resolve it for himself.[18] Obviously the

---

[17]Cf. M. Henri Bois, *Le Dogme Grec*, pp. 110-117: "Christianity is, therefore, without being this exclusively, a combination of facts and ideas. . . . The fact does not suffice. The fact by itself is nothing, serves no purpose. That it should avail anything, there is needed the interpretation of the fact, the idea. . . . Who will tell us in what the true interpretation of the Christian fact consists? . . . Jesus Christ himself and those whom he himself chose, prepared and inspired to make him known to the world. . . . The mission of the apostles was to recount and interpret the Christian facts to the world. . . . If God wrought certain definite acts for the whole of humanity together, it seems to us altogether natural that he should have given also, in a definite fashion, by his Son, Jesus Christ, Author of these acts, and by the apostles, witnesses of these acts, formed in the school of Christ and penetrated by his Spirit, an interpretation of these acts, valid for all humanity. God acted once for all, in a definite fashion: but the first essential sense of this act does not change, since the act itself, the past act, remains accomplished, immutable. There are therefore definitive ideas by the side of definitive facts. . . . We affirm, therefore, that the writings of the witnesses of the Christian facts, their accounts and their interpretations, have authority."

[18]Prof. Henry Wace, in his Bampton Lectures on *The Foundations of Faith* (p. 121), neatly exhibits the nature of the frequent assertion that the Bible contains no "dogmas" in a characteristic instance or two. "It is the favorite contention of those who impugn the faith of the Church," he says, "that the teaching of the Sermon on the Mount is purely moral and independent of theology. 'It is undeniable,' says the author of *Supernatural Religion*, with characteristic strength of assertion, 'that the earliest teaching of Jesus recorded in the gospel which can be regarded as in any degree historical is pure morality, almost, if not quite, free from theological dogmas. Morality was the essence of his system; the-

Bible does not give us a bare list of "naked facts": but a rich account and development of significant facts held in a special meaning—of facts understood and interpreted. With the interpretation of these facts, rather than with their mere record, a large part of the Bible is solely employed, as, for example, the Epistles of Paul: and even when the immediate object is the record of the facts themselves, they are not set down nakedly, but in a distinct doctrinal context. Dr. James Denney is thoroughly justified in his rebuke to expositors who would neglect this context:

> A mere exegete is sometimes tempted to read New Testament sentences as if they had no context but that which stands before him in black and white; they had from the very beginning, and have still, another context in the minds of Christian readers which it is impossible to disregard. They are not addressed to minds in the condition of a

ology was an afterthought.' Two pages later this writer states with perfect correctness, but with complete unconsciousness of inconsistency, that Christ's system 'confined itself to two fundamental principles, love to God and love to man.' But is there no theology involved in teaching love to God? No theology in the belief that God is, and that he is the rewarder of them that diligently seek him, and that in spite of all the difficulties, perplexities and cruelties of the world, he is worthy of the whole love and trust of our hearts! Why, this is the very theological problem which has racked the heart and brain of man from the dawn of religious thought to the present moment. On these two commandments—to which, in the curious phrase just quoted, Christ's system is said to have 'confined itself,' as though they were slight or simple—on these two commandments hang all the law and the prophets. They are the germ from which has sprung the whole theological thought of the Christian Church, and to which it returns; and no theologian can wish to do more than to deepen his own apprehension of them and to strengthen their hold upon others. With similar inconsistency, M. Renan declares that 'we should seek in vain for a theological proposition in the gospel,' and yet states elsewhere that 'a lofty notion of the Divinity was in some sort the germ of our Lord's whole being.' 'God,' he adds, 'is in him; he feels himself in communion with God; and he draws from his heart that which he speaks of his Father.' These are strange inconsistencies. But there is nothing, perhaps, more fitted to warn a thoughtful mind, at the threshold of skeptical speculations, of their essential shallowness, than the manner in which the vastest conceptions and the profoundest problems are thus passed over, as it were, dryshod by such writers as have just been quoted." The fine passage on pp. 194-198 on the influence of doctrine on life should also be read.

tabula rasa; if they were, they could hardly be understood at all; they were addressed to minds that had been delivered —as Paul says to the Romans: a church, remember, to which he was personally a stranger—to a type or mold of teaching; such minds have in this a criterion and a clew to the intention of a Christian writer; they can take a hint, and read into brief words the fulness of Christian truth. I have no doubt that it was in this way such expressions were interpreted as we find all through the New Testament: "Christ was once offered to bear the sins of many"; "he loosed us from our sins by his blood"; "Behold the Lamb of God that taketh away the sin of the world"; "he is the propitiation for our sins." To say that words like these express a fact but not a theory—a fact as opposed to a theory—is to say they mean nothing whatever. A member of the Apostolic Church would be conscious of their meaning without any conscious effort; what they suggested to him would be precisely that truth which is so distasteful to many of those who plead for the fact as against "theory," that in Christ's death our condemnation was endured by him. This theory *is* the fact; there is nothing else in these various expressions either to accept or to contest.[19]

If there be any justice in these remarks at all—and surely their justice lies on their face—it would be truer to say of the Bible that it contains nothing but "dogmas," than to say that it contains only "facts" and no "dogmas": all the facts given to us by Scripture are given as "dogmas," that is, as facts that have a specific meaning for our souls. Doubtless part of the extremity of such deliverances as M. Astié's is due to a failure on the part of their authors to strip the Christian facts bare enough. It is the fact as interpreted and not the naked fact itself that they call the fact. But it will scarcely do to prove that Christianity consists in facts to the exclusion of "dogmas," by calling all the dogmas which enter into the essence of Christianity facts. No doubt they are facts, but not in the sense intended by these writers: and thus the whole center of the debate would be shifted. The contention would no longer be that no "dogmas"

---

[19]*Studies in Theology,* pp. 119, 120. Cf. the wise remarks of Dr. Cairns, apropos of Semler, in his *Unbelief in the Eighteenth Century,* Lecture V. ii, near the beginning.

enter into the essence of Christianity, but merely that only such "dogmas" enter into the essence of Christianity as are rooted in fact, to the exclusion of such as have no basis in fact—in other words, of myths and lies. This no one will dispute. But it does not avail to show that Christianity consists of facts and not dogmas, but only that the dogmas which enter into Christianity are true.

The antipathy to external authority in religion is much too deeply rooted, however, to die with the mere exhibition of the necessity of interpretation to render facts of any import or value to man. There are some to whom it will still seem that the necessity of interpretation may be allowed and yet the existence of an external doctrinal authority be denied. M. Rivier may be taken as an example of this type of thought. "Certainly," he says, "to verify a historical fact is far from comprehending its religious and supernatural sense. An event whose significance remains foreign to us cannot have the least direct importance for our salvation, even though it may be ineffably rich in divine lessons and in religious motives. In order that we may know God, it evidently is not sufficient that he should act, it is necessary further that he should speak."[20] So far, everything runs along satisfactorily: it is just the contention we have been making. But M. Rivier proceeds at once to take the significance out of his admissions. "Only," he continues, and the word "only" is ominous: "Only it is necessary that he should speak to *us*. For we could never recognize his activity in a historical fact unless its explication made us personally verify a divine element in it. Now this interpretation God commonly gave, according to the Biblical narratives, to the witnesses of the events. Whilst we, in order to understand these facts, are to be reduced to the more or less exact report of their authentic interpretation!" "Therefore," comments M. Henri Bois, with his inimitable point:

Therefore, in what the Bible and history transmit to us,

---

[20]*Étude sur la révélation chrétienne*, p. 44; quoted in H. Bois's *Le Dogma Grec*, p. 114.

there is nothing but the raw facts for us to take into consideration. The rest is of no value: it is of little consequence to us what God has said to others; that alone is of
consequence to us which has been said to *us*. . . . Nevertheless, it is allowed that the facts without ideas are of no
value for salvation. . . . Consequently what history and the
Bible transmit to us has no value for salvation: value resides principally, fundamentally, in what God says to us,
at present, in our revelations, in our illuminations, in our
fantasies, in our dreams. For having wished to discard the
apostolic explications of the historic fact, we find ourselves
quite naturally brought to discarding the historical fact
itself.

And, indeed, we shall ask M. Rivier: Why this different
mode of treating the fact and the idea? "In order that we
may know God, it evidently is not sufficient that he should
act: it is necessary further that he should speak. Only it
is necessary that he should speak to *us*." So far so good.
But why not say also: "Only it is necessary that he should
act for *us*, by *us*, and in *us?*" It is of no use to make God
speak historically? Be it so. But why make him act historically? Are we to be reduced to the more or less exact
and more or less authentic reports of the facts of which
certain men were witnesses many centuries ago? No, it is
necessary that God should act for *us* and in *us*. The apostolic interpretation of the Christian facts is given us by
tradition, that fatal tradition, that nightmare of so-called independent minds? It is true. But by what, then, if you
please, are you furnished with the facts, if not by this same
tradition? You declare that tradition reporting ideas needs
later commentaries, and you exclaim, "Is the latest commentary too clothed with a divine authority?" We should
like you to tell us if tradition reporting facts has no need of
criticism: will criticism perchance, then, be clothed with a
divine authority?

In short, he who says fact, history, says at the same time
witness, tradition, authority. The more authority, the more
tradition—the more fact.[21]

We could scarcely have a neater or completer refutation by
the method of reduction to absurdity. The pity is that every-

---

[21]*Le Dogme Grec,* pp. 114 f.

body does not see that the reduction is to absurdity. For the absurd position to which M. Bois would thus drive M. Rivier— that very position is voluntarily assumed by others. Would M. Bois show that by parity of reasoning with that by which M. Rivier would refuse to be bound by the doctrines of the Bible, the facts, too, may be refused? Undoubtedly, replies, for example, Mr. G. Frommel: religion cannot consist of or rest upon external facts any more than upon external doctrines.

> By their very nature historical facts lack the special evidence which is indispensable for faith. The most certain of them are only probable. Their probability, by the accumulation of evidences and the weight of the testimony, may increase until it grazes certitude, but it never attains it. The best evidenced historical facts rest on intermediary witnesses, with regard to whom doubt remains permissible. Were they even absolutely proved, they would remain in essence incapable of forming authority for faith, the object of which cannot in any case be a historical fact—and, above all, not a past fact—and which demands for its establishment the discernment in history of a divine activity, the initiative and permanent character of which forms upon one a directly accessible impression.[22]

That is to say, past facts can enter into the essence of Christianity just as little as past dogmas: the essence of Christianity must be found wholly in what is present to the soul here and now. In reducing to absurdity the position of those who cry that Christianity consists of facts, not dogmas, M. Bois has only driven them to the position of another class who equally refuse to allow the validity of Christian doctrine—those whose cry is that Christianity consists in life, not doctrine. This position comes before us thus as the logical outcome of the demands of those who will have Christianity consist only of facts and not at all of dogmas.

Before we turn to the consideration of this new position, however, there is an extreme form of the contention that Christianity consists of facts, not doctrines, which claims our

---

[22]"La Crise du protestantisme," in *Évangile et Liberté*, May 27, 1892; quoted by Henri Bois, *Le Dogme Grec*, p. 72.

attention. This is that curious religious positivism which has gained such vogue of late through the vigor of the followers of Albrecht Ritschl, and which occupies a sort of transitional position between the type of thought which declares that Christianity consists in facts, not dogmas, and that which represents it as consisting in life, not doctrine. The extremity of this position resides in the circumstance that, while it agrees in general that Christianity consists not in dogmas but facts, it reduces these facts to a single fact: Christianity consists, it says in effect, in one sole fact.

That no dogmas lie at the root or enter into the essence of Christianity the proper Ritschlite is perfectly assured. Religion is one thing, he tells us, and metaphysics is another: and Christianity is in essence religion, while dogmas are metaphysical products. The service which Jesus did the world was not that he presented it with a revealed metaphysic, but that he gave it a religion. The metaphysical element came into historical Christianity when, in its advance from its primitive center and from its primitive simplicity, it came into contact with and bondage to the Greek mind, which at once seized upon it and, according to the inherent Greek tendency, philosophized it, and thus wrought out what we call the fundamental Christian dogmas. These, therefore, so far from being essential to Christianity, are corruptions of Christianity. And if we would have Christianity in its purity, we must strip off from it every remnant of "Greek dogma," or, to speak more broadly, every "metaphysical" element which has in the course of the ages attached itself to it. More, if we would save Christianity from entire destruction in the searching criticism of these modern times, we must separate from it those metaphysical accretions by its connection and consequent confusion with which it is brought into conflict with modern knowledge. If it is to be entangled with an outworn metaphysics, it cannot live in the light of modern thought. But let it be freed from all such entangling alliances, we are told, and stand forth in its purity as a simple religion, and philosophy and science will find that, as Satan found with Christ, they "have nothing in it." The effect desired to be obtained by this sharp distinction between the religious and the metaphysical, it will be seen, is the security of Christianity in the forum of the world's thought. The whole realm of the metaphysical is at once abandoned to the world, while that of the purely religious alone is retained for Christianity; and the two spheres are represented practically as mutually exclusive. Religion cannot properly intrude into the region of metaphysics, and metaphysics cannot invade the region of pure religion. Thus Christianity will be safe from attack on this side. But it is not only on the side of metaphysics that Christianity is attacked in these days. It is attacked also on the side of history. It is not only her "dogmas" that are assaulted, but also her "facts." When we yield up her "dogmas" to the mercy of the metaphysician, are we to defend at all hazards her "facts"? Is Christianity to be represented as standing or falling with them? No, says the Ritschlite. Christianity has no more need of its so-called "facts" than of its so-called "dogmas": one fact alone will suffice for it, the one great fact of Christ. Let historical criticism do its worst; let it evaporate into the mist of myth every fact on which men have been accustomed to found Christianity; Christianity will remain untouched: it is constituted by this one fact only—Jesus Christ.

Such, then, is the Ritschlite position, in, at least, its most characteristic form. That there are elements of truth and power in it is obvious on the face of the statement. It is much to protest against the identification of Christianity with the changing metaphysics of the schools: and it is undeniable that Christianity has often been confounded by the Hegelian with his Hegelianism, by the Aristotelian with his Aristotelianism, by the Platonist with his Platonism, and has thus been subjected to unwarranted suspicion and distrust. It is something also to realize that Christianity may survive the loss of many of her "facts"; that though her history is true and is worthy of her, and being worthy of her is part of her being and one of her supports and stays, yet she does not draw all her sap from this one root. Above all, it is a great thing to have our eyes focused on Jesus Christ as the great, the constitutive fact of Christianity, about whom all else gathers, from whom all else receives its significance, whom to have is indeed to have all. Through its insistence on such points as these, Ritschlism has often wrought a good work in the theological circles of Germany, and earned for itself a good degree. But unfortunately the theory it has put forward goes in its logical implications fatally beyond insistence on such points as these.

It is hard to take seriously the sharp discrimination that is proposed between religious and metaphysical knowledge; and it is hard to take patiently the complacent abandonment of the whole body of Christian doctrine which is proposed on the basis of this distinction. One is tempted to look upon it all as "playing to the galleries," as merely a clumsy flattery offered to the tendencies of an age essentially positivist. In an era when even our psychologists seek to steer clear of metaphysics, it is possibly not to be wondered at that a theology also should be attempted which shall be free from "metaphysical" conceptions. And certainly it cannot be wondered at that the failure is even more complete. M. Fouillée warns us that if we question those who reject "metaphysics" we shall very quickly discover that they reject it in the name of a metaphysical system—which naturally is their own.[23] It is so in the present case also. The whole Ritschlite system is the outgrowth of metaphysical theories drawn from Kant through the mediation of Lotze. On the basis of these metaphysical theories we are asked to eviscerate Christianity of its whole doctrinal content as being mixed with metaphysical elements! Nor do we, in saying the "whole doctrinal content" of Christianity, overstate the matter. For what truth concerning God and the soul can come to expression without involving metaphysical conceptions? Every religious truth, however primary, contains a metaphysical element. M. Bois is therefore within the limits of fact when he says that

---

[23]"Interrogez ceux qui rejettent la métaphysique; vous reconnaîtrez bien vite qu'ils la rejettent au nom d'un systéme métaphysique, qui est naturellement le leur." (Alf. Fouillée, *L'Avenir de la métaphysique fondée sur l'expérience*, p. 275; quoted by H. Bois, *Le Dogme Grec*, p. 51, note.)

"those who thus repel metaphysics do not understand themselves. For if it is certain that all that is metaphysical is not
on that account religious, it is no less certain that all that is
religious is on that account metaphysical. If you wish to be
rid of metaphysics at any cost, abstain from speaking of God.
Whoever says, 'I believe in God,' deals with metaphysics."[24]

It must be admitted, however, that the Ritschlites, having
placed their brand upon metaphysics in religion, do make the
boldest possible effort to cleanse their skirts of it altogether.
And herein, for us, lies their severest reproach. For at the
bidding of this theory, some have not hesitated to discard the
most elementary truths of religion. M. Bois says that we cannot
even say, "I believe in God," without a tinge of metaphysics.
We fully believe it. And the Ritschlite perceives it also, and
actually raises the question whether we may validly say even
so much as this, "I believe in God"! What do we, after all,
as Christian men, know of God, it is asked. That he is infinite?
Certainly not. That he is a person? No. That he exists? Not even
this. We only know that he is, as Ritschl himself once put it, a
"Hülfsvorstellung"—a useful postulate for the validating of our
practical ends.[25] "God, in other words"—as Mr. Denney

---

[24]*Le Dogme Grec*, pp. 51, 52.

[25]Prof. Otto Ritschl thinks that his father's former employment of
the term *Hülfsvorstellung* in this connection ought not to be remembered
against him. But with the excision of the term we do not see that the
conception has been changed. God still remains for Ritschl and Ritschlism a heuristic postulate. The case is the same, of course, with the deity
of Christ and its implications, as, for example, his preëxistence, which
Ritschl similarly spoke of as a *Hülfslinie* for the traditional conception—comparing it thus with the imaginary lines assumed in geometrical
reasonings, which have no reality and are intended to have none. We
note Prof. Otto Ritschl's welcome declaration that it might as well be
asserted of his father that he denied the existence of God and taught
atheism, as that he did not intend to teach the deity of Christ as a
reality; and we rejoice in this testimony to Ritschl's personal faith in two
matters which do indeed stand for him in similar relations. We rejoice,
too, in the concessions which Ritschlites have been led to make in the
matter of the proper deity of Christ (see them exhibited in Orr, as cited,
pp. 448 f.). But we are not here concerned with Ritschl's personal convictions, nor with the indications in his followers of a not unnatural
recoil from the full rigor of his teaching: but with the logical implica-

brings out Ritschl's idea—"is a necessary assumption of the Christian's view of man's chief end; but, scientifically—in its bearing on the interpretation of nature and history, for example —it may be left an open question whether there be a God or not."[26] In a similar spirit, Herrmann teaches that for "the maintaining of the impulse of religious faith," "it does not matter whether our conception of the world is theistic, pantheistic, or materialistic."[27] This is what we may come to when we refuse every metaphysical element in religion, and insist that all we need know of God is what is involved in the residuum of religious knowledge. It is the old idea of regulative truth brought back, in the extreme form which includes the implication that what is postulated as true for the needs of our practical life may in the sphere of theoretical knowledge be at the same time recognized as false.[28]

And this mode of dealing with the foundations of Christianity is carried by this school, also, as we have said, into the domain of "facts." Dr. Denney quotes[29] a characteristic example from Harnack when dealing with the miracles of Jesus. Harnack says,

The historian is not in a position to reckon with a miracle

tions of that teaching itself. And there is after all a considerable difference between God as a working hypothesis and the ἀληθινὸς θεός of the New Testament. For one thing, those to whom God is a working hypothesis are apt to conceive of him as their creature who cannot be permitted to wander from the place and function he was called into being to fill and serve. The extremity of this feeling was startlingly exhibited by Heine who, when asked in his anguish whether he had hope of forgiveness, replied, "Oh, certainly: that is what God is for." The distance between this attitude and the Christian conception of God is measured by the contrast between looking upon God as existing for us and realizing that we exist only for him.

[26]Studies in Theology, p. 8; cf. Orr, Christian View, etc., p. 45.

[27]See Orr, Christian View of God and the World, pp. 46 f.

[28]Cf. Orr, as above, p. 29: "Under the plea of expelling metaphysics from theology, the tendency is at present to revive this distinction in a form which practically amounts to a resuscitation of the old doctrine of a 'double truth'—the one religious, the other philosophical; and it is not held necessary that even where the two overlap they should always be found in agreement."

[29]Studies in Theology, p. 12.

as a certainly given historical event; for in doing so he destroys that very method of looking at things on which all historical investigation rests. Every single miracle remains, historically, entirely dubious; and no summation of the dubious can ever amount to a certainty. If in spite of this, the historian convinces himself that Jesus Christ has done what is extraordinary, and even in the strict sense miraculous, he argues from an ethico-religious impression which he has received of this person, to a supernatural power belonging to him. This inference belongs itself to the domain of religious faith. We may conceive, however, a strong religious faith in the teleological reign of the divine and the good in the world, which does not need such an inference.[30]

That is to say, as Dr. Denney points out, "since it belongs to the domain of religious faith, it cannot belong to the domain of assured fact," and it is only to those of little faith that the supernatural power and miracles of Jesus are not matters of indifference. From passages like this we may begin to learn the real import of the constant Ritschlite appeal to the historical Jesus—that fervent and devout appeal to the very central fact of Christianity which gives their writings such attractiveness to us all.

By the emphasis which they place upon the "historical Christ," who, according to them, is the one great constitutive fact of Christianity, the Ritschlites intend first of all to exclude from consideration the exalted Christ—the Christ who, according to his promise, is with his followers always, even to the end of the world, the living source of all their strength and the fountain of all their life. For this school of thought, which piques itself on its positivism, has no greater antipathy to what

---

[30]*Dogmengeschichte*, ed. 1, I. 50, note 4; cf. E.T. I. p. 65, note 3, where, however, the concluding words are quite different: "This conclusion itself belongs to the province of religious faith: though there has seldom been a strong faith that would not have drawn it. The German of ed. 1 (which alone is accessible to us as we write) runs: "Dieser Schluss gehört selbst dem Gebiet des religiösen Glaubens an. Es lässt sich aber ein starker religiöser Glaube an die Herrschaft und Zwecksetzung des Göttlichen und Guten in der Welt denken, welcher eines solchen Schlusses nicht bedarf."

it calls "metaphysics" in religion than to what it calls "mysticism." It would indeed be introducing "metaphysical" elements to conceive of Jesus, dead for two thousand years, yet ruling the world from the throne of God and instilling life by some magical process into the hearts of men. No! we can know nothing but the "historical Christ," the Christ who lived and died in Galilee, and by his life of pure faith has left an indelible impression upon the world. He, at least, is a fact: and a fact of such magnitude that face to face with him we cannot escape the conviction which was the spring of his life and which, from the spectacle of his life, is communicated to us, that there is a God who loves us, and that we are not merely the "step-children of time."

Yet we must guard ourselves from supposing that this historical Christ to which we have thus been pointed is the Christ of the historical documents which have preserved the memory of his life and deeds to us. For, by the emphasis which they place on the "historical Christ," the Ritschlites intend, in the next place, to exclude all "unhistorical" elements from the picture they would bring before us. It is not the Christ of legend to which they would direct our eyes, but the Christ of sober history: and they are willing to relegate to the domain of legend all that the most exigent criticism would ask of them. It is not the Christ who was born of a virgin, who was welcomed by angels, who wrought wonders, who, having died for our sins, rose again from the dead and ascended in bodily form into heaven—it is not this Christ who, according to them, is the one great constitutive fact of Christianity. It is the Christ of critical history: of whom we can say but this—that he lived and died and left behind him the aroma of a life of faith. This is the one fact of which Christianity consists. We cannot rid ourselves of the impression which this historical figure makes upon us, of the lesson of faith which his life teaches us: in its light we can walk our allotted pathway in life and see the hand of Jesus' God in the events that befall us, and so live, like Jesus, in communion with the God of providence: the religion of Jesus is thus ours, and we are Christians. Who Jesus was, what he

was, what he did—all this is indifferent to us: his life of love
in the world has begotten religion in our souls; and this is
enough. It is to this that the Ritschlite point of view would
reduce the "historical Christ"—the one fact that constitutes
Christianity. And if we find it hard to take patiently their
complacent abandonment of the whole sum of Christian doctrine on the plea that it is metaphysical, shall we not find it
impossible to take patiently their equally complacent abandonment of the whole series of Christian facts, on the ground that
it is unhistorical?

The inconsistency of the Ritschlite procedure here has
often been commented on. First, in their anti-metaphysical
bias, they insist on the historical character of Christianity:
Christianity is not metaphysics but fact; it is to the historical
Christ, and not to the Christ of theological construction, that
we are to go—the Christ that actually lived and died in Galilee,
not the Christ of the Nicene Creed or of the scholastics. And
then this historical Christ himself is calmly handed over to the
tender mercies of unbelieving critics, with permission to do
with him what they list. It is more to our present purpose,
however, to note the effect of this double dealing, in the evapo-
ration of the whole essence of Christianity. We all desire a
Christianity which is secure from the assaults of the unbelieving world, whether those assaults are made in the name of
philosophy and science, or in the name of history and criticism.
But this security is to be sought and can be found only in a
Christianity whose facts and doctrines are so intrenched against
the inevitable assault that, whatever else falls, they shall stand.
What fatuity it is to seek it rather by yielding to the assault all
it chooses to demand, and contracting Christianity into dimensions too narrow to call out the world's antipathy and too weak
to invite its attack. Such an eviscerated Christianity may no
longer be worth the world's notice and by that same token is
no longer worth the Christian's preservation. It has been reduced to a vanishing point, and is ready to pass away. It is
entirely fatuous to suppose that the spheres of religion and
thought, of religion and history, can be kept apart: what is

true in metaphysics is true in religion, and what is true in religion is true in history, or, in one word, we shall profess ourselves willing to confess a false religion. We may acquiesce in the implications of the persistent activity of our religious sentiment. Let metaphysics decide the problems of being as it may, let criticism decide the problems of history as it may, man is a religious animal. But to say that the special form and direction which have been given to the action of this religious sentiment by a specific body of convictions and a specific body of facts are independent of philosophical and historical determinations, passes beyond the apparent absurdity of paradox into the actually absurd. It sounds very well to ask, as M. Lobstein asks: "To declare that the full and complete satisfaction of the needs of the conscience and the aspirations of the heart is involved in the solution of a problem of historical criticism of *whatever importance*—is this not to cast souls into trouble and to expose them to the loss of that crown which they are exhorted to hold fast?"[31] But it is surely one thing for the soul to be sure with an immovable surety that the conceptions— that is, the "dogmas"—and the facts that underlie its faith and are implicated in it cannot be shaken by any criticism whatever: and quite another thing for one to imagine that he can lightly surrender them at the demand of any criticism you will and yet retain his faith undiminished. Accordingly, M. Bois justly fixes his eye on the extremity of M. Lobstein's language: that faith cannot depend on the solution of a problem of historical criticism, *no matter what its importance may be.*

> Will it be indifferent, then, to the Christian faith for it to be demonstrated that we do not possess a single authentic writing of Paul's, that the Fourth Gospel is the work of a forger, and that the Synoptics are only a tissue of legends and traditions without the least historical value? Will it, then, be indifferent to the Christian faith for it to be proved to us, for example, that Jesus Christ did not rise from the dead or even that he never existed? We should very much like to know what will remain to Christianity when there have been excluded from it the *ideas* (since metaphysics

[31]Quoted by H. Bois, *Le Dogme Grec*, p. 54.

must be excluded) and the *facts* (since we must be independent of historical criticism). Note that thus the person
of Christ is completely eliminated from Christianity, and it
is reduced to vague, obscure, doubtful sentiment—to sentiment in its pure estate. On the other side, do we not know
that the school of Ritschl does not wish to hear the *mystical
union* spoken of, that is to say, internal, personal, and living
relations between the soul and its Savior? What then is
left of Christianity? Nothing at all—except, perhaps, the
maxim of certain mediaeval monks: Bene dicere de priore,
facere officium suum taliter qualiter, sinere mundum ire
quomodo vadit. In all ways, the reaction against intellectualism, pushed to the complete proscription of doctrine,
of metaphysics, brings us to nihilism in the matter of
religion.[32]

Thus we see that the Ritschlian tendency also reduces itself
to absurdity in the extremes to which it must go in order to
save its principle. For to these extremes it must go or else admit
a metaphysical, a truly dogmatic, element at the very heart
of Christianity. Recoil from them ever so slightly, and the
center of the debate is at once shifted: we no longer are discussing *whether* "dogma" enters into the essence of Christianity,
but *what* "dogmas" may be rightly recognized as holding that
position. Jesus Christ alone constitutes Christianity; in him
is included all that can be asked for, for the perfect religion?
So be it. What Jesus Christ? The Jesus of the Gospels? Or
the Jesus of Strauss? The Logos Jesus of John's Gospel? The
heavenly Jesus of the Apocalypse? Or the purely earthly
Jesus of Pfleiderer and Renan? Or even perchance the entirely
imaginary Jesus of Pierson and Naber and Loman? It is an
insult to our intelligence to tell us that it makes no difference
to Christianity how these queries be answered. But the first
beginnings of an answer to them introduce the dogmatic element. From which it follows at once that Christianity cannot
exist without the dogma which it is the business of Systematic
Theology to investigate and state. As M. Henri Bois eloquently
puts it:

---

[32]*Le Dogme Grec*, p. 54.

Christianity is the person of Jesus Christ. Still we must enter into relations with this person. In order that two moral subjects should communicate with one another there must needs be manifestations between them. A person manifests himself clearly to us only by his acts and his words: and he has value for us only as we form for ourselves a certain idea of him. Christianity is, therefore, essentially, above all, a person: but on pain of reducing it to a magic, which would no longer possess any ethical and, consequently, no longer possess any religious quality, we must needs grant that Christianity, precisely because it is *essentially* a person, is *also* a body of *facts* and of *ideas*.

For the contemporaries of Jesus Christ, who could see and hear him, the teaching that fell from his lips and the deeds performed by him, constituted this necessary middle term between Jesus Christ and them. For us, with no wish, certainly, to deny the personal, present, and living relations of Jesus Christ with the soul of the redeemed, we cannot, without opening the door to the most dangerous mysticism, reduce Christianity to these relations, in derogation of the acts and revelations of the historical Christ, which we have neither seen nor heard, but which have been transmitted to us by tradition, by the Bible: this would be equivalent to cutting down the tree at its roots under pretext of being thus better able to gather its fruit.[33]

On pain, then, of cutting down Christianity at its roots under the pretext that we shall thus be better able to gather its fruits, we must admit a doctrinal element at its very basis. Christianity consists not merely of "Jesus Christ," but of that Jesus Christ which the apostles give us—in a word, of the Jesus of the apostolical "dogma," and not of any Jesus we may choose to fancy in this nineteenth century of ours.[34] Are there "metaphysical" elements in this apostolical dogma? Then metaphysical elements enter into the very essence of Christianity. Are there traces of Greek thought perhaps in these apostolical interpretations of the Christian facts? Of what importance is

---

[33]*Le Dogme Grec*, p. 107.
[34]"I determined to know nothing among you save Jesus Christ, and *him as crucified*," said the apostle, defining a special doctrine of Jesus as the essence of Christianity.

that to us? M. Bois says truly: "Whether there be, in these interpretations, Greek elements or not, is a very secondary question and one wholly without the importance that it is sought to give it. There is no good reason known to us for rejecting a teaching of St. Paul's or of St. John's, under the pretext that it has a Hellenic color." The apostolic interpretation is an inseparable element in the fundamental fact-basis of Christianity: and it cannot be rejected because a part of the providentially formed peculiarity of the apostolic mode of thought is distasteful to us.[35] Call it metaphysical, call it Greek, if you will. But remember that it is of the essence of Christianity.

By no means, the answer comes back to us at once: Christianity is a life, not a doctrine; he is a Christian man in whom this life is implanted; and the Bible itself is in the first instance a means of grace, not a textbook of theology. Thus we are brought back once more to that extremest of all anti-doctrinal positions, which proposes a Christianity which shall be independent of both facts and doctrines. We have already had a glimpse of it now and again; and it is probably clear by this time that, if the onset on doctrinal Christianity is to succeed at all, it must be under this banner. It is toward it, indeed, that every other tendency of thought inevitably drifts as it seeks to defend an anti-doctrinal position. According to its mode of thinking, the sole immediate purpose of the Bible is to quicken

---

[35]Dr. E. L. Hicks's suggestive paper on "St. Paul and Hellenism," which opens the fourth volume of the Oxford *Studia Biblica et Ecclesiastica*, will well repay consulting on this matter. "Greek thought," he says, "had provided for St. Paul a vocabulary, and a set of ideas as well as phrases, wherein to express his doctrine—a doctrine in nowise borrowed from Hellenic thought, but which could hardly be made intelligible to the minds of his time, or to our own minds today, unless Greek thought had prepared the human mind for such grand and far-reaching ideas: ὁ γὰρ φιλόσοφος συνοπτικός τις." "The influence of Hellenism began in fact with the first preaching of the gospel; and St. Paul is the foremost representative of the process. That influence was of course indirect and unconscious, and did not involve any deliberate adoption of Hellenic practices; but it had been a leaven working in the Church from the first."

life, not to satisfy curiosity, and we divert it from its proper use when we go to it as anything else than the living and abiding word through which we are begotten again—than the implanted word which is able to save our souls. When it has performed this function its immediate employment is at an end: its dogmas and its facts may alike be passed by in indifference when we possess the life—that Christ-life which, being once formed in us, surely renders us superior to all extraneous aid. And for the inception of this life we cannot be dependent on any book or on any dogmas or facts whatever, laid hold of by the intellect and embraced in knowledge. Its source can only be the Fountain of Life—our Living and Loving God himself: and he cannot be supposed to grant it only to shining intellectual gifts or to exceptional intellectual opportunities, or to the knowledge which is the fruit of these things. The poorest is as the richest before him, and poverty of understanding is no bar to his grace: while that poverty of spirit which is seldom conjoined with great knowledge—for knowledge rather puffeth up—is precious in his sight. Christianity is ill-conceived if it is thought to consist in or to rest upon either facts or dogmas: it is a life—and for this life we depend solely on God, the ever-living Source of all life.[36]

It will go without saying that a manner of thinking like this, which has commended itself to a multitude of the leading minds of our time and which has extended its influence so far beyond the circle of its own proper adherents that it may be truly said to have colored all modern religious thought, has much to say for itself. We need only turn over in our minds its characteristic modes of expression to find enshrined in them the deepest truths of Christianity. It is true that Christianity is a life: the life that is lived in communion with the Son of God, the life that is hid with Christ in God, the life of which it must be said that it is not we that live it but Christ that lives it in us. The whole series of Christian facts, the whole body of Christian doctrines, do exist only in order to this life. Christ did not

---

[36]Cf. Dr. Orr's discussion of this mode of statement in his *Christian View of God and the World*, pp. 18 f.

come into the world, die, and rise again merely that he might insert so many marvelous facts into the dull course of natural history: the constitution of the facts, the beautifying of the historical sequence, was not the end of his action: it was to save the souls of men— that they might have life and that they might have it more abundantly. And no single Christian doctrine has been revealed to men merely as a tenet in philosophy, to make them wise; each and every one is sent to them as a piece of glad tidings that they may be made wise unto salvation. Yet though all Christian knowledge is thus only in order to life and terminates on life, it is not in the power of all knowledge to give life. We live by the power of the Son of God, by virtue of a vital relation of our souls to him: and it is only because of the indwelling of the Spirit of God in our hearts that our ears are open to the truth or that our souls are amenable to its discipline. This Christian life that we live is not the creation of the doctrines or of the facts of Christianity: it is the working of the Spirit of God who, abiding within us, becomes to us a second and higher self. These are the fundamental elements of the gospel of Christ: and we count it a most happy thing that they are emphasized as the school of thought which we have now under view emphasizes them. Above all we rejoice that in the face of a positivist and materialistic age there have arisen men who so boldly proclaim the reality of the divine life, the actual presence of God in men, and the prevalent work of his Spirit in the heart. To the Ritschlite, of the extremer sort at least, it is as if there were no Holy Spirit; the spirit of the Christian community—that is, the general influence that exhales from Christians as a body—takes its place: it is as if there were no divine power within us working for righteousness; all that is allowed is a simply human ethicism, supported by a bare belief in a loving Providence—a bare belief which cannot reach the height of theoretical knowledge. But the very core of the teaching now engaging our attention is the great conception of the indwelling God: and we are profoundly grateful to it for making Christian mysticism once more a power in the world.

With the heartiest recognition, however, of the precious elements of truth which are embraced in this mode of thought, and of the service it has rendered in emphasizing them, we may still be unable to allow that it is able to do justice to Christianity, or even to those special elements of Christianity which it thus has taken up, when, in its preoccupation with the sharp separation which it institutes between life and doctrine, it declares that Christianity consists wholly in life and not at all in doctrine. It may possibly conduce to a clearer understanding of what the real implications of this contention are, if we will select some fair representative of the school of thought whose watchword it forms and seek through him to learn its fundamental ideas. Fortunately this has been rendered especially easy by the recent publication, on the part of the learned professor of Reformed theology at Paris, Prof. Auguste Sabatier, of certain documents apparently designed precisely to serve as a manifesto of his school.[37] In the discussion which necessarily arose among French Protestants around such utterances, the chief burden in behalf of the essential doctrines of Christianity was borne at first by the venerable Prof. Frederic Godet,[38] from whose expositions of Scripture we have all profited, and more latterly by the brilliant young professor of Montauban from whom we have already quite largely quoted in this paper, Prof. Henri Bois.[39] During the course of the controversy the postulates and implications of the mode of conceiving Christianity advocated by Prof. Sabatier have naturally been brought under a very searching light, with the result of exhibiting in the clearest way their utter inability to do justice to, or even to preserve the essence of, Christianity.

At the bottom of all M. Sabatier's religious thinking there

---

[37]Especially his *La Vie Intime des Dogmes et leur Puissance d'Évolution*, and his *Essai d'une Théorie Critique de la Connaissance Religieuse.*
[38]Papers in the *Chrétien Évangelique* for 1891 and 1892.
[39]Especially in his *Le Dogme Grec* and his *De la Connaissance Religieuse*. In the latter work, pp. 5 f., M. Bois gives an exact account of the primary literature in the controversy. An interesting narrative of the early stages of the controversy was given by the late Prof. Gretillat, in the *Presbyterian and Reformed Review* for July, 1892, and July, 1893.

proves to lie a crass philosophical empiricism, or, to be more precise, the empiricism of Mr. Herbert Spencer. Out of this empiricism there springs immediately the fundamental principle of his theory of knowledge, which is none other than the ordinary postulate of the sensational school—now being anew pressed upon our acceptance by certain of our physiological psychologists[40]—that sensation lies behind and is the source of all knowledge. In its strictness, M. Sabatier's contention is that "feeling comes first in time as well as in value: ideas come only afterwards and ideas cannot produce feeling, or, if they can produce it, this happens so imperfectly and so rarely that we need not take account of this in the role of ideas."[41] On the other hand, sensation does produce ideas, and all our ideas rest ultimately on and are the product of sensation: "our ideas are only the algebraic notation of our impressions and of our movements."[42] When carried over into the sphere of religion, this philosophical theory of knowledge becomes M. Sabatier's fundamental theological postulate. As sensation is the mother of ideas, so the Christian life is the mother of Christian doctrine. Life, then, is before doctrine, not merely in importance but in time: and doctrine is only a product of the Christian life. It follows, of course, at once that God does not reveal himself except through and by means of the Christian life: there is not and cannot be any such thing as an "objective revelation." "God reveals himself only in and by piety," and it "is faith that produces dogmas." A Christian life is first quickened in man: that Christian life effloresces into Christian action; and one form of action being intellectual action, Christian action ultimates among other things in Christian thought, knowledge, doctrine. As M. Dandiran puts it clearly: "We need a dogmatic; there is a Christian verity in Christianity; there is a

---

[40]"The tendency of physiological psychology is to make *feeling* the origin of intellect on the one hand, and of will on the other. . . . Sensation is the feeling that points towards the intellect. Desire is the feeling that points towards the will."—W. T. Harris.

[41]H. Bois, *De la Connaissance Religieuse*, p. 34.

[42]E. Gounnelle, in the Montauban *Revue de Theologie*, May, 1895, p. 299.

Christian philosophy; it is the most extensive of all philosophies. Only, *instead of placing it at the beginning, I place it at the end;* instead of making it precede the Christian life, we make it proceed from the Christian life. This is the difference between us and our opponents, but it is great enough to make us say, Here are two opposed theologies."[43]

All Christian doctrine being thus but the manifestation of precedent Christian life, doctrine will, of course, vary as the Christian life varies. And here M. Sabatier brings in and operates with the conception of evolution—the evolution of religion and with it the evolution of religious thought, and finally of Christian dogmas. In the course of human development, which has proceeded always naturally and normally, man has disengaged himself little by little from animalism and gradually created himself man. In the course of this upward growth he has slowly attained the free life of the spirit: his first religious stage was that of egoism, corresponding to the religions of nature; then came the stage of moralism; and lastly the stage of "the consciousness of Christ in which a new relation springs up between God and man, the relation of love." Thus as the religion of law succeeded the nature religions, the religion of love has succeeded the religion of law. But the stream still flows on; and as the stream of spiritual life still flows on, inevitably the stream of religious ideas dependent on the spiritual life also flows on, and our doctrines vary, age by age, in spite of ourselves. The children may speak the words of the fathers, but they cannot mean them in the same sense. The river of the underlying spiritual life, and the river of intellectual concepts and doctrinal ideas dependent on the fluctuations of the spiritual life, inevitably flow on forever.

This is, then, what M. Sabatier means when he says that Christianity is a life, not a doctrine. And it is quite clear that, when taken in its entirety, the theory amounts to the formal renunciation of Christianity as anything else than one stage in

---

[43]In *Évangile et Liberté*, Sept. 4, 1891; quoted by H. Bois in *Le Dogme Grec*, p. 28.

the religious development of humanity, having, like all other stages of religious development, in its life its relative fitness and value, and in its teachings its relative truth—relative to the times and the men to which it belongs and which have given it birth; but possessing as little absoluteness of value or truth as any stage of religious development which has preceded it. Religion, too, he tells us, is "subject to the law of transformation which dominates the manifestations of human life and that life itself"; and it is therefore folly for orthodoxy to wish to "elevate to the absolute what was born in time and must necessarily be subject to modification if it is to live in time":[44] we cannot bar the course of a river by building a dam across it. Thus, in M. Sabatier's conception, everything is in a flux: and the doctrines which Christianity proclaims, and even the form of life which underlies them and of which they are the expression, are only one evanescent moment in the ceaseless advance of mankind. As M. Godet has eloquently put it, from this point of view

> This religion is, like all those that have preceded it, only a temporary form of human development—"one of the day's works of humanity," as Lerminier said—a simple product of consciousness and reason on the road of indefinite progress, a form of the religious life of which it cannot be affirmed any more confidently than it may of all its predecessors, that it is the last. One who was in some sort the representative of this point of view, M. Scherer, expressed it thus: "Christianity, the fruit of a long elaboration of the human consciousness, destined to prepare for other elaborations, represents only one of the phases of the universal transformation." This is to proclaim, as sharply as possible, the perpetual banishment of authority in matters of faith. An authority intervening in this continuous work would mark in it a point of arrest, and would become a fetter upon the spontaneous progress which is looked upon as the supreme law of history. From this point of view the sacred books of the Christians have no other kind of value for religious thought than that which may be possessed for philosophical thought by the treatises of Aristotle or the

---

[44]Citations in H. Bois's *De La Connaissance Religieuse*, pp. 204, 205.

dialogues of Plato: interesting documents, no doubt, they could have no authority.[45]

That M. Sabatier has admitted to his mind such implications of his theory of evolution as applied to religion, inclusive of Christianity, as are here suggested, such sentences as the following assure us:

> The transformation of religious ideas does not always take place in a violent fashion. It is more frequently insensible, but it never pauses, whatever precautions may be taken or whatever barriers may be thrown up against it. The river of the spiritual life flows on continuously.

> The sons pronounce the same words with the fathers, but they no longer understand them in the same way.

> We continually speak of the inspiration of the prophets and apostles, of expiation, of the Trinity, of the divinity of Christ, of miracles, but we understand them, *peu ou prou,* otherwise than our fathers. The river flows on forever.

It is this last remark which gave occasion to the following comment of M. Godet's:

> You drop this phrase as in passing; but it rouses much thought. . . . What river flows thus continually on? No doubt that of doctrinal ideas, of intellectual concepts; that is [according to your conception] the "essentially variable element." It flows on continually, this doctrinal river, transforming itself, purifying itself, spiritualizing itself, from its source on the shores of the Lake of Genessaret to its present mouth on the Boulevard Arago. And who are these fathers of whom you speak, and with whom we are no longer in accord, we their children of the nineteenth century? Luther and Calvin? I comfort myself. Augustine and Athanasius, Polycarp and Ignatius? I still comfort myself. St. John, St. Paul? Now I do not so easily comfort myself. Jesus Christ? This time I do not comfort myself at all, and I even tremble, although fear is forbidden us. What! we understand the inspiration of the prophets and apostles otherwise than he did? Ah, well, pass on! But ex-

---

[45]*Chrétien Évangelique,* April 20, 1891, pp. 148, 149; quoted by H. Bois, *De la Connaissance Religieuse,* pp. 348, 349.

piation, the meaning of his own death? He made a very close connection between his outpoured blood and the remission of our sins. That is to be corrected! The Trinity? The conception of God, whom he called his Father and of whom he said: "No one knows the Son except the Father; neither the Father except the Son and him to whom the Son willeth to reveal him!" The Divinity of the Son? The conception which, according to the narrative of his disciples, he has given us of his own person! Miracles? Those facts which he considered the *witnesses of the Father* in his behalf, but which we know today to have been only the beneficent and natural effects of his personality! Yes, *peu ou prou*, we understand all this—and much else besides, of which I do not here speak—otherwise than he did. And when all this "Hebrew sediment" has been cast away so as to save only the "vital germ," what we have left is "the consciousness of the Son of God, which has been placed in the midst of history and in the bosom of humanity, as a power of life capable of engendering life after itself." For me, what strikes me in all this, is that in place of possessing, as I believe I do, a *fulness* in the Christ of the Gospels, I see form itself before me a *void* in which there disappears the Jesus of the Church, the Jesus of Jesus himself.[46]

It will, of course, go without saying, that M. Sabatier makes a vigorous effort to escape from this empty void to which his theory inevitably conducts him. Despite the necessary implications of his conception that Christianity is but one of the passing phases of the religious life of the race, and its doctrines but the evanescent expression of this passing phase, and Christ himself but the earliest typical form of this new phase of religious life: M. Sabatier cannot refrain from speaking of the religion of love, with which he identifies Christianity, as the perfect and definitive religion, and of Christ as having perfectly realized this perfect religion in his own life. But if ever an illogical thinker was fairly scourged out of his inconsistencies, we may believe that M. Sabatier's incoherences of this kind have been cured by M. Bois's lash. M. Bois refuses to believe that, on the theory of religious evolution put forth by

---

[46]*Revue Chrétienne*, April, 1892, p. 262; quoted by H. Bois, *op. cit.*, p. 208, where the above clauses from M. Sabatier will be found also.

M. Sabatier, there can be any necessity or place for such a one as Christians recognize in Christ, at all. He asks,

> Is it that evolution was not sufficient to guarantee the trans-
> formation of the religion of law into the religion of love?
> Why did the Spirit of God, enveloping, penetrating hu-
> manity, need anything else than his own universal and
> continuous action to reveal to us the true way? What nec-
> essity could there have been for Jesus Christ to come into
> the world? You tell me that Jesus Christ was simply the
> first man in whom evolution introduced the transformation
> of the religion of law into the religion of love. I reply, In
> that case it is evident that Jesus Christ represents the lowest
> degree of the religion of love; evolution has long ago passed
> him; we are superior to him by nineteen centuries of evo-
> lution. You wish to say that Jesus Christ perfectly realized
> the principle of love? That is inconceivable. How can we
> admit that the highest degree of the religion of love ap-
> peared suddenly in a people still entirely immersed in the
> religion of law? *Natura non facit saltus.* If Jesus Christ
> actually realized love perfectly, he must have been the end-
> term of an anterior evolution. It would be necessary to
> trace this evolution—not an easy task; and then it would
> be necessary to explain by evolution the spectacle which the
> nineteen centuries of Christianity present to us: evolution
> would demand that you should show us a new principle of
> subjective religion taking the place of the principle of love.
> But M. Sabatier does not desire this, since he declares that
> the religion of love is the perfect and definitive religion.

> The perfect and definitive religion! . . . a definitive, un-
> changeable religion! Have we read aright? Then, religion
> is not after all "subject to the law of transformation which
> dominates the manifestations of the human life and that
> life itself. . . ." The contradiction is flagrant. In order to
> justify the incomprehensible arrest which evolution under-
> went when it attained Christ, the ingenious critic declares:
> "It is very evident that we are morally able to conceive of
> nothing above the religion of love." A good reason, indeed!
> We, religious men of the nineteenth century, we cannot
> conceive anything better—that is very possible: but what of
> our descendants of the twentieth and twenty-first centuries?
> And then, methinks, this is strange language from the pen
> of our author and shows a singular forgetfulness of his
> own theories. We are morally able to conceive of nothing

above the religious experiences that we are having or have
had? Ah, it is too plain. Or does M. Sabatier renounce
his theory, according to which the idea, the conception,
follows on the experience? We cannot conceive anything
above the experience we have had—because we have had
only this experience. But when our posterity have had another experience (it is not my affair how; we know from
other passages that religious experience is a kind of inexplicable spontaneous generation), they will without trouble
conceive something superior to the religion of the men of
the nineteenth century. By what right do you erect into a
universal law your personal faculty of conceiving or not
conceiving that empirical product of the exercise and habi-
tudes of your own thought? By what right do you affirm
that our successors will not have experiences superior to
ours? No experience permits you such an affirmation.

It does not seem to me that our subtle theorizer can escape
from the objection drawn from his own premises to his
own point of view. If continuous transformation is the
universal law, if religion itself has evolved during so many
centuries, we cannot see why religion should suddenly become immutable and definitive—we do not see why Jesus
Christ should occupy the preponderant place which Christians attribute to him. M. Sabatier affirms that it is because in Christ and by Christ religion attained a certain
point of moral perfection: but how do we know that we
have not advanced far beyond what was for him morality
and religion? And otherwise, this does not remove the
contradiction. . . . If we place ourselves at the point of
view of M. Sabatier's theory of evolution, that theory absolutely interdicts that any symbol whatsoever, any religious
word whatsoever, even Jesus Christ, should preserve an
eternal value. The river flows on continuously—the river
of life, the river of doctrine, the river of the word. What
remains permanent? Logically, nothing![47]

But if M. Sabatier occasionally thus involves himself in
contradiction—whenever, namely, he speaks of Christ and
Christianity in the traditional manner, instead of according to
the demands of his theory; in the manner, that is, we may be
permitted to believe, in which he learned to speak of them

---

[47]*De la Connaissance Religieuse*, p. 203.

before he had worked his theory out, and which still occasionally tends to usurp its wonted place upon his lips—at other times, as we have seen, he frankly follows the implications of his theory to the legitimate result of really conceiving distinctive Christianity as of no importance to the Christian life. This comes out curiously even in utterances, the fervor and breadth of whose piety are apt to veil their extremity from the hasty reader. Take, for example, the following beautiful passage from his *Discourse on the Evolution of Dogmas*, where he is pleased to imagine

in one of our churches a great crowd come together for worship. There are, perhaps, in this auditory, poor old women, very ignorant and possibly superstitious, men of the middle class with a tincture of literature, scholars and philosophers who have conned Kant and Hegel, possibly even professors of theology, penetrated to the marrow with the critical spirit. All bow themselves in spirit and adore; all speak the same language learned in infancy; all repeat with heart and lips, "I believe in God the Father Almighty!" I do not know if there is on earth a more touching spectacle, anything more like heaven. All these spirits, so different from one another and perhaps incapable of understanding each other in the region of the intellect, really commune with one another; one identical religious sentiment penetrates them and animates them. The moral unity of which Jesus spoke when he said, "That they may be one as we are one," is for the moment realized on earth. But do you suppose that the same image is awakened in all these spirits by this one word "God," pronounced by all these lips? The poor old woman, who still remembers the pictures in the big Bible, has a glimpse of the figure of the eternal Father with a great white beard and bright and burning eyes like coals of fire. Her next neighbor would smile at this simple anthropomorphism. He has the Deistic idea, rationally established in his philosophical course at college. This notion in turn would appear rude to the disciple of Kant, who knows that all positive ideas of God are contradictory, and who, to escape from contradiction, takes refuge in that of the Unknowable. For all, however, the doctrine of God subsists, and it is because it is still living that it lends itself to so many different interpretations; but it is living—let it be well remarked—only because it serves to express a piety felt in common by all these believers.[48]

A true and affecting picture, we will all say, of the condition of Christianity in the world today, gathering in of every kind in order to elevate and purify their partial or wrong impressions of God and teach to all who and what really is the God and Father of our Lord and Savior Jesus Christ. Only this is not M. Sabatier's conception of the import of the scene he has brought so vividly before us. To him it is not a picture of Christian imperfections, passing away and to pass away for each of the worshipers as he better learns to know Christ. It is a picture of what is normal in the Christian life, and what most nearly approaches the heavenly state. It is the fulfilment of Jesus' prayer for Christian unity: a unity which exists and flourishes in the presence of the most extreme differences in even the most fundamental conceptions of religion. In a word, M. Sabatier places before us here only another picturesque plea for the extremest religious indifferentism. And therefore the rebuke which was administered to it by the late Prof. Charles Bois was fully deserved:

I avow myself not to have thoroughly understood how M. Sabatier can go into ecstacies over the communion of the souls which compose his assembly of superstitious devotees, deists, Hegelians, worshipers of the Unknowable—all repeating the "I believe in God, the Father Almighty," all prostrating themselves before him, all united in a moral and religious communion which can be compared to the communion of the Father and the Son, and in which we can see realized Jesus' prayer, "that they may be one as we are one." What idea does M. Sabatier have of the union of the Father and the Son? What! they are one as the Father and Son are one—they are morally and religiously one, these men, one of whom believes in a God who concerns himself about him, enters into the details of his life, knows his prayers and answers them; another of whom holds such belief to be superstitious and believes only in a God who directs the universe by general laws promulgated once for all, without special care for indi-

---

[48]Quoted in M. Henri Bois's *De la Connaissance Religieuse*, p. 35.

viduals; a third of whom thinks he can affirm nothing of
God without contradiction, unless we limit ourselves to
calling him the Unknowable; a fourth of whom, a pupil of
Hegel, does not even believe that God knows himself, and
confesses only that he exists! All these worshipers are
religiously one! But if they should discover to one another,
I do not say the bottom of their thoughts, but the bottom of
their hearts, they would perceive as great a contradiction
between their sentiments as between their convictions.
Their communion is only apparent—it is only in ritual, in
formula. And this is just the least touching and the least
admirable thing in the world.[49]

In fine, the goal to which M. Sabatier's theories have con-
ducted him, is just the popular latitudinarianism of the day.
The outcome of his theorizing is only to supply a reasoned
basis to the unreasoning indifferentism that vexes our time: and
we may best look upon his work as an attempt to justify this
indifferentism by placing beneath it a philosophical foundation,
in a theory of religious knowledge and a theory of religious
evolution. Its meaning to us will be, therefore, simply that if
doctrinal indifferentism is to stand, this is the basis on which
it must build itself: but, on the other hand, if, as we have seen,
indifferentism cannot remain Christian except at the cost of
admitting the claims of Christian doctrine and providing for
the essential work of that doctrine in forming a distinctively
Christian life, then, for the Christian man, this rational basis
for indifferentism must fall with it. The arguments against
M. Sabatier's theories, in other words, are the arguments
against indifferentism in religion: these arguments, indeed,
impinge more sharply against his theories than against un-
reasoned indifferentism, in so far as the points on which they
especially impinge were latent in it and are the explicit postulates of his theories.

Indifferentism, we will remember, does not precisely condemn Christian doctrine; it only neglects it. And, true to his
indifferentist results, M. Sabatier does not deny the possibility

---

[49]"Definition et Rôle de Dogme," in the *Revue Théologique*, 1890,
p. 166; quoted by H. Bois, *op. cit.*, p. 36.

or the right or even the necessity of Christian doctrines, or
even of Christian dogmatics. He confesses that a living religion must needs express itself in appropriate religious thinking and in those doctrines which embody this thinking. For
him this is only a special case under the general rule that faith
without works is dead. No faith is a living faith which does
not produce doctrine. It is not then exactly against the possibility or right of Christian doctrine that he protests: it is only
its usefulness that he denies.[50]   He conceives it not as the
former and director of faith, the occasion of its rise and determiner of its form, but as the product of faith, and therefore
as only the manifestation and index of the underlying life.
Life does not, therefore, fluctuate, and the nature of faith
change, according to doctrine: but doctrine fluctuates according
to the life-movements of which it is only a reflection. And
since life is movement, and vitality may be measured by richness of vital motion, it follows that changeableness in doctrine
is not an evil, but a sign of abounding life. The more unstable
a doctrine is, the more living it is: a really living Christianity,
we are told, renders its doctrinal product peculiarly supple and
malleable.[51]   In this, as it seems, we reach the very apotheosis
of religious indifferentism. We are prepared in its light not only

[50]It must be confessed that the writers of this school are not always
entirely consistent with themselves on this point. When M. Sabatier (*De
la Vie Intime des Dogmes*, pp. 25, 26) says: "In suppressing Christian
dogma, we suppress Christianity; in casting off absolutely all religious
doctrine, we kill religion itself. . . . A religious life which does not
express itself, would not be aware of itself, would not communicate
itself"—he is still speaking on the lines of his theory. But M. Astié
("La Fin des Dogmes," in *Revue de théologie et de philosophie*, July,
1891, pp. 372, 374) seems to pass beyond its bounds when he writes:
"A development of dogma is indispensable, of the very first necessity.
Practical piety by itself is insufficient. . . . Christian feeling, which is,
of course, the first factor, on pain of lapsing into fanaticism, into subjective fantasy, needs a Christian reason to give it tone, to lend it steadi-
ness." Here is a *use* to which dogmas can be put. Cf. H. Bois, *Le Dogme
Grec*, p. 34, and his criticism in *De la Connaissance Religieuse*, pp. 23 f.:
"M. Sabatier's affirmation comes to this obvious assertion: religion, if
it is not known, will not be known. But of what advantage is it to this
life itself to be known?"
[51]Cf. H. Bois, *De la Connaissance Religieuse*, p. 215, and note.

to look upon variations in doctrine with indifference; we shall anxiously seek for them as the mark of a deep and rich religious life. Periods of doctrinal unrest and uncertainty will become to us eras of faith, and periods of doctrinal stability—which we have hitherto called ages of faith—will seem to us to be times of deadness in religion.

It is of the greatest importance for us, however, to observe that these results are not dependent on M. Sabatier's theory of evolution in religion. That theory serves only to introduce order into the variations of doctrine consequent on the multiform activities of religious life: to postulate for them a goal: and to lay down for them a course through history. The results in question are the direct outgrowth of the fundamental postulate of the whole school of thought of which M. Sabatier is so brilliant a representative, and must follow from its principle that life precedes and determines doctrine, when proclaimed in the exclusive sense in which this school of thought proclaims it, independently of all further hypotheses which individuals may call in to complete their world-view. For if we are to define religion in this exclusive sense as a feeling, and to define Christianity as a religion in terms of the religious feeling alone, we have certainly identified Christianity with the religious sentiment, and have failed to institute any essential distinction between it and other religions, the products like it of the religious sentiment. The most that could be said on this ground would be that in what we call Christianity the religious feeling first comes to its rights, and for the first time expresses itself fully and freely in accordance with its truth. But even so, Christianity is represented as essentially one with all other religions, differing from them only as the perfect differs from the imperfect. All religions at once take their places as relatively true: they stand no longer in opposition to Christianity, as the false to the true, but in a hierarchy of relatively partial or complete. And above all, we lack all ground from this standpoint for declaring that in Christianity the religious feeling has at length succeeded in producing her perfect work: it may be as yet her masterpiece; but what is to assure us that in the coming ages there may not spring out of her depths some consummate flower of religion as much surpassing Christianity as Christianity surpasses fetishism? On this postulate, we cannot get beyond the judgment that Christianity is the purest and truest product of the religious feeling as yet known to us. Now no one doubts, of course, that religion is, among other things, a feeling: nor need we doubt that the implications of this feeling if fully drawn out and stated would give us a theology—and a theology, let us say it frankly at once, which would be true, and would enter into Christianity as the fundamental element of its doctrinal system. And no one doubts that Christianity, as a religion, is also, among other things, a feeling—a specific form which the religious feeling common to all men takes: or that, if the implication of this specific form of religious feeling which Christianity is were all brought out and stated, we should have a specifically Christian theology. But the very enunciation of these facts involves recognizing that behind the specific form of religious feeling which Christianity is, there are implications which are not common to it and other forms of religious feeling; and which have determined the religious feeling into this specific form. It might be conceivable that these implications should come to our knowledge only subsequently to Christianity, and as a result of an analysis of the Christian phenomena: but in the order of thought and of nature they are in any case precedent to Christianity and the producing causes of the specific form which the religious feeling takes in it.

Now, the pressing question is, What produces the specific form of the religious feeling which is distinctive of Christianity? Why is it that the Christian man feels, religiously speaking, specifically differently from the Buddhist, the Shamanist, the fetish-worshiper? The old answer was that the difference in the form which the religious sentiment takes in the diverse religions arises from the difference in the religious conceptions characteristic of these religions: and we do not see that any better answer has been or can be offered. There is something that is common to all religions, and this common element arises from the action of the religious nature of man: it suffices to prompt to a religion and it will secure that man, so long as he remains man, will remain a religious being, accessible to religious ideas and to religious training. What, however, is distinctive of the several religions arises from differences between them in religious conceptions, which mold and direct the action of the religious feeling into this channel or that. If this be so, a religion independent of conceptions, "dogmas," would be confined to a religion of nature and could possess nothing not common to all religions: and to proclaim Christianity independent of doctrine would be simply to cast off distinctive Christianity and revert to the fundamental natural religion. The only way in which Christianity is distinguished from other religions is through the different religious conceptions which animate it and which form for it a specific type of religious experience and religious life. But if this is so, then it is not true that life precedes doctine in the sense intended by this school of thought: doctrine precedes life and is the cause of the specific form which the religious life takes in Christianity, that is, of distinctive Christianity itself. To be indifferent to this doctrine as if it were only an index of the life flowing on steadily beneath it and independently of it, is therefore to be indifferent to distinctive Christianity itself.[52]

Of course, there is a sense less exclusive than that in which the school of thought at present under discussion uses the phrase, in which it is true that life precedes doctrine. We not only have no desire to deny, we rather wish to proclaim, the great truth involved in the watchword of the greatest of the fathers[53] and schoolmen, *Credo ut intelligam*, and adopted by the Reformers in the maxim of *Fides praecedit rationem*, and before the Reformers or schoolmen or fathers, proclaimed by Paul in the immortal words that "the natural man receiveth

---

[52]Cf. Prof. Orr's remarks on the relation of ideas to religion, *Christian View*, pp. 18 f.

[53]"Animus humanus, nisi per fidem donum spiritus hauserit, habebit quidem naturam Deum intelligendi sed lumen scientiae non habebit" (Hilary of Poictiers, *De Trinitate*, ii. 34). "Sic accepite, sic credite, ut mereamini intelligere: fides enim debet praecedere intellectum, ut sit intellectus fidei praemium" (Augustine, *Sermones de verb. Dom.*).

not the things of the Spirit of God, for they are foolishness unto him; and he cannot know them because they are spiritually judged" (1 Cor. ii. 14). None but the Christian man can understand Christian truth; none but the Christian man is competent to state Christian doctrine. There is a low ground on which this obvious proposition may be defended, which even Aristotle was able to formulate: ἕκαστος κρίνει καλῶς ἃ γίνωσκει, καὶ τούτων ἐστὶν ἀγαθὸς κριτής· καθ' ἕκαστον ἄρα ὁ πεπαιδευμένος, ἁπλῶς δ' ὁ περὶ πᾶν πεπαιδευμένος. But Paul has taught the Christian a much higher doctrine. It is only through the guidance of the Holy Ghost, dwelling within us, that we can reach to the apprehension of the deep things of God. Were this all that were meant by the assertion that life must precede doctrine, we would give it our heartiest assent. And so far as this assertion may be thought to mean that doctrine alone cannot produce life, we would welcome it, as has already been said, with acclamations. There is no creative power in doctrines, however true; and they will pass over dead souls leaving them as inert as they found them: it is the *Creator Spiritus* alone who is competent to quicken dead souls into life; and without him there has never been and never will be one spark of life produced by all the doctrines in the world. But this is not what is intended by the watchword that life precedes doctrine. What is meant by it is that the Christian life blooms and flourishes wholly independently of Christian conceptions, and that it is indifferent to the Christian life whether these conceptions—however fundamental—are known or not. Against this we protest with all the energy possible, and pronounce its proclamation a blow at distinctive Christianity itself. We fully accord, therefore, with M. Bois's strong words:[54]

> We conclude, then, that in religion the idea precedes life, knowledge precedes feeling (which does not at all prevent a certain knowledge following life). Even if we admit that it is feeling which constitutes the essence of religion—a feeling of dependence, of love, or of fear—it is still necessary for the feeling, no matter what it is, to have an object,

---

[54]Henri Bois, *De la Connaissance Religieuse*, p. 31.

known and thought. We are not able to love or fear what we have no knowledge of. We are not able to love what we do not think worthy of love, nor to fear what we do not think an occasion of fear. We are not able to feel dependent on something of whose existence we are ignorant. If religion is a feeling, this feeling supposes a certain knowledge which explains and justifies it; it is illusory and is condemned as such by conscience and reason, which command us to repel it and to eliminate it, if it has no object or if its object is not known. To make religion a feeling without precedent knowledge is to make it an illusion or a disease: its history is no more than the history of an illusion or of a disease, and the science which can be made of it is only a section of mental pathology.

But this is not all. We refuse to make religion consist solely and essentially in a feeling. . . . Thought is not an epiphenomenon superadded to piety; it forms an integral part of it. Doctrines are not something external and posterior to religion: they are an essential element of it. . . . Intellect and will have part in religion as well as feeling[55] —all the human faculties concur in it. . . . Without conscious ideas there might be obscure feeling, blind passion, fatalism, magic, all you wish: there would not be either morality or religion. Should there be emotions and feelings without ideas, those feelings and emotions would be neither moral nor religious.

But in proportion as we allow that feeling without a known object is blind and meaningless to us—and would be suggestive of disease rather than of the divine—in that proportion we give a place to doctrine at the root of religion and to Christian doctrine at the root of the Christian religion. As is the underlying

---

[55]Cf. Dr. Ladd's definition of religion: "Religion, subjectively considered, may be defined as an attitude of mind—intellect, feeling, and will— towards Other Being, on which I recognize my dependence for my being and my well-being, and to which I feel myself somehow responsible in the way of control" (*The New World*, Sept., 1895, p. 415). So also Prof. Laidlaw (*The Bible Doctrine of Man*, ed. 2, p. 130): "It is evident, on a general review of the facts, that we cannot assign religion to any single faculty or power in man as its exclusive function. The intellect, the affections, and the will are seen to be all concerned in it." He refers to Alliott's *Psychology and Theology*, pp. 54-59, for good remarks on the subject.

conception, so, then, is the feeling: and it becomes of the first importance for the Christian man rightly to conceive those fundamental ideas which give form and direction to the life. The right conception of these ideas it is the task of Systematic Theology to investigate and secure: and thus the right and function of Systematic Theology is already vindicated.

It will add greatly to the confidence with which we recognize this fundamental place of Christian truth with reference to Christian life, to remind ourselves that such was evidently the conception of the founders of the Christian religion concerning the relations of doctrine and life. This fact is written large over the epistles of Paul, for example, by the very distribution he makes of his matter: it is ever first the doctrine and then the life with him. The transition at the opening of the twelfth chapter of the Epistle to the Romans is a typical example of his practice in this regard. Eleven chapters of doctrinal exposition had preceded; five chapters of precepts are to succeed: and he passes from the one to the other with what has been called his "tremendous therefore": "I beseech you *therefore* brethren"—"therefore," because all this is so. In these "tremendous therefores" is revealed Paul's conception of the relation between truth and life. The same conception, it need scarcely be said, was that of his Master before him. How much Jesus makes of the Father's Word which had been given to him and which he had given to his followers, that they might know the truth and have eternal life, and that his joy might be fulfilled in them! His prayer for them was that they might be sanctified by the truth which God's Word was. There is, of course, clear recognition that faith rests upon a moral basis and is not to be compelled by the mere exhibition of truth. Gregory of Nazianzus did not go beyond the teaching of the founders of Christianity in his prescription how to become a theologian: "Keep the commandments: conduct is the ladder to theory—πρᾶξις ἐπίβασις φεωρίας." Our Lord himself declared, "If any one willeth to do the will of him that sent me, he shall know of the teaching whether it be of God, or whether I speak from myself"—that is, it is only in the good ground of a good heart that even the good seed of the gospel can produce fruit. But nowhere did he or any of his apostles ever teach that the good seed is unnecessary for the harvest—that the unsowed soil, however good, is competent of itself to produce the golden return. Knowledge of God's will with them was ever the condition of doing God's will, and lay at the root of all good conduct and true religion in the world.

And from that day to this, this has been the fundamental conception of the Christian religion among its adherents. The meaning of this is delightfully set forth at the opening of that eloquent book, Dr. James Macgregor's *The Apology of the Christian Religion*. Other religions have sought to propagate themselves in various ways, but this is what is characteristic and peculiar to Christianity: it made its appeal from the first to men's reason.

"No other religion," says Dr. Macgregor, "has ever seriously set itself . . . to *reason* the sinful world out of worldliness into godliness. The aspect of the new religion thus appearing towards the freedom of the human soul, in addressing itself to the reason in order to reach the man in his conscience and his heart, struck the intelligent heathens as a presumptive evidence of truth and divinity, since reason is 'the door' (John x. 1 f.)—the *lawful* way—of seeking to win and to control the manhood. And that aspect was given to the religion from the beginning by the author of it."[56] Christianity has thus from the beginning ever come to men as the rational religion, making its appeal primarily to the intellect. It has thus ever evinced itself not merely, as Dr. Macgregor puts it, preëminently as the apologetical religion, but also preëminently as the doctrinal religion. Above

---

[56]Compare also Dr. James Orr's remarks, *The Christian View*, p. 23: "If there is a religion in the world which exalts the office of teaching, it is safe to say it is the religion of Jesus Christ. It has been frequently remarked that in pagan religions the doctrinal element is at a minimum, the chief thing there is the performance of a ritual. But this is precisely where Christianity distinguishes itself from other religions—it does contain doctrine. It comes to men with definite, positive teaching; it claims to be the truth; it bases religion on knowledge, though a knowledge which is only attainable under moral conditions."

all other religions, it consists in doctrines: it has truth to offer
to men's acceptance, and by their acceptance of this truth it
seeks to rule their lives and save their souls.[57]

How else, indeed, would it propagate itself in the world?
We may speak of "spiritual contagion" and of the hidden work
of the Spirit of God in the heart; and each phrase enshrines
a precious fact without which Christianity could not live in the
world. Christianity does propagate itself from soul to soul, as
the prairie fire leaps from spear to spear of the tall grass: our
Lord himself tells us that the seed are the children of the kingdom. And all the religious life in the world is the creation
of the Spirit of God: the kingdom of God is like leaven hidden
in the meal, and works silently and unobservedly from within
till the whole mass is leavened. But the commission that the
Master has given us was not to depend on "spiritual contagion,"
but to sow the seed which is the Word of God: nor has he
promised that the Spirit should work his wonders of grace
apart from that Word. The commission is, *Go, preach:* and the
promise is to him that *heareth and obeyeth.* Are we, after all,
to suppose that this great duty laid on his followers is a mere
"spiritual exercise" of no value beyond themselves—a kind
of spiritual gymnastics for the manifestation and strengthening
of their own faith? Is the foolishness of preaching after all a
useless evil, inflicted on men? Was Paul mistaken when he
declared that Christ had sent him forth above all to preach the
gospel? We may think as we will; but it is very evident that
the founders of Christianity earnestly believed, not that the
so-called Word of God is the product of faith and its only use
is to witness to the faith that lies behind it and gives it birth,

---

[57]It is probably, then, not mere accident that in Rom. vii. 23, it is
from the νοῦς—the "mind"—that the conquest of Christianity over the
life proceeds outwardly to the members. Christianity makes its appeal
to the "mind" and secures the affection of the "inward man" first, and
thence advances to victory over the "flesh" and "members." Accordingly it is by the "renewing of their mind (τοῦ νοός)" that sinners are
to be so metamorphosed as to be no longer fashioned according to the
world, but to prove the will of God (Rom. xii. 2). Compare the rich
expressions of Eph. iv. 18-24. The noetic root of salvation is continually
insisted on in the Scriptures.

but that the veritable Word of God is the seed of faith, that faith cometh by hearing and hearing by the Word of God, or, in other words, that behind the Christian life stands the doctrine of Christ, intelligently believed. When, for example, the apostle asks the Galatians, "This only would I learn of you, Received ye the Spirit by the works of the law or by the hearing of faith?" he intimates with entire distinctness that it is in connection with the truth of God offered to faith that the Holy Spirit is given; and therefore elsewhere, although the gospel is naught save as it is attended with the demonstration of the Spirit and with power—and Paul may plant and Apollos may water in vain if God do not himself give the increase—yet this very gospel itself and its preaching is called the "power of God unto salvation" (Rom. i. 16; 1 Cor. i. 24).

In insisting, therefore, on the primacy of Christian doctrine, and on the consequent right and duty to ascertain and accurately to state this doctrine—which is the task of Systematic Theology—we have the consciousness of being imitators of Paul even as he was of Christ. How much the apostle made, not merely of the value of doctrine as the condition of life, but of the importance of sound doctrine! His boast, we will remember, is that he is not of the many who corrupt the truth, but that he, at least, has preached the whole counsel of God. He is not content that Jesus Christ should be preached, but insists on a special doctrine of Christ—Jesus Christ and him as crucified. He even pronounces those that preach any other gospel than that he preached accursed: and we should carefully note that this curse falls not on teachers of other religions, but on preachers of what we might speak of today as different forms of Christianity. In a word, in all his teaching and in all his practice alike, Paul impresses upon us the duty and the supreme importance of preserving that purity of doctrine which it is the aim of Systematic Theology in its investigation into Christian truth to secure.

16

THE INDISPENSABLENESS OF SYSTEMATIC THEOLOGY TO THE PREACHER*

Professor Flint, of Edinburgh, in closing his opening lecture to his class a few years ago, took occasion to warn his students of what he spoke of as an imminent danger. This was a growing tendency to "deem it of prime importance that they should enter upon their ministry accomplished preachers, and of only secondary importance that they should be scholars, thinkers, theologians." "It is not so," he is reported as saying, "that great or even good preachers are formed. They form themselves before they form their style of preaching. Substance with them precedes appearance, instead of appearance being a substitute for substance. They learn to know truth before they think of presenting it. . . . They acquire a solid basis for the manifestation of their love of souls through a loving, comprehensive, absorbing study of the truth which saves souls."[1] In these winged words is outlined the case for the indispensableness of Systematic Theology for the preacher. It is summed up in the propositions that it is through the truth that souls are saved, that it is accordingly the prime business of the preacher to present this truth to men, and that it is consequently his fundamental duty to become himself possessed of this truth, that he may present it to men and so save their souls. It would not be easy to overstate, of course, the importance to a preacher of those gifts and graces which qualify him to present this truth to men in a winning way—of all, in a word, that goes to make him an "accomplished preacher." But it is ob-

---

*From the *Homiletic Review*, Feb. 1897, pp. 99-105.
[1]As reported in *The Scotsman* for Nov. 13, 1888.

viously even more important to him that he should have a clear apprehension and firm grasp of that truth which he is to commend to men by means of these gifts and graces. For this clear apprehension and firm grasp of the truth its systematic study would seem certainly to be indispensable. And Systematic Theology is nothing other than the saving truth of God presented in systematic form.

The necessity of systematic study of any body of truth which we need really to master will scarcely be doubted. Nor will it be doubted that he who would indoctrinate men with a given body of truth must needs begin by acquiring a mastery of it himself. What has been made matter of controversy is whether Christian truth does lie so at the basis of the Christian hope and the Christian life that it is the prime duty of the preacher to possess himself of it and to teach it. It has been argued that the business of the preacher is to make Christians, not theologians; and that for this he needs not a thorough systematic knowledge of the whole circle of what is called Christian doctrine, but chiefly a firm faith in Jesus Christ as Savior and a warm love toward him as Lord. His function is a practical, not a theoretical one; and it matters little how ignorant he may be or may leave his hearers, so only he communicates to them the faith and love that burn in his own heart. Not learning but fervor is what is required; nay, too much learning is (so it is often said) distinctly unfavorable to his best efficiency. Engagement of the mind with the subtleties of theological construction excludes that absorption in heart-devotion and in the practical work of the ministry, which on its two sides forms the glory of the minister's inner life and the crown of his outer activity. Give us not scholars, it is said, but plain practical men in our pulpits—men whose simple hearts are on fire with love to Christ and whose whole energy is exhausted in the rescue of souls.

Surely, if the antithesis were as is here implied, no voice would be raised in opposition to these demands. If we are to choose between a chilly intellectualistic and a warmly evangelistic ministry, give us the latter by all means. A comparatively ignorant ministry burning with zeal for souls is infinitely to be preferred to a ministry entirely absorbed in a purely intellectual interest in the relations of truths which are permitted to exercise no influence on their own lives and which quicken in them no fervor of missionary love. But the matter cannot be settled by fixing the eye on this extreme only. What should we do with a ministry which was absolutely and blankly ignorant of the whole compass of Christian truth? Obviously it would not be a Christian ministry at all. Let it be admitted, then, that it is possible for men to become so occupied with the purely intellectual aspects of Christian truth as to be entirely unfitted for the prosecution of the Christian ministry. It must be equally allowed that they must have a sound knowledge of Christian truth in order to be qualified to undertake the functions of the Christian ministry at all. The possibility of the abuse of Systematic Theology has no tendency to arraign its usefulness or even its indispensableness to the preacher. A high capacity and love for mathematics may live in a sadly unpractical brain, and, for aught I know, the world may be full of pure mathematicians who are absolutely useless to it; but it does not follow that the practical worker in applied mathematics can get on just as well without any mathematics at all. In like manner, though there may be such a thing as a barren knowledge of even such vital truth as the Christian verities, there is not and cannot be such a thing as a fruitful Christian ministry without a sound and living knowledge of these verities. And it is very much to be deprecated that men should sometimes permit themselves to be driven, through their keen sense of the valuelessness of an inoperative knowledge, to speak as if no importance attached to that vitalizing knowledge of divine truth without which any true ministry is impossible. The warning given us by the lamented Aubrey Moore is sorely needed in our times. He says: "There are many earnest-minded Christians who are so morbidly afraid of a barren belief that they sometimes allow themselves to talk as if to hold fast to any form of sound words must be formalism; as if, in fact, the belief in a creed were rather dangerous than helpful. It is true, of course, as we all know well, that a right creed cannot save a man, and that when the bridegroom comes many may be found with lamps that have no oil; but surely if we discard our lamps, much of the precious oil we have may be lost."[2]

The fundamental principle on which the indispensableness to the preacher of a sound knowledge of Christian truth rests is not more surely rooted in a true psychology than it is illustrated by universal experience. That "conduct in the long run corresponds with belief," as Bishop Westcott puts it, "all experience goes to show." And certainly he is entitled to add that "this unquestionable principle carries with it momentous consequences." "Patient investigation," he continues, "will show that no doctrine can be without a bearing on action. . . . The influence of a dogma will be good or bad—that is an important criterion of dogma, with which we are not now concerned—but if the dogma be truly maintained, it will have a moral value of some kind. Every religion, and every sect of every religion, has its characteristic form of life; and if the peculiarities of these forms of life are smoothed away by time, it is only because the type of belief to which they correspond has ceased to retain its integrity and sharpness."[3] It is therefore that Principal Wace rebukes the "tendency of some modern historians to undervalue the influence upon human nature of variations in religious and moral principles," as "strangely at variance with the evidence before them."[4] "The history of the world," he adds, "would appear to be in great measure a history of the manner in which religious ideas, often of an apparently abstract and subtle character, can determine the future of whole races and of vast regions of the earth. . . . The facts of history thus afford conclusive evidence that the instinct of the Christian world, or rather the instinct of mankind, has not been mistaken in attributing extreme importance to those variations in faith, even on points apparently second-

[2]*Some Aspects of Sin*, p. 20.
[3]*The Gospel of Life*, pp. 48, 57.
[4]*The Foundations of Faith*, pp. 194-198.

ary, by which Christendom has been and is still so grievously divided." The whole case is most concisely put in a comprehensive passage in the *Systematic Theology* of the late Prof. John Miley:

> A religious movement with power to lift up souls into a true spiritual life must have its inception and progress in a clear and earnest presentation of the vital doctrines of religion. The order of facts in every such movement in the history of Christianity has been, first, a reformation of doctrine, and then, through the truer doctrine, a higher and better moral and spiritual life. . . . Such has ever been and must forever be the chronological order of these facts, because it is the logical order. When souls move up from a sinful life or a dead formalism into a true spiritual life they must have the necessary reasons and motives for such action. . . . If we should be consecrated to God in a life of holy obedience and love, it must be for reasons of duty and motives of spiritual well-being which are complete only in the distinctive doctrines of Christianity. These doctrines are not mere intellectual principles or dry abstractions, but living truths which embody all the practical forces of Christianity. The spiritual life takes a higher form under evangelical Christianity than is possible under any other form, whether ritualistic or rationalistic, because therein the great doctrines of Christianity are apprehended in a living faith and act with their transcendent practical force upon all that enters into this life.[5]

If there be any validity at all in these remarks, the indispensableness of Systematic Theology to the preacher is obvious. For they make it clear not only that some knowledge of Christian truth is essential to him who essays to teach that truth, but that the type of life which is produced by his preaching, so far as his preaching is effective, will vary in direct relation to the apprehension he has of Christian truth and the type and proportion of truth he presents in his preaching. As Bishop Westcott puts it: "Error and imperfection in such a case must result in lives which are faulty and maimed where they might have been nobler and more complete"; and, on the

---

[5]Vol. I, pp. 48-49. Cf. also p. 40.

other hand, "right doctrine is an inexhaustible spring of strength, if it be translated into deed."[6] In directly the same line of remark that saint of God, Dr. Horatius Bonar, urges that: "All wrong thoughts of God, whether of Father, Son, or Spirit, must cast a shadow over the soul that entertains them. In some cases the shadow may not be so deep and cold as in others; but never can it be a trifle. And it is this that furnishes the proper answer to the flippant question so often asked: Does it really matter what a man believes? All defective views of God's character tell upon the life of the soul and the peace of the conscience. We must think right thoughts of God if we would worship him as he desires to be worshiped, if we would live the life he wishes us to live, and enjoy the peace which he has provided for us."[7] And what is true of the doctrine of God is true of every other doctrine about his ways and works; as Dr. Westcott phrases it, "The same law which holds good of the effect of the ideas of God and of a future life and of the incarnation in their most general form, holds good also of the details of the view upon which they are realized."[8]

Accordingly Dr. Alexander Whyte testifies to the relation of right belief and all the highest devotion, in a striking passage which we cannot forbear quoting somewhat in full. He writes:

> One of the acknowledged masters of the spiritual life warns us against "an untheological devotion." "True spirituality," he insists, "has always been orthodox." And the readers of the *Grammar of Assent* will remember with what masterly power and with what equal eloquence it is there set forth that the theology of the Creeds and Catechisms, when it is rightly understood and properly employed, appeals to the heart quite as much as to the head, to the imagination quite as much as to the understanding. And we cannot study Andrewes' book [his *Private Devotions*], his closet confession of faith especially, without discovering what a majesty, what a massiveness, what a depth, and what a strength, as well as what an evangelical fervor and heartsomeness, his theology has given to his devotional life.

---

[6]*Op. cit.,* p. 58.
[7]*The Gospel of the Spirit's Love,* p. 22.
[8]*Op. cit.,* p. 55.

. . . In the *Grammar* its author says that for himself he
has ever felt the Athanasian Creed to be the most devotional formulary to which Christianity has given birth. We
certainly feel something not unlike that when Andrewes
takes up the Apostles' Creed, or the Nicene Creed, or the
Life of our Lord, or his Names, or his Titles, or his Offices.
When Andrewes takes up any of these things into his
intellect, imagination, and heart, he has already provided
himself and his readers with another great prayer and
another great psalm. So true is it that all true theology is
directly and richly and evangelically devotional.[9]

Readers of Dr. Palmer's *Life of Thornwell* will recall a parallel
testimony to what the reading of the Westminster Confession
did for Thornwell's soul; and we can ourselves testify from
experience to the power of the Westminster Confession to
quicken religious emotion, and to form and guide a deeply
devotional life. "So true is it," to repeat Dr. Whyte's words,
that "all true theology is directly and richly and evangelically
dovotional."

It cannot be a matter of indifference, therefore, what doctrines we preach or whether we preach any doctrines at all.
We cannot preach at all without preaching doctrine; and the
type of religious life which grows up under our preaching will
be determined by the nature of the doctrines which we preach.
We deceive ourselves if we fancy that because we scout the
doctrines of the creeds and assume an attitude of studied indifference to the chief tenets of Christianity we escape teaching
a system of belief. Even the extremest doctrinal indifferentism,
when it ascends the pulpit, becomes necessarily a scheme of
faith. As a bright writer in *The Atlantic Monthly* puts it, men
are always found believers in either the head or the tail of the
coin. Even "Renan's followers have their pockets crammed
with beliefs of their own, bawling to the public to try them;
they trundle their push-carts down the boulevard, hawking new
creeds: *'Par ici, mes amis, par ici! Voici des croyance neuves,
voici la Verité!'* "[10] Beliefs old or beliefs new, we all have

---

[9]*Lancelot Andrewes and His Private Devotions*, pp. 49-51.
[10]Henry T. Sedgwick, Jr., in *The Atlantic Monthly*, August 1896, p. 188.

them; and when we take our place in the rostrum in their behalf we perforce become their teachers. There may be Christian truths of which we speak as if they were of infinitesimally
little importance, because, as Aubrey Moore caustically puts
it, "from first to last we know infinitesimally little about
them";[11] but we need not fancy that we are teaching nothing
in so speaking of them, or are failing to preach a dogmatic
faith or by it to mold lives in essaying to occupy a position
of indifference. To withhold these truths from our hearers is
not merely a negative act, nor can their loss act merely nega-
tively upon their spiritual development. A mutilated gospel
produces mutilated lives, and mutilated lives are positive evils.
Whatever the preacher may do, the hearers will not do without
a system of belief; and in their attempt to frame one for the
government of their lives out of the fragments of truth which
such a preacher will grant to them, is it any wonder if they
should go fatally astray? At the best, men will be "driven to
a kind of empirical theologizing, attempting with necessarily
imperfect knowledge to coordinate for themselves the truths of
religion and those which follow as consequences from them";[12]
and so will build up an erroneous system of belief which
will mar their lives. At the worst, they will be led to discard
the neglected or discredited truths, and with them the whole
system of Christianity—which they see, even though the
preacher does not see, to be necessarily correlated with them;
and so will lapse into unbelief. In either case, they may rightly
lay their marred or ruined lives at the preacher's door. It is
not given to one who stands in the pulpit to decide whether or
no he shall teach, whether or no he shall communicate to others
a system of belief which will form lives and determine destinies.
It is in his power only to determine what he shall teach, what
system of doctrine he shall press upon the acceptance of men,
by what body of tenets he will seek to mold their lives and to
inform their devotions.

By as much, however, as the communication of a system of

---

[11]*Op. cit.*, p. 26.
[12]Aubrey Moore, *loc. cit.*, p. 25.

belief is the inevitable consequence of preaching, by so much is the careful formation of his system of belief the indispensable duty of the preacher. And this is but another way of saying that the systematic study of divine truth, or the study of Systematic Theology, is the most indispensable preparation for the pulpit. Only as the several truths to be presented are known in their relations can they be proclaimed in their right proportions and so taught as to produce their right effects on the soul's life and growth. Systematic Theology is, in other words, the preacher's true text-book. Its study may be undertaken, no doubt, in a cold and unloving spirit, with the mind intent on merely scholastic or controversial ends. In that case it may be for the preacher an unfruitful occupation. But so undertaken it has also lost its true character. It exists not for these ends, but to "make wise unto salvation." And when undertaken as the means of acquiring a thorough and precise knowledge of those truths which are fitted to "make wise unto salvation," it will assuredly bear its fruit in the preacher's own heart in a fine skill in rightly dividing the word of truth, and in the lives of the hearers as a power within them working a right attitude before God and building them up into the fulness of the stature of symmetrical manhood in Christ.

17

RECENT RECONSTRUCTIONS
OF THEOLOGY*

Strictly speaking, theology has not been "reconstructed" in recent, or, for that matter, even in modern, times. When men have thought themselves through the subject, and built up the fabric of their theology in a completed system, they have ordinarily been found to give us much what we have been familiar with for a couple of centuries. The Arminian probably remains today the latest real reconstruction of theology. The several treatises on dogmatics that come to us from time to time run on the essential lines of the old types and fall readily into place as Sacerdotal or Socinian, Arminian or Lutheran or Reformed dogmatics. The Decrees of Trent and the Racovian Catechism, the *Formula Concordiae* and the Remonstrance and its Apology, the Canons of Dort and the Westminster Confession have thrown up the dykes between which the streams of theological thought still flow. A brave attempt to open a new channel was indeed made by the "Mediating Theology," but its stream has dwindled to a trickle. Men like Ebrard and Dorner and Martensen, to be sure, will not soon cease to be read with profit; and the glamor of the conceptions which dominated their generation still dazzles eyes which strain to catch their light at some distance from its source. Thus in America we have quite recently had a system from Dr. Gerhart, of Lancaster, reflecting this light, and only the other day a handbook from Dr. Clarke, of Hamilton Seminary. But in the land of its birth the candle of the "Mediating Theology" has already gone out with a splutter; and everywhere it has come to be perceived that its precious

---

The Homiletic Review, March 1898, pp. 201-208.

"Christological" principle is little more than the old "Anthropological" principle of Arminianism, writ large. The Ritschlism which has sprung vigorously up in the field left barren by the wilting of this once flourishing plant, as yet lacks its thoroughly wrought-out system of dogmatics. When it comes, if it comes on the lines laid down by "the Master" and diligently worked by his most consistent and conspicuous followers, it will not create a new category of theological construction; the old category of Socinianism will be quite capable of receiving it. Meanwhile, however, we have no real "reconstructions of theology" of recent date which we may be expected to estimate. There are on every side of us tendencies, suggestions, tentative movements of thought; bundles more or less large and more or less miscellaneous of conceptions old and new; but scarcely "reconstructions of theology." I presume that what is asked of me is some estimate of the direction and value of these more or less strong, but certainly existent currents in theological thinking. Are they mere swirls and eddies on the surface of the great stream, or do they promise to combine after a while into a flood which shall break the barriers and perhaps cut out a new channel? From "the point of view of Systematic Theology," I am expected to make some estimate of the systematic value of these movements, of their effects on the system of truth concerning God and his relations to his universe—in a word, of the possibility of their flowing ultimately together into a system, and of the nature of the system which in such a case they will give us.

Our time is admittedly marked by a considerable confusion in its theological outlook. The currents that flow up and down in the theological world—sometimes apparently up and down within the limits of a single mind—seem to run very much athwart one another, and it is not always easy to attain a satisfying estimate of their value, either separately or in their various combinations. But there are some general characteristics which are shared by all, or nearly all, of those theological movements that can with any propriety of contrast be spoken of as recent, which have a very decided significance from the

point of view of systematization. And by withdrawing our attention from the confusing and often very confused details, and
focusing it for the time on these broad common characteristics
of "recent theological reconstruction," we may manage very
quickly to arrive at some sound estimate of them from "the
point of view of Systematic Theology."

1. I fancy that there is nothing more widely characteristic
of "recent theological reconstruction," in the sense defined, than
a tendency to cut loose from all "external authority." Our new
guides may differ in many things, some of them of fundamental
importance, not only in a systematic, but also in a vitally religious, aspect. But they all pretty much agree in looking with
some reserve, upon "external authority" as a source of knowledge of divine truth, and in readily substituting for it more or
less completely the authority of the human spirit in one or
another of its powers, or in one or another of its states. There
are differences in the completeness with which all appeal to
"external authority" is renounced; differences in the frankness
with which the appeal is made to the bare spirit of man. It
is comparatively rare, perhaps, that the baldly rationalistic
ground is taken up, and the naked reason openly looked to as
the sole source of truth. We hear it more commonly called
"the Christian consciousness," "the witness of the Spirit in the
heart," "the indwelling Spirit which is the common endowment of Christians." Nor are men always able to break so
sharply with the past as to turn their backs once and for all
upon all dependence on the guidance of the Scriptures. Even
when the logic of their thought, or even the express sense of
their assertion, abolishes all "external authority," they may still
be found clinging to its fragments, and building out of them
a foundationless house for their spiritual home. But it is undeniable that "recent theological reconstruction" holds at best
but a crumbling Bible in its hands. There may be some to
whom it is a supreme grief to see it crumble—whom we may
picture as appropriating to themselves the words of the poet:

> I stand amid the roar
> Of a surf-tormented shore,

And I hold within my hand
Grains of the golden sand—
How few! yet how they creep
Through my fingers to the deep,
While I weep—while I weep!
O God! can I not grasp
Them with a tighter clasp?
O God! can I not save
One from the pitiless wave?

But there are others whom we can equally easily fancy replying to the soul-cry of these, their weaker brethren, with a certain sardonic pleasure, that there is certainly not one atom of
that old "external authority" which used to tyrannize over
men that can be saved, and that for themselves they are
glad of it.

Look, for instance, at the jubilant tone of freedom with which
the last vestige of "Apostolical authority" is cast from them by
the whole school of Ritschl, whose teachings are just now invading our American churches, although already perhaps
beginning to show signs of waning influence in Germany.
Adolf Harnack has lately taken opportunity to make a quite
emphatic pronunciamento on this point, and to give it validity
for the whole school. Gustav Ecke had been seeking points of
conciliation between the Ritschlites and the Evangelicals, but
found himself ever confronted with the irreducible difference
that the Ritschlites, one and all, refuse to allow to the Bible the
authority which would attach to revelation. He is right! exclaims Harnack: no Ritschlite will accord revelation-value to
the Scriptures; no one of them will permit himself to be brought
(the emphases are his) "into *subjection* to *every* Bible doctrine," or will consent to look upon the teachings of the New
Testament as capable of being described any otherwise than
euphemistically as the "Apostolic confession of faith." Accordingly, we see Dr. A. C. McGiffert, the leading representative of the Ritschlian school in America, in his recent *History
of Christianity in the Apostolic Age*, not only laying aside
whole tracts of the New Testament as not in his judgment
apostolic in origin, or trustworthy in narrative, or authoritative

in teaching, but denying even to those parts the apostolic origin of which he can bring himself to allow, any peculiar authority in the Church—any more authority than belongs to the utterances of any Christian man who is led (as are all Christians) by the Holy Spirit.

At quite the opposite extreme from this open breach with the whole authority of the Scriptures stands such a writer as Dr. James Denney, whose attractive *Studies in Theology* rests throughout on the frankest use of Scripture, as if it were of authority in divine things. But even he at the end sets forth a "doctrine of Holy Scripture" which evaporates its authority, which speaks of it as "in the first instance" merely "a means of grace" and as only secondarily, through the medium of the new life quickened in the heart, becoming a source of knowledge, because, forsooth, "no religious truth, no spiritual truth, can be communicated" "by telling it in so many words." Thus he, too, throws back the spirit upon itself, under the euphemism of "the witness of the Spirit in the heart," for the source and test of all truth. One of the strange things in connection with this widely prevalent subjectivism is the tendency observed in many and very diverse quarters to represent it as a return to the attitude of the Reformers. It stands rather, of course, in direct contradiction to the Reformers' attitude. What they renounced was not "external authority," but "human authority," inclusive naturally of that of their own spirits; and what they fell back on was "Divine authority," which not only includes, but primarily exhibits itself in, the Scriptures. When it is "external authority" that is renounced, the authority of God goes with it, and we can revert only to the human authority of the individual soul. And *that*, conceal it under whatever honeyed phrases we may, is nothing but a return to the fundamental principle, not of the Reformation, but of "Rationalism."

2. A second very marked characteristic of recent drifts in theological thinking may be recognized as a direct outgrowth of its attitude of doubt and hesitation (when it is not an attitude of open denial) as over against the authority of the Scriptural

revelation. This is the general indefiniteness in doctrinal construction which seems to be coming in upon us like a flood. The outlines of doctrinal statement are becoming more and more blurred in the hands of our more recent guides. We are hearing more and more frequently sharp complaints of the "intellectualism" which is assumed to be inherent in any clear conceptions of doctrinal truths. Of one element after another of the Christian system, it is declared with ever-increasing emphasis that no "theory" of it can be attained, and that we must therefore fall back on the simple "facts," and renounce altogether the hope of understanding them. Here is the root of that general indifference to doctrine that is becoming so characteristic of our age. The constitutive doctrines of the Christian system are growing more and more doubtful, more and more shadowy things, and men are accordingly caring less about them. This is, of course, the inevitable effect of the increasing disregard of the authority of the Scriptures. For, if we are not to trust the Scriptures, where are we to go for information as to what is true about these tremendous problems? Such doctrines as those of the Trinity in unity, of the deity of Christ, of his work of expiation, of the supernatural redemption—such doctrines, in a word, as constitute the complex of what is known specifically as Christian theology—rest on Scripture and on Scripture alone; are drawn out of Scripture, or are not drawn out at all. And in saying this we have unveiled the seriousness of the drift into indefiniteness, consequent on the renunciation of the authority of the Bible. Speaking from the standpoint of the systematician, it portends the destruction of the whole system of Christian doctrine; speaking from the standpoint of the religious life, it means the destruction of Christianity itself. For all the Christianity of theology on the one hand, and all the Christianity in religion on the other, comes from the Bible. Apart from the revelation of God deposited for us in the Scriptures, there is no Christianity. Obliterate this revelation—theology may remain, but it is no longer a Christian theology; religion may remain, but it is no longer the Christian religion. In proportion, therefore, as faith in the Bible revelation is abolished, and the outlines of the doctrines dependent on trust in that revelation are washed out, in that proportion Christianity will be effaced. Our systems of theology will to this degree cease to be distinctively Christian, and our religion will lose its specifically Christian traits. In a word, if we are to follow our more recent guides, we shall inevitably drift toward a purely natural religion.

Copious evidence of this exists all about us. Perhaps none of it is more striking than the increasing deference which, in the construction of doctrine, is given on every side to what are called the data of "Science," as over against the data of "Revelation." Nothing is more characteristic of the mental outlook of our day. This was, for example, the note struck twenty years ago in such books as the notorious "Scotch Sermons." They essayed not to bring "Science" into harmony with Christianity, but Christianity into harmony with "Science." The note has become painfully iterant since. Scores of books appear every year with no other object than to conform Christianity to what are deemed the latest deliverances of "Science," that is, to the freshest and most untested products of speculation. Of the latest type of theological thinking which has acquired widespread influence, indeed—the Ritschlian—this point of view deserves to be called its very principle. Dr. James Orr has pointed this out very clearly in his recent informing little book on *Ritschlianism*. He says: "It would not be an unfair description of Ritschlianism to say that it is an attempt to show how much of positive Christianity can be retained compatibly with the acceptance of the modern non-miraculous theory of the world." And then he justly adds: "This is not to keep Christianity separate from modern thought, but to make a surrender to it. . . . It is the modern view which controls the Scripture statement."

Of course such a procedure can bear but one interpretation. The truth is, that our modern leaders are in ever-increasing measure turning away from revelation and turning to nature as the source of authoritative knowledge of divine things. And what that means is that men are more and more de-

Christianizing and more and more naturalizing our theology. After a while, if we proceed on this road, we shall have in our Systems of Theology only that knowledge of God which is derived from a study of his works. We shall have returned to a purely natural religion. We may designate it under whatever euphemism we may please, but the growing impatience with clear and sharp definitions of doctrine is a symptom of nothing other than a reversion to mere "Naturalism."

3. We may recognize as but one instance of this general drift toward the obliteration of the doctrines distinctive of Christianity, a third most marked characteristic of recent theological thinking. Perhaps we may call it its most strongly marked characteristic. I mean the widespread, the almost universal tendency to deprecate the uniqueness and the unapproachable majesty of the Son of God. It is undeniable that "recent theological construction" is restless over against the idea of a divine Christ. In its general theological indefiniteness it tends at least to indistinctness in its conception of the deity of our Lord. In its growing detachment from the authority of Scripture it feels itself on no firm foundations in speaking of incarnate divinity; for nature, of course, knows nothing of a divine Christ. In its renunciation of all "external authority" it cannot patiently brook the yoke of the God-man. Thus it comes about that there is no current in recent thinking that flows more broadly and strongly, or with a rush which promises to make a cleaner sweep of old conceptions, than that which impinges on the doctrine of Christ's Godhead.

The older Unitarianism—even in its extremest Socinian form—was not averse to leaving us at least "Christ our Prophet" and "Christ our Example." Our modern teachers would deny us even these. The Jesus they offer us is a Jesus who thought as a man of his day, who lived as a man of his day, and who ceases to be a trustworthy guide to us in either what he said or what he did. It may be still allowed that his living in the world marked an epoch in its history; that the impression which his life, and perhaps his teaching, made on men still reverberates down the ages. But it is denied that it is a valid inference from this that he was more than a remarkable man—of a type, though possibly the supreme instance, other examples of which we may discern in the Confuciuses, Sakya Munis, and Socrateses. Some words of a recent poet indeed quite exactly express what a sadly large number are thinking of Jesus:

> Then woke the world with sudden stir.
> "Whence came this power in our hearts to draw?
> Call ye this man a carpenter?
> He is a God!"—they cried in awe.

> Ah me, it was no God they hailed,
> No arbiter of life and death,
> But a poor man that dared and failed,
> A carpenter of Nazareth.

Of course such an attitude is that of extremists. It is, nevertheless, the attitude toward the "historical Jesus" which is inherent in the most recent influential type of theological thinking, the Ritschlian. A most startling indication of this has been lately given us in Dr. A. C. McGiffert's book, already mentioned, on the Apostolical Church. For the most distressing thing about that volume is not its destructive attitude toward the authority of the New Testament Scriptures, bad as that is. It is rather its terribly low estimate of Jesus. This estimate is such as to lead a quite independent critic, uninformed of Dr. McGiffert's ecclesiastical connections, to say in his simplicity: "We gather from the first two chapters that the author writes from the standpoint of Unitarianism, and, to a believer in the divine claims of Christ, his account of the Christian origins cannot fail to appear prejudiced and misleading." It is a mark of the times that such misjudgments can occur, and that such corrections as *The British Weekly* made in this case are possible and necessary. "*Literature*," it says, "in its review of Dr. McGiffert's *History of Christianity in the Apostolic Age*, concludes from internal evidence that Dr. McGiffert is a Unitarian. We believe that this is not so. Dr. McGiffert, if we are not mistaken, is a Presbyterian." How deeply the canker has eaten could not be better exhibited than that nowadays some Presbyterians write of Jesus in a manner that is indistinguishable from Unitarianism.

This, we say, is no doubt an extreme case. But it is far from an isolated one. And from this up it is rather a question of degree than of kind. In the more orthodox circles the driftage is strong at least in the direction of an extreme doctrine of *kenosis*. And what is that doctrine but a happy expedient by which we may lull our reverence to sleep by still speaking of Jesus as God, while we yet find nothing but what is purely human in his speech or action; by which we may decline his authority while offering him an empty homage? Our presses are groaning with treatises from the hands of those who have not forgotten how to call him their Lord and their God, the whole purpose of which is to find reason why they need not in this, that, or the other thing believe him, and ought not to be expected to follow him. Gloze it as we may, men today do not wish to have this Man to rule over them, to dictate what they shall believe or to show what they shall do; and the strongest drift in our theological thinking is toward the abolishing of the divine Christ. The flimsy artificial barrier of a *kenotic* theory can never hold back that flood; and the issue of the present theological movement can be nothing other than a new Socinian defection.

I beg my readers to understand that I am not assuming the role of a prophet. I am, indeed, told by our modern teachers that if I be a Christian at all, I am led by the same Spirit and have the same right to be heard as a Paul or an Isaiah. But I have myself more confidence in the prophetic gifts of those old, if somewhat outworn, writers than in my own; and I fall back gladly on their assurance that God will not permit his truth to perish out of the earth. I am criticizing tendencies, not predicting the future. And it is one thing to say that the current theologizing is in the direction of Rationalism, Naturalism, Socinianism; and another thing to say that Christianity is to sink in that slough. After all, the divine Christ is not abolished because men bid us cease to reverence him, or the

Christian system of truth destroyed because men ask us no longer to believe it, or the divine Word robbed of its power because we are warned no longer to bow to its authority. Men may come and men may go, but these are things that abide forever.

18

A REVIEW OF *Studies in Theology**

STUDIES IN THEOLOGY. Lectures delivered in Chicago Theological Seminary. By the REV. JAMES DENNEY, D.D. Second Edition. 12mo, pp. viii, 272. New York: A. C. Armstrong & Son, 1895.

This exceedingly attractive and stimulating volume has been made out of the lectures which were delivered by Dr. Denney to the students of the Chicago Theological Seminary in April, 1894, during a temporary vacancy in the chair of Dogmatic Theology in that institution. They well deserve the wider audience to which they appeal in their published form. A complete system of theology they do not offer us, as the author himself remarks in his preface. Possibly all the opinions expressed in them could not be wrought into an entirely consistent system. But they give us a series of exceptionally illuminating discussions of theological themes; and, as the subjects that are selected for treatment are the mountain masses of theological thought, he who follows Dr. Denney through his discussions ought to find little difficulty in divining the general topography of his system. The nature of the system which is thus revealed in its salient points is, in these days of loose speech and looser thinking, distinctly a reassuring one. It lies disposed about the great central facts of Christianity, which are firmly grasped and held with intelligent tenacity against all assault. A distinctively evangelical tone is thus cast over the whole exposition, and the emphasis is continually thrown upon the greater things—the curse and guilt of sin, a sin-bearing atonement, a divine Redeemer. There is nowhere visible a trace of that lightness in

*From *Christian Literature*, Oct. 1895.

dealing with such great verities which so frequently offends the serious mind in recent theological writing. Every line in Dr. Denney's lectures bears witness to solid learning and strenuous thinking, and every line is suffused with the glow of a truly Christian heart. He has not stinted intellectual labor in working out the problems that faced him; but with him, it is very evident, it is the heart that has made the theologian.

The method of presenting theological truth which Dr. Denney has adopted is not that of simple exposition or of mere positive statement and proof. He has chosen rather to set out what he holds as truth against a background formed by an erroneous system. There are obvious and important advantages in this method; and there are attendant upon it some disadvantages. Both the advantages and the disadvantages tend to reach their culmination, when the system of error chosen to serve as foil to the truth is a rather extreme form of error. The blacker the background, the more brightly the truth may be made to shine out against it; but also the blacker the background, the more readily may a dull gray, say, be mistaken, in contrast with it, for the white truth itself. That Dr. Denney has wholly escaped this natural illusion, in setting forth Christian truth partly by means of a running criticism upon the theories of Ritschl and his followers, we cannot affirm. In a number of cases the truth, as it seems to us, has appeared too glaring to him; in a few, his eyes seem to have been blinded before it altogether—as, for example, in the amazing instance where he actually adopts Harnack's thory of the primitive Church and its transformations, surely without fully considering its implications as to Christian doctrine, for the sake of which very implications, indeed, the theory was invented. But in general the reader will find it distinctly a ground of felicitation that Dr. Denney has selected the Ritschlite theories for his particular criticism. These theories are especially subtle and complete; they fall in with and are powerfully forwarded by some of the most prevailing tendencies of modern thinking; they have been wrought out and given form by masters of thought, furnished with the most adequate learning and endowed with the highest intel-

lectual force; and they are commended to us by a weight of
theological and historical authority which is well nigh overwhelming. Dr. Denney has rendered a very great service to the
English-speaking theological public by expounding to them
these theories in his singularly sympathetic and vital manner,
and at the same time exposing their essential shallowness and
their utter failure to do justice even to the fundamental elements
of Christian truth; and over against them he is able to throw
out in a very high light the greater verities of the gospel. We
have been especially struck with the two lectures on "the work
of Christ in relation to sin," in the former of which the New Testament doctrine of atonement is set forth, while the latter discusses certain current doctrines of atonement which are pronounced inadequate. But in these truly noble lectures we only
find at their best qualities of thought and treatment which are
in evidence throughout the volume.

A rather serious criticism must be passed upon the distribution of the material. This concerns the postponing to a
late point of all treatment of the authority of the Scriptures.
This is not the result of inadvertence, but of deliberate choice.
It is defended on the ground that "the Bible is, in the first instance, a means of grace," and its treatment belongs therefore
"under the rubric of means of grace"; and by an appeal to the
arrangement in certain Confessions, such as "the old Scottish
one and the new English Presbyterian one," which introduce
the topic of Scripture only at this late point and in subordination
to the doctrine of the Church. Surely, however, Dr. Denney's
usual acumen deserts him in this matter. There is an obvious
distinction between the religious and the theological use of the
Bible which he appears to have missed. Most assuredly the
Scriptures lie at the root of the Christian life, and therefore,
not only appropriately but necessarily, receive their treatment
as such under the rubric of "the means of grace." But do they
not also hold a place at the basis of Christian knowledge? And
how can a system of Christian knowledge be set forth—or even
a series of studies on items of Christian knowledge—without
presupposing the determination of all those questions which

concern the Scriptures as a source of Christian knowledge? The postponement of the topic of Holy Scripture in such formulas as the old Scotch Confession and the new Articles of the Presbyterian Church of England can be thought appropriate only if those creeds be conceived as dominated by a religious as distinguished from a theological purpose; and cannot in any way justify an attempt to set forth a body of religious knowledge without determining beforehand whence this knowledge is obtainable and how. Just as every system of philosophy presupposes a theory of knowledge, so a theory of religious knowledge—its nature, its mode, its sources—must underlie every theology. It is not a matter of choice, it is unavoidable, that prior to setting forth a body of Christian knowledge we must first establish the sources of that knowledge and investigate their trustworthiness.

It avails nothing to say in this connection that "the Bible is in the first instance a means of grace"—unless we are prepared to go the whole length with those with whom this mode of speech originated, and set aside altogether the direct use of the Bible as a source of Christian knowledge. Their meaning is clear enough, and is marred by no inconsistencies. Their meaning is that the single function of the Bible is religious, its entire work is to quicken religious life in the soul; and that this religious life, efflorescing into Christian thought, is the sole source of Christian knowledge. Thus the Bible is in the first instance solely a means of grace, and only in the second instance, through the medium of the Christian life quickened by it, does it become indirectly a source of Christian knowledge. Occasionally Dr. Denney speaks in language borrowed from this type of thought. This is so, for example, when he tells us that "no religious truth, no spiritual truth, can be communicated" "by telling it in so many words" (p. 25). But it does not appear that he has adopted this mode of thinking as his own. It would seem rather that he has only in this case, as in some others, taken up out of his broad reading points of view and modes of speech, without sufficiently considering their real implications. Certainly he repeatedly appeals to the Bible as if it were a direct source of Christian knowledge, uses its teaching as a test of Christian truth, and indeed, in immediate connection with the phrase under review, declares that "the Bible is *the* means through which God communicates with man, making him know what is in his heart toward him." In these circumstances, to say that "the Bible is in the first instance a means of grace" can mean nothing more in this connection than that *fides praecedit rationem*, that only a Christian can profitably discuss Christian truth (cf. p. 16). We grant it with all our heart. But this will scarcely exonerate the theologian in refusing to justify the sources of the knowledge he sets forth as such. If it be in any degree true, as Dr. Denney affirms with the emphasis of italics, that "the Bible is *the* means through which God communicates with man, making him know what is in his heart toward him," it would seem to be obvious that it is only with the Bible in his hands as the chief source of knowledge of God that a Christian man may fitly theologize; and this would seem to imply that the Bible should be established as such means before the Christian theologizes.

It is not meant, of course, that a writer on dogmatic theology, especially if he pretends to no formal completeness in his treatment of his subject, may not appropriately enough simply assume the doctrinal authority of Scripture, and build his whole system frankly on that assumption, treating of Scripture only as the primary means of grace when, in the consecution of topics, he arrives at the discussion of that *locus.* Such a procedure would merely imply that the establishment of the trustworthiness and authority of the Scriptures as a source of Christian knowledge is not conceived as a task of dogmatic theology, but will find its place in some preceding discipline—in the Prolegomena to Dogmatics, say, or better, in the preliminary discipline of Apologetics. Were this what Dr. Denney meant, we should be in hearty agreement with him. And this is what is conveyed by a quotation which he has done us the honor to make from a tract, in the preparation of which the late Dr. A. A. Hodge was good enough to associate the present writer. That quotation affirms that, among other things enumerated, "the general truth of Christianity and its doctrines" must be established before the question of the inspiration of the Scriptures is raised. The truth of the Christian religion in general is established by the discipline called Apologetics; the exact statement of the several Christian doctrines and of the system as a whole is the duty of Dogmatics. The fact of inspiration, in the sense of the tract quoted, is not presupposed in the former, but is presupposed in the latter task—that is to say, completeness and precision in doctrinal statement depend on detailed trustworthiness in the sources of knowledge. We might, to be sure, have a Dogmatics on the presupposition of no inspiration, and of no detailed trustworthiness of Scripture; and we might well, even in those untoward circumstances, have still a distinctively Christian Dogmatics. But such a Dogmatics would be relatively general and vague; and no more than any other Dogmatics could it avoid presupposing a theory of Christian knowledge and a determination of its sources. When Dr. Denney passes over all treatment of the doctrinal authority and trustworthiness of the Bible at the beginning of his lectures, however, it is by no means because he presumes these matters to have been already settled in the preliminary discipline of Apologetics. He simply postpones their discussion to a later point in his lectures, and meanwhile leaves his readers in suspense as to the guarantee he can give them of the propriety of his repeated appeals to Scripture in the progress of his doctrinal discussions—merely, for his part, expressing a "hope that the use which he makes of the Bible in passing will be such as to justify itself" (p. 21).

The formal objectionableness of this procedure remains the same, whether the use that is actually made of Scripture in passing does or does not "justify itself," or is or is not justified by the account given of Scripture when it afterward comes to be discussed. To us at least the frank and straightforward use which is frequently made of the Bible in these lectures very thoroughly "justifies itself"; and we have read the discussions of Bible doctrine and the references to Scripture as the source and norm of Christian doctrine, with the fullest acceptance and satisfaction. But we are not at all sure that this use of Scripture does not sometimes pass beyond the warrant of the theory of Scripture which is afterwards developed. The nerve of this theory is that Scripture is to be received as the word of God, in the language quoted from Professor Robertson Smith, "because the Bible is the only record of the redeeming love of God, because in the Bible alone I find God drawing near to man in Christ Jesus, and declaring to us in him his will for our salvation. And this record I know to be true by the witness of his Spirit in my heart, whereby I am assured that none other than God himself is able to speak such words to my soul." So far so good, we shall certainly say: here is assuredly unassailable reason for finding the voice of God in the Bible. In the Bible alone is there communicated to men the knowledge of God's redeeming love and of its outcome in the saving work of Christ; and to this, when it is once made known to a soul quickened by the Holy Spirit, that soul sets its seal, under that Spirit's gracious influence, that it is truly divine and divinely true. It was not left to Professor Robertson Smith to discover this fundamental argument; what was left to him was to counsel his followers to stop short at this point. And to stop at this point is, as Dr. Denney perceives and justly urges, to stop short of a justification of the detailed use of the Bible text for the ascertainment of Christian doctrine. What is given us by this argument, he tells us, "is really a doctrine of the word of God, or of the divine message to man," and it is therefore "not to be construed as if it were a doctrine of the text of Scripture" (p. 205). True enough. This palmary argument assures us unassailably that God speaks to us in Scripture; but it does not by itself assure us that the Bible itself is God's Word. If we stop with it and seek no further for evidence of the authority of Scripture as a source of knowledge of divine truth, we shall be very apt to find ourselves after a while evaporating the authority of the Scriptures altogether and substituting for it the authority of the Holy Ghost in the heart, by which alone the authority of the Scriptural word is validated for us. This happens also in Dr. Denney's case. "The real question," we observe him saying on one occasion, "is whether the characteristic teachings of the apostles, which constituted at once their theology and their gospel, are guaranteed by the witness of the Spirit" (p. 222). And on another occasion he tells us that "it is not very hard to give an exegetical statement of the whole subject" of eschatology; "what *is* hard is to say precisely what is of faith in the matter, what is made sure to the heart by the witness of the Spirit" (p. 229). Here certainly the authority of Scripture passes into eclipse and the authority of the individual soul under the guidance of the Holy Ghost takes its place. It is surely not necessary to point out that such was not the way the apostles understood the matter. With them the authority of Scripture was the test rather of the professed deliverances of the Spirit in the heart (1 Cor. xiv. 37). Nor ought it to be necessary to say that such was not the way the Reformers understood the matter. With them the formal ground of Christian knowledge was the written Word of God, and the testimony of the Spirit was his creative act upon the heart quickening it to the perception and acceptance of this truth. Let us rejoice that Dr. Denney's practice also is not conformed to his theory; and that his appeals to Scripture transcend his formally defended right to appeal to it. This circumstance may possibly exonerate us from the duty of exhibiting at length his doctrine of Holy Scripture, which seems to us seriously defective at a number of points—in its conception of revelation, of the origin and authority of the canon, of the nature and effects of inspiration, and of the nature and ground of Scriptural authority alike.

19

A REVIEW OF *Systematic Theology**

SYSTEMATIC THEOLOGY. By JOHN MILEY, D.D., LL.D., Professor of Systematic Theology in Drew Theological Seminary, Madison, N. J. Vol. I. New York: Hunt & Eaton; Cincinnati: Cranston & Stowe, 1892, 8vo, pp. xvi, 533, $3.

The high quality of the *Biblical and Theological Library*, now publishing by the Methodist Publication House, does honor to the great denomination which it represents. Dr. Miley's *Systematic Theology* is the latest issue in the series, and it is highly but not unduly praised when it is recognized as worthy to stand in company with Dr. Bennett's *Christian Archaeology* and Dr. Terry's *Biblical Hermeneutics*. It is clearly, directly, and strongly written; it is characterized by candor, restraint, and modesty; it is orderly in arrangement and lucid in discussion. It is altogether a good book, which the Arminian should find rarely satisfying, and with which the Calvinist should count it a privilege to join issue.

It is somewhat embarrassing to undertake an estimate of a half-finished book. When a treatise is occupied, as this is, with a well-known system of thought, the end is no doubt seen from the beginning; but something depends on individuality in the modes of statement and defense. In the present instance the embarrassment is increased by the fact that a number of detailed discussions, belonging to matters treated in this volume, have been postponed to an appendix, to be printed at the end of the second volume. We can scarcely fail, however, to catch from Dr. Miley's clear pages the elements of the doctrines which he would commend.

---

*From *The Thinker: A Magazine of Christian Literature*, April 1893; and *The Magazine of Christian Literature*, Feb. 1895.

An introduction of some fifty pages is occupied with the nature, sources, scope, and method of systematic theology. We miss here a satisfactory discrimination of the theological disciplines; and this has affected somewhat the contents of the volume. The great subject of "Theism," which Dr. Miley makes the first division of systematic theology, we should include in the preliminary discipline of apologetics. On the other hand, this introduction contains very illuminating discussions of such topics as these: the nature of scientific treatment; the scientific basis of Christianity; the right of systematization and the value of dogma: and the method of systematizing—under which occurs a very sensible criticism of the so-called "Christocentric" method. Dr. Miley despairs of attaining a single "unifying principle" in theology, and holds that systematizing must proceed "in a synthetic mode." He therefore follows the customary order of topics.

The sources of theology are distributed broadly into nature and revelation; and these sources are fruitfully discriminated on the basis of "modes of knowledge" (p. 9). Knowledge acquired "in the use of human faculties" is natural; that immediately communicated by divine agency is revealed. In the one case "the *mode of acquisition* is purely human"; "the discovery of truth is mediated by the use of our own faculties." In the other, "it is immediately given by the supernatural agency of God." "It is important," he adds justly, "thus sharply to discriminate these two modes of truth." For, if we lay the stress on source or agency alone, without taking into account also mode of knowledge, we may find ourselves embarrassed before the current pantheizing conception, which, by postulating immanent deity in all human thought, confounds the categories of reason and revelation, and thus does away with the category of revelation altogether, as readers of Dr. Whiton's recent little book, called *Gloria Patri,* have occasion to observe anew. We regret to note Dr. Miley, at a later point (p. 11), apparently deserting this ground. He there seems to posit a reception by heathen men of a divine revelation, which comes to them through their human faculties, and is not verified to the recipient as from God. Here he seems to step beyond the wall of his own definition, with the effect of throwing himself into the hands of the mystic rationalists. We must hasten to add, however, that when he comes to treat formally of mysticism (p. 16), he rejects the mystical path for attaining religious truth altogether, and deals very stringently with the modern doctrine of the Christian consciousness. We must confess that we know not how the views expressed at p. 11, as to a not uncommon revelation to heathen seekers, can be accorded with the criticism here; unless we are to suppose that God is nearer to heathen than to Christians, and deals more intimately with them than with Christians. We may take note, by the way, of the skill and success with which Dr. Miley treats the whole matter of the relation of reason and feeling.

The topics which fall under the head of theology proper are treated with logical power and self-restraint. The term "attribute" seems unduly limited in sense; but the distinction drawn between the "personal attributes" and all others is sound and fruitful. The divine intellect is discussed under the caption of omniscience; and the perplexities which emerge from it for Arminian thought are not disguised (pp. 189 f.). Dr. Miley refuses, however, to be led by these perplexities into a denial of the divine foreknowledge of free actions, which he defends unanswerably against the arguments of Dr. McCabe (p. 181). We cannot think, however, that he has followed out his own arguments to their legitimate conclusions. They not only involve the admission of the certainty (as distinguished from the necessity) of free actions (p. 183), which is all any Calvinist believes; but they distinctly imply the Calvinistic doctrine of predestination. For example, he acutely reduces the difficulties which are asserted to stand in the way of God's foreknowledge of the free acts of men to absurdity, by pointing out that the same difficulties would press equally against God's foreknowledge of his own free acts. This is unanswerable. But it will require an immeasurably more acute logic still to distinguish God's foreknowledge of his future choices, from a fore-intention to make those choices; and this is just the Calvinistic doctrine of predestination. And as it will be impossible to disentangle the future choices of God from those of his creatures, with which they are interwoven in the actual web of life, it will be exceedingly difficult to deny to these creature choices also a place in the comprehensive plan already fore-known in all its parts in eternity, and therefore pre-intended or predestinated. Again, the objection that it would be incon-sistent with the divine goodness to create souls whose rejection of salvation is certainly foreknown, is justly set aside with the remark that nescience will not obviate the objection; inasmuch as it presses almost equally against the creation of souls with the known possibility of their loss, and quite equally against the continuance of the race after the fact of such numerous losses has emerged in experience. But surely the bottom of the matter is not yet reached; for if God creates souls which he certainly foreknows will be lost, he must create them with the intention, in this sense, of their being lost; and this is the whole content of the Calvinistic doctrine of predestination in this case—of that *decretum horribile* to which men seem so unceasingly to object, but which is as surely a truth of reason as it is of Scripture.

The real difficulty here Dr. Miley finds in the very exist-ence of moral evil under the government of God. He con-siders that a complete theodicy is unattainable to human knowl-edge (pp. 429 f.); but we cannot consent to stop at the point at which he elects to stay his efforts to discover one. In this matter, as elsewhere, he appears to go upon a principle which is naturally very attractive to minds of the analytical power of his—the principle of *divide et impera*. The danger is that in the analysis the essence of the question may slip out be-tween the joints. This is what happens here. Dr. Miley shows in turn (1) that the creation of moral beings is per-missible; (2) that a probationary economy is permissible; and (3) that therefore the fall, which is necessarily contemplated as a possibility in a probationary economy, is permissible. Most excellent. But the question still remains for one who accepts, with the frankness of Dr. Miley, the doctrine of God's complete foreknowledge, how could it be permissible to create these moral beings and put them in this probationary economy, with the knowledge, not that they *might possibly* fall, but that they *certainly would* fall? The only tenable ground here is the Calvinistic ground that such action on God's part involves the divine intention, in this sense, of the fall—that is, its predestination. And the only conceivable direction in which to look for a theodicy is in that of an end great and glorious enough to justify the incidental evil arising from this course. Dr. Miley rejects out of hand all such theodicies, on the ground that "the fall itself," in that case, "must have been completely within the disposition of divine providence" (p. 439). But certainly we cannot exclude it from God's providence, as a single question will show. What required God to create just those free agents whom he foreknew would fall? Or shall we say that while he foreknew that some angels would stand and others fall, it was impossible for him to create a *human* free agent whose standing he could foreknow? In that case we must say either that *human* free actions cannot be foreknown (which Dr. Miley denies), or else that all possible *human* free agents would certainly fall, which would make human sin a necessity of nature without developing any theodicy for God's creation of such a nature.

In these remarks on the origin of evil we have, of course, passed out of the domain of theology proper into that of anthropology, leaving much behind of which we should like to speak. It is in the anthropology of the volume, of course, that the Calvinistic reader will find most which will seem to him open to question; and this the more that Dr. Miley occupies in this sphere the extremest Arminian ground. We find much, here too, in the way of care in statement and candor in treatment to admire; and we willingly bear witness to the fairness with which the Augustinian positions are stated. Dr. Miley divides the great question of original sin into three: whether there is such a thing as native depravity; whether it is penal; whether it is guilty. Only the first does he answer affirmatively. He teaches that all men are naturally depraved, and out of that depravity will certainly commit sin; but that this depravity does not come to them in any true sense by way of penalty, but only through the law of nature that "like begets like"; and that, because they are born with it and do not produce it, they cannot be held responsible for it, and it therefore is (as our New England brethren used to call it) "uncondemnable vitiosity." Of course we shall not commit the folly of attempting to refute this, as it seems to us, very refutable position, in the course of this brief notice. Let us only remark in passing that it passes the comprehension of our Calvinistically warped mind to understand how so close a thinker can, on the one hand, hang the whole weight of depravity on a "law of nature," or, on the other, deny the condemnability of a state of depravity which inevitably produces sin in every action into which it issues. What is a "law of nature"? and who made it a "law of nature"? and on what ground of right? To say that all that was threatened to Adam for sin—physical death and its precedent weaknesses and pains and spiritual death or depravity, with its inevitable issue into actual sinning—has been brought upon mankind simply on the basis of a "law of nature," so that the whole race is brought through the mediation of depravity into actual sin and guilt without possibility of escape, on the sole basis of a "law of nature"—is just no explanation at all: it is the deification of a phrase. And to say that a depravity which originally arose in personal action, and which is apparently the same in us as in Adam, and which is the inevitable spring of sin and the actual source of all sinning, is non-condemnable because it is only "a subjective quality"—is to antagonize the most intimate and ineradicable convictions of the human mind. If God looks upon Adam before the fall, and finds him with a "subjective quality" which is "excellent" and "pleasing to the divine mind," how should he not be pleased and show his pleasure? And if God looks upon us, after the fall, and finds us with a "subjective quality" which is not excellent, but depraved and displeasing to his holiness, how should he not be displeased and show his displeasure? Such teaching confounds all our ideas of God as a moral agent.

SYSTEMATIC THEOLOGY. By JOHN MILEY, D.D., LL.D. Volume II. New York: Hunt & Eaton, 1894. 8vo, pp. xix, 537. $3.00.

The second and concluding volume of Dr. Miley's *Systematic Theology* is conceived in the same spirit and executed with the same skill which characterized the first. The first volume included the topics which fall under the heads of Theology proper and Anthropology. This second volume discusses the remaining topics, under the heads of Christology, Soteriology, and Eschatology. Three appendices, on points of interest for which Dr. Miley's plan did not supply opportunity for treatment in the body of the work, conclude the volume. These discuss, respectively, the inspiration of the Scriptures, the angels, and the Arminian treatment of original sin. The material is handled in a masterly manner, and the volume as a whole sets forth the Arminian scheme of salvation in as powerful and logical a form as that scheme admits of. For Dr. Miley presents himself here as above all things an Arminian, and as above most Arminians ready to follow his Arminianism to its logical conclusions. Here, indeed, we find the highest significance of the book. It is the Arminian "Yea" to the Calvinistic declaration of what Arminianism is in its essential nature, where its center of gravity lies, and what it means with reference to that complex of doctrines which constitute the sum of Evangelical truth.

The Remonstrant controversy was a battle of giants. In its earnest grapple, the movement tentatively begun by Arminius tended rapidly toward its level in a distinctively Pelagian anthropology and Socinian soteriology. But in the great evangelical revival of the last century, the Wesleyan leaders offered to the world an Evangelicalized Arminianism. The rationalism of the Remonstrants, they affirmed, was not due to their Arminianism but to their Humanism. The essential elements of Arminianism, they asserted, were in no wise inconsistent with the great Evangelical doctrines of sin and atonement. On the contrary, they declared, the Arminian construction alone gave their full rights to the catholic doctrines of the condemnation of all men in Adam and the vicarious satisfaction for sin in Christ. An Arminianism zealous for these doctrines might well claim to stand on a higher plane than that occupied by the Remonstrants. The question, however, was a pressing one, whether the Evangelical elements thus taken up could consist with the Arminian principle. Calvinists earnestly urged that the union was an unnatural one, and could not be stable: that either the Evangelical elements ought to rule to the exclusion of the unharmonizable Arminian principle, in which case we should have consistent Calvinism; or else the Arminian principle would inevitably rule to the exclusion of the Evangelical doctrines forced into artificial conjunction with it, and we should have consistent Arminianism. After a century of conflict, Dr. Miley's admirably reasoned volumes come to tell us frankly that the Calvinists have been right in these contentions. Arminianism, he says, has no logical place in its system for a doctrine of race sin, either in the sense of the participation of the race in the guilt of Adam's first sin, or in the sense of the infection of the race with a guilty corruption. Arminianism, he says, has no logical place in its system for a doctrine of penal substitution of Christ for sinners and of an atonement by satisfaction. If the Arminian principle is to rule, he says, the doctrine of race sin must go, and the doctrine of vicarious punishment must go. And, as he thinks that the Arminian principle ought to rule, he teaches that men are not by nature under the condemning wrath of God, and that Christ did not vicariously bear the penalty of sin. Thus, in his hands, Arminianism is seeking to purify itself by cleansing itself from the Evangelical elements with which it has been so long conjoined.

The importance of Dr. Miley's attitude in this matter will not be properly estimated until we remind ourselves that he does not stand alone in it. Those who are familiar with recent Arminian theologizing will be aware that Dr. Miley in this is only a representative of a marked present-day drift in Arminian dogmatics. The nature of the impression which this drift will make upon us will doubtless depend, in part at least, upon whether our mind is upon the thinker or upon the thought. There is no one who will not feel regret to see one driven, by whatever stress of logic, from his hold upon fundamental Evangelical doctrine; it is better far to be inconsistently Evangelical than consistently Arminian. On the other hand, the line of thought by which Dr. Miley, for instance, clears away the Evangelical accretions from the Arminian core, commands our complete admiration. It is quiet logic, working its irresistible way to an irrefutable end. And as a matter of constructive reasoning it cannot be other than salutary. It is just as well that the world should come to know with the utmost clearness that these Evangelical doctrines are unconformable with Arminianism. It is just as well that the world should realize with increased clearness that Evangelicalism stands or falls with Calvinism, and that every proof of Evangelicalism is a proof of Calvinism. Dr. Miley's discussions of original sin and the atonement will help the world to perception of this salutary fact.

Under the caption of Christology, Dr. Miley includes only the doctrine of the person of Christ. The complicated questions which arise in the determination of this doctrine, he treats with eminent lucidity and acuteness, although we should dissent from what seems to us a Monothelite element in his own construction of the doctrine (pp. 9, 36, 40, 42). The usual topics which fall under the caption of Eschatology he discusses with sober good judgment under that head. We should dissent only from his difficulty in discovering rational grounds for the terrible indeed, but, as it seems to us, rationally reasonable, as well as Scripturally certain, doctrine of eternal punishment. The larger portion of the volume is given, however, to the great doctrines of Soteriology (pp. 65-419), which form thus, in every sense, the center of the volume. These doctrines are dealt with under the two sub-heads of "The Atonement in Christ" (pp. 65-240), and "The Salvation in Christ" (pp. 241-419). Those who are familiar with Dr. Miley's earlier volume on the Atonement (the discussions in which are here freely drawn upon) will not need to be told that, under the former of these sub-heads, the Governmental theory of the Atonement is expounded and advocated with great freshness and force. Under the latter of them, the "benefits of the atonement" are presented as "immediate" or "conditional," and the latter are developed under the influence of the Arminian principle of "freedom," a very thorough discussion of which is prefixed to the chapters on Justification, Regeneration, Assurance, Sanctification, and, finally, the Church. The whole forms, as we have already said, an unusually well-compacted, logically developed, and lucidly presented exposition of the Arminian system.

We have space only for a few remarks on the discussion of the atonement. The problem was to find a doctrine of atonement conformable to the Arminian *fundamentum*, which Dr. Miley does not hesitate to place in its psychology of the will. "Freedom," he says, "is fundamental in Arminianism. The system holds accordingly the universality and provisional nature of the atonement, and the conditionality of salvation" (p. 275). "The cardinal doctrines of the Wesleyan Soteriology" being thus determined—"that the atonement is only provisory in its character, rendering men salvable, but not necessarily saving them"; and that salvation is conditional in the sense of a real Synergism (p. 169)—"with these facts," Dr. Miley remarks, "the atonement of satisfaction must be excluded," and "the rectoral theory maintained as the only doctrine of a real atonement agreeing with them" (p. 169). The former part of this conclusion, at least, seems to us perfectly solid, and we go thoroughly with Dr. Miley in his clear proof (p. 122) of the untenableness of those schemes which seek to unite an atonement of penal substitution and conditional universalism. Whether the rectoral theory, on the other hand, is the only doctrine of atonement agreeing with the cardinal principles of Arminian Soteriology, or whether the rectoral theory can be properly described as a "doctrine of a *real* atonement," are questions whose answers admit of more doubt.

It is a question of some importance, to ask ourselves seriously whether the rectoral theory, which, as Dr. Miley justly perceives, is the highest form of atonement open to a consistent Arminian, is consistent with the foundation truths of religion.

Is it consistent, for example, with this foundation truth: that sin is inherently ill-deserving, and that God, the infinitely holy and just One, must react upon sin with a moral indignation which is exactly proportionate to its guilt, and which burns inextinguishably until it is satisfied by adequate punishment? Dr. Miley admits that it is not. "If justice," he says, "must punish sin simply for the reason of its demerit, penal substitution is the only possible atonement" (p. 169). That the rectoral theory of the atonement may be held, and with it the Arminian system, therefore, we must deny to God that moral indignation in view of evil, which we cannot help recognizing as one of the highest endowments of moral beings, and must transmute his "justice" into the merely public justice of a wise ruler; we must revise, in a word, all our natural notions of the relations of an infinitely holy being to sin. Dr. Miley attacks this problem at an early point (pp. 93 ff.), the result of his discussion being that he concludes that while punishment may not be inflicted where there is no sin, and may never go beyond the intrinsic demerit of sin—"and God has the exact measure of its desert" —yet sin need not be "punished according to its desert" (p. 97)—provided that the requirements of God's moral government are not endangered by the failure to punish it. In other words, while sin may not be punished beyond its desert, it may be punished below its desert, if it can be rendered "safe" to do so.

Here is certainly one of the watersheds between Calvinism and Arminianism. Those who believe that God must, by virtue of his all-perfect nature, visit sin with a punishment fitted to the exact measure of its desert—no more certainly, but just as certainly, no less—must, so far as logic can compel them, become Calvinists. But it does not seem to follow so stringently that those who take the other horn must hold to the rectoral theory of atonement. It does not seem obvious that, if it be once allowed that sin need not be punished, it is only under the provisions of the rectoral theory that it can be rendered "safe" for God to withhold his punishing hand. If it be "safe" to forgive sin on the ground of a "substitute for penalty," it would seem just as "safe" to make a sincere personal repentance that substitute as to make the suffering of an alien such substitute. In a word, Dr. Miley's argument seems to us to issue in setting aside all real necessity for atonement. He labors hard to exhibit its necessity. But its necessity for what? Not to enable God to forgive sin—that is grounded in his mere compassion, and in itself is always in his power. But to enable God to forgive sin *safely*. Forgiveness itself remains an act of pure grace. The rectoral theory does not appear to have any essential advantage here over those other theories which Dr. Miley so admirably sets aside as no theories of real atonement at all, because they lay no ground for forgiveness. Alike with them, the rectoral theory provides only a revelation of moral truths to men, and it differs from the common moral theory only in the way in which men are held to be affected by this revelation. We do not see that its advocates are in a position to cast stones at these other theories.

A book notice, however, is a narrow space in which to argue so great a question as the nature of the atonement. Let us close by simply pointing out that Dr. Miley is in error in supposing that Calvinists have an issue with him on the question of the extent of the atonement. No "limitationists," as Dr. Miley calls them, will doubt that the atonement does for all, all that a rectoral atonement is fitted to do for any. Dr. Miley has much to say of the "sufficiency of the Atonement." Is it sufficient for all? he asks. Sufficient for all, *for what?* we ask in return. No "limitationist" will doubt that it is sufficient to provide for all "a revelation of such moral truths as give the highest ruling power to the divine law" (p. 195). Every "limitationist" will be forward to assert that the atonement is sufficient to make known to all, God's infinite hatred of sin and his infinite love for sinners, and his infinite yearning that all should come unto him and live. But, if the question be whether it is sufficient to *save* all, it is Dr. Miley who speaks out at once the most emphatic No. It is not sufficient, he tells us, to save any; "it renders men salvable, but does not necessarily save them." Every "limitationist" will affirm that it actually saves many, and that it lays the ground for a free offer of salvation to all. Dr. Miley calls on "limitationists" to answer the categorical question, "Did Christ die for the non-elect?" None will hesitate to reply, Certainly he did, in all the stretch of purpose and effect which the atoning fact, as Dr. Miley conceives it, contains. Dr. Miley himself will not contend that he died for all with the purpose and effect of all that the atoning fact, as the "limitationist" conceives it, contains. There is, in a word, no issue between the parties as to the extent of the atonement. Their issue is as to its nature. Only among satisfactionists themselves has an issue as to the extent of the atonement any meaning: and here Dr. Miley correctly sees that the necessities of the argument are with the "limitationists." He himself solidly argues that an atonement of satisfaction cannot be conditional, and must save all for whom it is wrought.

20

REGENERATION*

Regeneration (from Lat. *re-*, again + *generare*, beget) is a theological term used to express the initial stage of the change experienced by one who enters upon the Christian life. It is derived from the New Testament, where the "new birth" (1 Pet. i. 3, 23; Titus iii. 5; John iii. 3 f.) is the beginning of that "renewal" which produces the "new creature." In the history of theology the term has been used with varying latitude of meaning. Among the Jews it was employed in an external sense to express the change of relation which took place when a heathen became a Jew; from them it was adopted in this sense by many of the Fathers, and is still so used by many advocates of "baptismal regeneration." It is used in the Latin Church to express the whole real change which corresponds to this external change of relation. The Reformers separated justification by itself as something wrought on, not in, the sinner, and employed regeneration to express the whole process of inner renovation in all its stages. In the development of Protestant theology the term has been still further narrowed: first, to express the opening stage of this subjective work as distinguished from its continuance in sanctification; and then, since the seventeenth century, to express the initial divine act in this opening stage itself, as distinguished from the broader term conversion, which includes, along with the act of God, revivifying man, also the act of man in turning to God.

The nature of regeneration is of course variously conceived by different schools, according to their various views of the nature of the soul and its relation to God, of original or habitual sin, and of divine grace.

---

*This article, from Johnson's *Cyclopaedia*, new ed. 1896, was written by "A. A. Hodge and revised by B. B. Warfield."

1. Pelagians, in accordance with their view of freedom and of sin, necessarily regard regeneration as a self-determined change in the general moral course of man's life, an act of the man himself, without any gracious assistance other than that involved in instruction and favorable providential conditions. This was the teaching of Pelagius in the early part of the fifth century; and although not adopted by a historical church, it has been reproduced in various combinations by Rationalists and Socinians.

2. The Semi-Pelagian doctrine taught by John Cassian (d. 440) admits that divine grace (*assistentia*) is necessary to enable a sinner to return unto God and live, yet holds that, from the nature of the human will, man may first spontaneously, of himself, desire and attempt to choose and obey God. They deny the necessity of prevenient but admit the necessity of co-operative grace and conceive regeneration as the product of this co-operative grace.

3. The Mediaeval and Papal doctrine, which is practically that of Thomas Aquinas, and is hence often called "Thomism," admits original sin and the necessity of prevenient grace, but places the efficacy of grace in the non-resistance of the subject.[1] But this grace is supposed to be exercised only through the instrumentality of baptism, which acts as an *opus operatum, ex vi actionis ipsius*, effecting regeneration and the entire removal of sin, and consequently of guilt, from every infant, and from every adult who does not willfully resist (*non ponentibus obicem*).[2]

4. The Arminian view of regeneration admits total depravity and consequent moral impotency, yet holds that man is not really responsible until there is redemptively bestowed upon him for Christ's sake sufficient grace to re-endow him with ability (gracious, substituted for natural) to do right, which grace becomes efficient when the sinner co-operates with it, and thus effects the end intended.

---

[1]See the *Council of Trent*, sess. 6, can. 4, chs. v and vi, and sess. 7, cans. 6 and 8.

[2]*Council of Trent*, sess. 7, can. 6; Bellarmin, *De Sacramentis*, 2, 1.

5. The Synergistic view was held by a party among the Lutherans, under the leadership of Melanchthon. At the Leipzig Conference (1548) Melanchthon said: "There concur three causes of a good action—the word of God, the Holy Spirit, and the human will assenting, not resisting the word of God."[3]

6. The Lutheran standard, the *Formula Concordiae*, teaches that: (1) human nature is spiritually dead; and (2) the Holy Ghost is the sole efficient agent who quickens the dead soul to life, without the least co-operation of the will of the subject; but the non-regeneration of the unbeliever is referred not to the absence nor to any deficiency of grace, but to the positive resistance of the man himself.[4]

7. The Reformed doctrine teaches as follows: (1) As to the nature of regeneration: (a) There are in the soul, besides its several faculties, habits or dispositions, innate or acquired, which lay the foundation for the soul's exercising its faculties in a particular way. (b) These dispositions (moral) are anterior to moral action, and determine its character as good or evil. (c) In creation God made the dispositions of Adam's heart holy. (d) In regeneration God recreates the governing dispositions of the regenerated man's heart holy. Regeneration is therefore essentially the communication of a new spiritual life, and is properly called a "new birth." (2) As to its efficient cause: It is effected by divine power acting supernaturally and immediately upon the soul, quickening it to spiritual life, and implanting gracious principles of action. (3) As to man's action: Conversion (*conversio actualis*) instantly follows, as the change of action consequent upon the change of character, and consists in repentance, faith, holy obedience, etc.[5]

What is called baptismal regeneration is held by members of the Church of England and others in various senses. (1) Some hold that the Holy Spirit through the instrumentality of baptism implants a germ of spiritual life in the soul, which may long re-

---

[3]*Loc. Com.*, p. 90.

[4]*Formula Concordiae*, pp. 662, 666, 582, 677.

[5]*Thirty-nine Articles*, art. 10; *Canons of Synod of Dordt*, ch. iii, art. 3; *Westminster Confession*, ch. x.

main latent, and may be subsequently developed (in conversion) or blasted. (2) Others hold that there are two regenerations— one a change of state or relation, and the other a change of nature; the first is baptismal and the second moral, though both are spiritual, since both are wrought by the Holy Ghost.

21

SANCTIFICATION*

Sanctification (from Lat. *sanctificatio* [deriv. of *sanctificare*, sanctify; *sanctus*, holy + *facere*, make], trans. of Gr. ἀγιάζειν, hallow, make holy, deriv. of ἄγιος, holy) is the work of God's grace by which those who believe in Christ are freed from sin and built up in holiness. In Protestant theology it is distinguished from justification and regeneration, both of which lie at its root, and from neither of which is it separable in fact; inasmuch as the term justification is confined to the judicial act or sentence of God, by which the sinner is declared to be entitled, in consideration of what Christ has done in his behalf, to the favor of God, and of which sanctification is the efficient execution; and the term regeneration is confined to the initial efficient act by which the new life is imparted, of which sanctification is the progressive development. Both regeneration and justification are momentary acts, and acts of God in which the sinner is passive; sanctification, on the other hand, is a progressive work of God, in which the sinner co-operates.

The nature of sanctification, as well as its method and the relation of the divine and human factors in its prosecution, is differently conceived by the several types of theology.

1. The Pelagian and Rationalistic view excludes the action of the Holy Spirit altogether; and makes sanctification to be nothing more than continued right action, in the native powers of the free moral agent, by which he gradually conquers evil tendencies, and builds up a holy character.

2. The Mediaeval and Roman view refuses to distinguish between justification and sanctification; and makes both jus-

---

*From Johnson's *Cyclopaedia*, new ed. 1896; it was written by "A. A. Hodge and revised by B. B. Warfield."

tification and sanctification to be the cleansing from sin, and the infusion of gracious habits by the Holy Ghost for Christ's sake by the instrument of baptism, upon which subjective change the removal of guilt and the divine favor is conditioned.[1] It is therefore held to be progressive, and to be advanced by good works, which possess real merit, and deserve and secure increase of grace;[2] as well as by penances, prayers, fastings, etc., which satisfy God's justice and purify the soul.[3] If the believer dies before the process of deliverance from sin is perfected, he must complete it in purgatory, the pains of which are expiatory and purifying; and there he may be assisted by the prayers and masses and dispensing power of the Church on earth.[4] But it is possible, even before death, for a believer perfectly to conform to all the demands of God's law as graciously adjusted to this life;[5] and it is even possible, out of love, to perform supererogatory service by obedience to the councils of Christ, which are advisory but not obligatory until voluntarily undertaken. These are voluntary poverty, celibacy, and obedience to monastic rule; and they merit more than the mere salvation of the person, and contribute to the "treasury of merits" at the disposal of the Church, which is imputable at the discretion of those holding the jurisdiction to believers on earth or in purgatory not yet fully justified.[6]

3. The Mystical view of sanctification, though never embodied in any church creed, has existed as a doctrine and as a tendency in all ages and among all Christian denominations. Christian mysticism more or less depreciates the dependence of the soul for light upon the objective revelation of the word of God, and the necessity of the means of grace and human effort, and emphasizes spiritual intuition, the regulative value of religious feeling, the physical communion of the soul with the substance of God, conditioned on quiet and passivity of

---

[1]*Council of Trent*, sess. 6, can. 7.
[2]*Council of Trent*, sess. 6, can. 32.
[3]*Council of Trent*, sess. 14, ch. viii; sess. 6, cans. 29 and 30.
[4]Bellarmin, *Purgator.*, ii. 9.
[5]*Council of Trent*, sess. 6, ch. xvi, can. 25.
[6]Bellarmin, *De Monachiis*, chs. vi and vii.

mind. Such views gained great currency in the Church through the writings of the Pseudo-Dionysius, which were published in Greek in the sixth century, and translated into Latin by John Scotus Erigena in the ninth century. They qualified the teaching of many eminent evangelical Schoolmen, such as Bernard of Clairvaux, Hugo and Richard of St. Victor, and subsequently Thomas à Kempis. They were taught with great influence among the early Protestants by Schwenckfeld (1490–1561), Paracelsus (1493–1541), Weigel (1533–1588), and Jacob Böhme (1575–1620); and among the Roman Catholics by St. Francis of Sales (1567–1622), Molinos (1640–1697), Madame Guyon (1648–1717), and Archbishop Fénelon (1651–1715). The original Quakers held similar views, as is seen in the writings of George Fox (d. 1691), William Penn (d. 1718), and Robert Barclay (1648–1690). A mystical conception is present whenever sanctification is conceived, not as the goal of effort, but as an immediate gift to the waiting soul.

4. The evangelical doctrine of sanctification common to the Lutheran and Reformed Churches includes the following points: (1) The soul after regeneration continues dependent upon the constant gracious operations of the Holy Spirit, but is, through grace, able to co-operate with them. (2) The sanctifying operations of the Spirit are supernatural, and yet effected in connection with and through the instrumentality of means: the means of sanctification being either internal, such as faith and the co-operation of the regenerated will with grace, or external, such as the word of God, sacraments, prayer, Christian fellowship, and the providential discipline of our heavenly Father. (3) In this process the Spirit gradually completes the work of moral purification commenced in regeneration. The work has two sides: (a) the cleansing of the soul from sin and emancipation from its power, and (b) the development of the implanted principle of spiritual life and infused habits of grace, until the subject comes to the stature of perfect manhood in Christ. Its effect is spiritually and morally to transform the whole man, intellect, affections, and will, soul, and body. (4) The work

proceeds with various degrees of thoroughness during life, but is never consummated in absolute moral perfection until the subject passes into glory.

In opposition to this doctrine a theory of perfect sanctification in this life has been taught from several distinct points of view, e.g.:

1. According to the principles of Pelagianism, a man is perfect who obeys the laws of God to the measure of his present natural ability, since the moral law is a sliding scale, adjusting its demands to the varying ability of its subject; and this is possible to every man.

2. According to the Mystical idea, perfection consists in absorption in the divine essence, or, in a less extreme form, in the absorption of human desires and will into the divine will, in a disinterested love; and this may be attained by anyone through persistent detachment from self and meditation on God.

3. According to the Roman or Ritualistic theory, perfection consists in perfect conformity to the law of God, graciously for Christ's sake adjusted to the capacities of the regenerated man in this life; and this perfection is attained by means of meritorious works and penances, prayers, fasts, acts of voluntary self-denial, and ecclesiastical obedience. Not only is this within the reach of men, but so is even the rendering of supererogatory service in the way of extra-legal self-denial from a principle of evangelical love.

4. The Wesleyan theory of perfection conceives that the satisfaction and merit of Christ have made it consistent with divine justice to offer salvation to men on easier terms than the old Adamic law of absolute perfection; and that perfection is attained when these lower terms have been complied with. "Christian character is estimated by the conditions of the gospel; Christian perfection implies the perfect performance of these conditions, and nothing more."[7]

---

[7]Wesley's tract, *Christian Perfection: Methodist Doctrinal Tracts;* Dr. George Peck's *Christian Doctrine of Perfection.*

22

HOW SHALL WE BAPTIZE?*

The broad simplicity which characterizes the allusions of
the New Testament to the sacraments stands in very striking
contrast with the anxious precisianism of the ecclesiastical prescriptions. A treatise on baptism, for example, especially if
it emanate from one of the sacerdotal Churches, is apt to insist
upon many details in the manner of applying the water which
are quite foreign to the New Testament notices of the rite.
We open, for instance, a recent Roman Catholic work on the
Sacraments, and read, broadly enough: "The proximate matter
of baptism is washing, which may be performed not only by
immersion, but also by affusion or aspersion."[1] But there are at
once added, with solicitous care lest the whole thing should fail
by defect, certain prescriptions of what is requisite to "true
washing." There must be, it seems, "(a) physical contact of
the water with the body, (b) successive contact by the motion
of the water over the body; and that, indeed, (c) in some quantity, that is to say, not in a drop or two, nor so that it has only
the form of unction." This concern for little things is not altogether a growth of time. The earliest of "Church Orders"—
the *Teaching of the Twelve Apostles*—already shows great
regard for such minutiae. We are to baptize, we are there told,
"in living water." "But," it is graciously added, "if thou hast not
living water, baptize in other water; and if thou canst not in
cold, in warm; and if thou hast neither, pour water thrice upon
the head in the name of Father, and Son, and Holy Spirit."[2]
Needless to say the New Testament has no care for such things.

---

*From the *Methodist Review Quarterly*, Oct. 1911, pp. 1-20.
[1]G. van Noort, *Tractatus de Sacramentis Ecclesiae*, I. 1905, pp. 135 ff.
[2]Chapter vii.

329

It simply commands that the disciples of Christ shall be introduced into their new relations by the rite of baptism; indicates
incidentally that the element with which this baptism is to be
performed is water; and, absorbing itself in the ethical and
spiritual significance of the rite, leaves its externalities to one
side.

We are not to infer, of course, that we are free to make of
baptism pretty much what we choose. The limitations imposed
upon our mode of administering such a sacred rite by the great
law of decency and order (1 Cor. xiv. 40) are not less stringent,
they are only less petty, than those exacted by that disease of
religion we call formalism. It is not to be denied that these
limitations have frequently been overpassed; perhaps as often,
certainly as seriously, through overvaluation as through contempt of the ordinance. We are all shocked when we hear of
such manifest disregard of what is becoming as is evinced in
the following anecdotes. John Mason Neale relates that a
clergyman "taking the duty" in a little English parish, on being
called upon to baptize an infant, found no water in the font.
"He thought it, of course, an accidental omission, and asked
for some. The clerk was in astonishment; however, he sent
for a glass of water, thinking the clergyman wanted it to drink.
And on conclusion, it came out that they never used it there."[3]
"At St. Martin's Church, Birmingham," writes Mr. A. C. Benson in his *Life of Archbishop Benson*, "on Sundays there were
held what were called 'public christenings,' at which persons to
be baptized were arranged round the communion rails, and
sprinkled from the font with a brush, like a Roman asperging
brush."[4] But thoughtless corruptions like these are, in the
nature of the case, exceptional.

The perversions of the rite which tend to become regular are
rather such as are dictated by a sense of its immense importance. Thus the Jesuit missionaries in Canada, urged on by
their belief that by the mere act baptism worked salvation, reduced it to a bald magical performance. "They had a special

---

[3]*Letters to John Mason Neale, D.D.*, 1910, p. 33.
[4]Vol. I, p. 6. The date of the occurrence is about 1830.

delight in baptizing dying infants, thus, as they believed, rescuing them from the flames of perdition"—we are quoting
Sir William Robertson Nicoll's account:

They did not hesitate to use equivocal methods in attaining
their end. Their practice of baptizing infants at the point
of death led the Indians to believe that baptism was a cause
of death. So when the priest entered a lodge where a sick
child lay in extremity, the scowling parents watched him
with jealous distrust, lest unawares the deadly drop should
be applied. How the Jesuits met the emergency is told with
great pride by one of themselves. He says that a Jesuit
Father baptized a little child two months old, in manifest
danger of death, without being seen by the parents, who
would not give their consent. "This is the device which he
used. Our sugar does wonders for us. He pretended to
make the child drink a little sugared water, and at the same
time dipped a finger in it. As the father of the infant began
to suspect something, and called out to him not to baptize
it, he gave the spoon to a woman who was near, and said
to her: 'Give it to him yourself.' She approached and found
the child asleep; and at the same time Father Pijart, under
pretense of seeing if he was really asleep, touched his face
with his wet finger, and baptized him. At the end of forty-
eight hours he went to heaven." Another of these naive
stories may also be told in the words of the missionary. A
little boy, six or seven years old, was to be baptized. "His
father, who was very sick, had several times refused to receive baptism; and when asked if he would not be glad to
have his son baptized, he had answered, No. 'At least,' said
Father Pijart, 'you will not object to my giving him a little
sugar?' 'No; but you must not baptize him.' The missionary gave it to him at once; then again; and at the third
spoonful, before he had put the sugar into the water, he let
a drop of it fall on the child, at the same time pronouncing
the sacramental words. A little girl, who was looking at
him, cried out: 'Father, he is baptizing him!' The child's
father was much disturbed, but the missionary said to him:
'Did you not see that I was giving him sugar?' The child
died soon after; but God showed his grace to the father,
who is now in perfect health." They would do anything to
get at a sick infant. No menace and no insult could repel
them from the threshold. They pushed boldly in and talked
till suspicion was lulled to sleep, and then, pretending to

observe the sufferer for the first time, approached it, felt its pulse, asked of its health, and then dexterously touched it with a corner of a handkerchief previously dipped in water. They murmured the baptismal words with motionless lips, and snatched another soul from the fangs of the infernal wolf.[5]

And what are we to say of the filthy habit of immersing, at the great baptismal seasons, multitudes of children, sick and well alike, one after another, in the same font? One does not wonder that "the contamination of the water by skin diseases" has been suggested as one of the coöperating causes which led to the giving way of the practice of immersion to affusion in the Latin Church.[6] The entire subject is discussed by the Russian Bishop Hermogen in a formal treatise, after a fashion which would be amusing were it not so distressing. The infant, according to him, is to be baptized preferably in cold water, and the plea that the cold water may injure it is not to be admitted—to add hot water "makes it no longer natural, but artificial."[7] If overtimid parents persist, then let the water be brought in some time before using it, that the chill may get off of it. How can there be any danger of the child taking cold and dying from the touch of the baptismal water, when it is immersed into it with the very object that it may receive from it new and spiritual life?[8] Timorous people may demur too to their children being immersed in the same font and at the same time

---

[5]*The British Weekly*, April 20, 1911, p. 158.

[6]J. Bellamy, in Vacant-Mangenot, *Dictionnaire de Theologie Catholique*, Vol. II. I. Abrahams, *Journal of Theological Studies*, July 1911, pp. 609-612, thinks sufficient cleanliness is secured, even when very small fonts are used, by the Jewish practice of the recipients bathing before their baptism one after the other in the same font.

[7]A translation of the treatise appeared in *The Church Eclectic* for August, 1900, pp. 431 ff.

[8]Similarly President A. H. Strong (*Systematic Theology*, ed. 1909, Vol. III, p. 940) bids those who doubt whether immersion can have been intended by Christ to be the universal mode of baptism, because, forsooth, it is often dangerous to health and life, to remember that "ardent feeling nerves even the body," and adds the lines: "Brethren, if your hearts be warm, ice and snow can do no harm." Can they not? And is it not written again, "Thou shalt not tempt the Lord thy God"?

with children suffering from contagious diseases. "To remove all such fears," let some of the water be drawn off into a separate receptacle, and let all the well children be baptized in the font itself, and *all those with diseases* (no matter how various!) be baptized, one after the other, in this separate receptacle! Surely fanaticism must hold the helm hard down, when the simplest laws of hygiene cannot be recognized as laws of God. Have we not good authority for saying, "The Sabbath was made for man, not man for the Sabbath"?

Clearly we cannot let either indifference or fanaticism determine for us how we should baptize. Not, however, because we particularly fear that our baptizing might be rendered invalid. A very indecent mode of baptizing may be a perfectly valid mode of baptizing. The method of baptizing which used to be practised at St. Martin's Church, Birmingham, will strike most of us as indecorous in the extreme. Yet it is precisely this way of baptizing which so sound a scholar and solid a thinker as the late Dr. Samuel J. Baird considered the right way to baptize, the way, he did not doubt, which was employed on the great Pentecost, when Christian baptism was inaugurated under such happy auspices—"the water being sprinkled with a hyssop brush, and the recipients of the rite presenting themselves in companies of suitable size, by scores or by hundreds."[9] We should not like to pronounce the mode of baptism seriously preferred by Dr. Baird no baptism at all. And who would have the heart to declare the poor little Russian babies to have passed through their infected bath in vain? If we are going to demand that our baptismal water shall be pure and clean, on pain of not being baptismal water at all, how pure and clean must we demand that it shall be? Must we have distilled water, fresh from the retorts? Would it not be better to remember that this water does not cleanse the flesh, but the soul, as Cyprian very patly reminds us, when discussing an analogous question—the question, to wit, whether a whole bath is required for valid baptism, or true baptism can be ad-

---

[9] S. J. Baird, *The Great Baptizer; A Bible History of Baptism*, 1882, p. 451.

ministered with only a little water sprinkled on the person? Does not the Lord himself say, he asks, "Then will I sprinkle clean water on you, and ye shall be clean" (Ezek. xxxvi. 25)?[10] To cleanse the soul, it is not a question either of the purity or of the abundance of the water, but of purity of intention and abundance of faith.

No doubt all perplexity would be at an end if the New Testament only prescribed a mode of baptism. But so would be at an end that evangelical freedom for which Christ has set us free; we should so far be entangled again in a yoke of bondage —and who knows how little leaven it may take to leaven the whole lump? We are not living under a legal dispensation, with its minute enactments and precise requirements. We are living in the freedom of the gospel (in which all things are summed up in holding fast the Head); and we should not wish to subject ourselves again to ordinances ("Handle not, touch not, taste not"), nor permit ourselves to be judged in the mere externalities of our observances. The simple breadth of the New Testament dealing with baptism is consonant with the whole spirit of the gospel, and if it leaves us without precise guidance as to how we are to administer the rite, this can cause us perplexity or distress only if we are not yet fully emancipated from a legalistic habit of mind. How shall he who has received the washing of regeneration and renewal of the Holy Ghost, poured out upon him richly by Jesus Christ his Savior, be solicitous, in publicly announcing this his great experience by means of an appropriate rite, how the symbolical water should be applied to his person? So only he sets forth openly that he is "washed," shall he not be satisfied? And may he not fitly remember the proverb with which our Lord once instructed one of his disciples: "He that has been washed [really *washed*, all over] has no need to lave [the reference is to bathing only a portion of the person]—except his feet"?

It may meanwhile be worth while to make clear to ourselves the little concernment the New Testament takes with the mode

---

[10]*Epistle lxix.* 12-14 (Hartel's ed., 1871, p. 760; E. T. in *Ante-Nicene Library*, Am. ed., V, p. 401).

of baptism. It is much understating the matter to say that it does not prescribe a mode of baptism. It does not even suggest one mode as preferable perhaps to another. It does not so describe any instance of baptism as to show interest in how it was performed, or to tempt us to look upon it as an example having normative value. It does not, indeed, in any of its allusions to baptism, make it unambiguously clear exactly how it was administered. In a word, not only can we not discover in the New Testament any authoritative directions for the right performance of the rite, but it is impossible to be quite sure precisely how the acts of baptism alluded to in the New Testament were performed. He who goes to the New Testament, therefore, in the hope of obtaining exact information as to how to baptize, is doomed to a quick disappointment. And he who affirms of any particular way of baptizing that it, and it alone, is valid baptism, has an immense burden of proof resting on his shoulders. He can produce no justification of his affirmation from the New Testament, in the way either of express assertion, or authoritative example, or unambiguous implication. And is it not a sound Protestant principle that only the Holy Spirit speaking in the Scriptures has the right authoritatively to order the things of the house of God?

Perhaps the place occupied by baptism in general in the New Testament is commonly exaggerated. It is not a subject on which the New Testament greatly enlarges. This does not prove that it is of little importance. But it does seem to show that there are few details concerning it which are of large importance. The New Testament considers it enough to establish it as the initiatory rite of Christianity, outline its significance in broad touches, and let it go at that. The terms "baptize," "baptism" occur, no doubt, with some frequency, in the pages of the New Testament.[11] But in a large number of these occurrences the reference is to the baptism of John the Baptist; in some others, to the Jewish lustrations; and in yet others the terms are used metaphorically. Comparatively few are left to

[11]The verb, seventy-four times; the noun, in its two forms, twenty-three times.

refer to Christian baptism. There is but one mention of the Christian rite of baptism in the Gospels.[12] This occurs in the "great commission" (Matt. xxviii. 19), in which the risen Lord sends forth his followers to make disciples of all the nations, incidentally adding that the disciples, when made, were to be baptized and instructed. In the book of Acts the baptism of Christian converts is currently mentioned—some ten instances occur in all[13]—but little is added to the mere notice of its administration. Then there are about the same number of allusions to baptism in the Epistles, chiefly in the Epistles of Paul; but these allusions are always incidental, and baptism is never mentioned for its own sake.[14] This is the entire material with which the New Testament supplies us with reference to the ordinance. The few passing allusions to it in passages where it is not named are not such as largely to advance our knowledge of it.[15]

What we are now to take note of is that in no one of this meager list of New Testament allusions to the Christian rite of baptism is there any prescription, recommendation, description, or even clear intimation of the mode in which the rite was to be, or was, administered. In the sole allusion to baptism made by our Lord (Matt. xxviii. 19), he simply commands that those gained to him by the preaching of his followers should be baptized "with reference to the name of the Father, and of the Son, and of the Holy Ghost," and adds absolutely not one word more on the subject. In all the ten accounts of baptizings in Acts, there is not a single description of the mode of its

[12]Mark xvi. 16 occurs in the spurious conclusion of Mark.

[13]Acts ii. 38, 41; viii. 12, 13, 16, 36, 38; ix. 18; x. 47, 48; xvi. 15, 33; xviii. 8; xix. 5; xxii. 16.

[14]Rom. vi. 3, 4; 1 Cor. i. 13-17; xii. 13; xv. 29; Gal. iii. 27; Eph. iv. 5; Col. ii. 12; Heb. ix. 10; 1 Pet. iii. 21.

[15]This would not be quite true if we could admit allusions to baptism in John iii. 5; Eph. v. 20; Tit. iii. 5; 1 Cor. vi. 11; Heb. x. 22 [Rev. i. 5]. This, however, we can by no means do. John iii. 5 was spoken before Christian baptism was instituted; and the "washing" of the other passages has no reference to the rite of baptism, concerning which this word is never employed in the New Testament (Acts xxii. 16 is no exception).

administration, nor even an incidental suggestion from which it may be confidently inferred how the baptism was performed.

Appeal has been made, it is true, to the graphic narrative of the baptizing of the Ethiopian chamberlain (Acts viii. 36 ff.) as implying immersion: "And they both went down into the water, both Philip and the eunuch; and he baptized him. And . . . they came up out of the water." That they went down (from the chariot) into the water for the baptizing is no proof, however, that the baptizing was by immersion. There are other modes of baptizing besides immersion, which can be administered only in the water. Affusion on the head of a recipient standing in shallow water, for instance, is the ordinary mode of baptism depicted in the early decorations of the Roman catacombs,[16] and it is more probable that it was this mode which was employed in the case of the Ethiopian eunuch (and in the baptisms of John the Baptist) than immersion. The situation and character of this "water," met with in the desert (of which we know nothing), may indeed have made it more convenient to enter the water for baptism in any mode, even that of sprinkling. The plain fact is that we are told nothing in this passage of the manner in which baptism was administered; we are only told of certain circumstances accompanying it, from which we can infer that immersion would be possible—provided the "water" was large enough and deep enough, and other circumstances of which we are told nothing concurred to make it suitable.

If we knew otherwise that immersion was the customary mode of baptism in the Apostolic Church, we should naturally infer that Philip and the eunuch went down into the water in order to immersion: in our actual situation of entire ignorance of how the Apostolic Church baptized, there is no ground for this inference. And this is the sole hint given us in any of the accounts of baptism, which even to this extent suggests an inference of immersion as the mode of administration. On the

---

[16]The whole subject of the archaeology of baptism is carefully discussed by C. F. Rogers in *Studia Biblica et Ecclesiastica*, Vol. V, Part 4: Oxford, 1903.

other hand, appeal has been made to the account of the baptism of Cornelius (Acts x. 47, 48) as implying baptism with a small quantity of water: "Can anyone withhold water, that these should not be baptized?" Certainly the question would be very natural if the water was to be brought. The inference is, however, scarcely stringent; and similarly, though it seems on the face of it unlikely that there were facilities for immersion in the Philippian jail, or that the immense number of converts on Pentecost were all immersed, these are not things that could be insisted upon were there reason to believe that immersion was actually employed. It remains true, therefore, that the accounts in Acts supply no data for confident conclusions as to the mode of baptism which was in use. When we have duly weighed every possible hint in them, we find ourselves still without knowledge.

Nor is it different with the allusions in the Epistles. Those who have been accustomed to think of baptism in the mode of immersion have, it is true, always not unnaturally seen that mode of baptizing alluded to in Rom. vi. 3, 4, Col. ii. 12, where we are said to be buried with Christ through or in baptism. There is no allusion in these passages, however, to the manner in which baptism was administered, as if by the very action the burial of the Christian with Christ, and his rising again with him (though this rising again is probably not connected with baptism in either passage), were visibly enacted in symbol. It is the spiritual experience of one who is in Christ Jesus which is adverted to, and baptism is mentioned only as the outward act by which the union of the soul with Christ is marked. Whoever has become united to Christ by that faith which is confessed in baptism, has ideally shared his death and resurrection (Rom. vi. 8, 9). He can say: "When Christ died it was my death. He died, and I died with him; he lay in the tomb for me, and I lay therefore buried there with him; and in his rising again, I, too, rose again to God." It is of this great spiritual fact that Paul is speaking in Rom. vi. 3, 4 and Col. ii. 12, and he has no more reference to the mode of administering baptism in these passages than he has in Gal. iii.

27, where he refers to the same great fact under another figure. "As many of you as were baptized with reference to Christ," he there exclaims, "did put on Christ." Does he imply that baptism was administered after a fashion which visibly symbolized changing one's clothes? As little in the passages now before us does he imply that baptism was administered after a fashion which visibly symbolized burial with Christ. He only asserts that every baptized person professes to be a participant in the death and burial and rising again of his Lord.

Indeed, the introduction of the symbolism of the external rite of baptism into the thought of these passages throws each of them into confusion. In one of them (Col. ii. 12) Paul is expressly engaged in warning his readers against permitting themselves to be drawn off into attaching importance to external ordinances. They had Christ: all the fulness of the Godhead dwells in Christ; and those who have Christ have in him everything. Why, then, should they be circumcised? They have already in Christ everything that circumcision stands for— "seeing that they have been buried with him in baptism," "in whom also they have been raised again through faith in the working of God who raised him from the dead." Is it possible to take this "burial in baptism" of the external symbol? Is it not necessarily the spiritual fact which is thus adduced? The other passage (Rom. vi. 3 ff.) is plainer still. "Or, know ye not that whosoever of us were baptized with reference to Christ Jesus—it was with reference *to his death* that we were baptized? We were buried, then, with him through"—what? Baptism? No. But "through this baptism *with reference to his death*." It is only by thus formally establishing a connection between baptism and the death of Christ, that Paul establishes a connection between baptism and burial with Christ. This he even labors to accomplish. Our baptism had special reference to *the death* of Christ, he argues, proclaiming a "blood theology"; and if it had thus special reference to *the death* of Christ, so that we may claim that he died for us and we therefore died with him—we may say we were buried with him in this baptism which has been shown to have special reference to his death.

Why should he make all this roundabout argument to connect our baptism with Christ's burial, if baptism in its very mode of administration was vocal with this connection? Is it not quite clear that Paul did not presuppose in his readers—or, indeed, hold for himself—a view of the external symbolism of the act of baptism which saw in it burial with Christ and resurrection with him vividly enacted in object lesson? We are not saying that we can learn from this passage that baptism was not to Paul an immersion. We are saying that we cannot learn from this passage that baptism was to Paul an immersion. He is not appealing in it to the symbolism of the external rite; so far from implying that the symbolism of the external rite was burial and resurrection with Christ, he clearly betrays that he knew of no such symbolism in it. He is appealing to the great spiritual fact which is signified by baptism, under one of the favorite figurative modes of expression by which he was wont to speak of it. The outcome is that we can learn nothing from these passages of how baptism was administered by Paul and his fellows. And that means, to put it briefly, that the New Testament nowhere either prescribes or suggests to us how this rite is to be administered; and nowhere does it even allude to the rite in such a way as to supply ground for a confident inference as to its mode of administration.

No doubt this complete silence of the New Testament on the mode of baptism is due in part to the absence of all need to instruct its original readers on such a matter. Everybody in the circles primarily addressed by the New Testament writers knew perfectly well how baptism was accustomed to be administered by the apostles and their helpers. The mere mention of baptism was enough for them; from their own daily experience they would supply all the details of the customary ceremony. We can scarcely suppose, however, that if great importance had been attached to some particular method of administering the ordinance, it would have been possible for the New Testament writers to allude to it cursorily and never drop a hint from which this important, perhaps indispensable, element in its administration could be inferred. That no such

hints have been dropped seems to imply that no great importance was attached to the externals of the rite, that the great
things about it were the things of which hints have been
dropped, to use no stronger language—its ethical and spiritual
significance. And meanwhile the effect of the failure—if we
may call it that—of the New Testament writers, in their allusions to baptism, to drop any hint of how it should be administered, has been for us (whatever it may have been for their
first readers) that we are left in ignorance of how they baptized
and of how they would have us baptize. If any real importance
does attach to the way in which the rite is administered; if any
special mode of administering it is essential to its validity, integrity, reality (call it what you will)—we are left not only
without intimation of this fact, but in the very unhappy condition
of never being sure we are administering the rite validly, in its
integrity, reality, because wholly without information of what
that mode of administering it is which is necessary to its validity,
integrity, reality. The natural inference surely is that the
silence of the New Testament writers as to the proper mode of
administering the rite means that they attached no great importance to the mode of administering it, but that their interest
in the rite lay elsewhere.

Of course it is easy to say that the New Testament writers
did not need to prescribe or intimate the mode in which baptism should be administered—because that service is performed
by the term itself. We are told that the baptism instituted by
our Lord was not a new thing invented by him, and needing to
be described elaborately in its mode of administration. It was
adopted from the baptism of John the Baptist, who had himself
adapted it from earlier rites, and, in its mode of administration,
it of course followed John's method of administering it. We
may therefore learn from John's baptism how Christian baptism
should be performed. The command to "baptize" carries with
it the command to do what "baptizing" was known to be—in
John's hands. Moreover (so we are told), the very term employed—"baptize"—has a perfectly definite meaning, and itself
conveys all the information needed to secure its proper ad-

ministration. We have but to do the thing which our Lord
told his followers to do when he instructed them to "baptize,"
and we shall find ourselves in possession of a perfectly definite
mode of baptism, varying from which we cease to "baptize."

How, then, did John baptize, if we are to get our method of
baptizing from him? And what is that mode of baptism which
is intimated to us by the very term itself? When we seriously
face these questions we find ourselves as much in the dark as
before. In plain fact we do not know precisely how John baptized; and the term "baptize" does not bring us any trustworthy
intimation of its mode.

Certainly, in the accounts that have come down to us of his
baptizing there are no detailed descriptions of how John
performed the rite. And any incidental hints which may occur in
the narratives from which we may fancy the manner of his
baptizing may be inferred, are both few and quite inconclusive.
They amount merely to intimations (1) that John chose places
for administering his baptism where there was abundance of
water: "all the region round about Jordan" (Luke iii. 3), or
Enon, "because there were many waters there" (John iii. 23);
and (2) an occasional ambiguous use of prepositions which
may be pressed to imply immersion. Abundance of water
might be needed, however, even though immersion was not
practised: much water was required, for example, for baptism
by pouring on the head of a recipient standing in the water—a
mode of baptism certainly very anciently in vogue. Might not
abundance of water, indeed, be desirable for places in which
crowds assembled, even if it were not necessary for the purposes of baptism itself? Who can tell whether the "many
waters" at Enon were of size and depth sufficient to allow
true immersion, or were otherwise convenient for the rite?
When we read, as we do in two instances (Matt. iii. 6; Mark
i. 5) that "John baptized in the river Jordan," we naturally
think of his taking the recipient into the water for the purpose;
and this impression is strengthened by the occurrence in one
passage (Mark i. 9) of a phrase which is rendered in our
Revised Version, "baptized into the Jordan." But this latter

phrase may just as well be rendered "in Jordan" and so conformed to the other passages; or it may be equally well rendered
"at Jordan," as it is rendered (for example) in Acts xxi. 13
"at Jerusalem"; and it is, after all, just as easy to baptize
a man "in Jordan" by affusion as by immersion. Nothing is
really gained by overpressing the implications of prepositions
which were, in point of fact, employed very flexibly at the stage
of the development of the Greek language when the New Testament was a-writing.[17] If we insist that, because the phrase
which, in the strictness of the original implication of the preposition, means to "come up out of the water," occurs in Mark
i. 10 (cf. Acts viii. 36), we must suppose that the persons so
spoken of were in the water, why not equally insist that, because in the parallel passage, Matt. iii. 16, the preposition
occurs which says only that "they came away from the water,"
we must suppose that the person spoken of was not in the
water? If we read that John's baptism was "in water," we cannot fail to remember that this expression may just as well be
rendered "with water," and that it is actually interchanged
with the simple "with water" in parallel passages, and that
in such a manner as to show that Matthew and John prefer
"in water" and Mark and Luke "with water"—that is to say,
the difference is merely a matter of style.[18] In a word, there
are no materials here on the ground of which a confident
decision can be reached as to how John baptized; all that we
are told of his baptizing would fall readily in with more than
one conjecture as to its mode. We may form an opinion of
our own in the matter, which may be more or less plausible;
but a dogmatic conclusion which we can impose on others as

---

[17]For a good account of the use of these prepositions in New Testament
Greek, consult Blass, *Grammar of New Testament Greek*, E. T. 1891,
p. 122. Conybeare and Stock, *Selections from the Septuagint*, 1905, p. 80,
illustrate the LXX usage. Perhaps the closest parallel to Mark i. 9 in the
New Testament is John ix. 7, "Go, wash at the pool of Siloam," where
the preposition designates merely the place at which the washing was to
be done, the washing of the eyes only being in question.

[18]"In water," Matt. iii. 11; John i. 26, 31, 33; "with water," Mark i.
8; Luke iii. 16; Acts i. 5; xi. 16.

authoritative determination of fact cannot be attained. Even if we were sure, then, that Christian baptism must needs follow that of John in mode—and of that we are far from sure—we could not learn from the notices of John's baptism how we should baptize.

Shall we fall back, then, entirely upon the intrinsic implications of the term itself? What are the intrinsic implications of the term itself? It has certainly been widely customary to say they are those of immersion; and this has even sometimes been sharpened into the assertion that the command to baptize is nothing but a direct command to immerse—"baptize" means "immerse," and when we are told to "baptize" we are just told to "immerse" and nothing else. This contention rests, however, upon a complete misapprehension of the philological facts.

It is quite true that the primitive root, to which the word "baptize" goes back, bears the sense of "to be deep"; and that the primary verb from which "baptize" is immediately formed has as its fundamental meaning "to dip," from which it advances, however, to express such secondary ideas as "moistening," "washing," "dyeing," "tempering," "imbuing," without the least implication that these effects have been produced by "dipping." It is even employed to express the "imbuing" of the mind with certain states—of course without any implication of "dipping"—as, for example, when we read of one "imbued with righteousness to his very depths," that is to say, taking all his color and temper from righteousness. "Baptize" is formed from this primary verb by the addition of a termination (represented in its English form by the syllable "-ize") which gives it a frequentative or intensive meaning. It might take its starting-point in any one of the senses—primary or secondary— of the verb from which it is formed. It might very well, therefore, mean originally "to dip," or "to moisten," or "to cleanse," or "to dye," and the like—only not "to dip," "to cleanse," and the like, simply, but, in accordance with the implications of its form, "to dip" or "to cleanse," and the rest, *repeatedly* or *effectually*, the emphasis falling, of course, in contrast with its primitive, on this added idea. In its usage it was rather an intensive than a frequentative verb, and in point of fact its common meaning in profane Greek is "to overwhelm," whether literally or metaphorically. "Baptized" ships are sunken ships; "baptized" sailors are drowned; cities are "baptized" in sleep; men are "baptized" with cares or debts, or with wine, so that "baptized" came to mean "drunken." The word does not occur, however, in this its common classical sense in the New Testament—unless we interpret from it the somewhat enigmatical use of it in Mark x. 38, 39, Luke xii. 50. It appears in the New Testament in a somewhat special sense, developed by Jewish tongues on the basis of the numerous lustrations required by the Jewish law, by which it came to mean just "to cleanse," "to purify." As the classical usage had taken its start from the idea of dipping effectually—with the effect, namely, of destroying, and so the word had come to express the idea of overwhelming without any implication of the process by which the overwhelming was accomplished; so the Jewish usage had taken its start from the idea of dipping effectually— with the effect of cleansing, and so the word had come to express the idea of purifying without any implication of the process by which the purification was wrought.

"Baptize," in other words, in the New Testament, expresses the single idea of purification, and does not connote any mode of the application of the water for the production of this purification. The notion of "dipping," which lay in the background of the development of the term, had passed as fully out of sight as the notion of a specifically *evening* meal has passed out of sight when we speak currently of the Lord's Supper, or the notion of *age* when we speak of the elders of the Church. "Baptism" appears on the pages of the New Testament just as the technical word for ceremonial purification, and does not contain in it any implication of the method by which this purification is wrought.

The process by which the word "baptize," as the technical term for ritual purification, displaced the word for "washing," which is employed of the Jewish lustrations in the Greek Old Testament, cannot be traced in detail for lack of material. It was in itself, however, a natural replacement to make. The implication which the intensive form, "baptize," bore of the efficacy of the "washing" for the object in view, gave the word an advantage over all other terms for designating ceremonial purification. In any event, the substitution was complete by the time the New Testament was written. In the Apocryphal books and in the New Testament—Ecclus. xxxiv. (xxxi) 25 (30); Mark vii. 4; Luke vi. 38; Heb. ix. 10—it is the standing term for the Jewish lustrations; and the designation of John's purificatory rite as a "baptizing," and of himself, its proclaimer, as, by way of eminence, "the baptizer," bears vivid testimony to the establishment of the term in its new sense. It is clear that, at this epoch, when men thought of a lustration which cleansed, they thought of it under the special designation of a "baptism." This was the "laving" which was effectual for the end in view. The broad language of Heb. ix. 10 in adverting to the lustrations of the law—"divers baptizings"— already brings us a suggestion of the width of the connotation of the term: however the Jewish lustrations were performed, they were all "baptizings." This is the term accordingly that is employed for the lustrations customary among the Jews before eating (Luke xi. 38, 39), by which are meant (according to Mark vii. 3 ff.) either the mere bathing of the hands (which was performed by affusion) or the "sprinkling" (for "sprinkling" is the right reading in Mark vii. 4, for which its synonym "baptizing" has been substituted by some copyist) of the person. Mark adds (vii. 4) that the Jews were accustomed to "baptize" also their (wooden) cups and pots and their brazen vessels—surely not always by immersing them; and some old copyist, who is at any rate a witness to the usage of his time, adds "couches" to the list, to immerse which would, of course, be out of the question, despite the mediaeval suggestion of Maimonides that "beds" (not quite the same thing) may be immersed in sections!

Possibly the most striking indication of the extension of the word to all modes of purification, however, is found outside the limits of the New Testament, in one of those few passages in which what is its settled usage in the New Testament crops out earlier. In the Apocryphal book of Ecclesiasticus, xxxiv. (xxxi) 25 (30), there is a warning against playing fast and loose with the laws of purification. When one became unclean by contact with a dead body, it was provided that he should be sprinkled with "the water of separation" on the third and on the seventh day, whereafter he should "wash his clothes and bathe himself with water" (Num. xix. 11, 19). Apparently the sprinkling with "the water of separation" was to cleanse him from the pollution of the dead body, and the bath, to cleanse him from the uncleanness which the "water of separation" seems to have brought upon all who were concerned with it (Num. xix. 1-22). Now what the Son of Sirach declares is that if anyone, after having had "the water of separation" sprinkled upon him, touches the corpse again, he cannot profit by the subsequent bath. This is the language in which he does this: "He that is baptized from a dead body and touches it again, what availeth his washing?" What, in other words, is the use of his proceeding to the bath, if he has defiled himself again after the sprinkling? The act of purification from the dead body, which was by sprinkling, is here distinguished, as a "baptism," from the subsequent bath, which is designated, in accordance with the usage of the Greek Old Testament, a "washing." "Baptism," of course, does not mean "sprinkling" here; but it is freely used of a purifying rite which was performed by "sprinkling." That is to say, it bears a sense wide enough to be used of all rites of purification, with entire indifference as to the mode of their performance; and the command to "baptize" is therefore not just a command to immerse, and would not have been understood as a command to immerse. There is in the term no intrinsic implication of any mode of applying the water, and we are left by the New Testament accordingly without any instruction as to how we are to baptize.[19]

How, then, are we to baptize? Lacking definite instruction

---

[19]The word accordingly appears in recently discovered Papyri, Christian and heathen alike, in the simple sense of ceremonial cleansing (cf. Moulton and Milligan, *The Expositor*, VII. vi. p. 377).

from the New Testament, and even clear example, it is obvious that we are thrown back upon the nature of the ordinance itself to suggest an appropriate mode of administering it, under the great law of decency and order. Baptism is, first of all, a symbolical rite; and its symbolism, naturally, should be the prime consideration in its mode of administration. By the washing of the body with water it represents the washing of the soul from sin in the blood of Christ. The first law of its administration is, therefore, that it shall be a washing. It is true, it has been common from an early date to insist upon another symbolism for it. In it, it is said, we are buried with Christ and rise again with him; and it is, therefore, to be so administered as to set forth this, its great lesson. To men accustomed to see baptism administered by immersion it has no doubt been not unnatural to interpret Rom. vi. 3 ff., Col. ii. 12, as suggesting such a symbolism for the rite. It has already been pointed out, however, that this is a manifest mis-interpretation of these passages; and outside of them no support can be found in Scripture for attributing such a symbolism to it. Throughout Scripture, baptism is, in its external nature, just a cleansing, washing, symbolizing the cleansing of the soul by the blood of Christ. It is the gospel of salvation, pictured forth in significant action—the "congealed Word." He who receives it, by that act confesses himself a sinner in need of salvation; recognizes full provision for that salvation in the blood of Christ; and in vivid object lesson represents this salvation as taking effect on him. It is not a mere part of the saving process which baptism symbolizes—not merely what we currently call "regeneration," for example; nor merely the cleansing of the soul from the pollution of sin, or its power, as distinguished from its guilt—the "subjective side" of salvation: but the whole of salvation, conceived as a cleansing—a cleansing from at once the guilt and the pollution and the power of sin. The two sacraments symbolize, not different parts or elements of salvation, but each the entirety of salvation, under its own particular figure. What distinguishes baptism from its companion sacrament is just that it symbolizes salvation as a cleansing; and therefore, we say, it should be so administered as vividly to set forth the act of cleansing.

In the symbolical rites of the Old Testament, cleansing is symbolized, now by a complete bath, now by affusion, now by sprinkling; and the symbolical rites of the Old Testament are not only our divine textbook in religious symbolism, from which we rightly derive instruction in the art, but they actually determined the form which the symbolical rites of the New Testament took. We are clearly within the bounds of decency and order when we follow their suggestions. Some, under the tutelage of passages like Ezek. xxxvi. 25, may consider the act of sprinkling the most significant possible symbol of the cleansing signified by baptism. Others, influenced by such passages as Joel ii. 28, may see in the act of pouring a more appropriate method of showing forth a cleansing the active agent in producing which is the Holy Spirit. Others still may prefer immersion as more fully picturing the completeness of the cleansing signified. Each of us may legitimately exercise his own preference, and within the limits set by the essential symbolism of cleansing, give effect to it in act. But surely no one, in the actual state of the case, is entitled to insist that his own preference must be adopted by all, on pain of being pronounced disobedient to the command of God and disregardful of the sacramental action which God has appointed.

So narrow an attitude with reference to the administration of this sacrament is a novelty of the modern Church; throughout the whole history of the ancient Church, the validity of baptism in more modes than one was never widely questioned. And oddly enough, the mode of baptism in the interest of which this narrow attitude has been taken up is itself a novelty of the modern Church. Certainly never in the ancient Church, and, for all that appears, never before the middle of the seventeenth century, was it customary to baptize by laying fully clothed recipients down on their backs in the water. But perhaps the oddest thing of all about this strange attitude of precisian scrupulosity in so slender a circumstantial of the sacrament of cleansing as the mode of applying the water in the symbolical bath, is that it is taken up by a body of Christians who show no tendency to such rigor in the minutiae of ritual detail in any other department of worship—who, for example, do not insist, in administering the sister sacrament, on anxiously preserving its character as specifically an *evening* meal (in accordance with its New Testament designation);[20] on receiving it always in a reclining attitude (as its first recipients received it); or even on administering it with unleavened bread (with which it was undoubtedly instituted). Surely this diverse dealing with the two sacraments is a mystery of inequality. Meanwhile those who have been called into freedom may safely go on their way and keep themselves clear of ordinances of men in the sacraments of our Lord's appointment, holding fast the Head, and publishing steadfastly the gospel of his salvation at once in the spoken Word and in the pictorial representations of the sacraments of his blood.

---

[20]Charles Chauncey, second president of Harvard College (1654–1672), was more consistent. He insisted both that baptism should be by immersion, and that the Lord's Supper should be celebrated only in the evening (Winthrop's *Journal*, ed. 1853, I. pp. 397-399; II. pp. 86, 87).

23

THE POSTURE OF THE RECIPIENTS AT THE LORD'S SUPPER*

A FOOTNOTE TO THE HISTORY OF REFORMED USAGES

What was revolted from by the Reformers as idolatry of the worship of the Church of Rome, culminated and found particular expression in the ceremonies of the mass. Much of the disputation at the Reformation centered, therefore, around the Lord's Supper; and the restoration of it to its original significance and mode of administration was one of the marks of the Protestant churches. The position of the recipients of the elements became, accordingly, among other matters of more intrinsic importance connected with this rite, an object of interest and even of controversy. The fundamental fact, determinative of all such questions for the Reformed, is that the Supper is a feast and is to be administered at a table. This fact is thus expressed by Heinrich Heppe in his summary of the Reformed doctrine of the Supper: "And since further the Lord's Supper is not an act of sacrificing, but a feast of communion resting on the sacrifice of Christ, it is not to be celebrated on an altar, but on a table, the table of the Lord."[1]

Heppe does not think it necessary to adduce any further voucher for the truth of the representation that this is the Reformed Doctrine, than the simple statement of Burmann's[2] that the first Supper was instituted "at the common table," and therefore the papists are wrong in erecting altars in the

---

*From the *Journal of the Presbyterian Historical Society*, June, 1922, pp. 217-234.
[1]*Die Dogmatik der evangelischreformirten Kirche*, 1861, p. 456.
[2]*Synopsis Theologiae*, 1699, VII. x. 45.

churches, and the Lutherans only less so in giving the tables the form of altars. That he confines himself to Burmann's testimony is not due to poverty of witnesses at his disposal; but to lack of occasion for adducing witnesses to a fact so notorious. From the very beginning of their existence, the Reformed churches had insisted that the Supper is a meal and is to be administered at a table. Philip Schaff describes for us "the first celebration," at Zurich, "of the communion after the Reformed usage . . . in the Holy Week of April, 1525, in the Great Minster." "The communicants were seated around long tables, which took the place of the altar, the men on the right, the women on the left. They listened reverently to the prayers, the words of institution, the Scripture lessons, . . . and to an earnest exhortation by the minister. They then received in a kneeling posture the sacred emblems in wooden plates and wooden cups."[3] Except for the circumstance that the elements were received kneeling, this might stand as a description of a typical Reformed celebration of any age.

The Reformed did not, it is true, consider the posture of the recipients in the Lord's Supper of intrinsically large importance.[4] Our Lord, they noted, at the institution of the Supper, distributed the elements to recumbent recipients. There is no reason, however, they thought, why we should perpetuate that posture; and it is probable that no one desires to do so. It was the primitive posture only because it was the customary posture of participants in a feast at that time and in that region. It belongs, therefore, to the accidents of the celebration; and naturally no other attitude substituted for it can take a higher

---

[3]*History of the Christian Church*, Vol. VII, p. 60. If anyone wishes to read a more vivid description of the scene, he will find it in J. H. Merle D'Aubigné's *History of the Great Reformation of the Sixteenth Century* (First American edition, Vol. III, 1842, p. 273): "The people then fell on their knees; the bread was carried round on large wooden dishes or platters, and everyone broke off a morsel for himself; the wine was distributed in wooden drinking cups; the resemblance to the primitive Supper was thought to be the closer." Cf. Rietschel, in Herzog (*New Schaff-Herzog*, Vol. VII, p. 38).

[4]We are summarizing in this paragraph the discussion of Bernard de Moor in his *Commentary on John Mark's Compendium*, Vol. V, p. 624.

than accidental place. The posture of the recipient is in itself
an indifferent matter, to be determined by the choice of each
church in accordance with the customs of its land and day.
We may very properly receive the elements standing, as was
done in antiquity[5] and is done now in some of the Reformed
churches, as, for example, in France.[6] They may properly be
received walking, as is done in the church of Leeuwaarden in
Frisia, in order to suggest readiness for service. They may
properly be received also sitting, as is usual in Reformed
churches, because this is the customary attitude at feasts in
the countries they inhabit, and the Lord's Supper is a feast
and should be celebrated as a feast. They may even, so far as
the posture itself is concerned, properly be received, in order
to express our humility, kneeling—though this surely is an
indecorous attitude at a feast. Not only is this posture that of
the Romanists, but it obtains also among many German
Protestant churches and in the Church of England, and, we
may add, also among the Bohemians.[7]

The elements may properly be received in any of these atti-

---

[5]Dionysius of Alexandria, third century, describes a participant of
the Lord's Supper as "standing by the table and stretching forth his
hands to receive the blessed food" (Eusebius, *Ecclesiastical History*,
VII. ix. 4; McGiffert's translation, p. 297). But De Moor need not have
confined himself to this instance. Samuel Cheatham (Smith and
Cheatham, *Dictionary of Christian Archaeology*, I, p. 416) sums up an
extended survey of the early notices by saying: "All the testimonies of
ancient writers adduced in this article, so far as they determine anything on the point, describe the communicants as receiving *standing*. As
this was the usual posture of prayer and praise on every Lord's Day and
during the Easter solemnities, the faithful would naturally communicate
standing on such days." Apparently the patristic posture of reception
may be broadly said to be standing.

[6]De Moor with apparent emphasis says he has himself seen them do it
thus in France; but it was not only in France that the custom was in
use.

[7]In the Bohemian Confession of 1609 (Müller, *Die Bekenntnisschriften der Reformirten Kirche*, p. 487) we read: "And after these things
have been done thus, the ministers with all reverence distribute the
sacrament; the people on their part receive it piously and religiously, as
far as possible [*ut plurimum*] kneeling, free from all idolatry and superstition, with thanks and praises."

tudes. But they are not equally desirable attitudes, and the complication of kneeling with the idolatry of the mass has rendered it now, though no doubt indifferent *per se*, eminently improper. Unsuitable in itself to the festival symbolism of the rite, it has become, through its association with the idolatry of the mass, at the least very compromising. There are really left, therefore, since the posture of walking is a mere local eccentricity, only the two postures of standing and sitting, to choose between. The National Synod of Dordt of 1578 gave its judgment in these terms: "We think standing or sitting in the administration of the Supper a matter of indifference (we omit kneeling on account of the superstition and peril of the adoration of the bread), and the churches may make use of whichever manner seems to them most convenient."[8] And the Hungarian Confession of 1562 (called by Müller the "Erlauthal Confession," that is, the Confession of "the true church" *in valle Agrina*), determines in the same sense. "*Stando sedendo libere sumimus,*" it says.[9] But, that liberty may not be carried too far, it adds: "We prohibit the superstition of kneeling, prostration, stretching out the hands, because they are signs of adoration." In accordance with this judgment, the customary posture of reception in the Reformed churches is either sitting or standing. In the Reformed German churches they stand;[10] in Scotland and Holland they sit.[11] A somewhat similar differ-

---

[8]Art. 69. De Moor quotes Beza and Voetius to the same effect.

[9]Müller, *Die Bekenntnisschriften der Reformirten Kirche*, 1903, p. 300.

[10]At the International Conference of the Evangelical Alliance at Basle in 1879 there was a united Communion Service in the Cathedral, "where a great crowd, of various nations, walked to the communion table, and there received (standing) the sacred elements from the hands of the clergy in their black gowns" (J. B. Figgis, *Keswick from Within*, 1914, p. 73). Cf. J. Westbury Jones, *Figgis of Brighton*, 1917, p. 114: "The vast congregation made up of representatives of the different churches, went up in files to the Holy Table; the communicants, according to the Lutheran form, received the elements standing, and a verger led them back to their seats." Standing is, no doubt, the general Lutheran form; but it is the form of the German Reformed also, and it is accordingly the form in use in the American German Reformed Churches.

[11]G. Rietschel in Herzog (*New Schaff-Herzog*, Vol. VII, p. 38) traces the custom of sitting in the Scotch and Dutch usage alike, to the in-

ence in custom obtains in the Lutheran churches, but there between standing and kneeling; in Wurtemberg and Bavaria they stand, in Schleswig-Holstein they kneel; and both postures are in use in the American Lutheran churches. In the Anglican Church the posture is kneeling.

The circumstance that the custom of receiving the sacrament kneeling has been retained from the old church by the Church of England, has given the history of the posture of reception an altogether peculiar character in Britain. The Scots followed the ordinary Reformed habit of sitting; and, working out in its support a fully developed theory, zealously propagated it, matching the gradually hardening English doctrine of the necessity of kneeling with an equally strong assertion of its complete inadmissibility. It was not the Scots only, however, who looked askance at the English custom. It was from the first alien also in England itself to the feelings of the more advanced Protestants; and it remained always an offense to the leaders of the more Reformed wing of the Church of England. We find William Tyndale, for example, speaking of the celebration of the sacrament, evidently from the point of view that conceived the proper posture of the recipient as sitting. "Come forth reverently unto the Lord's table," he says, "the congregation now set round about it and in their other convenient seats."[12]

Cranmer, on the other hand, insisted on retaining the posture of kneeling, and thus secured for this posture, in the end, the status of the prescribed mode in the Church of England. Until the framing of the second Prayer Book of Edward VI, in 1552, kneeling had not indeed been specifically ordered; and the injunction to it was inserted into that Book in opposition to growing criticism, and retained in the face of a vigorous assault upon it led by John Knox, who was then one of the King's Chaplains.

---

fluence of the orderly service drawn up by John à Lasco in 1550 for the church of the Dutch Refugees in London. "The communion bore the character of a family meal. The minister, elders, and members of the congregation sit around the table as far as there is room . . ." and this process is repeated as often as is necessary.

[12]"Of the Supper of the Lord"—*Works*, Parker Society Edition, Vol. III, pp. 265 f.

Through the influence of Knox, who came up to London after the Book had been printed, a supplementary rubric was, against the protest of Cranmer, inserted on a fly-leaf, in which it was explained that the posture of kneeling which was directed was not to be interpreted as implying that any adoration is done, or ought to be done, either unto the sacramental bread or wine then bodily received, or unto "any real and essential presence there being of Christ's natural flesh and blood." It was to be understood solely as a mark of thankfulness for the benefit received through the ordinance. This rubric, however, was expunged under Elizabeth; and although its restoration was repeatedly asked for by the Puritans, in the course of her reign[13] and subsequently, it was not restored until 1661, and then in a form which high Anglicans are accustomed to represent to themselves as somewhat weakened.[14]

The dissidents in the congregation at Frankfurt, even in their most extreme demands, we observe, did not get so far as "kneeling at the holy communion." "We gave up . . . kneeling at the holy communion," they say.[15] Indeed, the English clergy themselves seemed little inclined at the accession of Elizabeth to press the rubric which prescribed this attitude. There was even a suggestion made that standing and kneeling might be made alternative modes. Cecil proposed such a rubric to Bishop Guest, and Guest agreed that the two might be treated as indifferent alternatives. The motive lay, of course, in the fact that standing had Patristic warrant, and, as T. W. Perry says, "it was the external form of devotion in the Greek

---

[13]See, for example, *A View of Popishe Abuses yet Remaining in the Englishe Church*, 1572, one of the two admonitions prepared under the influence of Cartwright and presented to Parliament in that year. There is an allusion to it in Hastings' *Encyclopedia of Religion and Ethics,* Vol. X, p. 509a.

[14]Cf. F. Proctor and W. H. Frere, *A New History of the Book of Common Prayer*, 1901, pp. 83 ff.; and J. H. Blunt, *The Annotated Book of Common Prayer*, 1866, p. 199. Also L. Pullan, *The History of the Book of Common Prayer*, 1900, pp. 316 ff.

[15]Cox and others to Calvin in *Original Letters of the English Reformation*, 1754.

Church."[16] Later in Elizabeth's reign, it is interesting to observe, the despairing Puritans vainly petitioned to be permitted to receive the elements standing. They no longer cherished any hope of being allowed to sit; and standing commended itself to them as a practice in use in the Continental Reformed churches.[17] A proposition providing "that the order of kneeling" at the communion "may be left to the discretion of the ordinary" was rejected in the lower House of Convocation in 1562 by only a single vote, and that a proxy.[18] But the Queen was of less tolerant temper, and insisted on the posture of kneeling. In actual practice, we may be sure, throughout her reign as in those of her successors, the posture of reception varied from locality to locality, in accordance with the more or less marked Puritanism of the administrat or recipients.[19]

It must be borne in mind that this long controversy in the English Church concerned not the place but the attitude of the reception of the elements. Whether they were received kneeling or sitting, the people remained in their accustomed places in

---

[16]This notion comes strongly into view in Bingham's argument (*Orig. Eccles.*, Book XV, ch. v, no. 3; Vol. VI, pp. 406-451). He reaches the conclusion that "the ancients received the elements, sometimes standing, sometimes kneeling, never sitting."

[17]Cf. T. W. Perry, *Some Historical Considerations, relating to the Declaration on Kneeling Appended to the Common Office of the English Book of Prayer*, 1863, p. 64, citing Strype, *Annals*, Vol. I, p. 83. A great deal of interesting historical material has been gathered by Perry, whose purpose is to plead for an objective doctrine of the Presence in the Lord's Supper, and for the propriety of kneeling reception.

[18]Strype, *Annals*, Vol. I, pp. 336-339.

[19]The liberty claimed in this matter reached its culmination, of course, in the uproarious times of the mid-seventeenth century. The *Mercurias Rusticus* for 1646, p. 22, tells of the town of Chelmsford, that it was so full of sectaries, "especially *Brownists* and *Anabaptists*, that a third part of the people refuse to receive the blessed Sacrament, unless they may receive it in what posture they please to take it. They have among them two sorts of Anabaptists, the one they call the Old men or *Aspersi,* because they were but sprinkled; the other they call the New men, or the *Immersi,* because they were overwhelmed in their Rebaptism." It was particularly the Brownist protest against receiving the Lord's Supper kneeling which caused this difference as to the attitude of reception.

the church. The elements were consecrated at a small table so placed that all might see them, and were then taken by the minister and given to the communicants at their seats. It was part of the reactionary movement which culminated in the domination of Laud, to insist upon the table being placed altar-wise at the eastern end of the church, upon a raised platform, and railed in as a peculiarly sacred place, to which the people should be brought in order to partake of the sacrament. Under this rule, the railing in of the communion table was required under penalties, and there are, therefore, among the cases of maladministration reviewed by the Long Parliament and reversed, a number which concern the excommunication and arrest of church-wardens for refusing to rail in the communion table.[20] Parliament, in all cases of the sort brought before it, ordered the rails to be removed, the chancels to be leveled to the same plane with the rest of the church, and the tables to be removed to some other convenient place in the church.[21] The case of Dr. Layfield may be taken as a particularly instructive one for our purpose. He was reported to Parliament, as a delinquent, by the Grand Committee for Religion on November 25, 1640. Among the charges was that "he refused to give the sacrament to his people unless they came to the altar, though having offered reverently kneeling to receive the same in the body of the church." Further, he had "caused one Boulton to be excommunicated for not coming to the rails to receive, and refused to read his absolution." "He said he would not for £100 come from the rails to give the sacrament, nay, he would rather lose his living."[22] Here, kneeling in the body of the church emerges as the regular mode of receiving the sacrament, the statutory mode; while the requiring of the recipient to come to the rails is the reactionary innovation. The advanced Protestant mode of reception differed, therefore, from the statutory and more usual method in use in the Church of England, solely in the posture of the recipient. The re-

---

[20]Lords' Journal, IV. p. 56.
[21]Commons' Journal, II. p. 278; III. p. 220; cf. Rushworth, V. pp. 358 f.
[22]Commons' Journal, II. p. 35.

cipients in both methods remained at their seats; only, the more advanced Protestant—the Puritan—remained seated, while the Anglican assumed the attitude of kneeling. Accordingly, the Independents, who represented the advanced party in this, remained seated throughout the church at the celebration of the communion, and were served by the minister in this scattered distribution, to the great scandal of the Scots.

For the Scots revolted from the Independent method of celebrating the sacrament, as savoring of irreverence, with almost as much repulsion as from the Anglican method, as savoring of superstition. The "accommodation" proposed by the author of the tract, *Consilium de reformanda Ecclesia Anglicana* (London, 1643), published on the eve of the Second Reformation, which proposed to treat sitting or kneeling in the reception of the communion as an *adiaphoron*,[23] would have in no wise pleased the Scots, who would have been unable to content themselves with either method as practised in England. For the Scots had a way of their own of celebrating the communion of which they were very tenacious. This way required not merely that the recipients should sit, but that they should sit at the table as guests at the festival of the Lord.

The Scotch method, as we have seen, was in accord with that in use in the Dutch Reformed Churches,[24] and indeed even received support from the earlier English Reformers. Tyndale, for example, as we have seen, speaks of the people as seated "round about the table"; although he adds, "and in their other convenient seats." From this we may perhaps infer that in the custom he was commending, as many as could be

---

[23]See Mitchell, *Baird Lecture on The Westminster Assembly*, p. 118, note.

[24]This is the way the principle is expressed by A. Kuyper (*College-dictaat: Locus de Sacramentis*, p. 179)—the Dutch method being the same as the Scotch: "The Lord's Supper must be a feast. The Lutheran, Romanist, and Anglican Churches, which set out no table, go thus wholly wrong. It is not as mendicants that we are received. But Jesus spreads a feast for his friends, and as King invites his people to his table."

accommodated at the table sat there as a sort of object lesson; while the rest of the communicants sat throughout the room as convenience dictated—a mode of administering the rite to which Gillespie objects on the ground that "if some come to the table, and some not, this is not agreeable to that ἰσοτιμία, or equal honour and dignity, which all the communicants ought to have; natural decency, as well as scriptural warrants, are of equal concernment to all the communicants."[25] The Scots naturally found more support, however, from the custom of the foreign Reformed in England. For, as Henderson urged in the debate at the Westminster Assembly, "The Church of France, when it is in London, sits." It was so provided in John à Lasco's *Forma*, which was in use in 1551, and was printed at Frankford in 1555.[26] His description of his service, as held in London in 1555, closely resembles that of the Scotch tradition. The communion table, set in the sight of the congregation, with the recipients ranged on three sides, the *Ecclesiastes* in the middle, lies open on the fourth side to the view of all the people. To it, then, the people, each party in its turn, come, sit, receive, rise, and depart, one of the ministers reading the 6th chapter of John or other appropriate Scripture, as company gives way to company. "In the French Church at Canterbury," said Herbert Palmer, in the course of the debate at Westminster, "twelve hundred communicants receive it thus." And, he pleads, "we who have gratified one another for satisfaction

---

[25]*Miscellany Questions*, XVIII; *Works*, II. p. 956. In the debates at the Westminster Assembly of the Subcommittee on the Directory (Gillespie, p. 101) it is recorded that "Mr. Marshall, Palmer, Herle, and Goodwin, too, said it was enough that the elements be blessed on the table, *and that some sit at table*, but that the elements may be carried about to others in their pews or seats." To this Gillespie responded that Christ made use of a table and that with significance (Luke xxii. 30); that a table was used at Corinth and the apostle calls it "the Lord's table" and gives it a significance; and further, "The nature of a feast requireth that the guests be set at table, and that all the guests be set about it, for the use of a table is not for some, but for all the guests, else no table is necessary but a cupboard." These points are enlarged on in the discussion in his *Miscellany Questions*, XVIII.

[26]See *Opera*, ed. Kuyper, II. p. 10, and cf. pp. 62 f.

of particular brethren, ought to give satisfaction to the Church of Scotland" in this.[27]

Certainly the Church of Scotland was insistent for satisfaction in the matter. Kneeling, of course, it put out of the question. An attempt had been made to impose this on it in the Laudian persecution through which it had just passed; and that attempt had been resisted as requiring of it sheer idolatry. It is only necessary to read over the allusions to the matter in Samuel Rutherford's *Letters* to learn the uncompromisingness of the Scottish attitude. He warns his parishioners at Anworth, from whom he had been torn, to stand fast in the faith of Christ as they had received it—as in other things, so also in this, that they "should in any sort forbear the receiving the Lord's Supper but after the form that he had delivered it to them, according to the example of Christ our Lord, that is, that they should sit, as banqueters, at one table with our King, and eat and drink, and divide the elements one to another.[28] So, says he, they will escape "the superstition and idolatry in the instant of receiving the Lord's Supper."[29] The express idolatry of the kneeling reception he argues in formal Latin syllogisms,[30] and then throws these syllogisms into nervous passionate English in an attempt to hold back a wavering nobleman from guilty conformity. "I verily believe," says he, "that there was never idolatry at Rome, never idolatry condemned in God's word by the prophets, if religious kneeling before a

---

[27]Leishman, *The Westminster Directory*, 1901, p. 124, directs attention to a passage in Goulburn's *Life of Dean Bingham* (II. p. 16) from which it appears that something like the Scotch custom may not have been unknown in certain instances in the Church of England. Dr. Goulburn speaks of "those quiet Holy Communion services in the chancel of St. Mary's, where, according to old custom, we did not leave our seats, but the fair linen cloths were placed all around the chancel over the broad book-desks. He would come down, and as he administered," etc. But it does not appear that the recipients did not *kneel*. To receive each man in his place *kneeling* is indeed "according to old custom" in the Church of England.

[28]*Letters* (Bonar's ed., New York, 1850), p. 122.

[29]P. 357.

[30]P. 163.

consecrated creature, standing in the room of Christ crucified, in that very act, and that for reverence of the elements (as our Act cleareth), be not idolatry. Neither will your intentions help, which is not of the essence of worship; for then, Aaron, saying 'Tomorrow shall be a feast for Jehovah,' that is, for the Golden Calf, should not have been guilty of idolatry; for he intended only to decline the lash of the people's fury, not to honor the calf. Your intention to honor Christ is nothing, seeing that religious kneeling, by God's institution, doth necessarily impart religious and divine adoration, suppose that our intention were both dead and sleeping; otherwise, kneeling before the image of God, and directing prayer to God, were lawful, if our intention go right."[31] His exhortation to his correspondent is, therefore, "to refuse to bend his knee superstitiously and idolatrously to wood or stone, or any creature whatever." It would have been quite useless to cast oneself against this stone wall, and the English in truth had no impulse to do it.

Standing came as little into question here as kneeling, although many in the Assembly were not averse to it, and the Independents later made it an alternative with kneeling or sitting in their Savoy liturgy. Sitting, then, was agreed on, though with no great enthusiasm on the part of the English. But when it came to the demand that the sitting should also be at the table, there came a direct clash which promised to be final, and was overcome only by mutual concessions and ambiguities. Not only did Baillie asseverate that the Scotch would stand to their custom, as might be expected of one so deeply committed as he was to the "old ways," but even the more accommodating Henderson declared: "We, sent from the Church of Scotland, are all of one mind on this point: we can hardly part from it—nay, I may add we may not possibly part from it." The English were just as firm on the other side. Baillie gives this account of the situation in the Subcommittee of the Great Committee: "We agreed so far as we went except in a table. Here all of them oppose us and we

---

[31]P. 260; cf. pp. 343, 359, 376.

them. They will not; and saith the people will never, yield to alter their practice. They are content of sitting albeit not as a ryte institute;[32] but to come out of their pews to a table they deny the necessitie of it. We affirm it necessary and will stand to it."[33] In the Assembly itself the debate of this one point—the communicating at a table—consumed three weeks;[34] "the unhappie Independents insisting that there should be no coming up to any table, but a carrying of the elements to all in their seats athort the church."[35] The non-Independents, under appeals like that of Palmer, already quoted, were willing to yield the matter for the sake of the Scots, but the Independents persisted. "This day," says Baillie on one occasion, "we were vexed that in the Assemblie, we thought we had passed with consent sitting at the Table; but behold Mr. Nye, Goodwin, and Bridge cast all in the howes denying to us the necessity of any table, but pressing the communicating of all in their seats without coming up to a table. Messrs. Henderson, Rutherford, and Gillespie, all three disputed exceedingly well for it with arguments unanswerable, yet not one of the English did joine with us, only Mr. Assessour Burgess, who then was in the chair, beginning to speak somewhat for us but a little too vehementlie, and so mett with by the Independents that a shamefull and long clamor ended their debaite. This has grieved us that we fear the end of our worke, alwayes [however] we expect it shall be better."[36]

The truth was the debate was a struggle between the Scots and the Independents, the rest of the divines feeling no great personal interest in it, but being willing to favor the Scots as a piece of courtesy. The result was the formulation of the rubric in the words: "The communicants orderly sitting about the table"—which Baillie[37] correctly describes as "a general expression which by a benign exposition would infer our Church practice." Of course the Scots were not satisfied with this, and in the review of the Directory (having received instructions

---

[32]That is, they agree to accept sitting, but not by strict prescription.
[33]Ibid., II. pp. 148 f.
[34]Ibid., II. p. 204.
[35]Ibid., II. p. 195.
[36]June 28, 1644; Letters, II. p. 199.
[37]Ibid., II. p. 204.

from Scotland) they asked for a recommitment of the passage, or else that their sense might be expressed in the margin. This, says Lightfoot, "cast a long and large debate," at the close of which it was concluded thus to have it in the text, "about the table or at it as in the Church of Scotland," and so, adds Lightfoot, "they retain their custom and we of England are left at liberty." And "so"—this is his conclusion of the whole matter—"it was the sense of the Assembly that we might at liberty either cause the communicants to sit at the table or at some distance about it."[38] When the Book went up to Parliament, the words, "as in the Church of Scotland," were stricken out and the rubric left reading merely: "the Table being decently covered, and so conveniently placed, that the Communicants may orderly sit about it, or at it"—which certainly gives no direct prescription at all. Accordingly, when the Scotch Assembly came to establish the Directory and to put it into execution (February 3, 1645), it added this proviso: "Provided always, that the clause in the Directory of the Administration of the Lord's Supper which maintaineth the Communicants sitting about the Table or at it, be not interpreted as if, in the judgment of this Kirk, it were indifferent, and free for any of the Communicants not to come to, and receive at the Table; or as if we did approve the distributing of the elements by the minister to each Communicant, and not by the Communicants among themselves."

The upshot of the matter at the Westminster Assembly, then, it may be said, was that each party was left to enjoy its own custom. Only, the Scots have not, in point of fact, abided by their custom. They have on the contrary gradually assimilated their usage to the much disliked Independent method of distributing the elements to communicants seated "athort the church." In one of the chapters of his *Miscellany Questions* (XVIII), Gillespie argues the whole Scotch position with his wonted point; and indeed there was much to say for it. Centrally, this is to be said for it: that in this, above all other

---

[38]P. 306.

methods of administering the Lord's Supper, the main significance of the rite as a sacrificial feast is preserved. Gillespie
touches the very core of the question when he remarks that in
its general notion and nature the Lord's Supper "is an *epulum,
a banquet or feast*"—"no sacrifice but *epulum ex oblatis*, a
feast upon the body and blood of Christ, offered upon the
cross for us"; and "therefore we ought to come to the table of
the Lord to receive the mystical food in the sacrament, as well
as we come to our ordinary table for our ordinary food."[39]
Here is the very essence of the rite proclaimed and placarded
before us in the very mode of its administration; and this is
a very valuable thing to preserve.

But it may be said that necessity knows no law; and this
mode of celebrating the sacrament was doomed by its inconvenience. Whenever large companies were to partake, the
repetition of the tables interposed a strain upon both ministers
and people which was scarcely endurable: and the matter was
complicated by the break which the successive tables made in
the sense of communion in the participation of the sacrament.
How can that be thought of as a common feast shared in by
all, at which only small companies successively partake? The
desire for simultaneous communion of the whole congregation
thus powerfully reinforced the natural impulse to shorten and
simplify the service. The result has been that even in Scotland,
after all the strenuousness of the Scotch insistence upon this
mode of administering the sacrament, it has given way, and
passed practically out of use. It was no less a man than
Thomas Chalmers who was the instrument in giving it its
death blow.[40] In order to accommodate the large numbers of

---

[39]Pp. 94, 96.

[40]William Hanna, *Memoirs of Chalmers*, Vol. II, pp. 392 ff. Cf. Leish-
man, *The Westminster Directory*, p. xxxviii. The actual method of Chalmers' celebration seems to have been to spread white cloths on the
bookracks of certain pews so as to simulate a table. Chalmers draws a
very distressing picture of the confusion and inconvenience attending the
old way of celebration at successive tables, when the number of communicants was large. He himself tells us that he was not the originator
in the Scottish Establishment of the new method (*Memoirs*, p. 393).

communicants in his new church of St. John's, at Glasgow, to which he was transferred in 1818, "his people were allowed to communicate in their pews."[41] Those of the Tron Church, which he had left, followed their example. Complaint was made to the General Assembly,[42] which reaffirmed the old law of the Church. Attempts to enforce the law (1827), however, failed[43]—and that was the beginning of the end. "The tables" are today seldom seen in Scotland.

The Scottish and Irish Presbyterians and the English Independents, as was natural, each brought to America its own manner of administering and receiving the Lord's Supper. It is probably to the tenacious hold of the Presbyterians on their view of how it should be celebrated that Jonathan Edwards alludes in 1744, when he speaks of "some Presbyterians that. have lived with us, having desired baptism for their children, who yet lived in neglect of the ordinances of the Lord Jesus Christ, because of a difference in some trivial circumstances of the administration, from the method of the Church of Scotland."[44] No Presbyterian of that day would have permitted him unrebuked to call the difference trivial. It was a matter of principle with the Presbyterians to employ this manner of celebrating the sacrament and no other; their tenacity in it was part of their religion. It is interesting to observe accordingly that when churches in "the Western Country," which had been founded by Congregationalists, wished, under the "Plan of Union" of 1801, to become Presbyterian, they fully understood that their change of affiliation required a change also in their method of administering the Lord's Supper. The church at New Hartford, New York, for example, founded by immigrants

---

[41]Leishman, as cited.

[42]*Acts*, 1825, p. 34.

[43]This is the way Chalmers describes the result (*Memoirs,* p. 398): The Church "allowed me, the one party, to continue the table service in the way I had found to be most convenient, but, instead of laying aught like severity or rebuke upon the other, she, while disappointing them of their plea, dismissed them at the same time with a look of the most benignant complacency."

[44]See Dwight's *Life of Edwards*, p. 208.

of New England traditions, and organized as a Congregational-ist Church, in 1791, became Presbyterian in 1802. At the meeting when its Presbyterian organization was completed by the election of elders, October 9, 1802, it was "unanimously agreed that in the future, at the celebration of the Lord's Supper, the elements should be distributed to the communicants, being seated at tables spread in the aisles, and the congregation should not be dismissed until after the whole service was performed."[45] In the course of time this Presbyterian method of celebrating the sacrament ceased to be used by the congregation, now long Presbyterian. It is significant that the historian is compelled to note that there is no record in the minutes of the church session of such a change being made. Times changed and with them customs; so little was principle involved that the change was accomplished unobserved. Less and less insistence was placed everywhere upon usages which had sunk to the rank of mere habits, and the day came at last when the Scotch mode of celebrating the Supper had become merely an antiquarian curiosity to be observed rarely in the churches of Scotch origin. The usage of the other Reformed churches in America has made much the same history. In the larger churches today the old Reformed mode of celebration is to be found in use only in individual congregations which have preserved it as an old observance, to which they cling affectionately on sentimental grounds. And diligent inquiry has failed to reveal a single church, large or small, however intelligently concerned for the Reformed custom, or however conservative in temper, in which the new method of celebrating the Supper has not made inroads, and in which it does not promise ultimately to become customary.

It is not, however, by mere tradition, or merely on the grounds of sentiment, that the Reformed method of celebrating the Lord's Supper is commended. Wherever circumstances admit of its use, this is assuredly the ideal method of celebrating

---

[45]Oliver A. Kingsbury, *Centennial Day of the New Hartford Church, New York*, 1891, p. 33.

the Supper. But it would be visionary to hope that it can ever reëstablish itself or maintain itself in its integrity in large congregations, especially if, in obedience to an exhortation of the Westminster divines, they commune frequently. Perhaps a compromise between the two tendencies, toward perfect symbolism on the one hand and commodiousness of administration on the other, might more readily commend itself. Such a compromise we have seen recommended by William Tyndale and by the best judgment of the Westminster divines, excepting the Scots. We mean the serving of a table, to be occupied on three sides, leaving the fourth open to the congregation. At this table, as many as can be seated at it might be placed, while the elements might be conveyed from it to the rest. The "setting up a difference" between communicant and communicant, which George Gillespie very properly objects to in this method, might be measurably avoided by placing the office-bearers alone at the table, and having them, after themselves communing, arise and convey the elements to the participating congregation.

It will be said, and very properly said, that it is practically this which is done in the mode of celebrating the Supper which is now in ordinary use among us. When the minister takes his place behind the table bearing the elements, and the elders range themselves in front of it or at its sides, and thence convey the elements to the people—are we not all gathered about the table of the Lord? The difference between this actually employed method and the method of administration suggested is certainly not great. There is evidently more of the old Reformed method of administrating the Supper still remaining with us than, at first blush, we might be inclined to suppose. It is not apparent, indeed, why we should not recognize our customary method as essentially the same with the old Reformed—bearing the same significance and preserving the same implications. What has been done is in effect the conversion of the whole church, for the moment, into a table. This is made more apparent when, as in the case of the celebrations held by Chalmers and after him by very many (and also in the mode of celebrations described by Goulburn, as formerly customary at St. Mary's), white cloths are spread on the bookracks of the pews. But it is as real, even when this is not done. The whole church has become the Table of the Lord, and all seated in the one are seated at the other.

24

THE CONFESSION OF FAITH AS REVISED IN 1903*

That a revision of the Confession of Faith, on which it had been engaged for some years, was completed in 1903 by the Presbyterian Church in the United States of America, is, of course, a matter of universal knowledge. The exact nature of this revision does not seem, however, to be so universally understood. Attention has been vigorously directed to it again during the last few months by the part it has been made to play in the negotiations for union between the Presbyterian Church in the United States of America and the Cumberland Presbyterian Church; but it cannot be said that the public has been much enlightened by these negotiations. Some of the representations which have been made concerning the "Revised Confession" in the course of recent discussion have been, indeed, in the highest degree astonishing, not to say gravely misleading. The public mind appears in danger of being thrown into confusion about a matter simple enough in itself; and may acquire misapprehensions which, if permitted to take root, may prove hard subsequently to eradicate. It seems eminently desirable, therefore, that precisely what was effected by this revision should be exhibited in a plain and straightforward manner, from which even he who runs may gather enough to preserve himself from at least further misunderstanding.

We have said "what was effected," not "what was undertaken." This is not because we suppose these two questions would be answered very differently, but because we wish to confine ourselves for the moment to the matter of immediate practi-

---

*A pamphlet of 39 pages, published in Richmond, Virginia, 1904. See also the *Union Seminary Magazine*, Vol. XVI, No. 1.

cal importance. We do not purpose at present to trace out a piece of interesting history, instructive as that would be; but merely to exhibit the present condition of things—which is, after all, the matter of immediate concern. And we have used the word "exhibit," rather than "explain," because our purpose is not so much to set forth our own views of the "Revision of 1903," as to bring the Revised Confession itself as clearly as possible before the reader's mind, that he may see for himself what its revision has effected. Of course we are not disclaiming the office of interpreter. It is rather this office that we would fain assume, and that in its purity; for it is precisely the function of the interpreter to exhibit the meaning of his text in its integrity. We are simply renouncing for the moment every other duty but that of interpretation; and, leaving history and criticism alike to one side, confining ourselves to the establishment of the actual sense of the Revised Confession as it lies before us.

Scientific procedure in ascertaining the character of the Revised Confession coincides perfectly with the common-sense procedure of simply taking the Revised Confession up and reading it through consecutively, drawing out all its teaching in an orderly manner, and estimating it in its own light as a whole. The Revised Confession has just as much right to demand that it be read as a consecutive and consistent whole—part explanatory of part and the whole the resultant of all its parts— as has any other document. To it, as a constitutional paper in a given church, it is entirely immaterial whence its several parts have been derived, or in what debates they may have been beaten out. As they stand in the document, they form parts of its whole, affecting all the other parts and affected by them; and they must be dealt with accordingly. It follows, of course, that the meaning of no single clause of the Revised Confession can be determined in isolation, and that no one of its doctrines can be properly defined save as draw out, in balanced form, from the entire document. And it is obvious that this applies just as truly to passages newly inserted into the Confession as to portions which have been constituent parts of it from the beginning.

The readers whom we are at present addressing may be

thought to be sufficiently familiar with the unrevised Confession, however, to justify indulgence in a mode of procedure which would not otherwise be without its dangers. Instead of drawing out the teaching of "The Confession as Revised in 1903" as a whole, and then comparing this entire result with the teaching of the unrevised Confession, marking whatever differences emerge—which would be the scientific method of determining the difference between the two documents—we may permit ourselves here another method, less scientifically exact, no doubt, but more conducive to the comfort of the reader and sufficiently safe in the circumstances. We may begin rather with what has been called the "revision material," and seek to ascertain what each item of it has brought to the Confession, and then afterwards inquire what the effect of the whole mass of it is upon the teaching of the Confession into which it has been inserted.

This "revision material," from a purely formal point of view, parts into three classes: some of it makes alterations in the text of the Confession; some of it makes additions to the text of the Confession; some of it makes explanations of the text of the Confession. This purely formal division of it, naturally, carries us but a very little way into our problem, which is to determine the material effect of its insertion into the Confession. It will supply, nevertheless, a clear and useful order of treatment for the several portions of the material. Accordingly we shall take up these three portions in the order of their formal importance—first the material which merely explains the text; next that which adds to the text; and finally that which alters the text, substituting itself for greater or lesser portions of it. To the first of these classes belongs the "Declaratory Statement"; to the second, the two new chapters, entitled "Of the Holy Spirit" and "Of the Love of God, and Missions," together with which we may class, perhaps (materially if not formally), the final clause of the "Declaratory Statement"; to the last, the alterations which have been made in three sections of the Confession—XVI. vii, XXII. iii, XXV. vii. This is the whole mass of the "revision material."

THE "DECLARATORY STATEMENT"

The "Declaratory Statement," then, is not a "revision" of the text of the Confession, nor an "addition" to the text of the Confession; it is only an "explanation" of the text of the Confession. The text itself it leaves intact; and it not only leaves the text intact, it reaffirms that text. What it sets itself to do, in fact, is to protect this text from false inferences and to strengthen it by explication. That this is the real state of the case will be apparent if we give attention to the terms of the Preamble by which the "Declaratory Statement" is introduced. This Preamble is as follows:

> While the ordination vow of ministers, ruling elders, and deacons, as set forth in the Form of Government, requires the reception and adoption of the Confession of Faith only as containing the System of Doctrine taught in the Holy Scriptures, nevertheless, seeing that the desire has been formally expressed for a disavowal by the Church of certain inferences drawn from statements in the Confession of Faith, and also for a declaration of certain aspects of revealed truth which appear at the present time to call for more explicit statement, therefore the Presbyterian Church in the United States of America does authoritatively declare as follows.

It will be observed that the Preamble confines the "Declaratory Statement" to two things: (1) "a disavowal of certain inferences drawn from statements in the Confession of Faith"; and (2) "a declaration of certain aspects of revealed truth which appear at the present time to call for more explicit statement." All the "Declaratory Statement" does is ranged under these two categories. Now, the disavowal specifically of "certain inferences drawn from statements in the Confession" imports the retention of these statements. It is not the "statements" that are disavowed, but "certain inferences drawn from them." The disavowal of inferences is a protective measure designed to defend the statements themselves; and to defend statements is the precise contrary of disavowal of them. The "statements in the Confession of Faith," with which this "Declaratory Statement" deals, are, therefore, so far from being repudiated, that they are reaffirmed by it. Again, to speak of making a "more explicit statement" of "certain aspects of revealed truth," is to say that what already stands stated is "truth," and specifically "revealed truth"; and to imply that even the aspects of this revealed truth which it is now proposed to emphasize are already present in the existing statements implicitly at least, if not only somewhat less explicitly than it now seems desirable to state them. The fuller explication of certain aspects of statements is the very opposite of disavowal of these statements: it is, again, their reaffirmation.

It is perfectly clear, therefore, that the "Declaratory Statement" is as far as possible from antagonizing the passages of the Confession with which it deals. It does not even propose to state truths not already discoverable, in one way or another, in those passages; much less to state truths in any way contradictory to or inconsistent with anything found in those passages. What it proposes is summed up absolutely in these two things: to protect more carefully the Confessional statements against "certain inferences" sometimes drawn from them to their disadvantage; and to develop more fully in certain directions the truths contained in the Confessional statements. The passages with which the "Declaratory Statement" deals, now, are specifically the Third Chapter, *Of God's Eternal Decree*, and the Third Section of the Tenth Chapter, which sets forth the method of the salvation of infants, dying such. The "Declaratory Statement," therefore, reaffirms the Confessional doctrines of the Decree of God, and of the method of the Salvation of Infants, dying such; and undertakes to guard these doctrines from false inferences, affirmed to be sometimes drawn from them, and to explicate them in some of their aspects supposed to be less fully stated in the Confession than seems now desirable. Let us see how it does these things.

The Declaration as to the Decree of God

The first section of the "Declaratory Statement" has reference to the Third Chapter of the Confession, and to the doctrine of God's Eternal Decree therein taught. Its end, according to

the Preamble, is to guard this doctrine from certain false inferences, sometimes drawn from it as stated in the Confession,
and to explicate it more fully than is done in the Confession
in certain of its aspects. It runs as follows:

> The Presbyterian Church in the United States of America
> does authoritatively declare as follows:
>
> *First.* With reference to Chapter III of the Confession of
> Faith: that concerning those who are saved in Christ, the
> doctrine of God's eternal decree is held in harmony with
> the doctrine of his love to all mankind, his gift of his Son
> to be the propitiation for the sins of the whole world, and
> his readiness to bestow his saving grace on all who seek it.
> That concerning those who perish, the doctrine of God's
> eternal decree is held in harmony with the doctrine that
> God desires not the death of any sinner, but has provided
> in Christ a salvation sufficient for all, adapted to all, and
> freely offered in the gospel to all; that men are fully re-
> sponsible for their treatment of God's gracious offer; that
> his decree hinders no man from accepting that offer; and
> that no man is condemned except on the ground of his sin.

We observe that this declaration begins by very strongly emphasizing the reaffirmation of the doctrine of the Decree, which is
already implied in the Preamble. "With reference to Chapter
III of the Confession of Faith," it declares that "the doctrine
of God's eternal decree" therein taught—both "concerning those
who are saved in Christ" and "concerning those who perish"—
"is held." This doctrine it declares, we observe, "*is held.*" It
is not repudiated; it is not modified; it is not qualified; it is
not in any way weakened or diluted; it simply "is held." Reaffirmation could not be more explicit.

The purpose of the Declaration is not exhausted, however, by
this reaffirmation. Not only is the doctrine of the Decree as
defined in the Third Chapter of the Confession "held," but
certain other doctrines, which are now enumerated, are held
too; and the purpose of this Declaration is to assert the harmony
of this one doctrine that is "held" with these other doctrines
that are held along with it. The assertion is not, be it observed,
that these doctrines, here enumerated, are held in despite of

the doctrine of the Decree as set forth in the Third Chapter of the Confession, as some seem strangely to suppose. It is not even that the doctrine of the Decree as set forth in the Third Chapter of the Confession is held in despite of these other doctrines here enumerated, which are nevertheless recognized as also true. Much less is it that the doctrine of the Decree as set forth in the Third Chapter of the Confession is held so far only as it is— or may be thought by Tom, Dick, or Harry to be—in harmony with these other doctrines now enumerated, though there seems to be an inclination in some quarters to attempt to impose such a sense on it. The assertion is not that the doctrine of the Decree as set forth in the Third Chapter is out of harmony with the doctrines here enumerated, and therefore cannot be held, at least in its integrity, along with them, but must be modified to make room for them, if not wholly set aside that they may be held in its stead. On the contrary, the explicit assertion is that the doctrine of the Decree, as set forth in the Third Chapter of the Confession of Faith, both can be and actually is "held" by the signatories of the Confession, in harmony with these other doctrines, and therefore needs no modification in order to make room for them. In one word, what we have here is the most emphatic assertion possible of the harmony of the doctrine of the Decree as set forth in the Third Chapter of the Confession of Faith with the doctrines here enumerated. The edge of the implied polemic is directed not against the Third Chapter of the Confession, or the doctrine there stated, but against all who suppose that the doctrine of God's Eternal Decree there stated is not, and cannot be, held in harmony with the doctrines here enumerated; or needs any modification whatever in order that the doctrines here enumerated may be held, or may come to their rights.

Now, what are the doctrines of which it is here declared that they are in harmony with the doctrine of the Decree as set forth in the Third Chapter of the Confession, and may usefully be published now to refute false inferences drawn from that doctrine, or to bring out more clearly some of its implications? They are enumerated in two sets. The one set is to protect from false inferences, and to bring out the implications of, the doctrine of the Decree in its relation to the saved: the other in its relation to the lost. In the first interest the following propositions are enumerated: (1) that God loves all mankind; (2) that he has given his Son to be the propitiation for the sins of the whole world; (3) that he is ready to bestow his saving grace on all who seek it. In the second interest, it is declared: (4) that God desires not the death of any sinner; (5) that he has provided in Christ a salvation sufficient for all, adapted to all, and freely offered in the gospel to all; (6) that men are fully responsible for their treatment of God's gracious offer; (7) that his decree hinders no man from accepting that offer; (8) that no man is condemned except on the ground of his sin.

Here are eight doctrinal propositions, all of which are declared to be in harmony with the doctrine of the Decree as set forth in the Third Chapter of the Confession, and to be held by the signatories of the Confession in conjunction with that doctrine; enumerated here either to repudiate false inferences drawn from that doctrine as set forth in the Confession or to explicate more fully aspects of truth less fully brought to expression in the Confessional statement than may be now thought desirable. Obviously there is a polemic edge to the enumeration. Against whom is it turned? Of course, against those who deny that the doctrines here enumerated are harmonious with the Doctrine of the Decree as set forth in the Third Chapter of the Confession. And that is to say, against Arminian objectors to the Doctrine of the Decree as set forth in the Third Chapter of the Confession—the very essence of whose objections to that doctrine has ever been that it is inconsistent with the doctrinal propositions here enumerated, and is not and cannot be held in harmony with them. The first section of the "Declaratory Statement" appears, then, to be nothing other than a sharp repudiation of the ordinary Arminian assault on the doctrine of the Decree, as set forth in the Third Chapter of the Confession, and puts in a brief assertory form the common Calvinistic response to this assault.

This will appear in the plainest light when we go on to

observe, that as the assertion of the harmony of these propositions with the doctrine of the Decree is a commonplace of
Calvinistic polemics, so every item of doctrine affirmed in these
propositions is a commonplace of Calvinistic divinity. It cannot be necessary to pause to justify this remark to even the
most inattentive reader of Calvinistic literature. It will suffice
if we simply illustrate the matter by a series of cursory quotations from recognized Calvinistic divines, in which each of the
eight propositions will be found to be clearly asserted in turn.
We throw these quotations into small type to enable the reader
who is familiar with Calvinistic thought commodiously to pass
them over unread.

1. "The Heavenly Father loves the human race, and would not have
them perish."—Calvin, on John iii. 16.

"The Scriptures represent the redemption by Christ as . . . the fruit
of God's love to mankind."—Edwards, II, p. 462.

"The Scriptures plainly teach that God exercises a love of benevolence towards all men."—Girardeau, *Calvinism and Evangelical Arminianism Compared*, p. 275.

2. "The Scriptures plainly teach that God so loved the whole world
that he gave his only begotten Son to make expiation for the sins of
the whole world."—Shedd, *Presbyterian and Reformed Review*, I, p. 10.

"Augustinians do not deny that Christ died for all men. . . . He died
for all that . . . he might lay the foundation for the offer of pardon
and reconciliation with God on condition of faith and repentance. . . .
This is what is meant when it is said, or implied, in Scripture that
Christ gave himself as a propitiation, not for our sins only, but for the
sins of the whole world."—C. Hodge, II, p. 561.

3. "Now, like as God is ready to bestow these benefits on all and
every one, and that for Christ's sake, in case they believe; so Christ hath
merited pardon of sinne and salvation for all and every one, in case
they believe."—Twisse, *Riches*, etc., p. 109.

"An all-sufficient Savior has been held up before him, abundantly
able to save all that were ever invited to come; a door of access has
been opened to the throne of grace, so that he might have gone with
boldness and sought for the mercy which he needed with the certain
prospect of obtaining it."—Thornwell, II, p. 176.

4. "God delights in the conversion and eternal life of the sinner
rather than in his perdition, because this is a thing . . . congruous with
his own infinitely compassionate nature."—Turretin, IV. xvii. 33.

"According to the Scriptures communicating good to the creatures is what . . . God . . . delights in simply and ultimately. . . . Ezek. xviii. 32. . . . Ezek. xxxiii. 11."—Edwards, II, p. 242.

"The natural spontaneous desire of God towards all men . . . expressed in Ezek. xxxiii. 11, xviii. 32 . . . springs from the compassionate love of the Creator towards the soul of the creature."—Shedd, I, p. 452.

5. "Augustinianism teaches that a plan of salvation adapted to all men and adequate for the salvation of all is freely offered to the acceptance of all."—C. Hodge, II, p. 644.

"In the general offers of the gospel, God exhibits a salvation sufficient for and exactly adapted to all, and sincerely offered to every one without exception."—A. A. Hodge, *Outlines*, p. 229.

"We hold it perfectly consistent with this truth, that the expiation of Christ for sin—expiation of infinite value and universal fitness—should be held forth to the whole world."—Dabney, p. 533.

6. "The Doctrine delivered in the Gospell is such, and so confirmed, as may justly make them inexcusable that doe not believe. . . . If a man had a will to obey and believe but he could not, in such a case it were unreasonable he should be punished. But in the case of disobedience unto God we speak of, all the fault is in the will, voluntarily and wilfully."—Twisse, *Riches*, etc., pp. 169 f.

"The gospel offer, combined with the positive command of God, renders the duty of believing imperative upon all, and therefore leaves every unbeliever utterly without excuse in the sight of God. . . . The apostle was clearly of the opinion that the absolute and sovereign predestination of God did not take away responsibility from man or remove the guilt of his transgressions."—Thornwell, II, pp. 176, 181.

"Nothing but a sinful unwillingness can prevent any one who hears the gospel from receiving and enjoying it."—A. A. Hodge, *Outlines*, p. 229.

7. "God commanding all to [who?] heare the Gospell to believe, doth not hinder them from believing, when they are willing to believe." —Twisse, *Riches*, etc., p. 172.

"God makes no man an unbeliever. He commands and urges it upon all to believe, and debars none from the throne of grace."—Thornwell, II, p. 175.

"God, instead of hindering the sinner, is helping him."—Shedd, I, p. 454; cf. *Presbyterian and Reformed Review*, I, p. 18.

"The decree of election puts no barrier before men preventing them from accepting the gospel offer."—A. A. Hodge, *Outlines*, p. 229.

"His decree prevents no man from coming."—Girardeau, as cited, p. 369.

8. "For indeed, not any of our Divines was, I think, ever known to maintain that God did intend to damne any man but for sinne."— Twisse, *Riches*, etc., p. 186. (See also pp. 8, 14, 34, 44, 46, 106, etc.)

"God ordains none to wrath or punishment except on account of their sin."—Girardeau, as cited, p. 188; cf. pp. 186, 227.

"Everywhere it is sin which excludes from his favor, and sin alone." —Dabney, p. 240.

The insertion of this section of the "Declaratory Statement" into the Confession has, therefore, as its entire effect the re-affirmation of the doctrine of the Decree as expounded in the Third Chapter, together with the repudiation of certain well-known false inferences drawn from it by Arminian objectors; and the explicit assertion of its harmony with a series of precious truths with which these objectors have been accustomed to assert it to be inconsistent, but its consistency with which Calvinists have always strenuously asserted and solidly argued.

The Declaration as to Infant Salvation

The second section of the "Declaratory Statement" has reference to the Third Section of the Tenth Chapter of the Confession, and to the explanation there given of how children dying in infancy are saved. Its end, in accordance with the Preamble, is either to protect this explanation from false inferences, or to explicate truths implied in it, or both. It runs as follows:

> The Presbyterian Church in the United States of America does authoritatively declare as follows: . . .
>
> *Second.* With reference to Chapter X, Section 3, of the Confession of Faith, that it is not to be regarded as teaching that any who die in infancy are lost. We believe that all dying in infancy are included in the election of grace, and are regenerated and saved by Christ through the Spirit, who works when and where and how he pleases.

The particular false inference which it has been most common for adversaries to draw from the statement in the Confession in question is that according to it some infants dying in infancy are lost, or at least that some such infants may be lost. The gist of the "Declaratory Statement" therefore, as we observe, is to repudiate this inference in precise terms.

With this simple repudiation of a current injurious inference the "Declaratory Statement" might very well have paused. The statement of the Confession of Faith that is dealt with has nothing to do with the question of how many of those that die in infancy are saved. It confines itself strictly to explaining in what manner infants dying such may be reached by God's saving mercy. To draw any inference whatever as to "how many" from this explanation of "how" is wholly illegitimate; and the "Declaratory Statement" might well have contented itself with saying so with crisp brevity. But it does not do this. After repelling the false inference that has been so frequently drawn from this statement of the Confession, it proceeds to enunciate a positive doctrine of the salvation of all that die in infancy. Possibly the framers of the "Declaratory Statement," in doing this, understood themselves to be only explicating an aspect of revealed truth already implicitly contained in the section of the Confession they were commenting upon. In that case, the assertion of this doctrine would have a legitimate place in a "Declaratory Statement" professing a function of explication as well as of protection with regard to the passages of the Confession with which it deals. For ourselves, we must, however, confess inability to share the view of the implication of Chapter X. 3, which would be involved in this. To us the Confessional statement in question appears to confine itself strictly to the way in which dying infants are saved, without any implication whatever as to the number of them that are saved. We must look upon the enunciation of the doctrine of the salvation of all infants dying such, therefore, as, in a strict ordering, out of place in this "Declaratory Statement."

But apart from this merely formal question of order, there is nothing that can be objected from the Confessional or the Calvinistic standpoint to the new doctrine that is here enunciated, or to the form in which it is stated. It is a doctrine to which the Calvinistic system (and, we may add, the Calvinistic system alone) is logically altogether hospitable, and which has always been believed by some of the best of Calvinists, and for the last hundred years by practically all Calvinists. It is prudently and soundly expressed in this statement of it; and is placed in its right relations to the doctrines alike of birth-sin and birth-guilt, the sovereign election of God, and the purchase of redemption by Christ and its application by the Holy Spirit. Assuredly, therefore, there is nothing in this second section of the "Declaratory Statement" which in any way traverses any teaching or any statement of the Confession of Faith. On the contrary, it too, in essence and form alike, is a defense of the doctrine and the statement of the Confession against a current Arminian assault.

THE TWO NEW CHAPTERS

The formulation, in the closing words of the "Declaratory Statement," of a new doctrine—the doctrine of the salvation of all that die in infancy—may lead us by an easy transition to the formally new material which has been added to the Confession. This is included in two new chapters, which are numbered XXXIV and XXXV, and adjoined at the end of the Confession. They are entitled, respectively: "Of the Holy Spirit," and "Of the Love of God, and Missions." A brief Preamble introduces them, which runs as follows:

> *Whereas,* It is desirable to express more fully the doctrine of the Church concerning the Holy Spirit, Missions, and the Love of God for all men, the following Chapters are added to the Confession of Faith.

According to this Preamble, it will be observed, the new chapters do not profess to offer a correction of anything already found in the Confession on the topics with which they deal, but merely an expansion of the doctrine already given expression in the Confession. To undertake to "express *more fully* the doctrine of the Church," is to recognize that what already stands in the authoritative expression of the Church's doctrine to which these chapters are to be added is true as far as it goes, and needs, not modification, but supplementing. That is to say, these chapters come before us as reaffirming the doctrinal statements of the Confession on the topics with which they deal, and proposing to extend them.

The Chapter "Of the Holy Spirit"

The former of the two new chapters is entitled "Of the Holy Spirit," and is divided into four sections, which run as follows:

I. The Holy Spirit, the third person in the Trinity, proceeding from the Father and the Son, of the same substance and equal in power and glory, is, together with the Father and the Son, to be believed in, loved, obeyed, and worshiped throughout all ages.

II. He is the Lord and Giver of life, everywhere present in nature, and is the source of all good thoughts, pure desires, and holy counsels in men. By him the prophets were moved to speak the Word of God, and all writers of the Holy Scriptures inspired to record infallibly the mind and will of God. The dispensation of the gospel is especially committed to him. He prepares the way for it, accompanies it with his persuasive power, and urges its message upon the reason and conscience of men, so that they who reject its merciful offer are not only without excuse, but are also guilty of resisting the Holy Spirit.

III. The Holy Spirit, whom the Father is ever willing to give to all who ask him, is the only efficient agent in the application of redemption. He convicts men of sin, moves them to repentance, regenerates them by his grace, and persuades and enables them to embrace Jesus Christ by faith. He unites all believers to Christ, dwells in them as their Comforter and Sanctifier, gives to them the spirit of Adoption and Prayer, and performs all those gracious offices by which they are sanctified and sealed unto the day of redemption.

IV. By the indwelling of the Holy Spirit all believers being vitally united to Christ, who is the Head, are thus united one to another in the Church, which is his body. He calls and anoints ministers for their holy office, qualifies all other officers in the Church for their special work, and imparts various gifts and graces to its members. He gives efficacy to the Word, and to the ordinances of the gospel. By him the Church will be preserved, increased until it shall cover the earth, purified, and at last made perfectly holy in the presence of God.

It will be observed that the several sections of the chapter follow each other logically and develop the doctrine of the Holy Spirit in an orderly sequence. The first sets forth the nature of the Holy Spirit in his relations to the Godhead and to the rational creation. The second sets forth his general activities—cosmical, ethical, inspirational, evangelical. The third advances to his specifically soteriological activities and summarizes his work in the salvation of individuals. The last expounds his activities in the Church, by virtue of which the Church is constituted, edified, propagated, and perfected. The doctrine set forth in these several sections is the common doctrine of the Calvinistic churches, and may be found expounded at length in the body of divinity of any standard Calvinistic divine. The chapter is in effect, therefore, a compact summary of the ordinary Calvinistic doctrine of the Holy Spirit and his work.

As this chapter essays to put into brief compass a complete doctrine "Of the Holy Spirit," it necessarily repeats many elements of that doctrine which are already given expression in the Confession; and whenever the Confession has developed any items of this doctrine with fulness, the repetition of them in this chapter is much compressed. The first section of the chapter, for example, merely repeats what the Confession has already said in the following passages:

> In the unity of the Godhead there are three persons, of one substance, power and eternity, . . . the Holy Ghost eternally proceeding from the Father and the Son" (II. 3). "Religious worship is to be given to God the Father, Son and Holy Ghost; and to him alone (XXI. 2).

The third section is merely a very compressed summary of what the Confession has set forth in minute detail and with exceedingly rich development in that great series of chapters on the Application of Redemption, which constitutes its heart (Chaps. X–XVIII). This summary, certainly, evinces no great firmness or precision of touch. It fumbles a little alike with the conceptions it deals with and with the language in which it clothes them. But it is happily possible to tell the truth even with lisping tongue; and this section manages, even in its some-what bungling way, to set forth, from the phenomenal or ex-periential point of sight, a very tolerable account of the pro-gressive stages through which (in the Calvinistic view) a sinner passes as he is brought into the experience of salvation by the Holy Spirit, who is very properly described as "the only efficient agent in the application of redemption."

The several sentences of the fourth section likewise very largely repeat statements which have already found expression in the Confession. The following passages will illustrate this; they follow the order of the sentences in this section:

> All saints that are united to Jesus Christ the Head, by his Spirit and by faith, have fellowship with him, . . . and being united to one another in love, they have communion in each other's gifts and graces, and are obliged to the per-formance of such duties, public and private, as do conduce to their mutual good, both in the inward and outward man (XXVI. 1). The catholic or universal Church, which is invisible, consists of the whole number of the elect, that have been, are, or shall be gathered into one, under Christ the Head thereof; and is the spouse, the body, the fulness of him that filleth all in all (XXV. 1). Unto this catholic visible Church, Christ hath given the ministry, oracles, and ordinances of God, for the gathering and perfecting of the saints, . . . and doth by his presence and Spirit, according to his promise, make them effectual thereto (XXV. 3). The grace of faith . . . is the work of the Spirit of Christ, . . . and is ordinarily wrought by the ministry of the Word: by which also, and by the administration of the sacraments, and prayer, it is increased and strengthened (XIV. 1).

A certain effect of novelty is given to the restatement of the important truths contained in this section, however, by their marshaling in an orderly development of the doctrine of "the Holy Spirit in the Church"; and this is increased by the apparent absence from the Confession of any clause embodying, at least with the clearness and emphasis given it here, the inspiring truth enunciated in the last sentence. On the whole, then, this section may fairly be accounted a contribution toward the aug-mentation of the Confession with new doctrine. The doctrine of the work of the Holy Spirit in the Church is stated in it comprehensively, and not without point. The doctrine of the Church implicated is the common Reformed doctrine, and the statement here given homologates perfectly with the teaching of the Confession, whether in the main or in subsidiary points.

It is, however, in the second section that the really new matter of this chapter is presented. The second sentence of even this section, to be sure—which, moreover, is out of its logical place—is only a repetition of doctrine already set forth with fulness and emphasis in the First Chapter of the Confession. But the rest of the section is entirely new to the Confession, and gives a comprehensive statement of a great and distinctively Calvinistic doctrine not hitherto incorporated in detailed statement into the Confession—the doctrine, to wit, as it is currently designated by the systematizers, of "Common Grace." This important doctrine, first worked out by Calvin, passed from him into the systems of the Reformed divines in general, to be most richly developed in our own day by perhaps Dr. Charles Hodge[1] and two Dutch theologians who have won the admiration and love of the whole Reformed world by their sturdy support of the Reformed theology in the untoward conditions of present-day Holland—Dr. Abraham Kuyper and Dr. Herman Bavinck.

Of course this distinctively Reformed doctrine was not unknown to the framers of the Confession. It may be found more or less fully expounded in their private writings, and is always adverted to by them with a high sense of its value.[2] It is even incidentally alluded to in the text of the Confession itself.[3] But the framers of the Confession consecrated to it no separate section of their work, and indeed nowhere give it even incidental development. The incorporation of a statement of this doctrine into this chapter is, therefore, a real extension of

---

[1] Cf. Dabney, *Syllabus*, p. 577: "Dr. Hodge expounds with peculiar force and fulness the solemn fact that there is a 'common grace' of the Holy Ghost (which is not 'common sufficient grace')."

[2] Cf., e.g., Twisse, *Riches*, etc., pp. 243, 253.

[3] X. 4. "Some common operations of the Spirit."

the Confession by a new doctrinal definition; and the doctrine thus inserted is certainly one of large importance, if not to the integrity of the Calvinistic system or to its full statement for the practical ends of the religious life, yet certainly for its thorough elaboration and its complete development as a comprehensive world-view.

The statement which is here given to this important Reformed doctrine is, from the necessity of the case, succinct rather than elaborated, comprehensive rather than detailed. But it perfectly conforms to the teaching upon this topic of the best Reformed divines. The closeness of its conformity to the ordinary mode of stating the doctrine among accredited Reformed teachers may be fairly estimated by comparing this section with the exposition of the subject by, say, Dr. Shedd or Dr. Charles Hodge. Dr. Hodge, for example, says, among other things:

> God is everywhere present with the minds of men, as the Spirit of truth and goodness, operating on them according to the laws of their own moral agency, inclining them to good and restraining them from evil. . . . To the general influence of the Spirit (or to common grace) we owe all the decorum, order, refinement, and virtue existing among men. . . . The Scriptures speak of God's reasoning with men; of his teaching them, and that inwardly, by his Spirit; of his guiding or leading them; and of his coming, reproving, and persuading them. These modes of representation would seem to indicate a "moral suasion," an operation in accordance with the ordinary laws of mind, consisting in the presentation of truth and urging of motives. . . . These common influences of the Spirit are all capable of being effectually resisted. . . . We should above all things dread lest we should grieve the Spirit or quench his influence.

The resemblance between such teaching and the statement given in the section of the new chapter before us is patent.

The chapter "Of the Holy Spirit," then, besides reiterating the Confessional doctrines of the nature of the Holy Spirit and of his special activities, on the one hand, in the gift of the Scriptures, and, on the other, in the application of the redemption of Christ to individual sinners, develops and extends the

Confessional doctrine of the work of the Spirit in the Church, and adds to the Confessional statements the definition of a new doctrine, "Common Grace." In this further development of the one doctrine and fresh formulation of the other, it proceeds in full accord with both the spirit of the Reformed system and the very letter of the most accredited expounders of that system.

The Chapter "Of the Love of God, and Missions"

The latter of the two new chapters is entitled in the Revised Confession, "Of the Love of God, and Missions." This was not, however, its original title; and it is not perfectly appropriate to its contents. This chapter (like its fellow, in general) was borrowed by the Revision Committee which reported in 1902, and whose work, now incorporated into the Confession, constitutes the Revised Confession, from the work of a former revision committee, which reported in 1892, and whose work (including these two chapters) was at that time rejected by the Church. The title given the chapter by its framers was, "Of the Gospel"; and the chapter remains, despite the change of its title, distinctly a chapter on "The Gospel," that is to say, to speak in more technical language, on "The External Call." Of course it speaks of the "Love of God," and of "Missions"; for the "Gospel" is the expression of the love of God, and in its proclamation creates what we know as "Missions." But the chapter is in no sense a development of the doctrine of the "Love of God," which is introduced only incidentally as the source and burden of the "Gospel"; nor is it a development of the doctrine of "Missions," which, in the technical sense of that word, comes before us only in the closing section. It is a development of the doctrine of "the Gospel," which it very properly represents as originating in and proclaiming the love of God, and as issuing in missions. Our present purpose is not criticism, but exposition; but so much criticism of the misfitting title which has been attached to the chapter seemed necessary to its exposition. It runs as follows:

I. God, in infinite and perfect love, having provided in the covenant of grace, through the mediation and sacrifice of the Lord Jesus Christ, a way of life and salvation, sufficient for and adapted to the whole lost race of man, doth freely offer this salvation to all men in the gospel.

II. In the gospel God declares his love for the world and his desire that all men should be saved; reveals fully and clearly the only way of salvation; promises eternal life to all who truly repent and believe in Christ; invites and commands all to embrace the offered mercy; and by his Spirit accompanying the Word, pleads with men to accept his gracious invitation.

III. It is the duty and privilege of everyone who hears the gospel immediately to accept its merciful provisions; and they who continue in impenitence and unbelief incur aggravated guilt and perish by their own fault.

IV. Since there is no other way of salvation than that revealed in the gospel, and since in the divinely established and ordinary method of grace faith cometh by hearing the Word of God, Christ hath commissioned his Church to go into all the world and to make disciples of all nations. All believers are, therefore, under obligation to sustain the ordinances of religion where they are already established, and to contribute by their prayers, gifts, and personal efforts, to the extension of the kingdom of Christ throughout the whole earth.

It will be observed that the four sections of this chapter develop in logical sequence the doctrine of "The Gospel," or, in other words, "The External Call." In the first section the ground of the External Call or "the Gospel offer" is explained. In the second section, the contents of the External Call, or Gospel, are developed: thus, in effect, a definition of "the Gospel" its formulated. In the third section the effects of the External Call, or Gospel, are set forth. And in the last section the obligations growing out of the state of the case thus outlined are explained.

The doctrine thus developed is the ordinary doctrine of the "External Call" as expounded by the Reformed divines. The several declarations of the clauses are, indeed, but the commonplaces of the Reformed doctrine. It seems scarcely necessary to illustrate in detail so obvious a fact. One would need but to read over, say, Dr. Charles Hodge's section on "The External Call" to obtain not only a parallel to the general treatment, but parallel statements of the most express kind for each of the several clauses. The chief propositions announced, moreover, are so nearly the same with the propositions embodied in the first section of the "Declaratory Statement" that the quotations from standard Reformed divines given to illustrate them[4] will serve nearly as good a purpose for the clauses here.

It cannot be said, on the other hand, that these propositions merely repeat anything said, with full explication, in other parts of the Confession. No doubt the doctrine of the External Call underlies the whole of the Confession; and important elements of it are here and there clearly asserted, as, for example, in the Tenth Chapter, where its relation to the Internal Call is fully explicated. The whole of it, indeed, is crisply contained in such a declaration as that made in VII. 3, that God, in the covenant of grace, "freely offereth unto sinners life and salvation by Jesus Christ, requiring of them faith in him, that they may be saved." But the Confession was too busy developing the contents of the gospel to stay to expand into all its details the doctrine of "the Gospel" itself; it was too much absorbed with the inward call of the Holy Spirit and its great sequences of salvation, to care to do more than explicitly to recognize and indicate in outline the external call of the Word. It must be allowed, therefore, that this chapter, with its detailed explanation of the External Call, does make a substantial addition to the doctrinal definitions of the Confession. It incorporates into the Confession a rather full exposition of the doctrine of the External Call, sufficiently clear, calmly stated, and thoroughly sound. It is a pity that its significance is somewhat obscured to the careless reader by the unmeaning title that has been attached to it; and that its bearing on the general doctrinal exposition of the Confession is somewhat concealed by the illogical position given it at the end of the document. But what it brings in itself is just a sound bit of Calvinistic

---

[4] See above, pp. 378-380.

theology, which perfectly homologates with the total contents of the Confession.

THE TEXTUAL ALTERATIONS

We have yet to advert to the three instances in which "the Revision of 1903" has made alterations in the actual text of the Confession. To change the text of the Confession implies, of course, condemnation of the text that is changed—to the extent of the change which is made. The ground of this condemnation will naturally vary from instance to instance, and need not always be strictly doctrinal, or indeed doctrinal at all. But we need not enter upon that question here. After all, we are not directly concerned with the motives of the changes, but solely with the effect of them. Our business is not to determine what the doctrinal prepossessions of the revisers were, but what the doctrinal character of the Revised Confession is. For our present purpose, therefore, we might very well decline to consider at all what the change was *from*, and focus attention merely on what it is *to*. Something like this is, indeed, essential so far as that we must beware of interpreting the Revised Confession by way of contrast with the Unrevised. We must interpret it strictly according to its own language in its own context, and not imagine it to affirm the contradictory of what it may have omitted from a previous document.

The importance of this remark will become apparent when we observe that the textual changes made are either formally or at least essentially omissions. It cannot be reasonably assumed, however, that the Revised Confession denies all that it has omitted—much less that it asserts the logical contradictory of it. It may well be, for example, that its framers only shrank from affirming categorically what they omitted, and had no design whatever positively to deny it, much less to affirm its contradictory. And assuredly the Revised Confession is entitled to be understood according to its affirmations, and is not to be saddled with propositions which do not occur in it at all.

We may illustrate these remarks from the alteration made in Chapter XXII. 3. This consists in a simple omission, and the omission is of this single sentence: "Yet it is a sin to refuse an oath touching anything that is good and just, being imposed by lawful authority." It would certainly be illegitimate to say that by omitting this sentence the Revised Confession has denied that it is a sin to refuse such an oath. The fact is, the Revised Confession says nothing about the matter, one way or another. He who adopts this Confession adopts no expression on the subject. And silence is as favorable to one opinion as to another. "Oh! but," someone will say, "the *omission* of this declaration means something." Certainly it does. It means something relatively to the opinions of the revisers, though it is easy to attribute to them different motives from those which actually swayed them. But it means nothing relatively to the teaching of the Revised Confession. From the fact that its present form of statement has been reached by an omission from a previous form, we can infer nothing whatever as to the doctrine of the Revised Confession. Its teaching lies in what it says, not in what it does not say. Concerning the things of which it does not speak, it has no doctrine.

The same remarks apply also to the alteration made in Chapter XXV. 6. Here the revision takes the form of a reconstruction of the section; but the reconstruction appears to be nearly, if not altogether, in the interest of an omission. The motive of the revisers seems to have been to avoid calling the pope of Rome "that antichrist, that man of sin, and son of perdition, that exalteth himself in the Church against Christ and all that is called God"—which does seem rather strong language. Why the revisers wished to avoid applying these terms to the pope of Rome we can only conjecture. But their avoidance of it need not imply that they—some or all of them—felt prepared to deny that the pope of Rome is the antichrist of Scripture. Much less does the absence of these phrases from the Revised Confession commit its signatories to that position. It simply leaves its signatories free to believe what they choose in the matter. In saying nothing at all about it, it simply does not raise the question at all. It confines itself to saying that—

The Lord Jesus Christ is the only head of the Church, and

the claim of any man to be the vicar of Christ and the head of the Church, is unscriptural, without warrant in fact, and is a usurpation dishonoring to the Lord Jesus Christ.

This, it will be observed, is an expansion of the two first clauses of the old section. To this, and this alone, are the signatories of the Revised Confession committed.

These things are of comparatively little doctrinal importance. When we approach the third instance of revision by alteration, however, we touch on deeper concerns. This is a remodeling of the Seventh Section of the Sixteenth Chapter—the section in the chapter on "Good Works," which treats of the works of the unregenerate. It will be only frank to say at once that it seems to us a positively bad piece of work which the revisers have done here. We do not say, and we do not think, that the new section as it stands in the Revised Confession is untrue or "unsound." It is neither. But a comparison of the remodeled section with the section as it stands in the old Confession creates a suspicion that the determining motive for the remodeling may have been to avoid affirming that works done by unregenerate men "are sinful and cannot please God." It is difficult, no doubt, to divine what gain was expected to accrue from avoiding this assertion here, while not only were the Catechisms left untouched, but also the very strong assertions of human corruption and inability which appear elsewhere in the Confession—as in the chapters on Sin and Free Will— forming, as these chapters do, part of the context of the present section by which its meaning, as it stands in the Confession, must be determined. Nevertheless, it is hard not to suspect that the revisers were swayed, in avoiding the phrase in question here, by the influence of the "vanishing sense of sin" that is so unhappily apparent in much of modern thought.

All this, however, has no relevancy to the interpretation of the Revised Confession. We can infer nothing as to its meaning from any suspicion we may cherish as to the revisers' motives. It must be taken as it stands. And as it stands it also gives us a "form of sound words," in which all that is said is said fitly and truly. Something more might properly have been said;

and we, in whose minds some echoes of the old words linger, may miss something. But, after all, this something more is not obtruded on the consciousness of the reader of the Revised Confession itself, and will not ultimately be missed in this context. Indeed, it seems even to be suggested in what is said. For, if the works done by unregenerate men are not roundly declared to be sinful, they are at least said "to come short of what God requires," which assuredly itself comes very little short of saying they are sinful—unless the sinfulness of "sins of omission" be denied. The following is the new section, and its perusal will evince its essential soundness:

> Works done by unregenerate men, although for the matter of them they may be things which God commands, and in themselves praiseworthy and useful, and although the neglect of such things is sinful and displeasing unto God; yet, because they proceed not from the heart purified by faith; nor are done in a right manner, according to his Word; nor to a right end, the glory of God; they come short of what God requires and do not make any man meet to receive the grace of God.

The Effect of the Revision

Having thus passed in review the several items of the "revision material," let us seek now to form a general conception of what it as a whole has brought into the Confession.

(1) In the first place, then, its insertion into the Confession has brought into the Confession a reassertion of the formative doctrines of the Confession. It reasserts the doctrines of Revelation and Inspiration as set forth in the First Chapter of the Confession. It reasserts the doctrine of the Decree as developed in the Third Chapter. It reasserts the doctrine of Infant Salvation as explained in the Third Section of the Fourth Chapter. It reasserts the whole series of doctrines expounding the effectual application of the redemption of Christ to sinners by the Holy Spirit, as developed in the series of chapters from the Tenth to the Eighteenth. It reasserts, besides, the teaching of many fragmentary passages which is repeated in one or another clause of one or the other of the two new chapters, and may,

therefore, fairly be held to be covered by the reaffirmation clause in their Preamble.

(2) In the second place, the insertion of the "revision material" into the Confession incorporates into it a definite repudiation of the whole mass of assumptions on which has been founded an annoying assault upon certain important doctrines taught by the Confession, by which assault the adherents of the Confession have been vexed ever since its formulation. The method of this repudiation involves the distinct assertion of the inclusion in the Confessional system of a series of doctrinal propositions, complementary to or implied in those which have been the favorite mark of the assault in question. These implicated or complementary doctrinal propositions announce the love of God for all mankind, the gift of his Son to be the propitiation for the sins of the whole world, his readiness to bestow his saving grace on all who seek it, his desire that no man shall perish, his provision in Christ of a salvation sufficient for all, adapted to all, and freely offered in the gospel to all; the responsibility of men for their treatment of God's gracious offer, from accepting which no man is hindered by God's decree, as none is condemned save for his sin.

(3) In the third place, the "revision material" inserted into the Confession formulates certain new doctrines now for the first time, explicitly or in full exposition at least, made a part of the Confessional statement. These new doctrines include the doctrine of the salvation of all that die in infancy, the great doctrines of Common Grace and the External Call or "the Gospel," and the doctrine of the work of the Holy Spirit in the Church.

(4) In the fourth place, the incorporation of the "revision material" into the Confession removes from the Confession certain statements about the sinfulness of refusing a proper oath properly tendered, and the identification of the pope with the antichrist of Scripture; and somewhat reduces in one place the language in which the sinfulness of works done by the unregenerate is asserted.

What now is the total effect of all this on the Confession and its teaching?

The System of Doctrine Unaffected

Has it in any way affected the integrity of the system of doctrine taught in the Confession? How could it? We have just seen that it reaffirms the formative elements of that system, that what it adds is conformable to it and is added as conformable to it, and that what it takes away is, in the strict sense of that word, insignificant.

The system of doctrine taught in the Confession is the system that is known in history as the Reformed or Calvinistic system. The architectonic principle of this system is the doctrine of the Eternal Decree of God, which is set forth with notable purity and care in the Third Chapter, and into adjustment with which every other doctrinal statement of the Confession is brought. Not only are none of these adjustments disturbed by the revision, but it is precisely this doctrine that it has most emphatically reaffirmed, protected from false inferences and strengthened by explicit assertion of its harmony with certain complementary truths. The Revised Confession differs at this point from the unrevised Confession only in more elaborately buttressing the formative doctrine of the system. The unrevised Confession was content simply to state this doctrine with remarkable clearness and fulness: the Revised Confession adjoins a defense of this statement. That is all.

It may indeed be argued that the defense of this doctrine which the Revised Confession incorporates overreaches itself, and asserts a series of propositions as implicated in or complementary to the doctrine of the Decree, as set forth in the Third Chapter, which are really inconsistent with that doctrine, and, therefore, as now asserted, qualify it, modify it, or even neutralize it and wipe it practically out. It must be observed, however, first, that this is not the view of the Revised Confession itself; secondly, that it has been repeatedly expressly repudiated by the Church which has adopted this Revised Confession; thirdly, that it traverses the judgment of the whole body of the Reformed divines; and, fourthly, that it is merely the reassertion of the assault on the Confessional doctrine of the Decree which it is the very object of this enumeration of implicated and complementary doctrines to repel. The professed object of the Revision at this point is precisely to repulse this assault, and all the inferences that are accustomed to be drawn from it. Its professed object is to assert that the propositions here enumerated are implicates or complements of the doctrine of the Decree as set forth in the Third Chapter of the Confession. Whoever assumes that they are inconsistent with that doctrine takes up, therefore, a position not only outside of, but in direct antagonism to the Revised Confession; the Revised Confession expressly repudiates him, and by the necessity of the case he must repudiate the Revised Confession.

No Doctrines Modified

Must it not, however, at least be allowed that some of the doctrines of the Confession have been modified by the Revision? One would very much like to know what doctrines these can be. Not the doctrine of the Decree of God; that has been reasserted, defended from false inferences, and explicated. Not the doctrines forming parts of the Application of Redemption; these, too, have been reaffirmed. Not the doctrine of an Infallible Bible; that also has been reiterated. Certainly not the doctrines that have been left untouched. What doctrines, then, can have been modified?

There are, in fact, just three statements of the old Confession which have been modified in the new; and it is doubtful whether in any one of these cases any modification has been wrought in the doctrines themselves. The Revised Confession no longer asserts that it is a sin to refuse a properly required oath; or that the pope of Rome is the antichrist of Scripture; or, in so many words at least, that all the works of the unregenerate are sinful. We add the qualification, "in so many words at least," to the last instance, because not only does the Revised Confession still declare of all men that they are so corrupt that they are "utterly indisposed, disabled and made opposite to all good and wholly inclined to evil," and that this "corruption of nature itself and all the motions thereof are truly and properly sin," as well as a good deal more to the same effect; but in the revised statement itself it affirms, as we have seen, that the works of the unregenerate "come short of what God requires." It can scarcely be contended, therefore, that the Revised Confession no longer teaches that the works of the unregenerate are all sinful. It has merely modified one statement of this doctrine, not the doctrine itself. Elsewhere there are no modifications of even the statement of doctrines.

Extension not Alteration

At all events, new doctrines have been inserted into the Confession; and does not the insertion of new doctrines necessarily carry with it a certain modification of teaching, especially if these new doctrines be (as they are in this case) important? That depends on the nature of the new doctrines and their relation to the old doctrines already stated in the Confession. Certainly new doctrines have been inserted into the Confession by the Revision of 1903; and we have no disposition to minimize the importance of these new doctrines. But there is something else that must be said about them also. These new doctrines are true doctrines—good, sound, Calvinistic doctrines, which, taking their places in a statement of the Calvinistic system, simply expand it into greater completeness of treatment, and in no sense modify either it or any of the doctrines that enter into it.

What are these new doctrines which have been inserted into the Confession? The doctrines of "Common Grace," of the "External Call," of "Infant Salvation," of the "Holy Spirit in the Church." This is the entire list of them; for the doctrinal propositions included in the first section of the "Declaratory Statement" all recur in the chapter on the "External Call," and find their true doctrinal significance there. We have no wish, we repeat, to minify these doctrines or the significance of their addition to the Confessional statement of doctrine. Obviously they are important doctrines, and as obviously they are doctrines, speaking generally, of one special class, a class of doctrines to which comparatively little space was given in the Confession by its original framers. They supplement the teaching of the Confession, therefore, in a particular direction, the direction, to wit, of the general or universal aspects of grace. By their insertion into the Confession larger space has been given in it—larger emphasis, if you wish—to the universalistic side of the gospel. The Revised Confession, therefore, emphasizes the universalistic side of the gospel as the old Confession did not.

We must not, however, on the other hand, misconceive the meaning of this insertion into the Confession of a fuller treatment of the universalistic aspects of the gospel. Least of all must we fancy that its emphasis upon them in any way modifies the system of doctrine taught in the Confession, or any single doctrine that enters into that system. This it cannot do for the simple reason that the universalistic aspects of the gospel in question belong inherently to the system of doctrine taught in the Confession; were always present implicitly as the background of the Confessional statement of this system; were not only, therefore, allowed for in the statement of this system, but were repeatedly asserted in brief crisp passages which embodied over and over again their essence; and were left without fuller explication merely because the Confession confined itself to the development of the *cor cordis* of the system and left its outlying members to more allusive presupposition. The fuller treatment of these topics in the Revised Confession, accordingly, adds nothing whatever to the system set forth, modifies in no respect any of its doctrinal teachings, and only extends the circumference of its detailed discussion. Swell the Confession to even greater bulk still if you will, you will never change its character as a Calvinistic document so long as the newly incorporated materials remain elements in a developed Calvinistic system. Nor will you soon by thus expanding the Confession get beyond the necessity of selection in the material you incorporate into it. Even after the revision that has been accomplished there remain still many legitimate elements of

Calvinistic teaching which are not yet incorporated into the fabric of the Confession, and which may, after awhile, be inserted into it if anybody earnestly enough wishes to do so. Meanwhile it is important to remember that, however fully the Confession is gradually made to give expression to more and more Calvinistic doctrines, enlargement is not alteration, development is not revolution, elaboration is not correction.

OPPOSING VIEWS

Such, then, are the conclusions to which we have been led by an examination of the Revised Confession itself. They are conclusions which, we feel confident, will commend themselves in their own light to the candid reader. And they might well be left to do this. It is notorious, however, that very different conclusions have of late been now and again pressed upon the attention of the public, sometimes with much subtle argumentation, sometimes merely with much strong and repeated assertion. It may be well to direct attention to some of these, as we must believe, erroneous interpretations of the Revised Confession, with a view to pointing out the sources of their error.

We shall select for this purpose two typical instances, which have little in common except their common conclusion, proceeding as they do, the one from a strictly Calvinistic, the other from a definitely Arminian standpoint. The causes they seek to serve are in polar opposition to each other, and they pass very different estimates on the value of the "revision material." But they both argue that it has introduced into the Confession material which to a great degree neutralizes or tends to neutralize its Calvinism. We shall make some remarks on each in turn.

Dr. Webb's Criticism

The first of the criticisms which we propose to consider is embodied in a strongly written paper published in the *Presbyterian Quarterly* for April, 1904, from the accomplished pen of the Rev. Dr. R. A. Webb, Professor in the Theological School of the Southwestern Presbyterian University at Clarksville,

Tenn. Dr. Webb's zeal is for the integrity of the Calvinistic system, which he thinks is endangered by the new leaven that has been inserted into the Confession. The basis of his complaint is supplied by two passages of the "revision material," which he quotes as follows:

> CHAP. xxxv. 11—In the gospel God declares his love for the world, and his desire that all men should be saved.

> DECLARATORY STATEMENT—1. The doctrine of God's eternal decree is held in harmony with the doctrine of his love to all mankind, his gift of his Son to be the propitiation for the sins of the whole world. . . . Concerning those who perish, the doctrine of God's eternal decree is held in harmony with the doctrine that God desires not the death of any sinner.

The essence of his argument is compressed into the following statement in comment on the passages just quoted:

> Here we have three universal propositions which have been incorporated in the creed of Northern Presbyterians: (1) the universality of God's love; (2) the universality of God's desire; (3) the universality of Christ's atonement. God loves all men, God desires the salvation of all men, God has made propitiation for the sins of all men—these are the new doctrines which the revisers have added to Calvinism. We claim that they are substantive additions; that they are new doctrines; that they are out of harmony with the Calvinistic system; that they are radical and reconstructive; that they logically issue in universalism— universalism pure and absolute, or universalism conditional and hypothetical; that they are premises which cannot be made to yield that particularism which is the historic mark of Calvinistic soteriology.

What, now, is the flaw in this argument? This, briefly: that it seeks to ground a conclusion in a single premise, severed from its companion premises. Dr. Webb says of the sentences he quotes from the Revised Confession: "They are premises which cannot be made to yield that particularism which is the historic mark of Calvinistic soteriology." Of course they cannot—when taken by themselves! But they do not stand by themselves in the Revised Confession, nor even in the "revision material." In the Revised Confession they stand along with, say, the Third Chapter, "Of God's Eternal Decree," and all the other richly wrought out particularistic passages. In the "revision material" they are put forward as implicates and complements of these particularistic passages, and affiirmed to be held in harmony with them, and therefore not to be torn apart from them. Could they be taken by themselves, they might very possibly lead the unwary thinker "logically into universalism." Such universalistic passages in Scripture, when taken in isolation, have led many unwary thinkers before today into universalism. But when taken along with the particularistic passages along with which they stand in the Revised Confession (as in Scripture), they logically issue in—just pure Calvinism, with its harmonious adjustment of the particularistic and universalistic elements of the gospel.

The real question that is raised by the presence of these passages in the Revised Confession, then, is whether there is in the Calvinistic system a legitimate place for the universalistic aspects of the gospel. The Revised Confession declares that there is: and that not merely by inserting into its fabric these universalistic propositions, but by distinctly declaring, in doing so, that they are held in harmony with its doctrine of God's Eternal Decree and the like. No Calvinist has ever been found to doubt it; no Calvinist will ever be found to doubt it. Dr. Webb, we are sure, would be the last to doubt it. It has been, is, and ever will be, the glory of Calvinism that it does not oppose to the one-sided universalism of Arminianism an equally one-sided particularism; but knows how to do full justice to all the elements of the gospel revelation, and how to combine a true particularism and a true universalism in harmonious relations. Nobody, we are sure, more delights in this comprehensiveness of Calvinism, by which it evinces itself as just the gospel in its fulness, than Dr. Webb himself. Indeed, this comprehensive Calvinism is the Calvinism of the unrevised as truly as of the Revised Confession, and its universalistic side has not first been inserted into the Confession by the revision, but only more fully explicated by it.

If the universalistic passages that have been inserted into the Revised Confession are objectionable, therefore, it must be not on account of their mere universalism, but on account of the kind of universalism they express. Dr. Webb accordingly labors to make out that their universalism is the wrong kind of universalism. His argument here, too, however depends on dealing with them in isolation, apart from their context in the Revised Confession, by which their meaning is necessarily fixed. He seeks to strengthen his argument, moreover, by a mistaken application of the distinction between love of complacency and love of benevolence, as if the Revised Confession, when it says God loves all mankind, must perforce intend God's love of complacency. God's love of benevolence—perhaps he would prefer to call it "pity" (p. 656)—Dr. Webb himself would, questionless, allow to be universal. But, beyond all doubt, it is just God's love of benevolence which the Revised Confession signalizes when it says God loves the world, or loves all mankind— as appears, if from nothing else, then from this—that it is out of this love that God is represented as wishing and doing good to its objects, that is to say, as acting benevolently toward them.

While we are willing to say with Dr. Webb, therefore, that the doctrinal propositions inserted into the Confession in 1903 are "substantive additions" to the Confession, and so far "new doctrines" that they formulate aspects of truth not heretofore developed with fulness in its expositions of doctrine; we cannot agree with him—in disagreement with the whole Calvinistic world, with the unrevised Confession itself, and, we are sure, with Dr. Webb also when not considering these special propositions—that such assertions as that God loves "the world" or "all mankind," that he desires not the death of the sinner but that all should come unto him and be saved, and that he has given his Son to be the propitiation for the sins of the whole world, are "out of harmony with the Calvinistic system," are "radical and reconstructive" when inserted into a Calvinistic formulary, or, when read as constituent parts of such a formulary, "logically issue in universalism—universalism pure and absolute, or universalism conditional and hypothetical."

The universalism they issue in, when read in their context—
the context of their own "revision material," no less than the
context of the whole "Revised Confession," a part of which
they are and apart from which they cannot be read—is rather
that truly Calvinistic universalism which it is the just boast of
Calvinism that it alone can do justice to. By Calvinistic divines this Calvinistic universalism has had, no doubt, more or
less justice done to it, according as they have done more or less
justice to the Calvinistic system itself; but they have all in one
way or another recognized it as an element in the Calvinistic
system and sought to give it validity in proportion to the insight of each. We will ask a Calvinist of especially clear insight
to hint to us how justice may be done to it—a Calvinist whose
devotion to the historical particularism of the Reformed system,
we may add, Dr. Webb may emulate, but will hardly surpass.
This is how Dr. Kuyper presents the universalistic aspects of
the gospel:

> "God so loved the *world*, that he gave his only begotten
> Son, that whosoever believeth on him should not perish, but
> have everlasting life." The Mediator is called, "The Light
> of *the world*." The Lamb of God "bears the sin of *the
> world*." Christ is named, "the Savior of *the world*" (John
> iv. 42). He will give his flesh and blood "for the life of
> *the world*." "The fall of Israel," says Paul, "is the riches of
> *the world*" (Rom. xi. 12), and its rejection "the reconcilia-
> tion of *the world*." Accordingly, Christ is a propitiation
> "not for our sins only, but for the sins of *the whole world*."
> And the final triumphant cry at the return of the Lord is to
> be: "Now the kingdoms of *the world* have become our
> God's."

> To wish to infer from this, with the Arminians, that grace
> is not particular, and thus that the salvation of Christ is
> *for each and every man*, is, of course, out of the question.
> Nevertheless, the profundity of the rich declaration, "God
> so loved *the world*," is far from exhausted by saying that
> the world here means the elect. . . .

> Ask whether after the fall, God gave up this, his splendid
> creation, this human race with all its treasure of his image,
> in a word, *this his world*, in order that, casting it aside, he

might create something entirely new out of and for the elect. The Scripture answer is a decided negative. The Anabaptist and in part also the Methodist, may teach such a thing, but not one who through the Scriptures has become Reformed in all his thinking. Such an one knows full well that God has *not* deserted the work of his hands; has *not* given over his magnificent creation; has *not* permitted our race to fall away into the hell of destruction, as a miscarried product; and has *not* thrust away from him this his world as of no further use. But, on the contrary, that he loves the world, so loves it, because it is *his* creation, *his* workmanship, *his* production that he gave his only begotten Son for it; and has brought *his* creation triumphantly through all the terrible conflict, *recreating it*, not creating an entirely *new* thing—and so manifesting himself as *Savior of his own world*.

If we liken mankind, thus, as it has grown up out of Adam, to a tree, then the elect are not leaves which have been plucked off of this tree, in order that there may be braided from them a laurel-wreath for God's glory, while the tree itself is to be cut down, rooted up and cast into the fire; but precisely the contrary, the lost are the boughs, twigs, and leaves that have fallen away from the trunk of mankind, while the elect alone remain attached to it. Not the whole trunk goes to destruction, leaving only a few golden leaflets strewn on the fields of eternal light; but, on the contrary, the trunk, the tree, the race abides, and what is lost is broken off from the trunk and loses its organic nature. . . . And thus the elect come forward not as twigs and branches that have been broken off, but precisely as those that have been kept on. The recreated world is *theirs*. *They* shall inherit the earth.[5]

We may like, or we may not like, Dr. Kuyper's particular construction of Calvinistic universalism. We ourselves like it extremely well.[6] But, in any event, it will be a sad day for Christian theology when Calvinism forgets this, its universalistic

---

[5]*E Voto Dordraceno*, II, pp. 176-178. Cf. *De Gemeene Gratie*, II, pp. 91, 92; *Uit Het Woord*, 2nd Series, I, pp. 37, 237, 240, 245, 482.

[6]Hints of the same essential construction may be read in Drs. C. Hodge, Shedd, and Dabney, also. Cf., e.g., Dabney's *Syllabus and Notes*, p. 535. Cf. also Hasting's *Bible Dictionary*, IV, pp. 62, 63.

side, and hands over to the tender mercies of Arminianism that universality of God's love, of God's desire, of Christ's atonement, to which Arminian contingency is as little able to do justice as it is to the particularism of God's love, of God's desire, of Christ's atonement, that constitutes the core of Calvinistic soteriology.

The Cumberland Presbyterian Criticism

It is with great reluctance that we turn to the second typical instance of erroneous criticism of the Revised Confession which we think that we ought to notice. It is a criticism which has been very frequently repeated during the last few months. Its essence consists in an effort to impose upon the Revised Confession *vi et armis* the historically Cumberland Presbyterian view—which is the distinctively Arminian view—of the relation between the fundamental doctrines of Calvinism and such propositions as those enunciated in the "revision material"; and that, in the face of the explicit repudiation of this view by the Revised Confession in language and with reiteration which one would suppose could not be misunderstood or disregarded. The particularism which is the distinctive mark of Calvinism, says the Revised Confession, leaves ample room for such propositions, and claims the doctrines they announce as constituent elements of its own system. "Good!" cry the Cumberland Presbyterians. "You admit, then, these general propositions? That, we contend, is in effect a repudiation of the particularistic ones; and we propose to adopt your Confession on that understanding."

This is not a caricature. Incredible as it sounds, the columns of the *Cumberland Presbyterian* have been for months filled with just this assertion. Even the halls of the recent General Assembly of the Cumberland Presbyterian Church, met at Dallas, fairly rang with it. The Rev. Dr. S. M. Templeton, for example, in closing the debate on "Union," is reported to have given it such emphatic expression as this: "The revision of the Westminster Confession has been accomplished mostly by the declaration of doctrines contradictory to the objectionable ones; which necessarily implies the rejection of the latter." Semi-official authority has even been accorded this remarkable contention by its incorporation in a "Supplemental Report of the Committee on Fraternity and Union," presented to the Cumberland Presbyterian Assembly, received by it, spread on its Minutes, and frequently since commended to the Church for its guidance in the premises by the official church paper. We may most fairly found our remarks on this last-mentioned document.

Confusion worse confounded reigns throughout this strange paper, the outcome of which appears to be nothing but a plea for—and an astonishing illustration of—doctrinal indifference. Its jubilant refrain is, "Revision has revised"; and its main contention is that in its revising it has modified fatally "the genetic principle" of the Confession, viz., "Divine Sovereignty." To justify such a contention, it adduces as three elements of the Confessional doctrine of Divine Sovereignty unacceptable to Cumberland Presbyterians, "unconditional election," "limited atonement," and "irresistible grace," all of which it asserts have been "revised." For sole proof of this assertion, however, it culls a few sentences out of the "revision-material," torn from their context and diverted from their true meaning, partly by means of a series of remarkable comments. Perhaps the worst instance—though no doubt tastes will differ in the estimation of the relative badness of several bad instances—is the pleading of the passage in the second section of the new chapter "Of the Holy Spirit," which describes "Common Grace"—and carefully and explicitly limits itself to Common Grace—in proof that the Revision has "revised irresistible grace"! To drive the lesson home, to the declaration, that those who do not accept the gracious offer are, because of the fact of "common grace," "guilty of resisting the Holy Spirit," the triumphant comment is adjoined: "That which can be resisted is not irresistible." Which provokes us to ask how this proves that "that which is irresistible can be resisted." What are we to think of this constant tendency violently to twist the language of the "Revised Confession" into senses against which it itself loudly protests?

It is by such methods as these that our Cumberland brethren are seeking to persuade themselves that "the revision has revised" the Calvinism out of the Confession. No, even this document does not quite say that. Catching its breath as it closes, it reverts to the characteristic Cumberland contention that what the Revision has done is to fill the Confession with contradictions, thus leaving every signatory free to take his choice. "The old view," it says, "is not set aside, but the new, and we think the better, is set alongside." One would think that until the "old view" had been "set aside," those who do not believe the "old view" could not think of "adopting" the document. But no; they propose to adopt it and comfort themselves with the imagination that the "new view" has been "set alongside"! On this ground, supported as we have seen, this remarkable paper claims liberty under the Revised Confession for holding either Calvinistic (it would say "Fatalistic") or Arminian doctrines as each signatory lists!

We say, distinctly, Arminian doctrines. For whatever else this document leaves obscure or does its best to make obscure, this at least it makes clear: that the Cumberland Presbyterian Church is Arminian to the core—that is to say, so far as it is represented by this representative document. According to it, three of the constituent Calvinistic doctrines which were remonstrated against by the original Remonstrants and reaffirmed at Dordt, are decisively rejected by the Cumberland Presbyterians also. According to it, also, it is a distinctive Cumberland Presbyterian doctrine that the divine readiness to bestow saving grace is "conditioned upon human seeking"—than which no more extreme assertion of the central Arminian principle could be formulated.[7] If this is not an Arminian document, Arminianism is incapable of recognizable statement.

---

[7]Cf. on this Girardeau, *Calvinism and Evangelical Arminianism, passim,* e.g., pp. 35, 95, 141, 150, 304. Thus: "It is the specific difference of the Arminian doctrine so far as this question of the application of salvation is concerned, that in the last analysis the will of man must be

The real drift of the Cumberland contention concerning the Revised Confession is therefore now laid bare. It is not that the matter inserted into the Confession by the Revision of 1903 has somewhat modified its teaching—moderated its extremities —mollified its harshness—softened its outlines—or adjusted its details. It is that it has definitely Arminianized the Confession; or, at least, set the distinctive principles of Arminianism in it side by side with the distinctive principles of Calvinism—so leaving the two contradictory elements to be accepted, one or the other, as each signatory chooses—seeing that no man can possibly accept both! Certainly the extremity of this contention overreaches itself. Anyone who has read the Revised Confession, or only the "revision-material," however cursorily, will know—cannot fail to know—better than this. And everyone who will attend to the contention itself will perceive that it includes within itself an admission that the Revised Confession still teaches the old doctrines.

No doubt "Revision has revised." No one will wish to question that. But how has it revised? Not by eviscerating the Calvinism of the Confession; nor even by modifying it. But by reiterating it, repelling current assaults upon it, and explicating more fully certain implications of it which were left by the Confession in the comparative obscurity of merely recognized and not fully expounded doctrines. This, we claim, any unbiased reading of the Revised Confession will demonstrate. And this, we claim, the unbiased reading of it which has been given in this paper does demonstrate. The Revised Confession is, then, a Confession which every good Calvinist will recognize at once as his own. It is a Confession which no one, not a good Calvinist, can ever properly profess to make his own. For men who find the unrevised Confession unacceptable because of its Calvinism, to profess to "adopt" the Revised Confession because of the clauses by which it reiterates, defends, and explicates that Calvinism, is a procedure which, as the French say, "gives stupefaction." Or are we simply to infer that Calvinism

conceived as the determining factor." "Hence the decision of God's will is dependent upon the decision of man's" (pp. 150 f.).

can never be rejected when it is understood—that it requires only a little reiteration, defense, and detailed exposition to silence all its enemies and conquer the world? Let us hope that this is the true explanation of the remarkable phenomenon which is now forced on our observation. But certainly it is a very remarkable phenomenon, and requires a good deal of explanation.

25

CALVINISM*

Calvinism (like Pelagianism and Lutheranism) is a term used to designate, not the opinions of an individual, but a mode of religious thought or a system of religious doctrines, of which the person whose name it bears was an eminent expounder. It is synonymous therefore with what is technically called "the Reformed Theology." There have from the beginning co-existed in the Christian Church three specially well-marked and generically distinct systems of doctrine, or modes of conceiving and adjusting the facts and principles understood to be revealed in the Scriptures, under one or the other of which nearly every form of theological thought may be subsumed. One of these is the Pelagian, which denies the native guilt, pollution, and moral impotence of man, and makes him independent of the supernatural assistance of God. At the other pole is the Calvinistic system, which emphasizes the guilt and impotence of man, exalts God, and refers salvation absolutely to the infinite love and undeserved favor of God working in harmony with his justice, sovereignly selecting its objects, and saving them by the almighty power of grace. Between these comes the manifold and elastic system of compromise known in one of its earlier forms as Semi-Pelagianism, and in a more modern type as Arminianism, which admits man's original pollution but denies his native guilt, regards redemption as a compensation for innate and consequently irresponsible disabilities, and refers the

---

*This article, from Johnson's *Cyclopaedia*, Vol. II, pp. 17-25, is from the hand of A. A. Hodge and revised by B. B. Warfield. I have omitted the bibliography. For a later encyclopaedia article by Dr. Warfield, on the same subject, see the volume *Calvin and Calvinism*, 1932, pp. 353-369.

moral restoration of the individual to the co-operation of the human with the divine energy, the determining factor being the human will. The system to which this article is devoted was known historically, in its opposition to Pelagianism and Semi-Pelagianism, and is now designated more generally and indefinitely, by the title *Augustinianism*, from its earliest champion, the illustrious Augustine, Bishop of Hippo Regius in Northern Africa (A.D. 395–430); while the more modern and specific title is *Calvinism*, from the fact that it was developed into a perfect form, and infused into the creeds of the Reformed churches, and into the life of modern nations, through the instrumentality of John Calvin, the Reformer, of Geneva (1509–1564). The authentic statement of its constituent doctrines is not to be drawn exclusively from the writings of either of the great men mentioned, but from the public confessions of those churches which have professed this form of doctrine, and from the classical writings of their representative theologians.

The Reformed Confessions are very numerous—more than thirty in number—but they substantially agree in the system of doctrine which they teach. Those which have been most widely accepted as of symbolical authority are the Second Helvetic Confession, prepared by Bullinger, 1564, and adopted by all the Reformed churches of Switzerland (with the exception of Basel) as well as by the Reformed churches of Poland, Hungary, Scotland, and France; the Heidelberg or Palatinate Catechism, prepared by Ursinus and Olevianus, 1562, indorsed by the Synod of Dordt, and accepted as a doctrinal standard by the Reformed churches of Germany and Holland, as well as by their representatives in America; the Thirty-nine Articles of the Church of England; the Canons of the Synod of Dordt, 1618–1619, an Ecumenical Synod of the Reformed churches; and the Westminster Confession, with its accompanying Larger and Shorter Catechisms, prepared by the famous Westminster Assembly, 1644–1647, and accepted as a doctrinal standard by the Presbyterian churches and by British Calvinists in general. The Canons of Dordt are not so much a complete confession as a supplement to the previous confessions of the Reformed churches, which was necessitated by the rise of the Arminian controversy. The Westminster Confession is the only Reformed creed of wide acceptance which was framed after this controversy; it was prepared with the intention of exhibiting the harmony of the Reformed churches, and with ecumenical purpose and breadth; and it presents "the fullest and ripest symbolical statement of the Calvinistic system of doctrine.[1]

John Calvin remains the most representative theologian of Calvinism. Perhaps a list of representative theologians after him would include especially Bullinger, Aretius, Ursinus, Zanchius, Polanus, of the first age, with such others as Amesius, Voetius, Witsius, Heidegger, Turretin, and among English writers John Owen, John Howe, and Jonathan Edwards for the next age. Modern Presbyterian Calvinism "is best represented by the theological systems of Charles Hodge, W. G. T. Shedd, and Henry B. Smith."[2] The *vade mecum* of the Reformed pastors was in the early days Bucanus' *Institutiones;* this was supplanted later by Amesius' *Medulla;* and it in turn by Marck's *Compendium;* perhaps no handbook is more used today than A. A. Hodge's *Outlines.* Attempts more or less successful have been made to present the Calvinistic system from the writings of its representative theologians by, among others, Heinrich Heppe,[3] Alexander Schweizer,[4] and J. H. Scholten.[5]

It is proposed in this article to present, in necessarily meager outline, a statement (1) of the fundamental characteristics of the system; (2) of the history of its development and prevalence both before and after Calvin; and (3) of its practical moral influence upon individuals and upon communities.

---

[1]Schaff, *Creeds of Christendom*, Vol. I, p. 788.

[2]Schaff, *History of the Christian Church*, Vol. VII, p. 544.

[3]*Die Dogmatik der evangelisch-reformirten Kirche dargestellt und aus den Quellen belegt*, Elberfeld, 1861.

[4]*Die Glaubenslehre der evangelisch-reformirten Kirche dargestellt und aus den Quellen belegt*, Zurich, 1844–1847.

[5]*Leer der Hervormde Kerk, in hare grondbeginselen uit de bronnen voorgesteld en beoordeeld*, 1848–1850.

I. Statement of Principles

There is a very important distinction between the central, formative, or root principle of a system and its distinguishing features, which is not attended to when it is said, as it is sometimes said, that the "principle" of Calvinism is "the metaphysical principle of predestination." Predestination is rather a logical consequence of, and an essential element in, than the determining principle of, Calvinism. This is rather the glory of the Lord God Almighty. The formative idea of Calvinism is the conception of God; and it is its determination that God shall be and remain God in all its thought—to embrace God in the wholeness of his nature, and to do full justice to God in all his relations—which itself determines all those doctrines which have from time to time been mistaken for its "principle." On the practical side this is equivalent to saying that it is the effort of Calvinism to do full justice to the essence of religion. "Since all religion springs from the relation in which God the Creator has placed us, his creatures, to himself, it follows that the greatest religious height will be reached by him who at every point of his horizon views God as God, by honoring him in all things," as the Almighty Being who has created all things for his own sake, who is bound by nothing out of himself, and who determines for every creature both its being and the law thereof, both now and for eternity. And "as religion on earth finds its highest expression in the act of prayer," Calvinism in the Christian Church is simply that tendency which makes a man assume the same attitude toward God in his profession and life which he always exhibits in his prayer. . . . Whoever truly prays ascribes nothing to his own will or power except the sin that condemns him before God, and knows of nothing that could endure the judgment of God except it be wrought within him by the divine love. But while all other tendencies in the Church preserve this attitude so long as their prayer lasts, to lose themselves in radically different conceptions as soon as the amen has been pronounced, the Calvinist adheres to the truth of his prayer in his confession, in his theology, in his life, and the amen that has closed his petition re-echoes in the depths of his consciousness and throughout the whole of his existence."[6]

Those teachings which distinguish the Calvinistic from other systems of theology are simply the outgrowth of this fundamental attitude of mind. The Synod of Dordt defined the distinguishing doctrines of Calvinism as over against Arminianism in five propositions, which have therefore since been called "the five points of Calvinism," though they are rather the Calvinistic response to "the five points of Arminianism" than an independent statement of the differentiating elements of Calvinism. These five points affirmed absolute predestination, particular redemption, total depravity, irresistible grace, and the perseverance of the saints. If a single distinguishing principle is to be discriminated among these, it will not be found in "predestination," but rather in "irresistible grace." Predestination is acknowledged by both parties, and is indeed a necessary postulate of natural religion; the difference between the parties here lies in the conception of the *ground* of the predestinating decree. The distinguishing mark of Calvinism as over against all other systems lies in its doctrines of "efficacious grace," which, it teaches, is the undeserved, and therefore gratuitous, and therefore sovereign mercy of God, by which he efficaciously brings whom he will into salvation. Calvinism is specifically the theology of grace; and all are properly Calvinists who confess the absolute sovereignty of God in the distribution of his saving mercy. Two modifications of typical Calvinism have been attempted within the limits of the system, and have had considerable temporary and local influence. One of these, called Salmurianism from its place of origin (the theological school of Saumur, in France), sought to reconcile the sovereignty of grace with the doctrine of a universal atonement, which had been taught previously only by Pelagians and Arminians; this involved a modification of the doctrine of "particular redemption," and with it of the nature, purpose, and effect of the atonement, but left the doctrine of "irresistible grace" un-

---

[6]A. Kuyper, *The Presbyterian and Reformed Review*, II, pp. 378-382.

affected. The other modification sought to reconcile the sovereignty of grace with the Pelagian theory of the will and of man's power to the contrary; in its highest form (as taught by Bellarmine and certain Jesuit theologians) it has received the name of "the doctrine of congruity," and teaches that God adapts the amount and time of the persuasive influences of his Spirit to the foreseen state of mind of those whom he elects to salvation, and thus secures their free acceptance of his offers of mercy. This modification affects directly the doctrine of "irresistible grace," but remains Calvinistic so long as it makes God's selection of the recipients of the saving grace entirely sovereign, and his application of grace to them certainly efficacious. Typical Calvinism, which remains the faith of the great body of those who hold this type of doctrine, teaches that "efficacious grace" is the creative efficiency of the Holy Spirit operating beneath consciousness, not by moral suasion but "physically," the soul remaining passive therein until it has been quickened and renewed by the Holy Spirit and thereby enabled to act in the powers of its new life.

The following is an exposition of the chief features of Calvinism as a system of doctrine.

A. *The Relation of the Creator to the Creation.* There are three generically distinct views as to the relation of the Creator to the creation, each, of course, embracing many specific varieties under it. 1. The Deistical view, which admits a creation *ex nihilo*, and an original endowment of the elements with their active powers, and the subjection of the whole system of things to certain general laws, adapted to the evolution of certain fixed plans. The general plan and order of the creation is attributed to the Creator, and all events are referred to him in a general sense as the indefinitely remote First Cause, who inaugurated the ever-onflowing line of second causes. This view, however, denies the continued immanence of the Creator in the creation, and the immediate dependence of the creature on the Creator for the continuance of its substance, the possession of its properties, and the exercise of its powers. 2. The opposite extreme is the Pantheistic mode of thought, which identifies God and the universe as his existence-form, or at least so confines him to it as to deny his transcendence beyond the universe as an extra-mundane Spirit and conscious Person whose actions are rationally determined volitions. 3. Between these extremes stands Christian Theism. It emphasizes at once the transcendence of God beyond, and the immanence of God within, the world. He remains ever a conscious personal Spirit, without and above the world, able, in the exercise of his free volitions, sovereignly to exercise a supernatural influence (*potestas libera*) upon any part of that system of nature which he has established, ordinarily working through second causes, "yet free to work without, above, and against them at his pleasure." At the same time he continues to interpenetrate the inmost being of every element of every creature with the infinite energies of his free intelligent will, and his creatures momentarily continue absolutely dependent upon the energy of that will for substance and for the possession of the powers communicated to them as second causes in all their exercises.

All Christians, of course, are Theists in the sense thus defined; but the different schools of Christian theology take their points of departure here, as, on the one hand, they press the essential dependence of the creature upon the Creator in substance, properties, and actions, or as, on the other hand, they press the self-active power of second causes, and by consequence their self-sufficiency and independence. Here we have the ultimate antithetical grounds of Pelagianism and Augustinianism. Pelagius, who was characterized by a rationalistic habit of thought and a superficial religious experience, believing that power to the contrary is an inalienable attribute of every act of free will, necessary to render it responsible and therefore moral, maintained, in the supposed interests of morals, that every free agent is so adequately endowed by God as to be inalienably self-sufficient for action, each in a manner appropriate to his kind. Augustine, on the contrary, held that every creature exists and acts only as its substance is momentarily sustained, and its action conditioned, by the omnipresent and omnipotent energy of God. While affirming the free self-determining power of the human soul, he referred the moral character of the volition to the disposition which prompted it, and the persistence of the moral nature of man to the immanent influences of the Spirit of God. Even anterior to apostasy, therefore, the spirit of man depended for spiritual life and moral integrity upon the *concursus* of the Spirit of God, and the withdrawal of this would be the immediate cause of spiritual death and moral impotence. This divine influence, in one degree and in one mode or another, is common to all creatures and all their actions. This view of Augustine was subsequently elaborated by his disciples into the theory of the "previous," "simultaneous," and "determining" *concursus* of the Thomists and Reformed theologians.[7]

B. *The End or Design of God in Creation.* Every intelligent Theist must regard the universe as one system, and must therefore believe that the Creator had from the beginning one general end, for the accomplishment of which the whole and all its parts were intended. This general end must have determined the Creator in every step he has taken in the evolution of the universe, and hence our conception of it will give shape to any speculations we may form with respect to the relations of God and his works. It is evident that no solution of this transcendent question can be reached by reasoning from *a priori* principles, or by generalizations drawn from the comparatively few facts at present accessible to our observation, and that it can be rationally sought for only in a direct revelation. For the most part, this general end has been referred to the essential benevolence of God, prompting him to confer the greatest possible amount of blessedness, in the highest forms of excellence, upon innumerable objects of his love. Leibnitz, in his *Théodicée* (1710), which has exerted a wide influence on all modern speculation, lowered this view by emphasizing the "happiness" of the creatures as the great end of the creative goodness. The Scriptures, on the contrary, emphatically declare that the manifestation of his own glorious perfections is the actual and most

---

[7]See the *Summa* of Thomas Aquinas, II. i. 10, and Turretin, VI. vi. 6 and 7.

worthy possible end of the great Designer, in all his works of creation, providence, and redemption; and hence likewise the final end of all his intelligent creatures in all moral action. The recognition of this great principle, and its application to the interpretation of all God's dealings with man, and of all man's duties to God, has always been an essential characteristic of Calvinism. Pelagians and Semi-Pelagians, with more or less decision, place the general end of the system of things in the well-being of the creature: Calvinists place it absolutely in the glory of the Creator, which carries with it, not as a co-ordinate design, but as a subordinate yet certain effect, the blessedness of all loyal creatures.

C. *The Relation Which the Eternal Plan of God Sustains to the Actual Evolution of Events in Time.* Every Theist believes that the eternal and absolutely perfect intelligence of the Creator must have formed from the beginning a plan comprehending the entire system of creation and providence in reference to the great end for which they were designed. Pelagius himself admitted that the absolute foreknowledge of God embraced the future volitions of free agents, as well as all other classes of events, while he denied their foreordination. The Socinians, who have developed Pelagianism into a complete system, more consistently deny foreknowledge, as well as foreordination, since, if it is essential that a volition should be purely contingent in order that it should be responsible, it must be indeterminate before the event, and while indeterminate it cannot be certainly foreknown. The Arminians (though not without exceptions, such as Adam Clarke and the late Dr. McCabe) admit foreknowledge, but deny foreordination. The Calvinists argue that, in an intelligent being, prevision implies provision; and that the admission of God's infinite foreknowledge therefore necessarily involves the admission of his eternal foreordination.

In this matter they maintain the following positions: 1. In the case of an infinitely wise, powerful, and free Creator of all things *ex nihilo*, it is obvious that the certain foreknowledge of all events from the absolute beginning virtually involves the predetermination of each event, without exception; for all the causes and consequences, direct and contingent, which are foreseen before creation are, of course, determined by creation. As Sir William Hamilton asserts, "the two great articles of foreknowledge and predestination are both embarrassed by the selfsame difficulties."[8] 2. Since all events constitute a single system, the Creator must embrace the system as a whole, and every infinitesimal element of it, in one all-comprehensive intention. Ends more or less general must be determined as ends, and means and conditions in all their several relations to the ends which are made dependent upon them. Hence, while every event remains dependent upon its causes and contingent upon its conditions, none of God's purposes can possibly be contingent, because in turn every cause and condition is determined in that purpose, as well as the ends which are suspended upon them. All the decrees of God are hence called absolute, because they are ultimately determined always by "the counsel of his own will," and never by anything exterior to him which has not in turn been previously determined by him. 3. This determination, however, instead of interfering with, maintains the true causality of the creature, and the free self-determination of men and angels. The eternal and immutable plan of God has constituted man a free agent, and consequently can never interfere with the exercise of that freedom of which it is itself the foundation. However, according to the principles above stated, this created free will is not independent, but ever continues to have its ground in the conserving energies of the omnipresent Creator. Since the holiness of the created moral agent is conditioned upon the indwelling of divine grace, and its turning from grace is the cause of sin, it follows that all the good in the volitions of free agents is to be referred to God as its positive source, but all the evil (which *originates* in defect, privation) is to be referred simply to his permission. In this view, all events, without exception, are embraced in God's eternal purpose; even the primal apostasies of

---

[8]*Discussions*, Appendix 1, A.

Satan and of Adam, as well as all those consequences which have flowed from them. It is in view of these principles that Calvinism has been so often confounded with fatalism. It is, however, the antipodes of fatalism, preserving the real efficiency of second causes while subjecting their action to intelligent control. It teaches that the all-penetrating and all-energizing will of the personal Jehovah, who is at once perfect Love and perfect Light, constitutes and conserves our free agency, and through its free spontaneity works continually the ever-blessed counsel of his own will, weaving even rebellious volitions into the instrumentalities of his purpose, and making every consenting soul a conscious coworker with himself.

As to the bearing of this principle upon the question of the design of God in the application of redemption (predestination), see below.

D. *The Manner in Which the Divine Attributes of Benevolence, Justice, and Grace Are Illustrated in the Scheme of Redemption.* Arminians have generally held, with Leibnitz, that "justice is benevolence acting according to wisdom"— that is, inflicting a lesser pain in order to effect a greater or more general happiness. The necessity for punishment therefore lies not in the essential and inexorable demands of righteousness, but in its being the best means to secure the moral reformation of the sinner, and the best motive to restrain the community from disobedience. Grotius maintained that the moral law is a product of the divine will, and therefore capable of being relaxed by that will. In the gospel scheme, therefore, God, in the exercise of his sovereign prerogative, relaxes his law by forgiving sinners upon repentance and reformation, while as an administrative precaution he makes an exhibition of severe suffering in the person of his Son, in order that all other subjects of his moral government may be deterred from making the impunity of repentant men an encouragement to disobedience. The atonement, therefore, was an exhibition solely of the divine benevolence, but not of justice in the ordinary sense of that word.

Calvinists, on the contrary, hold that justice in the strict sense, as well as benevolence, is an essential and ultimate property of the divine nature, and hence lies back of, and determines the character of, all the divine volitions. By the perfection of God's nature he is always both benevolent and just in all his actions. The atonement accordingly was an act of infinite love, seeking and finding a way to be both just and yet the justifier of the sinner; it provides a divine substitute for the sinner, who undertakes for him and bears his penalties, and works out a perfect righteousness in his stead, with regard to which God may accept the person of the sinner as (judicially) righteous in his sight. While Arminians in their view of the gospel emphasize benevolence, Calvinists in their view emphasize justice and grace.

E. *The Degree of Guilt and Moral Damage Entailed Through the Apostasy of Adam upon His Posterity.* The answers respectively given to this question impose form and character upon all the various systems of theology.

1. Pelagius held that free will (*liberum arbitrium*), in the sense of an absolutely unconditioned power of choice between good and evil, is essential to responsible moral agency, and hence inalienable from human nature. Since, then, all men continue after the apostasy to be responsible moral agents, their nature in this essential respect must remain in the same condition in which it was created. The moral agency of a man at any one moment cannot determine the character of his moral agency at any other moment, and he possesses throughout his entire existence ability to will and to do all that God has any right to require of him. Hence Pelagians deny—(1) All original sin or corruption of nature, because sinfulness can be predicated only of free acts, and man in order to be responsible must always possess plenary ability to will aright. (2) All original guilt or desert of punishment common to the race, and prior to the actual transgression of the individual, since it would be a violation of justice to hold one moral agent responsible for the wrong volitions of another. (3) Hence men need redemption through Christ only to deliver them from the guilt of actual and personal transgression, and only those need it who have

thus sinned. Those dying in infancy are therefore worthy of neither reward nor punishment, and can be benefited by Christ only by being raised to a higher plane of blessedness than that belonging to nature—to the *regnum coelorum* as distinguished from the *vita aeterna*.

2. Augustinians and Calvinists, on the contrary, maintain— (1) That the entire soul, with all its constitutional faculties and acquired habits, is the organ of volition, the agent willing. (2) That this soul possesses the inalienable property of self-determination, the moral character of which determination always depends upon the moral condition of the soul acting. (3) That the holy moral condition of the soul, and hence its spontaneous disposition to will that which is right, depends upon the indwelling of the divine Spirit. The free agency of God is an absolute self-existent and self-sufficient perfection, self-determined to good and incapable of evil. The freedom of saints and angels confirmed in holiness is dependent upon divine assistance, but, like that of God himself, it is the very opposite to the "liberty of indifference" or "power to the contrary," being a *non posse peccare*, a *felix necessitas boni*. Adam was created in fellowship with God, and hence with a holy tendency of heart, with full power not to sin (*posse non peccare*), but also, during a limited period of probation, with power to sin (*posse peccare*). He did sin. As a punishment the Holy Spirit was withdrawn from the race, and he and his descendants lost the *posse non peccare*, and retained only the *posse peccare,* which thus became the fatal *non posse non peccare*.

This theological doctrine of total moral inability has nothing whatever to do with the psychological theory of "philosophical necessity" as an attribute of voluntary action, which, since the time of President Edwards, has been too frequently regarded essential to the defense of Calvinism. It has been conclusively shown by Principal Cunningham[9] that this metaphysical doctrine is not essential to Calvinism; while Sir William Hamilton[10]

---

[9]*Theology of the Reformers*, Essay IX.
[10]*Discussions*, Appendix 1, A.

and Sir James Mackintosh[11] propose to prove that it is absolutely inconsistent with Calvinism as historically taught. The phrases "bondage of the will," etc., so frequently used by all classes of Augustinian theologians, and above all by Luther in his treatise *De Servo Arbitrio*, are intended to apply only to the corrupt spontaneous tendency of fallen man to evil, which can be reversed only by a new creating energy from above. At the same time, every Calvinist holds devoutly to the free self-determination of the soul in every moral action, and is at liberty to give whatever psychological explanation of that fact may seem to him most reasonable.[12]

Hence Calvinists hold—First: as to original guilt. (1) Human sin, having originated in the free apostatizing act of Adam, deserves God's wrath and curse, and immutable justice demands their infliction. (2) Such, moreover, was the relation subsisting between Adam and his descendants that God righteously regards and treats each one, as he comes into being, as worthy of the punishment of that sin, and consequently withdraws his life-giving fellowship from him. Some refer this responsibility of Adam's descendants for his apostatizing act to a purely sovereign "divine constitution" (New England view); others hold that we all were in our generic essence guilty coagents with him in that act (Realistic view); while the common opinion is that God, as the guardian of our interests, gave to us all the most favorable probation possible for beings so constituted, in Adam as our covenant representative (Federal view). The whole race, therefore, and each individual it embraces, is under the just condemnation of God, and hence the gift of Christ, and the entire scheme of redemption, in its conception, execution, and application, are throughout and in every sense a product of sovereign grace. God was free to provide it for few or many, for all or none, just as he pleased. And in every case of its application the motives determining God cannot be

---

[11]*Dissertations on the Progress of Ethical Philosophy*, Note O.

[12]See *Confession of Faith*, ch. IX, and Calvin's *De Servitute et Liberatione Humani Arbitrii*.

found in the object, but only in the good pleasure of the will of the divine Agent.

Calvinists also hold—Secondly: as to original sin. (1) Since every man thus comes into the world in a condition of antenatal forfeiture because of Adam's apostasy, he is judicially excluded from the morally quickening energy of the Holy Ghost, and hence begins to think, feel, and act without a spontaneous bias to moral good. (2) But since moral obligation is positive, and the soul is essentially active, it instantly develops in action a spiritual blindness and deadness to divine things, and a positive inclination to evil. This involves the corruption of the whole nature, and absolute impotency of the will to good; is, humanly speaking, without remedy; and necessarily tends to the indefinite increase both of depravity and of guilt. It is therefore said to be total. Some Calvinists hold original guilt to be conditioned upon original depravity (e.g., the advocates of mediate imputation). Others, including the large majority, of all ages, hold original depravity to be the penal consequence of Adam's apostatizing act, and therefore to be conditioned upon original guilt (hence immediate imputation).

3. The advocates of the middle scheme have, of course, varied very much from the almost Pelagian extreme occupied by many of the Jesuits and of the Remonstrants, to the almost Augustinian position of the Lutherans and of the great Wesleyan Richard Watson. The Semi-Pelagians admitted that the nature of man was so far injured by the fall that he could do nothing in his own strength morally good in God's sight. But they held that man is able to incline himself unto good, though he is not able to effect it; so that in every case of spiritual reformation the first movement toward good may be from the soul itself, while the performance of it is the result of the co-operation of divine grace with the human will. They consequently denied the *gratia praeveniens*, but admitted the *gratia co-operans*. The modern Protestant Arminians (Limborch, Episcopius, etc.) admit original sin, while they deny original guilt, and regard innate corruption rather as a vice or fault of nature than as a sin in the full sense of that term. Dr. D. D.

Whedon[13] admits—1. That Adam and Eve by the apostasy morally corrupted their own nature and that of all their descendants. 2. That every child of Adam is born with an inherent tendency to sin which he cannot remove by his own power. 3. That Adam and Eve were fully responsible for their apostasy, because they sinned in spite of possessing power to the contrary, and therefore might justly have been damned. 4. Nevertheless, their descendants, although corrupt and prone to sin from birth, are neither responsible nor punishable until there has first been bestowed upon them redemptively a gracious ability to the right. 5. After Adam sinned, therefore, only one alternative was open to divine justice—either that Adam should be punished at once without issue, or that he should be allowed to generate seed in his own moral likeness, when equity required that an adequate redemption should be provided for all. 6. Hence Christ died for all men, and sufficient grace (including *gratia praeveniens* and *gratia co-operans*) is given to all men, which is essential to render them responsible, and they become guilty only when they abuse (by failing to co-operate with) that gracious power to the contrary (*posse non peccare*) which has been conferred on them in the gospel. Quoting the dictum of President Edwards,[14] "The essence of the virtue or vice of dispositions of the heart and actions of the will lies not in their cause, but in their nature," Whedon says: "To this we oppose the counter-maxim, that in order to responsibility for a given act or state, power in the agent for a contrary act or state is requisite. In other words, power underlies responsibility." The only limit he allows to this principle is in the case of that moral inability which results from the previous abuse of freedom by the agent himself. This he declares is the fundamental ground upon which all the issues between Arminianism and Calvinism depend. Thus while Calvinism exalts the redemption of Christ, in its execution and in each moment of its application, as an adorable act of transcend-

---

[13]*Bibliotheca Sacra*, April 1862.
[14]*Will*, pt. 4, par. 1.

ent grace to the ill-deserving, Arminianism, in its last analysis, makes it a compensation brought in by the equitable Governor of the world to balance the disabilities brought upon men, without their fault, by the apostasy of Adam. This difference is the practical reason that Calvinism has such a strong hold upon the religious experience of Christians, and that it finds such frequent irrepressible expression in the hymns and prayers of evangelical Arminians.

F. *The Nature and Necessity of That Divine Grace Which Is Exercised in the Moral Recovery of Human Nature.* Grace is free sovereign favor to the ill-deserving. It is the motive to redemption in the mind of God. It is exercised in the sacrifice of his Son, in the free justification of the believing sinner on the ground of that Son's vicarious obedience and sufferings, and in the total change wrought in that sinner's moral character and actions by the energy of the Holy Ghost. While the word *grace* applies equally to the objective change of relations and the subjective change of character, it is used in this connection to designate that energy of the Holy Ghost whereby the moral nature of the human soul is renewed, and the soul, thus renewed, is enabled to act in compliance with the will of God.

Pelagius found in his system neither need nor room for this divine energy, and confined the conception of grace to objective revelations and educational and providential influences.

Semi-Pelagians admitted its necessity to help man to complete that which he had himself power to commence, and held that it is actually given to all those who had thus prepared themselves for it and made themselves worthy of it.

Arminians admit that it is necessary in order that the corrupt will shall be even predisposed to good; but they regard it as a universal compensation for the irresponsible defects of an inherited nature, which restores the native power for either good or evil; and they make all further effects depend wholly upon the use made of it by the soul in which it acts. This is styled the theory of Co-operation as held by the Arminians and of "Synergism" as held by the followers of Melanchthon in Germany. Regeneration is the result of the coworking of two energies, but the determining factor is the human will. Hence grace is *sufficiens* in every case, and *efficax ab eventu vel congruitate.*

Augustinians and Calvinists, on the other hand, hold— 1. That, for Christ's sake, and in spite of all human demerit, a gracious influence is exerted on the minds of all men of various intensities. This is "common grace," and is a moral and suasory influence on the soul, tending to good, restraining evil passions, and adorning the soul with the natural virtues; it may be resisted, and is always prevailingly resisted by the unregenerate. 2. But at his pleasure, in certain cases, God exerts a new creative energy, which in a single act changes the moral character of the will of the subject, and implants a prevailing tendency to co-operate with future grace in all forms of holy obedience. This is *gratia efficax,* "effectual calling," which is always effectual because it consists in effecting a regenerative change in the moral nature of the will itself. The change which this grace effects is the "new heart" of Scripture, the *conversio habitualis seu passiva,* of which God is the agent and man the subject, which as a new habit of soul lays the foundation for all holy activities. Augustine has been generally followed in styling this grace "irresistible," because it cannot be resisted. Yet this is as incongruous a designation as it would be to call the creation of the world or the generation of a child "irresistible." Effectual calling consists in a new creative energy within the soul, making it willing, upon which it spontaneously embraces Christ and turns to God (the *conversio actualis seu activa*). It merges itself into the very spontaneity of the will, and enfranchises it from the corruption which had hitherto held it in bondage, and restores it to its normal equilibrium, in harmony with reason and conscience and the indwelling Spirit of God. 3. Afterward the divine Spirit continues to support the soul, and prepare it for, and to concur with it in, every good work. This grace is now prevailingly co-operated with by the regenerated soul, and at times resisted, until the status of grace is succeeded by the status of glory.

Calvinists hold that this "grace" in all its stages is purely undeserved favor, and therefore sovereignly exercised by God upon whom and at what time he pleases; hence it is called *gratia gratuita et gratis data*, otherwise grace would be no more grace. It also works in its various stages progressively, except in the single regenerative act. It is at first the *gratia praeveniens,* then the *gratia operans*, then the *gratia co-operans*, and finally the *gratia perficiens*, including the *donum perseverantiae*, infallibly securing perseverance in faith and obedience, unto the complete redemption of soul and body in glory.

G. *The Relation Which the Eternal Plan of God Bears to the Application of Redemption to Individuals.* Since the eternal plan, decree, or purpose of God includes all things that come to pass, none of which comes to pass without his prevision and provision, it includes also the destinies of all creatures. Predestination, in its restricted sense, is the term employed to express the purpose of God in relation to the salvation of individual men. Arminians maintain that this purpose of God is with reference to each man conditioned upon God's foresight of his possession or lack of faith and repentance; but Calvinists insist that since faith and repentance are the gifts of God and the fruits of his Spirit, their presence or absence cannot be the condition of predestination, but must rather be its predetermined and graciously effected result. The primary efficient cause of predestination is therefore God himself; the discriminating cause lies in the hidden counsels of his own will. Predestination therefore is the eternal, inscrutable, and unchangeable decree of God concerning the salvation of individual men; it consists of two parts—eternal election on the one side and eternal preterition on the other. It thus includes both the selection of one portion of the race to be saved and the leaving the rest to perish in sin. This act of discrimination is necessarily absolutely sovereign, and can find its cause on neither side in aught in the creature moving God to elect or pass him by; *ex hypothesi*, all stand in like condition before God prior to this act of discrimination, and what is common to the whole cannot be the ground of discrimination between the parts. But the subsequent treatment to which each section is subjected is not sovereign, but is conditioned on the one side on God's purpose of love to his elect, and on the other on the guilt of the sin in which the non-elect are left. The decree of election to eternal life is followed therefore by the foreordination of all the means thereto. And the purpose to pass by the rest and leave them in their sin is followed by the ordination of them to dishonor and wrath for their sin. A discrimination is thus drawn between the sovereign act of preterition and the judicial act of reprobation; or, as they are otherwise called, between the sovereign act of "negative reprobation" and the judicial act of "positive reprobation." So far all historical schools of Calvinism agree. Adherents of what is known as the school of Saumur are equally explicit and decided in these points with typical Calvinists.[15] Accordingly the Ecumenical Reformed Synod of Dordt (1619) and the broadly Calvinistic Assembly of Westminster (1644–1647) so define the doctrine.

In the further development of the subject, however, diverging schools of thought emerge within the limits of Calvinism. The great majority of Calvinists have always been what has come to be known as Infra- or Sublapsarians—that is, they hold that God's predestinating decree contemplates man as already fallen and resting under the curse of the broken law. God is conceived of as, moved by ineffable love for man, selecting out of the mass of guilty sinners a people in whom to show forth the glory of his grace, and then as providing redemption for them in order to carry out his loving purpose in election. The "order of decrees," as it is technically called, stands in this view thus: creation, fall, election, redemption by Christ, application of redemption by the Holy Spirit. A few Calvinists, whose inconsiderable number is balanced by their considerable learning and logical power, have always contended that on logical grounds it would be better to place the decree of election in the order of thought before that of the fall; they are therefore called

---

[15]See, e.g., Amyraldus, *Defense of Calvin*, ch. xiii, *Declaration against the Errors of the Arminians*, 1646, p. 6; and in this country James Richards, *Lectures on Mental Philosophy and Theology*, 1846, pp. 332 f.; Henry B. Smith, *System of Christian Theology*, 1886, p. 508.

Supralapsarians, and give the "order of decrees" thus: creation, election (or even election, creation), fall, redemption, application. This question did not come into discussion until the close of the sixteenth century, so that the position upon it of Calvinistic writers before that date is usually in dispute. There seems no good reason to doubt, however, that Augustine and Calvin were essentially Infralapsarian in their fundamental conceptions. On the other hand, the Supralapsarian scheme was adopted by men of such mark and influence as Beza, successor to Calvin in Geneva; Gomarus and Voetius, the great opponents to the Remonstrants in Holland; Twisse, the prolocutor of the Westminster Assembly. Ecumenical Calvinism ranged itself explicitly as Infralapsarian in the Canons of the Synod of Dordt (1619), and with less explicitness but no less reality, in the Westminster Confession (1644–1647). The difference between the two views is, however, almost entirely a logical one, and has little or no theological importance.[16] On the other hand, a departure from typical Calvinism was proposed by the school of Saumur in the first half of the seventeenth century in the opposite direction. In the effort to conceive of the work of Christ as having equal reference to all men indiscriminately, they proposed to place the decree of election subsequent in the order of thought to that of redemption, making the "order of decrees" the following: creation, fall, redemption by Christ, election, application of redemption by the Holy Spirit to the elect. This change is of greater theological importance, as it involves an entirely different view of the nature of the atonement from that taught by typical Calvinism. It has exercised far more influence than Supralapsarianism; but has left the great majority of Calvinists unaffected, chiefly on account of its inability to coalesce with a truly substitutionary doctrine of the atonement.

In all its forms alike Calvinism makes God the sole arbiter of the destiny of his creatures. But in no form does it make

---

[16]See Twisse, *The Riches of God's Love*, p. 35; Cunningham, *The Reformers*, etc., pp. 359-362; Dabney, *Syllabus on Systematic Theology*, p. 233.

him the author of sin, or the condemner of man irrespective of his sin. In all forms alike man is made the author of his own sin, and sin is made the ground of his condemnation. God positively decrees grace, and thus produces all that is good. He only determines the permission of sin, and punishes it because he forbids and in every way morally discountenances it. He elects of free grace all those he purposes to save, and actually saves them, while those whom he does not elect are simply left under the operation of the law of exact justice, whatever that may be in their case. Archbishop Whately, himself an Arminian, in his essays on *Some of the Difficulties in the Writings of the Apostle Paul*, honorably admits that the apparent harshness of Calvinism lies in the *facts* of the case as admitted by all Christians. It is obvious that all who are born sin and die, that all do not believe, and that all are not saved. Calvinistic "particularism" embraces the actual results of salvation in their widest scope, and refers all to the gracious purpose and power of God, but does not restrict it one iota within the limits determined by the facts themselves.

II. THE HISTORY OF CALVINISM

The Christian doctrines of sin and grace were, like other doctrines, brought to clear definition only through controversy. The intellectual energies of the Church were at first absorbed in the realization and definition of the doctrines of God and of the Person of Christ; and it was only after four centuries of controversy had brought these doctrines to clear expression that the Church could turn its attention to the more subjective side of truth. In the meantime all the elements of the composite doctrine of man were everywhere confessed: the evil consequences of the fall and the necessity of divine grace for salvation were as universally recognized as the freedom of will and the complete responsibility of man for sin. But the prevalent Gnostic and Manichaean heresies, which represented sin as a necessity of nature, led necessarily to a very special emphasis being thrown upon human freedom and responsibility by the Church teachers of the time. In necessary antagonism to these fundamental heresies, the early Fathers, especially Origen and his colleagues and followers of the Alexandrian school, were led to insist in a very unqualified manner upon the independent self-determining power of the human will, and to maintain that sin is the product of that freedom abused. They universally held that human nature was morally ruined by Adam's sin, and that it was redeemed by the blood and restored by the Spirit of Christ; but they conceived of these great principles in a crude and indefinite manner, without determining their relations to each other. But in the special attention to the defense of human self-determining power as the basis of responsibility, which all were in a manner forced to give, it was inevitable that sooner or later someone would arise who should so one-sidedly emphasize this element of the truth as consciously to deny its other hemisphere. As a general fact, the Greeks were especially distinguished for emphasizing the autocracy of the will, though without denying the need of grace. And the anthropology of the Greek Church has continued to preserve the same characteristics to the present day.[17] On the other hand, there was, during the third century, a marked tendency in the Latin Church to more profound views as to the moral and spiritual nature and relations of man. This characteristic was developed most obviously in Tertullian of Carthage (A.D. 220), who taught the propagation (*ex traduce*) of a corrupt nature from Adam to each of his descendants; in Hilary of Poitiers (368); and in Ambrose of Milan (397), the most explicit defender in that age of the sovereignty of God and the moral impotence of man, and the immediate teacher of Augustine.

The inevitable heresiarch came at the opening of the fifth century in the person of Pelagius (Morgan), a British monk, a man of pure life, clear practical intellect, and earnest zeal for the moral interests of human life. He was the moral author of the system which bears his name, while its intellectual con-

---

[17]Athanasius, *Expos. in Psalmos*, Ps. 1. 7, *Orthodox Confession of Peter Mogilas*, 1642.

structor was Coelestius, a youthful Roman advocate; and its most effective advocate was Julian, the deposed Bishop of Eclanum in Campania. The central and formative principle of Pelagianism was the inalienable plenary ability of man to do all that can righteously be demanded of him; from this principle it inferred that men are fully capable in their own powers to attain and maintain entire perfection of life, that they come into the world without entailment of moral weakness or sin from the past, and that they need and receive no divine aid in the sense of inward renewal and sustaining grace, to enable them to do their full duty. It was this denial of the necessity and reality of the inward operations of God's grace which most outraged Christian hearts, and Augustine lays the chief stress in the controversy on the reality of grace, and its necessity as arising out of original sin. In opposition to Pelagianism, the distinctive features of the theology of grace were developed out of the Scriptures and his own deep experience by this profound thinker, Augustine (354–430), a native of Tagaste, in Numidia, the son of a heathen father and of the sainted Monica, in turn a prodigal, unbeliever, Manichaean, Platonist, disciple of Ambrose, Christian of profound experience, preacher and teacher of transcendent genius, Bishop of Hippo Regius from 395 to 430, and the greatest theologian of all time. The result of the controversy was not doubtful. The opinions of Pelagius were universally condemned by the whole Church, Eastern and Western, at the councils held at Carthage A.D. 412 and 418, at the Council at Mileve, A.D. 416, by the popes Innocent and Zosimus, and by the Ecumenical Council held at Ephesus, A.D. 431. This rapid and universal condemnation of Pelagianism, after making all due allowance for extraneous influences, proves that, however indefinite the views of the ancient Greek Fathers may have been, nevertheless the system taught by Augustine was in all essentials the common and original faith of the Church. In the history of the entire Church to the present moment, Pelagianism has never been adopted into the public creed of any ecclesiastical body except that of the Socinians (*Racovian Catechism*, 1605), and it has prevailed practically only among Rationalists, whose Christianity was disintegrating into Deism.

But Pelagianism did not so die as to leave no "remainders" behind it. Already in Augustine's lifetime (as early as 428) we hear of a body of monastic leaders in southern Gaul seeking a middle ground between Augustinianism and Pelagianism by admitting inherited sin and the necessity of grace, but denying that this grace is either inevitable or necessarily prevenient. John Cassian, a disciple of Chrysostom, abbot of the monastery at Marseilles, was the leader of this middle system of compromise, whose advocates were at first styled Massilians, but during the Middle Ages and at present in the Romish Church Semi-Pelagians. His most influential supporters and followers were Vincentius of Lerinum (434), Faustus, Bishop of Rhegium (475), Gennadius, and Arnobius; and his opinions prevailed in France for a long time, and were confirmed by the provincial synods of Arles (472) and of Lyons (475). Against this party Augustine wrote his great works *De Praedestinatione Sanctorum* and *De Dono Perseverantiae*, and he was ably represented by Prosper and Hilarius, and the unknown author of the great work *De Vocatione Omnium Gentium*, ascribed to Pope Leo I (461); by Avitus, Archbishop of Vienna (490–523); Caesarius, Archbishop of Arles (502–542); and by Fulgentius of Ruspe (1533). Semi-Pelagianism was condemned by the decree of Pope Gelasius (496), and finally in the synods of Orange and Valence (529), which were confirmed by the edict of Pope Boniface (530); from which time a modified and softened form of Augustinianism became the recognized orthodoxy of the Western Church. It was taught by Gregory the Great, and held by the Emperor Charlemagne, the two persons who exerted the greatest influence in the reconstruction of Europe at the commencement of the Middle Ages. It was held throughout those ages by all the greatest church teachers and ornaments, as the Venerable Bede (673–735), Alcuin (804), and Claudius of Turin (839). The history of the persecution and condemnation of Gottschalk, under the influence of Rabanus Maurus and Hinckmar, with which Scotus

Erigena was involved (about 850), shows, however, how deeply the ever-increasing Semi-Pelagian leaven was affecting the whole Church. All the most illustrious teachers of the scholastic age, making allowance for the extravagance of many of their speculations, preserved, however, more or less of the tone of Augustinian thought, as, for example, Anselm, Archbishop of Canterbury (910); St. Bernard, Bishop of Clairvaux (1140); Peter Lombard, *Magister Sententiarum;* Hugo de St. Victor; and, above all, Thomas Aquinas, *Doctor Angelicus* (1247); and Thomas Bradwardine, Archbishop of Canterbury (1348). Thomas Aquinas fairly represents the result of the driftage of the Augustinian orthodoxy toward Semi-Pelagianism: his system is almost exactly intermediate between these two great types —with the one he affirmed that man since the fall had lost all ability to anything spiritually good, and without grace he could do nothing acceptable to God or which secured salvation; while with the other he represented original sin as rather a languor and a disease, and affirmed the power of fallen man to co-operate with grace. The distinctive point of Semi-Pelagianism is the denial of prevenient grace; the distinctive point of Thomism is the denial of "irresistible" grace—that is, of prevenient grace conceived of as a creative energy of God. The Dominicans as a class followed Aquinas, while the Franciscans followed their champion, Duns Scotus (1265), *Doctor Subtilis,* and in that age the ablest advocate of pure Semi-Pelagianism.

The controversies then revived have continued to agitate the Romish Church up to the present time. The Council of Trent (1546) attempted to satisfy both parties by indefinite decrees, and accordingly both Augustinians and Semi-Pelagians, Thomists and Scotists, have claimed that their respective views were sanctioned. The Jesuit society, whose doctrines and casuistry were ventilated in the *Provincial Letters* of Pascal, has always advocated Semi-Pelagianism. The illustrious thinkers of Port Royal, Paris, called Jansenists from Jansenius, Bishop of Ypres (Tillemont, Arnauld, Nicole, Pascal, Quesnel, etc.), were at the same time devout Catholics, and in the matters of grace

and predestination earnest Augustinians. They were persecuted by the Jesuits, and finally outlawed by the bulls of Popes
Innocent X and Alexander VII (A.D. 1653 and 1656), and
of Clement XI (1713). The present pope, Leo XIII, has
thrown the weight of his influence for Thomism, which indeed
is as nearly as may be the doctrine of the decrees of Trent.
This may be held, therefore, to be the formal doctrine of the
Church of Rome.

The great evangelical teachers and forerunners of the Reformers in the century immediately preceding the Reformation
were prevailingly decided Augustinians.[18] This is most con-
spicuously true of Wyclif (1384), Jerome of Prague, John Huss
(1415), John of Goch (1475), John of Wesalia, Jerome
Savonarola, a Dominican (1498), John Wessel (1499), "the
Light of the World," and his disciple, the great Grecian, John
Reuchlin, in his turn the teacher of Melanchthon, and Staupitz,
vicar-general of the "German congregation" Augustinians and
the spiritual teacher of Luther.

The Reformation was in all its leaders and in all its centers
as much a reaction from the growing Semi-Pelagianism as from
the tyranny of the papal Church. Zwingli of Switzerland,
Luther of Germany, Calvin of France, Cranmer of England,
and Knox of Scotland, although each movement was self-
originated and different from the others in many permanent
characteristics, were alike strictly Augustinian in doctrinal position. So that the Reformation was before everything else a
great Augustinian revival—the forerunner in this of nearly all
the great revivals which have refreshed the Church since.
Melanchthon, in the earliest editions of his *Loci Communes*
(1521), took extreme ground as to the moral impotence of the
human will and absolute predestination, which, however, he
gradually and radically modified in subsequent editions, until
he finally assumed synergistic ground. The personal followers
of Melanchthon excited the strong opposition of the stricter
Lutherans, and the struggle came to an explosion in the

---

[18]Neander's *History of Doctrine*, Vol. II, p. 609.

Weimar Confutation (1558). The result was that grandest monument of Lutheran symbolism, the *Formula Concordiae* (1580). This symbol sought to find a middle ground on the matter of predestination by teaching absolute predestination unto life (election), but denying predestination unto death (preterition); thus making the single predestination, as distinguished from the *praedestinatio duplex* of Augustinianism, confessional orthodoxy in the Lutheran Church.[19] In this illogical position the theologians of the Lutheran Church could not remain, and therefore, since Gerhard (†1637), they have cast off all remainders of Augustinianism and teach that predestination is based on foresight. A reaction led by a great theologian, C. F. W. Walther (†1887), has in our own day led the large Lutheran "Synodical Conference of America" (commonly called the "Missourians") back to the position of the *Formula Concordiae*. In most other respects, as to the guilt, pollution, and helplessness of the condition into which all children are born, as to justification, and the necessity and the efficacy of regenerating and sanctifying grace, the *Formula Concordiae* and Lutheran orthodoxy are at one with Calvinism.

By far the greatest of the Reformers, viewed either as a theologian, an interpreter of Scripture, or as a social organizer and founder of churches and republics, was John Calvin. His *Institutes* (1530), written when he was twenty-seven years old, the greatest work of systematic divinity the world has seen, has recast Augustinianism in its final Protestant form, and handed it over to the modern world stamped with its great author's name. His *Commentaries* are acknowledged by the most advanced modern scholars of every school to be the ablest exegetical work achieved in his generation. His *Tractatus* consists of various controversial treatises in defense of the truth, and his *Epistolae* consists of his voluminous correspondence with princes, nobles and commoners, statesmen and churchmen in every part of the Protestant world, concerning the important movements then revolutionizing Europe, both in

[19]See C. Hodge, *Systematic Theology*, Vol. II, pp. 721 f.; Francis Pieper, *Lehre und Wehre*, 36. 3.

Church and state. By him Calvinism and its correlates, presbyterianism in the Church and republicanism in the state, were not invented, but advocated and disseminated with transcendent ability and success. His doctrines have been most consistently developed and illustrated in the writings of such men as Bullinger, Martin Bucer, Theodore Beza, Diodati, Heidegger, Turretin, Witsius, Vitringa, Markius, De Moor, Pictet, John Owen, and Jonathan Edwards; in the deliverances of the international Synod of Dordt (1618–1619), of the national Assembly of Westminster (1648), of the French synods of Charenton and Alez, and in such creeds and confessions of the Church as the following: the Creed of the Waldensian pastors at Angrogne (1532), the two Helvetic, the Gallic, Belgic, and Scotch Confessions, the Thirty-nine Articles of the Church of England, the Lambeth Articles (1595), the Articles of Religion of the Dublin Convocation (1615), the Heidelberg Catechism, the Savoy Confession of the English (1658), and the Boston Confession (1680) of the American Independents. Calvinism is professed by all those Protestants of Germany who embrace the Heidelberg Catechism, the national (Protestant) churches of France, Switzerland, Holland, England, and Scotland, together with most of the free churches which have grown up in these lands, and the Reformed churches of Hungary and Bohemia, the Independents and Baptists of England and America, as well as the various branches of the Presbyterian Church in England, Ireland, and America.

From the time of Archbishop Laud (1644) a large proportion of the clergy and influential writers of the Episcopal churches have been Arminian, and it has even been disputed whether the Church of England was originally Calvinistic or not. The fact that the founders and leading ministers of that church were thorough Calvinists during the first hundred years of its history, and that its creed (the Thirty-nine Articles) remains such to this day, is as certain and as conspicuous as any other fact in history. The seventeenth article, "On Predestination," corresponds in spirit, design, and expression with all the other Calvinistic creeds. Tyndal, Frith, Barnes, who suffered under Henry VIII; Hooper, Latimer, Ridley, who suffered under Mary; Cranmer, the real author, and Jewel, who gave the finishing touch to the Thirty-nine Articles, were all Calvinists. "The same is proved by the whole history of the proceedings connected with the Lambeth Articles, the cases of Baro and Barret (1595), the Irish Articles (1615), and the Synod of Dordt (1619)" (Cunningham). The sources of information, and the arguments on both sides of this controversy, may be found in the *Works of the Parker Society*, Richmond's *Fathers of the English Church,* the *Zurich Letters,* the works of Heylin, Winchester, Daubeny, Tomline, and Lawrence on the Arminian side, and the works of Prynne, Hickman, Toplady, Overton, Goode, Principal Cunningham, and Alex. F. Mitchell on the Calvinistic side.

Over this vast area of time, and under all these various conditions of national and ecclesiastical life, Calvinism preserves its essential identity as a system of theological principles. It has, of course, undergone within these limits very various modifications as to details of structure and modes of statement. In Germany it has been rendered less thorough and definite through the influence of the compromising school of Melanchthon, and more lately under the modern tendencies brought in by Schleiermacher. In Holland, England, and Scotland it has been modified in form by the "Federal Scheme" introduced by the Westminster divines (1650) and the Dutch school of Cocceius. In France it was temporarily modified by the *Universalismus Hypotheticus,* or the universal impetration and limited application of redemption (1642), as held by Amyraldus, Daillé, and Placeus on the Continent, and by Baxter, Davenant, and in modern times by Wardlaw and others, in England. In America it has been coerced through more radical and more transient transformations in the speculations of Hopkins, the younger Edwards, Emmons, N. W. Taylor, and others of the New England school. But its vitality is ever exhibited by its power to take upon it various forms, and to live through periods of depression, and to enter the hearts of men as a power and new life after long epochs of religious death. It

was the inherent power of Calvinism which revived religious life
in Switzerland in the early part of this century, in the humble
teaching of Haldane and the powerful preaching of Malan,
Gaussen, Merle d'Aubigny, and other colaborers. And our
own days have seen a new exhibition of its power to awake to
new life in Holland, through the steady testimony of the Christian Reformed Church and the great leadership of Dr. Kuyper.
The history of Calvinism exhibits it not merely as a system with
great inherent vitality, but as the system of truth in which
abide the springs of religious life.

III. The Practical Effects of Calvinism on Personal Moral Character and upon the Social and Political Interests of Men

From the time of Coelestius and Julian, in the fifth century,
to that of Heylin (1659) and Tomline (1811), the *a priori*
objection has been brought against Calvinism that its principles
should lead either to licentious liberty or to abject subserviency,
to discouragement in the use of means, and to undue dis-
paragement and neglect of human reason. It is argued that the
doctrine of the absolute moral impotence of man's will should
destroy all sense of accountability, and that the doctrine of absolute decrees should cause the use of means to appear either
unnecessary or ineffectual, and lead to despair upon the one
hand or to licentiousness upon the other.

But the moral character of Calvinism is abundantly vindicated in two ways: 1. On the ground of reason. The recognition of the true (that is, actual) condition of man's nature
and relations to God, as this is revealed in Scripture and experience, must be more moral in its effect than the most
skilful misrepresentation possible of that actual condition can
be. The historian Froude, himself held by no trammels of sect or
party, says in his well-known address at St. Andrews (1871):
"If Arminianism most commends itself to our feelings, Calvinism is nearer to the facts, however harsh or forbidding those
facts may seem." Archbishop Whately, himself an Arminian,

acknowledges[20] that the ordinary objections against the moral attributes of Calvinism are in effect objections to the open *facts* of the case. That standard of morals which places the ground of obligation in the supreme will of the All-perfect, instead of in a tendency to promote happiness, and which utterly condemns fallen man, is obviously higher, and therefore more moral, than a more self-pleasing one which either justifies or excuses him. The system which teaches the total depravity and guiltiness of human nature from birth, its absolute dependence upon divine grace, together with the universal sweep of God's absolute decrees, at once maintaining the free agency of man and the infallibility of the divine purpose, must of course empty man of self, make all men equal before the law, and exalt the all-wise and all-powerful Father to the control of all events; such a system must make the highest attainments the condition and the fruit of God's favor, and must raise even the weakest believer to the position of an invincible champion for God and the right, "a coworker with God." 2. In the second place, Calvinists claim that on the ground of an illustrious and unparalleled historical record they can show that their system has been eminently distinguished by the effects produced by it upon all the communities which have embraced it in its purer forms, as to the following particulars: (a) the general standard of moral character practically realized in personal and social life; (b) the amount of rationally regulated liberty realized both in Church and state; (c) the standard of popular intelligence and education actually attained; (d) the testimony yielded to the power of the truth by the number and illustrious character of its martyrs; and (e) the zeal and devotion expressed in sustained missionary efforts for the extension of the kingdom of Christ.

1. As to the influence of Calvinism on the moral character of individuals, it is only necessary here to quote Mr. Froude's citation of the names of "William the Silent, Luther, Calvin, Knox, Andrew Melville, the regent Murray, Coligny, Cromwell,

[20]In his essay on *Some of the Difficulties in the Writings of St. Paul.*

Milton, John Bunyan—men possessed of all the qualities which give nobility and grandeur to human nature." As to its effect upon the general moral character of communities, it will be sufficient to cite the Waldenses; the little radiant state of Geneva, whose Protestant reconstruction began with the establishment of a Court of Morals; the Huguenots as compared with their Catholic fellow citizens; the Jansenists as compared with the Jesuits; the Dutch Protestants of their heroic period; the Scotch Covenanters; the English Puritans, whose very name signalizes their eminent moral character, in contrast with the corruption brought in at the Restoration;[21] and finally, all those sections of America settled by English Puritan New Englanders, by the Scotch and Scotch-Irish, and by Presbyterians from France and Holland. Mr. Froude says: "The first symptoms of its operation, wherever it established itself, was to obliterate the distinction between sins and crimes, and to make the moral law the rule for states as well as persons."[22] Pascal, the sublime avenger of the persecuted religionists of Port Royal, shows in the first nine of his *Provincial Letters* the connection between the infamous morality of the Jesuits and their Semi-Pelagian views as to sin and grace. Sir James Mackintosh vindicates at length the morality of the theological doctrine of predestination by a general review of the history of its most conspicuous professors.[23]

2. It appears superfluous to prove the tendency of Calvinism to promote freedom and popular government, both in Church and state. Its principles strip the ministry of all sacerdotal powers; they make all men and all Christians equal before God; they make God absolute and supreme over all, and the immediate controller and disposer of human affairs. Hence all churches accepting Calvinism, unless prevented by external conditions, have immediately adopted popular constitutions, either Presbyterian or Independent. This is true of all the churches of Switzerland, France, Holland, the Palatinate, Scot-

---

[21]See Macaulay's *Essays on Milton* and Hallam's *Constitutional History*.
[22]*Address*, p. 7. [23]Vol. XXXVI of the *Edinburgh Review*.

land, America, and the free churches of England and Ireland. The apparent exception is the English Establishment. The history of its political relations explains its prelatical character. Cranmer and the other Calvinistic founders of that church held, as did Archbishop Usher, a very moderate theory of the episcopate, and submitted to the constitution actually established only for state reasons. Afterwards, as Calvinism became more thoroughly incorporated in the public faith, presbyterianism was established by the Long Parliament, and independency by the Puritan army and Protector. It is a conspicuous fact of English history that high views as to the prerogatives of the ministry have always antagonized Calvinistic doctrine.

The political influence of Calvinism was at an early period discerned by kings as well as by the people. The Waldenses were the freemen of the ante-Reformation period. The republic was established at the same time with Presbytery at Geneva. The Hollanders, grouped around the sublime figure of William the Silent,[24] performed deeds of heroism against odds of tyranny unparalleled in all foregoing and subsequent history. This battle was fought by Calvinistic Holland, and the victory won (1590) completely, before the Arminian controversies had commenced. Add to these the French Huguenots, the Scotch Covenanters, the English Puritans in the Old and in the New World, and we make good our claim that Calvinists have been successful champions of regulated freedom among men.

Bancroft, the historian of the United States, attributes the modern impulse to republican liberty to the little republic of Geneva and to its Calvinistic theology.[25] He credits the molding of the institutions of North America chiefly to New England Independents, and to Dutch, French, and Scotch-Irish Presbyterians. "The Mecklenburg Declaration, signed on May 20, 1775, more than a year before that of July 4, 1776,

---

[24]*Calvinus et Calvinista.*
[25]*History of the United States of America*, Vol. I, p. 266; Vol. II, pp. 461-464.

signed in Philadelphia, was the first voice publicly raised for American independence. And the convention by which it was adopted and signed consisted of twenty-seven delegates, nine of whom, including the president and secretary, were ruling elders, and one, the Rev. H. J. Balch, was a Presbyterian minister." Tucker, in his *Life of Jefferson,* says: "Everyone must be persuaded that one of these papers must have been borrowed from the other"; and Bancroft has made it certain that the Declaration of Jefferson was written a year after that of Mecklenburg. The correspondence between the representative system and the gradations of sessions, presbyteries, provincial synods, and national general assemblies, developed in the Presbyterian system, to the federal system of state and national governments in the Constitution of the United States, seems too remarkable to have been accidental.

3. The relation of Calvinism to education is no less conspicuous and illustrious. The little republic of Geneva became the sun of the European world. The Calvinists of France, in spite of all their embarrassments, immediately founded and sustained three illustrious theological schools at Montauban, Saumur, and Sedan. The Huguenots so far surpassed their fellow countrymen in intelligence and skill that their banishment, on the occasion of the Revocation of the Edict of Nantes (1685), quickened the manufactures and trades of Germany, England, and America, and for a time almost paralyzed the skilled industries of France.[26] The fragment of marshy seacoast constituting Holland became the commercial focus of the world, one of the most powerful communities in the society of nations, and the mother of flourishing colonies in both hemispheres. The peasantry of Scotland has been raised far above that of any other European nation by the universal education afforded by her parish schools. The common school system of Puritan New England is opening up a new era of human history. In this country, for the first two hundred years of its history, "almost every college and seminary of learning,

---

[26]See Weiss's *History of French Protestant Refugees.*

and almost every academy and common school even, which existed, had been built up and sustained by Calvinists."[27]

4. The martyrology of Calvinism is pre-eminent in the history even of the Church. We call to witness John Huss and Jerome of Prague, who perished for their adherence to this faith one hundred years before Luther. The Waldenses, of whom were the "slaughtered saints whose bones lie scattered on the Alpine mountains cold," the victims of the reign of "Bloody Mary," John Rogers, and Bishops Hooper, Ferrar, Ridley, Latimer, and Cranmer, and their fellow martyrs, were all Calvinists; as well as Hamilton and Wishart, the victims of Claverhouse and the "Killing Time" of 1684 in Scotland, and the victims of the High Commission and of the "Bloody Assizes" of England (1685). Under Charles V and Philip of Spain, Holland had been made a spectacle to all nations by her sufferings, and had surpassed all other Christian communities with the number and steadfastness of her martyrs. When the Duke of Alva left the Netherlands, December, 1573, he boasted that within five years he had delivered 18,600 heretics to the executioner.[28] Moreover, Calvinists claim the victims of the Inquisition in Spain and Italy; the history of the Huguenots of France, from the martyrdom of Leclerc (1523) to the promulgation of the Edict of Nantes, 1598; the victims of the unparalleled atrocity of the massacre of St. Bartholomew, August 22, 1572, when some 20,000 princes, noblemen, and commoners perished at one time by the hand of assassins; and all the hundreds of thousands of the very flower of France who fell victims either to the wars which raged with comparatively short exceptions from the Reformation to 1685, or to the dragoonings, the galleys, and the expatriation which preceded and followed that dreadful time.

5. Calvinism has been proved an eminent incentive to all missionary enterprises, domestic and foreign. It is of course acknowledged that several Christian bodies not characterized by what are generally regarded as the peculiarities of Cal-

---

[27]See *New Englander*, Oct. 1845.
[28]Motley's *Rise of the Dutch Republic*, Vol. II, p. 497.

vinism have been in the highest degree distinguished by missionary zeal and efficiency. The most remarkable instances of this kind have been the Nestorians in western and central Asia from the fifth to the ninth century, the Moravians from 1732, and the Wesleyan Methodists from about 1769 to the present time. In the early Church, St. Patrick, the missionary of Ireland, fifth century; Augustine, the missionary of Gregory the Great to England; and Columba and his missionary college at Iona in the Hebrides, and his disciples the Culdees, in the sixth century, as well as the Lollards, the followers of Wyclif, in the fourteenth century, were all of the general school of Augustine. In 1555, through Admiral Coligny, Calvin sent two ministers to the heathen in Brazil. Cromwell in the next century proposed to appoint a council to promote the Protestant religion, in opposition to the congregation *De Propaganda Fide* in Rome. One of the principal objects of the promoters of the Plymouth and Massachusetts colonies was the conversion of savages and the extension of the Church. The charter of the Society for the Propagation of the Gospel in Foreign Parts was granted by the Calvinistic prince, William III. It is to the Calvinistic Baptists that the impulse to modern Protestant missions is to be traced, and the Calvinistic churches are today behind none in their zeal for a success in missionary work.

26

THE RITSCHLIAN SCHOOL*

There has been such a thing as "a Ritschlian school" in existence only for a matter of a short quarter of a century. Ritschl had taught for almost thirty years, first at Bonn and then at Göttingen, and had made no "pupils"; the issue of his work being not "a school," but "a theology." After much preliminary fragmentary publication, the first volume of his great treatise, *The Christian Doctrine of Justification and Reconciliation*, was issued in 1870. This contained only a critical historical sketch of the doctrine. It was followed during the year 1874 by the two remaining volumes, which dealt respectively with its Biblical and dogmatic aspects. At once "pupils" flocked to his standard. The "Ritschlian school" was thus obviously the creation of the "Ritschlian theology"; the "theology" once set fully before the public, the "school" came of itself.

The first public manifestation of the existence of the new school was given by the appearance in 1876 of Licentiate Herrmann's little book on *Metaphysics in Theology*, in which the fundamental postulate of the Ritschlian system, its attempted stripping of theology of all metaphysical elements, was brought to sharp expression. The discussion of this subject reached its climax in Ritschl's own polemic pamphlet bearing a similar title, *Theology and Metaphysics*, which appeared in 1881. Since then, the theological public in Germany has had no opportunity to forget the existence of the new school. Controversy after controversy has at its instigation torn the peace of the Church. First, there was the great

---

The New York Observer, Feb. 24, 1898.

excitement roused by Bender's extreme utterances in 1883; then the irritation caused by Bornemann's *Bitter Truths* in 1888; then the distrust and uncertainty produced by Kaftan's remarks on Dreyer's *Undogmatic Christianity* in 1889; and then the profound revulsion which was created by Harnack's assault on the Apostles' Creed in 1892.

There seems to have been at first a strong tendency in evangelical circles to look upon the new teaching with some favor. Such a tendency was, indeed, little creditable to either head or heart; and can be esteemed merely a fresh example of that shallow charity which "thinketh no evil," only because it lacks the mind to perceive or the heart to care for the evil that is flaunted in its face. For the Ritschlism of Ritschl himself was merely the old Socinianism in a new garment, cut from the cloth of Neo-Kantian speculation. Its views of sin and grace were of the lowest; it knew, as on its doctrine of sin it needed, no atonement and no divine Savior; it denied all living relation to an exalted Christ, and, indeed, all vital communion with God; and like the disciples that Paul found at Ephesus, it "did not so much as hear whether there is a Holy Ghost." When his new disciples, Haering and Kaftan, revolting from the barrenness of such teaching, asserted the need and reality, the one of some kind of atonement, and the other of some hidden life with God, Ritschl rebuked them sharply and asserted bluntly that one needed for salvation only to conduct himself morally in the kingdom of God.

Certainly any hopes that may have been cherished at the beginning that the new mode of thinking had any support to offer to either evangelical doctrine or vital religion were soon dashed. In the course of the controversies that have ensued it has been made abundantly evident that there is nothing dear to the Christian heart, nothing fundamental to the Christian system, which the Ritschlian solvent may not dissolve. It is, indeed, precisely those elements of religious thought and life which make them distinctively Christian, that the Ritschlian solvent must dissolve. For under its high-sounding proposal to cleanse Christianity of metaphysical accretions, precisely what Ritschlism essays is to reduce Christianity to a content against which a naturalistic philosophy, an unbelieving science, and a skeptical history cannot manage to raise objection. Along then with everything metaphysical, everything mysterious, everything mystical, everything to which the natural heart of man is averse, must go. As this has become clearer, and the Ritschlian polemic has grown sharper against every element of supernaturalism in redemption—from the virgin birth, miraculous life, and bodily resurrection of the Redeemer to the expiatory character of his redemption—and against every element of vital communion with God—from the regeneration of the Spirit down to the access of the individual to God in prayer—the reaction against it has become sharper, until, today, its influence seems distinctly on the wane in the land of its birth.

There are, of course, Ritschlians and Ritschlians. At the one extreme stand men like Haering, who has brought some softening and heightening to possibly every item of "the master's" teaching. Despite the ingrained naturalism of his thought, Herrmann again has not been able to escape from the deep religious feeling which became part of his very nature at his pious parents' knees, and which was fanned to a flame by his two years' residence with Tholuck; and has suffused the cold forms of Ritschlian Socinianism with a religious sentiment so deep and beautiful as almost to deceive the very elect.

Possibly the most orderly and legitimate development of the Ritschlian principles may be seen, on the other hand, in men like Johannes Gottschick, and, above all, in Adolf Harnack, who has consecrated powers and learning second to no man's of our generation to a historical vindication of the Ritschlian assault on the whole circle of distinctively Christian doctrine. As Loofs, of Halle, has pointed out, Harnack's great *History of Dogma* is therefore vitiated by the fundamental defect that it is at bottom simply a party document. All that favors "undogmatic Christianity" is set in the foreground, and the whole material is treated with the purpose and effect of presenting the distinctive doctrines of Christianity as corruptions of Christianity. It is a great book, full not only of learning, but of genius and stimulus. And through it, and his other writings, not only or mainly his controversial brochures, but also his splendid historical treatises, such as his as yet unfinished *History of Early Christian Literature*, Adolf Harnack is exhibiting himself as not only the most highly gifted church historian, but also one of the most destructive forces in the Christendom of today.

The fundamental evil of the Ritschlian movement lies in its attitude towards the authority of the teaching of the apostles. On the authority of the apostolic teaching, along with that of Jesus preserved by them, rests all that is really distinctive of Christianity. If that be cast away from us, Christianity in all its distinctive features goes with it. But the whole Ritschlian movement holds itself aloof from the apostolic teaching and treats it as merely the body of opinion held in the first age of the Church. Accordingly, Gustav Ecke justly finds at this point the hinge of the controversy. "If we will closely scrutinize," says he, "the present theological situation in its peculiarity, it will soon become clear to us that the decision of the conflict of the churchly tendency against the Ritschlian theology will not be reached through epistemological investigations—Ritschl's theory of knowledge retains little more than a historical interest—but through the decisive proof that, along with the teaching of Christ, the belief of the apostles concerning Christ is and must abide the basis and norm of the life of faith and of the spiritual knowledge of the Christian community."

This witness is true. And its meaning is that it is of no avail to join issue with the Socinianism of Ritschlism so long as the authority of the Scriptures is left in doubt. Without the authority of the apostolic teaching, Socinianism is inevitable; on that authority it is impossible.

PART IV

27

INCARNATE TRUTH*

"And the Word was made flesh, and dwelt among us, full of . . . truth" (John i. 14).

The obvious resemblance between the prologue to John's Gospel and the proem of Genesis is not a matter of mere phraseology and external form. As the one, in the brief compass of a few verses, paints the whole history of the creation of a universe with a vividness which makes the quickened imagination a witness of the process, so the other in still briefer compass traces the whole history of the re-creation of a dead world into newness of life. In both we are first pointed back into the depths of eternity, when only God was. In both we are bidden to look upon the chaotic darkness of lawless matter or of lawless souls, over which the brooding Spirit was yet to move. In both, as the tremendous pageants are unrolled before our eyes, we are made to see the Living God; and to see him as the Light and the Life of the world, the Destroyer of all darkness, the Author of all good. Here too, however, the Old Testament revelation is the preparation for the better to come. In it we see God as the God of power and of wisdom, the Author and Orderer of all; in this we see him as the God of goodness and mercy, the Restorer and Redeemer of the lost. Law was given through Moses; grace and truth came through Jesus Christ.

Through what a sublime sweep does the apostle lead our

---

*One of two sermons contributed by Dr. Warfield to the book *Princeton Sermons*, 1893, pp. 94-114. There are sixteen sermons in all, "chiefly by professors in the Seminary." Dr. Warfield edited the book, wrote the Preface (pp. iii-v), and contributed a second sermon entitled "The Christian's Attitude Toward Death" (pp. 316-337).

panting thought as he strives to tell us who and what the Word is, and what he has done for men. He lifts the veil of time, that we may peer into the changeless abyss of eternity and see him as he is, in the mystery of his being, along with God and yet one with God—in some deep sense distinct from God, in some higher sense identical with God. Then he shows us the divine work which he has wrought in time. He is the All-Creator—"all things were made by him, and without him was not anything made that hath been made." He is the All-Illuminator—he "was the true Light that lighteth every man that cometh into the world." And now in these last days he has become the All-Redeemer—prepared for by his prophet, he came to his own, and his own received him not; but "as many as received him," without regard to race or previous preparation, "he gave to them the right to become children of God, to them that believe on his name, who were born not of blood, nor of the will of the flesh, nor of the will of man, but of God." Then the climax of this great discourse breaks on us as we are told how the Word, when he came to his own, manifested himself to flesh. It was by himself becoming flesh, and tabernacling among us, full of grace and truth. He came as Creator, as Revealer, as Redeemer: as Creator, preparing a body for his habitation; as Revealer, "trailing clouds of glory as he came"; as Redeemer, heaping grace on grace.

It is clear that it is primarily in its aspect as a revelation of God that John is here contemplating the incarnation. Accordingly, he bears his personal witness to it as such: "The Word was made flesh, and tabernacled among us, and *we beheld his glory*, a glory as of an only-begotten of the Father." Accordingly, too, he summons the prophetic witness of the forerunner. And accordingly, still further, he closes the whole with a declaration of the nature of the revelation made, and its guarantee in the relation of the incarnated Word to the Father: "No man hath seen God at any time; God only-begotten which is in the bosom of the Father, he hath declared him."

In the special verse from which we have taken our text we

perceive, then, that John is bearing his personal witness: "And the Word became flesh, and dwelt among us, and *we beheld his glory*." He is telling us what of his own immediate knowledge he knows—testifying what he had heard, what he had seen with his eyes, what he had beheld and his hands had handled. An eye-witness to Christ's majesty, he had seen his glory and bears his willing witness to it. Nor must we fancy that he gives us merely a subjective opinion of his own, as if he were telling us only that the man Jesus was so full of grace and truth in his daily walk that he, looking upon him admiringly, had been led to conjecture that he was more than man. He testifies not to subjective opinion but to objective fact. We observe that the testimony is made up of three assertions. First, we have the fact, the objective fact, of the incarnation asserted: "And the Word was made flesh, and dwelt among us." Second, we have the self-evidencing glory of the incarnation asserted: "and we beheld his glory, a glory as of an only-begotten of the Father." And third, we have the characteristic elements which entered into and constituted the glory which he brought from heaven with him and exhibited to men, asserted: "full of grace and truth." Jesus Christ was incarnated love and truth. And precisely what John witnesses is, that the Word did become flesh, and dwelt among men, full of grace and truth, and that the blaze of this his glory was manifest to every seeing eye that looked upon him.

Now it seems evident, further, that John had a special form of the manifestation of love and truth before his mind when he wrote these words. He is thinking of the covenant God, who proclaimed himself to Moses on the mount when he descended on the cloud as "Jehovah, Jehovah, a God full of compassion, and gracious, slow to anger, and plenteous in mercy and truth." He is thinking of David's prayer, "O prepare lovingkindness and truth"; and his heart burns within him as he sees them now prepared. It is the thought of Christ's redeeming work which is filling his mind, and which leads him to sum up the revelation of the incarnation in the revelation of love and truth. Therefore he says, not "love," but "grace"—undeserved love to sinners. And in "truth" he is thinking chiefly of Christ's "faithful-ness." The divine glory that rested as a nimbus on the Lord's head was compounded before all else of his ineffable love for the unlovely, of his changeless faithfulness to the unfaithful. For in Christ, God commended his love to us in that, while we were yet sinners, Christ died for us.

Nevertheless, it would be a serious error to confine the words as here used to this single implication. This is rather the cul-mination and climax of their meaning than the whole extent and impletion of it. Christ is not only love as manifested in grace, but as the God of love manifest in the flesh he is love itself in all its height and breadth. Not only the loftiest reaches of love, love for the undeserving, find their model in him, but all the love that is in the world finds its source and must seek its support in him. His was the love that wept at the grave of a friend and over the earthly sorrows of Jerusalem, that yearned with the bereaved mother at Nain, and took the little children into his arms to bless them; as well as the love that availed to offer himself a sacrifice for sin. In like manner, that John has especially in mind here the highest manifestations of truth—our Lord's trustworthiness in the great work of salvation—in no way empties the word of its lower connota-tions. He is still the true Light that lighteth every man that cometh into the world; and all the truth that is in the world comes from him and must seek its strength in him. "We beheld his glory," says the apostle, "*full*"—complete, perfect—"of grace and truth." And perfection of love and truth avails for all their manifestations. This man, the man Christ Jesus, could not act in any relation otherwise than lovingly, could not speak on any subject otherwise than truly. He is the pure fountain of love and truth.

I. We confine ourselves on the present occasion to the latter of the two characteristics here brought together. And doing so, the first message which the declaration brings us is one so obvious that, in circumstances other than those in which we are now standing, it would seem an insult to our intelligence to direct attention to it. It is this, that since Jesus Christ our

Lord, the manifested Jehovah, was as such the incarnation of truth, no statement which ever fell from his lips can have contained any admixture of error. This is John's testimony. For let us remind ourselves again that he is here bearing his witness, not to the essential truth of the divine nature incarnated in our Lord prior to its incarnation, but to the fulness of truth which dwelt in the God-man: "And the Word became flesh, and dwelt among us, and we beheld his glory, full of . . . truth." More—it is the testimony of our Lord himself. "I," he declared, with his majestic and pregnant brevity, "I am the Truth." Nor dare we fancy that his plenitude of truth is exhausted in his witness to the great and eternal verities of religion, while the pettier affairs of earth and man are beyond its reach. His own norm of judgment is that only he that is faithful in the least may be trusted with the great. And it was testified of him not only that he knew whence he came and whither he went, but equally that he knew all men and needed not that any should bear witness of man, for he himself knew what was in man. He himself suspends his trustworthiness as to heavenly things upon his trustworthiness as to earthly things: "Verily, verily, I say unto you, We speak that we do know, and testify that we have seen; and ye receive not our witness. If I told you earthly things and ye believe not, how shall ye believe if I tell you heavenly things?"

Are we beating the air when we remind ourselves of such things? Would that we were! But alas! we are fallen on evil days, when we need to defend the truth of incarnate truth itself against the aspersions of even its professed friends. O, the unimaginable lengths to which the intellectual pride of men will carry them! Has one spun out some flimsy fancy as to the origin and composition of certain Old Testament books, which is found to clash with Jesus' testimony to their authorship and trustworthiness? We are coolly told that "as a teacher of spiritual truth sent from God and full of God he is universal," but "as a logician and critic he belongs to his times," and therefore had "a definite restricted outfit and outlook, which could be only those of his own day and generation." "Why should he be supposed to know the science of the criticism of the Old Testament," we are asked, "which began to exist centuries after his death?" Does another cherish opinions as to the interpretation of certain Old Testament passages which will not square with the use that Christ makes of them? He tells us at once that "interpretation is essentially a scientific function, and one conditioned by the existence of scientific means, which, in relation to the Old Testament, were only imperfectly at the command of Jesus." Has another adopted preconceptions which render our Lord's dealings with the demoniacs distasteful to him? He too reminds us that the habit of ascribing disease to demoniacal influences was universal in Jesus' day, and that we can scarcely expect him to be free from the current errors of his time. Let us cut even deeper. When one desires to break out a "larger hope" for those who die impenitent than Christ's teachings will allow, he suggests that in his efforts to lead his hearers to repentance Jesus spoke habitually as a popular preacher, and far more strongly than he could have permitted himself to do had he been an exact theologian. When another burns with a zeal for moral reform which is certainly not according to knowledge, he suggests that we have reached a stage of ethical development when "new and larger perceptions of truth" have brought "new and larger perceptions of duty" than were attainable in Christ's day, and are accordingly bound to govern our lives by stricter rules than would apply to him in that darker age. Or, to sum up the whole, we have been recently told plainly that "Christ in his manhood was not the equal of Newton in mathematical knowledge," and not "the equal of Wellhausen in literary criticism," because—so we are actually told—the pursuit of such sciences requires "much exercise of mind."

Is, then, the Light that lighteth every man that cometh into the world gone out in darkness? What is left us of the Truth Indeed, who proclaims himself no more the Way and the Life than the Truth, if his testimony cannot be trusted as to the nature, origin, authority, and meaning of the Scriptures of which his own Spirit was the inspirer; as to the constitution of that spiritual world of which he is the Creator and the King; as to the nature of that future state which it is his to determine as Judge; or as to the moral life of which he is the sole author? Yet these are devout men who are propagating such teachings; and each has of course his own way of saving himself from conscious blasphemy in erecting his own thought above the thought of the God-man. The most popular way at present is to suggest that when God became man he so surrendered the attributes of divinity as that, though God, he had shrunk to the capacity of man, and, accepting the weaknesses, become subject also to the limitations of a purely human life in the world. Thus it is sought to save the veracity of the Lord at the expense of his knowledge, his truthfulness at the expense of his truth. But who can fail to see that, were this true, the sorrowing world would be left like Mary standing weeping in the garden and crying, "They have taken away my Lord"? Where then would be Christ our Prophet? Who could assure us of his trustworthiness in his witness to his oneness with God, to his mission from God, to the completeness of his work for our salvation? Faith has received a serious wound, as it has been well phrased, if we are to believe that Jesus Christ could have been deceived; if we are to believe that he could— wittingly or unwittingly—deceive, faith has received its death blow.

Let us bless the Lord, then, that he has left us little excuse for doubting in so important a matter. To the law and the testimony. Is the man Christ Jesus dramatized before us in the length and breadth of that marvelous history which fills these four Gospels, as a child of his times, limited by the intellectual outlook of his times, or rather as a teacher to his times, sent from God as no more the power of God than the wisdom of God? Is he represented to us as learning what he taught us from men, or, as he himself bore witness, from God? —"My teaching is not mine, but his that sent me"; "I am come down out of heaven," and "he that hath sent me is true"; and "the things that I have heard from him, these speak I unto the world." Did he even in his boyhood amaze the doctors in the temple by his understanding (Luke ii. 47)? Did he know even "letters," not having learned them from man (John vii. 15)? Did he see Nathanael when, under the fig tree, he bowed in secret prayer (John i. 47)? Did he know without human informant all the things that ever the Samaritan woman did (John iv. 29)? Did he so search the heart of man that he saw the thoughts of his enemies (Matt. ix. 4); knew that one of the twelve whom he had chosen was a "devil" (John vi. 70); led Peter to cry in his adoring distress, "Lord, thou knowest all things, thou knowest that I love thee" (John xx. 17); and called out the testimony of John that "he knew all men, and needed not that any should bear witness concerning man, for he himself knew what was in man" (John ii. 25); as well as the testimony of all the disciples that they knew that he came from God, because "he knew all things" (John xvi. 30)?

But why need we go into the details that are spread from one end to the other of these Gospels? In our text itself John bears witness that the fulness of truth which dwelt in the incarnate Word so glorified all his life as to mark him out as the Son of God: "The Word became flesh, and dwelt among us, and we beheld his glory, the glory as of an only-begotten of the Father, full of truth." We surely need not fear to take our stand not only by the truthfulness but by the truth of our Lord. We surely need not shrink from, with the utmost simplicity, embracing, proclaiming, and living by his views of God and the universe, of man and the world. It was he that made the world; and without him was not anything made that hath been made. Who shall teach him how its beams were laid or how its structure has grown? It was he that revealed the Word. Who shall teach him how were written or what is intended by the words which he himself gave through his servants the prophets? It is he who is at once the Source and Standard of the moral law, and the Fount and Origin of all compassion for sinful man. Who shall teach him what it is right to do, or how it is loving to deal with the children of men? We need not fear lest we be asked to credit Jesus against the truth; we may confide wholly in him, because he is the Truth.

II. Nor let us do this timidly. Trust is never timid. Just because Jesus is the Truth, while we without reserve accept, proclaim, and live by every word which he has spoken, not fearing that after all it may prove to be false, we may with equal confidence accept, proclaim, and live by every other truth that may be made known to us, not fearing that after a while it may prove to contradict the Truth himself. Thus we may be led to the formulation of a second message which the text brings us: that since Jesus Christ our Lord, the Founder of our religion, was the very incarnation of truth, no truth can be antagonistic to the religion which he founded. John tells us that he was the true Light that lighteth every man that cometh into the world; and we may read this as meaning that as the Word of God, the great Revealer, it is he that leads man by whatever path to the attainment of whatever truth. There is, then, no truth in the world which does not come from him. It matters not through what channel it finds its struggling way into our consciousness or to our recognition—whether our darkened eyes are enabled to catch their glimpse of it by the light of nature, as we say, by the light of reason, by the light of history, or by the light of criticism. These may be but broken lights; but they are broken lights of that one Light which lighteth every man that cometh into the world. Every fragment of truth which they reveal to us comes from him who is the Truth, and is rendered great and holy as a revelation from and of him.

We must not, then, as Christians, assume an attitude of antagonism toward the truths of reason, or the truths of philosophy, or the truths of science, or the truths of history, or the truths of criticism. As children of the light, we must be careful to keep ourselves open to every ray of light. If it is light, its source must be sought in him who is the true Light; if it is truth, it belongs of right to him who is the plenitude of truth. All natural truths must be—in varying degrees indeed, but all truly—in some sense commentaries on the supernaturally revealed truth; and by them we may be led to fuller and more accurate comprehension of it. Nature is the handiwork of God in space; history marks his pathway through time. And both nature and history are as infallible teachers as revelation itself, could we but skill to read their message aright. It is distressingly easy to misinterpret them; but their employment in the elucidation of Scripture is, in principle, closely analogous to the interpretation of one Scripture by another, though written by another human hand and at an interval of an age of time. God speaks through his instruments. Prediction interprets prediction; doctrine, doctrine; and fact, fact. Wherever a gleam of light is caught, it illuminates. The true Light, from whatsoever reflected, *lighteth*.

Let us, then, cultivate an attitude of courage as over against the investigations of the day. None should be more zealous in them than we. None should be more quick to discern truth in every field, more hospitable to receive it, more loyal to follow it whithersoever it leads. It is not for Christians to be lukewarm in regard to the investigations and discoveries of the time. Rather, the followers of the Truth Indeed can have no safety, in science or in philosophy, save in the arms of truth. It is for us, therefore, as Christians, to push investigation to the utmost; to be leaders in every science; to stand in the van of criticism; to be the first to catch in every field the voice of the Revealer of truth, who is also our Redeemer. The curse of the Church has been her apathy to truth, in which she has too often left to her enemies that study of nature and of history and philosophy, and even that investigation of her own peculiar treasures, the Scriptures of God, which should have been her chief concern. Thus she has often been forced to learn from the inadvertent or unwilling testimony of her foes the facts she has needed to protect herself from their assaults. And thus she has been led to borrow from them false theories in philosophy, science, and criticism, to make unnecessary concessions to them, and to expose herself, as they changed their positions from time to time, to unnecessary disgrace. What has the Church not suffered from her unwillingness to engage in truly scientific work! She has nothing to fear from truth; but she has everything to fear, and she has already suffered nearly everything, from ignorance. All truth belongs to us as followers of Christ, the Truth; let us at length enter into our inheritance.

III. In so speaking, we have already touched somewhat upon a third message which our text brings us: that since Christ Jesus our Lord and Master is incarnate Truth, we as his children must love the truth.

Like him, we must be so single of eye, so steadfast in purpose, so honest in word, that no guile can be found in our mouth. The philosophers have sought variously for the sanction of truth. Kant found it in the respect a man owes to the dignity of his own moral nature: the liar must despise himself because lying is partial suicide—it is the renunciation of what we are and the substitution of a feigned man in our place. Fichte found it in our sense of justice toward our fellowmen: to lie is to lead others astray and subject their freedom to our selfish ends—it is ultimately to destroy society by destroying trust among men. From each of these points of view a powerful motive to truth may be developed. It is unmanly to lie; it is unneighborly to lie. It will destroy both our self-respect and all social life. But for us as Christians no sanction can approach in power that derived from the simple fact that as Christians we are "of the Truth"; that we are not of him who when he speaketh a lie speaketh of his own, who is a liar and the father thereof, but of him who is the fulness of truth—who is light and in whom is no darkness at all. As the children of truth, truth is our essential nature; and to lie is to sin against that incarnate Truth who is also our Lord and Redeemer—in whom, we are told, no liar can have part or share.

Bare avoidance of falsehood is far, however, from fulfilling our whole duty as lovers of truth. There is a positive duty, of course, as well as this negative one beckoning us. We have already noted the impulse which should thence arise to investigation and research. If all truth is a revelation of our Lord, what zeal we should have to possess it, that we may the better know him! As children of the truth we must love the truth, every truth in its own order, and therefore especially and above all others those truths which have been revealed by God for the salvation of the world. How tenacious we should be in holding them, how persistent in propagating them, how insistent in bearing our witness to them! "To this end was I born," said our Lord himself, "and for this cause came I into the world, that I should bear witness unto the truth." And we too, as his servants, must be, each in his place, witnesses of the truth. This is the high function that has been given us as followers of Jesus: as the Father sent him into the world, so he has sent us into the world, to bear witness of the truth.

We all know in the midst of what dangers, in the midst of what deaths, those who have gone before us have fulfilled this trust. "Martyrs," we call them; and we call them such truly. For "martyrs" means "witnesses"; and they bore their witness despite cross and sword, fire and raging beast. So constant was their witness, so undismayed, that this proverb has enshrined their eulogy for all time, that "the blood of the martyrs was the seed of the Church." They were our fathers: have we inherited their spirit? If we be Christians at all, must not we too be "martyrs," "witnesses"? must not we too steadfastly bear our witness to the truth assailed in our time? There may be no more fires lighted for our quivering flesh: are there no more temptations to a guilty silence or a weak evasion? Surely there is witness still to be borne, and we are they to bear it. The popular poet of the day sings against "the hard God served in Jerusalem," and all the world goes after him. But we—do we not know him to be the God of our salvation? the God who hath lovingly predestinated us unto the adoption of sons, through Jesus Christ, unto himself, according to the good pleasure of his will, to the praise of the glory of his grace? May God grant that in times like these, when men will not endure the sound doctrine, we may be enabled by his grace to bear unwavering witness to the glory of the Lord God Almighty, who "hath made everything for its own purpose, yea, even the wicked for the day of evil."

Need we pause further to enforce that highest form of the love of the truth, the love of the gospel of God's grace, which braves all things for the pure joy of making known the riches of his love to fallen men? The missionary spirit is the noblest fruit of the love of truth; the missionary's simple proclamation the highest form of witness-bearing to the truth. This spirit is no stranger among you. And I am persuaded that your hearts are burning within you as you think that to you "this grace has been given, to preach unto the Gentiles the unsearchable riches of Christ, and to make all men see what is the steward-ship of the mystery which from all ages hath been hid in God." You need not that I should exhort you to remember that above all else "it is required in stewards that a man be found faithful." May God grant that while you may ask in wonder, as you contemplate the work of your ministry, Who is sufficient for these things? you may be able to say, like Paul, "We are not as the many, corrupting the Word of God; but as of sincerity, but as of God, in the sight of God, speak we in Christ." May God grant that the desire which flamed in Paul may burn in you too:

> O could I tell ye surely would believe it!
>   O could I only say what I have seen!
> How could I tell or how can ye receive it,
>   How till he bringeth you where I have been?
>
> Give me a voice, a cry and a complaining—
>   O let my sound be stormy in their ears!
> Throat that would shout but cannot stay for straining,
>   Eyes that would weep but cannot wait for tears.

28

SPIRITUAL CULTURE IN
THE THEOLOGICAL SEMINARY*

It is natural that at the opening of a new session the minds of both professors and students, especially of those students who are with us for the first time, should be bent somewhat anxiously upon the matter which has brought us together. How are we who teach best to fulfil the trust committed to us, of guiding others in their preparation for the high office of minister of grace? How are you who are here to make this preparation, so to employ your time and opportunities as to become in the highest sense true stewards of the mysteries of Christ? Standing as you do at the close of your university work and at the beginning of three years more of mental labor—looking back at the conquests you have already made and forward at unconquered realms still lying before you— it would not be strange if your thoughts as they busy themselves with the preparation you require for your ministerial work should be predominately occupied with intellectual training. It is the more important that we should pause to remind ourselves that intellectual training alone will never make a true minister; that the heart has rights which the head must respect; and that it behooves us above everything to remember that the ministry is a spiritual office.

I should be sorry to leave the impression that it is questionable whether the Church may not have laid too strong an

---

*From the *Princeton Theological Review*, Jan. 1904, pp. 65-87. Also a pamphlet, Philadelphia, 1904. An opening address delivered to the incoming students at Princeton Seminary Sept. 20, 1903 (and, in an earlier form, at Western Seminary).

emphasis on the intellectual outfit that is needed for its minis-try. I must profess, indeed, that I am incapable of under-standing the standpoint of those (for such there seem to be) who talk of the over-intellectualization of the ministry. The late Dr. Joseph T. Duryea spoke rather strongly, but with substantial justice, when he declared it to be "high time that the question whether culture and learning do not unfit preachers for the preaching of the gospel to ordinary men and women, were referred back without response to the stupidity that in-spires it." It is not to be denied, of course, that there are learned men who are perfectly useless in the ministry; and even, what is more surprising, that there are men of broad and varied and, one would have thought, humanizing culture, who seem to be unable to turn their culture to any practical use. But it is yet to be shown that these same men, without knowl-edge and destitute of the culture which might have been ex-pected to humanize them, would have been any more useful. Are there no ignorant men, no men innocent of all culture, who are unpractical and of no possible use in the ministry? The fact is that when our Lord decreed that the religion he founded should be propagated by preaching, or, to put it more broadly, when he placed it in the world with the commission to reason its way to the hearts of men, he put a premium on intellectual endowments, and laid at the basis of ministerial equipment a demand for intellectual training, which no sophistry can cloud. The minister must have good tools with which to work, and must keep those tools in good condition.

You will find nothing in the curriculum which will be offered to you in this seminary, the mastery of which is not essential to your highest efficiency in your ministry. The intellectual train-ing at present provided for candidates for the ministry is not above either their prospective needs or the easy possibilities of their present powers. You will be wise to give yourselves diligently to making full account of it. It would not be easy to exaggerate the intimacy of the relation between sound knowl-edge and sound religious feeling: and the connection between sound knowledge and success in ministerial work is equally close. "Without study," says an experienced bishop of the Church of England, with his eye on the daily life of the minister it is true, but no less applicably to his preparation— "without study we shall not only fail to bring to our people all the blessings which God intends for them, but we shall gradually become feeble and perfunctory in our ministrations: our life may apparently be a busy one, and our time incessantly occupied, but our work will be comparatively fruitless: we shall be fighting as one that beateth the air."

So intimate is the connection between the head and the heart and hand, indeed, that it is not unfair to say broadly that if undue intellectualism exhibits itself in those preparing for the ministry, the fault is relative, not absolute: that, in a word, there is not a too muchness in the case at all, but a too littleness somewhere else. The trouble with those whom a certain part of the world persists in speaking of as over-educated for an effective ministry is not that they are too highly trained intellectually, but that they are sadly undertrained spiritually; not that their head has received too much attention, but that their heart has received too little. Of course I shall not deny that it is possible to find men who are naturally lacking in sufficient mental power to pursue a seminary course profitably: and I am far from saying that there are none of these "unlearned and ignorant men" who have been so baptized with the Holy Spirit that the Church may profitably induct them into the ministry to which God has obviously called them. But these are rare exceptions; and I do not think it characteristic of this humble but honorable class that they refuse to make the best use possible of the mental powers that have been vouchsafed to them. Certainly it would be perilous for us to make the existence of such a class the excuse for neglecting to stir up the gift that is in us. Rather I think it may be fairly inferred that when students for the ministry fail to take full advantage of the opportunities for intellectual culture offered them, the fault is usually to be found in the heart itself. When too much blood seems to have gone to the head, we may ordinarily justly presume that this is only because too little has gone to the heart; and similarly when little or none is thrown to the head, we may quite generally suspect it is because the heart has too little within it to supply the needs of any organ.

I

I have missed my mark in what I have been saying if, while insisting on the need of a strenuous intellectual preparation for the ministry, I have not also suggested that the deepest need is a profound spiritual preparation. An adequate preparation for the gospel ministry certainly embraces much more than merely the study of certain branches of learning. When Bishop Wilberforce opened Cuddesden College in 1854, he wrote: "Threefold object of residence here: 1. Devotion; 2. Parochial Work; 3. Theological Reading." The special circumstances of "candidates for holy orders" in the Church of England suggested, as we shall subsequently see, the order in which these three elements in their preparation are mentioned. In our special circumstances a different order might be suggested. But does it not, even on first sight, commend itself to you with clear convincingness, that any proper preparation for the ministry must include these three chief parts—a training of the heart, a training of the hand, a training of the head—a devotional, a practical, and an intellectual training? Such a training, in a word, as that we may learn first to know Jesus, then to grasp the message he would have us deliver to men, and then how he would have us work for him in his vineyard. We are told by the evangelist Mark (iii. 14) that when Jesus appointed his twelve apostles, it was first that they might be with him, and then that he might send them forth to preach. And surely we may believe that we who are the successors of the apostles as the evangelizers of the world have been called like them first of all to be with Jesus and only then to go forth to preach. It may not be without significance that out of the fourteen or fifteen qualifications which, according to the Apostle Paul, must unite in order to fit a man to be a bishop, only one requires an intellectual preparation. The bishop must be "apt to teach." But aptness to teach is only the beginning of his fitting. All the other requirements are rooted in his moral or spiritual fitness.

I am not going to lose myself in a vain—perhaps worse than vain—inquiry as to which of the three lines of preparation I have hinted at is the most essential. Why raise a question between three lines of training, each of which is essential both in itself and to the proper prosecution of the others? If intellectual acuteness will not of itself make a man an acceptable minister of Christ, neither will facility and energy in practical affairs by themselves, nor yet piety and devotion alone. The three must be twisted together into a single three-ply cord. We are not to ask whether we will cultivate the one or the other; or whether we will give our chief attention to the one or the other. We must simultaneously push our forces over all three lines of approach, if we are to capture the stronghold of a successful ministry at all. Doing so, they will interact, as we have suggested, each to secure the others. Do we wish to grow in grace? It is the knowledge of God's truth that sanctifies the heart. Do we desire a key to the depths of God's truth? It is the Spirit-led man who discerns all things. Are our souls in travail for the dying thousands about us? How eager, then, will be our search in the fountain of life for the the waters of healing. Is the way weary? Do we not know whence alone can be derived our strength for the journey of life? There is no way so surely to stimulate the appetite for knowledge as to quicken the sense of the need of it in the wants of our own spiritual life or in the calls of practical work for others. There is no way so potent for awakening a craving for personal holiness or for arousing a love of souls in our hearts, as to fill the mind with a knowledge of God's love to man as revealed in his Holy Book.

The reciprocal relation in which the several lines of preparation for the ministry stand to one another supplies me with my first remark as I address myself to the task immediately before me—of attempting to outline in a practical way some account of how your spiritual training may be advanced during your stay in the seminary. This remark takes a negative form and amounts to saying with some emphasis that your spiritual growth will not be advanced by the neglect of the very work for which you resort to the seminary. Such a remark may seem to some of you out of place; it is perhaps not so entirely unnecessary as it may appear. There is a valuable bit from his own personal experience given us by the late Phillips Brooks in his Yale Lectures (p. 43), which I shall repeat here for our admonition also. He is impressing on his readers the important truth that the first and most evident element in a true preparation for the ministry consists in a mastery of the professional studies leading up to it. He writes as follows:

Most men begin really to study when they enter on the preparation for their professions. Men whose college life, with its general culture, has been very idle, begin to work when at the door of the professional school the work of their life comes into sight before them. It is the way in which a bird who has been wheeling vaguely hither and thither sees at last its home in the distance and flies toward it like an arrow. But shall I say to you how often I have thought that the very transcendent motives of the young minister's study have a certain tendency to bewilder him and make his study less faithful than that of men seeking other professions from lower motives? The highest motive often dazzles before it illuminates. It is one of the ways in which the light within us becomes darkness. I never shall forget my first experience of a divinity school. I had come from a college where men studied hard but said nothing about faith. I had never been at a prayer-meeting in my life. The first place I was taken to at the seminary was the prayer-meeting; and never shall I lose the impression of the devoutness with which those men prayed and exhorted one another. Their whole souls seemed exalted and their natures were on fire. I sat bewildered and ashamed and went away depressed. On the next day I met some of these same men at a Greek recitation. It would be little to say of some of the devoutest of them that they had not learned their lesson. Their whole way showed that they had never learned their lessons; that they had not got hold of the first principles of hard, faithful, conscientious study. The boiler had no connection with the engine. The devotion did not touch the work which then and there was the work, and the only work, for them to do. By and by I found something of where the steam did escape to. A sort of amateur premature preaching was much in vogue among us. We were in haste to be at what we called "our work"! A feeble twilight of the coming ministry we lived in. The people in the neighborhood dubbed us "parsonettes." O, my fellow students, the special study of theology and all that appertains to it, that is what the preacher must be doing always; but he can never do it afterward as he can in the blessed days of quiet in Arabia, after Christ has called him, and before the apostles lay their hands upon him. In many respects an ignorant clergy, however pious it may be, is worse than none at all. The more the empty head glows and burns, the more hollow and thin and dry it grows. "The knowledge of the priest," said St. Francis de Sales, "is the eighth sacrament of the Church."

Well, it was not at Princeton Seminary that Dr. Brooks saw these evils. Perhaps they do not exist here: let us hope that they do not, at least in the measure in which he portrays them. Nevertheless his experience may fitly be laid to heart by us for our warning. The religious training which a minister needs to get in his days of preparation assuredly cannot be had by neglecting the very work he is set to do, in favor of any show of devoutness which does not affect the roots of his conduct, or of any show of zeal in another work which it is not yet his to do.

Of course there is another side to it. This religious training is not already obtained by the mere refusal to be led away from our primary work at the seminary by practical calls upon our energies. Our primary business at the seminary is, no doubt, to obtain the intellectual fitting for our ministerial work, and nothing must be allowed to supersede that in our efforts. But neither must the collateral prosecution of the requisite training of the heart and hand be neglected, as opportunity offers. Nor will a properly guarded attention to these injure the discharge of our scholastic duties; it will, on the contrary, powerfully advance their successful performance. The student cannot too sedulously cultivate devoutness of spirit. The maxim has been often verified in the experience of us all: *bene orasse est bene studuisse.* When the heart is thoroughly aroused, the slowest mind starts into motion and an impulse is given it which carries it triumphantly over intellectual difficulties before which it quailed afraid. And equally a proper taste of the practical work of the ministry is a great quickener of the mind for the intellectual preparation. We cannot do without these things. And the student must be very careful, therefore—even on this somewhat low ground—while not permitting any distractions to divert him from his primary task as a student, yet to take full advantage of all proper opportunities that may arise to train his heart and hand also. Preparation for ministerial service is very much like building a machine—say a locomotive. The intellectual work may have been accomplished and the machine may stand perfect before us. But it will not go unless the vital force of devotion is throbbing through it. Knowledge is a powerful thing: and practical tact is a powerful thing. And so is a locomotive a powerful thing—provided it has steam in it! Though I know all mysteries and all knowledge, and though I bestow all my goods to feed the poor, if I have not the love of God and man welling up in invincible power beneath it all and lifting it all and transmuting it all into effective working force—it profits me nothing.

II

But the question comes back to us, How are we to obtain this spiritual culture in the seminary? Well, theological students, in becoming theological students, have not ceased to be men; and there is no other way for them to become devout men than that which is common to man. There is but one way, brethren, to become strong in the Lord. That way is to feed on the Bread of Life! This is the way other men who would fain be devout take, and it is the way we, if we would fain be devout, must take. We are simply asking ourselves then, as theological students, what opportunities are offered us by our residence in the seminary for the cultivation of faith in Jesus Christ and obedience to him. What we are eager to know is how we can, not merely keep alive, but fan into a brighter flame, the fires of our love for our Lord and Savior. I desire to be perfectly plain and simple in attempting to suggest an answer to this question. I shall, therefore, only enumerate in the barest manner some of the ways in which the devout life may be assisted in the conditions in which we live in the seminary.

First of all, I must point you to the importance of a diligent use of the public means of grace. Public means of grace abound in the seminary. There is the stated Sabbath-morning service in the chapel; and no student who is not prevented from attending it by some imperative duty should fail to be in his seat at that service, adding whatever his presence and his prayers can bring to the spiritual forces at work there. Then there is our weekly Conference on Sabbath afternoon, in which we talk over together the blessed promises of our God and seek to learn better his will for the ordering of our lives. There have been those in times past whose hearts have been stirred within them at these Conferences; and they may be made by the seeking spirit very precious seasons of social meditation and prayer. Then, faculty and students meet daily, at the close of the day's work, to listen to a fragment of God's Word, mingle their voices in praise to God, and ask his blessing on the labor of the day. Indeed, we proceed to no one of our classroom exercises without pausing a moment to lift up our hearts to God in prayer. And every effort is made by all of us who teach, I know, in all our teaching—however it may appear from moment to moment to be concerned with mere parts of speech, or the signification of words, or the details of history, or the syllogisms of formal logic—to preserve a devout spirit and a reverent heart, as becomes those who are dealing even with the outer coverings that protect the mysteries of God. I need not stay to speak with particularity of the more rarely occurring stated services, such as the monthly concert of prayer for missions and the like. Enough has been said to suggest the richness of provision made in the seminary for public worship: and assuredly amid such abounding opportunities for the quickening of the religious life it ought to be a comparatively easy thing to cultivate devoutness of spirit.

You will doubtless observe that I have said nothing, so far, of additional opportunities for social worship afforded by public services open to the attendance of the students outside the boundaries of the seminary, or by voluntary associations for religious culture among the students themselves. These also are abundant, and have their parts to play in your edification. They may be justly accounted supplementary means of grace, useful to you, each in its own place and order. But what I am insisting on now is something which no such services, whether without or within the seminary walls, can supply: something which by the grace of God can go much deeper into the bases of your religious nature and lay much broader foundations for the building up of a firm and consistent and abiding Christian character. I am exhorting you to give great diligence to the cultivation of the stated means of grace provided by the seminary, to live in them and make them the full and rich expression of the organic religious life of the institution. I am touching on something here that seems to me to be of the utmost importance and which does not seem to me to have received the attention from the students which it deserves. Every body of men bound together in as close and intimate association as we are, must have an organic life: and if the bonds that bind them together are fundamentally of a religious character, this organic life must be fundamentally a religious one. We do not live on the top of our privileges in such circumstances unless we succeed in giving this organic religious life full power in our own lives and full expression in the stated means provided for its expression. No richness of private religious life, no abundance of voluntary religious services on the part of members of the organism, can take the place of or supersede the necessity for the fullest, richest, and most fervent expression of this organic religious life through its appropriate channels. I exhort you, therefore, brethren, with the utmost seriousness, to utilize the public means of grace afforded by the seminary, and to make them instruments for the cultivation and expression of the organic religious life of the institution. We shall not have done our duty by our own souls until we find in these public services the joy of our hearts and the inspiration of our conduct.

Let me go a step further and put into plain words a thought that is floating in my mind. The entire work of the seminary deserves to be classed in the category of means of grace; and the whole routine of work done here may be made a very powerful means of grace if we will only prosecute it in a right spirit and with due regard to its religious value. For what are we engaging ourselves with in our daily studies but just the Word of God, the history of God's dealings with his people, the great truths that he has revealed to us for the salvation of our souls? And what are we doing when we engage ourselves day after day with these topics of study and meditation but just what every Christian man strives to do when he is seeking nutriment for his soul? The only difference is that what he does sporadically, at intervals, and somewhat primarily, it is your privilege to give yourselves to unbrokenly for a space of three whole years! Precious years these ought to be to you, brethren, in the culture of the spiritual life. If such contact as we in the seminary have the privilege of enjoying with divine truth does not sanctify our souls, should we not infer either that it is a mistake to pray in Christ's own words, "sanctify us in the truth; thy word is truth," or else that our hearts are so indurated as no longer to be capable of reaction even to so powerful a reagent as the very truth of God?

I beseech you, brethren, take every item of your seminary work as a religious duty. I am emphasizing the adjective in this. I mean do all your work religiously—that is, with a religious end in view, in a religious spirit, and with the religious side of it dominant in your mind. Do not lose such an opportunity as this to enlighten, deepen, and strengthen your devotion. Let nothing pass by you without sucking the honey from it. If you learn a Hebrew word, let not the merely philological interest absorb your attention: remember that it is a word which occurs in God's Holy Book, recall the passages in which it stands, remind yourselves what great religious truths it has been given to have a part in recording for the saving health of men. Every Biblical text whose meaning you investigate treat as a Biblical text, a part of God's Holy Word, before which you should stand in awe. It is wonderful how even the strictest grammatical study can be informed with reverence. You cannot read six lines of Bishop Ellicott's *Commentaries, Critical and Grammatical,* on Paul's epistles without feeling through and through that here is a man of God studying the Word of God. *O si sic omnes!* Let us make such commentators our models in our study of the Word, and learn like them to keep in mind whose word it is we are dealing with, even when we are merely analyzing its grammatical expression. And when, done with grammar, we begin to weigh the meaning, O let us remember what meaning it has *to us!* Apply every word to your own souls as you go on, and never rest satisfied until you feel as well as understand. Every item of God's dealing with his Church to which your attention is directed, contemplate reverently as an act of God and search out the revelation it carries of God and his ways with man. And the doctrines— need I beg you to consider these doctrines not as so many propositions to be analyzed by your logical understanding, but as rather so many precious truths revealing to you God and God's modes of dealing with sinful man? John Owen, in his great work on Justification, insists and insists again that no man can ever penetrate the significance of this great doctrine unless he persistently studies it, not in the abstract light of the question, How can man be just with God? but in the searching light of the great personal question, How can *I,* sinner as I am, be accepted of God? It is wonderful how inadequacies in conceiving what is involved in Justification fall away under the illumination of this personal attitude toward it. And is it conceivable that it can be so studied and the heart remain cold and unmoved? Treat, I beg you, the whole work of the seminary as a unique opportunity offered you to learn about God, or rather, to put it at the height of its significance, to learn God—to come to know him whom to know is life everlasting. If the work of the seminary shall be so prosecuted, it will prove itself to be the chief means of grace in all your lives. I have heard it said that some men love theology more than they love God. Do not let it be possible to say that of you. Love theology, of course: but love theology for no other reason than that it is THEOLOGY—the knowledge of God—and because it is your meat and drink to know God, to know him truly, and as far as it is given to mortals, to know him whole.

There is yet another aspect of the seminary life the value of which as a means of spiritual development cannot easily be overestimated. I do not know how better to express what I mean than by calling the seminary a three years' retreat. The word "retreat" may strike somewhat strangely upon our Protestant ears: though even our Presbyterian ministry has been learning of late what a "retreat" is. Well, that is what a seminary life very largely is—a period of three years' duration during which the prospective minister withdraws from the world and gives his time exclusively to study and meditation on God's Word, in company with a select body of godly companions.

> Here man more purely lives, less oft doth fall,
> More promptly rises, walks with stricter heed.

Possibly with our natural Protestant objection to all that in the remotest way savors of the monastery, we may be prone to take little account of this feature of seminary life—much to our hurt. Much to our hurt, I say; for a "retreat" is what a seminary life is, and it will have its effect on us as such—one way or another, according as we do or do not prepare for it, and are or are not receptive of it.

Our brethren of the Church of England, who have only comparatively lately taken to multiplying distinctively theological colleges, because they look to the universities as the places where their candidates are to be educated for the holy office, consider this element in the life at a theological college one of its most characteristic and helpful features. It was because he viewed it thus that Bishop Wilberforce declared the three objects of residence at Cuddesden to be: 1. Devotion; 2. Parochial Work; and 3. Theological Reading. It is as a matter of fact inevitable that the practical withdrawal from the world and the congregation together of a hundred or two young men, all consecrated to the work of the Lord, and living in that closeness of intimacy which only community life can induce, should have a very powerful effect on their religious development. What, brethren, can you draw coals together without creating a blaze? I beseech you, esteem very highly and cultivate with jealous eagerness this unique privilege of long and intimate association with so many of God's children. No such opportunities of interaction of devout lives upon one another can ever come to you again in all your life. If no fire of Christian love breaks out among you, look well to yourselves: you may justly suspect there is something wrong with your souls. In the daily intercourse of scores of Christian men there must arise innumerable opportunities of giving and receiving spiritual impressions. See to it that all you give shall conduce to the quickening of the religious life, and that all you receive shall be food on which your own hearts feed and grow strong in the Lord. When you leave the seminary you will miss this intercourse sorely: but by God's help you may so use it while here that in the strength derived from it you may go many days.

III

But we must penetrate beneath even such means of grace as those I have enumerated before we reach the center of our subject. It is not to the public ordinances, not to your professors, and not even to your companions, that you can look for the sources of your growth in religious power. As no one can give you intellectual training except at the cost of your own strenuous effort, so no one can communicate to you spiritual advancement apart from the activities of your own eager souls. True devoutness is a plant that grows best in seclusion and the darkness of the closet; and we cannot reach the springs of our devout life until we penetrate into the sanctuary where the soul meets habitually with its God. If association with God's children powerfully quickens our spiritual life, how much more intimate communion with God himself. Let us then make it our chief concern in our preparation for the ministry to institute between our hearts and God our Maker, Redeemer, and Sanctifier such an intimacy of communion that we may realize in our lives the command of Paul to pray without ceasing and in everything to give thanks, and that we may see fulfilled in our own experience our Lord's promise not only to enter into our hearts, but unbrokenly to abide in them and to unite them to himself in an intimacy comparable to the union of the Father and the Son.

Lectio, meditatio, oratio, the old doctors used to say, *faciunt theologum.* They were right. Take the terms in the highest senses they will bear, and we shall have an admirable prescription of what we must do would we cultivate to its height the Christian life that is in us.

Above all else that you strive after, cultivate the grace of private prayer. It is a grace that is capable of cultivation and that responds kindly to cultivation; as it can be, on the other hand, atrophied by neglect. Be not of those that neglect it, but in constant prayer be a follower of Paul, or rather of our Lord himself; for, God as he was, our blessed Lord was a man of prayer, and found prayer his ceaseless joy and his constant need. Of course the spirit of prayer is the main thing here, and the habit of "praying without ceasing," of living in a prayerful frame, is above all what is to be striven for. But let us not fall into the grave error of supposing this prayerful habit of mind enough, or that we can safely intermit the custom of setting apart seasons for formal prayer. Let me read you a few appropriate words here from one of Dr. H. C. G. Moule's delightful devotional treatises:

> To speak in terms of the simplest practicality, the living Christian will do anything rather than make his "life" an excuse for indolence, and for want of method and self-discipline, in secret devotion; or for want of adoring reverence in the manner of it; or for neglect of the Written Word as a vital element in it, and as the one sure guide and guard of it all along. He will most specially take care that Christ is thus "in his life," in respect of *morning* intercourse with him. His "morning watch" will be a time of

sacred necessity and blessed benefit. He will not merely confess the duty of "meeting God before he meets man." He will understand that he cannot do without it, if indeed he would deal with the unfolding day as it should be dealt with by one whose "life is hid with Christ in God"; one who possesses the priceless treasure of the blessed Union, "joined to the Lord, one Spirit," and who has his treasure at hand, in hand for use. And he will be not less watchful over his *evening* interview with him who is at once his Master and his Life; coming with punctual reverence *to* him who meanwhile liveth *in* him, to report the day's bond-service, to confess the day's sins in contrite simplicity, to look again deliberately upon his Master's face mirrored in his Word, to feel again the bond of the Union, tested and handled through the promises and then to lie down in the peace of God. And will he not see whether some *mid-day* interval, if but for a few brief minutes, cannot be found and kept sacred, for a special prayer and watch half-way? Such stated times are not substitutes for the spiritual attitude in which the "eyes are *ever* toward the Lord," but they are, I believe, quite necessary in order to the proper preparedness of the soul for that attitude, and for the right use, too, of all public and social ordinances. Nothing can annul the vital need of secret and deliberate communion with him in whom we live, by whom we move.[1]

Next to the prayerful spirit, the habit of reverent meditation on God's truth is useful in cultivating devoutness of life. It is commonly said around us that the old gift of meditation has perished out of the earth. And certainly there is much in our nervous fussy times which does not take kindly to it. Those who read nowadays like to do it running. It is assuredly worth our while, however, to bring back the gracious habit of devout meditation. Says Jeremy Taylor in the opening page of his *Holy Living,* in his quaint old-world words: "The counsels of religion are not to be applied to the distempers of the soul as men used to take hellebore; but they must dwell together with the spirit of a man, and be twisted about his understanding forever: they must be used like nourishment, that is, by a daily care and meditation; not like a single medicine, and upon

---

[1]*Life in Christ and for Christ,* p. 37.

the actual pressure of a present necessity." It is the same lesson that Mr. Spurgeon expounds in his illuminating way in a passage like the following:

> We ought to muse upon the things of God, because we thus get the real nutriment out of them. Truth is something like the cluster of the vine: if we would have wine from it, we must bruise it; we must press and squeeze it many times. The bruisers' feet must come down joyfully upon the bunches, or else the juice will not flow; and they must well tread the grapes, or else much of the precious liquid will be wasted. So we must by meditation tread the clusters of truth, if we would get the wine of consolation therefrom. Our bodies are not supported merely by taking food into the mouth, but the process which really supplies the muscles and the nerve and the sinew and the bone is the process of digestion. It is by digestion that the outer food becomes assimilated with the inner life. Our souls are not nourished merely by listening awhile to this, and then to that, and then to the other part of divine truth. Hearing, reading, marking, and learning all require inwardly digesting to complete their usefulness, and the inward digesting of the truth lies for the most part in meditating upon it. Why is it that some Christians, although they hear many sermons, make but slow advances in the divine life? Because they neglect their closets, and do not thoughtfully meditate on God's Word. They love the wheat, but they do not grind it; they would have the corn, but they will not go forth into the fields to gather it; the fruit hangs upon the tree, but they will not pluck it; the water flows at their feet, but they will not stoop to drink it. From such folly deliver us, O Lord, and be this our resolve this day, "I will meditate on thy precepts."[2]

Meditation is an exercise which stands somewhere between thought and prayer. It must not be confounded with mere reasoning; it is reasoning transfigured by devout feeling; and it proceeds by broodingly dissolving rather than by logically analyzing the thought. But it must be guarded from degenerating into mere daydreaming on sacred themes; and it will be wise in order to secure ourselves from this fault to meditate

---

[2]*Morning by Morning*, p. 256.

chiefly with the Bible in our hands and always on its truths. As meditation, then, on the one side takes hold upon prayer, so, on the other, it shades off into devotional Bible reading, the highest exercise of which, indeed, it is. Life close to God's Word is life close to God. When I urge you to make very much while you are in the seminary of this kind of devotional Bible study, running up into meditation, pure and simple, I am but repeating what the General Assembly specifically requires of you. "It is expected," says the *Plan of the Seminary*, framed by the Assembly as our organic law, "that every student will spend a portion of time, every morning and evening, in devout meditation and self-recollection and examination; in reading the Holy Scriptures solely with a view to a personal and practical application of the passage read to his own heart, character, and circumstances; and in humble fervent prayer and praise to God in secret."

And do we not find in the practice here recommended the remedy for that lamentable lack of familiarity with "the English Bible"—as it is fashionable now to speak of it—which is distressing us all in candidates for the ministry? Brethren, you deceive yourselves if you fancy anyone can *teach* you "the English Bible" in the sense in which knowledge of it is desiderated. As well expect someone to digest your food for you. You must taste its preciousness for yourselves, before you can apply its preciousness to others' needs. You must assimilate the Bible and make it your own, in that intimate sense which will fix its words fast in your hearts, if you would have those words rise spontaneously to your lips in your times of need, or in the times of the need of others. Read, study, meditate on your Bible: take time to it—much time; spend effort, strength, yourselves on it; until the Bible is in you. Then the Bible will well up in you and come out from you in every season of need.

It is idle to seek aids for such reading and meditation. The devout and prayerful spirit is the only key to it. Nevertheless there are helps which may be temporarily used as crutches if the legs halt too much to go. Dean Alford has a couple of little books on *How to Study the Scriptures,* and Dean Goulburn has a little volume on *The Practical Study of the Bible* which may be profitably consulted for general direction. Our fathers used to read their Bibles with Thomas Scott's *Family Bible with Notes,* or Matthew Henry's *Exposition of the Old and New Testaments,* or William Burkitt's *Expository Notes on the New Testament* (which turns every passage into a prayer) on their knee; and a worse practice can be conceived. The pungent quaintness of Henry especially remains until today without a rival: and no one can read his comments with his heart set on learning of God without deriving from them perennial profit. Direction for your thoughts in meditating on divine truth may be sought also in the numerous books now in such general use for morning and evening religious reading. Bogatzky's *Golden Treasury* is the book of this sort our grandfathers used. William Jay's *Morning and Evening Exercises* is still one of the most useful of them. By its side may be fairly placed at least Spurgeon's *Checkbook on the Bank of Faith.* And the little books of Frances Ridley Havergal have won for themselves a good report. In the use of such aids it is wise to be constantly on guard lest, on the one side, we permit the aid to supplant the direct use of the Word of God as the basis of our meditation, and, on the other, we grow so accustomed to the crutch that we never learn to walk alone. Let neither Matthew Henry nor Charles Spurgeon supplant either the Word of God or the Spirit of God as the teacher of your soul.

IV

In speaking of such aids to the devotional study of Scripture and prayerful meditation, we are already making the transition to a further class of helps to which I must advert before closing. "Every student," says the *Plan of the Seminary,* "at the close of his course . . . must" (I beg you to observe that "must") "have read a considerable number of the best practical writers on the subject of religion." Even without such admonition we certainly could not have failed to recognize this source of quickening for the religious life. The question that is pressing is, Which are "the best practical writers on the subject of religion"? In the multitude clamoring for our attention, some good, many bad, and not a few indifferent, the need of guidance in the choice of our practical reading becomes very acute.

Four great movements have been especially prolific in books of edification, each, of course, after its own fashion and with peculiarities of its own. These are the great mystical movement which runs through all ages of the Church; the Puritan movement of the seventeenth century; the Evangelical movement in the latter part of the eighteenth and early nineteenth centuries; and more lately and to a less extent the Anglican revival of the nineteenth century. The characteristic mark of the works which have emanated from the mystical writers is a certain aloofness combined with a clear and piercing note of adoration. The Puritan literature is marked by intense devotion to duty and strong insistence on personal holiness. Its message is apt to be couched in a somewhat unadorned literary style. But when the graces of style happen to be added to its clear good sense and profound piety, nothing could be more charming. I can never forget my "discovery" of John Arrowsmith, for example, when, reading a mass of Puritan literature for another purpose, I suddenly passed from the plain goodness of Anthony Burgess to his delightful pages. The evangelical fervor of the writers of the great awakening, and the churchly flavor of the Anglican writers are naturally their most marked characteristics. Our task is to select from this varied literature just the books which will most feed our souls.[3]

---

[3]We have no good history of edifying literature in English. The amazing diligence of Hermann Beck has given the Germans two admirable books in this department of knowledge: *Die Erbauungsliteratur der evang. Kirche Deutschlands* (Erlangen: Deichert, 1883, Part I) and *Die relig. Volksliteratur der evang. Kirche Deutschlands in eine Abriss ihrer Geschichte* (Gotha: Perthes, 1892). A volume on *Books of Devotion,* by the Rev. Charles Bodington, has lately appeared in the series of practical treatises called *The Oxford Library of Practical Theology,* edited by the Rev. W. C. E. Newbold, M.A., and the Rev. Darwell Stone, M.A. (London and New York: Longmans, Green & Co., 1903). It is written from an extreme Anglican point of view: and I am afraid

Thinking that in the multitude of counselors there was likely to be strength, I made bold a few years ago to write to a number of religious teachers, each of them justly famous as a writer of books of devotional character, and asked their aid in making out a short list of "the best practical writers on the subject of religion" for the use of the students of the seminary. I will give you one or two of the answers I received, and these may serve as preliminary guides to your practical reading. Dr. James Stalker, now a professor in the United Free Church College, Aberdeen, thought the following, on the whole, the five most helpful books of practical religion: Thomas à Kempis' *Imitation of Christ*, Richard Baxter's *Reformed Pastor*, Jeremy Taylor's *Life of Christ*, John Owen's *Holy Spirit*, Adolph Monod's *Saint Paul*. The late Rev. Dr. William M. Taylor, of New York, gave the preference to the following five: Dean Goulburn's *Thoughts on Personal Religion*, Phelps's *Still Hour*, Tholuck's *Hours of Christian Devotion*, Alexander's *Thoughts on Religious Experience*, Faber's *Hymns*. Our own Dr. William M. Paxton recommends especially: Hodge's *Way of Life*, Bishop Ryle's *Holiness*, Doddridge's *Rise and Progress of Religion in the Soul*, Owen's *Spiritual Mindedness*, and Faber's *Thoughts on Great Mysteries*. These are all good books and would richly repay your loving study. A hundred others could be added just as good.

It would be useless, however, to draw out a long list of books to be especially recommended. I shall venture to set down the titles of just a round dozen, which I look upon as indispensable. Each must be read for what it can give us: and in none of them shall we seek inspiration and instruction in vain. They come from every part of the Church and from every age, and they include representatives of every type of Christian thought, from the Mariolatrous Romanism of Thomas à Kempis or the bald Pelagianism of Sir Thomas Browne to the penetrating mysticism of the *Theologia Germanica* and the

---

I shall have to add that it is high and dry to a degree and, beyond giving some account of the contents of a number of books of devotional tenor in English, largely of Romish origin, is of little value.

plain evangelicalism of John Newton. But they all are veritable devotional classics, and each of them has power in it to move and instruct the heart of whoever would live in the Spirit. Get at least these dozen booklets, keep them at your elbow, and sink yourselves in them with constant assiduity. They are: Augustine's *Confessions;*[4] *The Imitation of Christ;*[5] the *Theologia Germanica;*[6] Bishop Andrewes' *Private Devotions;*[7] Jeremy Taylor's *Life of Christ;*[8] Richard Baxter's *The Saints' Everlasting Rest;*[9] Samuel Rutherford's *Letters;*[10] John Bunyan's *Pilgrim's Progress;*[11] Sir Thomas Browne's *Religio Medici;*[12] William Law's *Serious Call,*[13] John Newton's *Cardiphonia,*[14] Bishop

---

[4]The editions are numerous. The best Latin text is that of Pius Knöll, which is accessible in the Teubner series of Latin texts (Leipzig, 1898). Of the English translations of the whole work, Dr. Pusey's is best both for the translation and its admirable notes. Dr. Shedd's edition of Watt's version contains an interesting Introduction. An excellent new translation of the first nine books, with introduction and notes, by Dr. C. Bigg, was published by Methuen in 1898.

[5]The editions are numerous and easily accessible in both Latin and English. Much the best English translation is that by Dr. Charles Bigg, published in Methuen's series of Devotional Books. A new departure was made by the publication at Berlin in 1874, by Dr. C. Hirsche, of an edition the text of which is presented "metrice." The English version of this metrically arranged text, published by A. D. F. Randolph, New York, 1889, is somewhat diffuse but interesting.

[6]Get the edition in Macmillan's *Golden Treasury Series,* edited by Dr. Pfeiffer, and translated by Susanna Winkworth.

[7]There are many editions. The best is *The Preces Privatae of Bishop Andrewes,* edited by F. E. Brightman, M.A. (London: Methuen, 1903). I recommend for the English reader also Dr. Alexander Whyte's edition (Edinburgh: Oliphant, Anderson & Ferrier, 1896), to which is prefixed an admirable "Biography" and still more admirable "Interpretation."

[8]Printed in Vol. II of Heber's edition of his *Works.*

[9]An edition is published by the Presbyterian Board of Publication, and another in Methuen's series of Devotional Books.

[10]Dr. Bonar's edition is the best (New York: Carter); cf. Dr. A. Whyte's *Samuel Rutherford and Some of His Correspondents.* The Messrs. Longmans publish an excellent selection from the letters, edited by Miss Lucy M. Soulsby, under the title of *Christ and His Cross.*

[11]A good edition is issued by the Presbyterian Board of Publication.

[12]*The Golden Treasury* edition (Macmillan) is particularly to be recommended.

[13]Get the edition in Dent's *Temple Classics.*

[14]An edition is printed by the Presbyterian Board of Publication.

Thomas Wilson's *Sacra Privata*.[15] To these twelve I should add two or three others which have peculiar interest to us as Princetonians, and which I am sure are worthy of association with them—Jonathan Edwards' *Treatise Concerning Religious Affections,* Archibald Alexander's *Thoughts on Religious Experience,* and Charles Hodge's *Way of Life.*

I have purposely omitted from this list collections of hymns and (in general) of prayers, in order that I might recommend the use of both to you in a separate category. I strongly advise you to make yourselves familiar with the best religious verse, and occasionally to support your devotions with the best prayers to which saintly men have given permanent form. Faber's *Hymns* have a quality of intense adoration in them which recommends them to many as the best for such a purpose; Miss Rossetti's devotional poems are unsurpassed for elevation of feeling; many prefer the quieter note of Keble's *Christian Year;* others still love best the evangelical sobriety of *The Olney Hymns,* or the exotic flavor of Miss Winkworth's *Lyra Sacra Germanica;* others find more attractive the variety afforded by such a book as Dr. Schaff's *Christ in Song.* On the whole, I fancy most of you will find that Palgrave's *Treasury of Sacred Song* will meet your needs as well as any other single volume; it is a veritable treasure-house of the best of English religious poetry. As to collections of prayers, nothing is more inspiring than Lancelot Andrewes' *Private Devotions,* which I have already named in the general list of recommended devotional books, unless it be Anselm's *Meditations and Prayers,*[16] which, despite the deforming hagiolatry which sometimes invades them, remain an example for all ages of how a great heart lifts itself up greatly to God.

---

[15]Keble's edition (Oxford, 1860) is the standard. A good edition is Bishop Wilson's *Sacra Privata,* edited by A. E. Burn, B.D. (London: Methuen, 1903).

[16]An English translation, with prefatory matter by Dr. Pusey, was published at Oxford in 1856. A good edition is that of London, 1872. The latest edition, *The Devotions of St. Anselm,* edited by C. C. J. Webb, M.A. (London: Methuen, 1903), contains only (along with the *Proslogion* and some letters) four each of the *Meditations* and *Prayers.*

There is yet another branch of religious reading which I think you will scarcely be able to neglect, if you would build yourself up into the full stature of manhood in Christ by the example of his saints. I refer to religious biography. Only let us remember that in selecting religious biographies to read with a view to our spiritual improvement, we must bear in mind that the adjective must be understood as qualifying the Life as well as the life: it must be the biographies themselves that are religious. It must be confessed that many of the greatest saints have been unfortunate in their biographers. Not only are their lives often written without a particle of literary skill, but equally often much of the religious impression of their holy walk has evaporated in the telling. Nevertheless from at least the time when the great Athanasius himself edified the Church with a life of Anthony—written, we fear, not without some imitation in form and content alike of the popular romances of the time[17]—the Church has never lacked a series of religious biographies which have in them the promise and potency of religious life for their readers. Dr. Stalker thinks the best of these for your use are Augustine's *Confessions,* Baxter's *Reliques,* Hanna's *Life of Chalmers,* Blaikie's *Life of Livingstone,* Witte's *Life of Tholuck,* and Brown's *Life of Rabbi Duncan.* The late Dr. William M. Taylor recommended Bonar's *Memoirs of McCheyne,* Hanna's *Life of Chalmers,* Arnot's *Memoir of James Hamilton,* Guthrie's *Memoirs,* Blaikie's *Life of Livingstone,* J. G. Paton's *Autobiography,* and Dr. Prentiss' *Life and Letters of Mrs. Prentiss.* You will not fail to observe how Scotch Dr. Taylor's list is. Tastes will differ: the late Dean Goulburn wrote me simply that there were no religious biographies equal to Isaac Walton's. I shall not undertake to add a list of my own, which doubtless would have its peculiarities also. I shall content myself with a bare hint that you must not miss reading the great books. Such, for example, is Bunyan's *Grace Abounding*—the seventeenth century replica of

---

[17]See a very interesting essay on "Greek and Early Christian Novels," pp. 357 ff. of Mr. T. R. Glover's *Life and Letters in the Fourth Century* (Cambridge, 1901).

Augustine's *Confessions*. Such also is John Newton's *Authentic Narrative*. Such also is Boston's *Memoirs* which can now be had in a worthy form.[18] Such, also, is probably Doddridge's account of James Gardiner's remarkable life. And such certainly is Edwards' *Life of David Brainerd*. And if I am to judge by my own experience of its religious impression, such also is the *Life of Adolph Monod* by one of his daughters.

Along with religious biography may I venture to mention also religious fiction—the portrayal of the religious life under the cover of imagined actors? Take the *Chronicles of the Schoenberg-Cotta Family*. Take the *Heir of Redcliffe*. Who in the face of the experience of a generation can doubt the quickening influence of such books? A book that has played a part such as that played by the *Heir of Redcliffe* in the lives of men like Dr. A. Kuyper and Mr. William Morris is surely worthy of our serious attention as a religious force in the world. And speaking of these books brings to my lips the exclamation, What women the Church of Victorian England gave the world! Elizabeth Rundell Charles, Charlotte Mary Yonge, Frances Ridley Havergal, Dora Greenwell, Dora Pattison—the Lives of all of these are accessible to you as well as their writings—though some of them, I am sorry to say, are rather dully written. Put them by the side of the *Life of Mrs. Prentiss* recommended to us by Dr. Taylor, and learn from them what women Christianity is still making all around us.

Of *Sermons* I shall say nothing: they form a department of religious literature by themselves. But I have reserved for the last mention a class of religious literature which, for my own part, I esteem the very highest of all for spiritual impression. I refer to the great Creeds of the Church. He who wishes to grow strong in his religious life, let him, I say, next to the Bible, feed himself on the great Creeds of the Church. There is a force of religious inspiration in them which you will seek in vain elsewhere. And this for good reasons. First, because

---

[18]Edited by Rev. G. H. Morrison (Edinburgh: Oliphant, Anderson & Ferrier, 1899).

it is ever true that it is by the truth that sanctification is wrought. And next, because the truth is set forth in these Creeds with a clearness and richness with which it is set forth nowhere else. For these Creeds are not the products of metaphysical speculation, as many who know infinitesimally little about them are prone to assert, but are the compressed and weighted utterances of the Christian heart. I am not alone, of course, in so esteeming them. You will remember with what insistence Cardinal Newman warns us against "an untheological devotion," and with what force he expounds in his *Grammar of Assent* the spiritual import of the Creeds and Catechisms of the Church. For himself, he tells us, the Athanasian Creed has always seemed the most devotional formulary that Christianity has ever given birth to: and certainly readers of Dr. Gore's beautiful exposition of it as "the Battle-hymn of Christians" will not be slow to feel the truth of Dr. Newman's estimate. Dr. Alexander Whyte, in commenting on Andrewes' *Private Devotions,* takes up the theme afresh and remarks on the exemplification it receives in Andrewes' treatment of the Apostles' and Nicene Creeds. "When Andrewes takes up any of these things," he observes, "into his intellect, imagination, and heart, he has already provided himself and his readers with another great prayer and another great psalm. So true is it that all true theology is directly and richly and evangelically devotional."

I do not think I go astray, therefore, when I say to you in all seriousness that the second and third volumes of Dr. Schaff's *Creeds of Christendom* have in them more food for your spiritual life—are "more directly, richly, and evangelically devotional"—than any other book, apart from the Bible, in existence. Nor can I think myself wrong in directing you specifically to the Reformed Creeds as, above all others, charged with blessing to those who will read and meditate on their rich deposit of religious truth. Our Scotch forefathers turned for spiritual nourishment especially to "the Sum of Saving Knowledge and the Practical Use Thereof," which had come to be a stated portion of the current editions of the

Confession of Faith, just because that volume circulated at first chiefly as a devotional book and a directory for practical religion. This treatise has never been a part of our "Church book." But in the Westminster Confession we have something even better. Read what Dr. Thornwell tells us of what the study of the Confession did for his soul[19] and then ask yourselves whether it may not do the same for you too. By the side of the Westminster Confession put the Heidelberg Catechism: where will you find more faithful, more probing Christian teaching than this? I beg you, brethren, feed your souls on the Christian truth set forth with so much combined clearness of apprehension and depth of feeling in these great formularies.

And so we come around at the end to the point from which we took our start. Religious knowledge and religious living go hand in hand. "It might be instructive to inquire," writes good Dr. Andrew A. Bonar,[20] "why it is that whenever godliness is healthy and progressive we almost invariably find learning in the Church attendant on it: while, on the other hand, an illiterate state is attended sooner or later by decay of vital godliness." We deceive ourselves if we think we can give a portion of our being only to God. If we withhold the effort requisite to learn to know the truth, we cannot hope to succeed in any effort to do his will. Unknown truth cannot sanctify the soul; and it is by the truth that we are to be sanctified. Mind, heart, and hand—true religious cultivation must embrace them all and carry on their training all together. We must indeed rebuke the lordly understanding if it essays to supersede the necessity of holy living. Our heart thrills responsively when the monk of Deventer, at the opening of his pungent book, asks us pointedly, How will it advantage you to know all things if you have no love?

> What is the profit of high argument on the Trinity if you lack humility and are offensive to the Trinity? Great words assuredly make no man holy and righteous; but by virtuous

---

[19]See Palmer's *Life of Thornwell*, pp. 162, 165.
[20]Introduction to his edition of *Rutherford's Letters* (New York, 1851), p. xvi.

living he becomes dear to God. Far better feel compunc-
tion than have skill in defining it. Though you know the
whole Bible and all the sayings of the philosophers, what
would it all advantage you without God's love and grace?
. . . It is natural to man to desire knowledge; but knowledge without the fear of God—of what avail is it?

Yes, yes, our hearts reply: it is all true, greatly true! But beneath our assent does there not lurk an underlying sense, as
we read on deeper into the exhortation, that there is something
of the narrowness of mysticism in the sharp "either—or" that
is thrust upon us? If we must choose between knowledge and
life, why of course give us life! But why put the alternative
so sharply? Must it be knowledge *or* life? Must it not rather
be knowledge *and* life? *Non comprehenditur Deus per investi-
gationem sed per imitationem,* says Hugh of St. Cher. Ah, but
"investigation" is the first step in "imitation"; for how shall
I strive to be like God, except by first discovering what God
is like? And "imitation" itself—is it after all the key-word of
Christianity? It is, no doubt, a great word. But it is not the
greatest. "Trust" is greater. And by the side of "trust" there
stand but two others. "But now abideth," says Paul, "faith,
hope, love, these three; and the greatest of these is love."

Happily we have not been left to ourselves to make the
correction. The Church has had greater teachers than even
Thomas à Kempis. And a greater than he begins a greater book
than his with greater words than he could give us:

Great art Thou, O Lord, and highly to be praised; great is
Thy power and Thy understanding is infinite. Yet Thee
would man praise—though but a little particle of Thy
creation: even man, who bears about with him his mor-
tality, bears about with him the proof of his sin, even the
proof that Thou resistest the proud: yea, Thee still would
man praise, this little particle of Thy creation. 'Tis Thou
that dost excite us to delight in Thy praise; for Thou didst
make us for Thyself and our heart is restless till it find its
rest in Thee. Grant me, Lord, to know whether I should
first call upon Thee or praise Thee; whether I should first
know Thee or call upon Thee. . . . Alas! Alas! tell me for
Thy mercies' sake, O Lord, my God, what Thou art unto

me. Say unto my soul, "I am thy salvation." So speak that I may hear. Behold, the ears of my heart are before Thee, O Lord: open Thou them and say to my soul, "I am thy salvation." Make me to run after Thy voice and lay hold on Thee. Hide not Thy face from me. Let me die that I die not: only let me see Thy face. Narrow is my soul's house; enlarge Thou it, that Thou mayest enter in. It is fallen into ruins: repair Thou it. There is that within it which must offend Thine eyes: I confess, I know it. But who shall cleanse it? Or to whom but to Thee shall I cry?

Here, I venture to say, is the essence of all true religion. Humility of spirit is here rather than depreciation of intellect: trust in the mercy of God to sinners rather than dependence on deeds of man. There is no such note struck here as this: "Even though I knew everything in all the world and were not in charity, what would it advantage me in the sight of God, who will judge me *ex facto*." *Ex facto* indeed! Who that is judged by his works shall stand? It is not an antithesis of knowledge and works that Augustine draws. It is an antithesis of man and God: and its note is, "In Thee only do I put my trust, O Lord, for in Thee only is there salvation." *Dic "Habeo,"* says he tersely, *sed, "Ab Eo."* It is an execrable word-play, but excellent theology, and the very quintessence of religion. And when we have learned this well—learned it so that it sounds in all the chambers of our hearts and echoes down through all the aisles of our lives—we shall have learned the great lesson of practical religion.

29

SOME PERILS OF MISSIONARY LIFE*

I suppose we all recognize that missionaries are the cream of Christians. They may say with Paul, in the whole length and breadth of his meaning, that unto them the grace has been given to preach unto the heathen the unsearchable riches of Christ (Eph. iii. 8). They are the bold and faithful spirits who bear the banner of the cross courageously to the front. We who abide at home hope that we are at home by the will of God and to his glory; but we cannot withhold our admiration from those whom God has chosen to form the advance-guard of his conquering host. We recognize that these "picked men" are the *elite* of the army of the cross. Their bearing justifies this recognition. There is no body of men in the world of equal numbers who so thoroughly meet the trust reposed in them and the lofty sentiments entertained toward them by their fellow Christians.

So exalted is our well-founded appreciation of the character of missionaries in general that it comes with something of a shock to us to discover, as we are now and then led to discover, that even missionaries are, nevertheless, men, and are sometimes liable to the temptations, and shall we not even say, the failings, that are common to men. In the difficult situations in which they have been placed, they have exhibited, in general, a wisdom, a faithfulness, a power of adaptation, a devotion, which seems almost superhuman, and which can be accounted for only as the fulfilment of the promise with which the Lord accompanied their marching orders—that he would be with

---

The Presbyterian Quarterly, July, 1899, pp. 385-404. Dr. Warfield says this was "an address to a body of prospective missionaries" (*Opuscula*, Vol. VIII, art. 20).

them to the end of the world. But in the midst of this general marvelous success, we find just enough of shortcomings to warn us that there are dangers attending the work of the missionary which it is requisite to face and to guard against. I do not here speak of such dangers as that of spiritual pride, which may be thought to lie very close to a calling which is recognized among us as one which in a special manner undertakes the work of God and may lay particular claim to his smile, and which may be peculiarly near to men who are everywhere esteemed, and may haply come to esteem themselves, as the *elite* of Christians. I am bound to testify that I have seen very little of anything resembling spiritual pride among missionaries, though doubtless it here and there exists, as how could it fail to exist? The dangers I wish to speak of are not those which spring from the very essence of the calling, but rather such as attend the work missionaries are called on to do, and such as show themselves in the manner of its prosecution. Here, too, the greatest danger is that we may fancy there is no danger. To be forewarned is to be partially, at least, forearmed; at all events it places it in our power to forearm ourselves.

Let us spring at once *in medias res* and mention at the beginning the supremest danger which can attend a missionary in his work—the danger that he who has gone forth to convert the heathen may find himself rather being converted by the heathen. The idea is monstrous, you may think. But the danger is an actual and a real one, and its working is not unillustrated by sad examples. It is no doubt exceedingly rare that a missionary is so fully converted to heathendom that he lays aside his Christian profession and adopts in its entirety the religion of those whom he was sent to convert, though even this is not absolutely unexampled. Dr. A. J. Behrends, for instance, in his little volume of missionary addresses delivered on the Graves's Foundation at Syracuse University (*The World for Christ,* p. 102), tells of a classmate of his own to whom even this occurred. He says:

I had a classmate in the Theological Seminary who, thirty

years ago, went as a missionary to China. He abandoned his calling and his faith, became a Mandarin of the "third button," and for many years has been associated with the Chinese legation in the courts of Europe. He writes of the "iced champagne" which he drinks when the heat of summer is oppressive, and talks flippantly of the "so-called" Holy Land and of the "historic cross of the carpenter philosopher," which annoys him at every step from Munich to St. Petersburg. He has developend into a Confucianist.

It much more frequently happens, however, that the impact of the heathen mind upon his thought has led the missionary only to modify his belief until he has laid aside the fundamentals of Christianity, or even now and then, under the ethical influences of his surroundings, has made shipwreck of faith in a practical sense and adopted the ethical views and fallen into the debased modes of life of his community. All this, of course, unhappily occurs to the pastor at home exceedingly frequently, despite the conserving energies of the society in which home pastors are immersed. The forces of the world impinging upon them, and reinforced, it may be, by native tendencies of thought and feeling, draw them away from their adopted lines of thought and gradually assimilate them to worldly views and modes of life. That it happens comparatively rarely among the missionaries in the far severer strain to which they are subjected, isolated as they are from the Christian community, and surrounded by a society the very grain of which is heathen, is only another proof that they are the *elite* of Christendom. But it does happen occasionally among them, too.

A classical example of a missionary becoming thus the convert, or at least the pervert, of his catechumens, is supplied by the famous Bishop Colenso, the pioneer of the present outbreak of rationalistic Biblical criticism in England. Bishop Colenso was bred in the evangelical faith of the Low-Church party of the Church of England, and had received in his youth the essentials of the faith as held by that body of nobly witnessing Christians, though certainly in a somewhat traditional way. When he went to Natal as a missionary, however, he had never given that deep and careful study to the elements of his faith which alone would guarantee their stability. It happened thus that his mind was first thoroughly awakened to the difficulties of his religion through the questions and objections of the "intelligent Zulu," to whom he sought to teach it. Under these objections he gave way, first discarding the fundamentals of evangelical religion, and then his belief in the Bible as the infallible Word of God; and thus became the protagonist of critical rationalism on English ground. Here is his own account of the final stage of his perversion:

> Since I have had charge of this Diocese, I have been closely occupied in the study of the Zulu tongue, and in translating the Scriptures into it. . . . In this work I have been aided by intelligent natives, . . . so as not only to avail myself of their criticisms, but to appreciate fully their objections and difficulties. Thus, however, it has happened that I have been brought again face to face with questions which caused me some uneasiness in former days, but with respect to which I was then enabled to satisfy my mind sufficiently for practical purposes, and I had fondly hoped to have laid the ghosts of them at last forever. Engrossed with parochial and other work in England, I did what, probably, many other clergymen have done under similar circumstances—I contented myself with silencing, by means of the specious explanations, which are given in most commentaries, the ordinary objections against the historical character of the early portions of the Old Testament, and settled down into a willing acquiescence in the general truth of the narratives, whatever difficulties may still hang about particular parts of it. . . . Here, however, as I have said, amidst my work in this land, I have been brought face to face with the very questions which I then put by. . . . I have had a simple-minded, but intelligent, native— one with the docility of a child, but the reasoning powers of mature age—look up and ask, "Is all that true?" . . . I dared not, as a servant of the God of Truth, urge my brother man to believe that which I did not myself believe, which I knew to be untrue, as a matter-of-fact historical narrative. I gave him, however, such a reply as satisfied him for the time, without throwing any discredit upon the general veracity of the Bible history. But I was thus driven —against my will at first, I may truly say—to search more

deeply into these questions. . . . And now I tremble at the result of my inquiries.[1]

The circumstances of this wonderful conversion to disbelief in the Christian Scriptures are no doubt capable of being looked at from two points of view—according as our attention is engrossed with the high and noble honesty of heart which considered not the humbleness of the questioner, or with the previous neglect of duty which left the questioned the prey of the first restless spirit which should attack him. Bishop Colenso's sympathetic biographer, Sir G. W. Cox, contemplates it from the first point of view, and this is his account of it:

> There can be but little doubt, rather there is none, that the choice of Mr. Colenso for missionary work in a heathen land, was a blessing not only to the heathen to whom he was sent, but to his countrymen, to the cause of truth, to the Church of England, and to the Church of God. Up to this time, his moral sense and spiritual instincts lacked free play; and, had he remained in England, those circumstances probably would never have arisen, which were made the means of evoking the marvelous strength of character evinced in the great battle of his life. It was just that appeal of the honest heart which was needed to call into action the slumbering fires. That appeal, and his instantaneous obedience to that appeal, were sneered at as stupid, childish, and contemptible; but the questions of the "intelligent Zulu" became for him questions like those which led Luther to nail his theses on the church door at Wittenberg, and enabled him to break with the force of a Samson the theological and traditional withes by which he had thus far been bound.[2]

Our own Dr. W. H. Green, in his trenchant review of Bishop Colenso's first book on the Pentateuch, contemplates it from the other point of view, and this is the way he puts it:

> The difficulty is in the whole attitude which he occupies. He has picked out a few superficial difficulties in the sacred

---

[1]*The Pentateuch and Book of Joshua Critically Examined,* by the Right Rev. John William Colenso, D.D. (New York, 1863), pp. 4-7.
[2]*The Life of John William Colenso, D.D., Bishop of Natal,* by the Rev. Sir George W. Cox, B.A., M.A. (London, 1888), Vol. I, 50 pp.

record, not now adduced for the first time, nor first discovered by himself. They seem, however, to have recently
dawned upon his view. He was aware, long before, of certain difficulties in the scriptural account of the creation and
deluge; and instead of satisfactorily and thoroughly investigating these, he was content, he tells us, to push them off,
or thrust them aside, satisfying himself with the moral
lessons, and trusting vaguely, and, as he owns, not very
honestly (p. 4), that there was some way of explaining
them (pp. 4, 5). The other difficulties, which have since
oppressed him, he then had no notion of; in fact, so late
as the time when he published or prepared his Commentary
on the Romans (p. 215), he had no idea of ever holding
his present views. As there is nothing brought out in his
book which unbelievers had not flaunted and believing expositors set themselves to explain long since, we are left to
suppose that his theological training as a minister and a
bishop, and his preparation as a commentator, could not
have been very exact or thorough. . . . His mission to the
Zulus, however, fortunately or unfortunately, as the case
may be, broke the spell. He went out to teach the Zulus
Christianity, and now at length he is obliged to study the
Bible on which that religion is based.[3]

I have been thus lengthy in exhibiting the fundamental
elements of the case of Bishop Colenso, because I desired to
bring out the source from which the danger to which he suc-
cumbed arose. Clearly its roots were set in this: he became a
teacher before he was himself taught. The remedy is that
missionaries should not fancy that a zeal for God and a love
for Christ is all the furnishing they need to enable them to win
the world to Christ; if they do, they may haply find themselves
like Bishop Colenso, rather won to the world. Those who expect to go forth as missionaries can read themselves the lesson.
As certainly as men go, mentally unprepared for their task and
its dangers, so certainly will they expose themselves to unnecessary peril and their work to unnecessary likelihood of
failure.

It is the same lesson that is read us by the somewhat parallel

---

[3]*The Pentateuch Vindicated from the Aspersions of Bishop Colenso,*
by William Henry Green (New York, 1863), 112 pp.

case of Francis W. Newman, whose autobiography detailing the changes in his belief, published under the title of *Phases of Faith,* created quite a sensation half a century ago. He was the brother of John Henry Newman, equally or more highly gifted, and, like him and Colenso, was bred in the evangelical faith. It is perfectly evident, however, to the reader of his own account of his religious life, that he never gave that labor and thought to the faith which he professed which were its due, and by which alone it could be firmly anchored in his soul. In one of the phases of his faith he joined Mr. Groves (in 1830) in his mission at Bagdad, and it is plain that he was led to give up the doctrine of the Trinity—one of the earlier stages of his drift away from the truth—by the pressure of Mohammedan objection. He felt uneasy from the first, as with his foundations in Christian thinking one fancies he well might feel uneasy, whenever the thought crossed his mind: "What if we, like Henry Martyn, were charged with polytheism by Mohammedans, and were forced to defend ourselves by explaining in detail our doctrine of the Trinity?" (p. 32). Then he discovered that religion was not the *peculium* of Christianity. There is a vividly drawn scene in a carpenter's shop in Aleppo which, one feels, must have had a significant place in his development.

> While at Aleppo I one day got into a religious discussion with a Mohammedan carpenter, which left on me a lasting impression. Among other matters, I was peculiarly desirous of disabusing him of the current notion of his people, that our Gospels are spurious narratives, of late date. I found great difficulty of expression, but the man listened to me with much attention, and I was encouraged to exert myself. He waited patiently till I had done, and then spoke to the following effect: "I will tell you, sir, how the case stands. God has given you English a great many good gifts. You make fine ships, and sharp pen-knives, and good cloth and cotton; you have rich nobles and brave soldiers; you write and print many learned books (dictionaries and grammars); all this is of God. But there is one thing that God has withheld from you and has revealed to us, and that is, the knowledge of the true religion, by which one may be

saved." When he had thus ignored my argument (which was probably unintelligible to him) and delivered his simple protest, I was silenced, and at the same time amused. But the more I thought it over the more instruction I saw in the case.[4]

The instruction he got out of the case was that, as the possession of a deep religious experience was not dependent on the possession of any one form of religious teaching, therefore all forms of religious teaching are alike useless or worse, and the religion of the individual's own consciousness is the only true religion. He was in other words converted to heathenism by the discovery that man has universally a religious nature.

Something of the same kind seems to have happened to James Macdonald, a missionary of the Free Church of Scotland, to Africa, and author of a readable book called *Light in Africa*. He has more recently published a more pretentious and really very instructive volume called *Religion and Myth*,[5] from which it appears that he has been deeply moved by the discovery that even the lowest savages may have a religious consciousness, exercise religious faith, and enjoy religious certitude. By this discovery he has been led, theoretically at least—let us hope it is wholly unassimilated theory with him—to confound all religions together as being higher or lower stages of the development of man's religious capacities and insight, dependent not on objective revelation but on growing intelligence and the progressive working of human thought upon religious material. Pressed to its legitimate meaning this is pure naturalism, elevated heathenism. Here is the conception of the origin of Christianity to which Macdonald has been brought: Religion began in reverence for a human king, to whom men looked for good, issuing in the conception that the king controlled natural forces; then from habit they still looked to the king for help after he had died, and hence arose a doctrine of souls; thence sprang a conception of personal and separate divinities, slowly gravitating toward the idea of

---

[4]*Phases of Faith,* by Francis William Newman (London, 1870), p. 52.
[5]London, 1893.

one Supreme God; after a while the conception arose that this one Supreme God became incarnate in time, by the substitution of the idea of a single incarnation revealing the will of God for the multitude of prophets—from rain-doctors up—who claim to hold converse with the unseen. Students of the literature of the subject will easily recognize this sketch. To us it seems that instead of converting the Africans to Christianity, Macdonald has himself been converted to a form of scientific heathenism.

The lesson of all these instances is obviously the same. The missionary is not prepared for his work until he has been forced to face all those problems raised by modern criticism and by modern thought—problems of comparative religion, of critical analysis, of philosophical unbelief; has faced them at home, worked through them, and mastered them. Unprepared by this mental discipline, he goes forth at his peril. There is danger in the foreign field for a man who has been too indolent at home to meet the difficulties of unbelief prevalent at home, fairly and squarely, and reason himself through them. He may quiet the doubts that rise in his own soul, but the heathen are not amenable to his lazy Peace! peace!—they will press these doubts upon him. If he parries them, they will justly despise him and he loses all fruit of his work. If he entertains them he is unprepared to deal with them, and—well, some men have lost their faith by that road. We would better prepare ourselves earnestly before we go.

If we fancy that so extreme a peril as that we have been picturing must be rare, let us glance at an analogous danger which necessarily attends all mission work, and which is at bottom only a less acute form of the same evil we have been discussing, though it often grows out of a different root—the danger namely that in striving to commend Christianity to the heathen and to remove their stubborn and abounding difficulties in accepting it we really accommodate Christianity to heathen thought—in a word we simply explain Christianity away. This too is an evil which is by no means confined to missionaries. It may properly be called the deepest danger of pastoral life. Few of us escape it altogether. It is the root of the concessive habit of stating truth, which is the bane of all Christian society. It is distressingly easy to fall into it, as a measure of charity—seeking to be all things to all men that we may gain the more. But what is it in effect but corrupting the truth? It is as if an army sent to protect the frontier against an invading host, should suddenly wheel and place itself, with flags flying and bands playing, and drum majors in full regalia performing, in front of the opposing ranks, and proudly lead them over the land—evidently conquering because now leading! This concessive habit is in other words only an expedient by which we can make it seem as if we had gained others to our side, when we have really placed ourselves at their side. It saves appearances at the cost of realities. It is therefore as I say, only a less acute and obvious form of conversion from Christianity wherever it shows itself—among pastors or among missionaries. For it does show itself occasionally even among those select warriors of the cross, the missionaries. I have met more than one missionary from Mohammedan lands, for example, who had learned to state the doctrine of the Trinity "so genially and so winningly" (as they expressed it), that it roused little or no opposition in the Mohammedan mind. And when I heard how they stated it, I did not wonder; they had so stated it as to leave the idea of the Trinity out—much as Dr. James Morris Whiton, in his recent attempts to show how Unitarians and Trinitarians can unite on a common formula, certainly succeeds in providing an explanation of the Trinity to which no Unitarian should object. You may see his efforts in a recent paper in *The New World,* and in his little book called *Gloria Patri.* The trouble is you look in vain in the explanations for a Trinity.

Without pausing to illustrate this very common danger, let us glance next at another danger attending the missionary in his work, analogous to this, from its opposite side. The method of conversion by concession is really, at bottom, an attempt to deceive men into a profession of Christianity; to make them believe that Christianity is not what it appears to be, and does not involve in its profession all that it seems; that it is much "easier to take" than men have been accustomed to think. Now there is another way of attempting to deceive men into professing Christianity which sometimes presents temptations to missionaries, especially those working among the simpler and less advanced races. We are accustomed to think of dubious miracles as the specialty of the more corrupt ages and localities of Romanism. It may behoove us to have a care, lest we fall victims to what may differ from appeals to dubious miracles by a very narrow ethical line indeed. There is a distinct temptation confronting the missionary at times to make use of his superior intelligence or superior acquirements to impress the ignorant with the divine character of his religion; a distinct temptation to overreach his less well informed brother men by an exhibition of the marvels which learning and science have put within his reach, as if these marvels were something more than proofs of advanced science, and were somewhat of the nature of signs from heaven of the justness of his claims and the validity of his apostleship; sometimes at least a willingness to permit the heathen to deceive themselves as to the purport of what to them are marvels. Take a passage like the following, from one of the noblest, purest, most Christlike missionaries which the Church has yet produced. I should be far from criticizing the motives or methods of such a man of God. I should not like to be understood as suggesting that the limit of the permissible were passed in this particular incident. But are they not at least so nearly approached that the incident may stand as a warning to us of how easy it may become, in somewhat like situations, to pass beyond the limits and attempt to deceive men into accepting the truth? I quote from one of the most thrilling narratives of missionary work our day has produced:

But I must here record the story of the Sinking of the Well, which broke the back of heathenism on Aniwa. Being a flat coral island with no hills to attract the clouds, rain is scarce there as compared with the adjoining mountainous islands; and even when it does fall heavily, with tropical profusion, it disappears . . . through the light soil and porous rock, and drains itself directly into the sea. . . . At certain seasons the natives drank very unwholesome water. . . . My household felt sadly the want of fresh water. I prepared two large casks to be filled when the rain came. But when we attempted to do so at the water-hole near the village, the natives forbade us, fearing that our large casks would carry all the water away, and leave none for them with their so much smaller cocoanut bottles. The public water-hole was on the ground of two Sacred Men, who claimed the power of emptying and filling it by rain at will. The superstitious natives gave them presents to bring the rain. If it came soon, they took all the credit for it. If not, they demanded larger gifts to satisfy their gods. Even our Aneityumese teachers said to me, when I protested that surely they could not believe such things: "It is hard to know, Missi. The water does come and go quickly. If you paid them well, they might bring the rain and let us fill our casks!"

I told them that, as followers of Jehovah, we must despise all heathen mummeries, and trust in him and in the laws of his creation to help us.

Aniwa having, therefore, no permanent supply of fresh water, in spring, or stream, or lake, I resolved, by the help of God, to sink a well, near the Mission premises, hoping that a wisdom, higher than my own, would guide me to the source of some blessed spring. . . . One morning I said to the old Chief and his fellow Chief, both now earnestly inquiring about the religion of Jehovah and of Jesus: "I am going to sink a deep well down into the earth, to see if our God will send us fresh water up from below."

They looked at me with astonishment in a sort of sympathy approaching pity. . . .

I started upon my hazardous job. . . . The old Chief and his best men . . . remonstrated with me very gravely. . . . I toiled on from day to day, my heart almost sinking sometimes with the sinking of the well, till we reached a depth of about thirty feet. And the phrase, "living water," "living water," kept chiming through my soul like music from God, as I dug and hammered away. At this depth the earth and coral began to be soaked with damp. I felt that we were nearing water. My soul had a faith that God would open a spring for us; but side by side with this faith, was a strange terror that the water would be salt. . . . One evening I said to the old Chief: "I think that Jehovah God will give us water tomorrow from that hole!"

The Chief said, "No, Missi." . . . I still answered, "Come tomorrow. I hope and believe that Jehovah God will send you the rain up through the earth." At the moment I knew I was risking much, and probably incurring sorrowful consequences, had no water been given. . . .

Next morning, I went down again at daybreak and sank a narrow hole in the center about two feet deep. The perspiration broke over me with uncontrollable excitement, and I trembled through every limb, when the water rushed up and began to fill the hole. Muddy though it was, I eagerly tasted it, and the little "tinny" dropped from my hand with sheer joy. . . . It was water! It was fresh water! It was living water from Jehovah's well. . . . The Chiefs had assembled with their men, nearby. They waited on in eager expectancy. It was a rehearsal, in a small way, of the Israelites coming round, while Moses struck the rock and called for water. By and by, when I had praised the Lord, and my excitement was a little calmed, the mud being also greatly settled, I filled a jug which I had taken down empty in the sight of them all, and ascending to the top, called for them to come and see the rain which Jehovah God had given us through the well. They closed around me in haste and gazed on it in superstitious fear. The old Chief shook it to see if it would spill, and then touched it to see if it felt like water. At last he tasted it, and rolling it in his mouth with joy, for a moment, he swallowed it, and shouted, "Rain! Rain! Yes, it is rain! But how did you get it?" I repeated, "Jehovah my God gave it out of his own earth in answer to our labors and prayers. Go and see it springing up for yourselves."[6]

Graphically told, is it not? The scene is brought vividly before us. What I ask is, if you would have been, in such a situation, superior to the temptation—I do not say of announcing the well as a miracle from God—but of permitting those poor superstitious folk to take it for a miracle. But surely,

---

[6]John G. Paton, *An Autobiography,* edited by his brother (London, 1890), pt. II, pp. 176-178.

surely, the proclaimers of the gospel of truth must not in even
so slight a degree sink to the level of those medicine men, who,
"if the rain comes, take all the credit for it."

Oddly enough in that stirring romance of missionary adventures which Mr. Rider Haggard has given us, he makes his
missionary hero first catch the attention of the people by an
incident precisely similar in its import with this which Dr. Paton
describes. The Rev. Thomas Owen has given himself with
entire faith and devotion to an exceedingly hazardous piece of
missionary work. The chief medicine man of the tribe among
which he is laboring has prepared for him a fatal trap; having
administered a deadly poison to the king for which there is but
one antidote, he contrives that all of Owen's credit and his life
itself shall be staked upon his power to recover the monarch.
Owen, meanwhile, has become possessed (in a supernatural
way, as Mr. Haggard would have us think) of the secret of the
poison and its antidote, and has taken care to provide himself
with the latter. Called to the king's side in the presence of all
the people, he prepares the curing draught, and "this done, he
clasped his hands, and, lifting his eyes to Heaven, he prayed
aloud in the language of the Amasuka. 'O God,' he prayed,
'upon whose business I am here, grant, I beseech Thee, that
by Thy Grace power may be given to me to work this miracle
in the face of these people, to the end that I may win them
to cease their iniquities, to believe Thee, the only true God,
and to save their souls alive. Amen.' " So he administered the
draught and reaped the natural effect.[7] Can we condemn the
novelist for so representing the practices of missionaries, when
missionaries so represent their own practices? But the oddest
thing is yet to say. Mr. Rider Haggard feels the unworthiness
of the part he has made his missionary to play. He does not
betray consciousness of it here, indeed. But later in the story
he makes him refuse to avail himself of a like transaction.
"But I say that I will not use it," are the words that he puts
in his mouth. "Are we witch-doctors, that we should take

---

[7]*The Wizard,* by H. Rider Haggard (New York and London, 1896),
p. 77.

refuge in tricks? No, let faith be our shield; and if it fail us, then let us die."[8] It is strange to turn to Mr. Haggard for a lesson in missionary morals. But as we read his pages and blush to think that authentic missionary annals may justify him in attributing deceit of this grave kind to a missionary, we may rejoice that missionary faithfulness has also suggested to him that a good missionary would refuse such a temptation; and in any event we may learn that missionaries must not be like the witch-doctors, and take refuge in tricks.

And is there not yet another form of moral danger to which the missionary may be exposed, suggested to us here—a danger lest in his zeal for propagating Christianity, he may be misled into the use of doubtful means of obtaining access to the heathen? Those who are acquainted with heathen lands, or even those who have a tolerable knowledge of missionary history, will understand at once what an ever present temptation stands before the messenger of glad tidings to obtain an opportunity to make them known by some act of *finesse,* which may all too easily pass into an act of deceit. Sometimes the country is closed to the open proclamation of the gospel, and the temptation arises to obtain access to its population under color of some other profession. One may at least go as teacher or physician, and while pretending to impart only secular learning, convey also that knowledge which is unto salvation; while pretending to no more than heal the body, minister also to the diseases of the soul. There is no one of us, doubtless, who would contend that the messenger of Christ is bound by human law in matters of this kind; it is for us, too, in this late day, to say with all boldness, "We must obey God rather than men" (Acts v. 29). But we must see to it that we do obey God, and must not cast aside his great law of truth, in order to carry the truth to others. The point is not whether we shall boldly proclaim the gospel in the face of all adverse force, or quietly propagate it in defiance of all adverse human enactments; but the point is whether we shall teach it under

---

[8]*Ibid.,* p. 119.

color of doing something else, under an implied or even express promise not to teach it. A missionary, we will say, has
long tried to gain entrance into a land closed to the gospel; an
offer comes to him to take charge of a Royal University, we
will say, with the express provision that if he takes charge of
it he obligates himself not to make his position a means of
Christian propagandism. Ought he to accept such an offer?
That is *prima facie* itself a serious question. How far does it
involve an open renunciation of his Christian duty? But the
point now is, if he does accept it, can he permit himself still to
teach Christianity? A more subtle form of the same danger
faces multitudes of missionaries. Take the case of Korea a
few years ago:

> It should be premised here that every one of the ministers
> from the United States to the Court of Korea has construed
> the treaty between the two countries to mean that the work
> of teaching and preaching Christianity is not allowed. It
> provides that men may live in the capital for the purpose of
> studying the language, and it is under cover of this pro-
> vision that missionaries are now resident in the country.[9]

That is an ominous and disagreeable word: "under cover
of." And the narrative runs on to point out that the first Presbyterian missionary to Korea "was not known at first as a
missionary," but "went ostensibly to practise his profession
as a physician"; that his standing as a missionary was unknown even to the United States minister, under whom he
served as physician to the American legation; that it was by
his "shrewdness" and the "discretion" of his immediate successors that a beginning of Christian missions was made—and
so on. I have no intention of passing a condemnation on these
brethren. One would better, before doing such a thing as that,
examine all the circumstances on the ground. But is there not
an unpleasant flavor in the mouth as we read such an account?
Do we not feel that it would require great discretion indeed—
possibly more than you or I possess—to preserve our integrity

---

[9]So writes George W. Gilmore, in his bright work on *Korea From Its
Capital* (Presbyterian Board, 1893), p. 294.

as servants of the God of Truth, in such trying circumstances? No wonder that the narrator calls it "a hard position in which to be placed." Its hardness consists, however, not in the choice of whether we will break the law of the land in order to preach Christianity, but whether we will keep the law of Christ in preaching it.

Take the situation in Japan. For traveling in the interior, passports have been necessary—to be secured from the central government. "A very uncomfortable thing about these passports," writes the Rev. M. L. Gordon, M.D., "is that they are granted only 'for health or scientific purposes.' Because of this fact, some missionaries are unwilling to use them for evangelistic touring, and so confine themselves to the vicinity of the open ports."[10]

All honor, we say, to such missionaries. A keen and high sense of honor is itself an evangelizing endowment. We condemn no one. But if you and I were there, might we not find ourselves in danger of "doing an evil that a good might come"? And may we not be sure that God will smile on those who seek to serve him, though even to the apparent hurt of the cause they love?

I must bring these desultory remarks to a close. I have no intention to seek to mention all the dangers to which missionaries are exposed. It may even be truly said that missionaries are no more exposed to the dangers that I have mentioned than to others which are precisely opposite to them. A missionary may be so hard and dry in his mode of proclaiming the truth that so far from being in danger of letting go the distinctive principles of Christ, he is in danger of forgetting to place those principles within the reach of his hearers. He may be so very careful of his own personal integrity that he fails to enter open doors, and prevents the spread of true Christianity by his litigious persistence in pressing petty points of no moral value—"losing his life" by his own attempts to "save" it. But all this only the more emphasizes the multiplicity of

---

[10]In his *An American Missionary in Japan*, p. 88.

the dangers amid which he walks, and shows us in increased clearness how circumspectly a missionary needs to walk if he is to adorn, as well as proclaim, the gospel of the grace of God. It also increases our admiration for our missionaries who, amid so many and such subtle dangers, do walk so circumspectly as to adorn the gospel. We do not think we could do it.

But that they do it, even those least in sympathy with them seem forced to admit. I have lately read, for example, a somewhat flippant book which gives an account of the ordinary mode of life among the British residents in Calcutta, from the point of view of a woman of the world. In it a missionary appears. Here is the description of him:

> The missionary padre receives his slender stipend from the S.P.G., or from some obscure source in America. It is arranged upon a scale to promote self-denial, and it is very successful. He usually lives where the drains are thickest and the smells most unmanageable, and when we of the broad river and the great Maidan happen to hear of his address, we invariably ejaculate, "What a frightfully long way off." The ticcagharry is not an expensive conveyance, but the missionary padre finds himself better commended by his conscience if he walks and pays the cost of his transportation in energy and vitality, which must be heavy in the hot weather and the rains. For the rest, he lives largely upon second-class beef and his ideals, though they don't keep very well either in this climate. . . . Those who are married are usually married to missionary ladies of similar size and complexion, laboring in the same cause. . . . The official padre's wife looks like any other memsahib; the missionary padre's wife looks like the missionary padre. I believe that chaplains sometimes ask missionary padres to dinner "quietly," and always make a point of giving them plenty to eat. And I remember meeting a married pair of them. . . . It was in the hot weather and they spoke appreciatively of the punkah. They had no punkah, it seemed, either day or night; but the little wife had been very clever and had made muslin bags for their heads and hands to keep off the mosquitoes while they were asleep. We couldn't ascertain that either of them had been really well since they came out, and they said they had simply

made up their minds to have sickness in the house during the whole of the rains. . . . They knew little of the Red Road or the Eden Gardens, where the band plays in the evenings; they talked of strange places—Khengua Pattoo's Lane—Coolestollah. [The wife] told us that her great difficulty in the zenanas lay in getting the ladies to talk . . . and [the husband] had been down in the Sunderbunds, far down in the Sunderbunds, where the miasmas are thickest, and where he had slept every night for a week on a bench in the small room with two baboos and the ague. . . . He was more emaciated than clever. . . .[11]

Not an attractive picture, you will say? That depends, however, on your point of view. From the world's point of view it is a very unattractive picture—though we cannot help fancying that even the authoress intended it partly as a compliment to missionaries. From God's point of view I should think it would be very attractive—for after all what "is required in stewards is that a man be found faithful" (1 Cor. iv. 27). A caricature, no doubt it is, but a caricature which would not have been possible were not the average missionary both strenuous and faithful.

And bearing such a description of his ways in mind, perhaps we may say in conclusion, that the greatest danger to which the missionary is exposed is that, in the zeal for souls that burns in his bones like a fire, and in his yearning desire to reap the fruits of his labors, he may forget the weakness of the human frame and wear himself out in toils that are too abundant, or cast himself away through sicknesses that are avoidable. The conditions of life in most mission fields are so different from those to which the missionary is accustomed at home, that a serious strain upon his physical system is unavoidable. It will be well if he does not unduly increase the strain and thus unduly decrease his usefulness by assuming burdens which no flesh can bear. Here, too, the rule is applicable that our zeal for God requires tempering with knowledge. Not that the missionary should not hold himself ready

---

[11]*The Simple Adventures of a Memsahib*, by Sara Jeannette Duncan (New York: D. Appleton & Co., 1895), 238 pp.

to give his life, if need be, for the cause to which he has devoted it; for here, too, is it true that he who would save his life shall lose it, and he who would lose his life for Christ's sake shall gain it. But that he should never be ready to throw away so valuable a life as his, through impatience with the limitations of human powers. In this matter, too, let us listen to the traditional saying of our Lord, which Dr. Westcott has adopted as his motto in life: "Be ye good money-changers." Let the missionary set high store on his life and strength—barter with them, sell them dearly—see to it that when they go down under the accumulated labors that will fall upon them, they bring a great price—the greatest price procurable—in souls. They have been given him not to be flung away as things of little value; they are his capital—let him put them out at long interest, that they may earn great gains to present the Householder when he comes and asks for an account of his stewardship.

30

AFRICA AND THE BEGINNINGS
OF CHRISTIAN LATIN LITERATURE*

In bringing his sketch of the African provinces to a close, Theodore Mommsen magnifies their significance for the history of Christianity. He represents the part played by Africa in the development of Christianity as very distinctly a leading one. He even seems to intimate that it was in and through Africa that Christianity received its character as a world-religion: it had its origin, no doubt, in Syria, but it was only through the translation in Africa of its sacred books into the popular language of the world-empire that it was given a world-wide mission.[1] There is some exaggeration here; and were the meaning that the universality of Christianity was a contribution to it of North Africa, the exaggeration would be gross. To Christianity, as to the leaven with which its author compared it, expansion belongs as an inherent quality; and the instrumentalities by which its dissemination was accomplished lay at its hand apart from any gift which North Africa could bestow upon it. With far more insight, though without the advantage of writing after the event, the author of the Book of Acts points to its establishment in the imperial city as giving the promise of its extension throughout the world.

Nevertheless, the possibility of such an exaggeration is a striking indication of the great part which was actually played by North Africa in the history of Christianity. In Africa rather than in Rome the roots of Latin Christianity are actually

---

*This article is from the *American Journal of Theology*, Jan. 1907, pp. 95-110.
[1]*Römische Geschichte*, Vol. V (2nd ed.), p. 657; English translation, Vol. II, p. 373.

set. It is from African soil, enriched by African intellect, watered by African blood, that the tree of Western Christianity has grown up until it has become a resting-place for all the nations of the earth. If we abjure speculation upon what might have been on this or that supposition, and give attention purely to what actually has been and is, we must needs confess that there is a true sense in which North Africa is the mother of us all. Christianity is what it is today, in all its fruitful branches at least, because of what North Africa was a millennium and a half ago, and because of what was done and thought and felt there. The very language in which it still defines its doctrines and gives expression to its devotion is of African origin; and the doctrines and aspirations themselves bear ineffaceably impressed upon their very substance the African stamp.

The great part played by North Africa in fixing the type of Western Christianity was of course no mysterious accident. It was the natural result of the dominating influence of Africa in the Roman world[2] throughout the period when Christianity was establishing itself in the West and fitting itself for its world-wide mission. This dominating influence was manifested in every sphere of life and was fairly symbolized by the ascension of sons of Africa to the imperial throne—not merely in such shadows as Didius Julianus and Albinus, Macrinus, Aemilianus, and Memorius, but in a founder of a dynasty like Septimius Severus. The senate is spoken of by Fronto[3] as in his day crowded with Africans, and at the same period the consulate appeared almost their peculiar possession.[4] It was, however, in the domain of the intellectual life that African dominance had become most apparent.[5] The eagerness with

---

[2]Cf. Gregorovius, *Hadrian,* English translation, p. 90.

[3]*Epist. ad amic.,* ii (p. 201, ed. Naber; p. 214, ed. Neibuhr).

[4]Cf. Monceaux, *Les Africains,* p. 347.

[5]"The Roman province of Africa had for centuries taken a leading place in the literature of the imperial period; and from Hadrian to the beginning of the third century it had set the fashion even for Italy."— Norden, in Hinneberg's *Die Kultur der Gegenwart,* volume on "Die griechische und lateinische Literatur und Sprache" (1900), pp. 38 f.

which letters were cultivated in the country of the Atlas, from the earliest days of the settlement of the provinces, is attested by the allusions which Roman writers make to the African taste for books and oratory. Horace tells us[6] that whenever the first vogue of a poem was over in Rome, the booksellers had to but pack off "the remainders" to Ilerda or Utica; the Spaniard and African took them up with avidity. Similarly Juvenal, despairing of Rome where employment went by favor, advises barristers who had brains to sell, to betake themselves to Gaul, or "rather," says he, to "Africa, that nurse of advocates."[7] The term he employs may bear a tinge of contempt in it, like Carlyle's "gentleman of the attorney species"; but the fact attested is that the art of speech and the science of pleading were cultivated in Africa with special zeal and met there with their appropriate reward. Such assiduity in the pursuit of letters could not fail to bear fruit; and after a while, when Latin literature was languishing in Rome, it was from Africa that new life came flowing in.

There is a somewhat remote sense, indeed, in which Africa may be said to have been midwife to the birth of all Latin literature worthy of the name. It was certainly to the stimulus given to the national life by the Punic Wars that the first great impulse to write in Latin must be traced.[8] But the only direct contribution of Carthage to that flowering of undefiled Latinity —the elegant and even exquisite Terence, whose delicate handling of the language became the model and despair of all subsequent stylists—was of course only one of those remarkable accidents with which the history of letters is filled. Meanwhile this primary impulse, having blossomed in the great republic and fruited in the Augustan age, had in the early years of the Christian era run hopelessly to seed. Rome was once more, so far as literature was concerned, a Greek city; and continued life was infused into specifically Latin literature only by fresh

---

[6]*Epist.*, i. 20, 13.
[7]*Sat.*, vii. 147-149: *nutricula causidicorum Africa.*
[8]Cf. Simcox, *Latin Literature*, Vol. I, p. 11.

sap flowing in from the provinces. The language of culture in Africa too was at this epoch chiefly Greek.[9] The extensive compilations of King Juba, whose half-century's reign centers at the birth of Christ, were made in that language. Cornutus, Fronto, Apuleius, Tertullian, the Emperor Severus, all were Greek as well as Latin authors. There is extant even a single piece of Apuleius, composed partly in Greek and partly in Latin. Something similar occurs in the *Passion of Perpetua and Felicitas,* which has come down to us in both Greek and Latin, leaving the scholars divided as to which form is original, many holding that both are original,[10] or that parts of the original were in each tongue.[11] But the traditions of Greek culture were already slowly dying out in Africa, as indeed this bilingual habit itself testifies. While lettered Rome remained still essentially Greek, a vigorous Latin literature was already growing up at Carthage. It was not yet quite ready, however, to enter upon its wider career.[12]

African rhetors and jurisconsults had begun to invade Rome, no doubt, from the days of the Caesars. Lucius Annaeus Cornutus of Leptis, for example, taught the Stoic philosophy at Rome under Claudius and Nero, and earned the loving admiration of pupils like Lucan, and above all Persius, whose panegyrics of his dear master quite touch the stars.[13] Shortly afterward his fellow countryman, the rhetorician Septimius Severus, won equal affection and praise from pupils as well worth having, such as Statius and Martial. He is said to have acquired a perfection in the use of the Latin tongue (as it was spoken in Rome—that "native speech of the Quirites" which

---

[9]Monceaux (*Histoire littéraire de l'Afrique chrétienne,* Vol. I, p. 51) would bid us be cautious lest we overstate this. Cf. also Norden, in Hinneberg, as cited, p. 376; and Leclercq, *L'Afrique chrétienne,* Vol. I, pp. 90 f. On the general subject of the use of Greek in the West, see Harnack, *The Expansion of Christianity,* Vol. I, pp. 19, 20, n. 1; Vol. II, pp. 380, 381; and for Africa, Vol. II, p. 412.

[10]Hilgenfeld, von Gebhardt, Harnack (1893).

[11]Monceaux, *op. cit.,* Vol. I, p. 83.

[12]Cf. Norden, *Die antike Kunstprosa,* Vol. II, pp. 594, 597.

[13]Cf. Oldsmith, *The Religion of Plutarch,* p. 53.

Apuleius professes to have found beyond his reach),[14] to which his imperial descendants could never attain. At least Statius declares of the rhetorician that no one would have believed he had drawn his origin from barbarous Leptis or had passed his youth away from the collines of Romulus, and greets him has an Italian of the Italians, to whose appearance and speech, or even mental habits, clung not the least taint of provincial ways.[15] It is recorded of the emperor, on the other hand, that he never learned to speak Latin without a strong Punic accent, and of his sister that, when she came to visit him at Rome, he was constrained to send her back to Leptis because of the mortification her abominable Latinity caused him.[16] Only a little later the place that had been filled by Severus was occupied by another African, P. Annius Florus, a man of apparently indefinitely less genius, but of no less lofty reputation. The combined careers of these celebrated teachers cover the period from Claudius to Hadrian; and meanwhile the Africans had conquered for themselves also the leading place in the more serious study of law. Hadrian's great jurist, Salvius Julianus, the author of "the perpetual edict," was from Hadrumetum; the high tradition which he established was carried on by his pupil, Sextus Caecilius Africanus, likewise an African; while he found no unworthy rival in Pactumeius Clemens from Cirta.[17]

All this was, however, but the prelude of what was to come. The real hegemony of Africa in Latin letters begins only in the second third of the second Christian century. It was from Spain, not from Africa, that in the first Christian age new life flowed in to invigorate the languishing stem of Latin literature. Seneca, Lucan, Tacitus, Martial—these are all Spanish names; and the whole literature of the period bears

---

[14]At the beginning of the *Metamorphoses* (the *Quiritium indigenam sermonem*).

[15]*Sil.*, iv. 5, 45: *Non sermo poenus, non habitus tibi, | Externa non mens: Italus, Italus.*

[16]Spartianus, *Severus*, 15 and 19.

[17]Cf. Monceaux, *Les Africains,* pp. 74, 345, 346.

the stamp of the Spanish character. But as the middle of the second century approaches, the supremacy passes finally from Spain, and what to the Roman ear seemed the *stridor punicus*[18] began to fill the world. No name of the first repute, it must be confessed, adorns the annals of secular Latin literature under the sway of African influence; it is a period of literary decay. At the opening of the period the chief writers that meet the eye are Cornelius Fronto, the tutor and friend of Marcus Aurelius, and Sulpitius Apollinaris, the grammarian, about whom gathered a crowd of fellow Africans, among them perhaps Aulus Gellius himself, while off in Carthage Apuleius was introducing a new genre in literary form. Its single poet worthy of the name, Dracontius, sings the swan-song of the African influence at the end of the period, at the court of the Vandals. Mommsen reproaches it with not having produced throughout the whole of its dominance "a single poet deserving to be remembered,"[19] and its prose tradition was but little higher. The only great poet of the age—Claudian—was, like the African Terence of an earlier time, one of those happy accidents, sprung from other blood and formed in other molds. The most important prose writer of the age—Ammonius Marcianus—was also Greek in origin. The mass of writers who jostle each other through these years were mostly "schoolmasters turned authors," over all whose work the "trail of scholasticism" runs; rhetors who, though become writers, still mouthed it in their pages with balanced cadences and elaborately constructed rhythms, in which the sense too often was neglected in straining after effects of sound. It is thus not a very attractive literature which Africa contributed to the secular Latin world. But for a period of at least two centuries it constituted all the Latin literature that existed; and throughout this whole period it not only flourished luxuriantly, but commanded the unbounded admiration of men. To those who

---

[18]The phrase is Jerome's (*Epist.*, 130, 5), but he refers by it to the voice and speech, not to a literary manner. On "African Latin" cf. F. Skotch in Hinneberg, as cited, pp. 433, 434.

[19]*Roman Provinces*, E. T. Vol. II, p. 373.

lived under its spell it did not suffer in comparison with the literature of the Augustan age itself. Septimius Severus may have made it the reproach of his rival aspirant to the purple (Clodius Albinus, an African like himself—and like Apuleius) that he found in the *Golden Ass* his favorite reading;[20] but this suggests an exceptional, perhaps not even an honest, judgment. The men of the time sincerely admired the literature of the time and felt themselves living in the heyday of literary art. Carthage seemed to them to have earned a right to the title of second mother of Latin letters. Even Augustine, with the utmost naïveté, declares that the two cities, Rome and Carthage, stand side by side as sources of the stream of Latin letters.[21] The bad poets of the day looked upon one another as touching the summit of literary accomplishment. "This at least is certain, Luxorius," said one to another with charming directness, "you have outdone all the ancients."[22] In one of his delightful letters,[23] Apollinaris Sidonius tells us that, if a manuscript were found lying by a lady's chair, it was pretty sure to prove to be a treatise on religion; if by a gentleman's, on eloquence. He adds: "I do not forget that there are some writings of equal literary excellence in both branches, that Augustine may be paired off against Varro, and Prudentius against Horace." Here, to be sure, we are introduced to the great Christian writers who adorned the time; and into their writings a new life had been infused, by virtue of which a really great literature was produced under African influence. But the main point is nevertheless illustrated: the characteristics of the literature of the age were the characteristics of the age, and the men of the age found themselves expressed in it and sincerely admired it.

It was in the midst of this period of African dominance that Christianity began to find a voice for itself in a Western tongue.

---

[20]Capitol., *Vita Albini*, 12 (cf. Boisier, *L'Afrique romaine*, p. 241).

[21]*Ep.*, 118, 9, near end (Migne, XXXIII, 468). Cf. Norden, *Kunstprosa*, Vol. II, 592; Crutwell, *Latin Literature*, p. 546.

[22]*Anthologie* (Riese), 87: *certum est, Luxori, priscos te vincere.*

[23]See ii. 9; cf. Hodgkin, *Italy and Its Invaders*, ed. 1, 1880, Vol. I, p. 319.

In its earliest stages Western Christianity had been Greek. With the single exception of that of the African Victor (188 or 189-199), the names of all the Roman bishops up to the death of Callistus in 223 are Greek. The earliest Christian writers in the West wrote in Greek—Clement, Hermas, Irenaeus, Hippolytus, and their contemporaries. The change came so swiftly that it can scarcely be spoken of as a transition, and the change was wrought at the hands of the Africans. Latin Christian literature burst upon the world with the suddenness of a tropical sunrise in the burning tracts of Tertullian. Jerome tells us, to be sure, that before Tertullian, Victor and Apollonius wrote in Latin. Such exceptions, even were they substantiated, would only prove the rule. Jerome, however, seems to be in error as regards Apollonius; and the literary product of Victor, who was himself an African, was in any case insignificant. The learned world was startled a few years ago, it is true, by the suggestion that an interesting tract, *Against Gamblers*, which has been preserved among the works of Cyprian, was really the composition of Victor, and in that case probably the earliest Christian Latin writing which has come down to us. The suggestion has not, however, been verified; the tract seems pretty clearly post-Cyprianic in date, and although its provenience cannot be said to be determined with equal certainty, it may very well be African in origin.[24] A much more striking exception would be furnished by the *Octavius* of Minucius Felix, who also was an African, could we suppose it, as many do, to have been produced during the lifetime of Fronto, say about A.D. 181. This much-admired tract is written with all of Fronto's "virtuosity" in the handling of the Latin language, and is crowded with archaisms, bookish allusions to the poets—Vergil, Horace, Lucretius—and reminiscences of the old Greek and Latin Sophists. Its true character is given it, however, by its skill in the new sophistical artifices which characterize all the literature of the African period, and which it never relaxes even in the warmest glow of its

---

[24]Harnack (*Chronologie*, Vol. II, pp. 370-387) now allows its post-Cyprianic origin, but still holds it to be Roman.

Christian indignation. It certainly would fitly enough stand at the head of that series of great but somewhat artificially written Christian writings which are the glory of the Latin literature of the African period, of which it would be an unworthy example only in its somewhat traditional contents and its undeveloped theology. But every internal consideration justifies Jerome's assignment of its origin to a period later than Tertullian.[25] In whatever way such questions may be settled, however, in any event the great stream of Christian Latin literature takes its rise in the height of the African influence, and in any event from apparently African-born writers; and thus in any event it must be accounted the gift of Africa to the world. If we see its rise, as apparently we must, in Tertullian, we add merely that this Christian African literature not only rose out of African influences and through African-born agents, but sprang up also on African soil.

From the end of the second century Christianity was the ferment of all cultural and literary development, and the poverty in great names of the secular literature of the period is offset by the richness in them of the Christian literature, from its very origin. For the stream of Christian Latin literature does not begin as a little rivulet which only gradually grows to a river; it bursts out at its source as a great flood. Its earliest examples set for it at once the highest of traditions. Their authors were of course, however, men of their times, imbued with the literary taste of their times. There are exceptions among them, no doubt, as there are exceptions among the secular writers of the period. Lactantius is a shining exception. The noble calmness of his truly classical Latinity knows no rival in the literary product of his day, whether in Christian or heathen circles.[26] Hilary of Poictiers is an equally shining exception; and indeed the writers of Aquitaine at large were justly famous for their command of the "Roman speech." No Latin of any age is superior in chaste elegance to that of

---

[25]So Massebieau, Monceaux, Neumann, Funk, Harnack.
[26]Cf. Norden, *Kunstprosa*, Vol. II, p. 582.

Hilary at his best.[27] But, taken as a whole, the same false taste ruled the great Christian which ruled the small heathen writers of the age. The finically embroidered diction which had been introduced by the Greek Sophists, Gorgias, Hegesias, Himerios—the so-called Asianism or "new rhetoric"—had conquered also the Latin world.[28] As it has been pungently expressed,[29] the reigning canon of beauty in style had become that "article of faith of all barbarism, that a man must tattoo himself in order to be handsome." Apuleius remains, of course, the supreme example. In him an incredible bombast unites with a painful fastidiousness: alliterations, paronomasiae, assonances, homoioteleuta, balanced clauses, rhythmic terminations, and rhymed endings, simply riot through his pages, in which, as it has been justly said, "a style celebrates its orgies which has degenerated into a mere bacchanalian dance of phonetics."[30] But it was not for nothing that the great Christian writers of the African period had all been rhetors before they became theologians, and had received their rhetorical training in the "new style." There is nothing in the way of virtuosity in the use of language in Apuleius which may not, without much searching, be matched in Tertullian. All the fiery impetuosity of that *ardens vir* did not carry him beyond the fashionable artifices; and at his worst—his contemporaries would have said at his best—his style is indistinguishable from that of Apuleius. The same is true, each in his measure, of all the other authors of the period. It is true of Minucius Felix and Cyprian, though of course the graceful elegance native to the one, and the unctious suavity of the other,[31] modify their use of the rhetorical devices common to all. It is true of Ambrose and of the Gallic writers who adorn the age at a little later time. It is true even of Jerome, whose taste was markedly pure and who knew how to recognize the "Asian tumor" in others, and unsparingly ridiculed the contemporary

---

[27]*Ibid.*, p. 583.   [29]By Bernays.
[28]*Ibid.*, p. 587.   [30]Norden, *loc. cit.*
[31]*Beatus Cyprianus*, says Cassiodorus, *velut oleum decurrens in omnem suavitatem.* Norden says he is the first Latin writer who has *unction.*

fashion. Augustine himself, who even in the matter of style towers so much above his age as almost to redeem it, nevertheless never emancipates himself from the traditions of his rhetorical school. In his greater works, where the gravity of the matter absorbs his attention, the wretched artifices, especially word-plays,[32] which constitute the signature of the "new style," may retire somewhat into the background. But they are absent from none of his compositions, and in his more popular pieces, where he is most at his ease and is thinking more of the effect he is producing, they obtrude themselves in painful abundance. He knew well enough the beauty of simplicity, but, as he himself would have said, *facilius est errorem definere quam finere.* His pages are studded with such turns of speech as *cetera onerant, non honorant,*[33] *dic "habeo," sed "ab eo";*[34] *o munde immunde;*[35] *est enim severitas quasi saeva veritas.*[36] If Apuleius can scarcely be opened without exposing the most astonishing examples of elaborate trifling with sequences of sound, and in the matter of balanced clauses and rhyming endings at least—"the sprightly dance of the Asian cola," as it has been called[37]—Tertullian even surpasses Apuleius, and Augustine will provide us with examples of precisely the same artifices of which we must at least acknowledge that Apuleius and Tertullian might have envied him them. Apuleius may give us such sequences as this:

> aut ara floribus redimita,
> aut quercus cornibus onerata,
> aut fagus pellibus coronata.

Tertullian may provide us with untold numbers such as this:

> tot pernicies
> quot et species,

---

[32]Cf. Hoppe, *Syntax und Stil des Tertullians,* p. 149: "Augustine makes use of all the artificial devices which Tertullian employs, and of the 'play on words' in even greater measure than Tertullian."

[33]*Sermo,* 85, 5: *h* is silent in Augustine's mouth.

[34]*Sermo,* 94, 14.

[35]*Sermo,* 105, 6.

[36]*Sermo,* 171, 5.

[37]Usener: *der rasche Tanz asianischer Kola.*

> tot dolores
> quot et colores;[38]

or, taking a wider sweep, as this:

> quam nec nationibus comparaverat,
>   ne consuetudine deputaretur,
> quam absens judicarat
>   ne spatium reus lucaretur,
> quam advocata etiam domini virtute damnaverat,
>   ne humana sententia videretur.[39]

But it is Augustine who writes, almost as if by force of habit, thus:

> eo nascente superi novo honore claruerunt,
> quo moriente inferi novo timore tremuerunt,
> quo resurgente discipuli novo amore exarserunt,
> quo ascendente coeli novo obsequio patuerunt.[40]

Such flowers of speech, with their elaborate assonance, balance, rhythm, and rhyme, cannot, of course, be transplanted into other tongues. Take, however, only the one item of rhyme, and how would it sound in English prose to be constantly tripping upon passages like this: "When he was born, to heaven a new honor was given; when away he was torn, all hell with new terror was riven; when he arose, the disciples with new love were affected; when he ascended, the angels were to new service subjected"?[41] It strikes us with a shock to observe that the

---

[38]*Scorp.*, I.

[39]*Pud.*, 14 *fin.* Many other examples are given by Hoppe, *op. cit.*, p. 166.

[40]*Sermo*, 199, 2, *ad fin.* (Migne, XXXVIII, 1028). Norden, *Kunstprosa*, adduces other examples.

[41]English Euphuism (like, no doubt, Spanish Guevaraism before it) which, as Mr. Morley (*English Writers*, Vol. VIII, pp. 316 f.) points out, was "an outcome of the revival of the study of Demosthenes and Cicero, and of the Greek and Latin works upon the art of speaking," can scarcely be looked upon as anything else than a revival of Asianism. John Lyly would not be inaptly described as an English Apuleius; and Dr. Landmann's description of his style would stand very well for a characterization of that of Apuleius: "a peculiar combination of antithesis with alliteration, assonance, rhyme, and play upon words, a love for the conformity and correspondence of paralleled sentences, and a tendency to accumulate rhetorical figures, such as climax, the

very martyrs in the mines cannot return their thanks for supplies sent by charity to their necessities without lapsing into the literary preciosity of the times.[42]

Despite their common preoccupation with such rhetorical devices, however, the greatest possible difference in tone and spirit obtains between the heathen and Christian writers of the period. In the case of the one this bizarre rhetoric entered into—or, perhaps we may say, constituted—the very essence of their work; they wrote in a true sense for its sake. In the case of the other, it was a mere accident of form, marring the dignity of their presentation indeed, but never concealing the earnestness of their purpose, or destroying the vigor or inherent eloquence of their product. In other words, Latin literature was fast sinking to the level of a mere rhetorical exercise when Christianity entered in with regenerating breath and once more recalled it to serious concernment with the matter of discourse. We may perceive the revolution even in the brutal pages of Arnobius, or perhaps we may more pungently say even in the polished periods of Minucius Felix. We do not need to go beyond Tertullian, however, to observe the whole contrast in its most striking manifestation. We have noted how deeply imbued Tertullian was with the artificial rhetoric of the day. His treatise on *The Mantle,* for example, almost outdoes Apuleius himself and has been described as simply "an oratorical debauch in which are prodigally expended all the resources of rhetorical invention."[43] Nevertheless, Tertullian never made rhetorical effect his chief object in writing, nor was the machinery of rhetorical artifice, however freely employed, ever permitted to put shackles upon either his thought or his passion. He even speaks shamefacedly of lapses into rhetorical devices as unfitting in the bearers of such

---

rhetorical question," etc. (*Der Euphuismus,* Giessen, 1881). Some interesting remarks on what may similarly be thought "the Asian rhetoric" in Arabic prose—the so-called *Al Saj'a* or *Al-Badi'a*—may be found in Lady Burton's edition of R. F. Burton's *Arabian Nights,* I. xiv; VI. 338.

[42]Cyprian's letters, *Ep.* 77, 3.

[43]Boissier, *L'Afrique romaine,* 259.

a message as Christians had committed to them, and due merely to the exigencies of debate. "We rhetoricize, just as we philosophize," he says, "only on the provocation of the heretics."[44] Despite its frequent artificiality of form, accordingly, his speech remained ever a speech of flame, and before the intense energy of his expression the rhetorical framework continually gives way. It has been justly pointed out[45] that the Latin language was never carried to a higher pitch of passionate expression, or made the vehicle of a fuller, richer, or more poignant emotional life, than in the hands of this most subjective and individual of all Latin writers. He strains the capacity of the language to the breaking-point in his determination to give full vent to the intensity of his feelings. With the utmost license he coins new words, imposes new senses upon old ones, crowds Latin forms into Greek idioms, elevates, intensifies the implications of terms and constructions alike—until there emerges from his hands what is really a new tongue, that Christian Latin of which he more than any other single author is the creator.[46] It was a veritable miracle that he wrought, and we need not wonder that it was not accomplished without some violence and recklessness. In a period of decadence the Latin tongue acquired in the hands of this linguistic genius a power of adaptation in giving expression to ideas hitherto unknown to it, such as it scarcely was able to exhibit in its most flexible period, when Cicero sought to popularize it in the Greek philosophy.[47]

Speaking broadly, Christian literature differentiated itself from the heathen, indeed, precisely as the literature of content from the literature of form. The heathen literature of the time

---

[44]*De res. carn.,* 5: *ita nos rhetoricari quoque provocant heretici, sicut etiam philosophari.*

[45]Norden, *Kunstprosa,* Vol. II, pp. 610, 611; cf. Hoppe, *op. cit.,* p. 2.

[46]Cf. Harnack, *Chronologie,* Vol. I, p. 667, and Norden in Hinneberg, p. 389. The latter says: "His style is without moderation like his nature; he breaks through the traditional forms instead of adjusting himself to them; but it is just in this that his greatness lies in this sphere too; he was the creator of a Latin ecclesiastical language."

[47]So Hoppe, *op. cit.,* p. 2.

was ruled by the maxim of art for art's sake. The maxim of the Christians was truth for truth's sake. In theory at least, the Christians were ready to carry their distinctive principle, indeed, to absurd extremes. From the first they defended the proposition that a sober and homely dress alone comported with the great truths they had to communicate; and they professed fear lest the meretricious charms of form should distract attention from the tremendous import of the matter. Here too the only suitable adornment seemed to them to be the inner adornment inherent in the beauty of naked truth. It was their constant contention, therefore, as Gregory the Great expresses it in his unmeasured way,[48] that it were an indecency to straiten the words of the heavenly oracle even under the rules of Donatus. Like the Master himself, they urged, the message should be without form or comeliness. So fanatical a theory, of course, could not be reduced to practice; and they who gave it its most extreme expression, like Gregory the Great himself—whose whole rhetorical form is cast in the Asian mold—were the last to attempt to put it into practice. Men wrote, if they wrote at all, to be read; and to be read they needed to write more or less in accordance with the canons of the art they affected to despise. At first, no doubt, a real simplicity of speech came naturally to the lips of Christians. The writers of the New Testament and the Apostolic Fathers are comparatively innocent of conscious rhetorical art,[49] and the popular sermons, particularly in the West, preserved for

---

[48]*Moral.*, praef. I.

[49]How important it is to exercise caution in speaking thus even of the New Testament writers may be learned from F. Blass, *Die Rythmen der asianischen und römischen Kunstprosa* (Leipzig, 1905), in which he endeavors to show that not only the Epistle to the Hebrews but the Epistles of Paul are written under the rules of the Asian cola (cf. also his *Textkritisches zu den Korintherbriefen* in Schlatter and Lütgerts *Beiträge zur Förderung christl. Theologie*, Vol. X, no. 1, 1906, pp. 51-63; and J. Dräseke, in *Zeitschrift für wissensch. Theologie*, 1906, Vol. I, pp. 133 f.). On the other hand, compare the review of Blass by A. Deissmann in the *Theologische Literaturzeitung*, April 16, 1906, no. 8, pp. 231 f. (also, more briefly in the *Theolog. Rundschau*, Vol. IX, no. 5, June, 1906, pp. 227 f.).

a considerable period more or less reminiscence of this early relative stylelessness. But already the Apologists, addressing heathen rather than Christian readers, began inevitably to write more after the fashion in vogue among the heathen. After them the barriers were broken down; and every device known to heathen rhetorical art became the ordinary medium of expression for Christians also. These unmeasured expressions of contempt for form which characterize the whole series of Christian writers must be read, therefore, only as a natural reaction of mind against the equally unmeasured riot of rhetoric which marked the times. And the reaction went only far enough to supply a much-needed corrective of the rage for superficial ornament; and secured only that the matter should not be lost in the form. Its effect was not to separate the Christian from the heathen as a mass of formless writers standing over against the formed. Its effect was only to infuse earnestness of purpose into their literary product, to recall attention from the externals of speech to its burden, and to save Latin literature from rotting down into a mere idle song of an empty day.

Certainly no personality could be imagined better fitted than Tertullian, by training, natural gifts, and temperament, to break out the channel for this new literature of substance in the West. In him Christian Latin literature attained the summit of its greatness at a leap.[50] And it was fortunate in the successors which it gave to Tertullian, who worthily carried on the tradition begun by him. For a full century they were all, like Tertullian, Africans. Until the opening of the fourth century, with the exception of the Greek, Irenaeus, there existed no Christian literature at all in Gaul;[51] and, with the exception of Novatian (who wrote in the middle of the third

---

[50]Cf. the somewhat varying estimates of Tertullian by Monceaux and Hoppe. Norden (Hinneburg, p. 38) strikingly says: "Passion which knew no measure is stamped on his nature; hardly any other fanatic has known as he knew how to hate; he almost never spoke in tones of love, that most beautiful fruit of Christianity; therefore we cannot love him, however much we may admire him."

[51]Monceaux, *Cyprian,* p. 132.

century), no Latin Christian literature in Italy. The great
Christian writers, in the meantime—Cyprian, the suave eccle-
siastic, and Lactantius, the "Christian Cicero"—and the small
ones too—Minucius Felix the elegant, Arnobius the inelegant,
and Commodian the first Christian poet—were all alike Africans of the Africans. Nor did the scepter depart from Africa
when a Christian Latin literature had sprung up elsewhere.
Pannonia furnished the first Latin Christian commentator in
Victorinus of Petau, and the greatest of all Latin Christian
men of letters in Jerome. Gaul in Hilary of Poictiers gave the
world a rare theologian. Italy offered in Ambrose the typical
ecclesiastical statesman of all time. Spain in Juvencus and
Prudentius opened up the stream of Christian Latin poetry.
But Africa still held the palm in philosophy in the person of
Victorinus, and in Augustine[52] set the capstone on Christian
Latin literature as she had laid its foundations in Tertullian.
From Tertullian to Augustine—the two hundred years which
stretch between constitute the period of African supremacy in
Christian Latin letters—the names themselves mark the supremacy of Africa in Christian thought. They are the names
of the two greatest forces in Western theology; and perhaps
we should omit the qualification "Western." What Western
Christianity is today is largely what Tertullian and Augustine
have made it—Tertullian as the initiator, Augustine as the
consummator. The whole history of Latin Christian thought
runs up to and down from Augustine as its water-shed. All
that precedes him was preparation for him; all that follows
him only registers the effects of his labors. And Augustine
was but the ripe fruitage of African theology. After him the
studium might well depart to Gaul, as it did, while Africa lay

---

[52]Norden (Hinneberg, p. 391) appreciatively says: "Yes, we dare to
say it, Augustine was the great poet of the ancient church, though, just
as little as Plato, does he write in verse. These two belong together as
the great poet-philosophers of all time." Cf. the eulogy of Eucken,
Lebensanschauungen der grossen Denker, 2nd ed., pp. 216 f., beginning:
"Augustine is the single great philosopher on the basis of Christianity.
All the results of the past and all the suggestions of his own time he
takes up into himself in order to create of them something new again."

crushed under the heel of the Vandal.[53] But it carried to Gaul with it only African problems; and the whole history of Christian thought in the West for the next thousand years is determined by the efforts of the Church to adjust itself to African Augustinianism—efforts which did not cease until Augustinianism was cast finally out of the old Church and created a Church for itself in what we know as the Reformation.[54]

[53]Cf. Norden, *Kunstprosa*, Vol. II, p. 587.
[54]Cf. Harnack, *History of Dogma*, Vol. V, p. 3.

PART V

31

THE AUTHORITY AND INSPIRATION
OF THE SCRIPTURES*

Christianity is often called a book-religion. It would be more exact to say that it is a religion which has a book. Its foundations are laid in apostles and prophets, upon which its courses are built up in the sanctified lives of men; but Christ Jesus alone is its chief corner-stone. He is its only basis; he, its only head; and he alone has authority in his Church. But he has chosen to found his Church not directly by his own hands, speaking the word of God, say for instance, in thunder-tones from heaven; but through the instrumentality of a body of apostles, chosen and trained by himself, endowed with gifts and graces from the Holy Ghost, and sent forth into the world as his authoritative agents for proclaiming a gospel which he placed within their lips and which is none the less his authoritative word, that it is through them that he speaks it. It is because the apostles were Christ's representatives, that what they did and said and wrote as such, comes to us with divine authority. The authority of the Scriptures thus rests on the simple fact that God's authoritative agents in founding the Church gave them as authoritative to the Church which they founded. All the authority of the apostles stands behind the Scriptures, and all the authority of Christ behind the apostles. The Scriptures are simply the law-code which the law-givers of the Church gave it.

If, then, the apostles were appointed by Christ to act for him and in his name and authority in founding the Church— and this no one can doubt; and if the apostles gave the Scriptures to the Church in prosecution of this commission—

---

*From the *Westminster Teacher*, Sept. 1889.

and this admits of as little doubt; the whole question of the authority of the Scriptures is determined. It will be observed that their authority does not rest exactly on apostolic authorship. The point is not that the apostles wrote these books (though most of the New Testament books were written by apostles), but that they imposed them on the Church as authoritative expositions of its divinely appointed faith and practice. Still less does the authority of the Scriptures rest on the authority of the Church. The Church may bear witness to what she received from the apostles as law, but this is not giving authority to that law but humbly recognizing the authority which rightfully belongs to it whether the Church recognizes it or not. The puzzle which some people fall into here is something like mistaking the relative "authority" of the guide-post and the road; the guide-post may point us to the right road but it does not give its rightness to the road. It has not "determined" the road—it is the road that has "determined" the guide-post; and unless the road goes of itself to its destination the guide-post has no power to determine its direction. So the Church does not "determine" the Scriptures, but the Scriptures the Church. Nor does it avail to say in opposition that the Church existed before the Scriptures and therefore cannot depend on them. The point is, whether the Scriptures are a product of the Church, or rather of the authority which founded the Church. The Church certainly did not exist before the authority which Christ gave the apostles to found it, in virtue of which they have imposed the Scriptures on it as law.

Apostolicity thus determines the authority of Scripture; and any book or body of books which were given to the Church by the apostles as law must always remain of divine authority in the Church. That the apostles thus gave the Church the whole Old Testament, which they had themselves received from their fathers as God's word written, admits of no doubt, and is not doubted. That they gradually added to this body of old law an additional body of new law is equally patent. In part this is determined directly by their own extant testimony. Thus Peter places

Paul's Epistles beside the Scriptures of the Old Testament as equally with them law to Christians (2 Peter iii. 16); and thus Paul places Luke's Gospel alongside of Deuteronomy (1 Tim. v. 18). Thus, too, all write with authority (1 Cor. xiv. 37; 2 Cor. x. 8; 2 Thess. ii. 15; iii. 6-14)—with an authority which is above that of angels (Gal. i. 7, 8), and the immediate recognition of which is the test of the possession of the Holy Ghost (1 Cor. xiv. 37; 2 Thess. iii. 6-14). In part it is left to be determined indirectly from the testimony of the early Church; it being no far cry from the undoubting universal acceptance of a book as authoritative by the Church of the apostolic age, to the apostolic gift of it as authoritative to that Church. But by one way or another it is easily shown that all the books which now constitute our Bible, and which Christians, from that day to this, have loyally treated as their divinely prescribed book of law, no more and no fewer, were thus imposed on the Church as its divinely authoritative rule of faith and practice.

Now it goes, of course, without saying, that the apostles were not given this supreme authority as legislators to the Church without preparation for their high functions, without previous instruction in the mind of Christ, without safeguards thrown about them in the prosecution of their task, without the accompanying guidance of the Holy Spirit. And nothing is more noticeable in the writings which they have given the Church than the claim which they pervasively make that in giving them they are acting only as the agents of Christ, and that those who wrote them wrote in the Spirit of Christ. What Paul writes he represents to be "the commandments of the Lord" (1 Cor. xiv. 37), which he therefore transmits in the name of the Lord (2 Thess. iii. 6); and the gospel that Peter preached was proclaimed in the Holy Ghost (1 Peter i. 12). Every Scripture of the Old Testament is inspired by God (2 Tim. iii. 16), and the New Testament is equally Scripture with the Old (1 Tim. v. 18); all prophecy of Scripture came from men who spake from God, being moved by the Holy Ghost (2 Peter i. 20) and Paul's Epistles differ from these older writings only in being "other"; that is, newer Scriptures of like kind (2 Peter iii. 16). When we consider the promises of supernatural guidance which Christ made to his apostles (Matt. x. 19, 20; Mark xiii. 11; Luke xxi. 14; John xiv and xvi), in connection with their claim to speak with divine authority even when writing (1 Cor. xiv. 37; 2 Thess. iii. 6), and their conjunction of their writings with the Old Testament Scriptures as equally divine with them, we cannot fail to perceive that the apostles claim to be attended in their work of giving law to God's Church by prevailing superintending grace from the Holy Spirit. This is what is called inspiration. It does not set aside the human authorship of the books. But it puts behind the human also a divine authorship. It ascribes to the authors such an attending influence of the Spirit in the process of writing, that the words they set down become also the words of God; and the resultant writing is made not merely the expression of Paul's or John's or Peter's will for the churches, but the expression of God's will. In receiving these books from the apostles as law, therefore, the Church has always received them not only as books given by God's agents, but as books so given by God through those agents that every word of them is God's word.

Let it be observed that the proof of the authority of the Scriptures does not rest on a previous proof of their inspiration. Even an uninspired law is law. But when inspiration has once been shown to be fact, it comes mightily to the reinforcement of their authority. God speaks to us now, in Scripture, not only mediately through his representatives, but directly through the Scriptures themselves as his inspired word. The Scriptures thus become the crystalization of God's authoritative will. We will not say that Christianity might not have been founded and propagated and preserved without inspired writings or even without any written embodiment of the authoritative apostolic teaching. Wherever Christ is known through whatever means, there is Christianity, and men may hear and believe and be saved. But God has caused his grace to abound to us in that he not only published redemption through Christ in the world, but gave this preachment authoritative expression through the apostles, and fixed it with infallible trustworthiness in his inspired word. Thus in every age God speaks directly to every Christian heart, and gives us abounding safety to our feet and divine security to our souls. And thus, instead of a mere record of a revelation given in the past, we have the ever-living word of God; instead of a mere tradition however guarded, we have what we have all learned to call in a unique sense "the Scriptures."

32

THE DIVINE AND HUMAN IN THE BIBLE*

There is probably no problem more prominently before the minds of Bible students of today than the one which concerns the relation between the divine and human elements in the Bible. Recent discussion of the authenticity, authorship, integrity, structure of the several Biblical books, has called men's attention, as possibly it has never before been called, to the human element in the Bible. Even those who were accustomed to look upon their Bible as simply divine, never once thinking of the human agents through whom the divine Spirit spoke, have had their eyes opened to the fact that the Scriptures are human writings, written by men, and bearing the traces of their human origin on their very face. In many minds the questions have become quite pressing: How are the two factors, the divine and the human, to be conceived as related to each other in the act of inspiration? And, how are the two consequent elements in the product, the divine and human, to be conceived to be related to each other in the Scriptures?

It would be a mistake to suppose such questions as these of little practical importance. It is true enough that Christian men are more concerned with the effects of inspiration than with its nature or mode. But men will not rest in their belief in effects which are not congruous with their conception of the nature and mode of inspiration. Inadequate or positively false conceptions of the nature and mode of inspiration are being continually suggested, and wherever they are in any degree accepted, they bring forth their natural fruit in a modified view of the effects of inspiration. Men are continually striving to

---

*From the *Presbyterian Journal*, May 3, 1894.

be rid of the effects which are ascribed to inspiration in the Scriptures and the formularies of the Church, on the plea that inspiration is not to be so conceived as to require these effects. The question of how inspiration is to be conceived having been thus raised, it becomes of very serious importance to go at least so far into it as to exhibit the untenableness of those theories which, when accepted, wholly overthrow the Biblical conception of the effects of inspiration. It is a matter, then, of importance, and not merely of curious interest, to ask, how are the two factors, the divine and human, to be conceived to be related to each other in the act of inspiration? And how are the two consequent elements in the Bible, the divine and human, to be conceived to be related to each other in the product of inspiration?

1. In the first place, we, may be sure that they are not properly conceived when one factor or element is so exaggeratingly emphasized as to exclude the other altogether.

At one time there arose in the Church, under the impulse of zeal to assert and safeguard the divinity of Scripture, a tendency toward so emphasizing the divine element as to exclude the human. The human writers of Scripture were conceived as mere implements in the hands of the Holy Ghost, by which (rather than through whom) he wrote the Scriptures. Men were not content to call the human authors of Scripture merely the penmen, the amanuenses of the Holy Spirit, but represented them as simply his pens. Inspiration, in this view, was conceived as a simple act of dictation; and it was denied that the human writers contributed any quality to the product, unless, indeed, it might be their hand-writing. This, properly so-called, mechanical theory of inspiration was taught by a number of seventeenth century divines, in all Protestant communions alike—by Quenstedt, Calov, Hollaz, among the Lutherans; by Heidegger and Buxtorf, among the Reformed; by Richard Hooker, among the Anglicans; and by John White among the Puritans. The obvious marks of human authorship in the Biblical books, however, prevented it from becoming dominant, in its extreme form. Recognition of these marks of human authorship—as for example, differences in vocabulary, style, and the like—was recognition of a human element in the Bible; and involved so far the substitution of a theory of co-authorship by God and man for the Scriptures, in the place of the strict theory of the sole divine authorship. In this form alone has the theory of dictation persisted in the Church; and in this form it no longer belongs to the class of theories under discussion. Probably no one today so emphasizes the divine element in Scripture as to exclude the human altogether.

The opposite fault, however, is exceedingly common today. Nothing, indeed, is more common than such theories of the origin and nature of the Scriptures as exclude the divine factor and element altogether, and make them purely human in both origin and character. Historically, this mode of thought is an outgrowth of Rationalism; but it takes every form which is required by a change of philosophical basis. A Hegelian, like Dr. Whiton, adapts himself to it as readily as a Deist; a mystic like R. H. Horton as readily as a vulgar Rationalist. The modes of statement given to it are very various, but they all agree in holding the Bible to be a purely human book. They differ only as to whether there has been any divine preparation for the book at all, or if this be allowed, whether this divine preparation included a revelation which men have recorded in this book, or whether it was only gracious or indeed only providential. The book market is flooded at present with treatises teaching this hopelessly one-sided theory. Dr. Washington Gladden's *Who Wrote the Bible?* is a very crude instance in point. To him God had the same sort of care over the production of the Bible that he has over the growth of an old apple tree. Dr. John DeWitt's recent book on *What Is Inspiration?* is another crude instance. According to him the prophet was left to express himself in human language "as well as he could." A slightly higher conception is taken by T. George Rooke in his *Inspiration and Other Lectures;* and a higher one still by a recent German writer, Leonard Staehlin, who thinks that God specifically prepared the Biblical writers for their task, but left them, when prepared, to execute their task in a manner so "free" as to be without continued divine guidance. Throughout all these modifications the germinal conception persists that it was man and man alone who made the Bible; and that it is, therefore, a purely human book, although it may contain a human report of divine deeds and words.

2. We may be equally sure that the relation of the divine and human in inspiration and in the Bible are not properly conceived when they are thought of, as elements in the Bible, as lying over against each other, dividing the Bible between them; or, as factors in inspiration, as striving against and excluding each other, so that where one enters the other is pushed out.

This hopelessly crude conception seems to have become extraordinarily common of recent years. It is this point of view which underlies the remark, now heard very frequently, that the human element in the Bible is coming to be recognized as larger than we had supposed—with the implication that, therefore, the divine element must be acknowledged to be smaller than we had supposed. Even so thoughtful a writer as Dr. Sanday falls into this mode of speech: "The tendency of the last 50 or 100 years of investigation," he tells us, "is to make it appear that this human element is larger than had been supposed."[1] So, too, Prof. Kirkpatrick says: "In the origin of Scripture there has been a large human element, larger than there was at one time supposed."[2] The underlying conception is that what is human cannot also be divine, and that wherever the human enters there the divine disappears. Thus Dr. Sanday speaks of his thesis as an apparent contention "for an encroachment of the human element upon the divine," and Dr. G. T. Ladd even speaks of the chief difficulty in the matter being the determination of "the exact place where the divine meets the human and is limited by it."[3]

On such a conception it is easy to see that every discovery

_____

[1]*The Oracles of God*, p. 161.
[2]*The Divine Library of the Old Testament*, p. 53.
[3]*What Is the Bible?* p. 437.

of a human trait in Scripture is a disproving of the divinity of Scripture. If, then, it be discovered that the whole fabric of the Bible is human—as assuredly is true—men who start with this conception in mind must end with denying of the whole fabric of the Bible that it is divine. As a preliminary stage we shall expect to meet with efforts to go through the Bible and anxiously to separate the divine and human elements. And if these elements are really so related to one another that when one enters the other is pushed out, this task will not seem a hopeless one. We may be warned, as Dr. Sanday does warn us, that it is "a mistake to attempt to draw a hard and fast line between the two elements." Men will feel that, on this conception of their relation to each other, it is a greater mistake not to make such an attempt. How shall we consent to leave confused such very diverse elements? We need not be surprised, therefore, that men like Horton and Gess have made the attempt. Nor need we at least, who perceive the folly of the underlying conception of the mechanical relation of the two elements to each other, feel surprised over the destructive nature of their results. They do not fail to find the human element entering almost everywhere, and therefore the divine element almost nowhere.

3. Justice is done to neither factor of inspiration and to neither element in the Bible, the human or the divine, by any other conception of the mode of inspiration except that of *concursus,* or by any other conception of the Bible except that which conceives of it as a divine-human book, in which every word is at once divine and human.

The philosophical basis of this conception is the Christian idea of God as immanent as well as transcendent in the modes of his activity. Its idea of the mode of the divine activity in inspiration is in analogy with the divine modes of activity in other spheres—in providence, and in grace wherein we work out our own salvation with fear and trembling, knowing that it is God who is working in us both the willing and the doing according to his own good pleasure. The Biblical basis of it is found in the constant Scriptural representation of the divine and human co-authorship of the Biblical commandments and enunciations of truth; as well as in the constant Scriptural ascription of Bible passages to both the divine and the human authors, and in the constant Scriptural recognition of Scripture as both divine and human in quality and character.

The fundamental principle of this conception is that the whole of Scripture is the product of divine activities which enter it, however, not by superseding the activities of the human authors, but confluently with them; so that the Scriptures are the joint product of divine and human activities, both of which penetrate them at every point, working harmoniously together to the production of a writing which is not divine here and human there, but at once divine and human in every part, every word and every particular. According to this conception, therefore, the whole Bible is recognized as human, the free product of human effort, in every part and word. And at the same time, the whole Bible is recognized as divine, the Word of God, his utterances, of which he is in the truest sense the Author.

The human and divine factors in inspiration are conceived of as flowing confluently and harmoniously to the production of a common product. And the two elements are conceived of in the Scriptures as the inseparable constituents of one single and uncompounded product. Of every word of Scripture is it to be affirmed, in turn, that it is God's word and that it is man's word. All the qualities of divinity and of humanity are to be sought and may be found in every portion and element of the Scripture. While, on the other hand, no quality inconsistent with either divinity or humanity can be found in any portion or element of Scripture.

On this conception, therefore, for the first time full justice is done to both elements of Scripture. Neither is denied because the other is recognized. And neither is limited to certain portions of Scripture that place may be made for the other, nor is either allowed to encroach upon the other. As full justice is done to the human element as is done by those who deny that there is any divine element in the Bible; for of every word in the Bible, it is asserted that it has been conceived in a human mind and written by a human hand. As full justice is done to the divine element as is done by those who deny that there is any human element in the Bible; for of every word in the Bible it is asserted that it is inspired by God, and has been written under the direct and immediate guidance of the Holy Spirit. And full justice being done to both elements in the Bible, full justice is done also to human needs. "The Bible," says Dr. Westcott, "is authoritative, for it is the Word of God; it is intelligible, for it is the word of man." Because it is the word of man in every part and element, it comes home to our hearts. Because it is the word of God in every part and element, it is our constant law and guide.

33

THE NEW TESTAMENT USE
OF THE SEPTUAGINT, AND INSPIRATION*

In 1855 a very able sermon on *The Inspiration of the Holy Scriptures* was preached by appointment before the Synod of New York and New Jersey, by Dr. Henry B. Smith, a most highly and most deservedly honored professor in Union Seminary. In this, he mentions and disposes as follows, of an objection at that time frequently adduced against that doctrine of the plenary and errorless inspiration of the Scriptures which in this sermon he propounded and defended.

A special argument is made against inspiration on the score of the citations from the Old Testament in the New, on the ground that the citations are incorrect, being often made from the Septuagint instead of the Hebrew, and sometimes differently made. . . . As to inaccuracy in citations, and the use of the Septuagint, a careful examination seems to show that in no case is the real sense of the original improperly conveyed or implied, even where the exact terms are not employed. A freedom is allowed in citing *ad sensum,* and not *ad verbum,* such as is found in all literature, and such as has force only against a mechanical theory of inspiration. Thus the difficult passage, "a body hast thou prepared me" (Heb. x. 5), is from the Septuagint, while the Hebrew reads, "Mine ears hast thou bored"; yet both express the state of a servant, which is the idea for which probably the citation is introduced. Sometimes there is a deviation from both the Hebrew and the Septuagint, to bring out the sense of the passage yet more fully. Nor can any instance, says Mr. Lee, be adduced in which they quote merely from memory, if that means that they so quote as to give an incorrect idea. These citations,

*The Presbyterian Journal, Dec. 8, 1892.

while they disprove a mechanical, prove a real, inspiration"
(pp. 32 f.).

Readers of Lee's *The Inspiration of Holy Scripture* (pp.
301-325) will perceive that Dr. Smith's statement is simply
an abstract of Lee's discussion, to which a further reference
is made in a footnote, and to which Dr. Smith thus gives his
adherence as sound and conclusive.

But doubting criticism of the plenary inspiration of the Bible
(like Rome's methods if not her doctrines), is *semper eadem;*
that is to say, it is ever bringing forth "novelties" from the
waste basket of the past. We cannot express surprise, therefore, that the old argument from the use of the Septuagint by
the New Testament writers in citing from the Old, and their
manner of using it, has been refurbished to do duty against
the doctrine of plenary inspiration, in the unhappy attack which
is now being made upon "the Scriptures of truth." We cannot
even express surprise (though we may be allowed perhaps to
express regret) that this argument, discredited long ago by
Dr. Smith, is now deemed capable of "shivering hopelessly into
pieces" that doctrine of inspiration against which he found it
innocuous, in the very halls of learning where for so long he, his
colleagues, and his successors taught that doctrine. We can
only express surprise that it should appear to anyone formidable against the truthfulness of the inspired Scriptures after it is
resuscitated. That it has within the past year, however, been
put forth twice in popular theological magazines, and under the
sanction of two names of repute among us—Dr. James M. Ludlow of East Orange, New Jersey, writing in *The Homiletical
Review* (for July, 1892, pp. 11-15) and Dr. Marvin R. Vincent, of Union Theological Seminary, writing in *The Magazine
of Christian Literature* (for April, 1892, pp. 11-17)—must
needs advise us that it is looked upon in some quarters even
yet, as something more than an antiquarian curiosity. It may
be worth our while to observe how an argument for so long a
time well dead and buried, looks when brought back "to the
light of earth."

There is a curious similarity in the form of these two articles.

The larger part of both is occupied with a historical account of the origin, character, and history of the Septuagint (in the course of which it becomes evident that Dr. Ludlow, at least, does not write history with what Dr. Vincent would call "verbal inerrancy"), and with a statement of the relation of the New Testament quotations from the Old to the Septuagint. In both articles, the bearing of the facts thus stated on the Church's doctrine of the inspiration of the Scriptures occupies but a little space in statement, and indeed, scarcely passes beyond mere statement. The assertion is strong enough in both instances. Dr. Ludlow says that the dealing of the New Testament with the Old, as thus exhibited, "is a great gulf in which the verbal theory is swallowed up as effectually as were Korah, Dathan, and Abiram." Dr. Vincent says that "upon such facts as these I have not a moment's hesitation in affirming that the theory of verbal inerrancy shivers hopelessly into pieces." But how these facts perform these feats, neither writer cares to occupy more than a few lines in attempting to show.

The points of similarity between the two articles go deeper, however, than this.

1. Thus, first, the arguments of both writers are based on a fundamental misapprehension of the doctrine of inspiration which they write to oppose. Both so express themselves as to fall under the scornful rebuke of Dr. H. B. Smith: "Many argue against inspiration as if they supposed a painful accuracy in writing down particular words was the chief office of the Spirit." Dr. Vincent is the chief sinner in this. He has even gone so far as to introduce an entirely new terminology to describe the doctrine which he opposes, and his pages are therefore thickly strown with such phrases as "literally inerrant," "verbally inerrant," "verbally accurate," "verbal inerrancy." Thus his paper leaves the impression that the doctrine of a plenary inspiration, extending to the choice of the words and securing the communication of truth without error, is a doctrine not of *real* inerrancy but specifically of *verbal* inerrancy. This may be a telling controversial device and may be necessary to prepare the way for the assertion that when the New

Testament writers quote the Old Testament "freely, and without regard to strict verbal accuracy," this is inconsistent with the doctrine of "verbal inspiration." But it is not in accordance with the facts. The doctrine of verbal or plenary inspiration (for these are but two names for the same thing) does not assert a "verbal inerrancy," but a real inerrancy; it does not imply that the quotation should be found verbally accurate, but really to the point. It asserts, not exactness but truth in every Scriptural statement. As Dr. H. B. Smith puts it: "The statement of each writer, it is well said by Dr. Alliott, may be partial and imperfect in point of fulness, while complete and perfect in point of truthfulness." The subintroduction of the idea of "verbal inerrancy," in the place of the real inerrancy claimed by the doctrine they are opposing, may be taken as the testimony of our authors' consciousness that their arguments do not avail against the doctrine itself, but that the doctrine needs caricaturing before it can be successfully opposed.

2. The arguments of both writers are based on an inaccurate apprehension of the nature of the problem raised by the use of the Septuagint by the writers of the New Testament in quoting the Old. It is doubtless a comparatively easy task to compare the mere wording of these quotations with that of the Septuagint, and classify them as verbally exact or inexact quotations; and the difficulty of the task is not greatly increased when the third element of the Hebrew is introduced in the same spirit and investigated in the same external way. As nobody holds a doctrine of inspiration which requires strict "verbal" or "literal" "accuracy in quotation," such an investigation, however, has little bearing on the question at issue. What we wish to know and what is of importance to know in the present debate, is whether, though using the Septuagint as the immediate source of their quotations, and varying often from its phraseology, the New Testament writers ever so quote as to falsify the sense of the passages quoted—as to adduce them in support of propositions which they do not support—as "to give an incorrect idea" of the original meaning of the passages, as Dr. Smith expresses it. We have seen that

Dr. Smith asserts that this never happens. It simply confuses
the issue to dwell as Drs. Vincent and Ludlow do, on the verbal
form and to fail to look beneath the wording to the sense
conveyed. "In the freedom of the Spirit of truth," says Beck
most admirably, "the question is not whether divine sayings,
already promulgated, have been quoted with rigid adherence
to their mere *letter,* but whether they have been given ever
true to their *spirit.*"

3. The arguments of both writers are even on their own
ground logically without validity. These arguments are different. They are alike only in that neither possesses any validity
for what it is adduced to prove.

(1) Dr. Ludlow's argument is as follows: "Now the fact
that the Septuagint was practically the Bible of Jesus, the
apostles, and the Church during all the ages of its planting,
raises the question whether any features in which the Septuagint
differs from the Hebrew can be essential to real inspiration."
Emphasizing the fact that the Septuagint is not a *literal* or
verbal translation of the Hebrew, Dr. Ludlow proceeds to
draw the immediate conclusion that, therefore, inspiration cannot be verbal. How far this amazing argument is, in any case,
from applying to the matter in hand, the reader who has
attended to what has already been said in elucidating the
status quaestionis, may be trusted to divine for himself. But
what a trenchant argument it is in itself; and how deeply it cuts!
For the Septuagint does not differ from the Hebrew only in
verbal expression. It differs in general contents, including a
number of whole books not included in the Hebrew. It differs
in the general contents of some of the books included in both
Hebrew and Septuagint, for example, of Daniel. And where
the books are the same in general contents, it often differs most
seriously in the sense conveyed: how seriously let Dr. Vincent
tell his coärguer. Characterizing the Septuagint, Dr. Vincent
says: "The prophets are often quite unintelligible." "It is full
of intentional as well as unintentional departures from the
original." "The Septuagint translation, in use in the time of
Christ and of the apostles, was, therefore, far from being a

faithful rendering of the original Hebrew. It was rather a corrected edition, a running commentary, freely manipulating the text according to the exegetical traditions of the day." On Dr. Ludlow's canon that no "features in which the Septuagint differs from the Hebrew can be essential to real inspiration"—we ask what then *is* inspired? Dr. Ludlow seems inclined to answer, "the general thoughts." Very "general" thoughts indeed, in those frequent portions of the prophets where the Septuagint is "quite unintelligible"! The plain fact is that Dr. Ludlow has asserted a canon which proves too much; to discredit plenary inspiration he argues in a way which, if it has any validity at all, discredits all inspiration. If inspiration does not touch "any features in which the Septuagint differs from the Hebrew," we simply have no inspiration, properly so called, at all. Reverting to the confusion of revelation and inspiration, the distinction between which Dr. Smith in 1855 hoped had been at length too firmly established to be again neglected, he would be forced to confine acknowledgment of the divine in the Scriptures to the revelation of not much more than the general ideas.

(2) Dr. Vincent's sole argument is, if possible, even more inconsequent than Dr. Ludlow's. After stating the facts as to the freedom with which the New Testament writers quote the Old Testament through the medium of the Septuagint, he remarks that upon such facts "the theory of verbal inerrancy"— his phrase, it will be remembered to misdescribe the doctrine of plenary inspiration—"shivers hopelessly into pieces." When we ask why? we only learn: "This matter of New Testament citation bears directly upon the question, because the theory of inerrant verbal inspiration carries with it as its corollary, the fact of inerrant transmission." The shivering into pieces is to be accomplished, then, not directly on the facts, but indirectly through the mediation of a shivered corollary, just as a St. Rupert's drop we suppose is shivered by the breaking of its tail. But suppose the broken tail has no connection with the St. Rupert's drop; suppose no such corollary follows from the theory in question? Dr. Vincent certainly labors to show that

it ought to follow. But it is difficult to follow his reasoning here; the average man being quite able to understand the distinction (which seems invisible to Dr. Vincent) between God's seeing to it that his revelation is once put purely into the hands of men, and God's interfering by a perpetual miracle to prevent man from ever afterwards corrupting his gift. Dr. Vincent might as well argue that God may as easily be supposed to have created man a sinner, as not to have interfered by his almighty power to prevent him from ever becoming a sinner, after he had been created. His whole argument is capable, *mutatis mutandis,* of being applied with equal cogency to this case. Immediately after the words just now quoted, he continues: "That is to say, that theory assumes that verbal inspiration is God's own ideal of inspiration; that when God undertook to give a written revelation to the world, he deemed it essential and imperative that that revelation should be verbally accurate. That being the case it is for the advocates of that theory to explain how it is that God has never carried out this ideal: that assuming that he gave this revelation originally in inerrant autographs, the human race from the beginning has never had the benefit of that inerrant autographic revelation." Shall we say, then, to one who asserts that God created man upright, that that cannot be true, because it would carry with it the corollary that God would have preserved him upright; and then argue, "that is to say, that perfect holiness is God's own ideal of humanity; that when God undertook to place a human being in the world, he deemed it essential and imperative, that that human being should be perfectly holy. That being the case, it is for the advocates of that theory to explain how it is that God has never carried out this ideal; that assuming that he created man originally perfectly holy, the human race from the beginning has never had the benefit of that perfect holiness." Could confusion in argument be worse confounded? God's creation of man holy did not involve his keeping him holy: and no more does his giving the Scriptures errorless to man, involve "an inerrant transmission" as a corollary.

We do not wonder that Dr. Vincent does not himself seem entirely convinced by his argument. How soon his ground is shifted from the assertion that the New Testament use of the Old is fatal to plenary inspiration, because it would involve an inerrant transmission, to a burning philippic against "the doctrine of originally inerrant autographs," on the ground that the errant copies are good enough for him! In this philippic he is once more in conflict with Dr. Henry B. Smith, who sets aside such arguments from various readings as Dr. Vincent seeks to raise here, with the remark: "The question of inspiration refers, in its most direct relations, only to the original Scriptures." And when Dr. Vincent speaks so fervently of not being "warranted in assuming the possibility of a better Bible than the one we have"—one feels like asking him what Bible is it that he has? Is it the King James Version? Is it unwarranted to suppose that in that case he could obtain a better one than "the one he has" for a small sum, by buying a copy of the Revised Version? Or, as a student of the Greek Testament, he may possibly have a copy of Stephens' text. Can he not be persuaded to get a better one "than the one he has," by purchasing a copy of Westcott and Hort? But the Revised Bible and Westcott and Hort's Greek Testament are recent books, which came to us only a decade or so ago. They are the product of the labors of those who, not satisfied with the Bible that they chanced to have, deformed as it was in its transmission by copyists' failings and printers' errors, gave themselves unwearyingly to obtain a Bible better than that they had, *because closer to the original autographs.* And Dr. Vincent, if he means these by the Bible he has, need not despair of getting, after a while, even a better Bible than these—*better because brought even closer to the original autographs.* This is what textual criticism is laboring for; and this is what it is accomplishing; and this is in essence the answer to Dr. Vincent's whole argument. God's ideal of a written revelation *is* an errorless one. He has said so himself in the doctrine of Holy Scripture given us in the teachings of his Son and his apostles. God's desire is that the human race shall always have the benefit of this errorless revelation. It is man's fault if he loses it. And it is man's fault if, having once lost it, he does not diligently use the materials preserved by God's providence for his use, in castigating "the Bible he has" back to the "Bible as God gave it." The providence of God in preserving so good a text in constant use; in preserving material for its improvement; in raising up men of scholarly minds and critical powers to give themselves to the task of reforming the text; it is in these and such things as these, that God's hand is seen by his singular care and providence keeping his Word pure in all ages for the use of man. We are sorry to see Dr. Vincent refusing to profit by the divine goodness, and taking his stand among the traditionalists who do not believe any better Bible is attainable than the one they happen to have. The argument is as absurd as it would be for one who had destroyed half the pages of his Bible to light his cigar with, to contend that it evidently was not God's intention to give man a perfect Bible, or he would have restrained him from mutilating it in this manner; and as for him he thinks it more reverent to be content with the half Bible he already has rather than to take the trouble and incur the expense of procuring an unmutilated one. The inerrant autographs were a fact once; they may possibly be a fact again, when textual criticism has said its last word on the Bible text. In proportion as they are approached in the processes of textual criticism, do we have an ever better and better Bible than the one we have now.

Dr. Vincent's attitude toward textual criticism leads us to animadvert on the curious vacillations which advocates of an errant Bible exhibit in dealing with subjects of critical importance. Now the Septuagint, for example, is glorified at the expense of the Hebrew text. That is to rebuke the "traditionalist" who objects to arbitrary dealing with the Hebrew text. Anon the Septuagint is depreciated as a translation of the Hebrew text. That is to rebuke the "traditionalists" who think Christ and his apostles better guides to a doctrine of Holy Scripture than an extreme school of modern critics. So of textual criticism; it is alternately glorified and depreciated. The latter is the attitude of Dr. Vincent in this article. He speaks despairingly of the possibility of obtaining a correct Septuagint text. "Under these circumstances we are obliged, as in the case of the New Testament, to fall back upon what we can get." That is not a very hopeful note as to the text of the New Testament. Accordingly he tells us that "the most searching scholarly criticism of modern times has left an eighth of the words of the New Testament still open to criticism." If we despair of these modern times of ours, what have we left? Does Dr. Vincent have no hope of the future doing what we have not done? But the case is not precisely as he represents it. He is quoting Dr. Hort here; and what he quotes is not all that Dr. Hort says. What he says is that various readings exist on about one word in eight, of sufficient importance to make us pause and look at it; but that only about one word in sixty has such various readings on it as to make decision difficult; while only one in a thousand has disputed various readings on it, which are difficult to decide between. We already have practically the autographic text in the New Testament in nine hundred and ninety-nine words out of every thousand; and Dr. Vincent can have it as well as the rest of us, if he can only be induced to part with "the Bible he has" for a better.

But we must not permit ourselves to wander from the main question. What shall we say finally of these new attempts to make the use of the Septuagint by the New Testament writers, in their quotations from the Old Testament, into an argument against plenary inspiration? What except that they miss the point altogether? The New Testament is written in Greek, and was written to Greek-speaking peoples. The Old Testament is written in Hebrew. If it was to be quoted at all in the New Testament—as, for example, by Paul in writing to the Corinthians or the Galatians—it could not be quoted *verbally,* that is, in the inspired *Hebrew* words; but only in a translation. Starting from this obvious and obviously fundamental fact, we need only ask further: What sort of a translation must this be? And we must obviously reply: It must be faithful. Faithful to what? Obviously, not to the mere verbal form, but to the sense. May it then be a free, as distinguished from a literal, translation? Who can doubt it, if only the amount of freedom allowed is consistent with the conveyance of the correct sense? But whose translation shall it be? The New Testament writers no doubt might have translated for themselves; but were they required to? Might they not legitimately and properly avail themselves of an existing translation ready at hand, so long as it both served their purpose and, for the purpose for which they adduced it, represented the meaning of the original sufficiently correctly? Undoubtedly. Now, this is just what the writers of the New Testament have done. Is it inconsistent with inspiration? inconsistent with plenary inspiration extending to the choice of the words and producing a record without error? The matter may be settled in a word. Is not such a procedure the very procedure employed by truth-loving ministers of the gospel today, in preaching to their flocks? And is it in them inconsistent with their truthfulness? Well, as inspiration secured only *truth*—not "*verbal inerrancy*," but *real truth*—how can a procedure that is confessedly not inconsistent with the truth of the uninspired man, be presented as a fact on which this theory of inspiration "shivers hopelessly into pieces"—or a "gulf in which it is swallowed up as effectually as were Korah, Dathan, and Abiram"? The inconsequence is nothing less than colossal.

34

THE WESTMINSTER DOCTRINE
OF HOLY SCRIPTURE*

"If any chapter of the Westminster Confession of Faith," says Prof. Mitchell, "was framed with more elaborate care than another, it was that which treats 'Of the Holy Scripture.' It was considered paragraph by paragraph—almost clause by clause—by the House of Commons, as well as by the Assembly of Divines, before it was finally passed, and its eighth paragraph was deemed worthy to be made the subject of a special conference between certain Members of the House and the Divines of the Assembly." The rather meager notes given in the "Minutes" of the Assembly bear out this statement in general, while they do not suggest that any special or unusual discussion was given to this chapter. There are no great debates recorded concerning it; and the divines appear to have been very much at one concerning its propositions, so that the event, for this chapter at least, justified Bailey's prevision that the Confession would be brought by the committee before the Assembly in a form that would rouse little discussion and cost but little time. We are surprised, indeed, by the rapidity and unanimity with which the work was done. The whole first draft of the chapter passed through the Assembly between July 7 and July 18, 1645, and debates are signalized only on the knowledge of the divine authority of the Scripture (sect. 5), the need of supernatural illumination for the saving understanding of the Word (sect. 6), and the literal sense of Scripture

---

*The New York Observer, Apr. 23, 1891, and The Independent, Apr. 23, 1891. A fuller treatment may be found in The Westminster Assembly and Its Work, 1931, pp. 155-257 (Vol. VI of the Oxford edition).

(sect. 9), to which may be added the conference with the House of Commons on the eighth section.

The most important proximate source of the Confession in this chapter, as well as elsewhere, was, as Dr. Mitchell has shown, those Irish "Articles of Religion" which are believed to have been drawn up by Usher's hand, and which were adopted by the Irish Convocation in 1615. But it belonged to the historical situation of the Westminster divines that their work should take much the form of a consensus of the Reformed theology, and of this chapter, too, the main source can be easiest found in the general doctrine of Holy Scripture which had been wrought out by the Reformed theologians of the preceding hundred years. How close a transcript the Westminster statement is of this general doctrine is oddly illustrated by comparing it with Heppe's effort to state the Reformed doctrine of Scripture on the basis of its chief Continental exponents. Except for the anachronism of two hundred years, one might be tempted to affirm that the Westminster divines had formulated their doctrine from Heppe's statement. The same conceptions, the same order, much the same language, are used. From this we may learn the conscientious care with which the Assembly sought to fulfil their commission, to secure in their dogmatic statements a "nearer agreement with the Church of Scotland, and other Reformed Churches abroad."

It is in accordance with the fundamental idea and the ordinary practice of the Reformed theology, that the Confession begins its exposition of doctrine with the doctrine of Holy Scripture, as the root out of which all doctrine grows, just because the Scriptures are the fountain from which all knowledge of God's saving purpose and plan flows. And as we have already said, the Confession follows, in stating the doctrine of Scripture, that natural and logical order of topics which had been wrought out by and become fixed in the Reformed theology. First, the necessity of Scripture is asserted and exhibited (sect. 1). Then Scripture is defined as the Word of God, both extensively, or in relation to its general contents, or, in other words, as to the Canon (sect. 2a), and intensively or in relation to its essential character, or, in other words, as to inspiration (sect. 2b); and this definition is applied to the exclusion of the apocryphal books (sect. 3). Then, what are called in theological language the three great properties of Scripture are taken up: its authority (sects. 4, 5), its perfection or completeness (sect. 6), and its perspicuity (sect. 7). The chapter closes with certain important corollaries as to the use of Scripture, with special reference to its transmission and translation (sec. 8), to its interpretation (sect. 9), and to its use in controversies (sect. 10).

It is, of course, true of the Confession as of other documents that its deliverances can be properly understood only when read in context, that is, in accordance with its structure. From failure to do this, many strange misapplications of passages in this chapter have been made, to the subversion sometimes of its whole point of view. For example, because the apocrypha are declared, in sect. 3, not to be part of the canon of Scripture on the ground that they are "not of divine inspiration," it has been inferred that the method of the Confession is to prove inspiration first and canonicity from it; whereas, the Confession itself settles the canon (sect. 2a) before it asserts inspiration (sect. 2b). Attention to the order of thought would have shown that the apocrypha are excluded simply by the application to them of the definition of Scripture settled in sect. 2. So again, sect. 5 has been strangely appealed to as outlining the Confession's mode of determining the inspiration and consequent canonicity of Scripture; whereas the Confession had already settled these matters in sect. 2, and is here professedly treating an entirely different matter, viz., how we are brought practically to yield to it the authority which this inspired and canonical book ought to exercise over us. Again, sect. 5 is confused with the preceding sect. 4, as if the authority itself of the Scriptures already asserted in the earlier paragraph was grounded on the testimony of the Spirit appealed to in the later—although the earlier one gives distinctly a different account of the matter.

The remedy against such perversions of a document is the

simple one of reading it only in context, that is, as we repeat, according to its structure. Following this rule, let us briefly outline the teaching of the Confession "of the Holy Scripture."

1. First, then, the Confession expounds the necessity of Scripture in a paragraph that has always been admired, not less for the chaste beauty of its expression than for the justness of its conception. The reality and trustworthiness of the natural revelation of God is recognized; and its scope defined as embracing "the goodness, wisdom, and power of God": though it is not so fully stated here as is afterwards done in chapter xxi. 1. The insufficiency of this natural revelation to give "that knowledge of God and of his will, which is necessary unto salvation," is next explained, in the same sense that is afterward repeated more at large in chapter x. 4, and the parallel question 60 of the Larger Catechism. The consequent gift, in the goodness of God, of a supernatural revelation, making known "his will, which is necessary unto salvation," is next affirmed; and the manner of this revelation suggested. To this is immediately attached the explanation that God has committed this supernatural revelation of his saving will "wholly unto writing"—not as a necessary step, but "for the better preserving and propagating of the truth, and for the more sure establishment and comfort of the Church." Thus the Scriptures are made the record of God's revelation; and the value of the making of such a record is moderately and winningly stated. All this is the groundwork of the proof of the necessity of the Scriptures. This comes in the further statement: "Which maketh the Holy Scripture to be most necessary; those former ways of God's revealing his will unto his people being now ceased." The necessity of Scripture thus rests on the insufficiency of natural revelation and the cessation of supernatural revelation—the record of which latter Scripture is, though a record of such sort that it itself is a revelation of God, since it was God and not mere man who "committed his will wholly unto writing."

The Confession thus speaks of Scripture as one of the ways in which God revealed his will, co-ordinate in this with his other supernatural ways of revealing himself: "those *other* ways of God's revealing his will unto his people being now ceased." According to the Confession, then, the Scriptures are not merely the record of revelation, but part of revelation, and not merely useful but necessary to salvation. It states, in a word, moderately and justly, the same doctrine of the necessity of Scripture which Edmund Calamy, one of its framers, states somewhat immoderately in the words: "There are two great Gifts that God hath given to his people: The Word Christ and the Word of Christ. Both are unspeakably great; but the first will do us no good without the second."[1] Yet even Calamy was not a "bibliolater," but means just what Paul does in Romans x. 14.

2. Having thus exhibited the necessity of Holy Scripture, or the written revelation or Word of God, the Confession naturally proceeds to define this "Holy Scripture or the Word of God written," which is so necessary unto salvation. This is done of course first extensively, by the enumeration of the writings that enter into it, which are first designated generally as "all the books of the Old and New Testament," and then to prevent all mistakes, enumerated one by one, by name. Of these books it is then affirmed, by way of intensive definition, that they are, one and all, "given by inspiration of God, to be the rule and faith of life." The canon and inspiration of Scripture being thus set, this definition, finally, is applied to the exclusion of "the books commonly called apocrypha," which, "not being of divine inspiration, are no part of the canon of Scripture." They are therefore declared, in accord with the ordinary Reformed doctrine, to be "of no authority in the Church of God, nor to be any otherwise approved or made use of other than human writings."

From this we learn (1) that those books that are of "divine inspiration and part of the canon of the Scriptures" do not belong to the category of "human writings," a broad line of demarcation being drawn between them and the apocrypha on this very

---

[1] *The Godly Man's Ark,* 7th ed., 1672, pp. 55 f.

ground; and (2) that the authority of a book of Scripture rests on its being of divine inspiration and part of the canon as previously settled facts—the apocrypha being declared to be "therefore of no authority," on the express ground that they are "not of divine inspiration," and "no part of the canon of the Scripture." According to the Confession then the order of procedure in ascertaining Scripture is to settle first the canon, then its inspiration, and then, as a corollary, its authority. And according to the Confession all the books of the canon of Scripture "are given by inspiration of God." This is, of course, not a formal definition of the nature of inspiration, but only a strong assertion of the fact of inspiration. This section is a definition of what Scripture is, not of what inspiration is. Nevertheless the Confession does not leave the nature of inspiration unaffirmed. There was, however, the less need for any formal remark here as to it, (1) because it was not in dispute at the time; and (2) because it had already been asserted in the preceding paragraph, when it was declared that it was God who constituted Scripture by himself committing his will wholly unto writing, thereby making another way of revelation. In conformity with this the Confession declares that these divinely inspired books are not "human writings" (sect. 3), but have "God (who is truth itself)" for their "author" (sect. 4), and in the originals are "immediately inspired by God" (sect. 8); so that they are the "very word of God" (Larger Catechism, Q. 4), "his own revealed will" (xxi. 1), "entirely perfect, infallibly true, and divinely authoritative" (sect. 5). As the historical meaning of the word "inspiration" as used in the Confession is not doubtful, so neither is the meaning of these phrases, further describing its sense. Take but a single one of them. John Ball, than whom no one probably was more highly esteemed as a judicious divine by the fathers of the Assembly, asks: "What is it to be immediately inspired?" and answers: "To be immediately inspired is to be as it were breathed and to come from the Father by the Holy Ghost, without all means." And again: "Were the Scriptures thus inspired?" and answers: "Thus the Holy Scriptures in the Originals were inspired both for matter and words."[2] The doctrine of the Confession is the doctrine of Ball, moderately stated, and is expressed in the same words; and similarly the doctrine of Featley, who declares that "in the undoubted word of God there can be no error," and calls it "blasphemy" to deny "the letter of the text to be Scripture"—replying to the Anabaptist assertion that "the letter of the Word of God is not Scripture without the revelation of the Spirit of God: the Word revealed by the Spirit is Scripture" —"Very fine doctrine; if God reveal not to us the meaning of the Scripture, is not the letter of the Text Scripture? By this reason, the greatest part of the Revelation, and other difficult Texts of Scripture, should not be Scripture, because [God] hath not revealed to us the meaning of them."[3] But neither are Ball and Featley "bibliolaters," but mean only to say what Paul says in 2 Tim. iii. 16, and our Lord in John x. 35.

3. Having thus defined Scripture as the very Word of God, the Confession naturally proceeds next to exhibit the properties which flow from its divine origin (sects. 4-7).

a. The first of these properties of a divine book to be adduced is, properly, its authority (sects. 4, 5). Just because the book is God's book revealing to us his will, it is authoritative in and of itself; and it ought to be believed and obeyed, not on the ground of any authority lent it from any human source, but on the ground of its own divine origin, because it is the Word of God and God (who is truth itself) is the author of it. So the Confession asserts (sect. 4) in unison with the whole body of Protestant polemics, not as if it held that Scripture is to be believed and obeyed as God's Word before we know it to be such, but as grounding its authority on the previously established fact of its inspiration. Because inspired, Scripture is the Word of God; and because the Word of God it exercises lawful authority over man. But men are not so constituted as readily to yield faith and obedience even to lawful authority. So the Confession devotes a paragraph of almost unsurpassed nobility of both thought and phrase, to indicating how sinful men may

---

[2] *A Short Treatise,* 15th ed., 1656, pp. 7 f.
[3] *The Dippers Dipt,* 1660, pp. 1, 16.

be brought to a full practical persuasion and assurance of the infallible truth and divine authority of Scripture (sect. 5). The value of the external testimony of the Church is recognized; the assurance of the Church may move and induce us to a high and reverent esteem for the Scriptures. The greater value of the witness of the contents of Scripture itself is affirmed; by the miracle of Scripture itself "it doth abundantly evidence itself to be the Word of God." But it is further pointed out that something more still is needed to persuade us wholly to commit ourselves to Scripture with full persuasion and assurance, trusting its every word as true and obeying its every command as of divine authority; namely, in ordinary language, a new heart, or in the Confession's language, "the inward work of the Holy Ghost, bearing witness by and with the Word in our hearts." According to the Confession, then, as according to the whole Reformed theology, man needs something else than evidence fully to persuade him to believe and obey God's Word —he needs the work of the Holy Spirit accompanying the Word, *ab extra incidens.* This is but to say that faith in God's Word is not man's own work, but the gift of God, and that man needs a preparation of the spirit as well as an exhibition of the evidences in order to yield faith and obedience. As Edward Reynolds, one of the Westminster men, puts it: "This light in the Word is manifested unto us: 1. By the manuduction and ministry of the Church, pointing unto the star, which is seen in its own light. 2. Because we bring not such an implanted suitableness of reason to Scripture as we do to other sciences . . . therefore, to proportion the eye of the soul to the light of the Word, there is required an act of the Spirit, opening the eyes and drawing away the vail, that we may discern the voice of Christ from strangers: for, having the mind of Christ, we do, according to the measure of his spirit in us, judge of divine truths as he did."[4] This is just the teaching of 1 Cor. ii. 14.

b. The second property of Holy Scripture adduced is its perfection or completeness (sect. 6). Here the absolute ob-

---

[4]*Works*, 1826, Vol. V, p. 154.

jective completeness of Scripture for the purpose for which it
is given is affirmed, and the necessity of any supplements,
whether by traditions or new revelations, denied; the need of
spiritual illumination for the saving understanding of the Scriptures—the analogue in this sphere of the witness of the Spirit
affirmed in section 5—is asserted, and the place for reason and
Christian prudence is defined. The doctrine is here also the
ordinary Reformed doctrine. John White, for example, in exact
agreement with it, writes: "Now things may be contained in
Scripture, either expressly or in plain terms, or by consequence
drawn from some grounds that are delivered in Scripture, and
one of these two ways all grounds of faith, or rules of practice,
are to be found in these holy writings." "Every godly man
has in him a spiritual light by which he is directed in the understanding of God's mind revealed in his Word, in all things
needful to salvation."[5]

c. The third property of Scripture adduced is its perspicuity
(sect. 7). What is affirmed is, that though all parts of Scripture
are not alike plain in themselves, or alike clear to all, yet all
that is necessary to salvation is somewhere plainly revealed,
and is accessible to all in the use of the ordinary means. This
again is simply the common Reformed doctrine. Arrowsmith
thus expresses it: "Scripture is so framed as to deliver all things
necessary to salvation in a clear and perspicuous way. There
are, indeed, some obscure passages in it to exercise our understandings, and prevent our lothing of overmuch plainness and
simplicity; yet whatsoever is needful for us to satisfy hunger
and nourish our souls to life eternal, is so exprest (I do not
say that it may be understood, but so) as men who do not wilfully shut their eyes against the light, cannot possibly but understand it."[6]

4. Finally, the Confession adduces certain important corollaries from its whole doctrine of Scripture as to its use, with
special reference, as we have already pointed out, to its trans-

---

[5]*A Way to the Tree of Life*, 1647, pp. 65, 161.
[6]*A Chain of Principles*, 1659, p. 96.

mission in text and translation, to its interpretation, and to its use in controversies.

a. As to the former matter, the Confession (sect. 8) asserts that final appeal in all controversies is to be made to the original Hebrew and Greek Scriptures, which are alone safeguarded in their accuracy by divine inspiration, and it asserts that these originals have been, "by God's singular care and providence, kept pure in all ages." Nevertheless, it vindicates the right of all to the possession and use of vernacular versions. The Confession does not mean here to deny that any corruptions have entered the text of Scripture in the process of its transmission, which require the care and study of men to remove. It only means to affirm the adequately exact preservation of Scripture in the original texts, and the transference of the "Word of God" into translations so far forth as to make it available to their readers. This general position is illustrated sufficiently by Lyford: "I lay down these two conclusions: First, that Divine Truth in English is as truly the Word of God as the same Scriptures delivered in the Originall, Hebrew or Greek; yet with this difference, that the same is perfectly, immediately, and most absolutely in the Originall Hebrew and Greek, in other Translations, as the vessells wherein it is presented unto us, and as far forth as they do agree with the Originalls."[7]

b. As to the interpretation of Scripture the Confession rejects the notion of manifold senses, and affirms that "the true and full sense of any Scripture is one"; and finds the only infallible rule of interpretation in parallel clearer Scriptures (sect. 9). So Richard Capel says: "The sense of the law is the law; and of the Word of God, there is but one sense; it is the easier found out, because there is but one sense."[8] And so John Arrowsmith, quoting Romans xi. 2, adds: "The infallible meaning whereof may be gathered from that in Peter: 'Elect according to the foreknowledge of God the Father.' "[9]

c. The whole is closed with the assertion that the Holy Spirit

---

[7]*The Plain Man's Senses Exercised*, 1657, p. 49.
[8]*Tentations*, 1655, p. 243.
[9]*A Chain of Principles*, p. 333.

who speaks in every part of Scripture (compare xiv. 2) is the Supreme Judge in all controversies of religion, so that they all are to be determined, not on the ground of decrees of councils, opinions of ancient writers, doctrines of men or asserted private revelations—under whatever name they may masquerade, whether as traditions, deliverances of reason or of the Christian consciousness, individual or corporate—but on the ground of the unrepealable "thus saith the Lord" of Scripture itself (sect. 10). Accordingly, in the Confession's sense, whenever the doctrine of Scripture is ascertained all religious strife is ended, and in its sentence we are to rest. As Rutherford says: "The Scripture makes itself the judge and determiner of all questions in religion."[10] Or, as Reynolds puts it: "The Scriptures . . . are the alone rule of all controversies. . . . So then the only light by which differences are to be decided is the Word, being a full canon of God's revealed will, for the Lord doth not now as in former times make himself known by dreams, or visions, or any other immediate way."[11] Or, if we may look beyond the immediate circle of Westminster men to a Puritan divine whose praise is in all the churches, as Richard Sibbes says: "What is the supreme Judge? The Word, the Spirit of God in the Scriptures. And who is above God? It is a shameless ridiculous independency of men that will take upon them to be judges of Scripture."[12] Shall we not say Amen to this, though it may condemn much modern practice and mayhap entail on us the charge of "bibliolatry"?

Such a reverence for God's Word as God's Word is no doubt an act of worship; but whom shall we worship if not the God of the Bible? At any rate, the Confession closes the chapter on Scripture which it began by declaring Scripture "most necessary," by declaring it also final and decisive in all questions of religion. We cannot do without the Scriptures; having them we need no other guide. We need this light to light

---

[10]*A Free Disputation*, 1649, p. 361.
[11]*Works*, Vol. V, pp. 152 f.
[12]*Works*, 1862, Vol. II, p. 493.

our pathway; having it we may well dispense with any other. Are we making it the light to lighten our feet? Are we following it whithersoever it leads? Are we prepared to test all religious truth by it, while it is tested by none? Are we prepared to stand by it in all things on the principle that it is God's Word and God will be true though every man be a liar?

35

THE WESTMINSTER DOCTRINE
OF INSPIRATION*

The question, What is the doctrine of inspiration taught by the Westminster Confession? is a purely historical one and should be investigated in a purely historical spirit. Whether we agree with it or not, after it is ascertained, may indicate our conception of the truth; but in the process of ascertaining it, we ought certainly to exhibit our loyalty to truth. We must be tolerant enough, whatever we believe, to allow the Westminster divines also their belief. And we must be sufficiently imbued with the historical spirit to be able to apprehend and state the doctrine of the Westminster Confession as a pure question of scientific symbolics, without coloring derived from our own point of view. Certain indications that these obvious principles may be partially lost sight of in discussions now in progress, render it desirable that attention should be called to what the Westminster doctrine of inspiration really is, as stated from the purely historical point of view, that the truth of fact at least may be preserved amid the conflict of opinion as to what is the truth of doctrine.

1. The most outstanding fact concerning the mode in which the Westminster Confession deals with inspiration, is that while it formally and emphatically asserts the *fact* of inspiration, it does not equally formally define the *nature* of the inspiration thus asserted. After having expounded the necessity of Scripture in the first section of the chapter, "Of the Holy Scripture," it is led naturally to define, in the second section, what this Holy Scripture or "Word of God written" is, which has been de-

*The Independent, Apr. 23, 1891.

clared to be so necessary. The definition is given both extensively and intensively. Extensively, Holy Scripture consists of "all the books of the Old and New Testament," which are then enumerated by name. Intensively, all these books "are given by inspiration of God, to be the rule of faith and life." Here there is no definition of inspiration; but Scripture is defined by means of inspiration. Or, in other words, the term "inspiration" is treated as a term of settled and well-known connotation, and is employed to define the nature of Scripture, already defined as to its extent by the preceding list of books. This advises us that the Westminster divines did not look upon the nature of inspiration as in dispute, but conceived that the assertion of the fact carried with it, in the very term employed, also the definition of the thing. They do not define because they are not conscious of the need of definition; and in asserting the fact they are to be understood as asserting the thing which the terminology employed conveyed to the minds of those making use of it.

2. What the Confession means, therefore, in asserting that "all the books of the Old and New Testament" "are given by inspiration of God" is to be determined by a historical inquiry into what these words expressed at the time they were written. We are not entitled to attribute to the word "inspiration" a nineteenth century sense—much less a sense current in any one school of nineteenth century thought; and to say that that is what is affirmed by the Confession. We are not entitled, for example, to say that by "inspiration" we mean "no inspiration," and that therefore in affirming that all the books of the Bible are inspired by God, the Confession only affirms that there is no inspiration in the case. We must deal with the Confession just as we would deal with Paul, when he says that "all Scripture is *theopneustos*." As in the one case we go to our Greek lexicons, the transcript of Greek usage, and seek to discover what *theopneustos* meant to Paul by ascertaining what it meant in contemporary speech; so in the other we must go to the contemporary usage to determine what the Confession meant to affirm when it affirmed that all Scripture is "given by

inspiration of God." In other words we are to understand the Confession's assertion of inspiration for the Scriptures, in its sense of that word, not in any sense we have chosen to make ours; and in the absence of contrary definition in the Confession itself we are obliged to take as its sense of the word the common current sense at the time it was composed—the sense in which its framers used the word in their most careful speech.

3. It cannot be doubtful, however, to anyone familiar with the theological literature of the first half of the seventeenth century, whether Lutheran or Reformed, whether Continental or British, whether Anglican or Puritan, what doctrine was conveyed in the speech of the time by the emphatic asseveration that all Scripture is "given by inspiration of God." This was especially the age of high doctrine on the subject. It would be difficult to believe that there was a single member of the Westminster Assembly who did not attach the sense of verbal inerrant inspiration to this phraseology. Certainly no one of them has been pointed out who in his published writings betrays doubt as to the truth of this doctrine. All through their writings we find such passages as the following, which we choose at mere random in order to convey a general idea of the state of consciousness out of which these divines affirmed the inspiration of the Scriptures:

"I answer, Although the pen-man did not, the inditer, viz., the Holy Ghost did exactly know whose names were written in the book of life and whose were not. Now he it was that in the history of the Acts suggested and dictated to his secretary both matter and words."[1]

"In the undoubted word of God there can be no error."[2]

"It is certain that all Scripture is of *Divine Inspiration,* and that the *holy men of God spake as they were guided by the Holy Ghost.* . . . It transcribes the mind and heart of God. A true Saint seeth the *Name, Authority, Power, Wisdom,* and

---

[1] Arrowsmith, *A Chain of Principles,* 1659, p. 299.
[2] Featley, *The Dippers Dipt,* 1660, p. 1.

Goodness of God in every letter of it, and therefore cannot but take pleasure in it. It is an Epistle sent down to him from the God of Heaven." "The Word of God hath God for its Author. . . . There is not a word in it but breathes out God, and is breathed out by God. It is (as Irenaeus saith) κανῶν τῆς πίστεως ἀκλινής, an invariable rule of Faith, an unerring and infallible guide to Heaven." "Therefore, let us bless God for the written Word, which is surer and safer (as to us) than an immediate Revelation. . . . For it is the same God that speaks by his written Word, and by a voice from Heaven. The difference is only in the outer cloathing; and therefore if God's speaking by writing will not amend us, no more will God's speaking by a voice."[3]

"If Solomon mistooke not (and how could he mistake in that, which the Spirit himself dictated unto him)."[4]

"The Word of God written is surer than that voyce which they heard in the Mount. . . . More sure is the Word written than that voyce of Revelation; not *ratione veritatis,* not in regard of the Truth uttered, for that Voyce was as true as any word in the Scripture; but more sure *ratione manifestationis,* more certain, settled, established." "Observe, keep, and hold fast the Letter of it; for though the Letter of the Scripture be not the Word alone, yet the Letter with the true sense and meaning of it, is the Word. . . . If ye destroy the Body, ye destroy the Man; so if ye destroy the Letter of the Scripture, you do destroy the Scripture; and if you deny the Letter, how is it possible that you should attain to the true sense thereof, when the sense lies wrapped up in the Letters, and the words thereof."[5]

These passages, we repeat, are chosen at random; they might be multiplied without other limit than that imposed by the amount written by the Westminster men on the subject. And if we are to interpret their words in the Confession historically, we cannot do otherwise than say that they meant by the em-

---

[3]Calamy, *The Godly Man's Ark,* ed. 7, 1672, pp. 55, 80, 93.
[4]C. Burgess, *Baptismal Regeneration of Elect Infants,* 1629, p. 277.
[5]W. Bridge, *Scripture Light the Most Sure Light,* 1656, pp. 4, 46.

phasis they laid on inspiration, to assert an all-pervasive divine character for Scripture as the product of inspiration, extending to the words and securing inerrancy. Thus only can we read their words in their sense.

4. But although we could, as historical students, only interpret the expression in which the Westminster divines declare the inspiration of Scripture, in the sense which they certainly attached to the terms they used, we are not left merely to this line of investigation in order to determine their doctrine. They felt no need of formally defining the meaning of a term used by them only in one settled sense; but as they wrote out of a clearly conceived doctrine of inspiration, they have not failed so to express themselves throughout this chapter and the whole Confession, as not only to imply but to assert the high doctrine which they intended to inculcate. We thus learn not only from their private writings, but also from the face of the Confession itself, what doctrine they teach when they declare the books of the Bible to be one and all "given by inspiration of God." Let us note what they teach, from section to section, of the nature of inspiration, its mode, and its effects.

a. The Confession teaches that by their inspiration the Scriptures are made not only to contain but to be *the Word of God*. In i. 2 the alternative name of Holy Scripture is "the Word of God written." In i. 4 it is declared that Holy Scripture "is the Word of God"; in i. 5 it is pointed out how it evidences itself "to be the Word of God." This phraseology pervades the whole document (cf. iii. 13; x. 1, 4; xiii. 1; xiv. 1, 2; xvi. 1; xx. 2; xxi. 5, 6, 7; xxii. 7; xxiv. 4; xxx. 2; Shorter Catechism, Q. 2, 99; Larger Catechism, Q. 3, 4, 67, 156, 157, 158, 159, 160, etc.). The Holy Scripture which is thus declared to be the Word of God is defined to be itself "all the books of the Old and New Testament"; and cannot, therefore, be thought to be only selected passages in those books. It is called the "Word of God written" to distinguish it by its accidents from the spoken Word of God, as given to the prophets aforetime, in the sense of i. 1, and as explained above in the citation from Calamy. Finally, when we read in the Shorter Catechism of "the Word of God, which is contained in the Scriptures of the Old and New Testaments," we are not reading of a distinction within the limits of the Scriptures between a word of God and a word not of God, as if it were only asserted that the former is to be found indeed within the Scriptures; but we are reading an anti-Romish and anti-Mystic declaration that the only Word of God that is recognized is that contained in the Scriptures. This, everyone acquainted with the literature of the times will perceive at once; it may be sufficiently demonstrated for our present purpose by adducing the wording of the original catechism undertaken by the Assembly and set aside when it was determined to frame two catechisms instead of one. The answer there runs: "The only rule of faith and obedience is the written Word of God, contained in the Bible or the Scriptures of the Old and New Testament." As simple historical students, we must admit that the Westminster Confession is committed to the position that the Bible not only contains but is the Word of God.

b. Accordingly, we observe that the Confession explicitly teaches that the nature of inspiration is such as that thereby *"God (who is truth itself)"* becomes *"the author thereof."* Nor is this conception of the divine authorship of Scripture a mere phrase with its writers—once used somewhat carelessly and forgotten; it is the exact expression of their innermost conviction as to the nature of inspiration as attributed to the written word. Accordingly, in i. 10 they speak of the Scriptures as in such a sense God's word that, when we appeal to them, we are really appealing to the Holy Ghost who speaks in them. For that this clause does not mean merely that the Holy Ghost speaks somewhere in the Scripture, but that all Scripture is his speaking, is sufficiently plain from the expression itself and the known opinions of its authors, and is placed beyond doubt by the parallel phrase in xiv. 2. There we read that "a Christian believeth to be true, *whatsoever* is revealed in the Word, for the authority of God himself speaking therein." According to which, God speaks *whatsoever* is in the Word; and all that stands written is true because, as our third section has it: "God (who is truth itself) is the author thereof." As simple historical students, then, we must hold that the Confession teaches that God is in such a sense the author of Scripture that he speaks all that stands written in it; and all that stands written in it is, therefore, true.

c. According to this conception, of course, the Scriptures are thought of as themselves a *revelation* of God's will. And this the Confession not only assumes but asserts and even proves. It repeatedly assumes and asserts it, not only in such phrases as occur in i. 6; iii. 8; xxi. 1; Larger Catechism, Q. 3, but also in such striking combinations as occur in Larger Catechism, Q. 157, or in xiv. 2, where we have "whatsoever is revealed in the word" placed in the immediate mouth of God. But apart from such assertions we have the whole matter logically developed in i. 1, where we read of God, and not man, committing the whole will of God to writing, "which maketh the Holy Scripture to be most necessary; those former ways of God's revealing his will unto his people being now ceased." The context and sense confine "those former ways of God's revealing his will," to the supernatural revelations added in the goodness of God to the natural revelation of his goodness, wisdom, and power; so that the Scriptures, committed to writing by God, are paralleled (in the term "former ways," implying that they are a "later way") with the open revelations of God through his prophets, as, not less than they, a revelation, and differing from them only as *another way of revelation,* viz., by the written rather than the spoken word. According to the Confession, therefore, the Scriptures are not merely the record of God's revelation, but are themselves God's revelation, by virtue of the fact that God has himself committed them to writing, that is, by virtue of the fact that he is in such a sense their author as that they are his Word, and he speaks whatever stands written in them.

d. This understanding of the matter implies, of course, that God is not only mediately but *immediately* concerned in the production of Scripture. And this again the Confession affirms in the ordinary locution, asserting in i. 8 that "The Old Testament in Hebrew . . . and the New Testament in Greek . . . are immediately inspired by God." What this phrase means we may learn as well as elsewhere from the Puritan writer, John Ball. He asks in his Greater Catechism the following questions:[6]

"*Q. What is it to be immediately inspired? A.* To be immediately inspired is to be as it were breathed, and to come from the Father by the Holy Ghost, without all means. *Q. Were the Scriptures thus inspired? A.* Thus the holy Scriptures in the Originals were inspired both for matter and words."

In the use of this term the Confession only repeats its assurance that God's committing Scripture to writing made him in the highest sense the author of it, and made it his revelation, direct and immediate.

e. The effects of this immediate inspiration are partly assumed and partly drawn out at length. We have already noted that the Confession teaches that since the author of Scripture is God (who is truth itself), therefore a Christian believeth as true whatsoever is contained in this revelation (xiv. 2). We note as marks of the same point of view that it speaks of the Scripture as "infallibly true" (i. 5, cf. i. 9); "divinely authoritative" (i. 5); and "entirely perfect" (i. 5); and requires us to rest "in its sentence" as against all decrees of councils, opinions of ancient writers, doctrines of men and private spirits (i. 10).

But in this paper we have in mind to draw out more the doctrine of the nature than of the effects of inspiration, as taught by the Confession. And doubtless enough has been said to show that the Confession teaches precisely the doctrine which is taught in the private writings of its framers, which was also the general Protestant doctrine of the time, and not of that time only or of the Protestants only; for, despite the contrary assertion that has recently become tolerably current, essentially this doctrine of inspiration has been the doctrine of the Church of all ages and of all names.

---

[6]See. ed. 10, 1656, p. 7.

36

THE INERRANCY OF
THE ORIGINAL AUTOGRAPHS*

Our Lord and his apostles looked upon the entire truthfulness and utter trustworthiness of that body of writings which they called "Scripture," as so fully guaranteed by the inspiration of God, that they could appeal to them confidently in all their statements of whatever kind as absolutely true; adduce their deliverances on whatever subject with a simple "it is written," as the end of all strife; and treat them generally in a manner which clearly exhibits that in their view "Scripture says" was equivalent to "God says."

Following this example and teaching, the Westminster Confession of Faith calls "all the books of the Old and New Testament," in their entirety, "Holy Scripture or the Word of God written" (i. 2), "all which," it affirms, "are given by inspiration of God," who is "the author thereof," being himself "truth itself" (i. 4). Accordingly, it declares all these "books of the Old and New Testament," in their entirety, to be "of infallible truth and divine authority" (i. 5), and asserts that "a Christian believeth to be true whatsoever is revealed in the Word, for the authority of God himself speaking therein" (xiv. 2). For the further clearing of difficulties, the Confession distinguishes between translations of Scripture and the originals, and with reference to the originals between the transmitted and the original text (i. 8). Of translations, it declares that they competently transmit the Word of God for all practical purposes. Of the transmitted text, it affirms that it has been providentially kept so pure as to retain full authoritativeness in all

*The Independent, Mar. 23, 1893.

controversies of religion. Of the original text, it asserts that it was "immediately inspired of God"—a technical term in common theological use at the time, by which the idea of divine authorship, in the highest sense of the word, is conveyed. To this original text alone, therefore, it is to be understood, are attributed, in their fullest sense, the various "qualities" of Scripture which are ascribed to it in the Confession, on the ground of its being the Word of God—such as divine authority, perfection, perspicuity, entire trustworthiness, and the like.

Efforts are at present being made to undermine the historical truthfulness of the Scriptural history, in the interests of a school of criticism whose view of the historical development of religious usages and doctrines in Israel is not accordant with that of the Biblical writers. The Presbyterian Church has thus been forced, under the constitutional provision of its Form of Government (xii. 5), to remind the churches of its communion of their confessional doctrine of Scripture, which is being attacked and endangered by this advocacy of a historically untrustworthy Bible. In the course of the controversy which has arisen, the phrase which has been placed at the head of this article has somehow been forced to the front, and a strong effort is being made to make it appear the sole "bone of contention." This is not at all the case. The present controversy concerns something much more vital than the bare "inerrancy" of the Scriptures, whether in the copies or in the "autographs." It concerns the trustworthiness of the Bible in its express declarations, and in the fundamental conceptions of its writers as to the course of the history of God's dealings with his people. It concerns, in a word, the authority of the Biblical representations concerning the nature of revealed religion, and the mode and course of its revelation. The issue raised is whether we are to look upon the Bible as containing a divinely guaranteed and wholly trustworthy account of God's redemptive revelation, and the course of his gracious dealings with his people; or as merely a mass of more or less trustworthy materials, out of which we are to sift the facts in order to put together a trustworthy account of God's redemptive revelation and the course of his dealings with his people. It is of the greatest importance that the Presbyterian Church should not permit its attention to be distracted from this serious issue.

Nevertheless, although the phrase "the inerrancy of the original autographs" is not an altogether happy one to express the doctrine of the Scriptures and of the Westminster Confession as to the entire truthfulness of the Scriptures as given by God, yet it is intended to express this doctrine, and does, in its own way, sharply affirm it; and the strenuous opposition to it which has arisen, has its roots in doubt or denial of this Scriptural and Confessional doctrine. It is important here too, therefore, that the true issue should not be permitted to be confused by the skilful manipulation of a mere phrase. It has therefore seemed proper to call attention to some of the curiosities of the recent controversial use of this phrase with a view to keeping the real issue clear.

It is certainly a curiosity of the controversial use of a phrase, to see the Church's *limitation* of her affirmation of the absolute truth and trustworthiness of the Scriptures in all their declarations, to those Scriptures "as they came from God," represented as an additional strain upon faith. Would these controversialists have the Church affirm the absolute truth of scribes' slips and printers' errors? If we were to take some of them "at the foot of the letter," they would seem to represent it as easier to believe in the infallibility of compositors and proof-readers than the infallibility of God. Everybody knows that no book was ever printed, much less hand-copied, into which some errors did not intrude in the process; and as we do not hold the author responsible for these in an ordinary book, neither ought we to hold God responsible for them in this extraordinary book which we call the Bible. It is *the Bible* that we declare to be "of infallible truth"—the Bible that God gave us, not the corruptions and slips which scribes and printers have given us, some of which are in every copy. Yet a recent writer,[1] with a great show of solemnity, calls upon the

---

[1]Dr. Henry Van Dyke of New York in *The Bible as It Is*.

Presbyterian Church for "a frank and full disavowal," "of any intention to make the inerrancy of the original autographs (as distinguished from *the Bible as it is*) a test of orthodoxy." But what is it that distinguishes "the Bible as it is" from the original autographs? Just scribes' corruptions and printers' errors; nothing else. And so this controversialist would have the Church "frankly and fully" disavow attaching more inerrancy to the Word of God, given by inspiration to men, than to the errors and corruptions of careless or bungling scribes and printers! Taken literally, this demand would amount to a strong asseveration of the utter untrustworthiness of the Bible.

It is another curiosity of the controversial use of a phrase, to find the Church's careful definition of the complete truth and trustworthiness of the Scriptures as belonging, as a matter of course, only to the genuine text of Scripture, represented as an appeal from the actually existing texts of Scripture to a lost autograph—as if it were the autographic *codex* and not the autographic *text* that is in question. Thus, we have heard a vast deal, of late, of "the first manuscripts of the Bible which no living man has ever seen," of "Scriptures that have disappeared forever," of "original autographs which have vanished";[2] concerning the contents of which these controversialists are willing to declare, with the emphasis of italics, that they know nothing, that no man knows anything, and that they are perfectly contented with their ignorance. Now, again, if this were to be taken literally, it would amount to a strong asseveration that the Bible, as God gave it to men, is lost beyond recovery; and that men are shut up, therefore, to the use of Bibles so hopelessly corrupted that it is impossible now to say what was in the original autographs and what not! In proportion as we draw back from this contention—which is fortunately as absurd as it is extreme—in that proportion do we affirm that we have the autographic text; that not only we but all men may see it if they will; and that God has not permitted the Bible to become so hopelessly corrupt that its restoration

---

[2] Drs. Van Dyke, McPherson, and Hamlin.

to its original text is impossible. As a matter of fact, the great body of the Bible is, in its autographic text, in the worst copies of the original texts in circulation; practically the whole of it is in its autographic text in the best texts in circulation; and he who will may today read the autographic text in large stretches of Scripture without legitimate doubt, and, in the New Testament at least, may know precisely at what rarely occurring points, and to what not very great extent, doubts as to the genuineness of the text are still possible. If our controversial brethren could only disabuse their minds of the phantom of an autographic *codex,* which their excitement has raised (and which, apart from their excited vision "no living man has ever seen"), they might possibly see with the Church that genuine text of Scripture which is "by the singular care and providence of God" still preserved to us, and might agree with the Church that it is to it alone that authority and trustworthiness and utter truthfulness are to be ascribed.

Another curiosity of controversy is found in the representation that the Church, in affirming the entire truthfulness and trustworthiness of the genuine text of Scripture, asserts that this text is wholly free from all those difficulties and apparent discrepancies which we find in "the Scriptures as we have them." Of course the Church has never made such an assertion. That some of the difficulties and apparent discrepancies in current texts disappear on the restoration of the true text of Scripture is undoubtedly true. That all the difficulties and apparent discrepancies in current texts of Scripture are matters of textual corruption, and not, rather, often of historical or other ignorance on our part, no sane man ever asserted. We must not, indeed, confuse *real* discrepancies and *apparent* discrepancies,[3] quoting Dr. Charles Hodge's confession[4] of his inability "to account for" some of the difficulties of the Bible, to justify our implication that they may very easily be accounted for—viz., as natural human errors in the genuine text of Scripture. The Church does indeed affirm that the genuine

---

[3]As Dr. Van Dyke and others do.
[4]*Systematic Theology*, Vol. I, p. 170.

text of Scripture is free from real discrepancies and errors; but she does not assert that the genuine text of Scripture is free from those apparent discrepancies and other difficulties, on the ground of which, imperfectly investigated, the errancy of the Bible is usually affirmed. The Church recognizes her duty to preserve the text of "the Scriptures of truth" committed to her keeping pure, and to transmit it pure to future generations; it is only that text that she trusts, and only on it will she hang the credit of her teachings. But she does not expect to be freed from the duty of studying this text, or from the duty of defending it against the assaults of unbelief. It would be a miraculously perfect text indeed with which imperfectly informed men could not find fault.

Still another curiosity of the present controversy is found in the constant asseveration which we hear about us, that the distinction drawn by the Presbyterian Church between the genuine text of Scripture and the current and more or less corrupt texts in general circulation, is something new. This is a rather serious arraignment of the common sense of the whole series of preceding generations. What! Are we to believe that no man until our wonderful nineteenth century, ever had acumen enough to detect a printer's error or to realize the liability of hand-copied manuscripts to occasional corruption? Are we really to believe that the happy possessors of "the Wicked Bible" held "thou shalt commit adultery" to be as divinely "inerrant" as the genuine text of the seventh commandment—on the ground that the "inerrancy of the original autographs of the Holy Scriptures" must not be asserted "as distinguished from the Holy Scriptures which we now possess"? Or, that those who read in their copies at 1 Cor. xv. 51 (as the possessors of one edition did), "we shall not all sleep, but we shall all be hanged," would violently defend "the Bible as it is" against the claims of the genuine text? Of course, every man of common sense from the beginning of the world has recognized the difference between the genuine text and the errors of transmission, and has attached his confidence to the former in rejection of the latter.

Richard Baxter was speaking no more for himself than for his whole age, and all the ages before him, when he defended the present position of the Presbyterian Church with such direct statements as these: "All that the holy writers have recorded is true (and no falsehood in the Scriptures but what is from the error of scribes and translators)"; "No error or contradiction is in it, but what is in some copies, by failure of preservers, transcribers, printers, and translators"; and many more passages of the same purport. In exactly similar manner Calvin and Luther repeatedly assign special difficulties to the corrupt form of transmitted Scripture as distinguished from the genuine text—no doubt sometimes without sufficient warrant; but that is so far from being the question that it is an additional evidence of their full recognition of the distinction in discussion. The Fathers, because they were dependent on manuscript (as distinct from printed) texts, in which corruption was unavoidably greater, were even more free in assuming that difficulties which they could not explain were due to corruption of text, rather than to lack of insight on their part, and much more rather than to aboriginal error in Scripture. Augustine's statement fairly represents the judgment of the Patristic Age: "I have learned to defer this respect and honor to the canonical books of Scripture alone, that I most firmly believe that no one of their authors has committed any error in writing. And if in their writings I am perplexed by anything which seems to me contrary to truth, I do not doubt that it is nothing else than either that the manuscript is corrupt, or that the translator has not followed what was said, or that I have myself failed to understand it."

From these facts alone, it is already apparent how seriously erroneous it is to say, as has been recently said, that the Westminster divines never "thought of the original manuscripts of the Bible as distinct from the copies in their possession."[5] They could not help thinking of them. I fancy I see John Lightfoot's face, on someone making that remark to *him,* just after he had

---

[5]Dr. E. D. Morris in *The Evangelist.*

risen from the composition—say of his *Harmony, Chronicle, and Order of the New Testament.* And I should vastly like to read his account of the remark and of his answer to it, as he might write it to one of his friends—say to "the great Mr. Selden, the learnedest man upon the earth," or to "the all-learned Mr. Wheelocke, to whom nothing is too difficult or unattainable," or to "the admirable Dr. Usher, the magazine of all manner of literature and knowledge"—who was just then helping Walton in the preparation of his great polyglot. I should like to see how such a remark would affect Samuel Rutherford, while the ink was still wet on the pages of his controversy with John Goodwin on the very point of the relation of the inspired autographs to the uninspired but providentially cared-for transmission. Why, this was the burning question as to the Scriptures in the Westminster age. Nobody in that circle doubted the plenary inspiration and absolute errorlessness of the genuine text; the question in discussion was in what sense and to what extent could there be posited a divine superintendence of the transmission, and how far could the current copies and translations be depended on as vehicles of the Word of God. The Westminster men took high ground in this controversy; and their writings are full of the echoes of it.

It is, therefore, thoroughly misleading to represent the distinction made in the Westminster Confession between the *immediate inspiration* of the original text of Scripture and the *providential supervision* of the transmission as either accidental or meaningless. The historical doubt really is not whether it may not mean less than is now attributed to it, but whether it must not mean more. And the declaration of the Presbyterian Church that her Standards teach that "the inspired Word as it came from God is without error," is a simple affirmation of the obvious meaning of those Standards, and certainly is accordant with the teachings of the Bible and within the limits of common sense.

37

THE WESTMINSTER CONFESSION
AND THE ORIGINAL AUTOGRAPHS*

In the assault on the trustworthiness of the Scriptures, with which the Presbyterian Church has been vexed for the last few years, two closely related but separable assertions have been made prominent. One of these concerned the gift of Scripture, or in other words the doctrine of Biblical inspiration. The other concerned the transmission of Scripture, or in other words the doctrine of Biblical preservation. In the course of the discussion attention has been chiefly concentrated upon the former topic. But the assailants of the trustworthiness of the Scriptures have no more sharply denied the plenary inspiration of the Bible as God gave it to men than they have denied the safe preservation of this Bible as God gave it to men. Their contention has ever been twofold: that God never gave an errorless Bible, and if he did, that errorless Bible is no longer in the possession of men. The air has been thick with satirical references to autographic copies which no man has ever seen, which are hopelessly lost, which can never be recovered. And the defenders of the trustworthiness of Scripture have been sarcastically asked what the use is of contending so strenuously for the plenary inspiration of autographs which have thus forever passed away.

The answer is very obvious that such a contention would be undoubtedly very foolish indeed; but that no one ever made such a foolish contention. It has not been those that have been defending the doctrine of the plenary inspiration of the autographs who have asserted the hopeless loss of this plenarily

---

*The Presbyterian Messenger, Sept. 13, 1894.

inspired text. The denial of the plenary inspiration of the autographs and of the safe preservation of the inspired text have rather gone hand in hand. The defenders of the trustworthiness of the Scriptures have constantly asserted, together, that God gave the Bible as the errorless record of his will to men, and that he has, in his superabounding grace, preserved it for them to this hour—yea, and will preserve it for them to the end of time.

So little has the necessity for this double affirmation been forgotten, that it has been formally made in all the official declarations of the Church on the questions at issue. It is its care to include both affirmations, for example, which constitutes the satisfactoriness of the now famous deliverance of the Portland assembly, and which has created the persistent criticism of and opposition to it in certain quarters. That deliverance reads:

> The General Assembly would remind all under its care that it is a fundamental doctrine that the Old and New Testaments are the inspired and infallible Word of God. Our Church holds that the inspired Word, as it came from God, is without error. The assertion of the contrary cannot but shake the confidence of the people in the sacred books.

Men have sought to make themselves merry over the sentence: "Our Church holds that the inspired Word, as it came from God, *is* without error." They have charged the "is" with being ungrammatical; with being nonsensical; with being ridiculous. It is, however, only a succinct and emphatic way of stating the whole truth: that not only *was* the inspired Word, as it came from God, without error, but that it remains so; that the Church still has this inspired Word and still has it without error. So, again, the deliverances of the Washington Assembly unite the two points, and affirm: "that the original Scriptures of the Old and New Testaments, being immediately inspired of God, were without error," and "that the Bible, as we now have it, in its various translations and versions, when freed from all errors and mistakes of translators, copyists, and printers, is the very Word of God, and consequently wholly without error."

According to the recent deliverances of the Church's supreme court, therefore, it is as truly heresy to affirm that the inerrant Bible has been lost to men as it is to declare that there never was an inerrant Bible.

If now the question is raised whether the Church is justified by her Standards in laying stress on the preservation as well as on the inspiration of Scripture, we do not know how it could be better answered than it has been in a recent editorial in *The Messenger;* and we beg leave to borrow from this editorial and make our own the following admirable exposition of the Confessional teaching on this subject:

> The language of the Westminster Standards on this subject is very plain and very full, as it says, "The Old Testament in Hebrew . . . and the New Testament in Greek . . . being immediately inspired by God and by his singular care and providence kept pure in all ages are, therefore, authentical; so as in all controversies of religion, the Church is finally to appeal unto them."
>
> This states two things clearly and distinctly: First, the original Scriptures were immediately inspired of God. Second, they were kept pure in all ages by his singular care and providence. Take these two statements and we have the solid rock on which to build our faith. Accepting fully these two statements, we can say that the Bible, as we now have it, is inspired of God, kept pure by his singular care and providence, and is the only infallible rule of faith and duty for men. Reject either statement, and the other is of little value. Reject the statement of original inspiration and the Scriptures are not worth preserving; reject the doctrine of divine preservation, and the original inspiration is of little value. It is when the two go together, explaining and interpreting each other, that we have the really valuable doctrine of the inspired Bible.

It is thus perfectly clear that, according to the Confession, the preservation of the Scriptures in their purity is of as vital importance to the Church as their original inspiration. The Presbyterian Church is committed by its Confession of Faith, no less than by its recent deliverances, to the doctrine that the inspired Scriptures have been preserved pure through the ages, as truly as to the doctrine that the Scriptures were given by the immediate inspiration of God.

Notwithstanding the clearness of the Confession upon this matter, however, it has not infrequently been seriously misinterpreted, and that in opposite directions. On the one side, its declaration has sometimes been all but evacuated of meaning. On the other, it has been pressed to convey a sense which is certainly far beyond its meaning.

It has not been uncommon to say, for example, that all that the Confession means is that the Scriptures have been, in the providence of God, kept "measurably pure," or, as it is otherwise phrased, "adequately pure," "pure enough to serve the purposes for which they were given." The Confession, however, does not say "measurably pure," or "adequately pure"; but "pure" without qualification or limitation. It adds, indeed, that because kept "pure" they are therefore still "authentical," which in the language of the day means "authoritative": but this does not suggest a limit to their purity, but is the proof of their perfect purity. Only the pure Word of God is simply authoritative. So far as it is impure, so far it loses its authoritativeness. We must take the language of the Confession as it stands, and in its natural and historical meaning. And so taking it here it affirms, without qualification, the preservation of Scripture in entire purity. Professor Henry Preserved Smith is quite right, then, when he says that the Confession does not declare that "the texts have been kept *singularly* pure, but that they have been kept pure"; and adds: "If the affirmation of truth means absolute truth, certainly the affirmation of purity means absolute purity. That one was attained by inspiration, the other by singular care and providence, does not affect the result, which is stated as sharply in one case as in the other."

But Professor Smith goes as far astray in the opposite direction, in misinterpreting the Confession, when he would urge us to believe that its language here asserts the absolute purity of every, or of any one, copy of Scripture. When he says, "What the Confession affirms, it affirms of the seventeenth century Hebrew and Greek editions which are more imperfect than our own," he puts into the Confession something which its authors did not put there. Thus he would drive us into a dilemma and force us either to modify the Confession's assertion of the truth of inspired Scriptures, or to declare, with what he affirms to be the meaning of the Confession, the "absolute purity" of every copy of Scripture. It is not difficult to decline so factitious a dilemma. The Confession knows nothing of it. It does assert the preservation of Scripture in "absolute purity": but it does not assert the "absolute purity" of "the seventeenth century editions," or of every copy, or of any copy of Scripture. We shall scan the text of the Confession in vain for any allusion to such a monstrous assertion. It would be to convict its authors (who had variant copies in their hands) of incredible folly to suppose them capable of such an assertion. The most cursory appeal to their writings on the subject will exonerate them from so unheard-of a charge. They do assert the preservation of Scripture to the Church in absolute purity by God's singular care and providence. But they did not find that Scripture, in all its purity, in any one copy or in any one printer's impression. They recognized the fallibilities of copyists and typesetters; and they looked for the pure text of Scripture, not in one copy, but in all copies. "What mistake is in one copy," they declared through one of their number, "is corrected in another." And so they proclaimed the perfect preservation of Scripture, in its absolute purity, through all ages, in entire consistency with the recognition that many copies might come from the press filled with corruptions, and that no copy would ever be made by men, wholly free from error.

Now it is easy to say that thus less than perfect assurance is given to each simple man as he looks into the pages of his own Bible, that he has before him the pure Word of God. This is indeed so far true. And the Westminster divines felt the necessity, therefore, of going on to declare the adequacy of the ordinary Bibles in use among Christian men, for all the purposes of the religious life and hope. This declaration occupies the latter portion of the same section (i. 8) from which we have already quoted. After declaring that the Scriptures were given by the immediate inspiration of God, and have been preserved by his singular care and providence, they go on to declare that the saving and sanctifying Word of God is competently contained for all the needs of the Christian life in the current vernacular translations, and to urge men to feed their souls upon it as there brought within reach of all.

There are, therefore, three parts to the Presbyterian doctrine of the Bible as brought out in this section of the Confession. The original Hebrew and Greek Scriptures are distinguished first of all from translations. The originals alone are declared to be inspired, and therefore authoritative for the determining of points of religious doctrine. The translations are declared, however, competently to represent the inspired Bible for all general purposes. When speaking of the originals, two things are affirmed. One concerns their origination: the other their preservation. The one declares that they came into being by the immediate inspiration of God: the other that they have been kept pure by his singular care and providence. The activities of God concerned in their original gift and in their preservation are distinguished. It was "*inspiration*" in the one case; "*providence*" in the other. Both are carried to their highest power by the accompanying adjectives. It was by "*immediate* inspiration" that God gave the Scriptures: it was by his "*singular* care and providence" that he has preserved them. But the two kinds of activity are not confused. And these distinctions must be preserved in our interpretation of the Confession. We must not confound inspiration and providence—either by reducing the inspiration by which the Scriptures were given to the level of providential guidance of the writers, or by raising the providence by which they have been preserved to the level of inspiration. The Confession intends the distinction to be taken at its full value: one was an immediate and the other a mediate activity of God. And the product corresponded to the difference: one produced the plenarily inspired Bible, every word of which is the Word of God; the other produced the safe transmission of that Word, but not without signs of human fallibility here and there in the several copies.

We thus have brought before us by the Confession, in turn, the original autograph of Scripture, produced by the immediate inspiration of God; the preservation of this autographic text in a multitude of copies whose production is presided over by God's singular care and providence; and the ordinary Bibles in the hands of the people, each of which conveys divine truth to the reader with competent adequacy for all the needs of the Christian life. And the Presbyterian doctrine of the Bible, therefore, embraces these three points: (1) the plenary inspiration of the Bible as God gave it, by which it is made the Word of God, trustworthy in every one of its affirmations; (2) the safe preservation of the Bible as God gave it, so as to be accessible to men, in the use of the ordinary means of securing a trustworthy text; and (3) the adequate transmission of the saving truth in every and any honest translation, so that the Word of God is accessible to all at all times for all ordinary purposes. The hearty acceptance of all three of these propositions is necessary, if we would range ourselves alongside of the Westminster Confession.

38

THE RIGHTS OF CRITICISM AND OF THE CHURCH*

We hear a great deal nowadays of the right of Criticism, spoken with a certain air of conscious heroism, as if Criticism (with a big C, doubtless because it is "Higher"), were being dreadfully oppressed by somebody. But we know no one who denies the right of Criticism. Everybody uses it; and everybody honors it. It is the instrument by which we test truth. And in proportion as the truth is important or the claims which it makes on us are supreme, is not only the right of Criticism allowed, but its duty insisted upon. The indifference with which we allow the claim of a book to be a romance of impossible life by Mr. Rider Haggard, or a romance of impossible canon-building by Mr. Herbert E. Ryle, passes, for the student of historical politics at least, into interested alertness to the evidence when it claims to be the lost work of Aristotle on the Constitution of Athens, and for all of us into something more than interest when it claims to be the Constitution of the land in which we live, with its declaration of our rights and its safeguarding of our liberties. It ought to, and it does, rise into the keenest and the most searching critical inquiry, when the book claims, or is claimed, to be the law of God binding on all our souls, and the discovery of the only way of salvation for lost sinners. So far from the Bible being less subject to criticism than other books, we are bound to submit its unique claims to a criticism of unique rigor. Criticism is the mode of procedure by which we assure ourselves that it is what it claims to be. Who will cast his soul's eternal welfare on an uncriticized way

---

*The Presbyterian, Apr. 13, 1892, pp. 7-8; and The Presbyterian Observer, Apr. 14, 1892, pp. 2-3.

of life? It is because we believe in criticism, and practise it with unflinching severity, that we reject the revelations of Mohammed, the book of Mormon, and the religion of Israel according to Kuenen and his fellows, and accept and rest upon the religion of Israel according to Moses and the prophets and the gospel of Christ according to the evangelists and the apostles. When such concerns are at stake, we wish to know the pure facts; and every one of us exercises all the faculties God has given him and exhausts all the tests at his command to assure himself of the facts. Criticism consists in careful scrutiny of the facts, and is good or bad in proportion to the accuracy and completeness with which the facts are apprehended and collected, and the skill and soundness with which they are marshaled and their meaning read. Deny the validity of criticism of the Bible! Nobody dreams of it. Abate the earnestness of our practice of it! At our soul's peril, we dare not. In proportion as we are awake to what the Bible means for man, will we search the Scriptures to see whether these things are so.

Whence, then, arises the plaint which we hear about us, that the right of Criticism is impugned and the rights of Criticism denied? From the ineradicable tendency of man to confound the right of Criticism with the rightness of his own criticism. We may safely recognize this to be a common human tendency; for, as all of us doubtless know by this time, *humanum est errare*. But as soon as our attention is directed to it, the way seems to be opened to remind ourselves of a few distinctions, which it will be well for the Presbyterian Church to attend to in the crisis which is at present impending over her—a crisis the gravity of which cannot be over-estimated for a church of Christ, to which has been committed the function of being the pillar and ground of the truth.

I

MISLEADING METHODS OF CRITICISM

It is not to impugn the right or the duty of criticism to declare that an untrustworthy and misleading method of criticism is not right but wrong. Criticism, we are justly told, is only a method. So is mathematics only a method. But this does not vindicate the correctness of every mathematical calculation, by every hand. Neither figures nor criticism will lie; but the men that use them may manage to reach very false conclusions through them despite their incorruptible veracity. And we soon discover, as there is mathematics and mathematics, so there is criticism and criticism. Because we believe in mathematics, we do not care to trust our weight on a bridge the strain of which has been calculated by a misleading method. An eminent professor of mathematics tells me that he can prove by an unexceptional process that one is equal to two. Some of the critics seem to have learned his method. Am I impugning the right of Criticism when I politely decline to believe that their criticism is right?

What is the present situation with regard to the criticism of the Old Testament? On the credit of a method of criticism which is discredited wherever it can be tested, we are being asked to believe that a large number of the books in the Old Testament are not the product of their apparent ages or their reputed authors, but the stratified deposits of the sea of time. On this evidence, at least, we respectfully decline. We point out the inconsequence of this method of criticism elsewhere. We recall the weary shadow-dance of similar methods in the sphere of the New Testament literature, and the recession of their boasted results into the realm of shadows whenever the light is fully turned on. We point to that admirable *jeu d'esprit* of the ingenuous Mr. McRealsham by which the very same methods applied satirically to the Epistle to the Romans are shown to yield parallel results—and lo! that logically compacted epistle falls apart into four underlying documents, discriminated from one another with a sharpness and a breadth which must make the Pentateuchal critic turn green from envy. Or, if we must have a real case, which is no *jeu d'esprit* but solemn earnest, we point to Scherer's brilliant analysis of the Prologue of Faust, which distributed its parts to their proper periods of Goethe's life, on the ground of deep-reaching differences of style and internal inconsistencies, such as were thought inexplicable save on the supposition of composition at different times and subsequent combination. But Ehrich Schmidt publishes the oldest manuscript of the poem, and lo! "it is the 'young Goethe' who wrote the prologue essentially as it now stands, in a single gush; it is the same 'young Goethe' who assumes the style at the same time of an effervescent youngster and of a cynical grey-beard." We point to the thorough refutation of this method in principle and in results by such Old Testament critics as possess enough independence of scholarship and judgment not to be swayed beyond their center of gravity by the reigning faction. Or if we glance at the method itself we are led to commend the insight of one of its founders, Graf, who already pointed out the danger of its degenerating into an argument in a circle, as we perceive that it first creates the documents it finds by distributing all the elements of one kind to each, and then proves their reality by the fact of this constant difference. We decline to be caught in this circle and whirled around until we mistake our giddiness for superior wisdom. It is not denying the right of Criticism to assert that this criticism is not right, and cannot lead to right, but only to wrong conclusions.

II

BIBLIOCLASTIC CRITICISM

It is not to impugn the right of Criticism to declare that such a misleading criticism, when used as an engine to undermine the divine authority of Scriptures, vindicated as that authority abundantly is by overwhelming evidence thoroughly tested by a sound and truth-eliciting criticism, is not only wrong but a serious wrong. That the effects of the current type of Old Testament criticism are of the nature of a disillusionment as over against the Bible, lies in the nature of the case, and has been illustrated lately by Horton—whose thoroughly disillusioned (and disillusioning) book on *Inspiration* Professor Cheyne recommends as the best he knows for these times of distress—from an old-fashioned clock which in youth he deemed to be of massive black marble with golden face, but which his wiser years have discovered to be only wood and gilt. Let any reader note the number of portions of the Old Testament which Dr. Driver in his recent sober *Introduction to the Literature of the Old Testament* adjudges to be "scarcely historical"; and then ask whether the authority of a historical revelation can be maintained when so large a portion of its historical record is "unhistorical." Then let him remember that the critical analysis which is the chief result of this method turns largely upon the discovery of disagreements and inconsistencies in the present texts. No wonder it has become common to speak of the authority of the Scriptures as belonging to, and their inspiration as residing in, not the form but the substance, not the husk but the kernel. It is a prophet of our own whose language runs: "The divine substance has been given in human forms, and no one will truly understand the Bible until he has learned to distinguish between the temporal, circumstantial, and variable form, and the eternal, essential, and permanent substance." We seem to have heard something like this before. But whether in the mouth of the old German Rationalist, or the new American "Critic," it is a position which must ultimate in the denial of inspiration properly so called altogether; since inspiration as distinguished from revelation necessarily concerns the form, or, as it is now commonly spoken of (not without an undesirable purpose), "the record of the revelation," not the "revelation itself." Accordingly, Professor Stapfer says frankly: "The doctrine of an inspiration distinct from revelation and legitimating it, is an error." And Dr. Washington Gladden, who desires us to note that he follows the leadership of "conservative criticism" only, with equal frankness says: "Evidently neither the theory of verbal inspiration, nor the theory of plenary inspiration can be made to fit the facts which a careful study of the writings themselves brings before us. These writings are not inspired in the sense which we have commonly given to that word." When we remember the strong tendency of these same "conservative critics" to reduce revelation itself to what they call "historical revelation," to *acts,* not *words,* or as Dr. Gladden expresses it again, to the "superintending care" of God over the progress of history, "his moral leadership in history"—we may estimate how nearly to a minimum the supernatural element has been reduced in a Bible a large portion of the historical record of which is "unhistorical."

Nor are we to be soothed by the assurance that though the authority of the Scriptures is gone for all else, it remains to it as a religious guide. In the nature of the case this can hardly be. Nor does this critical school find it possible to so conceive of it. We observe Dr. Samuel Ives Curtis writing: "We find in the theology of ancient Israel the divine revelation not only contained in earthen vessels, but also, on account of its temporal and educational character, containing incomplete and *even erroneous statements as to certain forms of religious thought.* That is, the revelation which has come from God is allowed to stand in juxtaposition with some forms of human error." Criticism must, therefore, discriminate among the distinctively religious teachings of the Bible, accepting some and rejecting others. We must thank a recent English writer, Mr. J. J. Lias, for permitting us to see with equal frankness whereto this must logically grow. "Even for matters of religion themselves," he tells us, the Bible has lost its authority, and we cannot "command assent to the contents of a volume which contains an infinity of propositions" further than "to require the acceptance of a few simple statements embodying all the essentials for salvation." We are not surprised to find on reading further that these "simple essential truths" are not according to the Gospels of either Matthew, Mark, Luke, or John, nor yet of Paul or Peter—but according to the gospel of Schleiermacher. Is it denying the right of Criticism to assert that this criticism is not only wrong, but is committing a serious wrong against the Church and the whole world lying in wickedness, in undermining confidence in the one charter of salvation?

III

ANTICHRISTIC CRITICISM

It is not to impugn the right of Criticism to declare that such a misleading criticism, when so far pressing beyond its mark as to curtail the trustworthiness of the witness of the Truth himself as a teacher of truth, is not only a wrong but an intolerable wrong to every Christian heart. Yet the current form of Old Testament criticism trembles on the verge of this gulf. The findings of its misleading method run athwart the implications of the words of him who spake as never man spake; and instead of adjusting its theories to accord with his teachings, it thinks of adjusting the God-man to its theories. Thus we have curious sustained efforts to minimize the amount and decisiveness of his teaching; new discussions of the propriety of "accommodation" in his teaching; and a whole new crop of studies on the limitations of our Lord's knowledge as man. When such a ball is once started rolling downwards, who knows to what it may grow? Not merely as a "critic" and as an "exegete," but also as a moralist and as a religious teacher, we shall find we have lost our Lord; if we cannot trust him as to the revelation of God (of which he, the Logos, was the revealer) of the past, how can we trust him as the revealer of God for the future? Are we indeed to say with one "critic" that "interpretation is essentially a scientific function, and one conditioned by the existence of scientific means, which in relation to the Old Testament were but imperfectly at the command of Jesus," and so rid ourselves of his authority in interpreting the Old Testament? Are we to say with another "critic" that as a logician or critic he belongs to his times, and as such had "a definite restricted outfit and outlook, which could be only those of his own day and generation"? But let us go at once to the bottom. W. Hay M. H. Aiken is reported to have permitted himself recently to use such words as these: "Literary criticism is a science, and one that requires as much exercise of mind as the pursuit of mathematics. You are not surprised that Christ, in his manhood, was not the equal of Newton in mathematical knowledge; why should you be surprised if he prove not to have been the equal of Wellhausen in literary criticism? The case may be put thus: In the truth of his manhood, Christ would naturally accept the views of his contemporaries as to the authorship

of the Old Testament Scripture, just as one of us would naturally accept the common view of the authorship of Shakespeare's
plays in spite of recent transatlantic theories on that subject.
The only thing that would induce on his part a view that was
something more than the popular opinion of the period in
which he lived would be an express revelation. Of course, if
God specifically revealed to Christ that the Pentateuch was
written by Moses, *cadit quaestio,* let God be true, and every
critic, if not a liar, at any rate mistaken."

But is not Christ himself God? Is it true that we could not
expect him to be a "critic," because criticism requires so much
exercise of mind? Are we rushing down to the pit of a new and
crasser unitarianism? What Christ is this that Aiken pictures
before us? Not the Christ of the Bible, who is our prophet
and our guide; who is the Truth itself incarnated; who is
dramatized before our eyes in the length and breadth of the
Gospels, not as a child of his times, limited by the mental
outlook of his day, but as a teacher to his and to all times,
sent from God as not more the power of God than the wisdom
of God; and whose own witness to himself was, "Verily, verily
I say unto you, we speak that we know, and testify that we
have seen; and ye receive not our witness. If I have told you
of earthly things and ye believed not, how shall ye believe, if
I tell you heavenly things?" Is it to deny the right of Criticism, to declare that a criticism which, starting on a wrong
path, rushes headlong into the very face of the Truth himself, is
an intolerable wrong which no Christian heart can calmly bear?

IV

THE CHURCH'S RIGHT TO CRITICISM

It is not to impugn the right of Criticism to declare that those
who adopt a misleading criticism as their guide to truth; and
draw from it conclusions inconsistent with what is held as
precious truth by the Church with which they are connected;
and teach these conclusions in opposition to the public Confession of the Church; may not rightly continue to receive the
endorsement of that Church as sound teachers of religion.

The refusal of the Church to remain responsible before the world for their teaching is no blow at the right of Criticism in the abstract, or even at the freedom of these "critics" to teach their special form of criticism. It is, on the one hand, only the assertion by the Church of *her* right to teach only what she believes, without infringing in the least upon the right of others to teach what they please on their own responsibility and in their own names; and on the other hand the liberation of the new thinkers from whatever trammels to their thought and speech they may recognize as growing out of the pledges they may have taken to believe and teach the doctrines of the Church. Or is the Critic only to be free and the Church bound? Let him exercise freely his right to criticize; and let the Church also be free to test not only the truth of the Scriptures as he does, but also the truth of his theories of the Scriptures, and to act accordingly. What Democrat would feel that his liberty of thought and speech were infringed by the refusal of a Republican club to become or remain sponsor of his political teachings? But, you say, no Democrat would desire to become or remain a member of a Republican club. That is the strangeness of the situation. One wonders that a new Criticism involving, as we are told, a wholly reconstructed theology should find so much attraction in a "traditionalist" Church of an "outworn" creed; or should care to do business under its trademark.

Hear the parable of the thistles. Thistles certainly have beauties of their own, and many virtues, which nobody would care to deny. But they do seem out of place in a garden designed for roses, even though they proclaim themselves more beautiful than any roses in the garden. And the husbandman seems to have a duty towards thistles growing in the garden, which even their irritable *noli me tangere* ought not to deter him from executing, with all due kindness indeed, but with that firmness of touch which becomes one in dealing with thistles. Otherwise, what will he say to the Lord of the garden, whom even the more luxuriant growth of the thistles may not please, when they are tossing their bold heads in the bed intended for roses?

39

A REVIEW OF THREE BOOKS
ON INSPIRATION*

THEOPNEUSTIA: the Plenary Inspiration of the Holy Scriptures. By DR. L. GAUSSEN, David Scott's Translation, re-edited and revised by B. W. CARR, with a preface by C. H. SPURGEON. London: Passmore & Alabaster, Paternoster Buildings, 1888. Crown 8vo, pp. 367.

THE BIBLE DOCTRINE OF INSPIRATION EXPLAINED AND VINDICATED. By BASIL MANLY, D.D., LL.D., Professor in the Southern Baptist Theological Seminary, Louisville, Ky. New York: A. C. Armstrong & Son, 1888. 12mo, pp. x, 266.

WHAT IS THE BIBLE? An inquiry into the origin and nature of the Old and New Testaments, in the light of modern Biblical study. By GEORGE T. LADD, D.D., Professor of Philosophy in Yale University. New York: Charles Scribner's Sons, 1888. 12mo, pp. xiv, 497.

We welcome the reissue of Gaussen's *Theopneustia,* under the auspices of Spurgeon, as an especially timely publication. The critical study of the Biblical documents, considered as literature, which has characterized our age perhaps more markedly than any other period, has a tendency, by calling repeated attention to the human origin and human qualities of the Biblical books, to make men forget their divine origin and divine characteristics. No book can be named which is better fitted to correct this than Gaussen's admirable volume, the mission of which is not to develop a well-rounded and carefully guarded doctrine of inspiration, but to prove the existence of an everywhere present divine element in the Scriptures. So strictly does it hold itself to this task, that the care-

---

The Presbyterian Review, Oct. 1888.

less reader has not infrequently misunderstood it and charged it with teaching a mechanical theory of inspiration, which, however, its author earnestly repudiates, declaring that "he has never, for a single moment, entertained such an idea," and that he "feels the greatest repugnance to it."[1] As a matter of fact, it ought never to have been misunderstood; it is simply and straightforwardly written, and though laying the emphasis on the divine side of Scripture, it yet not only never denies, but always allows for the human side, and it repeatedly asserts, in the most explicit way, that the human element is never absent: "We hold that every verse, without exception, is from men, and every verse, without exception, is from God"; "every word of the Bible is as really from man as it is from God." In a word, Gaussen is an advocate of that view of inspiration which considers the Spirit of God and the spirit of man as cofactors in the production of Scripture, working so together that the whole product is both human and divine in all its parts; a view which has been explicitly taught by nearly all the Reformed divines, and which has been from the beginning implicitly believed by the whole Church, and which is the immediate presupposition of all Biblical deliverances on the subject, all of which converge to the definition that the things which the human authors write are at the same time the commandments of the Lord (1 Cor. xiv. 37).

Dr. Manly's volume takes its place by the side of Gaussen's in the doctrine that it teaches, and is worthy of a place by its side also in the lucidity of its exposition and defense of his truly Biblical conception. He defines "inspiration" as over against "revelation," as "that divine influence that secures the accurate transference of truth into human language by a speaker or writer, so as to be communicated to other men" (p. 37). What is lacking in this definition is fully supplied by an earlier passage, in which just expression is given both to the fact of dual authorship and to the effect of that fact in both humanizing the resultant writings and clothing them throughout with divine

---

[1]See Gaussen's *It Is Written,* ed. 3, London, pp. i-iv.

authority, so as that they are, in a true sense, in all their parts God's word to man: "The Bible is God's word to man throughout; yet at the same time it is really and thoroughly man's composition. . . . The Word is not *of* man as to its source, nor dependent *on* man as to its authority. It is *by* and *through* man as its medium; yet not simply as its channel along which it runs, like water through a lifeless pipe, but *through* and *by* man as the agent voluntarily active and intelligent in its communication. . . . It is all unmistakably the work of man. It is all by singular and accumulated evidence declared to be the Word of God; all written by man, all inspired by God" (p. 27; compare also pp. 168, 169). Dr. Manly divides his book into three parts, in which he first carefully explains the doctrine, then offers proof for it, and then defends it against objections. The whole is vigorously written, and is well adapted to the popular audience for which it is designed. Now and then something seems to be lacking in close statement, and now and then the ordering of the proofs seems not absolutely the best, or their development seems somewhat less complete or cogent than might have been. One or two statements (e.g., on p. 102) are not perfectly clear; probably the name of Bishop Lightfoot on page 234 is a slip of the pen. But these are small matters; the work is an admirable one, and admirably expounds and defends the true doctrine.

The core of this doctrine is the assertion of the coactivity of both the human and divine authors in the production of Scripture. And one of the clearest passages in Dr. Manly's book expounds the essential incompatibility of the ideas of inspiration and dictation. "The act of committing to writing that which is dictated," he writes, "differs very much from what we understand to have occurred in writing or speaking what is inspired. The difference is this: that there is, when we dictate, no control over the will of the amanuensis; and also that there is no aid to his memory, reflection, imagination, or power of expression, on the supposition of his being willing but unable to give accurately what had been communicated to him. Both the control and the imparted power which we believe to belong

to inspiration are lacking" (p. 66). In the underlying contention of this passage, that God uses men in inspiration, through
the spontaneous activities of their own human powers, Dr.
Manly can claim Dr. Ladd as "of his part"; for no one has
given stronger or better expression to this great truth than
Dr. Ladd. "Inspiration," he says, "is a spiritual effect within
the human spirit, a quickening and elevating and informing of
the spirit; it must all necessarily take place in accordance with
the constitution of the being in whom the effect takes place.
It follows from what has just been said that all the different
faculties of human nature, as they are employed in the service
of divine self-revelation and inspiration, must remain true to
the fundamental laws of their being. Indeed, senses, sensi-
bilities, intellect, and moral and religious powers can be
occupied in the process of revelation and inspiration only as
they conform to these laws. . . . If the senses act at all in
revelation, if the revelation be through a vision, for example,
they must act as senses; they must act under all those conditions of limitation which belong to the very constitution of
sense. . . . We note, further, that in the realizing of divine
revelation and inspiration the faculties of man act together as
a living unity. . . . The inspired man is always a man with a
brain and a body, with a characteristic experience, and so a
characteristic memory, with a certain attainment of intellect
and range and quality of judgment. . . . Inspiration receives
the whole man as its subject; it affects the whole man by the
quickening and elevating influences which it introduces into
the soul. . . . The memory of man is influenced by and employed in the work of revelation and inspiration, but always
according to its fundamental laws. . . . The powers of reflection
are also influenced by the work of inspiration, and yet they, too,
are influenced in accordance with their constitution as powers
of the human soul. . . . We see, then, that the true subject of
all inspiration, the producer of the Biblical literature as sacred
and inspired, is *man*. . . . Therefore, the revelation and inspiration of each prophet and apostle will have its peculiar
characteristics; and these characteristics will depend both

upon the circumstances amid which each prophet and apostle lives and also on the personal character of each" (pp. 125-131). This is most excellently said, and would be as acceptable to Dr. Manly and to Gaussen as it is to Dr. Ladd himself. Where they part company with him is not in any failure on their part to do full justice to the human in the authorship of the Scriptures, but in failure on his part to do justice to the divine in it. Dr. Manly was speaking of Dr. Ladd's earlier work, the *Doctrine of Sacred Scripture,* when he named him as "certainly the most elaborate and probably the ablest of all the recent assailants of the strict doctrine of the inspiration of sacred Scripture" (p. 47); but the description fits as well the present volume, which is professedly but a popularized abstract of its more bulky predecessor.

We do not quarrel with definitions. We are as ready to clothe our conception of the methods in which the divine and human have entered into the genesis of the Scriptures in the terms of Dr. Ladd's definitions as in those of our own. We could readily accept the threefold discrimination of "revelation, inspiration, utterance" (p. 114), and inquire what is the teaching of Scripture and right reason as to the divine influence exercised on the human authors of Scripture in each. What we emphatically dissent from in Dr. Ladd's treatment of the subject is his sustained effort to minimize the divine element at every stage of the process of the production of Scripture, to limit it by the human, and to remove it more and more into the background, until in large portions of Scripture it is all but completely dissipated. The agent of "revelation" he unhesitatingly declares to be God, and its form to be "manifold; it is by history, . . . law, prediction, and doctrine, but is preeminently in and by the God-man Jesus Christ" (p. 411). But he everywhere speaks of its mode in such a way as to magnify the human element in the product and to reduce the divine as nearly as possible to the level of providential care. It is described as in essence, a "stirring up of some thought in human minds" (p. 413); as a "planting and growth within the soul, of certain great moral and religious ideas" (p. 232); as resulting from "a spirit of revelation moving in history with varying degrees of illuminating and purifying, as well as working and dwelling in the minds of chosen disciples" (p. 330). In a word, revelation is the work of genius; "from time to time God brought before the nation of Israel, through its great geniuses of a moral and religious kind, the more abstract statement of truths regarding his own mysterious Being and mode of action" (p. 409), just as he reveals great principles of other sorts . through geniuses of other kinds; for "the differences between the two concern chiefly the nature of the truth divinely imparted" (p. 429; yet compare p. 439). Even the phenomena of prediction appear to Dr. Ladd to require no further explanation. With him, foresight is the result of insight (p. 116); and while prediction is a divine work within the soul (pp. 232, 249), it is so only as the result of the prophet's own forecast of God's plan, founded on the moral and religious ideas which have been planted within him. In order to account for it, it is "unwarrantable" "to resort to a theory of 'remarkable coincidences' and 'shrewd calculations,'" when everything shows that it is the direct effect in the minds of the prophets of those feelings and ideas with which they were inspired" (p. 243). No wonder that he thinks it illegitimate to look for precise fulfilments of these prophetic forecasts (p. 249), which were, indeed, often better fulfilled "in the breach than in the observance" (p. 249), and chides Matthew for thinking otherwise (p. 250). "Inspiration" with Dr. Ladd is simply the subjective condition of revelation, and is as such both in a sense prior to revelation (so that we read of "committing to writing certain revelations previously received by inspiration," p. 104), and in a sense the result of it (so that we read of it as arising "in connection with the disclosure" made in revelation, p. 114). It consists in essence of "spiritual insight and sympathy" (p. 228); it is "a spiritual effect within the human spirit, a quickening and elevating and informing of this spirit" (p. 425), "a moral quickening and elevating of soul," such as "includes the illuminating of" the recipient's "faculty of insight, the purifying of his moral emotions, the strengthening of his purpose to further the ends of righteousness" (p. 116). As such, it is common to all believers (p. 424, and especially 439); but varies in intensity with different individuals, even within the limits of the authors of Scripture (p. 441). It is of course inconceivable that a purification and elevation of moral consciousness should have no effect on "utterance." So Dr. Ladd admits that when the apostles taught the truths of the gospel, they taught as inspired messengers, and in an authoritative way, whether it was by word of mouth or by writing (p. 98). He can see that "the words of the prophet who speaks prophetically are *per se* words of the Lord," and "if these words are faithfully recorded, the record will naturally, it will almost necessarily be regarded as sacred and inspired" (p. 112); so that "the faithful record of prophetic utterances may be considered, *in a secondary way,* as worthy to be called inspired" (p. 120). He can see that the spiritual awakening which he calls inspiration may result in something worthy of being called "a suggestion of words" by the Holy Ghost. "For the words of a writer under a strong spiritual impulse are born of that impulse as truly as they are the product of his own previous education and of the culture of the race to which he belongs" (p. 362). Not only will "the character of the thought thus influence the words in which it is itself expressed," but we even read: "Nor can it be denied that the indwelling divine Spirit may often suggest to the minds under its influence a new combination of terms, or a new use of a word, the better thus to give to future generations the ideas of God's revelation of himself as the Redeemer of man" (p. 426). Thus, " it is necessary to regard the Bible as something more than 'a record' of Biblical revelation"; it is at least "the bearer or 'vehicle' of a unique and incomparable form of revelation"; and even more: "In some sort we must speak of the Bible as being itself a revelation of God . . . that is, it is a result reached by giving written form to the truth which has been revealed" to the minds of its authors (p. 419). While Dr. Ladd is thus far from excluding the divine from the Scriptures, he nevertheless admits it by as indirect a route as possible and limits it to the smallest possible amount. He is sure that it is not there in such a sense that the Scriptures are the Word of God, or in such a sense as to render them errorless or infallible, or as the result of any special divine influence given to anyone to fit him for the work of writing (p. 98).

We get to the root of Dr. Ladd's conception of the relation of the divine and human in the production of Scripture when we see him speak of the difficulty of the task of determining "the exact place where the divine meets the human and is limited by it" (p. 437). He apparently conceives of the divine seeping into the Scriptures with difficulty, and as everywhere limited, contracted, and debased by the pressure and admixture of a vigorous human element. But why should we think of the union of the divine and human here as if there had been a conflict between them, and each had seized what it could, and so made the product prevailingly divine or human; and not rather as a harmonious and free flux of both into every part alike, making it all divine-human? Why should we accept a theory of inspiration which is the analogue of the deistic rather than one which is the analogue of the divine-immanence theory of God's relation to the universe? Why may we not believe that the God who brings his purposes to fruition in his providential government of the world, without violence to second causes or to the intelligent free agency of his creatures, so superintends the mental processes of his chosen instruments for making known his will, as to secure that they shall speak his words in speaking their own? A careful exegesis reveals this as the view of the writers of Scripture; and surely it need yield to no other in point of philosophical completeness or simplicity.

The compass of Dr. Ladd's book is broader than the question of the divine inspiration of the Bible. Its object is to convey its author's whole conception of what the Bible is to the popular reader. As a piece of scholarly popular statement, it attains a very high level; it is so crowded with matter as to be sometimes hard reading to "the general," but it cannot fail to awaken that confidence in the reader which the "full man," sometimes not altogether deservedly, usually commands. The

order in which the topics are treated does not seem very
natural; but if we may take the summary at the end of the
volume (p. 476) as our guide, we may say that Dr. Ladd
proposes to answer the questions that concern the origin and
composition of the Biblical books, their "literary and other
more obvious characteristics," the process by which they were
collected and canonized, and their religious qualities and value.
On the first of these topics he holds very advanced ground
(p. 294), and frankly admits that his position is inconsistent
with any theory of "infallible inspiration" (p. 296). His view
of the origin of "the canon" is also, as he is frank to say,
inconsistent with its being a divine gift to the Church in any
other than a providential sense (pp. 66, 329). His modes of
argumentation are often rather odd, and the reader must make
up his mind to puzzle now and then over ambiguities and un-
distributed middles. But nowhere, probably, do we meet with
a more curious confusion than the often repeated argument
which is intended to lower the authority of the Canonical Scriptures to the level of the authority of the Church, on the ground
that the "canon" was made by the Church.[2] When Dr. Ladd
writes that "as a collection it can claim no infallibility which
is not dependent upon the authority by which the collection
came to be made" (p. 363), meaning the Church, he speaks
as if some authority were attributed to it *as a collection* other
than and above what is attributed to its several parts, and he
utterly mistakes the authority which guarantees the canon.
This is not the Church, but the inspired apostles who gave the
sacred books one by one to the Church, thus at once creating
and filling up the total contents of the class of sacred books.
It is an odd confusion by which he is led to deny that the Bible
cannot witness to what it is. When the Bible tells us what
"scripture" is, and then asserts itself to be "scripture," it is not
a far cry to determine what is its witness to itself. If Dr. Ladd
were not prepossessed by the theory of the gradual formation
of the Christian canon, he would know better how to interpret

---

[2] See pp. 5, 17 f., 329, 363 f., etc.

the fact that the Church never, even in its earliest days, appealed to criticism, but always to tradition, to validate it and its parts, and would not write of a "selection being made on the grounds of fitness." There never was a "selection" of a canon; the "Church" never had anything to do with it but to receive it; and the authority which validates it as the law-code of the Church antedates and is the same authority which founded the Church itself.

40

INSPIRATION*

The words *inspiration* and *inspire* are employed in technical theological usage to translate the terms *inspiratio* (inbreathing) and *inspirare* (to breath into) in theological Latin, which rests, through the medium of the Patristic Latin, on the Latin Bible. Their meanings in technical theological usage, therefore, are grounded upon such passages in the Latin Bible as Job xxxii. 8, where *inspiratio* stands for the Hebrew *n'shâmâh,* and above all 2 Tim. iii. 16, where the Greek word θεόπνευστος is translated *divinitus inspirata.* This Greek word first appears in literature in this passage, and may have been coined by Paul, as expressing the fact that the inbreathing with which he had to do was from God more explicitly than the current terms, such as ἔμπνευστος (ἐμπνέω), which he might have adapted to his purpose. Its application to the Hebrew Scriptures apparently describes those Scriptures as having been breathed into by God in the process of their origination, in such a manner that they have been clothed with divine qualities and breathe out God to every reader. It is in this sense that the word inspiration has been applied to the Bible.

---

*From Johnson's *Universal Cyclopaedia*, Vol. IV, ed. 1909. This clear compact but comprehensive article was not included in the Oxford edition of Dr. Warfield's Works, no doubt because the Editorial Committee considered the later article from the *International Standard Bible Encyclopaedia* preferable (see *Revelation and Inspiration*, 1927, pp. 77-112, or *The Inspiration and Authority of the Bible*, 1967, pp. 131-166). But it is an admirable article, worth preserving for its structure, sections not found in other articles, and because it is a companion article to "Revelation" from the same encyclopaedia which is included in the Oxford edition (see *Revelation and Inspiration*, pp. 37-48).

I. Definition of Inspiration

In its theological usage, the word inspiration was at first employed to express the entire divine agency operative in producing the Scriptures. In the process of theological analysis, however, the various modes in which the divine has entered into the production of the Scriptures have been more clearly distinguished. Throughout the whole preparation of the material to be written and of the men to write it; throughout the whole process of gathering, and classification, and use of the material by the writers; throughout the whole process of the actual writing: divine influences of the most varied kinds have been at work, extending all the way from simply providential superintendence and spiritual illumination to direct revelation and inspiration; and entering into and becoming incorporated with the human activities producing Scripture in very various ways—natural, supernatural, gracious, and miraculous. In distinguishing thus between the various modes in which the divine enters into the production of Scripture, the several terms formerly used synonymously to designate the entire process have acquired each a distinct sense, connoting one element in the process. The general question of the "divine origin of the Scriptures" is now distinguished from the special questions of revelation and inspiration. "Revelation" and "inspiration" are sharply distinguished from each other; the former being used to denote the divine activity in supernaturally communicating to certain chosen instruments the truths which God would make known to the world; while the term "inspiration" is reserved to denote the continued work of God by which— his providential, gracious, and supernatural contributions being presupposed—he wrought within the sacred writers in their entire work of writing, with the design and effect of rendering the written product the divinely trustworthy Word of God.

Exact writers no longer use the term inspiration either in so broad a sense as to make it inclusive of all the divine activities operative in the production of the Scriptures, or in a sense synonymous with or inclusive of revelation; but confine it to the definite and fixed sense of the particular divine activity exerted in securing a trustworthy record. Discussion of the subject is, however, very greatly confused by the persistence of the older and more inexact usage of the word in many, even recent, works; together with the recent introduction of a newer usage by a special school of thinkers, who would make inspiration merely the correlate of revelation, expressing the divine preparation of the mind of the prophet for the reception of the revelation destined for him, or in some way the subjective factor corresponding to the objective revelation in the case of the recipient of a revelation.

The following are some recent definitions: "Inspiration was an influence of the Holy Spirit on the minds of certain select men, which rendered them the organs of God for the infallible communication of his mind and will."[1] "By the inspiration of the Scriptures we mean that special divine influence upon the minds of the Scripture writers, in virtue of which their productions, apart from errors of transcription, and when rightly interpreted, together constitute an infallible and sufficient rule of faith and practice."[2] "Defining inspiration positively, it may be described as the influence of the Holy Spirit upon a human person, whereby he is infallibly moved and guided in all his statements while under this influence."[3] "Revelation is that direct divine influence which imparts truth to the mind. Inspiration is that divine influence that secures the accurate transference of truth into human language by a speaker or writer, so as to be communicated to other men."[4] "The specific question with reference to the inspiration of the Bible presupposes a revelation as given, and asks whether the *record* of that revelation be inspired. . . . It has special reference to the Sacred Scriptures, and it thus embraces much of history, fact, and detail which is not a matter of direct revelation, but which came to the writers from other sources, from personal experience

---

[1] C. Hodge, *Systematic Theology*, Vol. I, p. 154.
[2] A. C. Strong, *Systematic Theology*, p. 95.
[3] W. G. T. Shedd, *Dogmatic Theology*, Vol. I, p. 88.
[4] B. Manly, *The Bible Doctrine of Inspiration*, p. 37.

or testimony. . . . It is a special divine influence for a special purpose. Its object is the communication of truth in an infallible manner, so that when rightly interpreted no error is conveyed."[5]

II. The Doctrine of Inspiration

The formation of a doctrine of inspiration in the Christian Church was conditioned by the circumstance that a specific doctrine on this subject was commended to it by the fact that it was held by the writers of the New Testament and by Jesus as reported in the Gospels. The Jews at the time of the rise of Christianity looked upon their Scriptures as in such a sense the utterances of God that every word of them was divinely guaranteed to be true, and was clothed with plenary divine authority. With characteristic exaggeration, this idea was given most startling expression by some of the rabbis, and extreme inferences were drawn from it. The writers of the New Testament and Jesus, as reported by them, without committing themselves to these extremer inferences, yet obviously shared the fundamental conception from which they were drawn; and looked upon the Old Testament as divinely safeguarded in even its verbal expression, and as divinely trustworthy in all its parts, in all its elements, and in all its statements of whatever kind. That this is the state of the case with reference to the New Testament writers is generally recognized by competent scholars of all schools of thought, not only by those who accept the authority of the New Testament in delivering this doctrine to us, but also by those who, whether of evangelical or of unevangelical convictions, reject this particular doctrine.[6]

It is this fact which accounts both for the immediateness of the

---

[5]Henry B. Smith, *The Inspiration of the Holy Scriptures*, pp. 8, 9.

[6]See Tholuck, "Old Testament in the New," in *Bibliotheca Sacra*, XI, p. 612; Rothe, *Zur Dogmatik*, p. 177; Farrar, *Life of Paul*, Vol. I, p. 49; Sanday, *Inspiration*, p. 407; Stuart, *Principles of Christianity*, p. 346; Pfleiderer, *Paulinism*, Vol. I, p. 88; Schultz, *Grundriss der evangelischen Dogmatik*, p. 7; Riehm, *Der Lehrbegriff des Hebräerbriefes*, Vol. I, pp. 173, 177; Reuss, *History of Christian Theology in the Apostolical Age*, Vol. I, p. 352; Kuenen, *Prophets*, p. 449.

adoption of this doctrine by the Christian Church, and for the tenacity of its hold upon it. From the very beginning, and unbrokenly since, this has been distinctly the vital belief of the Christian people as well as the formal doctrine of the organized Christian Church, as to the divine character of their Scriptures. It is this doctrine that was held and taught by the Church throughout the whole patristic age[7] and throughout the whole mediaeval age; and that was given expression by the Church of Rome in the Tridentine deliverance that God is the author of the Scriptures and that they were written *Spiritu sancto dictante.* The same doctrine was held and taught by all the Reformers, and underlies all the creeds of the Protestant churches, finding its fullest expression in the later creeds of the Reformed churches, such as the Westminster Confession and the Formula Consensus Helvetica.[8] Despite great divergences of opinion among recent theological writers, it is this same church doctrine that remains not only the confessional doctrine of the Church at large, but the fundamental conviction of the body of Christian people.

That this doctrine, as confessed by the Church of all ages, pertains as much to the New Testament as to the Old, is not due merely to a natural extension to the New Testament writings of the inspiration which the New Testament writers themselves accorded to the Old. This extension itself is rooted in the authority of the apostles. And that, not alone in the sense that it was simply on the authority of the apostles, embodied in their writings, that the Church received the doctrine of the inspiration of the Old Testament, so that the inspiration of the former underlay that of the latter; but also in the sense that the New Testament writers claim for themselves the same inspiration which they attribute to the Old Testament. They did not for a moment allow that they, as ministers of a New Cove-

[7]See John Delitzsch, *De Inspiratione,* and the catena of passages in Appendix B of Westcott's *Introduction to the Study of the Gospels.*

[8]See on the doctrine of the Reformed Creeds, A. A. Hodge, *Presbyterian Review,* 1884, p. 282; and on the Westminster Confession, B. B. Warfield, *Presbyterian and Reformed Review,* Oct. 1893, p. 582, and *Presbyterian Quarterly,* Jan. 1894, p. 19.

nant, were less sufficient than the ministers of the Old; they asserted that the Holy Spirit was the author of their teaching, both in matter and in form; they demanded entire credit and claimed divine authority for all their deliverances; they placed one another's writings in the category of that Scripture the whole of which they asserted to be inspired of God. It is thus simply on the authority of the apostles that the church doctrine attributes this complete inspiration to the entire Bible.

In the whole history of the Church there have been only two lines of influence making for a lower doctrine of inspiration which are of sufficient importance to require notice in a general review:

(1) With forerunners among the Humanists (e.g., Erasmus), the Socinians introduced a method of thought which sought to distinguish between inspired and uninspired elements in the Scriptures. This was taken up by the Arminians (e.g., Grotius, Episcopius) and culminated in Le Clerc.[9] Le Clerc's views were introduced into England by the publication in 1690 of *Five Letters Concerning the Inspiration of the Holy Scriptures, Translated out of the French*; and called forth a number of replies, in which a lower view of inspiration was conceded in the effort to defend matters of even greater importance.[10] In Germany, George Calixtus (d. 1656) had enunciated opinions essentially identical with the lower view which was thus propagating itself in England, but with little effect until they were reannounced by Baumgarten (1725). Since the beginning of the nineteenth century great vogue has been obtained for such opinions; chiefly in the two forms which affirm, the one that only the *mysteries* of the faith—that is, things undiscoverable by the unaided reason—are inspired, and the other that the Bible is inspired only in *matters pertaining to faith and practice*. But though appearing in a great number of writers, and affecting the thought of large and perhaps increasing numbers of Christians, this view has failed to supplant the common

---

[9]*Sentiments de quelques théologiens*, 1685, and *Défense des sentiments*, 1686.

[10]E.g., in Lowth's *A Vindication of the Divine Authority and Inspiration of the Old Testament*, 1692.

church doctrine either in the creeds of the Church or in the hearts of the people.

(2) Thinkers of a mystical type have in all ages tended to erect the "inner light" which they seemed to themselves to enjoy from the direct work of the Holy Ghost in their hearts, to a position co-ordinate with or superior to the external light afforded by the divine revelation in the Scriptures. Hitherto thinkers of this type have stood somewhat outside the ordinary currents of Christian doctrine, and when advocating extreme views have tended to form separate sects. But in the nineteenth century, through the genius of Schleiermacher, a strong stream of essentially mystical thought entered into and affected more or less profoundly the whole body of Protestant theology. From this point of view man is conceived of as having, either as man or as Christian man taught by the Holy Ghost, a divine source and criterion of truth in himself, to the test of which every "external revelation" is to be subjected. Accordingly, the whole contents of the Bible, religious and ethical as well as historical and scientific, the "mysteries" of faith as well as "rational" facts, such as are attainable by the unaided action of the human understanding, are subordinated to the judgment of human reason under such names as "the spiritual instinct," "the Christian consciousness," "the witness of the Holy Spirit in the heart," and the like. Adherents of this type of thinking define inspiration not as an activity of God rendering the Scriptural writings as such infallible and authoritative, but as the correlate of revelation in the process of the attainment of truth by the prophet himself—the subjective factor in the conception of divine truth by this chosen instrument of God. This tendency of thought has naturally assumed many forms and exists in various stages of development; sometimes it appears as only an undefined tendency, sometimes in a form distinguishable from vulgar rationalism only in the terms employed. It has become very widespread and influential in recent theological literature; but it has neither affected creed expression nor supplanted the ordinary church doctrine in the convictions of the Christian people.

The effect of both of these attempted modifications of the church doctrine of inspiration is to reduce the authority of Scripture. The former confines its authority to certain specified subjects—the undiscoverable mysteries of faith, or specific matters of faith and practice. The latter, in principle, sets aside its authority altogether in the general subordination of all "external authority" to "internal authority." The church doctrine looks upon the Bible as throughout a divine book, and as such authoritative in and of itself, in all its declarations of whatever kind.

III. Theories of Inspiration

It will be impossible to enumerate here all of the divergent theories of inspiration which have been enunciated, especially in the nineteenth century, even by writers of name and influence. The attempt to frame a conspectus of even the more important of them is greatly complicated by the differences that exist even among modern writers in their definition of terms. Some sort of order may be introduced into the enumeration by separating the theories into three classes, according to the attitude they take concerning the relation of "inspiration" to the production of the actual books which constitute our Bible. Those points of view which deny that there is any specifically divine element in the religion of the Bible may, of course, be left out of account; they deny all "inspiration" and cannot take a place among theories of "inspiration." Among those, however, who allow that the religion of the Bible is in some sense from God some confine the divine agency, which they call "inspiration," to the origin and growth of the Biblical religion itself, and deny that it was active in the actual production of the writings (our Biblical books) in which that religion has come to literary expression and record; others allow that God was in some way and to some extent concerned in the production of the writings themselves which compose our Bible, but deny that he was so concerned in their production as to become the responsible author of all their contents; while still others maintain that the Biblical books themselves have been in such a sense written under the inspiration of God as to be constituted in themselves the Word of God written, to every word of which divine truth and authority attach. Most of the theories of inspiration will be found to take their places naturally in one or another of these classes.

A. Theories which confine inspiration to the divine agency in the production of true religion, denying that it directly enters into the production of the Biblical books as such. In this class is included a great variety of theories very different from one another in everything except the one common tenet, that although they attribute a divine origin to the Biblical religion, they look upon the Biblical books, as such, as the product of unaided human powers. Writers of this class therefore deny inspiration altogether in the more exact and proper sense of that word; and for the most part define it as the correlate of revelation—as in one way or another a part of the process of revelation, the subjective factor in revelation, the preparation of the mind of the "prophet" to receive or assimilate the revelation, and the like. Thus Morell makes it merely the elevation of the religious consciousness, involving an increased power of spiritual vision by which religious truth is apprehended: "Revelation and inspiration indicate one united process, the result of which upon the human mind is to produce a state of spiritual intuition." And thus Rooke makes it "the inward spiritual preparation of a man to know and to feel what God chooses to communicate of his divine thought and will"; inspiration and revelation being "correlative terms, twin factors of knowledge in some human consciousness, inspiration being the subjective factor and revelation being the objective factor."

Theories of this class differ from one another therefore according to their conceptions of the nature and processes of revelation; and these are largely determined by the philosophical preconceptions which underlie them. They range all the way from theories which differ from pure pantheism in little more than words, to theories which form the transition between the present and the higher classes afterward to be enumerated. They are all characterized by speaking of inspiration as "personal" and "non-biblical"—that is, as belonging to the prophet and not to the book. And in even their highest form the nearest they can approach to speaking of "inspired *Scriptures*" is to say that an inspired man will of course write (as he does everything else) as an inspired man—that is, any books he may write will bear the impress of his character and attainments. The following are some of the leading forms which this general conception has taken:

1. The lowest form reduces the divine influence exerted in inspiration to something which is essentially common to all men, and has received the names, appropriate to its several modes of expression, of the *natural,* the *intuitional*, or the *providential* theory. According to this point of view, the inspired man is simply the religious *genius,* and differs from his fellowmen only in the degree in which his religious insight or susceptibilities have been excited under influence common to all, or only providentially different from those enjoyed by his fellowmen. Sometimes this is so expressed as to be indistinguishable from pantheism. All life and thought are said to be divine—"the unfolding of the life and thought of God within the world." All human thought of God is therefore divinely inspired. "God is everywhere immanent and everywhere expressive; and expression, as soon as recognized, becomes revelation."[11] At other times it takes forms of expression which are not only theistic, but make inspiration dependent on providential contact with Christ, and therefore tend to confine it to Christ's immediate followers. In one of its lower forms it is taught by F. W. Newman and Theodore Parker, and it grades upward to such teachers as Morell and Scherer (in one of his stages of development).

2. It is a higher form of the same general position which identifies inspiration with those influences of the Holy Ghost which are common to all Christians, and which has received the names, therefore, of the *gracious* or the *illumination* theory. According to this point of view, the inspired man is

---

[11]Whiton, *Gloria Patri,* p. 138.

simply the Christian man of special spiritual attainments, and inspiration is nothing other in kind than *spiritual discernment*. This is the view of the more evangelical wing of the followers of Schleiermacher and of the followers of Coleridge. "To us, as to the holy men of old," says F. W. Farrar, "the Spirit still utters the living oracles of God." This is the view of such writers as Tholuck and Neander, as Arnold, Hare, F. W. Robertson, Maurice.

3. It is still but a higher form of the same general position, when the peculiarity of the prophetic office is recognized, so that revelation and its correlate, inspiration, are confined to a special body of chosen men; but a sharp distinction is drawn between the revelation given by the inspiration of God and the record of that revelation which has been left to unaided human powers. One form in which this point of view is presented is represented by T. George Rooke, who calls it the "theory of sufficient knowledge." He teaches that God by revelation communicates sufficient knowledge to every Biblical writer to enable him to produce the portion of Scripture committed to him, in which case "these writers could be trusted to express themselves in appropriate words, and there was no need for the Holy Spirit to supply the form as well as the matter of their utterance in every case, or even to superintend and check that utterance in its spoken or written form."[12] It is more common for writers of this class, however, simply to say that after God had communicated his will to the prophet, the prophet was left "to express in human language the divine conception, with which he was inspired, as well as he could."[13] It is a somewhat higher point of view when Leonard Stählin represents the Holy Spirit as not only by his inspiration communicating to the recipients of revelation the matter to be expressed, but as by the same act "fitting" them "to express that which they say, exactly in those particular words which appear in their writings."[14] Thus God's preparation of the sacred writers for writing was

---

[12]*Inspiration*, p. 158.
[13]So De Witt, *What Is Inspiration?*, p. 82.
[14]*Neue Kirchliche Zeitschrift*, 1892, no. 71.

specific, but it only provided a basis for their writing; the writing itself was "free," and was not *accompanied* by any superintending or directing activity of God.

B. Theories which teach that God was directly concerned in the production of the Biblical books, as such, so that it is true to say that the Bible contains the Word of God, and is therefore, as such, of divine origin; but which confine inspiration to certain portions or elements in the Bible, and thus deny that God is the responsible author of the whole book. Writers of this class are agreed that inspiration is the peculiar property of certain chosen instruments of the revelation of God's will, and that it attaches to their written product, the Biblical books. But they usually define inspiration as synonymous with or the inseparable accompaniment of revelation, and are thus led to deny inspiration to all parts and elements of the Bible which are not direct "revelations." They differ from one another in the matters and elements which they severally determine to be inspired or uninspired in the Scriptures. Three well-marked sub-classes may be distinguished:

1. *The Theory of Partial Inspiration.* This holds that some distinct and separable *portions* or *parts* of the Bible are inspired and others not. Sometimes the line is drawn broadly between the Old and the New Testament. Sometimes (as, for example, by Coleridge, in some of his utterances) an inspiration is attributed to the Law and the Prophets which is denied to the rest of the Bible. At other times the larger portion of the whole book is thought of as inspired. Dr. G. T. Ladd thinks "a large proportion of its writings inspired,"[15] and with reference to the New Testament, that it is inspired "in nearly all its extent."[16] R. F. Horton has even undertaken to go through the Bible and point out generally what is inspired and what not,[17] and W. Fr. Gess has carried out this process in such detail that he is prepared to separate the inspired and uninspired portions down to the very sentences and clauses.

---

[15]*Doctrine of Sacred Scripture*, Vol. I, p. 759.
[16]Vol. II, p. 508.
[17]*Revelation and the Bible.*

"In the blessing of Jacob," he says, for example, "only the prophecy concerning Judah is a real word of God."[18]

2. *The Theory of Limited Inspiration.* According to this point of view, the Bible is inspired indeed throughout, but only in certain of its *elements;* in other of its elements it is not from God. a. Some limit inspiration to what they call the *mysteries,* that is, to things not discoverable by unaided human powers, while what man could come to know by his natural faculties rests only on human authority. Walter R. Browne argues that the "supernatural element" in Scripture alone is inspired, since, on the principle of economy, God will give only such aid as is *necessary.*[19] b. Others limit inspiration to what they call *matters of faith and practice,* that is, to religious doctrines to be believed and moral precepts to be obeyed, while in the whole sphere of philosophical, scientific, and historical fact the writers are said to have been left to their unaided powers, either absolutely or with the exception of such of these facts as are inseparably involved in "matters of faith and practice." This, as has already been pointed out, is a very common theory, especially among apologetical writers seeking to mark out the *minimum* to be defended. c. Others limit inspiration to the *ideas, thoughts, concepts,* while the writers are held to have been left to their unaided powers in bringing these "concepts" into expression. It is obvious that this theory passes very readily into the one enumerated above under A, 3; it is differentiated from it in that it posits the continued operation of the Spirit in the whole process by which the material to be written is thought out by the sacred writers, and leaves them to themselves only in the actual "wording." This seems to be the theory of Dean Alford; and many others hold it somewhat confusingly in conjunction with other conceptions.

3. *The Theory of Graded Inspiration.* According to this point of view the Bible is indeed inspired in all its parts, but some portions of it are more inspired than others. This mode

---

[18]*Die Inspiration der Helden der Bibel und der Schriften der Bibel.* Cf. especially p. 426.
[19]*The Inspiration of the New Testament.*

of statement originated in the Jewish schools and has had large popularity, especially among English writers of a generation or two ago, such as Daniel Wilson, Philip Doddridge, John Dick, Enoch Henderson. It is obvious that it is the result of the confusion—common to the writings of this whole class B—between inspiration and the other processes by which a divine element has entered the Bible. If we are to subsume all the divine influences, providential, gracious, and supernatural alike, revelation as well as inspiration in its stricter sense, under the one name of "inspiration," then it is undeniable that some portions of the Bible are more inspired than others. More of these processes have been operative in the production of some portions of the Bible than others. Writers of this type need not differ therefore from those of class C otherwise than in definition. Most of them have, however become confused in their distinctions, and have thus been the means of propagating a lower view of inspiration than that held by class C.

C. Theories which maintain that God was in such a sense concerned in the production of the Biblical books, as such, that his providential, gracious, and supernatural activities attending the preparation of the matter to be written and the men to write it, were supplemented by his co-operation in the very writing of the books themselves; so that he is the responsible author of the Scriptures in all their parts, in all their elements, and in all their statements of whatever kind; and they are the Word of God written and as such are infallibly true and divinely authoritative in all their declarations. It is evident at once that this theory is identical with the church doctrine of inspiration. It has received the name of the doctrine of *plenary* inspiration, in contradistinction from the several theories of incomplete inspiration enumerated under B; and in contradistinction from that form of the theory of limited inspiration, which confines inspiration to the thoughts, ideas, or concepts and denies that it extends to the choice of the words in which these thoughts, ideas, and concepts are expressed (B, 2, c), it has received the name of the doctrine of *verbal* inspiration. It exists in two forms, which differ in their conception of the mode in which the divine activity has worked in the production of Scripture. These are:

1. *The Theory of Dictation.* According to this mode of conception the whole of Scripture has been dictated by God to the human writers, who thus are to be thought of not as authors but as amanuenses, penmen, or even, as some writers affirm, merely pens, instruments in the divine hand, acting mechanically in the production of the resultant writing. From this point of view God alone is the author of the Scriptures. Its characteristic contention is that the human writers have contributed no quality of their own to the product, save as a musical instrument may contribute a quality to the music played upon it. It "excludes the working of the natural faculties of man's mind altogether, . . . so that both the understanding and the will of man, as far as they were merely natural, had nothing to do in this holy work save only to understand and approve that which was dictated by God himself unto those that wrote it from his mouth, or the suggesting of his Spirit."[20] The obvious marks of human authorship in the Biblical books as, for example, the differences in vocabulary, style, and the like, have led to modifications of the stringency of this contention; until, as Dr. Henry B. Smith says, "there is little room left for objection," and the dispute between this form of the doctrine and the next to be mentioned "becomes a verbal one."[21] An instance of this moderate manner of stating the theory may be found in Rohnert, *Die Inspiration der heiligen Schrift* (p.46). While he is sure that "in the act of inspiration the self-moving activity of the holy men of God entirely receded," yet he is equally sure that "the dictation of the Spirit was not a mechanical repeating of words for mechanical record," but that the persons who wrote were used *as persons* and not as dead utensils, and acted as the willing instruments of the Spirit's activity, working "freely according to their individual peculiarities." In every age of the Church there have been representatives of the theory of dictation. Only in the

[20]John White, *A Way to the Tree of Life,* p. 60.
[21]*The Inspiration of the Holy Scriptures,* p. 24.

Protestant theology of the seventeenth century, however, did it tend to become dominant. At that time it found more or less clear expression in many of the chief doctrinal treatises of the Lutheran and Reformed bodies alike, and in Britain as fully as on the Continent (e.g., Quenstedt, Calov, Hollaz, Heidegger, Buxtorf, Hooker, White, Lightfoot). In our own day this theory has been revived in the Lutheran Church, in reaction against the prevalent lower theories, chiefly through the example of a great theologian of the United States, C. F. W. Walther; it is represented in Germany by such writers as Kölling and Rohnert.

2. *The Theory of Concursus.* According to this mode of conception the whole of Scripture is the product of divine activities, which enter it, however, not by superseding the activities of the human authors, but confluently with them; so that the Scriptures are the joint product of divine and human activities, both of which penetrate them at every point, working harmoniously together to the production of a writing which is not divine here and human there, but at once divine and human in every part, every word, and every particular. The philosophical basis of this theory is the Christian conception of God as immanent in his modes of working as well as transcendent. It is this theory, as has already been pointed out, that underlies the church doctrine of inspiration and constitutes, indeed, the church doctrine of the mode of inspiration. It was the conception of the greatest of the Fathers (e.g., Augustine) and of the Reformers, and it remains the conception of the great body of modern theologians. It is, for example, the theory of Gaussen, Lee, Bannerman, Manly, Dieckhoff, of A. C. Strong, A. Cave, C. Hodge, A. A. Hodge, H. B. Smith, and Shedd.

IV. The Relation of the Divine and the Human in Inspiration

That the Scriptures are a human book, written by men and bearing the traces of their human origin on their very face, is obvious to every reader. That they are a divine book as well is the contention of every theory of inspiration. How are these two factors, the divine and the human, to be conceived as related to one another in the act of inspiration? And how are the two consequent elements in the product, the divine and human, to be conceived to be related to one another in the Scriptures? This is one of the fundamental problems in working out a conception of inspiration, and it has received very varied treatment.

A. Some writers have emphasized one factor or element in so exaggerated a way as to exclude the other altogether. At one time the divine element was commonly so emphasized. This produced the seventeenth century theory of dictation. This is not common today. The opposite fault of emphasizing the human factor or element so exaggeratingly as to exclude the divine, which is an inheritance from rationalism, is, however, very widespread. The effect remains the same, though the underlying philosophy be altered to one of a pantheizing type, which speaks, indeed, of the Scriptures as wholly divine, but adds that so also is all thought and all expression of thought. Nor is the effect altered when men allow a divine element of preparation for the book, but deny a divine factor in the immediate production of the book itself as such, and consequently deny any divine element in the book itself as such.[22]

B. Others appear to conceive of the two factors in inspiration as striving against and seeking to exclude each other, and of the two elements in the product as lying over against each other, dividing the Bible between them. Crude and mechanical as it appears, such a conception seems extraordinarily common, and makes itself heard in the most unlikely places. It is this point of view which leads to the declaration concerning a given element in the Bible, that because it is human it is therefore not divine; and which underlies the quite common remark that in the prosecution of Biblical science it is becoming ever more certain that the "human element" in the Bible is larger than we supposed—with the implication that the divine element is therefore

---

[22]E.g., Gladden, *Who Wrote the Bible?*; Horton, *Inspiration and the Bible*.

smaller.[23] So Dr. Ladd speaks of the difficulty of determining "the exact place where the divine meets the human, and is limited by it."[24] This conception naturally is held with different degrees of crudity, and sometimes results even in an attempt to separate the inseparable, and to point out in detail what elements or parts of the Bible are divine and what human.[25]

C. Justice is not done to the two factors in inspiration or to the two elements in the Scriptures by any other theory than that of *concursus*. On this theory the whole Bible is recognized as human, the free product of human effort, in every part and in every word—with the exception of the comparatively small portion which came by direct revelation. And at the same time the whole Bible is recognized as divine, to the smallest detail. The human and divine factors in inspiration are conceived of as flowing confluently and harmoniously to the production of a common product. And the two elements are conceived of in the Scriptures as inseparable constituents of one simple and uncompounded product. On this theory, of every word of the Bible in turn, it is to be affirmed that it is divine and that it is human; and all the qualities of divinity and of humanity are to be sought and may be found in every portion and element of the Scriptures. This is the church doctrine on the subject, and it has underlain the thought of all the great church teachers of all ages, and finds more or less full expression in their extant writings.

V. THE EVIDENCE OF INSPIRATION

It will not be possible to present even an outline of the evidence for the inspiration of the Christian Scriptures here. All that can be attempted is to indicate the sources from which it is drawn. It is necessary even for this purpose, however, to discriminate between the several definitions of inspiration. If

---

[23]Sanday, *The Oracles of God;* Thayer, *The Change of Attitude toward the Bible.*

[24]*What Is the Bible?*, p. 437.

[25]Gess, *Die Inspiration;* Horton, *Revelation and the Bible.*

we are to define it as the correlate of revelation, the evidence for it is the evidence for supernatural religion. If we are to define it as a wide term, including all the divine activities which have entered into the production of the Bible, the evidence for it is the evidence for the general divine origin of the Hebrew and Christian Scriptures. In these two bodies of evidence the whole ground of Christian apologetics is covered. If, on the other hand, we define inspiration, with exact writers, as the activity of God in producing a divinely safeguarded record of his will in written documents, all this mass of evidence for supernatural revelation and for the divine origin of the Scriptures is presupposed. Inspiration, in its more exact sense, cannot come into discussion until theism, the reality of revelation, the authenticity and historical credibility of the Scriptures, the divine origin and character of the religion which they present, and the general trustworthiness of their presentation of it, have been already established. It is the crowning attribute of these sacred books, and is inconceivable and would not be affirmed if they were not previously believed to be the trustworthy records of a divinely given religion. When inspiration is said to be independent of the authenticity or historical credibility of the Scriptures, or of their trustworthiness in their presentation of the facts or even the doctrines of Christianity, or even independent of the truth of theism itself, it is because a different definition of inspiration is in mind from that which is used by exact writers, and in which it is affirmed by the church doctrine.

It is obvious that the primary source of evidence for inspiration, in this its exact sense, is the declarations of Scripture itself. (1) This is not reasoning in a circle: the question of inspiration does not come into discussion until the general trustworthiness of the Scriptures as sources for Christian doctrine has already been established; and the establishment of this belongs to the general "evidences of Christianity," and not to the specific evidence for inspiration in its more exact sense. (2) Nor is it to be objected to on the ground that the nature of the inspiration of the Scriptures is to be inferred by induction from the phenomena of Scripture, and not learned from the teaching of Scripture. This could be true only on the supposition that the general trustworthiness of the Scriptures as sources of Christian doctrine had not already been established by the general "evidences of Christianity." Immediately on the establishment of this, any phenomena of Scripture which may seem to be inconsistent with its teaching as to its own origin and character, pass into the category of "difficulties" not yet explained; and can set aside or modify the doctrine derived from the teaching of Scripture only in case they raise an objection to it formidable enough to neutralize the whole body of evidence for the general trustworthiness of the Scriptures as sources of Christian doctrine. The actual phenomena of Scripture—phenomena, as is asserted, of "error" and "discrepancy"—which are pleaded in this reference, are, however, of a kind which are far from being able to raise so formidable an objection to the truth of Scriptural teaching. These "discrepancies," as Prebendary Row says truly, "have been exaggerated to an extent that is absurd. A large number of them admit of an easy reconciliation under the guidance of common sense. Others arise from the fragmentary nature of the narrative, and our ignorance of the entire facts. Not a few of the remainder owe their origin to the fact that the events have been grouped in reference to the religious purpose of the author, rather than to the order of direct historical sequence. Of a few the reconciliation is difficult." None of them are such as would justify a rejection or modification of the teachings of the New Testament, coming to us authenticated as that teaching as a whole is. (3) Nor yet is it to be objected to this appeal to the Scriptures that equal testimony is not borne by all parts of the Scriptures to their inspiration, and specifically that it is only in the later and more "scholastic" portions of Scripture that a fully developed doctrine of Scripture can be discerned. This is just what would be expected from the progressiveness of the delivery of doctrine, and from the manner in which Scripture is written (occasional writings); and it is much in favor of the doctrine as derived from Scripture that it is only developed gradually in the progress of revelation, and finds its clearest and fullest expression in the New Testament, from the mouths of Christ and his apostles—and, among them, from the mouths of those most didactic and logical in their expression of doctrine.

It has already been pointed out that the Church has always, acting on these principles, derived her doctrine of inspiration from the Scriptures, and primarily from the New Testament. As Dr. Sanday truly says: "The one proof which in all ages has been the simplest and most effective as to the validity of that idea was the extent to which it was recognized in the sayings of Christ himself."[26] It has also already been pointed out that it is really not a matter in dispute among untrammeled scholars that the doctrine of inspiration which underlies the whole New Testament's dealing with the Old, and which is expressed in all the New Testament declarations upon the subject, is one quite as high and strict as that which the Church has adopted. As Hermann Schultz (*loc cit.*) expresses it: "For the men of the New Testament the Holy Scriptures of their people are already God's word, in which God himself speaks"; and the doctrine of a "verbal inspiration" both underlay all Christ's dealings with Scripture and is formally recognized by the "scholastic men of the apostolic circle" "in express words, as well as in the way in which they cite" the Old Testament books. It will not be possible to draw out here the details of evidence on which is based this general judgment of modern scientific exegesis as to the New Testament conception of Scripture. It must suffice to say that it rests on a wide induction from all the phenomena of the use made of the Old Testament by the New: inclusive not only of such direct assertions of divine infallibility and authority for Scripture as those of Christ in John x. 35, of Paul in 2 Tim. iii. 16, and of Peter in 2 Peter i. 21, but also of the obvious assumption of the divine inspiration, trustworthiness, and authority of the Scriptures in the whole dealing of the New Testament with them. This comes

---

[26]*Inspiration,* p. 393.

to expression, for example, in the titles given to Scripture, such as "Scripture," "the Scriptures," "the oracles of God"; in the formulas of quotation, such as "it is written," "it is spoken"; in the mode of its adduction, by which "Scripture says" and "God says" are made equivalents (Rom. ix. 17; x. 19; Gal. iii. 8), and even the narrative portions of Scripture are quoted as utterances of God (Heb. iv. 4); in the ascription of Scripture to the Holy Ghost as its source, and the recognition of the human writers as only his media of expression (Matt. xxii. 43; Acts ii. 34); in the reverence and trust shown toward the very words of Scripture (Matt. xxii. 32, 43; John x. 34; Gal. iii. 16); and in the attitude of entire subjection to Scripture which characterizes every line of the New Testament books. That the New Testament books were in the estimate of their writers equally "Scripture" with the Old Testament is evinced by the claim to equal authority which is made for them (2 Cor. x. 7; Gal. i. 7; 1 Thess. iv. 2; 2 Thess. iii. 6-14); by the similar ascription of their inspiration to the Holy Ghost (1 Thess. i. 5; ii. 13; iv. 2; 1 Cor. ii. 16; vii. 40); and by the inclusion of New Testament books along with the Old Testament under the title "Scripture" (1 Tim. v. 18; 2 Peter iii. 16).

There can be no question that what has been outlined above as the church doctrine of inspiration is grounded in the conception of Scripture held by Christ and his apostles. It will necessarily be accepted as true by those to whom the authority of Christ and his apostles is supreme. It will be rejected by those who refuse the authority of Christ and his apostles in matters of doctrinal truth. And it may be avoided by those who, while accepting this authority in general, yet suppose that on a principle of "accommodation," or on a principle of "incomplete knowledge," as applied to Christ and his apostles, they may modify the application of that authority in detail. The first of these attitudes toward the authority of Christ and his apostles is the historical attitude of the Christian Church; and it is the only attitude from which the "plenary inspiration" of Scripture can even come into discussion. If Christ and his apostles are not of infallible authority, even in the matter of their doctrinal teaching, the question cannot be raised whether they have been rendered by the Holy Ghost infallible, not only in the matter, but also in the very form of all their communications, of whatever kind.

PART VI

41

WHY FOUR GOSPELS?*

No complete biography of our Lord has ever been or will ever be written. For such a work, the writer must needs fully comprehend the person whose life he has undertaken not only to outline but also to portray and explain; he must, in a word, be sufficiently on a level with him to understand him and to know the working of his heart and to be able to trace out the complications of his motives and actions, refer each to its source and measure each in its potency and results. Dr. Holmes reminds us of a universal truth when he records his experience in writing the life of Emerson: "No matter how much superior to the biographer his subject may be," he says, "the man who writes the life feels himself, in a certain sense, on the level of the person whose life he is writing." It follows that if the distance between the writer and the subject is immeasurable, a biography in this full sense is impossible. It is only from above that the whole mountain can be seen. We may turn the worn pebble of some human life about in our fingers and give its exact measurements and estimate its narrow powers; but who can so deal with the Rock of Ages? Who can comprehend the height and depth and length and breadth of that which passeth knowledge? Who track out his paths whose ways are past finding out?

Least of all men, were those who stood most closely about Jesus likely to think that they could comprehend or portray their Lord unto perfection. What Peter proclaimed were such things as, it seemed to him, angels might well desire to look into (1 Peter i. 12); and John, the most high-visioned of all,

---

*From *The Westminster Teacher*, July 1887, pp. 245-246.

despairs of doing more than recording a slender selection of Jesus' "signs" and "deeds," that those who read might believe him to be the Christ, the Son of God, and, believing, might have life in his name (John xx. 30 f.; xxi. 25). That Spirit that was in them and whose mouthpieces they were, no doubt searched all things, even the deep things of God. Of him we may justly affirm that he was "on the level of the person whose life he was writing." But he searched the depths of man, too; and he knew it was not well to pour the ocean through the narrow channels of any man's soul. This would have been to do away with the evangelist and to speak in his own divine person directly to man. Who could listen to the thunders of his voice? Nay, man needs a mediator between him and God, and it is God's way to speak to man in human words and through human lips. Thus, we could not have one complete biography of Christ, one full account of all that he was and did in working out our redemption. This, "the world could not contain."

But if no one man could stand above this mountain of grace and write out for us a description of what it is and of all the streams that flow from it to make glad the country spread at its base, neither were we to be confined to the view of it that one man, from his lower standpoint, could obtain. This would indeed have been an inestimable blessing. What one man, illuminated in his spirit by the Spirit of God, could understand of the signs and deeds that Jesus did, and, directed in his hand by the same Spirit's inspiration, could record of what he saw, would be enough to make us believe that Jesus is the Christ, the Son of God, and to bring us life in his name. But this was not all that the Spirit could give; and it is not all that he has given. He has, as it were, stationed Spirit-led men around the foot of the mountain and bidden them look and write. And one tells us what it is on this side, and one, what it is on that, until through their eyes we may catch, piecemeal indeed, but with truth and perspective, some shadowy glimpse of the perfect whole. Our eyes cannot bear the blinding glory of the Sun of Righteousness, but we are not, therefore, forbidden more than one color of its spectrum. Our finite ears cannot receive the whole diapason of this divine life, but we are given not one part only of the tremendous strain, but a divine fourfold harmony—a *Diatessaron,* as the first harmonist over 1800 years ago called his *Harmony of the Four Gospels.* In this divine song each evangelist has his part to sing, and each part is complete in itself; while the Holy Ghost is the composor of all, the author at once of their diversity, suiting the part to the voice that is to sing it, and of their concordant harmony by which we may get a foretaste of that vaster music which it shall be ours to hear "when we shall see him as he is."

This, then, is why we have four Gospels. No one Gospel could suffice to tell us what Jesus was and did. It is that we may get what has been called a "stereoscopic" view of his life and person—for alas! we cannot as yet see him, but only some image of him "in a glass darkly"; and that, looking on the picture, we may perceive that we have before us the image of a real man, a man of many sides and of infinite sympathies, a man who comes to all hearts with a special message to each, and who demands from all hearts alike something more than homage, even as he is visibly something more than man.

From this reason why four Gospels were given us, it is easy to learn how we should study them. We ought to study them both separately and together. A patchwork narrative made out of the events recorded in these four precious volumes is far from being a suitable substitute for the four books themselves. This would be to attempt to make without the aid of the Spirit what no evangelist essayed under his guidance. No mechanical arrangement of these events can give us a complete view of the life of Christ; and in such an arrangement, useful as it is in its own sphere, we have left out just the most important thing that each Gospel contains—its individual conception of Christ and his work. To obtain the view of Jesus that the Holy Spirit intended when he gave us "a fourfold Gospel bound together by one Spirit," we must combine in one view the views of the four, not the fragments of facts that go to make up those views. We must first understand each Gospel as a whole and catch the full revelation of the

Master given by each, in order that we may then combine these revelations into one great conception of Jesus' person and work. The Gospels are not bundles of facts to be shaken apart like so many bundles of sticks, and then bound together into one greater fagot. They are rather like the several portraits which Van Dyke painted from various points of view of Charles I, that the sculptor might combine them into one rounded statue—not part by part, but as so many wholes. That a full and proper use may be made of them, we must begin by knowing each separately in its individuality and point of view, that we may end by knowing the Jesus of all alike to be the one divine Savior of the world.

42

THE GOSPEL OF JOHN*

Whenever we turn from one of the other Gospels to John's, we feel ourselves at once in a changed atmosphere. The very impression of the language is different. That of the other Gospels is sufficiently simple and direct. But John's is even more so. We seem here to look straight into the thought without the intermediation of words. Only, as we look, the sense of simplicity gives way to an ever increasing consciousness of profundity. Just as, often, gazing at the bright face of the full moon on a clear night, it seems almost within reach, until suddenly a sense of its distance enters the eye and it is seen sailing majestically through immensity. All the evangelists tell us of the same Jesus. But each in his own way; and what John has to tell is that which, though spoken in words which a child can understand, yet passes all human understanding.

Like the other evangelists John tells us much that Jesus did: and sometimes the same things that they tell us—though this rarely, for he had the others before him and meant, among other things, to supplement their account, not to repeat it. And they, like him, tell us much that Jesus said. But even in the mere external matter of the proportion between these elements there is an obvious difference. They are predominantly Gospels of Christ's deeds: John's is the Gospel of Christ's words. And when we look at the matter of the discourses recorded, the difference widens into a broad contrast. Not that there is not much that is Johannine in the sayings of Christ reported in the other Gospels. But the very recognition of this element in them as Johannine, is the sufficient proof of the general contrast be-

*The Westminster Teacher, July 1891.

tween the matter reported in the two. It makes it evident, indeed, that it is the same Christ that all are reporting: but also that each is giving us from the riches of the common store that which his soul found most congenial or which his purpose most demanded.

It is a small matter—though doubtless revealing to us an important fact, with its historical significance—that John reports chiefly the discourses of Christ in Judea; the others his sayings and doings in Galilee. It is of more, yet not yet of most, importance—though again not without its significance for the matter in hand—that John repeats chiefly our Lord's private discourses, with the inner circle of his disciples or with individual souls; the others chiefly his public discourses. What is of prime moment is, that John busies himself little with the external side of truth, but reports chiefly those discourses which go to the heart of things, and is ever concerned with the central and fundamental truths of the gospel. This is John's peculiarity. And this it is that led to his Gospel being called by one of the early Fathers, "the spiritual Gospel." "John," says Clement of Alexandria, "perceiving that what had reference to the body [i.e., probably to outward events] was clearly set forth in the other Gospels, composed a spiritual Gospel."

All the Gospels are written out of devout adoration of the divine Savior, and portray our Lord as divine. But the adoration shining in the pages of the others is the adoration of the subject, the follower, the servant. They picture Christ as the divine Messiah, the divine Benefactor, the divine Savior, and are busied with his earthly relations. Matthew paints him in his relation to the past of God's kingdom, Mark to its present, Luke to its future, as the Savior of the world. John is thinking of him as the infinite God, and paints him in his relation to eternity. Accordingly he begins, not, as Matthew does, with his messianic descent; nor, as Mark does, at once with his beneficent activity; nor, as Luke does, with his historical setting and human relationships; but with his relation to God as having from all eternity been with him and one with him and as having come forth from his bosom to reveal him to men and to gather back to communion with him all those given to him by the Father.

Accordingly John's Gospel is first of all the *Gospel of the Logos*. That the man Christ Jesus is the Word of God, who was in the beginning with God and was God—this is the central thought of the whole. It is with the formal exposition of this great teaching that the Gospel opens: and it is our Lord's self-witness to his oneness with God that, like a golden thread, binds all the discourses together. So that we are prepared to hear at the end, that the book was written that we might believe that Jesus is the Christ, the Son of God. Next to this, this is the *Gospel of Light*. The Word to whose glory it witnesses, is the light that lighteth every man that comes into the world; who came into the world to reveal by word and work and above all by his own person, the God of light. No less, however, is it the *Gospel of Life*. From beginning to end it is the Gospel of redemption, and according to it the incarnate Logos has been given to have life in himself that he might be the life of men. Finally, it is the *Gospel of Love,* in which, above all others, there is made known to us our divine Father's heart (John iii. 16), and our divine Shepherd's devotion (John x. 4).

In his Gospel too, therefore, John stands before us as the apostle of love. He is not therefore, however, the type of indiscriminate benevolence and easy good nature. This belongs rather to indifference than to love. It is because God is love, that he is also a consuming fire; and it is because John is the apostle of love that he is also a son of thunder. This love dares all, and *cannot bear* the evil (Rev. ii. 2). John was not the apostle of action: that was Peter or Paul. He was the apostle of loving contemplation, who, like Mary, hid everything in his heart and sought to make it *his* before making it *others'*. And his Gospel is not the Gospel of action: that is Mark's, which is also Peter's. Rather, in the highest and best sense of the word, John's is the Gospel of passion. It is the Gospel of passionate, never-failing, brooding love. He who wrote it understood his Master as only love can understand. Long years he had kept him, and what he did and what he said, treasured up not merely in his mind but in his heart; and his understanding had ripened as the years fled by—for "it is the heart that makes the theologian." In his old age, he brings out of the treasures of his teeming memory, words of life for the healing of the nations. Would these things have perished from the memory of man, had it not been for him? This Gospel could not have been written save by him who leaned on Jesus' breast. It can be understood only by those who lean on Jesus' breast.

43

JOHN'S GOSPEL OF ETERNAL LIFE*

Eternal life! In these two pregnant words are summed up, in the teaching of our Lord, all the blessings of salvation. Whether we look into the record, which Matthew, Mark, and Luke have preserved for us, of his occasional utterances, or into the record which John gives us of his more intimate discourses, in both alike, we shall find these great words on the Master's lips as a comprehensive epitome of all that he came into the world to bring to men.

There are, to be sure, some slight differences of emphasis in the two records. In the sayings recorded in the earlier Gospels our Lord's employment of the phrase is less frequent than in the discourses preserved by John. And there is a more prevailing reference in them to that future when the promised life shall be enjoyed in its perfection. Its characteristic presentation in these Gospels is as the heritage of those "righteous ones" who have followed Jesus in this world, when they shall receive their reward. The gate to it may be narrow, and the way straitened, but it is worth the toil and trials of the journey: it is good to enter into it, even maimed, that so escape may be made from that "eternal punishment" of "destruction" which is described as the "unquenchable fire." In the discourses preserved in John, this reference to the future is not absent. It rather underlies all allusions, and is, indeed, embedded in the very term. It occasionally also comes to direct expression, as when our Lord admonishes us even to hate our soul "in this world" that we may keep jt "unto life eternal." But the prevailing emphasis in these discourses is on the present

---

*The Westminster Teacher, May 1908, pp. 260-261.

possession of this life by all who are in "the Way." For, all who have the Son (who is the Way, the Truth, and the Life), not shall have but already have, eternal life. Wherever faith in him is, there, our Lord assures us, eternal life is already in real and indefeasible enjoyment.

It follows, of course, that wherever faith in Jesus Christ is not, there is no life at all. The gospel of eternal life is thrown up, in other words, against a background of universal death. It is just because men are dead that they need life; that life is such a boon to them; that Jesus Christ has come to bring them life. The whole world lies in the evil one; but God so loved the world, that he gave his only begotten Son that whosoever believes in him should not perish, but have eternal life. It is not merely that men are in danger of perishing; or merely that they are in the way of perishing. It is that they are already dead and can live only when the hour strikes when the dead hear the calling voice of the Son of God, and, hearing, live. And therefore, he tells us with plain faithfulness, those that disobey the Son shall not see life, but the wrath of God, not comes, but "abides," remains on them. They do not first incur the wrath of God by their disobedience; they only fail to escape it by obedience to him in whom alone is life and who graciously quickens whom he will.

This is the reason why the gospel of life is so great a gospel. It is a gospel of life out of death. It is not enough to say that those who receive it receive in it life. We must say, if we will do it justice, that they have "passed out of death into life." They have been dead, but now they live; yea, and they shall live forevermore. For, as we must take the death out of which they have passed in its full significance, so we must take the life into which they have passed in its complete meaning. This life is an "eternal" life. It did not need the adjective "eternal" to tell us so. In its very nature, the life which is brought to men by the Son of God is an imperishable life; and, therefore, the simple term "life" and the compound term "eternal life" are used quite interchangeably in our Lord's discourses. Those who, hearing the word of the Son of God, believe him who sent him, have definitely passed out of death into life, can never come into judgment. Of them it must always be said, they have—not may possibly have, may perchance, after a while, attain to, but *have*—"eternal life."

Manifestly, then, this "eternal life," thus received from the Life Indeed, is not a mere endless extension of the life we live in the world. When it is called "eternal" it is indeed declared to be of endless duration. But it is not thereby implied that in this lies its sole or even its chief contrast with the life which we live "in the world." This natural life, in contrast with the life in Christ, is rather no life at all; it is death. It would be no boon to continue it endlessly: that would be eternal death, and the very thing we are delivered from in Christ Jesus. No extension of death, into however infinite a duration, can make it life. Life is not only something specifically different from death, but its express contradiction. When, then, we pass out of death into life, we have once for all left the world and all that the world stands for behind us. We have entered into a specifically new kind of existence.

But although we enter at once on this new existence, it is not to be supposed that we receive at once all that the new life has in store for us. The gulf that separates life and death is an absolute one; and we have sprung this gulf once for all. But there is much yet before him who has sprung it. He is still in the world though no longer of it; and the world is the seat of evil, and he that remains in the world is assailed by this evil and is subject to temptation and sin. It would assuredly be better to be with Christ, where he is. Meanwhile, there is a course to be run, and there is a goal to strive after; and there is the promise of the holy keeping of the Father; who, though he takes us not yet out of the world, will guard us from the evil one. It is a great change we have experienced, passing out of death into life; but though all that is yet to come is contained in principle in this change, all the changes we are to experience are not exhausted in it. It is not yet manifest even to ourselves all that we shall be.

But the principle of the new life we have received is from the first manifest to us—the principle out of which, we know, all else is to flow. For here is the astonishing fact which illuminates our whole consciousness and transfigures our whole living; we now know God and live in communion with him, and with his Son, Jesus Christ. For this is life eternal, that we should know the only true God, and him whom he has sent, Jesus Christ. That we should *know* God and Jesus Christ! We do not know a person when we merely are assured that he exists. We do not really know him when we merely have a speaking acquaintance with him. We do not know him when we are merely accustomed to look to him for benefits and to receive favors from his hands. When we say we "know" a person, we mean that he is our familiar friend, with whom we have an intimate intercourse and constant companionship. The life which Christ brings his people is the introduction of them into this close and continuous communion with God.

And this is the reason why the gospel of eternal life is so precious a gospel. Because, this eternal life with which our Lord endows his people is just the everlasting continuance of blessed existence in unbroken communion with God. That we may take as a definition of "eternal life" as it is used in the discourses of our Lord in John's Gospel. Is it not also the definition of all the human heart can long after and aspire to?

44

THE APOCALYPSE*

It would be idle to deny that the Apocalypse is a very difficult book. It is probable that very many of the readers who,
under the spur of the great hope held out to them (Rev. i. 3),
turn to its pages for instruction, lay it aside again with unsatis-
fied longings and puzzled minds. But it is also certain that
the difficulty is largely of our own making, and not very hard to
unmake. Shortly, the enigma of the book arises from two
causes: chiefly from the wrong traditions as to its nature, which
have grown up around it, and under the influence of which we
approach it with so firm a belief that we shall find it what it is
not that we cannot see it as it is; and after that, from the
unwonted form in which it is cast.

We do not write and read apocalypses in these days. Few
of us have any acquaintance with this literary form, save as
it is exemplified in the Apocalypse of John. Nevertheless, John
did not strike out a totally new form of composition in this
book. The Holy Spirit simply adopted for it the most popular
literary vehicle of the age when it was written. It is strange to
us, not because it is unique or unhuman, but because fashions
in literature have so far changed in the course of eighteen centuries of time and the passage from the Jewish East to the
Anglo-Saxon West, that what was natural and lucid as a form
of expression then has become almost unintelligible now.
Fancy what a matter-of-fact and downright man, who had
never heard a fable, would make of one of Aesop's or La
Fontaine's gems, if suddenly confronted with it. This is what
has happened to us with the Apocalypse. Fables we know,

The Westminster Teacher, Nov. 1886, pp. 405-406.

and allegories, and, thanks to the Gospels, parables; but apocalypses we do not know, and when we are placed face to face with one in the Revelation of John we do not know what to make of it.

The remedy is simple. We must acquaint ourselves with the literary laws that govern the composition of apocalypses, and then read this apocalypse in accordance with them. This is what we do instinctively with a poem, a parable, an allegory, or a fable. We know how artistically a sonnet is framed, and, of late years, we have learned what marvels of art a rondeau or ballad can be. We know what to do with the form of a fable, and what to understand behind the figurative language of an allegory. What may be called the external art of an apocalypse surpasses that of a sonnet or a ballad; and in the case of the Revelation of John this symmetry of parts is more perfectly wrought out than in any other known example. But deeper than any matter of mere arrangement lies the basal principle of all apocalyptics, which is more far-reaching, moreover, than the principle of either fable or allegory. The apocalypse is a book of symbols. The whole action of the book and every detail of the representation, alike, is wrought out not directly, but through a symbolical medium. And as nothing is stated, so nothing is to be taken, literally; but every event, person, and thing, that appears on its pages is to be read as a symbol, and the thing symbolized understood. This is not to say one thing and mean another; it is only to say what is said through the medium of a series of symbols, and to mean nothing but the things symbolized. This may be strange to modern readers; but it is a thoroughly legitimate literary method, and no admirer of Bunyan or Dante can seriously object to it.

What it is to be an apocalypse being once understood, an apocalypse will be easy or difficult in proportion to the obviousness of its symbolism to us. If we have the key to its scheme of symbols it is easy. And this is why John's Apocalypse need not be other than easy: all its symbols are either obvious natural ones, or else have their roots planted in the Old Testament poets and prophets and the figurative language of Jesus and his apostles. No one who knows his Bible need despair of reading this book with profit. Above all, he who can understand our Lord's great discourse concerning the last things (Matt. xxiv), cannot fail to understand the Apocalypse, which is founded on that discourse and scarcely advances beyond it.

But in order to its understanding we must consent to read the book simply and in accordance with its structure. This implies that: (1) We should apply its symbolism consistently throughout. For instance, the number seven is not a designation of a literal "seven," but of a divine perfection, and we readily read it so when we read of the "seven" spirits that are before the throne, the "seven" seals of the book, the "seven" golden candlesticks, and the like. We must not forget this in xvii. 9, and understand the "seven" mountains as literally seven in number. (2) We should not forget that the purpose of this prophecy, as of all prophecy, is ethical and not chronological. All truth is in order to holiness. And the truths here revealed are not in order to enable us to read the detailed history of unborn ages, but to comfort the persecuted, encourage the tried, and succor the despairing. We are not to expect to find, therefore, pedantic descriptions of the special petty crises that have visited this people or that, or are yet to visit them; but a splendid revelation of the position and fortunes of the Church of Christ in the world and an enheartening assurance of the certain eventuation of the conflict in victory. (3) We should not try to force the book to deliver a continuously progressive prophecy from beginning to end. Nothing is clearer than that it constantly returns on itself. And it is probable that, with a prologue (i. 1-8) and an epilogue (xxii. 6-21), it is framed in seven parallel sections (the divisions falling at iii. 22; viii. 1; xi. 19; xiv. 20; xvi. 21; xix. 10), each of which independently unveils the great principles that rule the conflict between Christ and Belial, and glance at it in its whole extent from inception to victorious conclusion.

It cannot be denied that the unlettered Christians who have gone to the book for comfort and strength amid dark days have understood it better than the scholars. The scholars are still puzzling over it and wresting it to their will. The simple child of God has never failed, in a time of spiritual crisis, to go to it with wondering love or to return from each draught with new heart and power. And thus, for its chosen readers, it has always proved to be as Godet says, "the precious vessel in which *the treasure of Christian hope* has been deposited for all ages of the Church, but especially for the Church under the cross."

45

DOUBT*

The Hebrew of the Old Testament seems to lack an exact equivalent to our term "doubt," when used in a religious reference. Some have, indeed, understood "doubters," "skeptics" to be meant when the Psalmist, who loves God's law and hopes in his word and delights in keeping his commandments, declares that he "hates them that are of a double mind" (Ps. cxix. 113, סֵעֲפִים). Apparently, however, it is rather hypocrites, what we should call "double-faced men," who are meant; and it seems to be hypocrisy, rather than doubt, which is in mind also in 1 Kings xviii. 21, where the kindred term סְעִפִּים occurs, and in 1 Chron. xii. 33, Ps. xii. 2, where the similar phrase "double heart" (לֵב וָלֵב) appears, as well as in Hos. x. 2, where the commentators differ as to whether the words חָלַק לִבָּם are to be translated "their heart is divided," or, perhaps better, "their heart is smooth," that is, deceitful.

In the New Testament, on the other hand, we meet with a series of terms which run through the shades of meaning expressed by our words, perplexity, suspense, distraction, hesitation, questioning, skepticism, shading down into unbelief.

Perplexity is expressed by the verb ἀπορέω (Mark vi. 20; Luke xxiv. 4; John xiii. 22; Acts xxv. 20; 2 Cor. iv. 8; Gal. iv. 20), with its strengthened compound, διαπορέω (Luke ix. 7; Acts ii. 12; v. 24; x. 17), expressing thorough perplexity, when one is utterly at a loss, and the still stronger compound ἐξαπορέω (2 Cor. i. 8; iv. 8), in which perplexity has passed into despair. This perplexity is never assigned in the New Testament to the sphere of religion. Even in such instances as Luke xxiv. 4, where we are told that the women, finding the Lord's

---

*Hastings' *Dictionary of the Bible*, Vol. I, pp. 618-619.

tomb empty, "were perplexed thereabout"; Mark vi. 20, Luke ix. 6, where Herod's perplexity over John's preaching and the subsequent preaching of Jesus and his followers is spoken of; and Acts ii. 12, where the extreme perplexity of those who witnessed the wonders of the Day of Pentecost is adverted to, it is not a state of religious doubt but of pure mental bewilderment which is described. The women merely had no explanation of the empty tomb ready, they were at a loss how to account for it; Herod simply found John's preaching and the reports concerning the preaching and work of Jesus and his disciples inexplicable, he had no theory ready for their explanation; the marvels of Pentecost, before Peter's explanation of them, were wholly without meaning to their witnesses; and, similarly, in Acts x. 17, Peter was just at a complete loss to understand what the vision he had received could mean, and required a revelation to make it significant to him. It was this state of mind, a state of what we may call objective suspense due to lack of light, which the Jews claimed for themselves when in John x. 24 they demanded of Jesus: "How long dost thou lift up our soul (τὴν ψυχὴν ἡμῶν αἴρεις)? If thou art the Christ, tell us plainly." They would suggest that they were in a state of strained expectation regarding his claims, and that the lagging of their decision was due, not to subjective causes rooted in an evil heart of unbelief, but to a lack of bold frankness on his part. Jesus, in his reply, repels this insinuation and ascribes the fault to their own unbelief. They were not eager seekers after truth, held in suspense by his ambiguous speech: they were men in possession of full evidence, who would not follow it to a conclusion opposing their wishes; they were therefore not perplexed, but unbelieving.

For the doubt of the distracted mind the New Testament appears to have two expressions, μετεωρίζεσθαι (Luke xii. 29) and διστάζειν (Matt. xiv. 31; xxviii. 17). This state of mind is superinduced on faith, and is a witness to the faith which lies behind it; only those who have faith can waver or be distracted from it. But the faith to which it witnesses is equally necessarily an incomplete and imperfect faith; only an imperfect faith can waver or be distracted from its firm assurance. The exhortation, "Be ye not of a wavering mind," is appropriately given, therefore, in Luke xii. 29, to those who are addressed as "of little faith" (ὀλιγόπιστοι), of whom it is the specific characteristic. It is to trust in God's providential care without carking anxiety as to our food and drink and clothing that the Savior is exhorting his hearers in this context—to fulness of faith, which, according to its definition in Heb. xi. 1, is absorbed in the unseen and future in contrast with the seen and present. Those who have full faith will have their whole life hid with God; and in proportion as care for earthly things enters, in that proportion do we fall away from the heights of faith and exhibit a wavering mind. It was a similar weakness which attacked Peter, when, walking, by virtue of faith, upon the water to come to Jesus, he saw the wind and was afraid (Matt. xiv. 31); and, accordingly, our Savior addressed him similarly, "O thou of little faith, wherefore didst thou doubt (ἐδίστασας)?" Here, again, is real faith though weak, but a faith that is distracted by the entrance of fear. The same term, and surely with similar implications, is used again and on an even more interesting occasion. When the disciples of Jesus came to the mountain where he had appointed them and there saw their risen Lord, we are told (Matt. xxviii. 17), "They worshiped: but some doubted (ἐδίστασαν)." It is this same doubt of imperfect and distracted faith, and not the skeptical doubt of unbelief, that is intended. All worshiped him, though some not without that doubt of the distracted mind which is no more "psychologically absurd" here than in Luke xii. 29 and Matt. xiv. 31. Whence the distraction arose, whether possibly from joy itself, as in Luke xxiv. 41, or from a less noble emotion, as possibly in John xx. 25, we do not know. But the quality of doubt resulting from it, although manifesting the incompleteness of the disciples' faith, was not inconsistent with its reality; and the record of it is valuable to us as showing, along with such passages as Luke xxiv. 37, 41, John xx. 25, that the apostles' testimony to the resurrection was that of convinced rather than of credulous witnesses.

A kindred product of weak faith, the doubt of questioning hesitation, is expressed in the New Testament by the term διαλογισμός (Luke xxiv. 38; Rom. xiv. 1; Phil. ii. 14; 1 Tim. ii. 8). It is the nemesis of weakness of faith that it is pursued by anxious questionings and mental doubts. Thus, when Christ appeared to his disciples in Jerusalem, "they were terrified and affrighted, and supposed that they had beheld a spirit" (Luke xxiv. 36), provoking their Master's rebuke, "Wherefore do questionings arise in your heart?" And in St. Paul's Epistles, the timid outlook of the weak in faith is recognized as their chief characteristic. This seems to be the meaning of Rom. xiv. 1, where "he that is weak in faith" is to be received into full Christian brotherhood, but not "for the adjudication of questionings" (cf. the κρινέτω of vs. 3 and the κρίνων of vs. 4): here is a man whose mind is crowded with scruples and doubts —he is to be received, of course, but not as if his agitated conscience were to be law to the community; he is to be borne with, not to be obeyed. The same implication underlies Phil. ii. 14, where the contrast between "murmurings and disputings" seems to be not so much between moral and intellectual rebellion, as between violent and timid obstacles in the Christian pathway—a contrast which appears also in 1 Tim. ii. 8. It would seem that those who are troubled with questionings are everywhere recognized as men who possess faith, but who are deterred from a proper entrance into their privileges and a proper performance of their Christian duties by a settled habit of hesitant casuistry, which argues lack of robustness in their faith.

The New Testament term which expresses that deeper doubt which argues not merely the weakness but the lack of faith is the verb διακρίνεσθαι (Matt. xxi. 21; Mark xi. 23; Rom. iv. 20; xiv. 23; James i. 6 bis; Jude 22). Wherever this critical attitude toward divine things is found, there faith is absent. The term may be used in contrast to that faith by which miracles are wrought, or in which God is approached in prayer (Matt. xxi. 21; Mark xi. 23; James i. 6 bis); in either case it implies the absence of the faith in question and the consequent failure of the result—he that "doubteth" in this sense cannot expect to receive anything of the Lord. It may be used of a frame of mind in which one lives his life out in the Christian profession (Rom. xiv. 23); in this case, the intrusion of this critical spirit vitiates the whole course of his activities—because they are no longer of faith, and "whatsoever is not of faith is sin." Or it may be used as the extreme contrast to that fulness of faith which Abraham exhibited in his typical act of faith; and then it is represented as the outgrowth of unbelief (Rom. iv. 20). From the full description of its opposite here, and the equally full description of it itself in James i. 6 ff. (see Mayor's note), we may attain a tolerably complete conception of its nature as the critical self-debating habit of the typical skeptic, which casts him upon life like a derelict ship upon the sea, and makes him in all things "double-minded" and "unstable." Such a habit of mind is the extreme contradiction of faith, and cannot coexist with it; and it is therefore treated everywhere with condemnation—unless Jude 22 be an exception, and there the reading is too uncertain to justify its citation as such.

46

THE SIGNIFICANCE OF THE WESTMINSTER STANDARDS AS A CREED*

The significance of the Westminster Standards as a creed is to be found in the three facts that: historically speaking, they are the final crystalization of the elements of evangelical religion, after the conflicts of sixteen hundred years; scientifically speaking, they are the richest and most precise and best guarded statement ever penned of all that enters into evangelical religion and of all that must be safeguarded if evangelical religion is to persist in the world; and, religiously speaking, they are a notable monument of spiritual religion.

1. The gospel of the grace of God, or evangelical religion as we call it today, is, of course, the whole burden of the Scriptural revelation. But the Scriptural revelation does not supply the starting point, but the goal of the development of doctrine in the Church. There is a great gulf cleft between the writings of the apostles and their immediate successors, which is in nothing more marked than just in the slight grasp which the latter have on the principles of evangelical religion. It was not until Augustine, in opposition to the audacious assaults of Pelagianism, recovered for it the treasures of the gospel of grace that the Church grasped them with any fulness or firmness. Nor even then was it able to retain them in their purity. The light which Augustine kindled faded again steadily until it was rekindled by the Reformation. It was once more obscured for the Lutheran churches by Melanchthonian syn-

---

*This is a summary of an address "delivered, on its appointment, before the Presbytery of New York, Nov. 8, 1897" (from the *Princeton Press,* Nov. 13, 1897); published in book form, with the same title, New York, 1898, 36 pp.

ergism and the subsequent developments. Only among the Reformed was it retained in all its brightness, and that not without a struggle against not merely external foes but internal treason. In these struggles, however, the gem of the gospel was cut and polished, and it is on this account that the enunciation of the gospel in the Reformed Confessions attains its highest purity; and that among other Reformed Confessions the Westminster Confession, the product of the Puritan conflict, reaches a perfection of statement never elsewhere achieved.

2. It is incident to this, its historical origin, that the statement given the gospel in the Westminster Standards touches the high-water mark of the scientific statement of the elements of evangelical religion. For, a higher scientific quality of doctrinal statement is attainable through the vital processes of controversy than through the cool efforts of closet construction. The scientific character of the Nicene and Chalcedonian definitions are due to this cause; and the Westminster Standards are the products of a similar history, and can lay claim to like finality in their sphere. The perennial foes of evangelical religion— sacerdotalism and humanitarianism—received not only their most powerful embodiment but also their most insidious and subtle manifestations in the age in which the Westminster theology was being prepared; and, in conflict with them, the most perfect statement of evangelical religion was necessarily wrought out. As truly as in the cases of the Nicene and Chalcedonian formularies, the Westminster Standards mark an epoch in the history of human reflection on the truths of the gospel— an epoch in the attainment and registry of doctrinal truth; and as truly in the one case as in the other the statements they give of the truths that fall in their sphere are scientifically final. All attempts at restatement must either repeat their definitions or fall away from the purity of their conceptions or the justness of their language.

3. A scientific statement of vital truth, originating in organic controversy, cannot possibly lack in spiritual quality. It is the product of intellect working only under the impulse of the heart, and must be a monument of the religious life. This is

true of all the great creedal statements, and preëminently true of the Westminster Standards. Their authors were men of learning and philosophic grasp; but above all of piety. Their interest was not in speculative construction, but in the protection of their flocks from deadly error. It results from the very nature of the case, therefore, that it is a religious document which they have given us; and the nicety of its balance in conceiving and the precision of its language in stating truth, will seem to us scholastic only in proportion as our religious life is less developed than theirs. It requires a well-closed vessel to keep out all corrupting germs; and it requires a wide experience and a nice appreciation of what true holiness is to estimate at their true value the expedients used for the exclusion of the corrupting germs. In proportion as our own religious life flows in a deep and broad stream, in that proportion will we find spiritual delight in the Westminster Standards.

Surely blessed are the churches which feed upon such meat! May God Almighty infuse their strength into our bones, and their beauty into our flesh, and enable us to justify our inheritance by unfolding into life, in all its completeness and richness, the precious gospel which they have enfolded for us in their protecting envelope of sound words!

47

THE DOGMATIC SPIRIT*

What is called the dogmatic spirit is not popular among men. It is characterized by an authoritative method of presenting truth; by an unwillingness to modify truth to fit it to current conceptions; by an insistence on what seem to many minor points; and above all by (what lies at the root of most of its other peculiarities) a habit of thinking in a system, and a consequent habit of estimating the relative importance of the separate items of truth by their logical relation to the body of truth, rather than by their apparent independent value. Such a habit of mind seems to be the only appropriate attitude toward a body of truth given by revelation, and committed to men only to embrace, cherish, preserve, and propagate. It seems to be, moreover, the attitude toward the body of revealed truth commended to those who were to be its "ministers" and not its masters, by the Lord and his apostles, when they placed it as a rich treasure in the keeping of stewards of the mysteries of God. But it is irritating to men. They would discuss rather than receive truth. And, if they must receive it, they would fain modify it here and there to fit preconceived opinions or permit cherished practices. Especially in a busy age in which Pilate's careless question, "what is truth?" represents the prevailing attitude of men's minds, the dogmatic habit is apt to fare somewhat badly.

An illustration of what is meant by the dogmatic spirit may be found in a passage in the biography of that great servant of Christ, Caesar Malan, who is forgotten already in the land which he served so nobly in the gospel of Christ, but to whom,

---

*The Presbyterian Journal, Oct. 11, 1894, p. 648.

under God, along with his compeers, Merle D'Aubigne and
Louis Gaussen, Switzerland owes her awakening to the light
of truth in this century. It is, perhaps, none the worse as an
illustration that it presents the dogmatic habit in an extreme
form, and, in the opinion of the biographer at least, in perverted action. The biographer is pointing out what he believed
to be Malan's greater fitness for the missionary than for the
pastoral office. He thinks his habit of mind, firing him with
zeal for the whole truth, eminently fitted him for the one function and somewhat unsuited him for the other. "Called to be
a witness, a confessor, an apostle," he says, "we may say of
him what the chief of the apostles scrupled not to say of himself, that 'he was not sent to baptize, but to preach the gospel.'
. . . Looking at everything from the most serious point of view,
tracing each offense not to its secondary or accidental source,
but to those abstract principles which his spirit so rapidly
divined, and the issues of which he so vividly apprehended,
it was too probable that with him every act of heedlessness
would be a crime, every unenlightened sentiment a heresy,"
[the spirit by] which the dogmatic habit is exposed. It may be
misled into harsh judgments of individuals by its own clear
view of the consistency of truth, and its own vivid realization
of the significance and issue of special errors and shortcomings.
But its essential virtue is also here presented before us. Its
clear insight into truth as a body and in its parts; its rapid
perception of and firm grasp upon determining principles; its
vivid apprehension of the logical and ultimately the inevitable
practical effects of this and that apparently unimportant modification of truth; its consequent zeal to preserve the truth from
corruption and its devotion to its propagation: these are the
elements of the true dogmatic spirit. It is, accordingly, as
Malan's biographer forcibly points out, the true missionary
spirit—the spirit of the Apostle Paul.

We may observe its working in Paul, in the Epistle to the
Galatians. Here burns the purest zeal for that gospel which he
had been sent to preach. Doubtless the preaching of the
Judaizers appeared to the Galatians as but a slight modification

of that of Paul—a modification which did not affect the essence of the gospel, and which presented many advantages. The Judaizers also preached Christ. They preached Christ as the promised Messiah of Israel, only through the acceptance of whom could entrance be had into the messianic salvation. To them, too, therefore, the promised redemption was unattainable save through the promised Messiah. But though they preached that only in his name could salvation be had, they denied that it could be had in his name alone. Something else was requisite. Men must accept the Messiah; but men must also be circumcised—men must keep the law—men must enter into life by the gate of Judaism. It was this teaching—not the proclamation of an entirely anti-Christian system—which Paul brands as a different kind of gospel or rather no gospel at all, but only a troubling of Zion by those who would pervert the gospel of Christ.

Was Paul narrow-minded and over-severe in this? Evidently there were many Galatians who thought so. Why harshly pronounce those "accursed" who taught fundamentally the same doctrine of the Messiah; and only differed in this, certainly very minor, point of whether the keeping of the law was not necessary too? How can the violence of asserting that if circumcision be received Christ will profit nothing, be possibly excused? Is not this the very embodiment of narrow-minded fanaticism yielding to the *odium theologicum?* There are apparently many today who would sympathize with the Galatians in so arguing. Paul, however, thought in a system; traced apparently small differences back to their principles; perceived clearly the issues to which they tended; and condemned according to fact and not according to appearance. He is the type of the dogmatic spirit. And we who would be followers of Paul, even as he was of Christ, may learn some very valuable lessons from him.

Primarily, we may learn this lesson: that it is not a matter of small importance whether we preserve the purity of the gospel. The chief dangers to Christianity do not come from the anti-Christian systems. Mohammedanism has never made inroads upon Christendom save by the sword. Nobody fears that Christianity will be swallowed up by Buddhism. It is corrupt forms of Christianity itself which menace from time to time the life of Christianity. Why make much of minor points of difference among those who serve the one Christ? Because a pure gospel is worth preserving; and is not only worth preserving, but is logically (and logic will always work itself ultimately out into history) the only saving gospel. Those who overlay the gospel with man-made additions, no less than those who subtract from it God-given elements, are not preaching "the gospel" in another form, but are offering a different kind of gospel, which is essentially no gospel at all. They are troublers of Israel, who are perverting the gospel of Christ.

Then, we may learn this lesson: that it is not a matter of small importance for the servant of Christ to begin to seek to please men in the gospel which he offers them. Doing so, he ceases to be Christ's servant, performing his will; and becomes the slave of men, veering hither and thither according to their beck and call. So doing, he is no longer the teacher of the truth to men, but the learner of falsehood from men. It doubtless seemed to the Judaizers very proper to adapt the mode in which they presented Christ to man, to the views of the community on which they had to depend for their first hearing in every fresh city. Paul says that in so doing they won not the blessing of God but his curse. After all, what is required of stewards is that they be found faithful.

And then we may learn this supreme lesson above all: that it is of the very gravest importance to keep clearly before our and others' minds and hearts the great fact that in Christ alone is there salvation. In Christ alone; and that in both senses of the word "alone." Not only can there be no salvation except in him; but in him is all that can be needed for salvation. Jesus only! Paul determined to know nothing in Corinth but Jesus Christ and him as crucified. The only saving gospel is to find in him *all*. There needs no supplement to his work. His work admits of no supplement. To depend on aught else—aught else, however small it may seem—along with him is as truly to lose him as to depend on aught else instead of him. The solemn words of Paul, "Behold I, Paul, say unto you that if you receive circumcision, Christ will profit you nothing," have their multiform application in these modern times. And it behooves us so to live and so to preach, today, that we can say now, as he said then, that our only trust and our only glory is in the cross of Jesus Christ; and that we find in him and his work alone the beginning and the middle and the end of salvation. He is not only the author but also the finisher of our faith.

> A Christless cross no refuge is for me;
> A Crossless Christ my Savior may not be;
> But, O Christ crucified! I rest in thee.

48

AUTHORITY, INTELLECT, HEART*

The exact nature of the intimate relation between religion and theology is not always perceived. Sometimes religion is made the direct product of theology; more frequently theology is conceived as directly based on religion. The truth is that while they react continually upon each other, neither is the creation of the other. They are parallel products of the same body of truths in different spheres. Religion is the name we give to religious life; theology is the name we give to the systematized body of religious thought. Neither is the product of the other, but both are products of religious truth, operative in the two spheres of life and thought. Neither can exist without the other. No one but a religious man can be a true theologian. No one can live religiously who is innocent of all theological conceptions. Man is a unit; and the religious truth which impinges upon him must affect him in all his activities, or in none. But it is in their common cause—religious truth—that religion and theology find their deepest connection. The truth concerning God, his nature, his will, his purposes is the fundamental fact upon which both religion and theology rest. The truth of God is, therefore, the greatest thing on earth. On it rest our faith, our hope, and our love. Through it we are converted and sanctified. On it depends all our religion, as well as all our theology.

There are three media or channels through which the truth of God is brought to man and made his possession, that it may affect his life and so make him religious, or that it may be systematized in his thinking and so issue in a theology. These

---

*The Presbyterian Messenger, Jan. 30, 1896, pp. 7 f.

three media or channels of communication may be enumerated briefly as *authority,* the *intellect,* and the *heart.* They are not so related to one another that any one of them may be depended upon to the exclusion of the others. In any sound religion and in any true religious thinking, that is theology, all three must be engaged, and must work harmoniously together as the proximate sources of our religion and of our knowledge. The exaltation of any one of the three to the relative exclusion of the others will, therefore, mar our religious life and our religious thought alike, and make both one-sided and deformed. We cannot have a symmetrical religious life or a true theology except through the perfect interaction of all three sources of communication of the truth.

It may, indeed, be plausibly pleaded that the three reduce ultimately to one; and this one channel of truth may, with almost equal plausibility, be found in each of the three in turn. Thus it may be urged that our confidence in the processes of our intellects and in the deliverances of our feelings, rests ultimately on the trustworthiness of God; so that, after all, authority is the sole source of our information concerning God. We know only what and as God tells us. Similarly it may be argued that all the dicta of authority are addressed to the intellect, which, also, is the sole instrument for ascertaining the implications of the feelings; so that all our sources of knowledge reduce at last to this one source—the intellect. We know only what our intellect grasps and formulates for us. Still again, it may be contended that not the logical reason but the facts of life, our upward strivings, our feelings of dependence and responsibility, supply the points of contact between us and God, without which all the thunders of authority and all the excursions of thought into the realm of divine things, would be as unintelligible to us and as inoperative upon us as a babbling of colors would be to a blind man. There is truth in each of these representations; but they do not avail to show that we have but one means of access to divine things, but rather emphasize the fact that the three sources so interlace and interact that one may not be exaggerated to the exclusion of the others as our sole channel of knowledge concerning God and divine things.

The exaggeration of the principle of authority to the discrediting of the others would cast us into *traditionalism,* and would ultimately deliver us bound hand and foot to the irresponsible dogmatism of a privileged caste. This is the pathway which has been trodden by the Church of Rome, and we have as the result a nerveless submission to the dicta, first of an infallible church, then of an infallible class, and lastly of an infallible person. Here neither the heart nor the intellect is permitted to speak in the presence of lordly authority; but men are commanded docilely to receive, on authority alone, even what contradicts their most primary intuitions (as in the doctrine of transubstantiation) or what outrages their most intimate feelings (as in the use of indulgences).

The exaggeration of the principle of intellect to the discrediting of the others would bring us to *rationalism,* and leave us helplessly in the grasp of the merely logical understanding. This pathway has been followed by the rationalists, and we have as the result any number of *a priori* systems built up on the sole credit of the reasoning faculty. Here neither revelation nor the conscience is permitted to raise a protest against the chill processes of intellectual *formulae,* but all things are reconstructed at the bidding of *a priori* fancies, and men are required to reject as false all for which they have not a demonstration ready even though God has spoken to assert its truth (as in the doctrine of the Trinity) or the heart rises up and answers, I have felt (as in original sin).

The exaggeration of the principle of the heart to the discrediting of the others would throw us into *mysticism,* and deliver us over to the deceitfulness of the currents of feeling which flow up and down in our souls. This pathway has been traveled by the mystics, and we have as the result the clash of rival revelations, and the deification of the most morbid of human imaginations. Here neither the objective truth of a revealed word nor adherence to rational thinking is allowed to check the wild dreaming of a soul that fancies itself divine,

or the confusion of our weakest sentiments with the strong voice
of God; and men are forbidden to clarify their crude fancies
by right reason (as in the doctrine of absorption in God), or to
believe God's own testimony to his real nature (as with reference to his personality).

Thus authority, when pressed beyond its mark and becoming traditionalism, intellect when puffed up into rationalism,
and the heart when swamped in mysticism, alike illustrate the
danger of one-sided construction. Authority, intellect, and the
heart are the three sides of the triangle of truth. How they interact is observable in any concrete instance of their operation. Authority, in the Scriptures, furnishes the matter which is received
in the intellect and operates on the heart. The revelations of
the Scriptures do not terminate upon the intellect. They were
not given merely to enlighten the mind. They were given
through the intellect to beautify the life. They terminate on
the heart. Again, they do not, in affecting the heart, leave the
intellect untouched. They cannot be fully understood by the intellect, acting alone. The natural man cannot receive the things
of the Spirit of God. They must first convert the soul before
they are fully comprehended by the intellect. Only as they
are lived are they understood. Hence the phrase, "Believe
that you may understand," has its fullest validity. No man can
intellectually grasp the full meaning of the revelations of
authority, save as the result of an experience of their power
in life. Hence, that the truths concerning divine things may
be so comprehended that they may unite with a true system of
divine truth, they must be: first, revealed in an authoritative
word; second, experienced in a holy heart; and third, formulated by a sanctified intellect. Only as these three unite, then,
can we have a true theology. And equally, that these same
truths may be so received that they beget in us a living religion,
they must be: first, revealed in an authoritative word; second,
apprehended by a sound intellect; and third, experienced in an
instructed heart. Only as the three unite, then, can we have
a vital religion.

49

HERESY AND CONCESSION*

In Dr. G. P. Fisher's recently issued *History of Christian Doctrine* there is a very suggestive passage in which he tells us how heresies usually originate, and gives us an insight into their nature. He says:

> When Christianity is brought into contact with modes of thought and tenets originating elsewhere, either of two effects may follow. It may assimilate them, discarding whatever is at variance with the gospel, or the tables may be turned and the foreign elements may prevail. In the latter case there ensues a perversion of Christianity, an amalgamation with it of ideas discordant with its nature. The product then is a heresy. But to fill out the conception, it seems necessary that error should be aggressive and should give rise to an effort to build up a party, and thus to divide the Church. In the Apostles' use of the term, "heresy" contains a factious element.

He then proceeds to remark that " 'heresy' meant originally 'choice'; then an opinion that is the product of choice or of the will, instead of being drawn from the divine Word"; that it is, in a word, "a man-made opinion" as distinguished from a divinely taught doctrine.

It does not require the wide and detailed acquaintance with the history of religious thought which Dr. Fisher has at his command to enable the reader to appreciate the aptness of this generalization. Possibly Dr. Fisher would not himself present it as the formula by which every heresy has been compounded. It obviously fairly describes, however, the origin of most of the greater heresies which have vexed the Church. The early gnostic systems were but varied attempts to baptize

---

The Presbyterian Messenger, May 7, 1896.

oriental pantheistic and dualistic speculations. Each of the christological constructions of the ante-Chalcedonian Church was but an effort to pour the teachings of the Scriptures as to the person of the Redeemer into the molds of some human philosophy. The Pelagian exaltation of human ability and consequent denial of the necessity of the inner work of the Holy Ghost was but (as Hefele says) "the rehabilitation of that heathen view of the world," in accordance with which Cicero declared that men do indeed thank God for gold and lands, but never for their virtues; and Jerome accordingly speaks of it accurately as "the heresy of Pythagoras and Zeno." The subsequent semi-Pelagianism which has stained the thought of the whole Latin Church, and the Arminianism which has sapped the purity of so large a section of Protestant thought, are but less acute forms of the same exaggeration of human rights and powers as over against the sovereign right and absolute power of the Ruler of the universe. And just as the pagan considers his idol as his property, and requires of it the services which he asks of it—beating it when it fails to give according to his desires, and destroying it when it no longer fulfils his expectations—so modern "thinkers," still considering themselves Christians, look upon their God as the product of their intellection, keep him strictly to the activities for which they have invented him, and require at his hands all that they have made him for. So poor Heine was sure of forgiveness, for, as he said, "that is what God is for"; and so our new Kantians acknowledge God only so far as they have need of him to harmonize their intellectual difficulties or solve their moral doubts. Like the idols of the heathen, he is the work of their hands, and exists only to serve their ends. They never imagine that they are the work of his hands and exist only to serve his ends.

Let us look a little more closely, however, at Dr. Fisher's fruitful description of how heresy arises.

True Christian doctrine is the pure teaching of the divine Word. Whatsoever is revealed in that Word the Christian believes to be true for the authority of God himself speaking in it. There may be other sources of knowledge from which he may learn what is true, but there is no source of knowledge which will rank with him in authority above the written Word of God, or to which he can appeal with superior confidence. It is a mark of the Christian man that the Word is his source and norm of truth, and wherever it has spoken he asks no further evidence, nor can he admit any modification whatever of its deliverances, no matter from what quarter they may be drawn.

But Christianity is immersed in the world. And the world has its own modes of thought and its own teachings, which are their products. And the Christian man necessarily comes into contact with them. What attitude shall he assume with reference to them? What welcome shall he accord them? Of one thing certainly he is sure—that all truth is God's. All truth comes forth from him; all truth leads back to him. No one should greet truth from whatever source with more readiness and more enthusiasm than he. And it is only simple justice to say that in all the history of thought no one has ever shown himself more hospitable to truth in every sphere, more eager to seek and embrace it, than the Christian man. Zeal in investigation, success in wresting nature's secrets from her, unwearied diligence in the study of the past—these are marked characteristics of Christian civilization.

An attitude of eager hospitality toward the researches of the world is becoming in the Christian man; he serves the God of truth. Such an attitude is safe for him; he has in his hands the norm of truth, in the Word of God. This is the Ariadne clue by means of which he can thread his way through the labyrinths of the world's thought; this is the touchstone by the art of which he may choose the good and refuse the evil. So long as he clings to it he will build up the temple of truth, whencesoever he quarries the stones. When he loses hold of it, however, he descends into the arena and takes his hap with other men; and going his own way, it is not strange that he is often found with his back turned to God. The condition of right thinking —or "orthodoxy"—is, therefore, that the Christian man should look out upon the seething thought of the world from the safe standpoint of the sure Word of God. The fertile source of wilful thinking—or "heresy"—is that, on the contrary, he is often found looking at the teachings of God's Word from the standpoint of the world's speculations.

It is to be observed that it is to the very prevalent habit of "concession" to the world's thinking, that Dr. Fisher's words point us, as the fruitful mother of heresy. And it must be admitted that the temptation to "concession" is often very strong.

For one thing, the world is very confident of its own conclusions, and it is very sure of the infallibility of its own methods of research. It does not call its tenets "opinions," "views," "conjectures." It dignifies them in the mass by the abstract names of "philosophy," "science," "learning," "scholarship." It does not offer them to the Christian for testing and trial; it thrusts them upon him as the perfect expression of final knowledge. He is not requested to subject them to his touchstone, the Word of God, or sift from them the good and reject the bad. He is required to substitute them for the teachings of the Word of God as the only really solid basis of all his thinking.

For another thing, the Christian teacher is very anxious to conciliate the world. His primary interest is in the souls of men. May he not smooth the passage of many to the ark of safety by clothing himself in the garments of their thought? And, after all, why should he distrust either their methods or their conclusions? Would it not be better to take up a position shoulder to shoulder with them, stand on their platform, and concede to their demand everything which can be conceded while yet the central citadel be held? Has not the *minimum* of assertion after all its own strength? and is it not better to claim no more than we must? In any event, what is the use of flinging into the face of an unbelieving world as truth that which the *consensus* of scholarship or of scientific investigation proclaims impossible? Let Tertullian, if he will, "believe because it is impossible," and such paradoxists as Sir Thomas Browne train their faith by posing it with incredible things. We cannot expect men of common sense to look upon such procedure with allowance. Nay, as men of common sense ourselves, we cannot profess to nourish a faith strong enough to believe to be true what all science or all philosophy or all criticism pronounces unbelievable.

For still another thing—let us confess it with what shame we may—the Christian man is often painfully aware that he himself, that the Christian community, is no match for the world in varied knowledge, in power of dialectic, in diligence of literary production; and so feels too weak to hold his position in the face of the world's assaults. Had not an apostle foretold to us that not many wise would be called, and warned us that the wisdom of men would be arrayed against the truth of the gospel, we might indeed be often dismayed, if not beaten down, by the superior vigor, brightness, acumen, force of the world's thinking. As it is, we are often puzzled; and good men have sometimes thought it necessary, as they account for the unapproachable majesty and calm security of the apostolic writings by the inspiration of God, so to call in an evil inspiration to account for the brilliancy of the world's attack on the religion of Christ. Thus good John Newton suggests that evil men must be credited with what he calls a "black inspiration."

"After making the best allowance I can," he writes, "both for the extent of human genius and the deplorable evil of the human heart, I cannot suppose that one-half of the wicked wit, of which some persons are so proud, is properly their own. Perhaps such a one as Voltaire would neither have written, or have been read or admired so much, if he had not been the amanuensis of another hand in his own way."

Whatever account we may give, however, of the power of the world's thought over Christian men, it seems pretty clear that the "concessive" attitude which leads men to accept the tenets which have originated elsewhere than in the Scriptures as the foundation of their thinking, and to bend Scripture into some sort of conciliation with them, is the ruling spirit of our time, which may, therefore, be said to be dominated by the very spirit of "heresy." "Modern discovery" and "modern thought" are erected into the norm of truth, and we are told that the whole sphere of theological teaching must be conformed to it. This is the principle of that reconstruction of religious thinking which we are now constantly told is going on resistlessly about us, and which is to transform all theology. What is demanded of us is just to adjust our religious views to the latest pronouncements of philosophy or science or criticism. And this is demanded with entire unconsciousness of the fundamental fact of Christianity—that we have a firmer ground of confidence for our religious views than any science or philosophy or criticism can provide for any of their pronouncements. It is very plain that he who modifies the teachings of the Word of God in the smallest particular at the dictation of any "man-made opinion" has already deserted the Christian ground, and is already, in principle, a "heretic." The very essence of "heresy" is that the modes of thought and tenets originating elsewhere than in the Scriptures of God are given decisive weight when they clash with the teachings of God's Word, and those are followed to the neglect or modification or rejection of these.

It probably requires to be confessed that the form which has been taken by much recent apologetics has played into the hands of this "concessive" habit, and may therefore be held responsible for some of the "heresy" in the Church of the day. Apologetics is in its nature a conciliatory science, and it is often the best apologetics to find and stand on the *minimum*. This is often the best apologetics, we say, but not always; and it can never be good apologetics to lead men to suppose that the *minimum* is all, or all that is worth defending, or all that is capable of defense. Yet it is undeniable that some recent apologetics has left on the minds of men some such impression. Perhaps we may even say that some recent apologists have been emphatic in proclaiming that this *minimum* is the entirety of defensible Christianity. At its best, however, this method of apologetics needs to be warily used; when it becomes a fixed habit of mind, it is very liable not only to be abused but to prove the prolific parent of many evils.

For one thing, it is found, in practice, that he who is accustomed to defend only the *minimum* is singularly apt to come to undervalue the undefended *maximum*. A truth not worth defending very soon comes to seem to him not worth professing. For another thing, the *maximum* left undefended is very apt to be also forgotten, and the defended *minimum* pieced out into some sort of apparent completeness, with scraps borrowed from the tenets elsewhere originating than in the Word of God; and so "a perversion of Christianity" arises, "an amalgamation with it of ideas discordant with its nature." For still another thing, he who only defends the *minimum* renounces the strongest and best of all the evidences of Christianity. That great demonstration of the truth of Christianity which springs at once from an apprehension of it as a whole, as a perfect and perfectly consistent system of truth: the evidence of the gospel itself as the grandest scheme of thought ever propounded to the world, is entirely lost. So that it may not unaturally happen sometime that the defense of the *minimum* alone will turn out to be the *minimum* defense of the gospel. Finally and above all, there may easily enter into the habit of defending a *minimum* of the gospel alone a certain unfaithfulness to the truth committed to us, which may go far to forfeit the testimony of the Holy Spirit, which needs to attend all defense of the gospel if it is to prevail with men. After all, God wishes a large trust in him and in his power, and will honor those who are not afraid to make great drafts upon him. In this sphere, too, it may well prove true that he who speaks boldly in God's name all the truth that has been entrusted to him will have cause to admire God's power. Here too, mayhap, he is saying to us:

> O, that my people would hearken unto me;
> That Israel would walk in my ways!
> I should soon subdue their enemies,
> And turn my hands against their adversaries.
> The haters of the Lord should submit
> themselves unto him.

In a time deeply marked by "concession," at all events, it is worth our while to remember on the one hand that "concession" is the high road to "heresy," and that "heresy" is "wilfulness in doctrine"; and on the other, that God has revealed his truth to us to be held, confessed, and defended, and that, after all, he is able to defend and give due force to the whole circle of revealed truth. And surely it is worth our while to recognize the most outstanding fact in the conflicts of our age—this, namely, that the line of demarcation between the right-thinking and the wilfully-thinking lies just here—whether a declaration of God is esteemed as authoritative over against all the conjectural explanations of phenomena by men, or whether, on the contrary, it is upon the conjectural explanations of phenomena by men that we take our stand as over against the declaration of God. In the sphere of science, philosophy, and criticism alike, it is the conjectural explanations of phenomena which are put forward as the principles of knowledge. It is as depending on these that men proclaim science, philosophy, and criticism as the norm of truth. We are "orthodox" when we account God's declaration in his Word superior in point of authority to them, their interpreter, and their corrector. We are "heretical" when we make them superior in point of authority to God's Word, its interpreter, and its corrector. By this test we may each of us try our inmost thought and see where we stand—on God's side or on the world's.

50

EVADING THE SUPERNATURAL*

Dr. James Macgregor, who, twenty years ago, was teaching Systematic Theology in the Free Church College at Edinburgh, has of late been sending forth from his new home in Southern New Zealand a series of solidly thought and breezily written works on Christian Apologetics, which ought to be more widely known. The second of these works bears the title of *The Revelation and the Record*,[1] and traverses the fundamental aspects of the current controversy as to the supernatural, inspiration, and the canon, with a vigor, a directness of touch and a force of argumentation which soon shake the reader's mind free of illusions and recall it to a proper estimate of the essential elements of fact on which well-grounded opinion must turn. It comes to us like a cooling waft of refreshment from the other side of the world.

Near the opening of this treatise, Dr. Macgregor finds it necessary to allude somewhat caustically to what he calls "Christian Evasions of the Supernatural," as one of the factors which must be reckoned with by the apologist just as surely as anti-Christian denials of it. How sadly all experience bears him out! "This evasion," he tells us, "may be perpetrated through simple avoidance of the point of supernaturalism in fact or doctrine—as the priest and Levite passed by on the other side. Or it may be accomplished through ambiguity of expression, ostensibly affirming the supernaturalism in question, but really not affirming it, perhaps rather suggesting an explanation that explains it away." Every reader who has followed the controversies of the day will set his seal to it that

---

The Presbyterian Journal, Sept. 13, 1894.
[1]Published by T. and T. Clark, Edinburgh.

this description is just. And when Dr. Macgregor goes on to give illustrative samples of this evasion, and places among the evasions of the question of the supernatural Book the use of such expressions as these: "The Bible contains the Word of God; it records a revelation that came from him; its inspiration is the highest of all literature"—while all the time the real question of whether the Bible *is* God's Word is ignored—it may seem to some of us that he is writing specifically to bring light to some darkened minds in our own Presbyterian Church.

Now, that such evasions should continually arise among Christian men in the course of any strong attack upon the supernatural foundation of Christianity, is not at all to be wondered at. Many men are fairly carried off their feet by such an attack, and their only thought is to save what they can, however little, out of the destruction which seems to them to have been wrought. With them, "evasion" is the result of the desperate clutching of a drowning man for some support in the deep waters. With others, it is the result of sheer timidity before the world or before the swelling claims of unbelieving learning; they dare not assert what their hearts still tell them is true in the face of scoffing unbelief. With others, still, it is the mark of an illogical mind, which, as George Eliot says, in its extreme hospitality, "readily entertains contradictory propositions together": these are self-deceived rather than deceivers of others. The wonder is not, then, that it constantly shows itself anew in every controversy of Christianity with unbelief. There must always be a neutral territory between the contending parties, where the remnants of supernaturalism which still cling to minds already fundamentally anti-supernaturalistic will seek to hold out their helpless hands to both parties to the strife; and unhappily there are also always likely to be some who would fain cover their nakedness from the observation of their fellows with the clothing of better days, no longer properly theirs.

The wonder is that Christian people, after so long an experience with the phenomenon, should not yet know how to estimate it. It certainly is not in any of its aspects a new phenomenon. Every phase of it, as exhibited, for example, in the present contest over the supernatural Book, has been over and over again experienced by the Church. Does Dr. Briggs represent his assault upon the Bible as only a breaking down of barriers which have barred men away from its proper and profitable use?[2] So did Ernest Renan before him. We were only yesterday told by Dr. Neubauer that Renan's aim was only "to make the Scriptures popular among his readers."[3] Does Dr. Driver tell us that the dealing accorded to the Old Testament by the type of criticism which he represents, leaves its inspiration untouched?[4] We cannot forget that this was the sort of language to which poor Edouard Scherer was accustomed to treat his readers, as he made his easy descent from evangelical Christianity to utter unbelief. "I do not see what harm there is," he said, "for the piety of the Christian, to exchange the letter of a code for the living products of apostolic individuality, an authority for a history, a cabalistic ventriloquism for the noble accents of the human voice." This harm— in vain the Christian might reply—that with the sinking of the divine into a merely human voice, all real authority has forever gone out of the Bible. Do again, Adolf Harnack and his followers assure us that all their onslaughts on the most precious doctrines of Christianity offer no real danger to Christian faith, because forsooth faith rests not on propositions but embraces a person, and is not a crediting of all sorts of statements but the vital response of the soul to the manifestation of God's fatherhood in Christ? Accents like these, too, have fallen upon our wearied ears before. Can we forget reading in the preface of Strauss's *Life of Jesus:* "The author is aware that the essence of the Christian religion is perfectly independent of his criticism. The supernatural birth of Christ, his miracles, his resurrection and ascension, remain eternal truths, whatever doubts may be cast on their reality as historical facts. . . . The dogmatic significance of the life of Jesus remains inviolate."

---

[2]Inaugural Address on *Authority of Holy Scripture.*
[3]*Jewish Quarterly Review*, Jan. 1893, p. 202.
[4]Preface to his *Introduction to the Literature of the Old Testament.*

How can so many, after so many like experiences, exercise still such a *sancta simplicitas* as not to take instructed note of their repetition? The dogmatic significance of the life of Jesus remains inviolate! What dogmatic significance? Not that which the Church has recognized in it, and by which alone the soul of man may live, but that which the modern rationalist chooses to permit to it. The "inspiration" of the Old Testament remains unaffected! What inspiration? Not that which the Church ascribes to it and by which alone a man may be justified in pinning his faith to its declarations. But such "inspiration" as the critics of the day may find it convenient to allow to it. Thus we "palter in a double sense." And by the aid of such paltering, as Dr. Macgregor puts it, a Strauss is kept from being intruded into the Chair of Theology at Zurich—the canton of Ulrich Zwingli—only by a political revolution; and a Baur actually dispenses unbelief from the Tübingen of Albert Bengel for a whole generation. American cheeks used to burn with indignation at the thought of such things. We have grown used to something like them at home, now.

A notable instance of these "evasions," by which all the phraseology of Christianity is retained to veil an entirely naturalistic scheme of thought, is given by Prof. Pfleiderer,[5] who has been lately discrediting supernatural Christianity to an Edinburgh audience. Prof. James Orr, of the Divinity Hall of the United Presbyterian Church in Edinburgh, has done wisely in exposing this feature of his modes of representation.[6] "He is never weary of assuring us," he tells us, "that if his theories are accepted, religion, so far from being destroyed, will be put upon a firmer basis than ever. It is only the accidents, the excrescences, the drapery and embellishments of religious ideas that disappear; the essence, the kernel, the rational, the imperishable truth remains; and what could any reasonable mind wish more?" A wonder-working thing is this preservation of the "kernel," while the husk is discarded; and in this century, as well as in the last, it has served as a notable device for re-

[5]Gifford Lectures.
[6]*The Supernatural in Christianity*, pp. 39 f.

taining the prestige of the Christian name and phraseology for a purely natural religion. Prof. Orr properly reminded his listeners of the use to which such asseverations have been put, adducing in illustration other words of Strauss's, in which he says:[7] "But we have no fear that we should lose Christ by being obliged to give up a considerable part of the Christian Creed. He will remain to all of us the more surely the less anxiously we cling to doctrines and opinions that might tempt our reason to forsake him. But if Christ remains to us, and if he remains to us as the highest we know and are capable of imagining within the sphere of religion, as the person without whose presence in the mind no perfect piety is possible, we may fairly say that in him we do still possess the sum and substance of the Christian faith." But did Christ so remain with Strauss, after he had stripped away from him all the drapery of supernaturalism with which his own hands had clothed himself? History answers that question most grimly; and the sequel of the *Colloquies* is written in the *New Life of Jesus.*

The echoes of such words as Strauss's are about us now every day. A tendency to the minimizing of the importance of the high supernaturalism of the creeds of the Church has taken possession of the world. In this regard such a book as the recent brochure on *The Divinity of Christ,* published by the Andover professors, is most painful. The end cannot be other than it has been in such circumstances in all the past. Christianity, in its very essence, is supernaturalism. To attempt to evade the one, in whatever degree, is to permit the other, just so far, to escape us.

---

[7]Quoted from the *Colloquies*, E.T. p. 65.

51

ABRAHAM THE FATHER
OF THE FAITHFUL*

Abraham was the father of the Hebrew nation. This alone would give him a high place in the records of men. That the historian should be able definitely to trace to him the origin of a great people, differentiated by national peculiarities and a special national destiny, would necessarily give him a position of the first importance in the history of the race.

How little the quality of Abraham's greatness is measured by this, however, is manifest at once from a single fact. He was not only the ancestor of the Jewish race, but the promise was literally fulfilled to him that he should be the "father of a multitude of nations" and kings should come out of his fruitful loins; yet his importance in ethnological science or national history we feel to be the least of his claims to greatness. Abraham was the father not only of one or of many of the world's peoples; he was the father of one of the world's religions. He takes his place not only as the most noble and the most substantial of those often somewhat shadowy figures to which the several peoples trace, in legend or history, their origin; but also among those world-movers whose spiritual aspirations have begotten a new religion among men, or whose enthusiasms have kindled among them the fires of a new faith in the unseen. Abraham was the father of the Jewish religion. And through that religion he has become the father of much beyond. To give him his loftiest title from this point of view, Abraham was the father of monotheism. As such "he stands," as Professor Max Müller says, "as a figure second only to One in the whole history of the world."

*The Westminster Teacher, Feb. 1894.

But even here we have not reached the climax of his greatness. It is not enough to say of him that he "is the Zoroaster of the Semitic race," even though we add at once (as Baron Bunsen does, in so characterizing him), that he was greater than Zoroaster, inasmuch as his sense of the divine was more spiritual. To uncover his greatness, we must paradoxically rob him of his claims to greatness. He was not a great conqueror and organizer, who founded a great nation, though many a legend of his descendants so represents him. He was not a great thinker, in the powerful solvent of whose thought old faiths dissolved and their purer elements crystalized into higher forms. He was but the humble instrument through which God wrought his will. Abraham did not produce the Hebrew nation. Out of his dead body, God Almighty created the people of his choice. Abraham did not discover monotheistic truth. The Everlasting God was not known of him. He knew him that he might teach the world to know the way of the Lord. Abraham is great, not because of the place he holds in the history of peoples, or of the world's religions. He is great because of the place he held in the favor of God. He is great because God "chose him" and "called him," made himself known to him, and initiated in him that course of gracious dealing with men by which all the nations of the earth have been blessed. He is great not because the Hebrew and the Arab call him father, or because the Jew and the Mohammedan point back to him as the first preacher of the primary principle that there is but one God. The title that reveals his greatness is the title that inspiration gives him, the Father of the Faithful.

It is back to Abraham as their father that all those look, who, whether in circumcision or uncircumcision, walk in the steps of that faith which Abraham had, when in hope he believed against hope, and, looking unto the promise of God, wavered not through unbelief, but waxed strong through faith, giving the glory to God, and being fully assured that what God had promised he was also able to perform. There have been many heroes of faith since his day. There were some before it; the Epistle to the Hebrews tells us of Abel and Enoch and Noah.

Yet Abraham was as none were before him, and has remained for after ages the typical man of faith, of tested faith, of triumphant faith. His whole life was ordered that it might stand as the example of faith. In him we see faith's high aspirations, which not content with what the world gives, hearkened to the heavenly call. In him we see faith's consequent disengagement from the world, not only from its pleasures but from its ties; faith's pilgrim-life on earth. In him we see faith's other-worldliness. In him we see faith's homesickness for heaven, its longing for the city that hath the foundations, because its builder and maker is God—because, in a word, it is the Father's city and therefore our home. In him, above all, as his life ran through its stages, we see faith's budding, faith's testing, faith's assured confidence in God—God Almighty, God Everlasting, God the See-er, God the Provider—who quickeneth the dead and calleth things that are not as though they were.

But in a much deeper sense than even this typical one is Abraham the Father of the Faithful. Through the course of divine dealings which, though announced from the beginning of the world, commenced with him, faith is supplied with its special object. In him God begins to train fallen man for heaven, and through him God begins to prepare heaven for fallen man. Abraham is no more the father of the faithful in the sense of those who believe, than he is the father of the Faithful One in whom we believe. In his seed all the nations of the earth are blessed; "and he saith not, And to seeds as of many, but as of one, And to thy seed, which is Christ." In Abraham begins that line of direct preparation which culminated in the advent into the world of that Son of Abraham, who was also the Son of God, whom, true anti-type of Isaac, his own Father laid upon the altar for the life of the world. Abraham's life is indeed, when looked at on one side, the example to all those who would live by faith, but also, when looked at from another side, the pledge to all such, that the faithful God will provide. His supremest glory is that in his faithfulness he has supplied to men a revelation of the heart of God.

52

JESUS THE MEASURE OF MEN*

The Greeks had a proverb: "By the straight is judged both the straight and the crooked; the rule is singly the test of both." Wherever the straight is brought to light, there inevitably is the crookedness of the crooked also made visible. Let the builder hang his plumb-line over any wall; and if the wall be not straight, every wayfarer may perceive it. Let the carpenter lay his straight-edge alongside of any board, and every crook and bend is brought to the instant observation of all. This is what is meant when the Scriptures tell us that by the law is the knowledge of sin. The law is for moral things what the plumb-line and the straight-edge are for material things. It is the rule by which our hearts are measured, and in the presence of which what we really are is made manifest. We may sin and scarcely know we sin, until the straight-edge, the law, is brought against us. How evidently, then, do we fall away from its line of rectitude!

Now, our blessed Savior, as the Perfect One, full of all righteousness and holiness, is the embodiment of the law, in life; and more perfectly and vividly than any law could—though it should be holy and just and good—does his presence among men measure men and reveal what men are. The presence of any good man in our midst acts, in its due proportion, as such a measure. Accordingly, from the beginning of the world, men have been stung by the presence of a good man among them into hatred of him. Therefore Plato supposed that if ever a divine man should come into the world men would assuredly crucify him. And an observant modern novelist

*The Presbyterian Messenger, Jan. 18, 1894.

remarks that "there is certainly a 'tyrannous hate' in the world for unusual goodness, which is a rebuke to it." But no man ever so feels his utter depravity as when he thinks of himself as standing by the side of Jesus. In this presence even what we had haply looked upon as our virtues hide their faces in shame and cry, "Depart from us, for we are sinful men, O Lord."

Lay open the narrative in the Gospels of how the Son of man went about among men in the days of his sojourn on earth; and note on the one hand the ever-growing glory of the revelation of his perfect life, and on the other the ever-increasing horror of the revelation of human weakness and of human sin. It could not be otherwise. When we see Jesus it must be in the brightness of his unapproachable splendor that we see those about him; just as it is in the light of the sun that we see the forms and colors and characters of all objects on which it shines. Especially when we see him in conflict with his enemies we cannot escape the spectacle of his utter perfection, and in that light the spectacle of the utter depravity of men. Men are revealed in this presence in their true, their fundamental natural tones, with a vivid completeness in which they are never seen elsewhere.

Let us look, for example, at that marvelous trial scene which closes his life on earth.

Here the priests, the rabble, the Roman governor, the Jewish king, are all brought into sharp contrast with that one calm figure of a perfect man, looking down unmoved upon all their turbulence and folly and wickedness. Open the commentaries on this passage; turn to the multitudes of sermons that have been preached upon it. Is it an accident that they are all found to busy themselves at once with analyses of the character of Pilate, exposures of the inconsistencies of the priests, measurements of the immeasurable fickleness of the mob? No; the plumb-line of perfection is here let down into the seething mass of imperfect men, and a great day of the revelation of character is come. Exactly what each person is, in the ground principles of his being—what he is, not what he would like to be—is thrown prominently into observation, by the simple fact that he is brought into immediate contact with the utter perfection of Jesus. The awful necessity of the hour drives each one on to the legitimate outcome in act of what, in the inner springs of his nature, he is.

Look, for instance, at the priests. Doubtless they were a reasonably respectable body of priests. They might have gone on deceiving the people and deceiving themselves until they were laid in their honored graves, had not the figure of Jesus been thrust in their way. Once face to face with him, how soon their real character emerges! The crust of artificial legalism which had seemed the very essence of the Pharisee is shivered by the touch of real law-abidingness. No law could restrain the inflamed legalist from wreaking his frenzy upon embodied Law. Mock piety insatiably thirsted for the blood of real holiness.

The smooth, indifferent Sadducee could not tolerate the meek Jesus. All the real intolerance of his superficial and skeptical nature burst into flame as he faced incarnate Love.

And the people—shall we say, *vox populi, vox dei*, when we hear them rejecting Christ and choosing Barabbas? It was probably not a worse crowd than other crowds. They had come to the Praetorium on an errand of mercy. They won a double popular victory, and doubtless departed full of the self-congratulations with which we are accustomed to felicitate ourselves when we have overreached our neighbor. But they had cheated justice out of a criminal and hounded an innocent man to a hideous doom. It was simply their careless good nature that did it; in the thoughtless mood of the populace they were actuated by no real pity, by no zeal for right—they were intent upon their holiday and on their popular rights. On another occasion we might possibly be seduced into a certain sympathy with their mood. But Jesus is here: and by that touchstone what a revelation is made of the essential cruelty of mobs, their dreadful levity in matters of life and death, of truth and righteousness.

Alongside the typically Roman character of Pilate the straight-edge is also laid. How clearly are exhibited at once the shallowness of his good impulses, the singleness of his regard for personal interests, his entire disregard for human suffering, truth, divine right.

Nearly every stratum of society, every rank in life, every type of man are brought before us in this pitiful scene, vying with one another in the revelation of their depravity. In the spectacle is unveiled before us the juggernaut march of human selfishness, to which the agonies of the best and the noblest are as naught in its mad grasp after its own. In what a clear light is the depravity of man set by the presence of that patient suffering figure in the midst! All the analyses of the theologians do not so sharply bring home to us the corruption of human nature. It is the mystery of iniquity.

It is worthy of note, also, how unexpectedly the exhibition of his character is thrust upon each. When each was least looking for it, lo! Jesus stood by him, and all men could see just what manner of man he was. The priests had decided not to arraign Jesus during this feast. They had determined not to enter into the ordeal, when an unexpected opportunity drives them with breathless haste to the betrayal of the whole wickedness of their hearts. The mob is apparently only accidentally (so to speak) at Pilate's gate at the fateful moment when he is himself face to face with Jesus, and nervously anxious to escape the test. They surge up to the palace with no thought of Jesus, demanding the release of a prisoner. Pilate seizes the apparent opportunity and offers them Jesus. So unexpectedly are they too cast into the trying fires.

In this great trial scene we may see a type of human life. Such a crisis Jesus is bringing into the life of every man upon whom the light of the knowledge of him shines. No man can escape the test. Christ Jesus has come into the world full of grace and truth; and he confronts us all with the spectacle of his perfect humanity. When men are least thinking of him, lo! there he stands by their side. Every time his name is mentioned in the assemblies of men, every time his image arises in a brooding heart, the great crisis comes anew to human souls. They may not recognize the trial; they may prefer it should not come; they may determine not to enter into it. They cannot escape it. Against their wills they are tried and tested every moment they live in the presence of this Light. Some, like the priests, may burn with ungovernable rage at every thought of the supreme claim he makes upon their homage; and with all violence declare they will not have this man to reign over them. Others, like Pilate, may yield a cold and languid recognition to his goodness and worth, while choosing the pursuit of pleasure and gain above the service of him. Others, like the rabble, may, with easy indifference, prefer some other leader, though he be a murderer and a robber. But a crisis he is daily bringing to every heart; and a revelation of man in his native depravity is the inevitable result. As he moves through the world the whole race lies at his feet, self-condemned. We shudder, as in the light of his brightness we see man as he is. Can we wonder that his visible return to earth, once more to stand visibly in the midst of men, is made in Scripture the Day of Judgment—that day when the thoughts of every heart shall be revealed and the work of each shall be made manifest, for the day shall declare it?

53

INTRODUCTION TO
SAMUEL G. CRAIG'S
*Jesus As He Was and Is**

It gives me great pleasure to respond to Dr. Craig's request that I should say a few words which may serve as an introduction to this book. The book seems to me to meet admirably a very distinct need. We live very busy lives nowadays. And in the hurry and fret of these busy lives we are sometimes in danger of permitting to grow dim to us things which are too precious to let slip from our minds. In a direct and telling way Dr. Craig calls some of these back to our memories. He reminds us of who Jesus is, what he has done, and what he is to us. It is good to listen to him and through his quiet words to hear the voice of Jesus himself speaking to our souls. We shall scarcely be able to read the book without feeling that we have gained in the clearness and firmness of our knowledge of our Lord.

Dr. Craig calls his book, *Jesus As He Was and Is.* He means by that to remind us that Jesus is today all he ever was. That there is nothing he has been to any past generation, back to the first—the generation which knew him in the flesh—that he may not be, that he is not, to this generation—the generation in which we live and which we may be sometimes tempted to fear has begun to forget him. That there is nothing he has ever been to even the greatest of his saints, that he is not to the weakest one of us who would fain believe himself his. We are inevitably reminded of that great triumphant shout which we find imbedded in the Epistle to the Hebrews—"Jesus Christ yesterday and today the same—and forever!" No better motto

---

*Introduction to Dr. Samuel G. Craig's book *Jesus As He Was and Is: a Modern Attempt to Set Forth the Abiding Significance of Jesus Christ,* New York, 1914, pp. xiii-xx.

could be found for the book and I think I could do nothing better in the way of an introduction to it than simply to write this motto on its forefront.

What the author of the Epistle to the Hebrews was doing when he put on record for us this great declaration, was exhorting his readers to bear in mind those notable Christian men who had taught the gospel to them, and to mold themselves, whether for living or for dying, on their shining example. As truly as that great cloud of witnesses which he had lately summoned from the records of the Old Testament to cheer them in their struggles, these men had been heroes of faith. He bids his readers to note with care how they had borne themselves in the troubles and trials which filled their lives—up to the very end. He urges them to imitate the faith which had brought them so triumphantly through them all. And then to encourage them in this high endeavor, he suddenly raises their eyes from the servants to the Master, crying aloud: "Jesus Christ, yesterday and today the same—and forever!" As much as to say that if they repeated the faith of their teachers they could not fail to repeat also their victory. It was to no doubtful experiment that he called them, but to a sure triumph. Jesus Christ remained the same through every change and chance of time. He was as accessible to them as he had been to their predecessors, and as ready and as able to sustain and to succor. They had but to trust in him and they could not be put to shame.

The appeal is made, we may say, to the faithfulness of Christ. But something deeper than faithfulness is meant. We do not speak of the faithfulness of the rock, the house that is built upon which will stand, though the floods come and the winds blow and beat upon it. Jesus Christ not only will be faithful but cannot but be faithful. The appeal is made, we may say again, then, to the unchangeableness of Christ. But something higher than unchangeableness is meant. It is not merely to a passive quality of being that we are pointed, but to an active principle of conduct. Jesus Christ is not merely abstractly incapable of change, but unalterably constant in his dealings with his people. Put the two together, then, and we may say that the appeal is made to the immutable steadfastness of Christ. But we still fall below this great declaration. These words are too cold and impersonal. We must pour more emotion into them, and relate them more closely to our hearts. Instead of "immutable" we must say at least "unfailing," for "steadfastness" we must say at least "trustiness." What those old Hebrew Christians were assured was that Jesus Christ is unfailingly trusty; and there is included in that the implication not only that he will but also that he can. They might safely trust him as those great men did whose lives and deaths they reverently looked back upon; for he remains the same trusty Lord and Savior now that he was then. The appeal, in a word, is to the love of Christ; to his changeless love; to his almighty changeless love. We do not get its full force until we emphasize each of these three ideas in turn. What the writer was telling his readers is that the same Christ was theirs in whom their revered teachers had trusted—the same Christ in the same almighty changeless love; and therefore to trust in him would bring them to the same victory, the contemplation of which in their teachers filled them with mingled awe and rejoicing.

This great assurance, now, does not belong to the Hebrew Christians of two thousand years ago alone. It comes to us today with as direct an application and as clear an encouragement as it brought to them. There is nothing about it which can confine it to any one time, or to any one state of circumstances, or to any one body of hearers. Rather, it is expressly made universal. It does not say merely, Jesus Christ is yesterday and today the same: though, had it said only that, it still would be impossible to bind it to only one yesterday and only one today. It adds to this declaration the further words, "and forever." And this addition can mean nothing else than that the assurance given was expressly and emphatically intended to be of universal application. Not only could the first readers of the Epistle be sure that they would find Jesus Christ all that they had seen their venerated teachers find him. All, everywhere, throughout all ages, have but to taste and see his like preciousness to them. For "Jesus Christ is yesterday and today the same—and forever."

There is even reason to suspect that the declaration was not first framed for the occasion on which we find it here used, and was not first made to these Hebrew Christians, as an incitement to them to imitate the victorious faith of their teachers. The suddenness with which it is introduced, the compact vividness of its language, its completeness in itself, the absence from it of all connectives, its exclamatory form, the stately grandeur of its manner—more like a trumpet blast than an argument: all give it the appearance of one of those crisp proverbial announcements, in which the first Christians early learned to crystalize the essence of their faith, and by the repetition of which they were accustomed to exhort and encourage one another in their temptations and trials. We meet with these golden nuggets of compressed Christian confession in the so-called Pastoral Epistles, set off to our observation as "faithful sayings." "This is a faithful saying," says Paul and reminds his readers of one of the maxims of fundamental Christian faith, which he thus adopts and adapts to his momentary purpose. We meet with them also, however, elsewhere, scattered through the Epistles without any formal intimation being given of their origin in the general heart of the Christian community or of their proverbial character. Surely we meet with one of them in this stirring battle cry of the Christian life: "Jesus Christ, yesterday and today the same—and forever!" In point of compressed pregnancy of language it rivals the Moslem's cry, "No God but God!" or the old Jewish "confession," "Jehovah our God, Jehovah One," while for depth of emotional appeal it passes far beyond either: "Jesus Christ, yesterday and today the same—and forever!" Here vibrates a passionate assertion of the unfailing trustiness of Jesus Christ, the Christian's support and stay, the eternal refuge of his people.

If this be at all the case, then, in claiming this great assurance for ourselves, we do not so much apply to our needs words spoken first to the Hebrew Christians of two millenniums ago to encourage them to increase of faith. The writer of the Epistle rather applies to their needs words put together first for us and by us—by the general Christian community, for every Christian of that and of every time reminding himself of the Rock on which he builds the house of his life. And in that case the words must be taken in their most unlimited meaning, and come to us today, after all these years, as the embodiment of our common Christian assurance. They remind us that Jesus Christ is the strong Son of God who has come into the world to save sinners, and who, through all the world's life, as age passes on into age, abides the same strong Savior—yea, forever. In the midst of the trials of life and its perplexities, its temptations and its failures, its errors and its sins, what we want to know—what we want with all the strength of our hearts to believe—is that Jesus Christ is the same, yesterday, and today, and forever; that we can safely venture on him with our all—whether for this life or for the life to come. It is this assurance that this great Christian battle cry gives us.

And it is because Dr. Craig's book seems to me to tend to bring this assurance to the men and women of today that I am glad to commend it to them.

54

THE IMPORTUNATE WIDOW AND
THE ALLEGED FAILURE OF FAITH*

It is quite usual to treat Luke xvii. 20–xviii. 8 as practically a connected discourse, divided into its parts, no doubt, but dealing with a single subject. There seems to be no sufficient ground for this. The whole material from xvii. 12–xviii. 30, it is true, belongs together as recounting incidents of the journey "through the midst of Samaria and Galilee" on the way up to Jerusalem (xvii. 12). Some of the incidents recounted occurred also, as we know from Matthew and Mark,[1] in immediate sequence, though this is not modified in any case by Luke. Some of the paragraphs in this section, moreover, are internally connected by the common lesson which they inculcate;[2] and there is no intrinsic reason why the three paragraphs which make up the section xvii. 20–xviii. 8, might not be similarly bound together. In point of fact it seems possible to trace in them a certain, if not exactly sameness, yet community of teaching; and this perhaps accounts for their preservation by Luke together. But on the face of them they give us three distinct utterances of our Lord, different alike in subject and in reference. The first of them, drawn out perhaps by a testing inquiry of the Pharisees, has to do with the kingdom of God, and declares it either spiritual in its nature or a present fact in the world, according as we interpret its key-phrase, "The kingdom of God is within—or among—you" (xvii. 20 f.).

Expository Times, Nov. 1913, pp. 69-72, and Dec. 1913, pp. 136-139.
[1]Those recounted in xviii. 17 f. and xviii. 18-20; cf. Mark x. 17; Matt. xix. 14 f.
[2]The teaching of the last three paragraphs, xviii. 9-14, 15-17, 18-20, is alike to the effect that the kingdom of God is a gift, not an achievement.

The second treats of the "days of the Son of man," and declares them definitely in the future and not a thing the signs of the coming of which are anxiously to be watched for (xvii. 22-37). The theme of the third, as Luke expressly tells us in its preface, is the necessity of persistent prayer (xviii. 1-8). The kingdom of God now present in men's hearts; the second advent to come unexpectedly in the undefined future; the necessity of perseverance in prayer: we could scarcely find three subjects of discussion which would seem more distinct. They appear to have in common only a tendency to withdraw the mind from engagement with the future and to focus it upon the duties of the present life.

Luke introduces the Parable of the Importunate Widow and the Unjust Judge without any intimation of close connection with the preceding paragraph. He presents it only as a further item of Jesus' teaching at this general time. He says simply, "And he spoke a parable to them. . . ." Even were the "also" genuine, on which stress is sometimes laid as a proof of a close connection here[3]—"And he spoke *also* a parable to them"— that conclusion would not follow. The meaning would be only that Luke was adjoining this parable to what he had already recorded, as an additional item of Jesus' teaching.[4] Much less is a close connection implied in the mere "to them"—"And he spoke a parable *to them*"—as is also sometimes pleaded.[5] This "to them"—which no doubt could have been omitted (as at xiii. 6)—merely intimates that the parable was spoken, like the item of teaching immediately preceding it, to the disciples rather than to the Pharisees, say (xvii. 20), or any other special circle (xviii. 9). Nor is there anything in the contents of this paragraph to suggest a close connection with that which precedes it. It has been argued, indeed,[6] that it presents itself as the conclusion of the preceding discussion by showing that despite the delay in the coming of the Son of man, intimated in

---

[3]E.g., by Godet and Göbel.
[4]On the frequency of δὲ καί in Luke, see Plummer on iii. 9.
[5]E.g., by Plummer.
[6]So, e.g., B. Weiss; cf. Holtzmann.

xvii. 22, the longing of those who are looking forward to it for the vindication of God's elect shall ultimately be gratified. But this rests on an interpretation of the application which Jesus gives the parable (vss. 6-8) which brings it into apparent conflict with its preface,[7] which finds no point of departure for itself in the parable itself, and which does not seem in itself necessary or even indeed possible.

In introducing the parable Luke gives it a quite general reference. "And he spake a parable unto them," he says, "to the end that they ought always to pray and not to faint." There is no intimation that the inculcation of perseverance in prayer has special reference to prayer for the second advent. It has the appearance, on the contrary, of being entirely generally meant. And with this general reference the parable itself perfectly accords. It presents simply a vividly drawn picture of persistency in petition, with the ultimate issue of its granting. If, then, the Lord in his application of the parable, gives it a narrower reference, there is an appearance at least of conflict between his application of it and the announced reference of the parable, with which its substance accords. It is, of course, open to us still to say that in his concluding remarks our Lord does not intend to develop the whole teaching of the parable, but only wishes to apply its general lesson of importunity in prayer to the special case of the second advent. The language of these remarks, which is at their hinge-point derived directly from that of the parable, does not, however, encourage this interpretation of them. The fundamental question, in any case, remains whether these remarks are rightly read as applying the parable specifically to prayer for the second advent. They run, as they are given in our Revised Version, as follows: "And the Lord said, Hear what the unrighteous judge saith. And shall not God avenge his elect, which cry to him day and night, and he is long-suffering over them? I say unto you, that he will avenge them

---

[7]Accordingly B. Weiss remarks: "On this very account the reference which Luke gives it in vs. 1 is much too general (against Meyer, Godet)." Cf. Holtzmann.

speedily. Howbeit, when the Son of man cometh, shall he find faith on the earth?" The passage bristles with difficulties. But there are some things about it which seem tolerably clear.

The phrase which is translated "avenge" is derived from the parable and must obtain its interpretation from it. There we read in our Revised Version that the widow's importunate demand took the form of "Avenge me of mine adversary!" while the judge's meditation ran in the words: "Because this widow troubleth me, I will avenge her." "Avenge" is, however, an unfortunate rendering of the Greek phrase here, and preoccupies the mind with wrong suggestions. What the widow was seeking was not fundamentally vengeance on her adversary, but rather relief from his oppressions. No doubt there was punishment sought for the evil-doer, and no doubt punishment was inflicted upon him.[8] But punishment was not the main end aimed at or obtained; it was only the means by which the real end of relief and protection was secured. "'Εκδικεῖν," comments Godet; "to deliver (ἐκ) by a judicial sentence (δίκη). This term does not therefore include the notion of vengeance, but that of justice to be rendered to the oppressed." More exactly still, Plummer paraphrases: "Give me a sentence of protection from; vindicate my right (and so protect me) from." He proceeds to quote in support Schleasner's, "Assere me jure dicundo ab injuria adversarii mei," and comments thus: The ἀπό "does not express the *penalty exacted from* the adversary, but the *protection afforded from* him, as in ῥῦσαι ἡμᾶς ἀπὸ τοῦ πονηροῦ. The meaning is "preserve me against his attacks," rather than "deliver me out of his power," which would require ἐκ.[9] Precisely the thing the widow demanded, and precisely the thing the judge tardily granted her,

---

[8]This should satisfy Jülicher's remark (Vol. II, p. 279), that "the afflicted widow does not merely wish to be quit of her adversary, like the man in xii. 58; she demands ἐκδίκησις, that vengeance should be wreaked on him, he should be punished. . . ."

[9]Similarly Göbel, and Weizsäcker; cf. J. Weiss. Plummer's comment rests partly on Trench's, whose paraphrase is: "Or, since men go not to a judge for vengeance, but for justice—Do me right on, deliver me from the oppression of, mine adversary."

was accordingly protection.[10] When then our Lord, taking up this phrase in a somewhat more emphatic form of expression,[11] declares, in his application of the parable, that God will "avenge his elect," he must be understood not so much as proclaiming the certainty with which the divine vengeance will be visited at the last day upon the oppressors of his people, as giving a gracious assurance to them of the unfailing protection of God amid the evils which assault them in this life.[12]

There are not wanting indications in our Lord's further words which bring support to this conclusion. One of them is found in the clause rendered in our Revised Version, "And he is longsuffering over them." It is not easy to be perfectly sure of either the construction or the exact sense of this clause. Its office is in any case, however, to deny that God is indifferent to the sufferings of his people; and in its most natural interpretation it declares that as his ears are always filled with their cries he will not be slow to act in their defense.[13] This declaration is immediately reinforced by the strong asseveration which follows upon the question, returning, with great energy of

---

[10]Hence James Moffatt, *The Historical New Testament,* 1901, translates: "And she used to come to him, saying, 'Grant me protection from my opponent'"; "Yet, since this widow disturbs me, I will give her protection."

[11]Jülicher says, "more solemn." Cf Göbel's comment: "It is self-evident that the fuller periphrasic form ἐκδίκησιν τινος ποιεῖν must have just the same meaning as ἐκδικεῖν previously, vss. 3-5, therefore = 'to effect the deliverance of one suffering injustice.'"

[12]Alfred Loisy's rendering of the several phrases is notably close: "Do me justice against my opponent"; "I will do her justice"; "Shall not God do justice to his elect?" Yet even here there is lacking the implication that is strong in the Greek text that this doing of justice issues in relief and protection. Loisy's rendering is closely followed in the paraphrase of *The Twentieth Century New Testament:* "Asking for justice against someone who has wronged her"; "I will grant her justice"; "Will not God see that his own chosen people who cry to him night and day have justice done them?" Cf. Weymouth's *The Modern Speech New Testament:* "Give me justice, and stop my oppressor"; "I will give her justice"; but in vss. 7-8 "avenge."

[13]The right reading is certainly μακροθυμεῖ, and Godet gives in general the right meaning of that reading. Translate: "And does he delay with respect to them?"—that is, in effect (Plummer remarks of

assertion, a decisive answer to both its inquiries: "I say unto you, that he will avenge them"—that is, "do them justice"— "quickly." A great strength of emphasis falls here on the word "quickly."[14] The outcome of the whole question and answer is thus the assurance that God will not—not merely leave his elect unavenged, but—be slow to rescue them from their distresses. He keeps an open ear to their cries and gives them quick deliverance.

It would be certainly difficult to refer so strongly stressed an assertion of the speediness of the succor which God will give to his distressed children to the ultimate vindication which shall come to them at the second advent, along with the final confusion of all their foes. This would be a strong assertion of the immediate imminence of the second advent, and an equally decisive reference of all the hopes of God's people in the mercy of God to that event. And that, to go no further, would read very oddly in immediate sequence to the paragraph xvii. 22-37, the whole office of which is to teach that the days of the Son of man are not immediately imminent, and to withdraw the minds of Christ's followers from the great engrossment with their coming. It may not be quite impossible to explain "speedily" as meaning really "suddenly"; and the resulting declaration may not be altogether inappropriate to the matter in hand: to promise the elect that the destruction which shall fall upon their oppressors, at last shall fall upon them unexpectedly, may have some imaginative value in the

μαχροθυμεῖ: "It is almost synonymous with βραδύνω"): "Is he slack concerning them." Van Oosterzee comments admirably: "With μαχρο-θυμεῖ it is not the idea of *forbearance* in general, but *delaying* of help that is to be adhered to, and the second half of the question, vs. 7, is, with Meyer, therefore, to be paraphrased: "And is it his way in reference to them to delay his help?" It appears from this that the first member of the question requires an affirmative, the second, on the other hand, a negative answer; and that the here designated μαχροθυμέα stands directly in contrast with the ἐκδίκ. ποιεῖν ἐν τάχει which (vs. 8) is promised in the most certain manner." Jülicher (p. 287) agrees in general with this interpretation, and cites for it already Clement of Alexandria, and among the moderns B. Weiss, Steinmeyer, Stockmayer, Weizsäcker, Holtzmann, Nösgen, and, for the main matter, Göbel.

[14]Plummer: "In any case the ἐν τάχει is placed last with emphasis."

way of comfort to them in their meanwhile unalleviated griefs. But all this is manifestly difficult. The term translated "speedily" does not naturally mean "suddenly."[15] Knowledge of the unexpected suddenness with which destruction shall fall upon one's tormentors, when they are at length destroyed, goes but a little way toward removing the sufferings which must be meanwhile endured. And, then, we shall still have to reckon with the clause in the question which demands whether God is slow to act in the defense of his elect, to which this strong declaration, "No, he shall act speedily," is a response. No doubt a meaning may be found for this clause also, which would bring it into line with the reference of God's promised succor to the second advent. But even when that is done, there still remains the conflict of this whole interpretation with the expressed purport of the parable given in the preface, to say nothing of the general difficulty under which it labors of leaving God's people without promise of help in their sufferings here and now—and that, for any generation except that which shall itself witness the coming of the Lord means nothing less than hopeless suffering to the end of their days. What requires consideration is the multitude of adjustments which need to be made in order to carry this interpretation through. An unlikely explanation of a single element in a statement might be endured. Each unlikely explanation added to this multiplies the difficulty of accepting the proposed interpretation. Can any interpretation survive so many unlikelinesses as are here accumulated?

We may take it as clear, then, that our Lord directs our eyes here not to the vindication which God's elect shall receive at the second advent, but to the constant succor which he gives them in the trials of their daily life. And this conclusion will be powerfully confirmed if we will permit his declaration to work upon us in its entirety, in its relation to the parable to which it refers. It does not bear the character of a special

---

[15]Jülicher (p. 286): "The sense of 'unexpected,' 'suddenly,' is not established." Göbel: "The words can on no account mean the *sudden* occurrence of an event in opposition to one expected and prepared for."

application of a general fact. It bears the character rather of the enforcement of a great fact by a parallel instance. Only, the argument here is by contrast—not so much *ex similitudine* as *ex dissimilitudine*. What God is declared to do is not so much like what the judge is pictured in the parable as doing, as unlike it: and the contrasts are thrown up into the strongest emphasis. Over against the unjust judge, the righteous God is set. Over against the unjust judge's long delay in rendering his suitor justice, the swiftness of God in responding to the cries of his elect is set. It does not appear that the widow had any personal claim upon the judge to whom she brought her case; it is intimated that God has a personal interest in those whose cries rise to him—they are "his elect." The widow may have wearied the judge with repeated appeals; the cries of God's elect to him are not merely repeated but continuous—they rise to him unbrokenly day and night. The whole representation is *a fortiori* and it gathers force as it proceeds from its repeated enhancements. "And the Lord said, Hear what the unjust judge says: and *God*—shall not *he* do justice *to his elect,* who cry to him *day and night,* and is he *slow* with respect to them? I say unto you that he will do justice to them *speedily!"* A wicked judge, the good God: a stranger suitor, God's own chosen ones: repeated demands, an unbroken cry: tardy justice, speedy succor. It is in this circle of contrasts that our Lord's declaration moves. And it is out of this series of contrasts that it must find its interpretation. How, for instance, should "speedily" here not mean just *speedily?* How could the point of the remark be that God would postpone his intervention for the relief of his elect—until the judgment day?

This remark of our Lord's is not, then, "eschatological"! It is not meant that it has no eschatological elements in it or is unconditioned by eschatological conceptions. It was the gospel of the kingdom that our Lord came preaching, and there is no part of his teaching which is not at its core eschatological. Eschatological elements lie on the background of his most uneschatological declarations and may be continually detected in the perspective. In our present declaration, for example, we hear of "God's elect," and when we say "God's elect," we have already said eschatology: this is an eschatological conception. Though, therefore, our Lord is speaking here of God's hearing of prayer in general, and in that sense the saying is not "eschatological," it does not follow that as he speaks his thought is free from eschatological suggestions. We cannot be surprised, then, that a direct eschatological allusion crops out before he is done. "Howbeit, the Son of man, when he comes," he asks in concluding his enforcement of the lesson of the parable—"shall he find faith on the earth?" Even when he is speaking of the trials of his people in this life, and of God's open ear to their cries, he is thinking no less of the term set to their evil days by his coming. During these days of distress his people are to live by prayer; through their prayers they shall obtain their relief. But afterwards—he comes; and this is the end of all. What will he find them doing when he comes to them to bring all their days of conflict to a close?

Precisely what our Lord means by this concluding question is, indeed, far from universally agreed upon. Of one thing, however, we may feel sure. He does not mean to assert, under the guise of a question, that all faith will have perished out of the earth before he comes again. And surely it would be even more impossible to suppose that he means to assert that faith will at least have almost perished out of the earth, or will have done so in great part, or, indeed, will have done so to any extent. There is no hint in his words of any such qualification of the catastrophe which he predicts—if he predicts any catastrophe. If our Lord's meaning is that faith will no longer be found on the earth when he comes again, it will be only right to take his assertion on its full meaning. But there is no reason to suppose he had any such meaning. Why should he, in the act of commending persistent prayer to his disciples and of promising God's unfailing and speedy help to his petitioning people in all their trials, suddenly turn to declare that after a while God will have no people in the world to care for; that the cries that rise to him now, day and night, will cease; and that his whole role of prayer-hearing and prayer-answering God will fall into abeyance? To ask whether the Son of man will find faith on earth when he comes—even if the form of the question suggests that an affirmative answer is doubtful[16]—is, after all is said, something very far from asserting that it will not be found.

In endeavoring to ascertain just what our Lord intends by the question, it may be well to begin by determining the sense which is to put upon the term "faith" here—or "the faith," we may say, since it has the article. On the face of it, it is clear that there is not meant by it the Christian religion; nor yet belief in Jesus as the Christ, nor yet the assurance that he will come again. Any one of these things the term might mean in a different context. But not here. Here it naturally means that faith which sustains, and manifests itself in, persistent prayer.[17] This parable was spoken to inculcate the necessity of persistent prayer with unabating confidence. And, in his words of application, our Lord reasserts, with the greatest emphasis, the sure basis of this confidence in the character and purposes of God. It is naturally of this confidence that he continues to speak, when, in his closing question, he demands whether "the faith"—the faith in question, the faith which he had been illustrating—shall still be found on the earth at his coming.

The question is, of course, a rhetorical one. Our Lord is not inquiring for information. But it is not, therefore, to be taken as a merely counterfeit one. Our Lord is not, in the form of a question, giving information. He neither expects to learn from his disciples, nor does he expect to teach them, by his question, whether such faith as he had been commending to them shall remain on the earth when he comes again: his object is neither to elicit nor to communicate information: it is

---

[16]Jülicher (p. 288): "ἄρα no doubt, as in Acts viii. 50, Gal. ii. 17, indicating doubt of an affirmation.

[17]Godet: "Not *some faith* in general, but *the faith*—that special faith of which the widow's is an image, which, in spite of the judge's obstinate silence and long apparent indifference, perseveres in claiming its right."

to rouse to effect. What he is aiming at is ethical impression. He wishes to encourage his disciples to preserve that attitude of confident trust in God which it is the purpose of the parable and all its accompanying words to indicate. He, so to speak, in this final question "puts it to" the disciples, whether "the faith" of which he speaks shall be a permanent fact in the world. God's ears are ever open to the cries of his people; he is faithful. Are they, on their part, equally to be depended upon? If God is not like the unjust judge, are they like the importunate widow? Or will they, as she did not, fail? The design of the question is thus to incite the disciples to the preservation of the attitude of confident trust in God which it is the object of the parable to commend. And thus it takes its place as an essential part of the discourse, without which the discourse would not be complete. The parable was spoken with reference to the necessity of the preservation by the disciples of an attitude of persistent prayer. The discourse could not find its end therefore in an assurance of the faithfulness of God. The point is not what God will do. The point is what will the disciples do? Will they always pray and not faint? What will the Son of man find when history has run its course out to the end, and he comes again to take account of the ages? God certainly is and will continue to be faithful; will the disciples be faithful too? Not till the lesson of the parable is clinched by this direct appeal to the disciples to preserve their confidence in prayer, could the discourse come to its end. Only in such an appeal is its lesson driven thoroughly home. For the lesson is not that God will hear the cries of his people and grant them deliverance from their distresses; but that his people must needs always pray and not grow weary.

Whether God's people will in point of fact always pray and not faint is outside the scope of discussion. It would have been inconsequent to raise that question here. But the very purpose of the whole discussion is to incite to that confident trust in God which will lead to persistent prayer to him for needed protection. And there could not easily be devised a way to give this incitement force and effectiveness, more pointed than our Lord's closing demand: "God is ever ready to hear the cries of his people—What about your faith? Will *it* abide? When I come again, what shall I find?" We cannot infer, then, from our Lord's stray question, as he turns suddenly upon his disciples and drives the lesson of his parable home, that faith will have perished—or almost perished— from the earth before he comes again. We can only infer that he would not have faith perish from the earth. It is therefore that by the great plea of the faithfulness of God, he urges his disciples to preserve it.

There are one or two points which seem to require brief notice in conclusion lest they should obtrude themselves as objections to the uneschatological interpretation of our paragraph.

It may be thought, for instance, that so strongly stressed a promise as we find here (vss. 7, 8a), of God's speedy intervention on behalf of his people in all the trials of life, would supersede the necessity of perseverance in prayer on their part, and so evacuate the parable of significance. We must bear in mind, however, that the promise is not made apart from, but in connection with, perseverance in petition. It is those who cry out to him day and night to whom the Lord promises that God will give them his speedy protection. The difficulty, moreover, if it be a difficulty, is inherent in the case and bears equally against any interpretation of our Lord's words. It might as easily be said that so strongly stressed a promise of the Lord's speedy coming to deliver his people would supersede the necessity of exhorting them to persevere in prayer for his coming. Whatever difficulty we find here rests really on our failure to estimate aright the inconstancy of our hearts: how quickly in the experience of trial we cease to trust God's promises and to pray to him for our relief. The measure of our need of encouragement to perseverance is not the length of time through which we must endure, but the lassitude of our faith and our proneness to faint.

It may be felt again that the introduction of the coming of the Son of man in verse 8b implies the dominating presence of that conception in the preceding context. That would be true, however, only if the Son of man and his coming were introduced in verse 8b as a matter of course. So far is that from being the case that they are thrown forward in the sentence with great emphasis.[18] Their appearance is therefore notably abrupt, and by its suddenness it is advertised to us that something new is brought into view. A startling turn is given then to the discussion with the effect of producing a revulsion of feeling and of calling the disciples sharply back to a contemplation of their own part in the matter. "Nevertheless, the Son of man when he comes—shall he"—I put it to you: shall he—"find faith on the earth?" This language admits indeed of no other explanation than that the coming of the Son of man had not been in thought before and is introduced here unexpectedly and with tremendous effect.

Finally, it may be asked whether, on the uneschatological interpretation of this parable, it is not made a mere doublet of the Parable of the Importunate Friend (Luke xi. 5-8). We need not dwell on the depreciatory adverb; for the rest the lesson of the two parables is, on the view taken, no doubt the same. But surely it is not contrary to our Lord's manner to enforce the lessons he would convey by more than one similitude. We have a couple of instances of such doublets from him in the narrow compass of Matthew's great chapter of Parables of the Kingdom—in the parables of the Mustard Seed and Leaven, and in those of the Hid Treasure and Pearl of Great Price. Obviously our Lord was fertile in similitudes, and no doubt he varied them endlessly in his daily teaching. We can infer from such doublets only on the one hand that the topic of which they treat was one to which he repeatedly adverted, and on the other that in the mind of his reporter as well as of himself it was a topic of importance.

---

[18]Plummer: "Note the emphatic order, with ὁ υἱὸς τοῦ ἀνθρώπου and ἐλθών being placed before the interrogative particle. So also Meyer and Weiss.

55

THE SPIRIT OF GOD
IN THE OLD TESTAMENT*

In passing from the Old Testament to the New, the reader is conscious of no violent discontinuity in the conception of the Spirit which he finds in the two volumes. He may note the increased frequency with which the name appears on the printed page. But he would note this much the same in passing from the earlier to the later chapters of the Epistle to the Romans. He may note an increased definiteness and fulness in the conception itself. But something similar to this he would note in passing from the Pentateuch to Isaiah, or from Matthew to John or Paul. The late Professor Smeaton may have overstated the matter in his interesting Cunningham Lectures on *The Doctrine of the Holy Spirit.* "We find," he says, "that the doctrine of the Spirit taught by the Baptist, by Christ, and by the apostles, was in every respect the same as that with which the Old Testament church was familiar. We nowhere find that their Jewish hearers took exception to it. The teaching of our Lord and his apostles never called forth a question or an opposition from any quarter—a plain proof that on this question nothing was taught by them which came into collision with the sentiments and opinions which, up to that time, had been accepted, and still continued to be current among the Jews." But if there be any fundamental difference between the Old and the New Testament conceptions of the Spirit of God, it escapes us in our ordinary reading of the Bible, and

*The Presbyterian Messenger, Oct. 3, 1895. A larger treatment of this subject may be found in *Biblical Doctrines*, 1929, pp. 101-129 (see pp. 102-104, 125-129), or *Biblical and Theological Studies*, 1952, pp. 127-156.

we naturally and without conscious straining read our New Testament conceptions into the Old Testament passages.

We are, indeed, bidden to do this by the New Testament itself. The New Testament writers identify their "Holy Spirit" with the "Spirit of God" of the older books. All that is attributed to the Spirit of God in the Old Testament is attributed by them to their personal Holy Ghost. It was their own Holy Ghost who was Israel's guide and director and whom Israel rejected when they resisted the leading of God (Acts vii. 51). It was in him that Christ (doubtless in the person of Noah) preached to the antediluvians (1 Pet. iii. 18). It was he who was the author of faith of old as well as now (2 Cor. iv. 13). It was he who gave Israel its ritual service (Heb. ix. 8). It was he who spoke in and through David and Isaiah and all the prophets (Matt. xxii. 43; Mark xii. 36; Acts i. 16; xxviii. 25; Heb. iii. 7; x. 15). If Zechariah (vii. 12) or Nehemiah (ix. 20) tells us that Jehovah of Hosts sent his word by his Spirit by the hands of the prophets, Peter tells us that these men from God were moved by the Holy Ghost to speak these words (2 Pet. i. 21), and even that it was specifically the Spirit of Christ that was in the prophets (1 Pet. i. 11). We are assured that it was in Christ, upon whom the Holy Ghost had visibly descended, that Isaiah's predictions were fulfilled that Jehovah would put his Spirit upon his righteous servant (Isa. xlii. 1) and that the Spirit of the Lord Jehovah should be upon him (Isa. lxi. 1; Matt. xii. 18; Luke iv. 18, 19). And Peter bids us look upon the descent of the Holy Spirit at Pentecost as the accomplished promise of Joel that God would pour out his Spirit upon all flesh (Joel ii. 27, 28; Acts ii. 17). There can be no doubt that the New Testament writers identify the Holy Ghost of the New Testament with the Spirit of God of the Old.

This fact, of course, abundantly justifies the instinctive Christian identification. We are sure, with the surety of a divine revelation, that the Spirit of God of the Old Testament is the personal Holy Spirit of the New. But this assurance does not forestall the inquiry whether this personal Spirit was so fully revealed in the Old Testament that those who were dependent on that revelation alone, without the inspired commentary of the New, were able to know him as he is known to us who enjoy fuller light. Whether this be so, or, if so in some measure, how far it may be true is a matter for separate investigation. The Spirit of God certainly acts as a person and is presented to us as a person, throughout the Old Testament. In no passage is he conceived otherwise than personally—as a free, willing, intelligent being. This is, however, in itself only the pervasive testimony of the Scriptures to the personality of God. For it is equally true that the Spirit of God is everywhere in the Old Testament identified with God. This is only its pervasive testimony to the divine unity. The question for examination is, how far the one personal God was conceived of as embracing in his unity hypostatical distinctions. This question is a very complicated one and needs very delicate treatment. There are, indeed, three questions included in the general one, which for the sake of clearness we ought to keep apart. We may ask, May the Christian properly see in the Spirit of God of the Old Testament the personal Holy Spirit of the New? This we may answer at once in the affirmative. We may ask again, Are there any hints in the Old Testament anticipating and adumbrating the revelation of the hypostatic Spirit of the New? This also, it seems, we ought to answer in the affirmative. We may ask again, Are these hints of such clearness as actually to reveal this doctrine, apart from the revelation of the New Testament? This should be doubtless answered in the negative. There are hints and they serve for points of attachment for the fuller New Testament teaching. But they are only hints, and, apart from the New Testament teaching, would be readily explained as personifications, or ideal objectivations of the power of God.

Undoubtedly, side by side with the stress put upon the unity of God and the identity of the Spirit with the God who gives it, there is a distinction recognized between God and his Spirit—in the sense at least of a discrimination between God over all and God in all, between the Giver and the Given, between the Source and the Executor of the moral law. This distinction already emerges in Genesis i. 2; and it does not grow less observable as we advance through the Old Testament. It is prominent in the standing phrases by which, on the one hand, God is spoken of as sending, putting, placing, pouring, emptying his Spirit upon man, and on the other the Spirit is spoken of as coming, resting, falling, springing upon man. There is a sort of objectifying of the Spirit over against God in both cases; in the former case, by sending him from himself God, as it were, separates him from himself; in the latter, the Spirit appears almost as a distinct person, acting *sua sponte*. Schultz does not hesitate to speak of the Spirit even in Genesis i. 2 as appearing "as very independent, just like a hypostatis or person." Kleinert finds in this passage at least a tendency toward hypostatizing—though he thinks this tendency was not subsequently worked out. Perhaps we are warranted in saying as much as that: that there is observable in the Old Testament, not, indeed, a hypostatizing of the Spirit of God, but a tendency toward it—that, in Hofmann's cautious language, the Spirit appears in the Old Testament "as a 'somewhat' distinct from the 'I' of God which God makes the principle of life in the world." A preparation, at least, for the full revelation of the Trinity in the New Testament is observable; points of connection with it are discoverable: and thus Christians are able to read the Old Testament without offense and to find without confusion their own Holy Spirit in its Spirit of God.

More than this could scarcely be looked for. The elements in the doctrine of God which above all others needed emphasis in Old Testament times, were naturally his unity and his personality. The great thing to be taught the ancient people of God was that the God of all the earth is one person. Over against the varying idolatries about them, this was the truth of truths for which Israel was primarily to stand; and not until this great truth was ineffaceably stamped upon their souls could the personal distinctions in the Triune God be safely made known to them. A premature revelation of the Spirit as a distinct hypostatis could have wrought nothing but harm to the people of God. We shall all, no doubt, agree with Kleinert that it is pragmatic in Isidore of Pelusium to say that Moses knew the doctrine of the Trinity well enough, but concealed it through fear that polytheism would profit by it. But we may safely affirm this of God the Revealer, in the gradual delivery of the truth concerning himself to men. He reveals the whole truth, but in divers portions and in divers manners; and it was incident to the progressive delivery of doctrine that the unity of the Godhead should first be made the firm possession of men, and the Trinity in that unity should be conveyed to them only afterward, when the times were ripe for it. What we need wonder over is not that the hypostatical distinctness of the Spirit is not more clearly revealed in the Old Testament, but that the approaches to it are laid so skilfully that the doctrine of the hypostatical Holy Spirit of the New Testament finds so many and such striking points of attachment in the Old Testament, and yet no Israelite had ever been disturbed in repeating with hearty faith his great Sch'ma, "Hear, O Israel, the Lord our God is one Lord" (Deut. vi. 4). Not until the whole doctrine of the Trinity was ready to be manifested in such visible form as at the baptism of Christ—God in heaven, God on earth, and God descending from heaven to earth—could any part of the mystery be safely uncovered.

The temporary withholding of exact information as to the relation of the Spirit of God to the Godhead did not prevent, however, a very rich revelation to the Old Testament saints of the operations of the Spirit of God in the world, in the Church and in the individual soul. Least of all could it prevent the performance by the Spirit of his several functions in the world, in the Church, and in the soul throughout the whole Old Testament dispensation. That too was a dispensation in which the Spirit of God wrought. What then is meant by calling the new dispensation the dispensation of the Spirit? What does John (vii. 39) mean by saying that the Spirit was not yet given because Jesus was not yet glorified? What our Lord himself, when he promised the Comforter, by saying that the Comforter would not come until he went away and sent him (John xvi. 7); and by breathing on his disciples, saying,

"Receive ye the Holy Spirit" (John xx. 22)? What did the descent of the Spirit at Pentecost mean, when he came to inaugurate the dispensation of the Spirit? It cannot be meant that the Spirit was not active in the old dispensation. We have already seen that the New Testament writers themselves represent him to have been active in the old dispensation in all the varieties of activity with which he is active in the new. Such passages seem to have diverse references. Some of them may refer to the specifically miraculous endowments which characterized the apostles and the churches which they founded. Others refer to the worldwide mission of the Spirit, promised, indeed, in the Old Testament, but only now to be realized. But there is a more fundamental idea to be reckoned with still. This is the idea of the preparatory nature of the Old Testament dispensation.

The old dispensation was a preparatory one and must be strictly conceived as such. What spiritual blessings came to it were by way of prelibation. They were many and various. The Spirit worked in providence no less universally then than now. He abode in the Church not less really then than now. He wrought in the hearts of God's people not less prevalently then than now. All the good that was in the world was then as now due to him. All the hope of God's Church then as now depended on him. Every grace of the godly life then as now was a fruit of his working. But the object of the whole dispensation was only to prepare for the outpouring of the Spirit upon all flesh. He kept the remnant safe and pure, but it was in order that the seed might be preserved. This was the end of his activity, then. The dispensation of the Spirit, properly so-called, did not dawn, however, until the period of preparation was over and the day of outpouring had come. The mustard seed had been preserved through all the ages only by the Spirit's brooding care. Now it is planted, and it is by his operation that it is growing up into a great tree which shades the whole earth, and to the branches of which all the fowls of heaven come for shelter. It is not that the work is more real in the new dispensation than in the old. It is not merely that it is

more universal. It is that it is directed to a different end—
that it is no longer for the mere preserving of the seed unto the
day of planting, but for the perfecting of the fruitage and the
gathering of the harvest. The Church, to use a figure of
Isaiah's, was then like a pent-in stream; it is now like that
pent-in stream with the barriers broken down and the Spirit of
the Lord driving it. It was he who preserved it in being when
it was pent-in. It is he who is now driving on its gathered
floods till it shall cover the earth as the waters cover the sea.
In one word, that was a day in which the Spirit restrained his
power. Now the great day of the Spirit is come.

56

THE LOVE OF THE HOLY GHOST*

The love of God for sinners is the main theme of the Bible, and forms the mainstay of the Christian. Christian speech is, as is natural, full of even repetitious assurances of this greatest and most precious fact. It is with such texts as these that every child of God strengthens and comforts his soul: "For God so loved the world that he gave his only begotten Son"; "Behold what manner of love the Father hath bestowed upon us"; "God being rich in mercy, for the great love wherewith he loved us"; "Hereby we know love, because he laid down his life for us"; "Greater love hath no man than this, that a man lay down his life for his friends." It is with the glorious truths that such texts certify us of, that God the Father loves us, and that Christ the Savior loves us, that we comfort one another in times of darkness and trial and establish our own souls in their moments of darkness and dismay.

But although it is equally involved in the great fact that God is love, and is of equal importance to the Christian in his earthly pilgrimage, it is to be doubted whether we so constantly

*The Presbyterian Messenger, Feb. 20, 1895. This material may also be found, not in the same order but with greater fulness, in the fifth sermon of The Power of God unto Salvation, 1930, pp. 121-148. One reviewer of this book of sermons writes: "Dr. Warfield is one of our most accomplished and honored scholars. He is also a devout and sweet-spirited Christian preacher. The very marrow of the gospel is condensed into these living pages" (Watchman, Boston, Mar. 3, 1904). Another reviewer writes: These sermons are "not dry metaphysical dissertations, but live, pungent, and refreshing discussions of the deep things of the Kingdom. They are full of doctrine, yet are alive with a rich experience and a practical bearing. They are meant for the heart as well as for the brain" (The Presbyterian, June 24, 1903). Among these sermons the one entitled "The Love of the Holy Ghost" is often singled out for special comment and commendation.

remember that God the Holy Spirit loves us. We remind ourselves daily, perhaps even hourly, of the love of God the Father, and of the love of God the Son. It is possibly only rarely that we dwell in grateful appreciation upon the love of God the Spirit. It may even be that, owing to its unwontedness to our thought, it may fail to move our spirits as it ought when it is suggested to us. We feel the lift of John's appeal, "Beloved, if God so loved us, we ought also to love one another." We feel the power of Paul's declaration, that "the love of Christ constraineth us." But do we feel equally the force of Paul's similar appeal, "Now I beseech you, brethren, by the love of the Spirit, that you strive together with me in your prayers to God"? Are we equally moved by James's challenge, "Or think you that it is an empty saying of Scripture, that the Spirit which God hath made to dwell in us yearneth after us even unto jealous envy?"

Doubtless the comparative infrequency with which we meditate on the love which the Holy Ghost bears to us is due in part to the infrequency with which the love of the Spirit is expressly mentioned in Scripture. There is, possibly, only a single passage where it is quite certainly the theme of the sacred writer, and this passage is so obscured in our ordinary translation that it is doubtful whether the average reader often penetrates its meaning. This is that great demand of James iv. 5, which has just been quoted. It stands in the Authorized Version thus: "Do you think that the Scripture saith in vain, the Spirit that dwelleth in us lusteth to envy?" This is not very clear. The text of the Revised Version is no clearer: "Or think ye that the Scripture speaketh in vain? Doth the Spirit which he made to dwell in us long unto envying?" But the Revised Version gives some marginal renderings which will enable even the English reader to put the sentence together so as to convey the sense which the Greek certainly expresses, thus: "Or think ye that the Scripture saith in vain, That Spirit which he made to dwell in us yearneth for us even unto jealous envy?" Read thus, in accordance with the context, it is not too much to say that we have here one of the most precious texts in the Bible. It is a declaration, on the basis of Old Testament teaching, of the deep yearning which the Holy Spirit, whom God has caused to dwell in us, feels for our undivided and unwavering devotion.

A simple glance at the context is enough to assure us that the phraseology of the whole passage is colored by the underlying presentation of the relation of the Christian to God under the figure of marriage. The Christian is the bride of God; and, therefore, any commerce with the world is unfaithfulness. There is not room in the relation of marriage for two lovers. Hence the exclamation of "Adulteresses!" which springs to James's lips when he thinks of the Christian loving the world. We cannot have two husbands, and to the one husband to whom our vows are plighted, all our love is due. To dally even in thought with another lover is already unfaithfulness. On the other side, God is the husband of the Christian soul; and he loves it with that peculiar, constant, changeless love with which a true husband loves what the Scriptures call his own body. Is the soul faithful? Who can paint the delight he takes in it? Is it unfaithful, turning to seek its pleasure in the world? Then, the Scriptures tell us that it is with envious yearning that God looks upon it. The essential meaning of the text is thus revealed to us as a strong asseveration of the love of God for his people, set forth under the figure of a true husband's yearning love for his erring bride.

When James presents this asseveration of God's love for his people as the teaching of "Scripture," he has, of course, the Old Testament in mind, as he was in the act of penning the earliest of New Testament books. And throughout the Old Testament there are scattered numerous passages in which the Lord has been pleased graciously to express his love for his people under the figure of the love of a husband for his chosen bride, or in which he has been pleased to make vivid to us his sense of the injury done his love through the unfaithfulness of his people by attributing to himself the burning jealousy of an injured husband. In its general meaning, then, there is nothing in our text which had not been the possession of the people of God concerning God's love for them from the days of Moses. But it has its own peculiarities in expressing this greatest of all revelations, and these peculiarities seem to be specially worthy of our consideration.

1. The first of them to claim our attention is the intense energy of the expression which James uses to declare the love of God for his erring people. God is said to "yearn for us even unto jealous envy." Modes of speech sufficiently strong had been employed in the prophets of the Old Testament in the effort to convey to men some adequate sense of the vehemence of the divine grief over their sin, and the ardor of his longing to recover them to himself. The attribution of the passion of jealousy to him is itself startling, and this representation is heightened in every conceivable way. Even in Exodus the very name of God is declared to be "Jealous," as if this were his characteristic emotion, which expressed his very being. While Zechariah tells us that the Lord is "jealous for Zion with great jealousy; that he is jealous for her with great fury." But the language of James rises above all Old Testament precedent. Not only does the verb he uses express the idea of eager longing as strongly as it is possible to express it, but its emphasis is still further enhanced by an adverbial addition of the strongest character. The verb is that which is employed by the Greek translators of the 42nd Psalm: "As the hart panteth after the water-brooks, so panteth my soul after thee, O God." It is with the thirst of the panting stag for water, says James, that God thirsts after his wandering people. The adverb is not the ordinary active term for "jealousy" which is elsewhere applied to God, but a term of deeper passion, nowhere else applied to God, but often employed in the classics to express the feeling cherished towards a rival. It emphasizes the envious emotion which tears the soul at the sight of a rival's success. With this sickening envy, says James, God contemplates our dallying with the world and the world's pleasures. The combined expression is astonishingly intense. God is represented as yearning after us even unto, not merely jealousy, but jealous envy.

2. Another peculiarity of the text lies in the clearness

with which it distributes the objects of this great love of God into individuals. When the Scriptures make use of the figure of marriage to reveal the quality of God's love to his people, it is commonly his people as a body which they have in mind. In the Old Testament is is the "house of Israel" to whom Jehovah is espoused; in the New Testament it is the Church which is the Bride, the Lamb's wife. Only occasionally do the individuals which constitute this body come prominently forward in the application of this figure. In our present passage, however, the reference is directly to the individual. The effect is to remind the Christian that it is he, individually, who is in covenanted vows to God, and who is guilty of spiritual adultery when he permits the least shade of love of the world to enter his heart. The effect is to assure the individual Christian that God jealously envies the world the love which he gives it, and yearns after the return of his love to him, the Lord, who "longeth after him even unto jealous envy."

3. A third peculiarity of the text lies in its direct attribution of this appropriating love of God for his people to God the Holy Ghost. In this, as has been already hinted, the text is probably unique in the whole range of Scripture. No doubt, it may be said that the love of the Spirit is implied in the undifferentiated expression of the Old Testament. When it pleases Jehovah to represent his love to his people under the figure of a husband's love for his wife, and to ascribe to himself the emotion of jealousy in view of his people's unfaithfulness, it is, of course, implied that God the Holy Ghost partakes in this love and shares this jealous indignation. It is indeed this fact which James undoubtedly has in mind when he sends us to the Old Testament as the source of his declaration. "Think ye," he asks, "that Scripture says emptily, the Spirit that he made to dwell in you yearneth jealously?" James has evidently in mind those passages which ascribe this emotion to God, especially, of course, those wonderful passages in Ezekiel and Hosea which represent God as never wearying in his bearing with Israel and as purposing its complete and eternal restoration, not only to his favor but to his duty. The Christian

doctrine of God justifies his use of these passages in this way: but it is equally true that his use of them renewedly justifies the Christian doctrine of God. It is a gain from the point of view of an intelligent apprehension of the truth concerning God's nature and modes of subsistence, to hear this explicit declaration that the passages which express God's intimate relations to his people are to be read, in the light of the supreme revelation of God in Christ, as expressions of the relations in which the Holy Spirit, no less than the Father and the Son, stands to the people of his choice. But surely it is a still greater gain from the point of view of the Christian life, to have this explicit declaration of the heart of the indwelling Spirit. What James chiefly tells our hearts is that it is God the Holy Spirit, whom God has caused to dwell within us, who is the subject of the unchanging love towards us, which is expressed in these words of unexampled strength, as a yearning after us even unto jealous envy.

Could there be presented to us a completer manifestation of the infinitude of God's love than is contained in this revelation of the love of the Spirit for us? Does not this greatest of all revelations take on new force to move our souls, when we are made to realize that not only does the Father love us and the Son love us, but the indwelling Spirit also loves us—that despite the foulness of our sin, he yearneth after us unto jealous envy? Could there be given us a higher incentive to faithfulness to God, than is contained in this declartion of the love of the Spirit for us? Can we dally with sin, forget our covenanted duties to God when the Spirit which he has caused to dwell in us is known by us to be yearning after us even unto jealous envy? Could there be afforded us a deeper ground of encouragement in our Christian life, than is contained in this revelation of the love of the Spirit for us? Can we doubt what the end shall be, despite all the world can do to draw us down, and the flesh and the devil, when we know that the Spirit which he hath made to dwell in us is yearning after us even unto jealous envy? Could there, then, be granted us a firmer foundation for the holy joy of Christian assurance than is contained in the revelation of the love of the Spirit for us? Surely though our hearts faint within us, and the way seems dark, and there are lions roaring in the path, we shall be able to look through and past all difficulties, see the open gates of pearl beyond, whenever we remember that the Spirit which he hath made to dwell in us is yearning for us even unto jealous envy.

57

INABILITY AND THE DEMAND OF FAITH*

One of the most difficult questions which the seeker after souls has to meet arises out of the doctrine of Inability. The sinner, with anxious earnestness, asks the great question, "What, then, must I do to be saved?" He cannot be put off, and he ought not to be put off, with a mere "You can do nothing." This is not the Scripture answer. The Scriptures certainly do not say, as many would have us say, "Go and pray, listen to the gospel, use the sacrament and strive to live a holy life." All this is needful. But many a man may say in reply: "All this have I done from my youth up; what lack I yet?— what must I do to be saved?" The Bible answers briefly and pointedly: "Believe in the Lord Jesus Christ, and thou shalt be saved." But may not the sinner answer that this is precisely what he cannot do? May he not reply that, being wholly dead in sin, the exercise of faith is just what he cannot attain unto?

Such a response may doubtless be nothing more than a theoretical difficulty raised by the sinner as an excuse for not obeying the command of God. In such a case it is enough, in reply to it, to point out that at bottom it is a cavil. The command to believe is explicit. And the object of faith is most winningly presented to the mind and heart. Our obvious duty is to believe: and if we do not do so the responsibility rests upon us. That we cannot do so is the result and index of our sinfulness. Inability is a sinful condition of the will, and the sole reason why a man cannot believe is that he is so exceedingly sinful that such a one as he cannot use his will for believing. He cannot will to do it because he loves sin too much. For such a "cannot" he is certainly responsible.

*The Presbyterian Messenger, Nov. 15, 1893.

725

But the objection is not a mere theoretical cavil, but a real practical difficulty, the expression of a soul despairingly conscious of its sin and of its sinful inability. In such a case it stands in the way of a soul seeking life, and must be dealt with in faithful gentleness.

1. Something may be done toward removing the difficulty by pointing out the nature of the puzzle into which the mind has fallen. The puzzle is a logical one, and concerns doctrine, not action; and it must not be permitted to stand as an obstacle to action. Regeneration is not a fact of experience, but an inference from experience; and inability is not a ground of quiescence, but an inference from quiescence. It passes away in regeneration; and no one can know that it is gone save by the change in activity. We reason back from our experience and call in the doctrine of inability to explain our actual conduct, and that of regeneration to explain the gulf between our conduct of yesterday and today. But that gulf is revealed in consciousness only by action. No man can know, then, whether he is unable save by striving to act.

We may point out, therefore, that the doctrine of inability does not affirm that we cannot believe, but only that we cannot believe in our own strength. It affirms only that there is no natural strength within us by which we may attain to belief. But this is far from asserting that on making the effort we shall find it impossible to believe. We may believe, in God's strength. Our case is parallel to that of the man with the withered hand. He knew he could not stretch it forth: that was the very characteristic of a withered hand—it was impotent. But Christ commanded, and he stretched it forth. So God commands what he wills and gives while he commands. Unable in ourselves, we may taste and see that the Lord is gracious. These very struggles of the soul are an evidence of the working of the Holy Spirit within us. So that we are justified in saying to every distressed sinner, in the words of Principal Gore: "Act against sin, in Christ's name, as if you had strength, and you will find you have."

2. In order to incite to the requisite action we may uncover

the frequent commands of God to believe and the frequent unlimited and universal promises of acceptance. We may show that
man has nothing to do with God's part in the work, but only with
his own; and pressing the commands and pleading the promises,
excite to the effort, depending on God's promises. This very
effort is already an exercise of the required faith. And thus
the sinner may be led to perform the act and claim the promise.

That faithful preacher and successful evangelist, Robert
Murray M'Cheyne, gives in his sermons many examples of
the dealings of a true minister of Christ with sinners. He never
glosses their inability. To the objection that the heart is hard
and cannot believe, he replies: "This does but aggravate your
guilt. It is true you were born thus, and that your heart is
like the nether millstone. But that is the very reason God
will most justly condemn you; because from your infancy you
have been hard-hearted and unbelieving." But he makes this
very inability a reason why we should look from ourselves to
a Savior for salvation. "You say you cannot look, nor come,
nor cry, for you are helpless. Hear, then, and your soul shall
live. Jesus is a Savior to the helpless. Christ is not only a
Savior to those who are naked and empty, and have no
goodness to recommend themselves, but he is a Savior to those
who are unable to give themselves to him. You cannot be in
too desperate a condition for Christ." Here is the essence of
the matter: Christ is needed as a Savior all the more because
we cannot do the least thing to save ourselves.

3. To drive home the appeal we may emphasize the dangers
of delay, and the roots of it in a sinful state. Dr. McCosh has
a striking sermon on "Waiting for God," in which a fine
example is given of this faithful appeal. "But I have a commission to proclaim," he says; "God's reign in your hearts
is pressed upon you. . . . But you say you can do nothing
without grace; you are waiting for it. Ah, there is reason to
fear that to all thy other sins thou art adding the sin of
hypocrisy. Thou art not waiting for grace, but in thy secret
heart for something very different. Determined to cherish thy
self-righteousness, thou art waiting for self-indulgence, waiting

for earthly goods and pleasures. God does offer thee grace, but thou wishest to remain graceless. Thou mightest be made humble, but thou art determined to remain proud. Thou mightest have thy self-righteous spirit subdued, and thou art resolved to lean on thine own deeds. Thou mightest have thy selfishness eradicated, but thou art resolute in pursuing thine own immediate worldly interests. Thou mightest become holy, but thou art bent on abiding unholy. Friend, I would strip you of these false pretexts by which thou art deceiving thyself, but by which thou canst not deceive God. Away with the delusion that thou hast been waiting for God, when thou hast been waiting for self-seeking ends. Let there be a surrender at once of thy self-will. Commit thyself at once and implicitly into God's hands. If thou knewest the gift of God, and how good he is to them that 'wait for him,' thou wouldst even now submit thyself to him to do with thee as seemeth to him good; to bend thee as thou requirest to be bent; to change thee as thou requirest to be changed; and to fashion thee anew after his own pleasure. And say not that thou art waiting for the movement of the Spirit, as the impotent man waited at the pool for the troubling of the waters. For the spiritually impotent are cured not by any wished-for movement of their spirits, but by Christ himself as he passes by; and he is now passing by and is ready to heal."

This seems to me an admirable specimen of faithful dealing with such souls: they are not to be argued with but pressed to come at once to Jesus.

58

UNDER ORDERS*

Rudyard Kipling, in one of his "Barrack-room Ballads," expresses the inner nature of heathenism, from what may be called the soldierly point of view. The characterization runs thus:

> The heathen in his blindness bows down to wood and stone.
> He don't obey no orders, unless they is his own.

The heart of these lines is of course the fine soldierly sense of the value of order and discipline which they utter. The soldier is conscious of not standing alone in weak isolation, but of being rather a member of an organism, a wheel in a machine if you will, but at all events in a machine much greater than the individual, and with work to do larger and more momentous than any which the individual's whims can emulate. His place in the organism lends worth and dignity to his individuality. Standing in it he is a factor in great designs and great accomplishments, all of which depend on him as one element in their completion. The symbol of his significance as part of this great organism and sharer in these great events, is the fact that he is "under orders." Obedience to orders, which is his duty as a soldier, does not appear to him a hard necessity; but has come to appeal to him, as a good soldier, as the source of all that is good and valuable, all that possesses dignity and worth in his position. His pride in being a soldier centers in this, that he is "under orders." It is the fact which has not only reduced chaos into order for him, but which has lent a real meaning and importance to his life and made him a

---

*The Presbyterian Messenger, Oct. 1, 1896.

fellow worker in great undertakings. He looks down on those who are not like him, "under orders," as occupying an inferior place. They are not "in it," and he is. The principle of "authority" is thus one of his most precious possessions, not only as an organizing but as an elevating principle.

And now, looking out on the religious world with that keen insight into relative values which belongs to those whose eyes are not blinded by occupation with too numerous a body of details, the simple soldier-man strikes on this as the essential difference between Christians and heathen. Christians are like soldiers; they are under orders. The heathen are like the disorganized rabble; they have no orders to obey, but each man is governed by his own caprices. It is not merely or chiefly the sense of the value of organization which he thus expresses. It is true that obeying orders does introduce objective order and the efficiency that comes from order into the mass. But it is not this objective ordering which is most prominent in this soldier-like judgment. The eye of the barrack-room philosopher is on his own interior life, and he transfers the judgment passed on that to the discrimination between Christian and heathen. Obedience to orders has made him a man. That he has orders to obey has been the chief elevating force in his life; it is this which has given all the dignity and value to his action which it has ever possessed. Without this he would have remained not merely a unit, uncorrelated with other units and able to accomplish only a unit's work; but he would himself have remained a subjective and disorganized unit. When he characterizes the Christian therefore as one who has orders to obey, and the heathen as one who is left to his own wilfulness, he does not intend merely to pass judgment on the power of organized Christianity or the weakness of disorganized heathendom. He means also to uncover the sources of the dignity and value of the Christian man, of the worthlessness and the inherent disorganization of the heathen. The Christian man possesses worth and dignity, and the reason is that he has orders to obey. The heathen man is without worth and dignity, and the reason is that he obeys no orders but his own. The soldier announces here his philosophy of life. To be under orders is to receive one's true value in the world. And he applies this to Christianity and heathenism. The reason why the Christian stands above the heathen is the same reason why the soldier stands above the hoodlum—he has orders to obey. The source of all the Christian's self-respect, dignity, force, and worth is thus to the soldier-man summed up in his having "orders" to obey.

Now it seems to us that this soldierly judgment really does cut with curious precision to the very root of the matter. The discrimination between Christianity and heathenism does actually turn precisely on the point that Christians have orders to obey, while the heathen are left to their own devices. We commonly express this by saying that Christianity is the only revealed religion. That is to say, Christians possess a body of instructions covering both what men are to believe concerning God and what duty God requires of man, by which they may order their lives; and the heathen lack this body of instructions. In this fact lies all the difference between the two. And this fact cannot be better expressed than by saying that the Christian man, like the soldier, enjoys the advantages which come from being under orders; and, like the soldier, acquires not only thus a place in the progressive successes of the power which he serves, but also an inward dignity and worth not attainable in any other way; while the heathen man, lacking the advantages of being under orders and being perforce a law unto himself, not only loses whatever force comes from union, but loses also whatever inward dignity and development come from conscious contact with and actual direction from higher powers. The principle of authority is inherent in the very idea of a revelation. Thus it emerges that the fact of being under an "external authority" is the source of the dignity and worth of the Christian man, and is ultimately the root of all the distinction between him and a heathen. The heathen obeys no orders but his own; he is self-governed; he is autocratic. The Christian has orders from above to obey; he is governed by a power without himself; he is under obedience to an external authority. And it is just because of this difference that the Christian is superior to the heathen.

This soldierly judgment runs oddly athwart much of the theological opinion of the day. Nothing is so little esteemed in our time as "external authority." Voices are never louder or more harsh than when they are raised to denounce subjection to "external authority," and to demand that the Christian man shall emancipate himself from it and be a law to himself. Our barrack-room philosopher finds this power to be the very characteristic of heathenism. Historically this demand has been known in the Christian Church as "rationalism." "Rationalism," in other words, is that tendency of thought which would discard all "external authority" in the government of Christian thought, belief, action, in favor of the authority of the man's own self—his reason, consciousness, ethical judgment, conscience, what not. It has passed through many phases, and runs naturally through a wide range—from cold intellectualism on the one side, to the warmest mysticism on the other. But in all its phases alike, it is characterized by this fundamental trait: it scouts "external authority," and makes its appeal to what is within the man himself. In other words, it refuses to be "under orders," and declines to obey any order except the individual's own. According to our barrack-room judgment, this is essentially heathen. And this judgment is right. The mark of Christianity is that it is a revealed religion; that is, its adherents march by orders from without, and not from within; they are under "external authority," and receive all that gives them worth and value in the world from that fact.

It is marvelous how subtly and persistently the essentially heathen attitude seeks to engraft itself on Christianity. Just now, we are called upon to face it most insidiously in the form given it by that antique system of half belief which loves to call itself the "New Theology." An appeal, it seems, is to be made hereafter not to an "external authority," but to the "Christian Consciousness," as it is to be called. This is specious enough, but there is involved in it the surrender of the whole

Christian position. For, after all, even a Christian's consciousness is himself; and the Christian man differs from the heathen
precisely in this—that he has a source higher and better than
himself to which to look for his orders. Our "New Theology"
friends may indeed seek to identify their "consciousness" not
with themselves but with Christ. They may tell us that in
looking to it for guidance they are not obeying, each man
himself, but all alike the one Christ who informs the spirit
of each. But is it so very certain that by looking thus within
themselves for him and his "orders," they will most surely find
Christ, and be most surely freed from the anarchy of each man
following his own devices? A Christ without us, speaks objectively to us in words heard and reported by his followers;
here indeed are "orders." But an assumed Christ within us—
is it not only too likely to be, has it not always historically
evinced itself to be, only another way of following our own
leading, to make our appeal to it? Let our "New Theology"
friends, then, tell us plainly whether they are prepared to take
their stand frankly with "Christians" and receive their orders
from a Lord and King, outside of and above them; or whether
they are determined to occupy the "heathen" standpoint and
obey no orders but their own. A writer in a recent number of
the Unitarian quarterly, *The New World,* whose theological
standpoint is precisely opposite to our own, and who fully
adopts the "heathen" principle of the set authority of the
individual reason, very sharply uncovers the ambiguous position which these "New" teachers have assumed. "They cannot
long deceive themselves or others," he exclaims, "by thus
playing fast and loose about the person of Christ. Will they
plainly tell us to what authority they bow? Do they mean by
the guiding Christ, words of Jesus or rather that inward light
which lighteth every man? Do they not, like other modern
minds, test and interpret the words attributed to Jesus by means
of this light of the Universal Reason? What teaching of Jesus,
as for instance about devils, or the last judgment, or the second
coming, or the final fate of the wicked, do they not translate
with perfect freedom into the terms of their own thought? Will

they point at a single teaching of Jesus which they accept simply because Jesus said it, and not rather because in their judgment it is true?"

The finger is put here directly upon the ulcer. It is possible to talk much about Christ and yet to betray him. The point is not to whom we attribute our guidance. The point is from whom we receive our orders. Do we accept Jesus' statements and obey his commands simply because Jesus affirms them and gives them? Or do we accept and obey because and only so far as we judge them ourselves to be wise and true? Are we under orders, and do we look upon it as a source of dignity and worth to ourselves that we are under the orders of such a Leader? Or, after all, are we in the position of the heathen, of whom it is said that "They don't obey no orders, except they is their own."

Let us look to ourselves closely; for it is just here that the Christian is really separated from the heathen standpoint. The Christian is a man under orders; the heathen obeys no orders but his own.

59

A CALM VIEW OF THE FREEDMEN'S CASE*

We already recognize it as a commonplace to say that the greatest work before the American people today is the elevation and civilization of the seven millions of blacks that form so large a section of its fifty millions of souls. But, like so many other commonplaces, it is easier to bandy this phrase from mouth to mouth than thoroughly to realize the very serious meaning that lies in it. Some appear to think that they have done all that can be required of them when they have yielded their assent to the assertion; though, at that rate, we cannot hope that the great work thus acknowledged will be soon overtaken. Almost nowhere, however, is its magnitude adequately appreciated, although it is difficult to see how anyone who has had much contact with the masses of the blacks, with his eyes and heart open to see and feel, can have escaped a certain amount of deep anxiety as to their future. He sees adequate capacities for rising in them; but he sees also great obstacles to their rising; and he asks himself, in doubt, whether any capacities can avail to lift a people upward on whom rests so great a weight of prejudice, evil custom, and sad fate.

We need not speculate as to the causes of so great an apathy in the face of so great a problem. Men are indifferent only because men are insufficiently acquainted with the true state of the case and have inadequately realized the difficulty of the task now set before the American people. For instance, the terrible legacy of evil which generations of slavery have left to our freedmen is scarcely appreciated by any of us. We are prone to represent the average slave to ourselves as a carefully

---

*The Church at Home and Abroad, Jan. 1887, pp. 62-65.

nurtured and taught inmate of a Christian household, sent out at last into the world to care for himself with almost the same preparation in character and moral training that was given to the sons of the house themselves. The foundation of this fancy is a no more than just recognition of the constant efforts of the slaveholders of the South to teach their bondmen the truths of religion and to frame within them a sound system of morals. But when we so state the results attained we forget two very important considerations: that the house-servants were but a small proportion of the whole body of slaves on the one side, and on the other that the very fact of slavery was the most potent of demoralizers.

The Southern slaveholders did what they could to teach a true Christianity to their slaves, and the results attained by them, which, all things considered, are nothing less than marvelous, are the sufficient proof not only of their own vital and yearning piety, but also of the strenuousness of their efforts to indoctrinate the souls which were in their charge with the truths of religion. But the masses of plantation hands could be only partially reached by any efforts; and, as a mere matter of fact, here as always elsewhere the fruit of slavery was ingrained immorality. When we grieve over the odd divorce of religion and morality which is so frequently met with among the blacks, let us not indeed blame the slaveholders for it, as if their Christian teaching was at fault, but let us equally remember that slavery itself is responsible for it. I do not forget what contact with Christian masters has done for the thousands of heathen savages which were being continually landed on our shores, up to the very outbreak of the war itself. Let anyone simply compare the average self-respecting Negro in America with the naked savage of the African forests, and thank God for the marvelous change. But I am concerned to have it clearly seen what the very conditions of slavery prevented this contact from accomplishing; and in what moral state it necessarily sent forth its millions of freedmen to cope with the world. Let us only remember that, by its very nature, slavery cannot allow to its victim a will of his own; that it leaves him master of none of his deeds; that it permits him ownership in nothing, not even in his honor or virtue. Who need ask after the moral effect of such a state of things? How could the moral instruction of one member of the family hope to overcome the immoral compulsion of others? I could name some colored women who were nothing less than martyrs of chastity. But the masses are never martyrs, and the curse of slavery eats to the roots of all life.

This, it is to be observed, is not to deny that slavery did form and compact a moral character in the bondmen. It is to point out what kind of moral character it compacted. There is an honor among thieves; and there is a strict and binding morality among slaves. But as in the one case it is a different honor from that which obtains among honest men, so in the other it is a morality of a different stamp and of a separate standard from what obtains among freemen. What is virtue in the slave is vice in the freeman, and this reversal of all moral principle is one of the chief characteristics of the terrible institution of human slavery. The task now before us would be easier had slavery only demoralized. As a matter of fact it did worse: it moralized on a false and perverted system. The freedman has his code of morals, and in his way and from the slave's point of view he is an intensely moral man. He is not unmoral; he is an enthusiast for an immoral ethic—an ethic that now that he is a freedman will not range with his new position and his new duties. In a word, slavery, so far from fitting its victims for freedom, unfitted them for it. The task before the American people in dealing with the blacks is nothing less, then, than the uprooting and expulsion of a settled and ingrained system of immorality, in order that a true morality may be substituted for it.

It is another result of the state of things which I have tried to point to as the inevitable effect of generations of slavery, that the freedman's sons are, morally speaking, a distinct deterioration from the freedman himself. That this is a fact every careful observer at the South recognizes, though it must not be misunderstood, as if it involved a denial of the very rapid growth upwards of those who have had the opportunity of growth. Unfortunately, however, it is the few of the new generation who have received this opportunity, while the many thus far have been caught in the toils of necessity and are working out their own destruction without help from without. We do not share fully in the distress of many that the old type of Negro is dying out with the generation which had the severe discipline of slavery; but it is a fact that it is dying out, and that, generally speaking, what it leaves behind it is something apparently worse. But the very reason of this sad phenomenon is that the old type was an artificial product. The slave was trained into and held in a bearing of dignity and self-respecting conduct by external pressure. He stood by virtue of props from without. When those props were removed he still stood by virtue of old habit. But there was no sufficient inner centripetal force to hold him together. He was like a barrel which has stood so long that its contents have solidified, and, when the hoops are knocked off, still retains its uprightness. The sons of the freedmen came into the world without hoops, and they simply betray to us the artificiality of the product which we have admired. Their morality is not only wrongly centered, but is in a fluid state; and it is our task to see that it crystalizes around some solid kernel of truth and righteousness. This were better than to gather it up and try, as of old, to tie it into shape by the pressure of outside institutions.

And here we are face to face with our problem; for it is with the sons of the freedmen that our generation has especially to deal. And we are face to face with the knottiest part of the task. What pressure can we bring to bear on these wandering souls to draw them within the formative influences of a true and sound morality? The strongest motive with most men is the hope of rising. The most degraded immigrant that reaches our shores is under this spell: the lure of hope dances ever before his eyes. However high above him others may stand, he has but to lift his eyes to see that the plain pathway runs from his feet to theirs, and it is only a question as to whether he is willing to climb—whether he will not stand by

their sides tomorrow. If he has no ambition for himself, he
has for his children; and it is rare indeed that the civilizing
influence of this single hope is not the sufficient excitement to
endeavor, self-respect, and growth. But this is lost for the
African. The class to which he belongs by birth is the class
with which he must make his home until death sets him free.
He bears a brand on his brow that closes all avenues of advance before him, and the despondency of his heart, that makes
him reckless of public opinion as to his deeds, is but the inward
answer to the stern outward fact that, become what he individually may, he cannot rise into the classes above him. It is
probably impossible for any of us to realize the deadening
burden of this hopelessness. It clips the wings of every soaring
spirit, and drives every ambition back to gnaw its own tongue
in unavailing pain. Yet an adequate appreciation of its is
one of the conditions of our understanding the gravity of the
problem that is before us, in our efforts to raise and educate
the blacks to take their proper place in our Christian civilization.

Those who expect, in such circumstances, the freedmen to
elevate themselves are building castles in Spain with a vengeance. And it is but little less unreasonable to expect the
South to take the whole burden of their training for the important duties of free men and women. To go no further, the
South has not the means in men or money for the task. Apparently illiteracy is increasing among the blacks, even now;
and it is certain that were Northern aid removed the burden
would be so hopeless that it could not even be undertaken. It
must be sorrowfully added (for I too am a Southerner, in
birth, training, and affiliations) that the Southern people are
not thoroughly awake either to the necessity of, or to their
duty in, this matter. Many individuals are already alive to it;
the Christian South has not lost its pity for these suffering
and ignorant claimants to its aid; and multitudes there are
ready for any personal sacrifice for their elevation and improvement—as they understand what their elevation and improvement
ought to be. But the spirit of caste (for it cannot be called
by any milder name) is practically universal, and colors

the opinions and paralyzes the efforts of the whole South to such an extent as to render it unfit for much useful work in this field. For it cannot be too strongly emphasized that it is not he who feels persuaded that the Negro was made a little lower than man, and who is graciously willing to train him into fitness for such a position, who can educate him into true and self-centered manhood. It is only he who is thoroughly persuaded that God has made of one blood all the nations of the earth, that has the missionary spirit, or that can serve as the hand of the Most High in elevating the lowly and rescuing the oppressed.

I am not saying that the spirit of caste is confined to the South; I have met with it in full bloom in the North also. But it is practically universal in the South. And the community is so entirely imbued with it that it can scarcely believe any other sentiment possible to self-respecting people and gravely asserts it when intending to deny it. "It has been charged," said a Mississippi delegate only the other day, to the General Conference of the Protestant Episcopal Church, held at Chicago, "that the colored race has been expelled from attending church by the white members. This is not so; they would be gladly welcomed, *and seats have been set aside for them in all the churches.*" The saddest thing about it is that the good brother actually seemed to suppose that he had made his point. "Only such a prejudice" exists against the colored people "as would exist against any uneducated and unrefined people," indeed! In what community are special seats set aside "in all the churches" for the "uneducated and unrefined"? It would be a marvelously instructive sight to see *this* division carried through by some sure touchstone! Ah, no! we are hand to hand here with the pure spirit of caste; a caste which we cannot call unnatural when all the circumstances are taken into consideration, and which I should be one of the last too sharply to blame the South for entertaining, but none the less a caste the existence of which we must explicitly and calmly recognize if we are ever to grasp all the contents of the problem of the elevation of the colored population of the South, and which it is painful to see in this nineteenth century anywhere out of India. I have myself known a Negro woman who had, in anxiety for her soul, ventured to enter a crowded church during a series of revival meetings, to be asked out by the elders. It would be unfair to say it is the settled policy of the South toward the Negro, but it is at least the inbred instinct of Southern men and women, whether in church or state, to make the Negro know what they are pleased to call "his place"—as if, forsooth, his place as a man was not side by side with men, and his place as a Christian was not in the midst of God's children. Are we today to reverse the inspired declaration that in Christ Jesus there cannot be Greek and Jew, circumcision and uncircumcision, barbarian, Scythian, bondman, freeman?

The harm that caste does toward those whom we would elevate cannot be overestimated. It kills hope; it paralyzes effort; it cuts away all of those incitements to endeavor that come of intimacy with those above us, and the example of those who, having trodden where our feet now walk, have passed into the regions beyond, leaving footprints for us to follow. It is a marvel to me that its dangers too are not more fully appreciated. Apart from all question of religion and the kingdom of God, is it good public policy to compact a lower class, escape from which, by reason of the indelible stain of color, cannot be had, into a solid phalanx of opposition to the ruling class, and by heaping, year after pear, petty injustices and insults upon it, to beget undying hatred in its heart and to perpetuate all the evils of race alienation into an indefinite future, if not even to treasure up for ourselves wrath against a day of wrath? For after a while this blind Samson must awake, and the issues which depend on these two things—that when he awakes he shall not be still unmoral, and that he shall not awake with a deep sore in his heart against his fellow citizens of another color—are simply tremendous, for the South and for the nation.

What I have said, I have said only with the purpose of outlining the seriousness of the problem now before the American people. But it seems to me that it will avail also to suggest the instrumentalities by which alone the problem can be successfully attacked. If it is a true moralization of the blacks that is needed, this can be secured only by a careful moral teaching such as can be furnished only by religious organizations which will educate as well as preach. Secular training will do small good; simple preaching of the gospel does not reach deep enough. We must have Christian schools everywhere, where Christianity as a revealed system of truth and of practice is daily taught by men and women whose hearts are aglow with missionary fervor—who find in every creature of God the promise and potency of all higher life. Can the Presbyterian Church safely neglect to do her part in this great work?

60

DRAWING THE COLOR LINE*

About three years ago Carl Schurz announced in his pamphlet on *The New South:* "I think it safe to say that whatever atrocities may have happened during that terrible period of sudden transition from one social order to another, the relations between the white and black races are now in progress of peaceful and friendly adjustment; and," he added, building hopes upon his view of the nature of the approaching adjustment—"that the disappearance of race antagonism on the political field will do more for the safety of the Negro's rights and the improvement of his position in human society than could be done by any intervention of mere power." The three years that have passed since this forecast have brought us little occasion for self-congratulation upon our progress toward so desirable a goal. The readers of Cable's admirable paper in the *Contemporary Review* for last March have been shown with photographic distinctness and depth of shadow, the disheartening picture, on the one side, of over a million American citizens, with their wives and children, still held in a position which makes them "virtually subjects and not citizens, peasants instead of freemen"; and, on the other, of a new generation of the ruling class with "no well-defined political faith beyond the one determination to rule without appeal to any consent but their own, and at all costs, spiritual and material, to others or themselves."

It may be that advance has been made toward an adjustment of relations between the two races, such as may promise an early truce if not a peace; but it has scarcely been along the

---

The Independent, July 5, 1888, with the sub-title "A Fragment of History": by a "Disinterested Spectator."

path of disappearance of race antagonism. The young men of the "new South," who have had no experience, or who preserve but a faint recollection of slavery, appear to cherish a vehemence of race antipathy to which their fathers were for the most part strangers. Unsoftened by the intimate association which formerly obtained with the slaves of the household, who constituted almost as much a part of the family as the children themselves, and who entered heartily into the family life, the family fortunes, and the family pride; and exacerbated by daily experience of what they consider the intolerable impudence of an inferior and menial race, they seem to be adding, day by day, the physical repulsion which is more proper to those who have had little contact with men of another race, to their inherited and passionate conviction that the safety of our state, of society, of the family itself, depends on the stern preservation of their supremacy over the degraded masses that swarm about them. Thus it has come about in Cable's striking phrase, that emancipation has abolished only private but not public subjugation; has made the ex-slave not a free man but only a free Negro. Meanwhile the black masses, who, taken as a class, emerged from slavery with no sense of wrongs to avenge, but rather with a lively appreciation of the manifold kindnesses which they had received from their masters, and with a true gratitude for the elevation which they had obtained at their hands through the generation or two that separated them from the dimly remembered savagery of Africa, have been gradually becoming, under the irritation of continually repeated injustices, great and small, more and more compacted into a sullen mass of muttered discontent, which promises to develop into full-fledged race-antagonism on their side also. Thus race seems to be arraying itself increasingly against race. Wearied with the apparently ever accumulating hopelessness of the task of breaking down the antipathy to conjoint public life, now rapidly becoming mutual, men have begun to seek after some method of formal segregation of the races into separate political units, as the sole hope of the establishment of a *modus vivendi* between them.

A bright side-light has been thrown, during the last few months, upon the present relation of the two races by some rather remarkable proceedings of two ecclesiastical bodies. The Protestant Episcopal Diocese of South Carolina has been distracted, through a period of thirteen years, over the apparently simple question whether a Negro clergyman who has fulfilled all the canonical requirements has right to a seat and vote in the Diocesan Convention. So fierce has been the determination to draw the "color line" in this religious assembly, that the very existence of the Convention was imperiled when a majority of the clergy could not be brought to follow the laity in demanding that the names of the colored members should be "cut off" from the list furnished by the bishop. Secession was freely resorted to until a large number of the most important parishes of the state were unrepresented in the Convention; and, at its assembling last spring, it was doubtful whether a quorum could be obtained. It might be thought that after such a purging the "faithful remnant" could be trusted to stand firmly for the equal rights of man, irrespective of color or race, in a Christian assembly. But not so. The most faithful are anxious to have it known that they "have not fought for color but for the rights of the clergy." Accordingly, although the colored clergyman was unanimously declared to be entitled to his seat, it soon became evident that this was rather a proclamation of the ideal Church than a declaration of a chosen line of policy in the actual Church. Lay delegates besought the Convention to save the diocese, the life or death hour of which was now come; and solemnly warned it that unless something decisive was done *now* to give relief, there would never again be a lay delegate seen on its floor. Under such pressure the rector of the colored church through which the crisis was precipitated, hastened voluntarily to anticipate what he saw would be imposed by force, and proposed a series of resolutions which declare that absolute necessity has arisen for the separate organization of the two races in the diocese, and appoint a committee to confer with the colored churches and clergy with a view to effecting "a complete separation into two organizations." The resolutions passed with effusion, and have been accepted as satisfactory by the colored church most particularly affected; while Bishop Howe expresses himself as thinking that "the attitude of the late Convention was altogether considerate of the colored Churchmen of the diocese."[1]

To turn from the Protestant Episcopal Diocese of South Carolina to the great national Presbyterian Church is to turn to a much broader and perhaps somewhat different constituency; but it brings no change in the matter now under consideration. In the movement toward bringing the two branches of this great Church into more cordial and closer relations, a new step toward which was taken last year in the appointment of committees of conference and inquiry by the respective bodies, it soon became apparent that the great difficulty lay in "the Negro question." The Southern Presbyterian newspapers were practically unanimous in the assertion that the Church which they represented could never consent to reunion unless pledges were given that the colored churches should be organized into a separate denomination. And when the committees came together this was the position taken by their committee, who say, "In our Church entire independence of the colored people in their Church organization is the policy which has been adopted; coupled with the largest possible measure of aid—spiritual, intellectual, and material—which can be given by our Church and people to our colored brethren." The furthest extreme to which they were prepared to go in modifying this position appears to have been a willingness to see the separate colored churches, presbyteries, or synods provisionally represented, through their presbyteries, in the common General Assembly, "with the hope and expectation" that the colored people will make such growth as will prepare them "to stand in their own strength, a Presbyterian Church,

---

[1]For the full text of the resolutions and the temper of the body, see the very interesting letter of Dr. Porter in *The Churchman* for May 19th last (pp. 596-601).

independent of all organic connection with any other Church."
Here is an attempt to draw the color line not only unfalteringly
but indelibly.

The conferring committee, representing a Church which has
a large and growing Negro constituency in the South, already
organized, of course, into presbyteries and synods, and represented equally in the General Assembly, objected only to the
indelibility of the line which it was thus proposed to them to
draw, while as to the line itself, they professed themselves of
the opinion that their Church would be willing indirectly to
conserve it. "We are of the opinion," they said, "that our
Assembly will agree to a basis of organic union by which the
present boundaries and constituencies of presbyteries and synods
in the South shall remain *in statu quo*, to be changed only with
the consent of the parties interested, and that all the new
churches and all new presbyteries hereafter established, shall
be organized by and received into connection with presbyteries
and synods respectively as the interested parties may mutually
agree." Nor did they deceive themselves. At the recent meeting
of the General Assembly at Philadelphia, it declared "its
hearty approval of the general principles enunciated in the
replies of the Committee to the inquiries propounded by our
Southern brethren, as furnishing substantially a reflection of
the views of this body touching the several subjects to which
they relate." Thus the whole Presbyterian Church, in both its
branches, stands as fully committed to the color line as the
Protestant Episcopal Diocese of South Carolina. It has, indeed, been sometimes doubted whether the plan propounded
by the Committee and approved by the Assembly is justly described as "drawing the color line"; but it was proposed in order
to satisfy the Southern Church on this very point; there is no
reason outside of this for the continuance of a double organization in the Southern States, and now that the approval of the
Assembly has been given, a prominent member of the drafting
committee, who happens to be also an editor, makes no difficulty in saying editorially: "The thing that was most emphatically done by the Special Committee and Assembly, was an

indorsement of the 'color line' proposition about presbyteries and synods."[2]

Can the story imbedded in such examples be missed? Christian men, under the pressure of their race antipathy, desert the fundamental law of the Church of the Living God, that in Christ Jesus there cannot be Greek and Jew, circumcision and uncircumcision, barbarian, Scythian, bondman, freeman. Episcopalians array themselves in open rebellion against bishop and clergy that they may be freed from the hated presence of the Negro in their councils. An ecclesiastical body which proclaims itself the champion of the exclusively spiritual functions of the Church demands, as the price of reconciliation with a sister body, the reorganization of the whole church organism on the lines of political and social cleavage.

But there is something else to learn from such strange phenomena, over and above the determination of the "new South" to secure and perpetuate a complete segregation of blacks and whites in all public concerns. We notice an apparent readiness of the professed friends of equal rights to betray by indirection the cause which they directly champion. The Diocesan Convention of South Carolina is eager for the separation if only it can be secured by the poor expedient of forcing an apparently voluntary action on the part of the colored people themselves. The General Assembly of the Presbyterian Church is willing to buy reunion with its Southern brethren at the fearful cost of affixing an unjust stigma upon a whole section of its own constituency, if it can only be done under the poorer expedient of a *status quo*. We notice further a tendency to plead the worst features of the case in extenuation of its visible injustice. We are repeatedly told that the Negroes themselves desire the proposed separation. The very special nature of their "voluntary" expression of desire in the diocese of South Carolina we have already seen. The case is similar in the Presbyterian Church. If the reunion is to be consummated,

---

[2]See *The Presbyterian Journal* for June 7th last (pp. 360 f.). The full text of the correspondence between the two committees was published in most of the Presbyterian weeklies of the second week in March.

they prefer not to be forced upon unwilling presbyteries. But, so far as their asserted desire is real, what does it argue but the awakening of race antipathy on their part also; but the sharp answering edge of the other side of the cleft which the wedge that is being so ruthlessly driven into the body politic is opening wider every day? Love answers to love, and hate soon gives its reply back to hate. Already in the Church the blacks are ready to draw off to themselves. The Presbyterian Negroes are said to be already giving their Board for Freedmen to understand that Negro pulpits are for Negro preachers. What will be before us when the seed so unsparingly sowing begins to bear a plumed harvest also in this state?

More than a hundred years have now glided away since a great genius wrote for us a history and a theory of the whole case, clothed in matchless prose, which we might well bind as a phylactery on our hands:

" 'When Tom, an' please your Honor, got to the shop, there was nobody in it but a poor Negro girl, with a bundle of white feathers slightly tied to the end of a large cane, flopping away flies—not killing them.'

" ' 'Tis a pretty picture,' said my uncle Toby; 'she had suffered persecution, Trim, and had learnt mercy.'

" 'She was good, an' please your Honor, from nature, as well as from hardships; and there are circumstances in the story of that poor friendless slut that would melt a heart of stone,' said Trim; 'and some dismal winter's evening, when your Honor is in the humor, they shall be told you, with the rest of Tom's story, for it makes a part of it.'

" 'Then do not forget, Trim,' said my uncle Toby.

" 'A Negro has a soul, an' please your Honor,' said the corporal (doubtingly).

" 'I am not much versed, Corporal,' quoth my uncle Toby, 'in things of that kind; but I suppose God would not leave him without one, any more than thee or me.'

" 'It would be putting one sadly over the head of another,' quoth the Corporal.

" 'It would so,' said my uncle Toby.

" 'Why, then, an' please your Honor, is a black wench to be used worse than a white one?'

" 'I can give no reason,' said my uncle Toby.

" 'Only,' cried the Corporal, shaking his head, 'because she has no one to stan' up for her.'

" ' 'Tis that very thing, Trim,' quoth my uncle Toby, 'which recommends her to protection, and her brethren with her; 'tis the fortune of war which has put the whip into our hands, *now;* where it may be hereafter, Heaven knows! But be it where it will, the brave, Trim, will not use it unkindly.'

" 'God forbid!' said the Corporal.

" 'Amen,' responded my uncle Toby, laying his hand upon his heart."